Library Use Only

CONTEMPORARY
*B*lack
*B*iography

CONTEMPORARY

Black

Biography

Profiles from the International Black Community

Volume 12

Shirelle Phelps, Editor

GALE

DETROIT · NEW YORK · TORONTO · LONDON

ISSN 1058-1316

STAFF

Shirelle Phelps, *Editor*

Carol Brennan, John Cohassey, Ed Decker, Ellen French, Simon Glickman, Robert Jacobson, Anne Janette Johnson, Mark Kram, L. Mpho Mabunda, James McDermott, Emily McMurray, Joan Oleck, Nicholas Patti, Joanna Rubiner, Julia Rubiner, Stephen E. Stratton, Amy Strumolo, Gillian Wolf,
Contributing Editors

Linda S. Hubbard, *Managing Editor, Multicultural Department*

Marlene S. Hurst, *Permissions Manager*
Margaret A. Chamberlain, Maria Franklin, Kimberly F. Smilay, *Permissions Specialist*
Diane Cooper, Edna Hedblad, Michele Lonoconus, Maureen Puhl, Susan Salas, Shalice Shah, Barbara A. Wallace, *Permissions Associates*
Sarah Chesney, Margaret McAvoy-Amato, *Permissions Assistants*

Mary Beth Trimper, *Production Director*
Shanna Heilveil, *Production Assistant*
Cynthia Baldwin, *Product Design Manager*
Barbara J. Yarrow, *Graphic Services Manager*
C. J. Jonik, *Desktop Publisher*
Randy Bassett, *Image Database Supervisor*
Pamela A. Hayes, *Photography Coordinator*
Mikal Ansari, Robert Duncan, *Imaging Specialists*

Victoria B. Cariappa, *Research Manager*
Barbara McNeil, *Research Specialist*
Julia C. Daniel, Tamara C. Nott, Norma Sawaya, Cheryl L. Warnock, *Research Associates*

∞™ This book is printed on acid-free paper that meets the minimum requirements of American National Standard for Information Sciences— Permanence Paper for Printed Library Materials, ANSI Z39.48-1984.

ISBN 0-7876-0100-4
ISSN 1058-1316

10 9 8 7 6 5 4 3 2 1

Contemporary Black Biography
Advisory Board

Contents

Introduction ix

Photo Credits xi

Cumulative Nationality Index 241

Cumulative Occupation Index 247

Cumulative Subject Index 257

Cumulative Name Index 287

Floyd Adams 1
The first black mayor of Savannah

Andrew C. Barrett 4
Former FCC leader

Jennifer Beals 7
"Flashy" Actress

Bill Bellamy 10
MTV's funnyman

Lonnie Bristow.. 14
AMA President

Marie Dutton Brown 17
Literary genius

Zora Brown 20
Crusading cancer awareness activist

Eugene Bullard 24
Unsung hero of aviation

Leonard Coleman 27
National League's leading man

Albert Collins 31
Blues musical "Iceman"

J. California Cooper 35
Notable fiction writer

Alison Davis 38
Insightful writer and anthropologist

Bessie Delany... 42
Pioneering dentist

Sadie Delany 42
Retired, aged teacher of knowledge

Marilyn Ducksworth 46
Publishing house wiz

Cesaria Evora 50
The Barefoot Diva

Willie Gary 53
Prominent, passionate lawyer

Nelson George 56
Versatile, ambitious writer

Nathaniel Glover 60
High-rising sheriff of the South

Lawrence Otis Graham 64
Controversial lawyer and writer

Ken Griffey, Jr. 68
Big "Junior" of baseball

Anthony Griffin 72
ACLU lawyer

Bethann Hardison 76
Modeling agency entrepreneur

Barbara Harris.. 79
The Episcopal church's first black female bishop

E. Lynn Harris 82
Intriguing author

Robert Hayden...85
Poet extraordinaire

Larry Irving..89
One of the leading blacks in the White House

Shirley Ann Jackson... 92
Scientific genius

Charles S. Johnson 96
Leading sociologist of his time

Amayla Kearse...101
Appealing judge

Flo Kennedy 105
    Crusading activist and lawyer

Chaka Khan..*109*
    Long-standing fruitful diva

Eriq La Salle 113
    ER's doctor love

Maria Liberia-Peters 116
    Queen of the Netherlands Antilles

Ken Lofton..120
    Near-Perfect baseball giant

Henry Lyons 123
    Leader of the National Baptist Convention USA

Ali Mazrui 126
    Prolific, controversial writer

Kaire Mbuende 130
    Independent diplomat

Lonette McKee 134
    Showboat's leading lady

Gilbert Moses 138
    Gifted director extraordinaire

Cecil Murray.....................................141
    Spiritually-conscious religious leader

Eddie Murray.....................................146
    Enduring baseball hero

Maria Mutola 150
    High-rising track and field star

Zena Oglesby 153
    Pioneer in the Black adoption market

Charles Ogletree 157
    Tenacious lawyer

Deval Patrick......... 161
    Civil Rights leading man

Frederick D. Patterson 166
    UNCF founder

Dennis Rodman.............................. 170
    Chicago Bull's "hairy," player

Al Roker 174
    TV's only ordinary weatherman

Patrice Rushen 177
    Multi-talented musician

Synthia St. James 181
    Fast-rising artist

Augusta Savage............................. 186
    World-renown sculptor

Leopold Sedar Senghor.....................191
    Respected political activist

Audrey Smaltz.................................196
    Coordinator of fashions

Roger G. Smith................................ 200
    Well-respected actor

Paul Stewart....................................204
    The West's newest advocate

Sheryl Swoopes 207
    Olympic Swoopster

Frank Thomas 211
    Baseball's Big Hurt

C. Delores Tucker 215
    Controversial association leader

Patrice C. Washington.....................219
    High-flying airline captain

Val Washington.............................. 223
    Advocate for the Republican party

Perry Watkins................................. 226
    High-profile military figure

Dorothy West.................................. 230
    Everlasting author of the 1990s

Conrad Worrill.................................234
    Million Man March organizer

Introduction

Contemporary Black Biography provides informative biographical profiles of the important and influential persons of African heritage who form the international black community: men and women who have changed today's world and are shaping tomorrow's.

Contemporary Black Biography covers persons of various nationalities in a wide variety of fields, including architecture, art, business, dance, education, fashion, film, industry, journalism, law, literature, medicine, music, politics and government, publishing, religion, science and technology, social issues, sports, television, theater, and others.

In addition to in-depth coverage of names found in today's headlines, *Contemporary Black Biography* provides coverage of selected individuals from earlier in this century whose influence continues to impact on contemporary life. *Contemporary Black Biography* also provides coverage of important and influential persons who are not yet household names and are therefore likely to be ignored by other biographical reference series.

Designed for Quick Research *and* Interesting Reading

- **Attractive page design** incorporates textual subheads, making it easy to find the information you're looking for.

- **Easy-to-locate data sections** provide quick access to vital personal statistics, career information, major awards, and mailing addresses, when available.

- **Informative biographical essays** trace the subject's personal and professional life with the kind of in-depth analysis you need.

- **To further enhance your appreciation** of the subject, most entries include photographic portraits.

- **Sources for additional information** direct the user to selected books, magazines, and newspapers where more information on the individuals can be obtained.

Helpful Indexes Make It Easy to Find the Information You Need

Contemporary Black Biography includes cumulative Nationality, Occupation, Subject, and Name indexes that make it easy to locate entries in a variety of useful ways.

Available in Electronic Formats

Diskette/Magnetic Tape. *Contemporary Black Biography* is available for licensing on magnetic tape or diskette in a fielded format. Either the complete database or a custom selection of entries may be ordered.

The database is available for internal data processing and nonpublishing purposes only. For more information, call (800) 877-GALE.

Online. *Contemporary Black Biography* is available online through Mead Data Central's NEXIS Service in the NEXIS, PEOPLE and SPORTS Libraries in the GALBIO file.

We Welcome Your Suggestions

The editors welcome your comments and suggestions for enhancing and improving *Contemporary Black Biography.* If you would like to suggest persons for inclusion in the series, please submit these names to the editors. Mail comments or suggestions to:

The Editor
Contemporary Black Biography
Gale Research, Inc.
835 Penobscot Bldg.
Detroit, MI 48226-4094
Phone: (800) 347-GALE
FAX: (313) 961-6741

Photo Credits

Floyd Adams, Jr.

1945—

City official

In November of 1995, Floyd Adams, Jr. became the first African-American to be elected mayor of Savannah, Georgia (population 137,000). Despite the fact that the city's civil rights movement was extremely peaceful, and that Martin Luther King once called Savannah "the most desegregated city in the South," actual change in the city's power structure had been slow in coming. Nevertheless Adams, a Democrat, has downplayed his achievement. "During the last few weeks, I've gotten many calls from across the country," Adams said in his inaugural address, as quoted by the *Savannah Morning News.* "They all say, `Floyd, congratulations on being the first black mayor of Savannah.' I really wished they would have said, `Congratulations, Floyd, on becoming the mayor of Savannah.' My race, or gender for that matter, has no bearing on how well I can lead Savannah during the next four years."

Adams was born in Savannah on May 11, 1945, and grew up on the city's west side. That same year, his father, Floyd "Pressboy" Adams, Sr., and his mother, Wilhelmina, cofounded the *Herald,* a weekly newspaper aimed at the black community. The paper, which bills itself as "Savannah's Black Voice," had a circulation of 8,400 in 1996.

Adams grew up in a segregated Savannah, where white schools, churches, theaters, beaches, and lunch counters were off-limits to blacks. By the time he became a young man, however, things had begun to change. After earning high grades at St. Pius X, a Catholic high school, Adams applied for admission to Savannah's historically white Armstrong College. In 1964, as a freshman, Adams was one of the first black students to attend the college, where he earned a degree in business.

After graduating in 1968, Adams took the position of editor at his family's newspaper, where he became known for encouraging heated political debate and controversial commentary. In 1983, after his father died, Adams became the organization's chief officer, a position he currently holds. The paper has remained a family business, where Adams' two grown children, Kenneth and Khristi, also work. Despite the fact that Adams is increasingly in the public eye, the paper has continued to publish controversial opinions. One recent opinion piece claimed that banning felons from schools will result in a "school ghetto," while another asserted

At a Glance...

Born May 11, 1945, Savannah, GA; son of Floyd Sr. (a newspaper publisher), and Wilhelmina Adams; children: Kenneth, Khristi. *Education:* received B.A. in business from Armstrong College. *Politics:* Democrat. *Religion:* Catholic.

The Herald, Savannah, GA, editor, 1968--, publisher and president, 1983--; alderman, Savannah City Council, 1982-95; mayor of Savannah, 1995--.

Member: Finance and Inter-Government Relations Committee of National League of Cities, Private Industry Council, Georgia Black Elected Officials Association, National Black Council of Local Elected Officials, Georgia Municipal Association, Savannah's Printers Association, NAACP, Savannah Branch, Prince Hall Masons.

Addresses: *Home*—Savannah, GA. *Office*—Office of the Mayor, P.O. Box 1027, Savannah, GA 31402.

that black Republicans are "dealing a death blow" to the black community.

Ran for City Council

In 1982, Adams made his first run for the city council, as representative of the west side-downtown first district. He defeated his rival after a bitter campaign. Adams would eventually serve three terms as an alderman, for a total of 13 years' experience in City Hall. As a member of the city council--which had been integrated for less than a decade--Adams made it a point to stand up for the rights of Savannah's majority black community. In 1989, he created a seat for himself on the Savannah Arts Commission, which he claimed overlooked black artists. In 1990, he urged the city not to renew a contract with Southside Fire Department, because it allegedly employed no blacks, and lacked an affirmative action plan. In 1992, he accused then-Mayor Susan Weiner, a Republican, of fostering "regressive" policies that divided the city racially. "We are in a war between the white community and the black community," he was quoted as saying in the *Savannah Morning Press.*

Though a lifelong Democrat, Adams also became known

for crossing party lines in debates, and for endorsing Republicans for office if he felt they were the stronger candidates. He has described his political philosophy as "moderate to conservative," while stressing that this stance does not make him a rarity among black politicians. "Most people want to automatically label blacks as liberal," he told Savannah's weekly entertainment paper *Creative Loafing.* "I'm very fiscally conservative--I don't believe in free-spending. When I air my views on a conservative level, some people think I'm Republican." Nevertheless, defecting to the Republican Party is out of the question. "I'm pursuing an independent mode overall. Partisan bickering can be too divisive," he continued. In 1991, Adams was elected alderman-at-large--the first African-American to win citywide election. The following year, he became the first black Mayor Pro Tem (vice mayor).

Elected Mayor of Savannah

In 1995, Adams announced that he planned to run for mayor against Weiner and two other candidates. Weiner, a former actress and business consultant, was Savannah's first woman mayor, and many expected her to win. In the initial election, held November 4, Weiner received 39 percent of the vote, while Adams received 37 percent. However, under Georgia law a candidate must garner a majority of the vote to take office. A runoff election between Weiner and Adams was scheduled for November 28.

At the time, few thought that Adams had a chance. Weiner spent $150,000 on her campaign--three times as much as Adams--and had the support of Savannah's influential business community. According to the *Washington Post,* during her campaign Weiner "played the race card," while attacking Adams' record in negative advertisements. Adams, however, did not return in kind, instead favoring the mild slogan, "It's okay to be for Floyd."

When votes were counted on November 28, Adams had received a 50.4 percent majority, winning by an extremely narrow margin of 256 votes. At a party that evening, Adams danced to "Celebration" by Kool and the Gang, while supporters cheered. "Nobody thought I could win," Adams told the *Washington Post.* He credited his victory to the fact that he targeted black women, who ran his grass-roots campaign, increasing voter turnout among blacks by almost 25 percent. Meanwhile, Weiner contested the result of the election, alleging voter fraud. For days after, her campaign volunteers searched the voter records for irregularities, but found nothing. Adams took office on January 2,

1996.

Strives to Be "Agent of Unity"

While Adams has stated that he is proud to be Savannah's first black mayor, he has continually stressed that he wants to be an agent of unity, not division, in the city. "We always talk about two communities. I don't want two communities, I want one community," he told *Savannah Scene.* One of his first moves as mayor was to inaugurate a Human Relations Committee, modelled after a similar committee established during the turbulent 1960s. "I felt that it was time for a healing process," Adams told *Creative Loafing.* "This is an effort to undo the tensions caused by racial and economic problems, as well as the atmosphere left by the former administration." The organization will have no punitive power, Adams explained, but will be a forum where people can discuss problems.

Adams has made also it clear that it is important to remember all aspects of the city's complex history. In January of 1996, he joined in the Martin Luther King Birthday celebrations; in April, he participated in events commemorating Confederate history. Nevertheless, Adams has acknowledged that he will never be accepted into Savannah's blue-blood society. "I've never been to the Oglethorpe Club," Adams told the *Washington Post,* referring to Savannah's exclusive all-white club. "Never been inside and I'll never be invited inside. But it doesn't bother me. I could care less." As an alderman, Adams had attempted to cancel the liquor licenses of private clubs, including the Oglethorpe Club, but the measure was defeated.

> "Most people want to automatically label blacks as liberals."

Adams has received a lot of attention for his strong anti-crime stance: he supports daylight curfews to curb juvenile crime, and encourages concerned citizens to turn in known drug dealers. "I advocate an aggressive harassment policy of drug dealers on the street by intimidation," he told *Savannah Scene.* "I realize that they have civil rights too, but they give up some of that by engaging in illegal activity." In combination with these anti-crime measures, Adams advocates increased vocational training in public schools, to offer young people an alternative to crime.

Adams has often stated that one of his main goals as mayor is to make sure that everyone shares in Savannah's prosperity. "The only way that the city is going to survive is to improve our middle class," he told *Savannah Scene.* "The 'haves' are gaining on the 'have-nots' and we need to reverse that trend." He hopes to accomplish this goal by encouraging new businesses to settle in Savannah. "The type of industry we want to attract is non-polluting industry that will bring in a decent salary, so that everyone can afford a home," he told *Savannah Scene.* Import/export companies, insurance companies, and shipping rank high on Adams' list.

Long-term goals aside, the most important event in Adams' first year will doubtless be the Summer Olympics of 1996. While most of the events will be held in Atlanta, the ten Olympic yachting events will be held off the coast of Savannah from July 22 to August 1. "I see Savannah benefitting from the world-wide publicity, but we've got to be ready for it," Adams told *Savannah Scene.* Adams is looking forward to the attention that will focus on Savannah, a city he obviously loves. "I've been on many trips, visited many places," Adams told *Savannah Scene,* "but I can't wait to get back to Savannah."

Sources

Creative Loafing, March 2, 1996, p. 1.
Herald, October 18-25, 1995, p. 2; December 6-13, 1995, p. 1; March 13-20, p. 3.
Jet, January 24, 1996, p. 12.
Savannah Morning News, November 6, 1991, p. C1; November 8, 1995, p. A1; November 28, 1995, p. A1; November 29, 1995, p. A1; November 30, 1995, p. A1; December 1, 1995, p. A1; January 2, 1996, p. A1; January 3, 1996, p. A4.
Savannah Scene, Winter 1996, p. 22.
Washington Post, January 14, 1996, p. A3.

Additional information for this profile was provided by the mayor's office, Savannah, Georgia.

—Carrie Golus

Andrew C. Barrett

1942(?)—

Attorney, former federal official

Andrew C. Barrett arrived in Washington, DC in 1989 determined to be much more than a mere government bureaucrat. Appointed to the Federal Communications Commission in 1989—and confirmed for a full five-year term in 1990—Barrett proved to be an outspoken and unpredictable force on the FCC. Barrett faced daunting tasks such as policing broadcast indecency, divvying up the financial rights to television re-runs, and charting the path of the "Information Superhighway." To these tasks he added the goals of bringing more minorities and women into television and radio station ownership, and pressing the Clinton administration to make the Internet and other computer-based information systems available to minorities and the poor. His strong opinions on such matters as foul language and violence on the airwaves assured Barrett a high profile during his tenure with the FCC—and his political clout with fellow Republicans remains high even though he has returned to the private sector.

Barrett was born in Rome, Georgia but was raised in the Hyde Park section of Chicago, where his father owned a bar. Barrett grew up Catholic, and his neighborhood was racially mixed. As a youngster he considered going into the priesthood until he "found out there were girls in the world," as stated by Barrett in an *Ebony* profile.

As he came of age in Chicago, Barrett drew benefit from the liberal social programs advanced by then-president Lyndon B. Johnson. "If it weren't for the Great Society programs, I couldn't have gotten a masters (from Loyola University of Chicago) and a law degree (from De Paul University)," he told the *Chicago Tribune* many years later. His education and early work experience influenced Barrett's political views, however. He grew disenchanted with the Democratic Party and what he saw as a welfare system that encouraged second-class citizenship for the poor. Therefore, he switched to the Republican Party in 1973.

State Government Service in Illinois

Barrett began the 1970s working for nonprofit national organizations, including the National Conference of Christians and Jews (NCCJ) and the Chicago Branch of the National Association for the Advancement of Colored People (NAACP). In his spare time he turned his

At a Glance...

Born ca. 1942 in Rome, GA; son of a bar owner. *Education:* Roosevelt University, B.A.; Loyola University, M.A.; DePaul University, J.D.

Attorney. National Conference of Christians and Jews (NCCJ), associate director, 1971-75; National Association for the Advancement of Colored People (NAACP), executive director of Chicago Branch, 1975-79; Illinois Law Enforcement Commission, Chicago, director of operations, 1979-80; Illinois Department of Commerce, Chicago, assistant director, 1980-89; Illinois Commerce Commission, commissioner, 1980-89; Federal Communications Commission, Washington, DC, commissioner, 1989-95; Edelman Public Relations, Washington, DC, associate, 1996—.

Addresses: *Office*—Edelman Public Relations Worldwide, 1420 K Street N.W., 10th floor, Washington, DC 20005.

legal acumen and organizing skills to the service of James Thompson, a Republican running for governor of Illinois. When Thompson won the governorship, he did not forget the help he received from Barrett. In 1980 Thompson named Barrett to the Illinois Commerce Commission. Barrett spent the next nine years as a commissioner with this state regulatory agency, becoming an expert on the telephone industry.

The ICC post was hardly a high-profile job, but Barrett nevertheless became known to a number of prominent Republicans, among them Senator Robert Dole of Kansas. In the summer of 1989, upon Dole's recommendation, President George Bush named Barrett to a vacant position on the Federal Communications Commission, thrusting Barrett into "a potentially intoxicating spotlight," to quote James Warren in the *Chicago Tribune.*

Member of the FCC

Barrett joined the FCC at a time when changes in technology and the abilities of the media were sparking a number of important regulatory and public policy questions. Expectations were that, as a newcomer to the commission, Barrett would make few if any original

contributions—and that he would make his decisions at the behest of his Republican colleagues in the White House and the Senate. Barrett had other ideas. "I'm a black first; a Republican second or third," he explained in the *Chicago Tribune.*

The FCC felt Barrett's presence almost immediately. He took his seat in the fall of 1989, just as the commission was struggling to change the financial interest and syndication ("fin-syn") regulations pertaining to the financial control of television re-run rights. "When I came [to Washington]," Barrett told *Ebony,* "I think people thought I was just going to be a vote, so nobody ever asked me how I felt about 'fin-syn.' Since they didn't ask me how I felt, I thought I'd devise my own plan and it ultimately won."

> "The haunting fact is that those unwilling or unable to join the electronic revolution will find themselves at an economic, educational, and cultural disadvantage."

Because "fin-syn" could have meant billions of dollars of revenue to the major television networks, Barrett found himself courted by lobbyists for the networks' interests, including such prominent players as publisher Rupert Murdoch, CBS, Inc. chairman Laurence Tisch, and even his former colleague Jim Thompson. If anything, this big-time lobbying only made Barrett more determined to forge what he felt was a truly equitable conclusion to the "fin-syn" debate. His was the swing vote in favor of a proposal he helped to craft that gave the networks far less financial interest in re-runs than they felt they deserved. "I'm not from Washington," Barrett later told the *Chicago Tribune,* "... I didn't go there to be anyone's vote, and I don't want people to be able to read me."

The Challenges of a Media Age

While with the FCC, Barrett also let his views be known on other media and technological issues. His concerns about indecency in broadcasting, for instance, were tempered by the opinion that government can hardly be expected to obliterate something that the general public seems to crave. Barrett explained in the *Chicago Tribune* that he found offensive language on the airwaves "deplorable ... but it doesn't exist in a vacuum. If there wasn't a market out there for it, it wouldn't exist." Children were finding role models, he insisted, not on television but around them in their own communities—for better or worse. Nevertheless, he helped the FCC to level fines against performers and radio announcers whose broadcasts were deemed offensive and indecent.

As the third black commissioner in the history of the FCC, Barrett committed himself to finding new opportunities for minorities and women in the media and on the Information Superhighway. He voiced strong concerns that many poor people of all races would suffer in the long run because they "wouldn't be able to afford the ticket price" to admit them to the computer-based information systems. He also pushed for greater minority and female ownership of American broadcast properties, helping to establish an auction process for wireless communications services.

Throughout his tenure with the FCC, Barrett maintained strong ties to the public and to his Chicago roots. A very private individual, he chose his Washington social activities with great care, preferring to make work-related headlines. Near the end of his term with the FCC, he spoke out most forcefully on the need for government to ensure that emerging technologies would be made available to the poor as well as the wealthy. In the *Los Angeles Sentinel,* he demanded that African Americans be included in the move towards cyberspace. "This technology will be the ticket for greater knowledge and access to new forms of entertainment," Barrett said. "The haunting fact is that those unwilling or unable to join the electronic revolution will find themselves at an economic, educational, and cultural disadvantage."

Barrett's term with the FCC expired in 1995. He has since been employed at Edelman Public Relations Worldwide in Washington, DC.

Sources

Black Enterprise, February 1990, p. 32.
Chicago Tribune, April 12, 1992, p. 2; February 20, 1994, p. 3.
Ebony, October 1991, pp. 64-67; January 1995, p. 98D.
Forbes, March 4, 1991, pp. 140-41.
Jet, June 18, 1990, p. 38; November 7, 1994, pp. 24-25; April 15, 1996, p. 5.
Los Angeles Sentinel, May 24, 1995, p. C6.
Washington Afro-American, February 19, 1994, p. A1.

Additional information supplied by the Federal Communications Commission, Washington, DC.

—Anne Janette Johnson

Jennifer Beals

1963—

Actress

With her starring role in the 1983 movie *Flashdance* Jennifer Beals became a household name virtually overnight. The unknown Yale University student, a former teen model, had been cast as a young woman who dreams of becoming a dancer while stuck in the rut of her Pittsburgh steel mill job. At the time, the media made Beals the freshest new celebrity of the year, with much ink spilled over her heritage, personal life, and acting skills; many commentators heralded the newcomer as a talent to watch for the 1980s. "But oddly, Beals, who managed to inject intelligence and unself-conscious sensuality into a character who was, on paper, little more than a sentimental cliche, practically disappeared from the pop landscape," noted *Elle*'s Diane Cardwell in 1995. Post-*Flashdance*, Beals's screen appearances over the decade dwindled precipitously--until a well-timed comeback with roles in several acclaimed art-house films of the mid-1990s.

Beals was born in 1963 in Chicago to Alfred Beals, an African American who owned several grocery stores, and Jeanne Beals, an educator and Irish Catholic. Jennifer joined brother Greg, five years her senior, and

a year after her arrival came a second brother, Bobby. Their father died when Beals was only nine, and Jeanne supported the children through her job as an elementary school teacher in Chicago. They lived in a predominantly African American neighborhood on the South Side, near 82nd Street and Indiana Avenue, and Beals was often teased because of her light skin; she said later that the ribbing made her a natural loner.

Later Jeanne Beals moved the family to the north side of the city, in another racially integrated neighborhood known as Uptown. As a teacher, Beals's mother knew the deficiencies of the Chicago public school system, and obtained scholarships for her bright children to the private Francis W. Parker School, also the alma mater of Darryl Hannah. Beals excelled in the progressive school geared toward the academically gifted, but in 1979, when she was 16, Beals began modeling for local print ads after ascertaining that she could "make a lot more money for college than by baby-sitting and working at Baskin-Robbins," she recalled for *People* magazine writer Jim Jerome. Eventually she began working with famed Chicago photographer Victor Skrebneski, an early force behind Cindy Crawford's successful ca-

At a Glance...

Born c. 1963, in Chicago, IL; daughter of Alfred Beals (a supermarket chain owner) and Jeanne Cohen (an elementary school teacher); married Alexandre Rockwell (a film director), 1986. *Education:* Earned degree from Yale University, mid-1980s.

Film actress. Worked as a fashion model with photographer Victor Skrebneski in Chicago, c. 1979; first film role as lead in *Flashdance*, 1983; also appeared in *The Bride*, 1985, *Vampire's Kiss*, 1989, *In the Soup*, 1993, *Mrs. Parker and the Vicious Circle*, 1994, *Devil in a Blue Dress*, 1995, *Four Rooms*, 1996, and *Let It Be Me*, 1996.

Addresses: *Home*—New York, NY.

reer, and during her last years of high school she did summer modeling stints in New York and Paris.

From Runway to Ivy League Library

Despite her success, Beals had more exciting plans for herself than a life on the catwalk. She applied to only one college, Yale University, and didn't tell her mother about her gamble until she was accepted. Before she started her freshman year, however, Beals auditioned for a role in a movie about a blue-collar female who dreams of a career in dance. As she was getting settled during her first few days at Yale, a call arrived notifying her that she'd won the lead. Her academic career was put on hold temporarily as she took time off for the filming.

Flashdance was released in the spring of 1983 to overwhelming box-office receipts, and Beals instantly became the celebrity du jour. In the movie, set in Pittsburgh, she plays a young welder in a steel plant who gives steamy dance performances in grubby bars by night. A tryout with a real ballet company is part of the plot, as is a romance with a handsome coworker at the factory. Yet Beals, only 19 when the movie was released, quickly alienated herself from producers and the Hollywood system when she spoke up about the actual dance sequences on film. She told the media about Marine Jahan, a French dancer who was used as her dance double, but then left out of the credits. Both Beals and Jahan would shoot the same dance sequences, and the producers and directors edited the film from the two.

Beals seemed to feel bad about Jahan's lack of credit. "Marine even helped to teach me," she told Jim Jerome in *People.*

But it wasn't really Beals's dancing, or lack of it, that made *Flashdance* such a success. "Even critics who dumped on the film drooled over Jennifer," wrote Jerome in *People.* "The movie ads showed her coyly perched with a ripped sweatshirt stretched over one lusciously bare shoulder, and that one image was enough to launch a fashion revolution that sent scissors slashing sweats all over the country," the magazine noted at year's end in its recap of 1983's hottest names. "Out of the blue, everyone wanted to look like Yale sophomore Jennifer Beals."

Became Fodder for Gossip Columns

Beals had to endure more salacious publicity, however. In the film, and perhaps in light of its predominantly blue-collar setting, the actress looks a bit Italian-American. At the time, articles about Beals openly discussed her heritage, yet, as *Vibe* magazine wrote years later, "[the media] delighted in revealing that the woman occupying pop culture's collective desire was half African-American. The black press, meanwhile, seemed determined to claim the successful actress as one of their own. It was later intimated that she'd denied her heritage in order to get the *Flashdance* role, and everyone--black and white--was left wondering what her 'racial allegiances' were."

Beals was absorbed in her studies at Yale, pursuing a degree in American literature, when this intense media spotlight was focused upon her. After her sophomore year, she took off to Europe to co-star in a remake of the Bride of Frankenstein story alongside British pop star Sting. The reported $500,000 she received helped defray some of the $12,000 annual tuition at Yale, but unfortunately *The Bride* fared only moderately well at the box office and poorly with critics. Worse for her future in Hollywood, Beals was tagged as difficult to work with. Franc Roddam, director of *The Bride*, defended the young actress against these charges at the time. "She considers herself very intelligent," he asserted to *People*'s Jerome after shooting had finished. "I instructed my department heads that she doesn't want a lot of noise or to be hassled on the set. That could be considered prima donna or just a modus operandi. Warren Beatty told me, 'If she hadn't chosen to be an actress, she could be President.'" Beals described herself to Jerome as "a paradoxical blend of willful and insecure.... Some days go better than others."

Film Career Fell Flat

After graduating from Yale, Beals married Alexandre Rockwell, a film director, but had difficulty in finding roles suited for her. In 1989 she co-starred opposite Nicholas Cage in a little-seen horror comedy called *Vampire's Kiss.* She played a sneaky bloodsucker and denizen of New York's underground nightclub culture whose liaison with the nebbish Cage convinces him that he is Dracula. Yet subsequent film roles were few and far between for Beals. She appeared in the 1992 television series *2000 Malibu Road* and in a 1993 made-for-TV film called *Night Owl.* Better opportunities came with 1994's *Mrs. Parker and the Vicious Circle,* in which she had a minor role as the wife of 1920s-era literary figure Robert Benchley, and in the film *Caro Diario.*

> "I think that America is going to have to wake up and realize that the dominant face of this country is not white."

Beals's comeback began in earnest when she was cast in the title role of the 1995 film *Devil in a Blue Dress* opposite Denzel Washington. An adaptation of the acclaimed 1990 debut novel from African American writer Walter Mosley, Beals later confessed that it was a part that she had fought to win. "[I] basically yelled and screamed my way into a reading," she told *Elle*'s Cardwell. Beals portrays a femme fatale and the object of Washington's character Easy Rawlins's search through the seedier corners of Los Angeles just after World War II. Preparing for the role entailed gaining a few pounds by eating lots of heavy food to better fill the blue dress as a white woman flirting with dangers in the city's African American community. *Rolling Stone* reviewer Peter Travers praised director Carl Franklin's efforts, calling the film "whip-smart and sexy," but faulted him for his treatment of Beals. "Franklin limits her chances to cut deeper. He also limits the book's torrid sex to an occasional hot look that fails to get at Easy's need to lose himself in her pale beauty. An odd choice for a film that hinges on questions of identity."

Polished and Confident

Devil in a Blue Dress was only one of a trio of films that heralded Beals's comeback. She was also cast in the quirky ensemble comedy *Four Rooms,* a project effort that included directorial stints by Beals's husband as well as Quentin Tarantino. Scheduled for release in 1996 was another dance-oriented flick--her first since *Flashdance*--a ballroom epic titled *Let It Be Me.* "I've learned to be more careful in picking roles," she told Cardwell in the *Elle* article, "finding scripts where I really love the character but the whole piece works, too. It's not as interesting unless you can marry the two." Clearly comfortable with her mixed heritage, Beals moves easily across color lines for her roles, an attitude she wished others also shared. "I think that America is going to have to wake up and realize that the dominant face of this country is not white," Beals told *Vibe.* "It's many things.... The whole country is changing, and the whole idea of race has got to change. I don't know how, but it surely can't stay as divisive as it is."

Sources

Elle, September 1995.
Esquire, March 1995, p. 43.
Maclean's, January 2, 1995, p. 50.
People, May 16, 1983, p. 98; December 26, 1983, p. 90; September 5, 1985, p. 85.
Rolling Stone, October 5, 1995, p. 75.
Vibe, April 1995, pp. 69-70.

—Carol Brennan

Bill Bellamy

1967—

Comedian, television host

As the host of the cable television show *MTV Jams,* Bill Bellamy has had a chance to enjoy what he described in *Chicago Weekend* as his "dream job." His breezy manner and elegant good looks have helped the young comic to become a staple on the music video network. Eschewing the profanity and raunch that characterize much comedy in the hip-hop era, he has pursued a gentler approach and won a sizable audience. Bellamy's trademark catchphrase--"I'm in the hooouse!"--became increasingly difficult to ignore by the mid-1990s.

Bellamy was born in New Jersey in the late 1960s, the eldest of three children. Though he was an ardent fan of comedian-actor Bill Cosby--whose relatively wholesome material also differed from the racier content delivered by his peers--the career goals he formulated growing up had little to do with nightclubs. Besides, he had more than a little urging in an academic direction. "My mother always said, `Make sure you get your education, because they can never take that away from you,'" he informed *Jet.* "She also said, `Dream as big as you can dream.'" After attending Seton Hall prep school, he went on to major in economics at Rutgers University. He told Shonda McClain of the *Indianapolis Recorder* that he "was so into economics because I was really into the stock market and stuff." His career path seemed obvious, under the circumstances: "I figured when I graduated I was going to work on Wall Street," he recollected in the *Los Angeles Times.* "That was the picture I had. A sweet job at a good firm and work my way up."

Stand-Up Success Determined Path

It was not to be. His friends noticed that he had a flair for comedy--"they would always say, `Bill, you're so stupid, man. You are retarded'"--and an experience in front of a crowd during his junior year convinced him that he had a shot. Entering a male beauty pageant at Delta Sigma Theta Sorority, Bellamy realized he needed an act of some kind. "Everybody else was dancin' and singin' and playing instruments for the talent segment of the program," he informed the Cincinnati *Call and Post,* "and I just came out there and made people laugh and it came off."

Though his coup at the pageant boosted his confidence as a stand-up comic, Bellamy for some time sought the traditional American dream. "I wanted to get a good job, get married, have 2.5 kids and 1.5 pets," he quipped in *Essence.* He realized after graduation, however, that he wanted to pursue a career in comedy and got his parents' blessing to do so. "I had a nine to five job as a sales representative for a tobacco company," he related in a publicity biography, "but in the evenings and weekends, I was at any club that would have me, perfecting my comedy."

He kept his job but performed at night all over New Jersey and New York, entering a series of amateur stand-up competitions and winning every one. "It was very surprising," he admitted in his publicity bio. "But

At a Glance...

Born c. 1967, in Newark, NJ. *Education:* Rutgers University, B.A. in economics, 1988.

Comic performer, c. late 1980s--. Performed at comedy clubs across the United States; appeared on television programs *Showtime at the Apollo, Def Comedy Jam,* and HBO's *15th Annual Young Comedians Special,* 1992-93; played small role in film *Who's the Man?,* 1993; made host of *MTV Jams* on Music Television (MTV) network, 1994; toured as opening act for singer Janet Jackson; wrote and performed comedy special *Booty Call* for Showtime network, 1995.

Addresses: *Publicist*—Sutton-Saltzman Public Relations, 8967 Sunset Blvd., Los Angeles, CA 90069. *Office*—MTV, 1515 Broadway, New York, NY 10036.

once I started winning I realized comedy was my calling." He eventually scored $5,000 in a comedy contest at the Manhattan club Sweetwater's. This victory landed him gigs at nightspots around the country, including Catch a Rising Star and The Original Improvisation in New York, and The Comedy Store in Los Angeles.

Spot Led to Bigger Things

Then came his first major break: a spot on the television program *Showtime at the Apollo.* Part of what differentiated him from other comics was his steadfast refusal to rely on profanity. "Funny is funny," he declared to *Essence* writer Deborah Gregory. "You don't have to curse people to death to get a laugh." The influence of Cosby in particular came through in Bellamy's comedic approach. "I try to make people see the lighter side of things," he mused in the *Los Angeles Times.* "Most stuff in life is so serious. Life can be so boring, that just going to work, getting by, raising kids can be very dull. I just bring out the fun part of what people do that we don't realize."

At the same time, Bellamy has dealt with fairly serious subject matter in his routines; his goal has been to temper the content with his typically upbeat comic spin. "It's possible to make people laugh and think at the same time without being heavy-handed," he insisted in his MTV bio. Yet he dismissed the idea that his material was too painstakingly crafted. "The things I talk about in

my comedy are my experiences," Bellamy added in his publicity release. "I don't make a conscious effort to do a certain kind of comedy. I just do what I know."

Bellamy's *Showtime at the Apollo* appearance made an impression on impresarios Bernie Brillstein and Russell Simmons, who eventually managed the young performer. "When I saw Bill on the Apollo, I was overwhelmed," Brillstein recalled in Bellamy's publicity materials. "His timing was impeccable. He grabbed the audience immediately and held them throughout his set. I knew he had the potential to be the next biggest comic."

In 1992, the two comedy producers gave Bellamy a spot on *Def Comedy Jam* on the HBO cable network; this led to an appearance on *Rascal's Comedy Hour* and *The Arsenio Hall Show,* then to HBO's *15th Annual Young Comedians Special,* a high-profile showcase hosted by *Saturday Night Live* star Dana Carvey. "When I got the call, I was blown away," Bellamy declared in his publicity bio. "It was all happening very fast. I had only been in comedy for two and a half years and I would be appearing on a show that launched the careers of famous comedians. It was kind of scary." His fears evidently didn't come across, since executives from MTV were impressed enough to offer Bellamy a small role in *Who's the Man?* a feature film comedy starring Dr. Dre and Ed Lover, the hosts of *Yo! MTV Raps.*

Given "Dream Job" on MTV

The biggest plum of all came in 1994, when MTV gave Bellamy the job of hosting *MTV Jams,* a daytime R&B/ Hip-Hop video and interview show that allowed him to banter with superstars and work his considerable charm on the video network's huge viewing audience. He joked to the *Los Angeles Times* that his interview for the position wasn't very rigorous: "It was like, `He can read the teleprompter! We love him!'" It was nonetheless clear that MTV saw big things for the unfailingly likable Bellamy, who was able to loosen up certain guests in a way other veejays couldn't. "Hosting `Jams' is a dream come true," he enthused in his publicity bio. "It's a job, but it doesn't feel like work at all. I get to interview people I've always admired, from [singer-actress] Janet Jackson to [actor-comedian] Eddie Murphy to [filmmaker] John Singleton, and listen to music I love."

A particularly noteworthy moment came when megastar Jackson appeared on the show with her coterie of dancers, who "writhed around him suggestively," as *Times* writer N.F. Mendoza put it. "It just happened,"

Bellamy claimed. "The chemistry was just right." He was the first member of the media to interview Jackson after the release of her milestone album *Janet,* and even performed as her opening act. "When I opened for Janet, I thought, `Oh God, please don't let them boo me!' but they enjoyed my being there," he noted with relief to *Chicago Weekend* writer Rodney Hudson.

"Eligible Bachelor"

Indianapolis Recorder correspondent McClain described Bellamy as "tall, dark and handsome" and "one of the country's most eligible bachelors." *Times* writer Mendoza took note of the veejay's "way of looking into the camera and addressing just you," not to mention his "flirtatious manner." The young comic--unencumbered by excessive modesty--has taken compliments from interviewers about his looks in stride. "Right now there aren't a lot of men for Black women to look at and admire," he reflected with apparent seriousness in the *Indianapolis Recorder.* "[Actor] Denzel [Washington] is it. It's got to be time for the new brother. It's my time and I'm happy." Anticipating new projects, he inaugurated his own production company, Bill Bellamy Entertainment. At the same, as he explained to Hudson, he wasn't taking his newfound status for granted: "Even when the staff on the show asks me how I want things it still is a bit moving," he said, "but I thank God always. I'm Baptist, and I firmly believe to direct and preserve, you've gotta have the Christ. That's how I keep my center, just staying real!"

> "Funny is funny... You don't have to curse people to death to get a laugh."

Bellamy's clean-living rhetoric hasn't been confined to the stage; he stepped comfortably into the position of role model for young viewers, and offered himself as an alternative to the violent lifestyle often associated with black culture in the mass media. "I'm willing to accept my role in doing the best I can to help turn some of the madness around," he asserted to Hudson. "I grew up in the hood like the average person. I'm pretty regular." At the same time, he urged kids to "Be positive" and was adamant that "There's gotta be other things that typify the Black experience than guns and drugs. Romance and values are my things. I'm trying to make a positive impact on some of the things that are going on out there through comedy and other ways to get it done."

He elaborated on the romance "thing" to McClain of the *Indianapolis Recorder.* "I like independent women; a woman who is very positive and supportive," he proclaimed. "I'm very supportive also. Just an uplifting person who can help me with the situation I'm going through." Even so, he averred, his schedule precluded any all-consuming relationships for the time being. "When you're in entertainment and your career is taking off," he explained, "it's a lot of phone calls."

"Booty" and Beyond

Bellamy starred in his own comedy special, *Booty Call,* for the Showtime cable network in 1995. "It's some of the funniest material I've written," he insisted in *YSB,*" and I thought it would have people going to work Monday morning talkin' 'bout, `Did you see that Bill Bellamy? He's a trip!'" *Entertainment Weekly* reviewer Caren Weiner, however, found the "trip" to be routine; she complained that Bellamy "wavers between trying to be a junior Bill Cosby and a junior Eddie Murphy. Though he's often funny, the homages end up making his limitations that much more apparent."

Nonetheless, *Booty Call* was--according to Bellamy's publicists--Showtime's highest-rated special in two years." Its release on video and his regular presence on MTV continued to boost his profile. By early 1996, the word was out that Bellamy sought a late-night talk show. He announced plans for a variety show produced jointly by MTV and Paramount, describing it in his publicity materials as "an `Ed Sullivan' with a 90s flavor," referring to the legendary variety show host of the 1950s and 1960s. He also claimed to be "mulling over scripts" for a possible series. Whether or not Bellamy would succeed in a more open-ended format remained to be determined, but his wholesome charisma would no doubt stand him in good stead. "I see a guy who is just happy and blessed that he can do what he wants to do," he remarked about himself in the *Indianapolis Recorder.* "Bill Bellamy is just a regular brother, good-hearted. It's like, hey man, this is me. People like me the way I am."

Sources

Call and Post (Cincinnati), April 7, 1994, p. 3B.
Chicago Weekend, November 10, 1994, p. 24.
Entertainment Weekly, November 24, 1994, p. 116.
Essence, May 1994, p. 60.
Indianapolis Recorder, February 25, 1995, p. B1.
Jet, May 15, 1995, p. 36.
Los Angeles Times (*TV Times*), January 2, 1994, p. 79.

Newsweek, January 29, 1996.
YSB, January 31, 1995, p. 17.

Additional information was provided by MTV and Sutton-Saltzman publicity materials, 1995.

—Simon Glickman

Lonnie Bristow

1930—

Physician

Dr. Lonnie Bristow has long been an advocate for patients and doctors alike, and, on June 21, 1995, he prepared to use his skills and energy to lead the largest society of physicians in the United States--the 300,000-member American Medical Association (AMA). On that day, Bristow made history by becoming the first African American to hold the top position in the association's 148-year history.

Bristow's interest in medicine dates from his youth. He was born and raised in the Harlem borough of New York City, where his father was a Baptist minister and his mother a nurse at Sydenham Hospital. As a teenager Bristow regularly met his mother at the hospital emergency room to walk home with her. "One of the things that most impressed me in those visits was the realization that many cultures were represented on the staff," Bristow recalled in the *American Medical News.* "That had a powerful impact on me, seeing several races and several ethnic cultures linked by the common goal of providing compassionate care to patients. It was one of the reasons I chose the medical profession."

At age 16 Bristow enrolled at Morehouse College, a predominantly black institution in Atlanta, where, in addition to his studies, he played quarterback for the football team. Academic success eluded him, however, and he quit school after two years. Following a stint in the U.S. Navy, a more mature Bristow returned to New York City to earn his bachelor's degree from the City College in 1953. Four years later he received his medical degree from the New York University College of Medicine. He interned in a hospital in San Francisco and fulfilled his residency requirements in New York City and San Francisco hospitals. Since 1964, he has practiced medicine as an internist with a subspecialty in occupational medicine in San Pablo, California, a small city east of San Francisco.

Shortly after entering private practice, Bristow became actively involved in organized medicine. "It doesn't take you long after you get out of a medical training program to realize that taking care of people one at a time is fine, but it's nice if you can take care of a whole community and do something that affects a whole lot of people," Bristow explained to Aura Bland of *California Physician.* Over the years, Bristow has been active with a number of state and national professional organizations,

At a Glance...

Born April 6, 1930, in New York, NY; son of Lonnie Harlis (a Baptist minister) and Vivian (a nurse; maiden name, Wines) Bristow. Married Margaret Jeter, June 1, 1957 (divorced August, 1961); married Marilyn Hingslage (a nurse), October 18, 1961; children: Mary (from first marriage), Robert and Elizabeth (from second marriage). *Education:* City College of New York, B.S., 1953; New York University, M.D., 1957.

Private practice in internal medicine, San Pablo, CA, 1964--; Brookside Hosp., San Pablo, staffer; CA. Dept. of Health Care in Prisons, Sacramento, consultant, 1976-77; Advisory Committee on Sickle Cell Disease, California State Dept. of Health Services, member, 1977-79; American Medical Assn., alternate delegate, 1978, delegate, 1979, board of trustees, 1985-90, exec. committee, 1990-93, chair of board of trustees, 1993-94, pres.-elect, 1994, became pres., 1995. Graduate Med. Education State Advisory Committee for California's Office of Statewide Health Planning and Development, member, 1980-84; Physician Discussion Group on Physician Reimbursement, appointed mem., 1983-85; Executive Committee of FORUM for Med. Affairs, 1984-87, 1991-92; National Visiting Committee, City Univ. of New York Med. School, 1986--; Interagency Committee on Smoking and Health of the Centers for Disease Control, appointed member, 1987-94; Centers for Disease Control Advisory Committee on the Prevention of HIV Infection, appointed member, 1989-93; Quadrennial Advisory Council on Social Security, appointed member, 1989-93.

Awards: Award of Excellence, California Medical Action Committee, 1976; elected to the Institute of Medicine of the National Academy of Sciences, 1977; Contra Costa County Humanitarian of the Year award, Contra Costa County Board of Supervisors, 1989; California's Most Distinguished Internist Award, California Society of Internal Medicine, 1990. Received honorary doctorates from Morehouse College School of Med., 1994, Wayne State University School of Med., 1995, and the City College of New York, 1995.

Member: American Medical Assn., American College of Physicians, Natl. Medical Veterans Soc., Federated Council on Internal Medicine, Joint Commission on Accreditation of Healthcare Organizations, California Medical Assn., California Society of Internal Medicine, East Bay Society of Internal Medicine, Alameda-Contra Costa Medical Assn.

Addresses: *Home*—3324 Ptarmigan Dr., Apt. 3B, Walnut Creek, CA 94395-3157. *Office*——2023 Vale Rd., San Pablo, CA 94806-3834.

often serving in leadership roles. He has also lectured widely and published often in professional journals, including the *Internist* and the *Journal of the American Medical Association.*

Bristow's involvement with the American Medical Association has a long history. As a model team player he rose rapidly through the organization's ranks. After serving as an alternate delegate to the association in 1978, he became a full delegate the following year. In 1985, he became the first African American to serve on the board of trustees, and eight years later he became the first black chair of the board. Bristow's election to the top spot in the AMA seemed inevitable to many. Association members and nonmembers alike celebrated Bristow's election as a symbol of the AMA's new stance--a stark contrast to its hundred-year history of excluding blacks.

While pleased, Bristow did not dwell on the meaning of his election. "The significance is that it means America is moving forward," Bristow noted in the *Detroit Free Press.* "I just wish the country would reach the point where [race is] no longer important." He also remarked in *Jet,* "I think my being elected shows it is possible to accomplish things through hard work and education."

The stated goals of the AMA are to inform its members of government decisions that affect health care and to represent the membership before Congress. In addition, the organization informs the public on medical issues. However, over the decades the AMA has earned the reputation as a self-serving organization, one that protects the level of physicians' salaries rather than safeguarding the public. Bristow hoped to change this negative perception, beginning with better communication. "We need some type of two-way communication, a way for the public to tell us what it thinks about what we're doing," Bristow explained to a *Jet* reporter. "I'd like to know about the public's hopes, desires, and fears regarding health care." Bristow enthused to Adams in the *Detroit Free Press,* "I'd love to see the day come when the people of America consider the AMA as their AMA."

Bristow has been instrumental in the AMA's long-term strategic planning. He has attempted to make the organization more responsive to the needs of Americans. As the board of trustees chair in 1993 and 1994, he worked to reform Medicare by promoting the AMA's health agenda: universal coverage, greater physician involvement, and antitrust relief. Bristow is concerned about the role of business in health care. "We now have health care being controlled by MBAs [persons with a master's degree in business administration] rather than by physicians committed to the Hippocratic oath [a pledge to a code of ethics taken by those about to begin medical practice]," Bristow told *Los Angeles Times* reporter Bettijane Levine. "And once health care becomes corporatized, and it has, and once it goes on the open stock market, then its major commitment is to Wall Street and the stockholders to maximize profits, rather than to give the best possible patient care." Bristow added, "Business principles are introduced that unfortunately put patient care second to corporate profits."

> "It has been very rewarding to be a part of organized medicine."

Hoping to rally physicians to the AMA, whose membership fell to 40 percent of doctors from 70 percent in the 1970s, in 1994 Bristow criss-crossed the country, giving speeches on a variety of medical issues. Another long-term goal of the AMA under Bristow has been to promote high ethical standards. Bristow told McCormick of the need for such standards, "At least one-fourth of U.S. medical schools have no formal courses in medical ethics…. No wonder so many physicians are having a hard time deciding what is right and what is wrong." Bristow hoped to make an impact by promoting the AMA Code of Professional Ethics, requiring ethics courses at medical schools and including ethics questions on licensing exams.

When Bristow became more involved in policy making and reform, he cut back his office hours to one day per week. "It has been very rewarding to be a part of organized medicine," Bristow told Bland. "You have the opportunity to promote your ideas and concepts and see if your peers accept them. When they become a policy of the organization and ultimately of the profession, it's very exciting."

Sources

American Medical News, June 5, 1995, p. 7.
Black Enterprise, October 1994, p. 18.
Boston Globe, June 13, 1994, p. 7.
California Physician, July 1994, pp. 22-25.
Chicago Defender, June 22, 1995, p. 1.
Detroit Free Press, June 19, 1995, p. 5A.
Jet, June 27, 1994, p. 5; July 10, 1995, pp. 38-40; August 21, 1995, p. 24.
Journal of the American Medical Association, January 13, 1989, pp. 284-285.
Los Angeles Times, July 18, 1995, pp. E1, E6.
New York Times, June 22, 1995, p. A12.
USA Today, June 13, 1994, p. A8; June 21, 1995, p. D3.
Washington Times, June 13, 1994, p. A7.

—Jeanne M. Lesinski

Marie Dutton Brown

1940—

Literary agent

Marie Dutton Brown's career in publishing has taken many turns. She began as a bookstore buyer and worked a long stint as an editor at a prestigious publishing house. These experiences helped inspire Brown to found her own literary agency in 1984, at its onset a shoestring operation out of her apartment. A decade later Marie Brown Associates boasts a staffed Greenwich Village office, and its namesake is one of only five African American literary agents in the country. The success of her business--the agency's client list has grown to over a hundred authors--reflects both her vision and drive as well as the corporate publishing world's belated realization that African Americans represent a huge book-buying market. Increasingly literate, increasing affluent, increasingly eager to read material that speaks to them in their own voice, African American readers are finding bookshelves loaded with a variety of new titles, many of which Brown helped pilot to success.

Brown was born Marie Dutton in 1940 in Philadelphia. The first of three children of a civil engineer father and a mother who was a high school English teacher, Brown came of age on college campuses in Virginia and Tennessee, where her father taught engineering. She often spent hours in the campus library. She inherited her love of books, along with a no-nonsense attitude, from her parents. Both had worked menial jobs to put themselves through college in leaner times, and, as Brown told Lisa Genasci of the *San Francisco Examiner,* "I knew something about standards, about hard work, and I knew I'd better not mess up."

The early 1960s found Brown enrolled at Penn State University, where she was part of the 1 percent of the student body's African American population. After earning a degree in psychology in 1962, she became a social studies teacher in the Philadelphia public school system, and two years later was promoted to coordinator of intergroup education, an office that was an early attempt to diversify the public school curriculum. When a publishing associate from New York visited Brown's office to sell some of her company's titles to the department, she told Brown to give her a call when she next came to New York. She did, and when they met for lunch the editor had brought along some of her colleagues from Doubleday--the lunch date had been set up as a job interview. Brown was hired at the publishing house as a trainee at a time when such companies were trying to

At a Glance...

Born Marie Elizabeth Dutton, 1940, in Philadelphia, PA; daughter of a civil engineer and a high school English teacher; married Kenneth Brown, c. 1969; children: Laini. *Education:* Penn State University, B.A., 1962.

Philadelphia (PA) public school system, high school teacher, 1962-65, coordinator of intergroup education, 1965-67; Doubleday & Co., New York City, publishing trainee and editorial assistant, 1967-69; freelance editorial consultant, Los Angeles, CA, and Washington, DC, c. 1969-70; Bronze Books, Los Angeles, manager, 1970-71; returned to Doubleday & Co. as an associate editor, 1972, became editor, 1974, became senior editor, 1978; founding editor, Elan magazine, New York City, 1981-82; Endicott Books, New York City, began as bookseller, became assistant buyer and assistant manager, 1982-84; Marie Brown Associates, New York City, founder and owner, 1984--. Consultant to the literary journal *American Rag,* the Louis Michaux Book Fair, and Howard University's Book Publishing Institute. Board member, Poets and Writers Inc., Coordinating Council of Literary Magazines & Presses, Studio Museum of Harlem, Frederick Douglass Creative Arts Center, The Friendly Place, and The Writer's Room.

Addresses: *Home*—New York City. *Office*—Marie Brown Associates, 625 Broadway, New York, NY 10012.

diversity their workforce.

Moved to the West Coast

Brown stayed at Doubleday for two years, then married Kenneth Brown and moved with him to Los Angeles when he began art school there. She found it hard to find a similar job in publishing in California, and so worked as a freelance editorial consultant and manager of a bookstore featuring third-world and ethnic American titles, which she happened upon one day on the way to the supermarket. She also gave birth to a daughter, Laini. In 1972 Brown returned to New York City and was rehired by Doubleday as an associate editor. Her

rise through the ranks during the rest of the decade coincided with a reawakening of interest in African American literary titles, spurred on by the civil rights and black identity movements of the 1960s and a continuation of the Harlem Renaissance literary tradition dating back to the 1920s. With the success of bestsellers like Alex Haley's *Roots,* publishing houses were eager to find and shepherd through the publication process works of both fiction and nonfiction geared toward African Americans. Brown was at the forefront of this trend at Doubleday and brought many titles into print, including Vertamae Smart Grosvenor's *Vibration Cooking* and Mari Evans's *Black Women Writers.*

Yet things had not changed that drastically in the tradition-bound halls of publishing, Brown recalled in the interview with the *San Francisco Examiner*'s Genasci. "It was difficult to try to bring into the mainstream thinking things that were part of the ongoing existence of African American people." Indeed, the "fad" seemed to be on the wane by the late 1970s, when publishing houses like Doubleday began losing interest in issuing such a diverse roster of titles. Additionally, this time also coincided with a cutback in public spending that had originally financed the large-scale purchase of such books for schools and libraries. Brown received direct orders to diversify her list of authors and titles, but did manage to champion the publication of one or two pet projects, such as Carolyn Rodgers's acclaimed *How I Got Ovah.* In 1980 she quit Doubleday to become founding editor of *Elan* magazine, an upscale, glossy magazine that focused on the cultural life of the international black community. After over a year in the job and seeing three issues launched, Brown was left jobless when *Elan*'s financial backers pulled out. She took a job in a bookstore on Manhattan's West Side, a job she has said gave her an important retail perspective of the publishing industry. Soon she had advanced to assistant buyer and assistant manager at the store, but left at the urging of a friend in mid-1984 to begin her own company.

Launched Own Venture

Marie Brown Associates opened its doors for business in the fall of 1984, but its doors were also Brown's Harlem apartment. The fledgling literary agency had some initial strokes of luck, including the signing of J. Randy Taraborelli, the biographer of Diana Ross and later Michael Jackson, onto its roster, yet times remained lean for several years. In 1987, Brown told *Essence* magazine's Judy Simmons about her worklife: "I am the company, the secretary, the copy center, the mail room. I go to the post office and the bank, do the typing." The long hours paid off, however, and by 1995 Brown was still working weekends, but this time at her offices in Greenwich Village. Her list of writers had grown to include several old friends and some new ones as well. Ed Bradley, the CBS news program *Sixty Minutes* correspondent whom she had known when they were both teachers in Philadelphia, was heeding Brown's directive to complete his autobiography. Vertamae Grosvenor was also part of the literary agency's talent roster, as were Alexis Deveaux and Eloise Greenfield, both friends from Brown's Doubleday years. New clients included mystery writer Barbara Neely, Spelman College president Johnnetta Cole, and acclaimed children's author Faith Ringgold.

Success Dovetailed With New Era

Brown's success in a field that is traditionally white--and long known for its Ivy-League-educated, East-Coast-bred air--is a testament to her years of hard work and determination, but in more recent times she has also been encouraged by the rise of a number of prominent African American authors. Alice Walker, Toni Morrison, and Gloria Naylor--all of whom achieved bestseller success in the late 1980s--helped pave the way for a second generation of African American writers in the 1990s. The popularity of novelists like Terry McMillan, Walter Mosley, and Bebe Moore Campbell seemed to be a sign that the long-locked corporate gate to publishing was now opening. The critical and financial success awarded these authors "delivers the same message to publishers: The African-American community can no longer be overlooked; in fact, it is one of the fastest growing segments of the book-buying market," as Carolyn M. Brown put it in *Black Enterprise.* When the larger publishing houses began courting African American writers, Brown's agency was at the forefront. Her established stable of writers and contacts within the African American literary world ushered in a new era of success and acclaim for both author and agent.

> "I knew something about standards, about hard work, and I knew I'd better not mess up."

Despite working seven days a week and rising at five a.m. every day in order to maintain control of her growing business, Brown still finds the time to contribute her talents to the community. She serves on numerous boards and is a consultant literary magazines as well as Howard University's Book Publishing Institute. Such outreach efforts win Brown the praise of her contemporaries. She sits on the board of the Studio Museum of Harlem, and its director Kinshasha Holman Conwill told the *Examiner's* Genasci that the literary agent "defines commitment. She is enormously gifted and creative, but she does what she does not only because she has the expertise but because she loves and believes in what she is doing." Journalist Ed Bradley also spoke glowingly of Brown's achievements, telling Genasci that "she is determined and hardworking, someone who every day is pushing a boulder uphill and never stops. She is bucking a tide."

Sources

Black Enterprise, February 28, 1995, p. 108.
Essence, May 1987, p. 135.
San Francisco Examiner, August 13, 1995, p. B3.

Additional information for this profile was provided by Marie Brown Associates publicity materials, 1996.

—Carol Brennan

Zora Kramer Brown

1949—

Cancer awareness activist

In the 15 years following her mastectomy Zora Brown has accomplished a great deal. She began by speaking at her own and other local churches about her own family's experience. Then, gathering momentum, she started keeping track of the latest advances in cancer research, and was appalled to learn from the National Cancer Institute that mortality rates for black victims had risen 13 percent since 1974, while white women under the age of 50 had seen an 11 percent decline. These alarming figures galvanized her into setting up the Washington, D.C.-based Breast Cancer Resource Committee, a dedicated organization which vows to lower the African American mortality rate by 50 percent the end of the century.

Zora Kramer Brown was three years old when her parents were divorced. The youngest of eight children, she suffered little deprivation as a result of the breakup. "I was spoiled rotten," was the memory those years left behind. Her mother, on the other hand, had to shoulder the hefty challenge of bringing up eight children on her own. But Helen Brown never bemoaned her fate. Instead, she found it more productive to develop a philosophy that would help her family to cope. "If you

see a problem and don't seek a solution, you have no right to complain," was the principle by which she lived.

A Family Tendency Towards Breast Cancer

Helen Brown's creed proved to be a literal lifesaver when the family's genetic tendency towards breast cancer revealed itself. Though mastectomies became a depressing routine after biopsies uncovered malignancies in Zora's grandmother, her mother, then sister after sister, the ingrained habit of dealing promptly with problems sent each patient to a gynecologist as soon as she felt a telltale lump. In most cases, this swift response was rewarded. Zora's grandmother lived to be 94 years old, as of 1996 her mother was 81, and two of her three sisters managed to recover from cancer. Only her late sister Belva "was not fortunate," as Zora puts it, having lost her 12-year battle in 1990.

Mindful of her family's dismal health record, Zora learned early to keep a vigilant eye on her own body. She checked for changes often, examined her breasts regularly, and stuck resolutely to a macrobiotic diet.

At a Glance...

Born March 20, 1949, in Holdenville, OK; daughter of Willie and Helen Brown. *Education:* Oklahoma State University, B.S., 1969.

Career: Secretary, Pharmaceutical Manufacturers' Association, 1969-70; secretary, Ford Motor Company, 1970-76; administrative assistant, The White House, 1976-77; staff assistant to U.S. House Majority Leader, U.S. House of Representatives, 1977; assistant director for public affairs, Federal Communications Commission, 1977-86; public affairs director, Broadcast Capital Fund, 1989-91; chairperson, Breast Cancer Resource Committee, 1989--. Member of National Cancer Advisory Board, 1991-98, President's Cancer Panel, Special Commission on Breast Cancer, 1992-94, District of Columbia Cancer Consortium, 1989--; board member of Breast Institute, Philadelphia, PA, 1992.

Awards: Marilyn Trish Robinson Community Service Award, Washington Association of Black Journalists, 1992; Community Service Award, Susan G. Komen Foundation, 1992; Cancer Control Service Award, National Cancer Institute, 1991; Breast Awareness Award, National Women's Health Resource Center, 1992; Gretchen Post Award, 1993; Citation, U.S. Senate, November, 1995.

Then, reasoning that there was little more she could do to control the future, she tried not to let her fear of contracting cancer stand in the way of normal life.

Yesterday and Today: Career Moves and Cancer

She graduated from Oklahoma State in 1969 with a bachelor's degree in business administration, then obtained a job as a secretary at the Pharmaceutical Manufacturers' Association. Next came a switch to the Ford Motor Company, where a six-year stint in the lobbying office taught her a great deal about the art of public communication.

In early 1976 Brown took an administrative assistant's post at the White House. The office to which she was assigned was concerned with women's programs, at a time of frantic nationwide efforts to find the necessary 38-state ratification for the Equal Rights Amendment (ERA) before its 1978 deadline. Brown's lobbying experience plus various assorted Washington internships had given her valuable knowledge of Capitol Hill bureaucracy, so she was unfazed by the prospect of working with the numerous women's groups invited to participate by First Lady Betty Ford, a staunch ERA supporter. The ERA deadline was ultimately extended to 1982, long after the Carters succeeded the Fords in the White House. Nevertheless, though the working relationship between Betty Ford and Zora Brown was ostensibly over, the acquaintance left an important connection between the two women.

The unlikely tie was too close a knowledge of breast cancer. But while Betty Ford's diagnosis of malignancy had ended with a mastectomy in 1974, Brown's own moment of truth did not arrive until 1981, when she had been married exactly one year. The long-dreaded symptom, a hard lump, was discovered during a breast self-examination. "It was no bigger than this," she told the *Washington Post* in 1990, picking up a crumb from the table during a lunchtime interview.

At the time she became ill, Brown was serving as Director for Minority Enterprise at the Federal Communications Commission, where her specific goal was stimulating minority interest in owning and operating television stations. Sensibly, she rearranged her priorities and entered the hospital for surgery as soon as the doctor confirmed the diagnosis. "My entire breast was removed in a modified radical mastectomy, and I didn't bother with reconstructive surgery," she said later. "Prosthesis products are widely available in terms of being able to dress fashionably. I have one for swimming, one for strapless dresses, and regular bras for other wear." Grateful to be alive, she soon went back to work, writing training programs for prospective television-station owners, giving speeches about ownership, and listing available financial opportunities and how to find them.

An Urgent Purpose

Brown's experience with cancer had given her life an urgent demand that she try to prevent the same kind of suffering in other black women. Reaching out, she began to speak in local churches in the District of Columbia area. She had a very specific agenda: to attack the long-held false notions of breast cancer as a "white women's problem;" to educate her audiences about the need for the regular medical care that might detect malignancies before they spread to other organs; and most of all, to serve as living proof that a diagnosis of breast cancer need not be an automatic death sentence.

The tragic exception was her own sister, Belva Brissett. A community activist herself, Belva helped to spread the word, though she had been stricken with breast cancer herself. In 1989 the disease began to spread. Zora drove her sister to doctors' appointments, sat with her in the hospital, read the newspaper to her, and supported her when she wearily remarked that the process of getting well was more daunting than the cancer. In her case, this proved to be correct—in 1990 the cancer won.

> "I'm always more comfortable with African-American women. I'm more relaxed … more forthright. We're on the same wavelength."

Today, Belva Brissett is remembered by two important things. One is the diary of her last months, which is in the possession of her family; the other is the Belva Brissett Advocacy Center within the Greater Southeast Healthcare System, which serves the District of Columbia and its surroundings. The center itself targets supermarkets, beauty shops, churches, and businesses in the inner-city area, with the express mission of educating women about breast cancer and encouraging them to treat regular screening as a top priority. Advocates are volunteers, who are trained by physicians, social workers, and other professional personnel working within the Southeast Healthcare system.

The Breast Cancer Resource Committee

The Belva Brissett Center is an offshoot of the Breast Cancer Resource Committee (BCRC), an organization formed in 1989 by Zora Brown herself. The central core of her life's mission, BCRC came about shortly after a summit meeting on mammography on Capitol Hill, at which Brown was shocked to see an attendance of black women so small that she was able to invite them all out to lunch after the conference ended.

The BCRC maintained Zora Brown's original mission: to achieve a 50 percent drop in Afro-American breast cancer deaths by the end of the century. Their chief weapon was education, with two main themes: that breast cancer does not choose its victims by race, and

that regular mammograms are the best path to both prevention and early detection. Their third main objective was to offer support to those who had already been stricken.

Once organized, BCRC got off to a brisk start. An initial error was asking Marilyn Quayle, wife of former Vice-President Dan Quayle and daughter of an unlucky breast cancer victim, to speak alongside Zora Brown at churches with African American congregations. Quayle gladly co-operated. But the turnout was invariably disappointing, because the inner-city black women Brown was trying to reach often felt more comfortable with women of their own race. Brown understood their feelings. "I'm always more comfortable with African American women. I'm more relaxed … more forthright. We're on the same wavelength." Secure in the knowledge that she had a cause that no educated person could turn down, Zora Brown did not let this initial failure deflect her from her purpose. She simply looked for another gateway through which she could reach her target audience.

Once a Year For a Lifetime

The Revlon Company is a concern that has always found loyal support in the African American community. Convinced that their support would give her cause exposure, Brown contacted their foundation for funding to make a movie explaining the benefits of regular mammography. Then, with the help of Lilly Tartikoff, wife of the NBC President, she contacted Phylicia Rashad, a familiar face to fans of the *Cosby Show,* and Jane Pauley, a highly-respected television news anchorwoman.

On November 16, 1990 the documentary movie *Once a Year … For a Lifetime* made its television debut, and was immediately followed by the simultaneous appearance of the National Cancer Institute's hotline number, together with an invitation to viewers to call with questions. The film carried a powerful message, made poignant by the use of Belva Brissett's diaries, which had been carefully incorporated by the scriptwriter.

By 1991 Brown's prominence as a personal health ambassador to Washington D.C.'s inner-city African American women was firmly established. Modestly she disclaimed any suggestion that this was due to her own determination to improve the security of their lives. "It has to do with the comfort level of me as a black woman," she observed. "They identify with me more."

This realistic, matter-of-fact statement found willing agreement on Capitol Hill. That year she was appointed by President Bush to the National Cancer Advisory Board of the National Cancer Institute, which helps to steer the institution's policy. The new appointment brought another benefit—a Congressional appropriation of $500,000 for breast and cervical screening for low-income, uninsured inner-city women.

Creating Public Awareness

Still, Brown was not satisfied. Anxious to reach black women nationwide, she invited 350 representatives from organizations such as the National Council of Negro Women to come to Washington for education and training on how to create public awareness campaigns. Then, she encouraged them to return to their own organizations and make even greater numbers of advocates from their own membership.

In 1992 she organized the Cancer Awareness Program Services (CAPS), to institute comprehensive educational and prevention programs focusing on cancers affecting women. The "coordinating" wing of the Breast Cancer Research Committee, CAPS compiles resources containing information about services available from federal, local and state agencies, and the medical and research communities, as well as makes it available to the public through the media and through public service messages.

By now, though all her efforts were beginning to take root, there was still one aspect of awareness that had yet to be covered. The Breast Cancer Research Committee was receiving constant requests for counseling sessions targeting only breast cancer victims. Initially reluctant ("there were so many other support organizations," she said), in 1993 Brown heeded the call for an all-black group by establishing Rise-Sister-Rise, a free Saturday morning gathering.

Rise-Sister-Rise

Like most other programs Brown initiated, Rise-Sister-Rise is meticulously organized. There is open enrollment, but participants are expected to attend eight sessions. Audiences listen to talks by nutritionists, psy-

chologists, and medical personnel, all of whom gear their lectures to problem-solving as well as discussion of the actual illness itself. In order to emphasize the Afrocentrist culture, the approach is very spiritual. "Even those of us who don't go to church have the same understanding of Biblical references, the same traditions, the same problems with our hair.... We speak a universal language," Brown explained.

Recognition for Brown's great efforts has been generous. In 1994 she had the satisfaction of seeing "Minority Breast Cancer Day" proclaimed by Washington, D.C. Mayor Sharon Pratt Kelly, and of watching 400 women gather there in support of mammograms, further research, and regular medical care. The meeting was a triumphant watershed, and a welcome contrast to the 1989 Capitol Hill summit that had sparked the whole effort.

The following year she was honored by Senator Fred Hollings of South Carolina, who invited her to become a board member of the Hollings Cancer Center at the Medical University of South Carolina; she also appeared in a *Washington Post* feature called "Portraits of the City," which lauded her for her work and for her goal—reducing cancer in African American women by 50 percent by the year 2000--now less than a decade in the future.

Sources

Books

Ford, Betty, with Chris Chase, *The Times of My Life*, Harper & Row, 1978.

Periodicals

Congressional Record, Volume 141, number 171, November 1, 1995.
Emerge, October 1992, p. 40.
National Cancer Institute, "Breast Cancer Deaths Decline Nearly 5 Percent," January 11, 1995.
U.S. Department of Health and Human Services, "Discovery of Breast Cancer Gene," September 14, 1994.
Washington Post, October 27, 1995, p. A28.

—Gillian Wolf

Eugene Bullard

1894–1961

Combat pilot

Though many think of the famed Tuskegee Airmen of World War II as the first African American combat fighters, they were simply the first to serve in the United States military. Eugene Bullard, a Georgia-born bon vivant who spent much of his life in France, was the first African American to fly a fighter plane--though World War I-era prejudices dictated that his missions be flown for France. Remembered as the "black swallow of death" for his in-air bravery, Bullard earned several decorations from the French government for his service and stayed on in Paris after World War I, even working for the French Resistance during World War II. Bullard eventually returned to the United States and lived a more sedate existence--for a time he even worked as an elevator operator in New York City.

Bullard was born in the heart of the South in 1894. His hometown of Columbus, Georgia, was typical of the geographic region in its extreme racial tensions. As a boy Bullard was witness to lynch mobs and other signs of Ku Klux Klan violence; his brother Hector was murdered by one such gang. Sometimes the family, like others in the community, was forced to hide from bands of marauding whites, and during those sleepless nights Bullard's father would regale the children with stories about their Martinique ancestry. On this French-held island in the Caribbean, the elder Bullard said, harmony between whites and blacks prevailed, as it did in France; all men were considered equal. Such talk inspired eight-year-old Bullard to leave home and sell his goat for

$1.50, assuming that with the proceeds he could make his way to France. Instead he joined a troupe of English Gypsies that traveled through the South, from whom he learned much about horses; he eventually found work as a jockey.

Europe-Bound Stowaway

During his teens Bullard hopped on a freight car to Newport News, Virginia, and from there stowed away on a German cargo ship bound for Scotland. When he was discovered, the captain first threatened to toss him overboard, but instead allowed him to work in the ship's coal furnaces. In Scotland and later in England, Bullard earned a living through a variety of colorful jobs, such as running errands for bookies and acting as a lookout for illegal gambling operations. As he grew into an adult, he became a boxer for a time, but found the compensation not worth the aggravation. One day a musical troupe called "Freedman's Pickaninnies" invited Bullard to accompany them to Paris, and he accepted, finally setting foot on the soil of a country whose principles had inspired him to look elsewhere for freedom from such an early age.

In 1914 longstanding tensions between neighbors Germany and France erupted in a war that would become World War I. Bullard enlisted in the French Foreign Legion, a legendary refuge of some of the world's most

At a Glance...

Full name, Eugene Jacques Bullard; born October 9, 1894, in Columbus, GA; died, 1961, in New York, NY; married Marcelle Straumann, c. 1920s; children: Jacqueline Hernandez, Lolita Robinson.

Worked odd jobs in England and France prior to World War I; enlisted in the French Foreign Legion, 1914; served in the French Army during World War I; wounded at the Battle of Verdun, 1916, and given a medical discharge; enlisted in the French Air Service and flew several missions, 1917; became jazz drummer and nightclub owner, Paris, France, 1920s; fought in French Army at the onset of World War II and later worked in the French Resistance; returned to United States and became perfume sales person in New York City, mid-1940s; RCA Building, New York City, elevator operator, early 1950s.

Awards: Received numerous military honors from the French government for his service during World War I, including the Legion of Honor, Croix de Guerre, and the Medaille Militaire; decorated for work in the French Resistance during World War II; honored posthumously by the Smithsonian Institution's National Air and Space Museum, 1994.

daring mercenary soldiers--as well as scoundrels on the lam. He was eventually transferred into the regular French Army, where he fought on the notoriously bloody battlefield of Verdun. He sustained injuries twice, but twice returned to the field. Finally French military authorities gave him a medical discharge because of his injured leg. Sitting in a Paris cafe on the Boulevard Saint Michel one day with a group that included another opinionated American, Bullard bragged that he could fly a fighter plane even with his bad leg. The American bet him a large sum of money that he couldn't, but Bullard pulled a few strings from among his friends who were now high-ranking French military officials. He enrolled in flight training school, and, upon earning his pilot's license, returned to the cafe and collected on the wager.

Accompanied by Pet Monkey

Combat aviation was a reckless pursuit in those years. The airplane itself was less than two decades old, and

pilots strapped themselves into open cockpits of tiny planes that were loaded with artillery guns; Bullard's Spad biplane was enhanced by the presence of Jimmy, a monkey he had bought in Paris. The commander of his flying regiment, the Lafayette Escadrille, often chastised him for flying behind enemy lines or making too-daring sorties in his attempts to shoot down German planes, and from this daredeviltry Bullard earned the nickname "the black swallow of death." It is known that the pilot chalked up one kill to his outstanding record of military service, downing a German plane known as a Fokker Dreidecker. There were other American pilots in the Lafayette Escadrille fighting on the side of France; when the United States formally entered the war against Germany, the Yankees applied for transfers, and all but Bullard's application were accepted.

> Probably the most unsung hero in the history of U.S. wartime aviation.

The American forces also put an end to what was surely an embarrassment--an African American flying a plane for France, while back home racial prejudices held that blacks were not intelligent enough for such endeavors. The Americans pressured Bullard's French superiors into ruling his injured leg a liability, and Bullard was grounded permanently. After the war, Bullard convinced a fellow African American to teach him how to play drums, and with his new profession became a fixture in the jazz nightclub circuit in Paris during the 1920s. He eventually owned two nightclubs as well as a gymnasium and married a French woman, but with the renewal of French-German tension in the 1930s things began to go awry for Bullard. His wife wished to relocate to the countryside, but he refused to leave Paris. She died unexpectedly, leaving him to raise their two daughters. When Nazi Germany invaded France, he became a part of the Resistance movement, an underground network that worked to undermine and sabotage both Nazi rule and French collaboration. He often eavesdropped on conversations between German military officers in both his bar and the gym--the prejudiced Germans seemed unaware that an African American could understand their language.

Cycled Across Europe

Eventually Bullard decided that he should return to America, and rode a bike to Portugal, where a Red

Cross ship was allowing evacuees. His daughters eventually joined him, and for a time he worked as a perfume salesperson in New York City. After the war he returned to France, and attempted to recover his nightclub that had been expropriated during the chaos of the war. He received a small settlement, and in New York City worked for a time as an elevator operator at the RCA Building. In 1954 the fledgling NBC *Today* show discovered Bullard and his colorful past, and featured him in an interview segment. He died in Harlem in 1961, forgotten as the only African American to pilot a plane during World War I. In 1994 the Smithsonian Institution's National Air and Space Museum honored Bullard, whom the *Chicago Tribune* called "probably the most unsung hero in the history of U.S. wartime aviation." The chair of the aviation museum, Dom Pisano, compared Bullard's achievements to that of the Tuskegee Airmen of the second World War, a unit created only when the War Department was threatened with a bias lawsuit. The Tuskegee unit "broke the color barrier and proved to everyone that [blacks] were the equal of white pilots," Pisano noted. "It was rough, but Eugene Bullard was the precursor of all of them. He must have been quite a man."

Sources

Books

Sammons, Vivian Ovelton, *Blacks in Science and Medicine,* Hemisphere Publishing, 1990, p. 41.

Periodicals

Chicago Tribune, October 11, 1992, sec. 1, p. 30.
Ebony, December 1967, p. 120.
Los Angeles Sentinel, December 7, 1994, p. A1.

—Carol Brennan

Leonard S. Coleman, Jr.

1949—

Sports administrator

When he assumed the presidency of baseball's National League in 1994, Leonard S. Coleman Jr. became the highest-ranking African American executive in professional sports. A native of New Jersey and a lifelong baseball fan, Coleman faces the task of restoring baseball's public image in the wake of a lengthy players' strike. He must also be the final arbiter in on-field disputes, whether they concern rival players, players and umpires, or managers. Coleman is deeply concerned that professional baseball has alienated its fans, who perceive both its owners and its players as greedy and concerned only with their own gains. As president of the National League, he plans to do what he can to restore the old-time feeling of baseball as a source of national pride and local identity. "We have to create a greater focus on the game for the fans so they can enjoy the game and not have to hear as much rhetoric about the business aspects of baseball," he told *Ebony* magazine. "We have to understand that the business of our game *is* the fans." One of those fans is Coleman himself. "The first thing I can ever remember loving is baseball," he noted in the *New York Times.* "There aren't too many people who get an opportunity to make their living at the first thing they ever loved."

Baseball and Politics

Coleman was born in Newark, but he grew up in Montclair, New Jersey, a village not far from New York City. He lived in a two-family home which his parents shared with an uncle, and everyone seemed to root for a different baseball team. Coleman and his mother liked the Brooklyn Dodgers. Coleman's father preferred the New York Giants. To make life interesting, the uncle cheered for the Yankees. "Everything in our house was politics and baseball," the league president recalled in the *New York Times.* "That's all we talked about."

At Montclair High School Coleman played baseball and football, becoming best known for his football skills. He was named All-State and All-American at halfback during his senior year, an accomplishment that he still points to with pride. "I was part of an all-state backfield with Joe Theismann, Franco Harris and Jack Tatum," he remembered in *Sports Illustrated.* "I'm the only one without a Super Bowl ring."

Coleman continued playing baseball and football as an

At a Glance...

Born February 17, 1949, in Newark, NJ; married, wife's name Gabriella Morris (an attorney); children: Leonard III, Christiana. *Education:* Princeton University, B.S., 1971; John F. Kennedy School of Government, Harvard University, M.P.A., 1975; Harvard Graduate School of Education, M.S., 1976.

Missionary in Africa for Protestant Episcopal Church, 1976-80; president, Greater Newark Urban Coalition, 1980-82; commissioner of New Jersey Department of Energy, 1982-86, and New Jersey Department of Community Affairs, 1986-88; municipal finance banker with Kidder, Peabody & Co., New York City, 1988-91; executive director of market development for Major League Baseball, 1991-94; president of National League, 1994--. Has served on numerous boards and commissions, including Martin Luther King Jr. Center for Nonviolent Social Change, Metropolitan Opera, Waterloo Foundation, and Reviving Baseball in the Inner Cities (R.B.I.).

Addresses: *Office*—National League, 350 Park Ave., New York, NY 10022-6022.

undergraduate at Princeton University, becoming the first black player ever to score a touchdown for that prestigious Ivy-League school. Still he felt that he was not being given enough opportunity to prove himself with the team--and he thought his race was the reason. As a sophomore, he joined two other black players in a protest, charging the Princeton football program with violations of the university's policy of equal opportunity for minorities. When the complaints drew national attention, Coleman and his two friends were dismissed from the team, but a panel charged with investigating the incident urged greater sensitivity toward minority students in the athletic program. Coleman told the *New York Times* that the experience "changed my life in many ways," especially helping him to develop a keen social consciousness.

After earning his bachelor's degree from Princeton in 1971 Coleman moved on to Harvard University, where he pursued dual master's degrees in public administration and education. With such stellar academic credentials he might have entered the work force on the fast track, but instead, in 1976, he accepted a position as

a missionary to Africa for the Protestant Episcopal Church. There he put his education and expertise to work as a consultant on health care, education, and community services. All told he spent four years in Africa, serving in 17 different countries and cultivating a close friendship with South African Archbishop Desmond Tutu. "I matured while I was overseas, and I found out about the warmth and affection of the people," Coleman recalled in *Ebony*. "Everywhere I went, there was a new and exciting experience."

Politics and Baseball

Returning to America in 1980, Coleman began to consider a career in politics. He first served as president of the Greater Newark Urban Coalition, an organization that sought to create liaisons between businesses, community groups, and government. In 1982 he was appointed commissioner of the New Jersey Department of Energy. There he became an important member of the administration of Republican New Jersey governor Thomas H. Kean. During this period he also married Gabriella Morris, an attorney.

Leonard Coleman was hardly the stereotypical public servant, however. Midway through his four-year appointment to New Jersey's Energy Department, at age 35, he worked his way into the Metropolitan Baseball League, a semi-pro affiliation catering to college players and other young pro baseball hopefuls. His late fling with baseball was the source of much joking in the governor's cabinet, but on the field Coleman was a serious competitor. Over two years of play, he compiled a .337 career batting average. He explained in *Ebony* that the semi-pro experience satisfied his aspirations as a baseball player. "I loved playing baseball, but I was realistic enough to know that I wasn't going to make it to the major leagues," he said.

Handsome and affable, Coleman proved to be a great asset to the Republican Party in New Jersey. He helped to promote Governor Kean among black voters in such cities as Newark, Trenton, and Camden, and indeed Kean earned more votes in those cities than any Republican had in years. In 1986 Kean named Coleman commissioner of the New Jersey Department of Community Affairs, another cabinet-level position with an annual budget of some $250 million. Coleman had greater ambitions as well, at one time entertaining the idea of running for a Senate seat. He was popular and well-known in New Jersey, especially among Republicans, but when the 1988 Senatorial campaign got underway, Kean supported Pete Dawkins, a white Republican. Dawkins was subsequently beaten soundly by Democrat Frank Lautenberg. Coleman never made an issue of the campaign, and in fact he supported Dawkins as well, but in 1988 he left the public sector for a job as an investment banker with the prominent New York firm Kidder, Peabody & Co. He has expressed no interest in returning to national politics since that time.

A Dream Fulfilled

Coleman eventually was named vice president of municipal finance for Kidder, Peabody, and he might have spent the rest of his career there. Instead, in 1991, he accepted his first position with Major League Baseball: director of market development. Coleman was charged with the task of reviving fan interest in baseball at a time when attendance was beginning to slip in many markets. He decided that the best way to prepare professional baseball for a bright future was to spark more interest in the game among youngsters. One program that caught his attention was Reviving Baseball in the Inner Cities (also known as R.B.I.), an initiative aimed at keeping city teenagers active in baseball after they leave the Little Leagues. The program began modestly but has--with Coleman's encouragement--expanded to more than 30 cities, bringing with it new playing fields, equipment, and organized baseball programs.

> "I was part of an all-state backfield with Joe Theismann, Franco Harris, and Jack Tatum.... I'm the only one without a Super Bowl ring."

In March of 1994, the owners of the National League baseball teams unanimously chose Coleman to succeed outgoing Bill White as president of the National League. Coleman described his new position in *Sports Illustrated* as "a dream come true." At first glance the job does look ideal. League presidents are paid to fly around and attend big-league baseball games. They get the best seats at any sporting event--not just baseball, but everything from the Super Bowl to the U.S. Open tennis tournament to the Olympics. Their philosophies shape the game in ways both large and small, governing everything from the fines levied for a fight between players to the image of the game itself. The National League presidency is a high-profile position, one of the most important in organized professional sports, and the job holder is treated accordingly.

The dream can become a nightmare, however. Coleman began his duties with the National League just as one of the worst players' strikes in history was taking shape. The strike brought cancellation of a good part of the regular season in 1994 as well as all post-season play, and tarnished the image of the national pastime. To Coleman fell the task of restoring baseball's image and promoting the game as wholesome family entertainment. Asked what he would like to accomplish as National League president by the *Sporting News,* Coleman replied: "In terms of fans, we want an exciting product on the field that they can be proud of and relate to." He added: "I think baseball historically has had the roots within our North American society as the national pastime. Baseball has had an impact off the field and on. I look at some of the problems in our country with education, with getting children immunized. We have a role as hopefully a community citizen to help where we possibly can."

With such a philosophy in place, it is not surprising that Coleman has proven to be a tougher disciplinarian than his predecessors. "Violence, certainly, has become much more prevalent in our society. And I don't think it has a place in our sport," he commented in the *New York Times.* Coleman has been decisive about handing out fines and suspensions to brawling players. He has joined current and former players in a much-publicized campaign against the use of chewing tobacco during games. And he has actively encouraged players to spend more time reaching out to fans, especially children. "Baseball is going to have to provide hope and provide some type of vision in society so that kids' lives in this country can be better because of this sport," he explained in *Ebony.*

Not surprisingly, Coleman has also been a crusader for the rights of African American baseball players. He was instrumental in persuading Major League Baseball to open its health insurance plan to the players and the spouses of players who participated in the Negro Leagues. He also helped to design a plan that provides pension money to former Negro League players earned from the sale of Negro Leagues merchandise that is marketed by Major League Baseball.

Baseball purists have been relieved to discover that Coleman has no plans to introduce the designated hitter rule to the National League. "I like the National League style of play," he said in the *Sporting News.* "It's not going to be leading any movements for any change." What Coleman *would* like to see change is the message professional baseball is sending to its viewers. "It used to be that baseball had a strong connection with society," Coleman explained in the *New York Times.* "It was always able to transcend the field in a variety of very positive ways. Now, though, the only message we have been communicating is money, money, money. That is not a message we should be communicating."

Instead Coleman envisions such improvements as less drug abuse among players, less fighting during games, and more promotion of baseball as entertainment for the whole family. "We need to be role models and try to encourage players to be such," he maintained in the *Sporting News*. "If you look at the game of baseball, it's been one of the great continuities of life.... There's a certain flow to it. You don't want to tinker with it on the field. But any ways you can enhance the fans' enjoyment, you do that."

Coleman continues to live in Montclair, New Jersey with his wife, son, and daughter. His busy schedule may take him to as many as five different American cities in as many days, and he sees as many ball games in person as he possibly can. "I am thoroughly enjoying my work at Major League Baseball," he told the *New York Times*. "I feel blessed that I've had several gratifying careers."

Sources

Black Enterprise, July 1995.
Ebony, June 1994, pp. 116-18; June 1995, p. 41.
New York Times, March 6, 1994, p. NJ3; May 6, 1995, p. A27; September 17, 1995, p. NJ4.
Sporting News, May 2, 1994, p. 9.
Sports Illustrated, March 14, 1994, p. 51.

—Mark Kram

Albert Collins

1932–1993

Musician, singer

Although he went largely unrecognized by the general public during most of his career, the Texas-born musician Albert Collins eventually was acknowledged as one of the most talented and distinctive blues guitarists of his era. He established his fame by creating a unique sound with his Fender Telecaster guitar that was based on unusual tunings and scorching solos. His nickname "Iceman" was bestowed on him because his guitar sounds were piercing and could scorch the ears, just as icicles were sharp and could burn.

Peter Watrous wrote in the *New York Times* that "Mr. Collins made his reputation by combining savage, unpredictable improvisations with an immediately identifiable tone, cold and pure." "In the Iceman's powerful hands," said Jas Obrecht in *Guitar Player,* "that battered Tele could sass and scold like Shakespeare's fire, jab harder than Joe Louis, squawk like a scared chicken, or raise a graveyard howl."

Musicians ranging from Jimi Hendrix to Canned Heat to Robert Cray have cited Collins as having a major influence on their styles. He was especially known for his frenzied live peformances during which he would often

stroll into the audience and dance with the fans, his playing arena extended by a 100-foot extension cord attached to his electric guitar. Often he would start talking a blue streak, regaling his fans with hilarious and lewd remarks.

While his crowd-pleasing improvisations made him an extremely popular performer over the years, his recordings sold erratically until late in his career. His ultimate fame was also delayed by the long-time domination of Chicago blues over the Texas-based version. While the Chicago blues of performers such as Muddy Waters and Howlin' Wolf emphasized group jam sessions, the Texas variety was more of a showcase for individual talent where guitarists tried to outplay each other. Few could compete with Collins in these "bouts," but his talent didn't bring him widespread fame until he was brought to the attention of rock fans in the late 1960s.

Relatives Were Noted Blues Guitarists

After moving to the Houston ghetto as a child, Collins first became interested in music while listening to the

At a Glance...

Born May 3, 1932, in Leona, Texas; died November 24, 1993, of lung cancer, in Las Vegas, Nevada; married Gwendolyn Collins, 1968.

Blues guitarist, singer, and songwriter. Born to a sharecropping family; moved to the black ghetto of Houston, TX, as a child; learned to play piano as a youth and grew up listening to big-band music of Jimmie Lunceford, Count Basie, Louis Jordan, and Tommy Dorsey; learned to play guitar from cousins Willow Young and Lightnin' Hopkins; began playing blues at local clubs with Clarence "Gatemouth" Brown, 1947; played with his own group, the Rhythm Rockers while working days on a ranch and driving a truck, 1949-51; played with Piney Brown's band, early 1950s; became session player, 1953; recorded and performed with Little Richard, Big Mama Thornton, and others, 1950s; recorded first single, "The Freeze," 1958; recorded million-selling single, "Frosty," 1962; released first major album, *Truckin with Albert Collins,* for Blue Thumb, 1965; signed with Imperial label, 1968; sang for the first time on an album (*Love Can Be Found Anywhere (Even in a Guitar),* 1968; toured extensively throughout California, late 1960s; performed at Newport Jazz Festival and Fillmore West, 1969; stopped performing and began working for a building contractor in Los Angeles, 1971; signed with Alligator record label, and formed the Icebreakers, 1977; performed at Montreux Jazz Festival, 1975; performed with George Thorogood at Live Aid Concert, 1985; was chief attraction at American Guitar Heroes concert at Carnegie Hall, New York City, 1985; performed on Musicruise Dayliner circling Manhattan on opening night of JVC Jazz Festival, 1987; appeared in film, Adventures in Babysitting; was subject of television documentary on PBS, Ain't Nothin' But the Blues, 1980s.

Awards and honors: W.C. Handy Award, best blues album (*Don't Blow Your Cool*), 1983; Grammy Award, best blues album (*Showdown,* with Robert Cray and Johnny Copeland), 1986; W.C. Handy Award, best blues artist of the year, 1989.

pianist in his church. He took piano lessons at school, then learned about playing guitar from his cousins, blues guitarists Willow Young and Lightnin' Hopkins. His cousins turned out to be major influences on Collins's trademark style. He emulated Young's style of playing

without a pick, and learned to tune the guitar in a minor key from Hopkins. By using his fingers rather than a pick, his playing developed a more percussive sound.

Collins claimed in *Guitar Player* that he made his first guitar out of a cigar box, using hay-baling wire for strings. Through his teen years he wanted to be an organist, but his interest in that instrument waned after his organ was stolen. While Collins said that his greatest influence was Detroit's John Lee Hooker, he spent much of his youth listening to the big band music of artists such as Jimmie Lunceford, Count Basie, and Tommy Dorsey. At one time he considered becoming a jazz guitarist, and his playing often shifted between blues and the horn-driven sound of a jazz big band.

After Collins switched form acoustic to electric guitar, he began listening to T-Bone Walker, Clarence "Gatemouth" Brown, and B.B. King to refine his talent. Brown was a key influence due to his horn-driven sound that Collins found especially exciting. Collins emulated Brown by starting to play with a capo and a Fender guitar, an insturment that would become inextricably linked to him. Since he couldn't afford to buy the guitar at that time, he started by having a Fender Telecaster neck put on another guitar.

By age 15 Collins was playing at local blues club with Brown. Then he formed his own group, the Rhythm Rockers, in 1949, with which he performed at honky tonks in Houston's all-black Third Ward on weekends while working during the week as a ranch hand and truck driver. Next on his career path was three years of touring with singer Piney Brown's band.

In the early 1950s, Collins's talent earned him positions as session players with performers such as Big Mama Thornton. He later replaced future guitar great Jimi Hendrix in Little Richard's band. By this time Collins had established himself as a great eclectic who could produce unusual sounds with his guitar playing. As David Gates wrote in *Newsweek,* Collins "tore at the string with his bare hands insted of the ostensibly speedier pick, used unorthodox minor tunings instead of the more versatile standard ones and unashamedly clamped on a capo (a bar across the fingerboard, which raises the pitch of the strings), making the already stinging Telecaster sound even more bright and piercing."

Established "Ice Man" Persona

Collins cashed in on the popularity of instrumentals ushered in by performers such Booker T., Duane Eddy, and Link Wray in the late 1950s. His first recording, an instrumental called "The Freeze," featured extended notes played in a high register. Collins told *Guitar Player* that the record sold about 150,000 copies in a mere three weeks.

> "That battered Tele could sass and scold like Shakespeare's fire, jab harder than Joe Louis, squawk like a scared chicken, or raise a graveyard howl."

Collins lost a chance to play with soul music star James Brown in the late 1950s because he couldn't read music. Meanwhile, he still didn't feel that he could make his living entirely from guitar playing, and he worked as truck drivers and as a mixer of paint for automobiles. Then he hit the blues big time with his recording of "Frosty," released in 1962, that sold over a million copies and became a popular blues standard. This song confirmed his reputation as a player of "cold blues," and his producer urged him to continue this theme in his song and album titles. He even named his backup band The Icebreakers.

With just his fingers and his capo that he would move up and down the neck of his guitar, Collins produced a wide range of effects ranging from the sound of car horns to footsteps in the snow. He released a series of singles for small record labels such as Kangaroo, Great Scott, Hall, Fox, Imperial, and Tumbleweed that had moderate success at the regional level. He continud playing through the 1960s, but recording very sporadically and was unable to tour because of his day job.

According to Peter Watrous in the *New York Times*, Collins' first significant album was *Truckin with Albert Collins* in 1965. The album featured what would become famous blues recording of his previously released "Frosty," "Sno-Cone," and other songs. Following the release of his compilation album, The Cool Sound of Albert Collins, he quit his paint job and moved to Kansas City in 1966. While there he met his future wife, Gwendolyn, who would become an important motivator for him as well the composer of some of his best-known songs. Among her compositions for Collins were "There's Gotta Be a Change" and "Mastercharge."

Gained New Popularity with Rock Fans

Blues music gained in popularity in the late 1960s due

to various rock performers such as Jimi Hendrix and Canned Heat stressing the importance of blues as inspiration for their work. A major boost to Collins' career came as the result of interest in him by Bob Hite. Hite recommended Collins to the Imperial, which was affiliated with Canned Heat's label, Liberty/USA. His understated singing style showed up on a recording for the first time on *Love Can Be Found Anywhere Even in a Guitar,* the first of three albums that he recorded for Imperial. Later he recorded albums for Blue Thumb, then Bill Szymczyk's Tumbleweeed label in Chicago in 1972.

Appearances at the Newport Jazz Festival and at Fillmore West in 1969 gained Collins more exposure and acceptance with young rock audiences. He also appeared at the Montreux Jazz Festival in 1975. While jamming in the 1970s in Seattle, he met and played with Robert Cray. More than a decade later, he teamed up with Cray and and Johnny Copeland on a Grammy Award-winning blues album, Showdown. As late as 1971, when he was 39 years old, Collins found it necessary to work in construction because he couldn't make a sufficient living from his music.

More comfortable playing for small audiences than mass gatherings, Collins nevertheless agreed to perorma in the 1985 Live Aid Concert which was aired to an estimated 1.8 billion viewers. Right into his fifties, he maintained his flamboyant stage presence. Eventually, Collins was well established as the leading blues celebrarity second to guitarist B.B. King.

Selected recordings

Singles:
"The Freeze," 1962.
"Frosty," 1962.
"Snow-Cone," 1962.

Albums:
Truckin' with Albert Collins, Blue Thumb, 1965.
Love Can B Found Anywhere (Even in a Guitar), Imperial, 1968.
Trash Talkin, Imperial, 1969.
There's Gotta B a Change, Tumbleweed, 1971.
Ice Pickin', Alligator, 1978.
Frostbite, Alligator, 1980.
Live in Japan, Sonet, 1984.
Showdown, 1985.
Molten Ice, 1992.

Sources

Books

Clarke, Donald, editor, *The Penguin Encyclopedia of*

Popular Music, Penguin????, pp. 262-263.

Kozinn, Alan, Peter Welding, Dan Forte, and Gene Santoro, *The Guitar, The History, The Music, The Music, The Players,* Quill, 1984, pp. 84-85.

Larkin, Colin, editor, *Guinnes Encylopedia of Popular Music,* Volume 1, Guinness Publishing, 1992, p. 531.

Periodicals

Audio, June 1988, p. 148.

Downbeat, February 1992, p. 48; February 1994, p. 14; May 1994, p. 56.
New York Times, November 25, 1993, p. D19; November 26, 1993, p. B23.
Guitar Player, May 1988, p. 87; July 1993, p. 30; April 1994, pp. 69, 70, 72, 75-77.
High Fidelity, May 1987, p. 79.
London Times, November 26, 1993, p. 23.
Los Angeles Times, November 25, 1993, p. A22.
Newsweek, December 6, 1993, p. 84.

—Ed Decker

J. California Cooper

19(?)(?)—

Author

In 1984, J. California Cooper's short story collection, *A Piece of Mine,* was the first book to be published by Wild Trees Press--a publishing company set up by African American novelist Alice Walker and her partner, Robert Allen. "Others will now have the opportunity to enjoy Cooper's talent, humor, and insight into character," Walker wrote in the introduction to the book. Praising Cooper's style as "deceptively simple and direct," Walker wrote that "in its strong folk flavor, Cooper's work reminds us of Langston Hughes and Zora Neale Hurston."

A Piece of Mine received many positive reviews. Diana Hinds, for example, writing in *Books and Bookmen,* described it as "an example of how colloquial storytelling can also be beautifully crafted." Since that first break, Cooper has written three more collections of short stories, *Homemade Love, Some Soul to Keep,* and *The Matter Is Life;* two novels, *Family,* and *In Search of Satisfaction;* and at least seventeen plays. *Homemade Love,* which appeared in 1986, won the American Book Award. Cooper's most recent short story collection, *Some Love, Some Pain, Sometime,* was published in 1995.

Cooper was born in Berkeley, California. As a child, she invented stories about her paper dolls. Once she turned 18, however, her mother decided she was too old to continue playing with dolls. Cooper had no alternative but to begin writing her stories down.

Name Inspired by Tennessee Williams

The "J" in her name stands for "Joan," "California" is for the state where she was born, and "Cooper" is her father's name. While she has at times moved away from her home state--living for a while in Alaska, and in Texas for seven years--Cooper later resettled in Oakland. Cooper told *Emerge* that she chose to call herself "California" in imitation of her favorite playwright, Tennessee Williams; some reviewers have mentioned a similarity in their work as well as their names. "You have to have a name, and I wanted something I could give to people. They can have California," she told *Emerge.*

This protective attitude toward her first name is typical of her skeptical view of publicity. While biographical details on Cooper are scarce, one of the few things that is well known is her unwillingness to allow her privacy to be invaded. "About seven years ago it looked like fame was catching up with me," she explained to the *Los Angeles Sentinel* in 1994. "Too many people wanted me to do things and wanted pieces of me. That sounds egotistical, but I don't like a whole bunch of people in my life." She claims that only two types of people suit her: the very old, who no longer care about the game of life, and the very young, who have not yet learned to play it. "I love God, and I know he said love people and I do. Just at a distance," she told the *Los Angeles Sentinel.*

Cooper worked as a secretary for most of her career, and has one daughter, Paris Williams, who lives in Northern California. She will not admit her age or the number of marriages she has had--though she has confirmed that she has been married more than once. She also insists that there are no autobiographical clues in her work, and none of her writing is based on her own experiences. "Everything is fiction because I don't like to write fact," she told *Emerge.*

Novels Explore Christian Morality

A common theme in Cooper's work is women's search for love. Another is Christian morality; in an interview with *Emerge,* Cooper described herself as " a Bible student." The Christian theme is particularly obvious in the book *In Search of Satisfaction,* in which Satan

appears in every chapter. Pearl Cleage, writing in the *Atlanta Journal-Constitution,* described the book as "an old-fashioned morality tale."

Typical of morality tales, the characters in the book have names that offer clues about their roles--just as Cooper's own name offers a clue about hers. According to Victoria Valentine, writing in *Emerge,* "Cooper manipulates the naming process (a traditionally symbolic endeavor in the black community) with the implications of some names influencing her characterizations." For example, the mixed-race character Yinyang is a union of opposites, well-meaning but greedy; Ruth demonstrates the faithfulness and obedience of the Biblical character; the Befoes arrived in the town before everyone else, while the Krupts are corrupt. Perhaps most interestingly, one of the characters is called Josephus Josephus, a name he invented for himself; Cooper writes in that novel that "He chose to take the name he hoped his mother had given him, twice, rather than take the name of the cruel owner he had lived under."

Cooper's fiction is often set in another historical period. *In Search of Satisfaction,* for example, stretches from the late 1800s through to the middle 1900s. "History is fascinating ... because history is people and that's what I am talking about. People," Cooper told the *Los Angeles Sentinel.* Other works, however, have settings that are deliberately vague: *Some Love, Some Pain, Sometime* offers no clues about time or geography. "I named this book what I think about life," Cooper told *Emerge.* "I know life is composed of many more things,... but in the meantime, love is what seems to make a person's world go 'round and it has some love sometime, and some pain sometime." Like her earlier fiction, *Some Love* also centers on issues of morality.

Writes Stories as Monologues

According to Terry McMillan, writing in the *New York Times Book Review,* the first rule of creative writing is to show, rather than tell. Cooper, however, "rejects this notion entirely." Instead, her tales are often narrated as monologues, in which one woman tells about a crisis in the life of another woman she knows. Many reviewers have praised her talent in capturing African American speech, while pointing out that the narrators of different stories often sound the same. A typical review of *Some Love, Some Pain, Sometime,* which appeared in *Publishers Weekly,* claimed that "Cooper's spirited use of the first person makes every tale engaging, even if the uniformity of voice makes the narrators largely indistinguishable." According to Cooper, who writes her stories in longhand, the characters in her fiction simply appear in her mind and begin telling her stories. "This happens during the rainy season, which I why I never write during the summer," Cooper told *Emerge*. "With the rain comes these people."

"Everything is fiction because I don't like to write fact."

Malaika Brown, writing in the *Los Angeles Sentinel*, described Cooper as a "lightning bolt of energy and enthusiasm, paced with little excess in about five feet of vertical space." During her promotional readings, Cooper always wears a Polynesian-style yellow and green muumuu. "All my characters fit in there with me," she told *Emerge*. "I've worn it for every single reading for every book for the last 10 years." In the future, Cooper told *Emerge,* she plans to write two collections of short stories--one with a religious theme, and one for women who don't know what to do with men. She also plans to write a novel set during the Reconstruction.

Selected writings

Short-story collections

A Piece of Mine, Wild Trees Press, 1984.
Homemade Love, St. Martin's, 1986.
Some Soul to Keep, St. Martin's, 1987.
The Matter Is Life, 1991.
Some Love, Some Pain, Sometime, 1995.

Novels

Family, 1990.
In Search of Satisfaction, 1994.

Sources

Books

Contemporary Literary Criticism, Volume 56, Gale, 1989.

Periodicals

Atlanta Journal-Constitution, October 20, 1994, p. D3.
Booklist, August 1994, p. 1987.
Emerge, October 1994, p. 64; November 1995, p. 88.
Los Angeles Sentinel, November 23, 1994, p. C4.
Publishers Weekly, September 12, 1994, p. 83; July 31, 1995, p. 66.

—Carrie Golus

Allison Davis

1902–1983

Social anthropologist, educator

On February 1, 1994, the late University of Chicago social anthropologist Allison Davis joined the prestigious ranks of such outstanding African Americans as Martin Luther King, Jr., A. Philip Randolph, Harriet Tubman, W.E.B. DuBois, and Jackie Robinson. The occasion was the issuance of a new United States postage stamp in Davis's honor--the 17th in the Postal Service's Black Heritage stamp series. "He challenged the cultural bias of standardized intelligence tests and fought for the understanding of the human potential beyond racial class and caste," a Postal Service announcement declared. "His work helped end legalized racial segregation and contributed to contemporary thought on valuing the capabilities of youth from diverse backgrounds."

Unfortunately, the late Dr. Davis's time in the spotlight was brief; the 29-cent stamp bearing his likeness was replaced a mere month later by the new 32-cent stamp. Yet, even this brief exposure introduced many Americans-- for the first time--to a man who wrote ten respected books, was one of the first black professors to be granted tenure at a major predominantly white northern university, and served on the President's Commission on Civil Rights—and so much more.

Indeed, Davis rose above the Jim Crow limitations of his youth to argue effectively and successfully that defective intelligence tests were excluding talented blacks from educational institutions and depriving the nation of untapped sources of human talent. What's more, his impassioned reasoning had enormous impact on the course of education in the United States. According to the Journal of Blacks in Higher Education: "[Davis's] thesis that social class, rather than race, was the determining factor in black educational inequality formed the basis for the federal antipoverty program's Operation Head Start, a major and durable achievement that seeks to get disadvantaged children started off on the right educational foot."

Rising Through the Academic Ranks

Born on October 14, 1902, Davis entered a life of unusual privilege for a black child at the turn of the century. As the son of John Abraham and Gabrielle Dorothy Davis of Washington, D.C., his parents, a federal employee and homemaker, encouraged young Allison to read Shakespeare and Dickens and to enroll at the prestigious Williams College in Western Massachusetts. Despite the fact that the college's system of rigid segregation did not allow Davis to live on campus, he rented a room in a black-owned boardinghouse down the street where he became the valedictorian of the Class of 1924. He went on to earn two master's degrees in comparative literature and anthropology from Harvard University in 1925 and 1932 respectively, and a Ph.D. from the University of Chicago in 1942. En route, he also studied at the London School of Economics.

He married the former Elizabeth Stubbs in 1929 and

fathered two sons, Allison and Gordon Jamison Davis. Gordon would go on to become the New York City commissioner of parks and recreation. He recalled his father's accomplishments in a telephone interview with *CBB.* Davis's obvious intellectual gifts won him a rapid rise through academia. He started out intending to become a poet and a writer. According to his son, these interests explain his M.A. in literature, but after teaching a few years, Davis shifted gears and devoted himself to the study of culture--particularly the racist culture that was firmly in place in America at that time.

Early in his career, he became codirector of field research in social anthropology at Harvard University, professor of anthropology at Dillard University in New Orleans, and research associate in psychology at the Institute for Human Relations at Yale University. He was also a visiting professor at other universities, but spent the bulk of his professional life—over 40 years—at the University of Chicago, starting there as a research associate at the institution's Center on Child Development in 1939. In 1940, he published his first book, *Children of Bondage: The Personality Development of Negro Youth in the Urban South,* for the American Council on Education.

Davis was beginning to attract attention for his theories of how cultural factors impact poor children and how learning takes place in different ways depending on social class and caste. Accordingly, he was hired by the University of Chicago in 1942 as an assistant professor in its Department of Education, where he became a full professor in 1948. In 1947, he and his colleague Abram Lincoln were the first African Americans to be granted tenure at the University of Chicago and were among the first such appointees nationwide. But there was more going on here than just an acknowledgement of Davis's intellectual gifts.

According to the *Journal of Blacks in Higher Education,* "Professor Davis taught at the University of Chicago for over 40 years at a time when most blacks in Chicago could aspire to do nothing higher than [take] a job working as a Pullman porter or a civil servant in the post office," According to the same article, Davis was hired only because the liberal Julius Rosenwald Fund offered to pay his salary. Then, once hired, he was unable to buy a house in the university's Hyde Park neighborhood. Even after obtaining tenure, Davis was unable to walk into the faculty Quadrangle Club until 1948, when the club also began admitting women.

How Black Americans Get Categorized

In 1941, *Deep South,* certainly Davis's most emotional book, was published with coauthors Burleigh B. Gardner and Mary R. Gardner and with research help from Davis's wife, Elizabeth Stubbs Davis. A study of the cotton plantation system and the color caste system in and around Natchez, Mississippi, *Deep South* would later help to shape Gunnar Myrdal's landmark volume on race relations, An American Dilemma. Davis's book was also the first effort to apply anthropological techniques to the American landscape and to critically analyze the roots of a racist culture.

In a retrospective chapter published in an updated edition of the book in 1965, Davis wrote with sadness that the conditions he had found in Mississippi in 1933 remained largely unchanged. People were born into a caste, depending on the color of their skin, and they literally died that way too: even cemeteries were as segregated as society, Davis reported.

"In the final empirical view, government rests upon power, upon physical, economic and political control of the governed by the governing, of those who submit to subordination by those who dominate. The Negro, whether in the deep South or in Chicago, is at the bottom of the power hierarchy. He exerts the least economic, political and physical power, although in 'black counties' and in northern cities he may be far from the least in numbers. Since the Negro in the deep South had little power except that of a laborer in a rather depressed labor market and that of a customer in a money economy, and since he had been trained by the economic and caste systems not to use the potential bargaining power he had, he remained the most severely subordinated group in the United States."

This caste system, Davis wrote, still rested on endogamy (legal regulation of marriage to prohibit black/white marriage), the interracial sex taboo and "the overwhelming proscription of all types of relations of social equivalence (eating together, visiting in the home, dancing together, courting) between whites and Negroes. This system of sexual and social control still is reinforced, as it has been for ninety years, since the end of Reconstruction, by economic, political, educational and physical subordination of Negroes to whites."

Worse yet, Davis wrote, if this control couldn't be peaceably enforced, violence inevitably ensued: In the 1930s even black women—who could hardly be accused of the widely feared "rape" of white women—were subject to lynching. The dangers of which Davis wrote weren't just something he observed; he lived them too, his son, Gordon, said in the telephone interview. ``They were like spies,'' he said of his parents' research trips to Mississippi. "They were dropped in from a foreign country into the heart of a segregated, racially segregated caste system of the Old South, which was still enforced, as the book described, by violence and extralegal means.

"If it had ever been discovered that they were collaborating with a white couple [the Gardners interviewed whites while the Davises, acting "undercover" as academics researching "the black church," interviewed blacks], they would have been in considerable danger."

In fact, Gordon Davis said, his father carried a gun in the car at all times and met with the Gardners only at isolated locations and at "safe" places like all-black

Tuskegee College in Alabama. "It was an an extraordinarily heroic and courageous act," the son said. "The work they did was foundational." Among Davis's subsequent books were: *Father of the Man; How Your Child Gets His Personality,* in 1947; *A Psychology of the Child in the Middle Class,* in 1960; *Compensatory Education for Cultural Deprivation,* in 1965; and *The Crisis of the Negro Intellectual,* in 1967.

"In terms of I.Q. tests," Gordon Davis said of his father, "he was the first person to systematically challenge and reveal that standardized testing in this country, particularly the focus on the I.Q. test, was culturally biased in a way that was detrimental to the lives and futures of millions and millions of lower-class, working-class, and black children. He was the first one who blew the alarm in a way that was heard." Allison Davis's last work, *Leadership, Love, and Aggression,* in 1983, examined the psychologist profiles of the African-American leaders Rev. King, Du Bois, Richard Wright, and Frederick Douglass. "He admired them particularly on account of their ability to use anger and aggression for creative and positive purposes," the Journal of Blacks in Higher Education stated.

In the 1960s, the upheaval that led to the fight for civil rights for black Americans was reaching its peak; by this time, Davis had developed a reputation that reached far beyond the University of Chicago. He served, under presidents Lyndon Johnson and Richard Nixon, as a member of the President's Commission on Civil Rights and as vice chairman of the Department of Labor's Commission on Manpower Retraining. He was also a member of the Conference to Ensure Civil Rights in 1965 and the White House Task Force on the Gifted in 1968. In 1967 he became the first scholar from the field of education to become a fellow in the American Academy of Arts and Sciences.

Sadly, his first wife, Elizabeth, did not live to share his successs; she died in 1966. Davis married for the second time, three years later, in January 1969; his second wife, the former Lois Mason, has outlived him. But the couple still had 14 years together. And according to reports, Davis in his private life was more than just a starchy academic. His son, Gordon, described him as a devoted and talented tennis player. And a Chicago Tribune article once described him as "a lover of Mozart and classical ballet, and a jazz fan who particularly admired Louis Armstrong. He'd recite Chaucer and Shakespeare from memory but wanted his children to understand and identify with the black experience."

In 1970, Davis was named the University of Chicago's John Dewey Distinguished Service Professor. He held visiting appointments at Columbia Univ, the University of Michigan, Smith College, the University of Pittsburgh, and the University of California at Berkeley. He also won MacArthur Foundation "genius" grants, in 1982 and 1983, to further his work on the life and career of Dr. King, and he established the Allison Davis '24 Lecture Series at Chicago in 1988, which annually brings to campus a distinguished African American scholar for a lecture and short residency.

Davis died on Nov. 21, 1983, at Michael Reese Hospital in Chicago, after undergoing heart surgery. He was 81-years old. On the tenth anniversary of his death, the Postal Service announced the issuance of the stamp honoring his contributions to ending racism in America. A large number of Davis's colleagues had joined together to promote this project before the Citizens Stamp Advisory Committee, which decides what stamps will be issued.

> "My father was a brilliant man who brought to bear his powers of observation and analysis, and he was a wonderful writer.
> —Gordon Davis

"My father was a brilliant man who brought to bear his powers of observation and analysis, and he was a wonderful writer," his son said, enumerating possible motivations for the stamp project. "His books are some of the most well-written social science books ever done. So what he brought to it was that he bored away at the system in the most positive and substantial way he knew how, which was to analyze it, expose it and try to begin to articulate ... how the society needed to be changed."

Selected writings

Leadership, Love & Aggression, Harcourt Brace Jovanovich, 1983.
Rebellion or Revolution, William Morrow, 1968.
The Crisis of the Negro Intellectual, William Morrow, 1967.
The Psychology of the Child in the Middle Class, University of Pittsburgh Press, 1960.
Deep South: A Social Anthropological Study of Caste and Class, University of Chicago Press, 1941.
Children of Bondage: The Personality Development of Negro Youth in the Urban South, American Council on Education, 1940.

Sources

Books

Davis, Allison, Citation from "Power and Caste," retrospective chapter, pp. 337-346.
Gardner, Burleigh B., Gardner, Mary R., *Deep South, A Social Anthropological Study of Caste and Class,* University of Chicago Press, 1965.

Periodicals

Amsterdam News, New York, Jan. 8, 1994, p. 8.
The Journal of Blacks in Higher Education, Spring 1994, p. 23.
New York Times, Nov.23, 1983, p. B8.
Time, Jan 31, 1993, p. 5.

Other

"Dr. Allison Davis Honored\17th in Black Heritage Stamp Series," *Postal News,* Jan 21, 1994.

Additional information for this profile was obtained through an interview with Gordon J. Davis, May 5, 1996.

—Joan Oleck

Bessie and Sadie Delany

Dentist, teacher

Miss Sadie Delany, aged 106, and her sister, Dr. Bessie Delany, deceased at 104, had definite rules for living a long and healthy life. Both exercised every single day, whether they felt like it or not. Both always downed chopped garlic and cod liver oil at breakfast, and ate at least seven vegetables at lunchtime. The sisters also made a habit of living as stress-free a life as possible. They steadfastly refused to install a telephone, preferring more personal methods of communication. Other strategies for the sisters' serenity were published in the *Delany Sisters' Book of Everyday Wisdom* in 1994. The sisters also shared reminiscences of their family--the Delanys (their late father's family) and the Logans, from their mother's side. Gathered together in their book, *Having Our Say,* these stories offer a glimpse into the lives of pre-Civil War black Americans and portray the harmful effects of racism, from the late-19th-century Jim Crow laws to the lingering discrimination and distrust that affects some black-white relationships almost a half-century later.

Bessie and Sadie Delany were able to claim a direct link back to the days of slavery more than 135 years ago.

Their father, Henry Delany, was a child of seven in 1865, when the end of the Civil War brought emancipation for his whole family. Educated at the North Carolina-based St. Augustine School, which had been established in 1867 to serve the needs of the newly-emancipated, he stayed on campus to become the institution's vice-principal as well as the country's first black elected Episcopal bishop. His role as a black intellectual demonstrated for the next generation how to reach professional goals despite the frustrating barriers of a segregated and discriminatory wider society.

He was no less in the vanguard as a parent. He brought his ten children up with deeply-rooted values, sheltered them from bigotry and danger as much as he could, and urged all of them to attend college at a time when most Americans, black or white, were content to forsake academic pursuits after high school. Possibly Henry's wife had much to do with his success. The two met as students at St. Augustine's school and shared the same general goals. The former Nanny James Logan efficiently buttressed her husband's career by working as the school's matron, and supported his child-rearing

At a Glance...

Born Sarah (Sadie) Delany, September 19, 1889, and Annie Elizabeth (Bessie), September 3, 1891, both in Raleigh, NC; Bessie died September 25, 1995; daughters of Henry Beard Delany and Nanny James Logan. *Education:* Sadie graduated from St. Augustine's in 1910, earned a B.A. from the Pratt Institute, New York, 1918, attended Columbia University Teachers' College, 1920, and received M.A. from Columbia University, 1925. Bessie graduated from St. Augustine's in 1911, recieved doctor of dental surgery degree from Columbia University, 1923.

Sadie: Worked as Jeanes Supervisor, Wake County, NC, 1910; taught domestic science first in elementary school, then at Theodore Roosevelt High School, Bronx, NY, at Girls High School, Brooklyn, NY, then at Evander Childs High School, Bronx; retired, 1960. Bessie: began to teach in Boardman, NC, 1911; moved to Brunswick, GA, 1913; establihsed dental practice, New York City, 1923; retired, 1956.

efforts by raising each member of her sizeable brood to become a fiercely independent, thrifty, and professional adult.

Sadie and Bessie, inseparable for more than a century until Bessie's death in 1995, were born in 1889 and 1891 respectively, just before the Jim Crow laws bloomed into full-blown viciousness in the mid-1890s. "Colored" railroad cars, lynchings, and other means of segregation became commonplace events to them, and so did the calculated insults of white storeowners who refused to wait on them. Their parents tried to teach them to stay out of trouble by sitting only on correctly labelled park-benches and staying away from potentially dangerous crowds--but the lessons were only partly successful. Always the more even-tempered of the two girls, Sadie complied docilely with such strictures. Ever-feisty "Queen Bess," on the other hand, understood the Jim Crow laws perfectly, yet often went out of her way to flout the rules. She boasted of such exploits as purposely drinking from the 'white' fountain to see whether the water tasted any better than that which came from the "colored" faucet. (It didn't.)

Aiming High

In 1910, Sadie graduated from St. Augustine's, after

earning herself a qualification that entitled her to a teaching post. Her father wanted her to further her studies at a four-year college. "You owe it to your nation, your race and yourself to go. And if you don't, then shame on you!" he said. But that was not all he had to say. He also wanted her to know that scholarships would be the wrong way to raise the money. "If you take a scholarship," he warned her, "you will be beholden to the people who gave you the money."

Sadie agreed. She started looking for a teaching post and eventually found one as a Jeanes supervisor. This was a position named after a white educator named Jeanes, who had started a fund to introduce home economics to nonwhite schools all over the South. Sadie's job was to travel from school to school, starting courses where none existed, and hiring teachers to continue her work. She often found that a school was an exaggerated claim for a church basement, where the children knelt on the floor and used pews as desks. Her travels revealed to her how the truly poor post-Reconstruction black family lived, and motivated her to help less fortunate colored people. In 1911, Bessie graduated from St. Augustine's and started teaching in Boardman, North Carolina, to save money for college. She stayed there two years, then moved on, to a slightly larger town in Brunswick, Georgia.

Civil Rights and Feminism

While Bessie was in Boardman she began to entertain the idea of staying single forever. Having helped to raise all her younger brothers and sisters before becoming a teacher, she found the overwhelming attention and love in her classroom too cloying for her independent soul. She made her choice to remain unmarried, and never regretted it. For Sadie, the idea of life as a dedicated single began at home, in the center of her over-protective family. It surfaced as a resentment of men's authority, which was displayed when her father and her older brother Lemuel decided that a certain beau was not suitable for her. She was given no choice in the matter, but was simply informed that "you won't be seeing any more of Frank for now." Neither she nor her sister quite dared to protest to her father, but Bessie said often that Sadie, as a professional woman in her mid-20s, should have been allowed to pick her own friends.

In 1915, both young women visited New York City for the first time. Once they visited trendy Harlem, they were eager to stay. So both set their sights on Columbia University and returned to New York City in 1919 to work towards entering classes there. Once arrived, they enjoyed Harlem's thriving culture but found that not everything in their new life was as pleasant. One painful experience affected their brother Manross, a World War I veteran, who came back to postwar America believing that military service by black soldiers would make a difference in the way they were treated. However the opposite turned out to be true; the willingness of black Americans to lay down their lives for their country had done nothing to alleviate the sting of racism. Manross' bitter comment showed his deep hurt: "What more do I have to do to prove I'm an American too?"

The Delany sisters were determined not to let prejudice from the outside world spoil their first taste of adult independence. Sadie started her first teaching job in 1920, and earned $1,500 her first year. Resourceful and anxious to save for post-graduate education, she earned money on the side by making cakes and candies and selling them at school, and hiring a second person to peddle her "Delany's Delights" all over New York until 1925, when she graduated from Columbia with a master's degree in education. She then started aiming for promotion to a high school post. She began by applying to the Education Department, then prepared herself to wait out the usual three years before reaching the top of the seniority list. She made meticulous plans to ensure that her chances of promotion could not be dashed simply to appease those parents who might object to her teaching in a white school.

First, knowing that the usual excuse for not hiring black teachers was "can't employ anyone with a Southern accent," she took speech lessons to subdue her Carolina lilt. She cleared the next obstacle by when she skipped her interview with the school principal by letting the interview date pass. She sent a letter of apology to the principal, and simply turned up to teach on the first day of school.

Meanwhile, Bessie was working her way through dental school. Having deferred her studies for so many years, she was far older than the other students, though few of them knew that. Reticent by nature, neither she nor Sadie ever discussed their past or responded to questions about their age or their previous teaching experience. "A lot of the girls were just looking for husbands," Bessie said later. "I wanted to be taken seriously."

By 1925, Bessie had embarked on a practice as New York's second-ever black female dentist. She shared a Harlem office with her brother Hap, but they each served their own patients. Although Dr. Bessie served prosperous patients, she never turned the poor away. Her generosity cost her more than her patients knew. Unable to afford a cleaning woman, she rose each workday at dawn and walked ten blocks to clean her office herself. She then walked home, showered and changed, and went back to her office as Dr. Bessie Delany.

Bessie spent her spare time participating in civil rights protests. Characteristically forthright, she agreed with W. E. B. DuBois about the need for forceful and visible protest, and she actively took part in such activities such as protest marches rather than the passive lunch-counter sit-ins preferred by many of her friends. However, she found the protests to be dominated by males who made their female counterparts feel distinctly unwelcome. Their attitude produced a conflict in her about whether she should fight first for first-civil rights or for the interests of women. Because she thought she was more visible as a colored person, the civil rights cause won out. Nevertheless she maintained her close interest in feminist affairs. Both she and Sadie were thrilled when women were given the vote in 1920, and neither of them ever missed a chance to cast their ballots at the polls.

The Great Depression

During the Depression years, life was not easy for anyone in Harlem. Many people lost their jobs and their homes; the sight of entire families picking through garbage dumps became a common one. People who formerly frequented playgrounds of the rich, like the Cotton Club, now did their part for the surrounding community by raising money for food baskets for the destitute. The Delany dentists were no better off than the rest. While Sadie always had a steady job for the New York Board of Education, on several occasions Bessie and her brother Hap were evicted for nonpayment of rent. But Bessie would not allow herself to lose hope. One day she went to the government service agency along with one of her patients. After her patient obtained a job, she landed a part-time post in a government clinic, which enabled her not only to keep her practice going in the afternoons, but also to help those less fortunate than herself--in her own words, to "contribute to America's well being." "We loved our country," she later recalled, "even though it didn't love us back."

Lifestyles Change

In 1950 the increasing feebleness of their elderly mother forced the sisters to change their lifestyle. It became obvious that one of them would have to stop working to give her continuous care. Together the sisters decided that Bessie would close her office, because her work as an independent dentist would not provide a pension at retirement. Sadie, however, would collect a pension from the Board of Education if she kept working for another ten years. The three women moved into a little cottage in the Bronx, and Bessie became a housewife, taking care of their mother and the many brothers and sisters who visited almost daily. Two of Sadie and Bessie's brothers died of heart disease between November 1955 and January 1956, just months before their 95-year-old mother died the following June.

Oral History: Slavery to Neighborhood Integration

Although Nanny Delany had no money to leave her children, she left them a valuable legacy in the form of a detailed oral history. The 75 years between the Revolutionary War and the Civil War came alive through stories of their great-grandparents, white Jordan Motley and his colored wife, Eliza, whose parents had been an unknown slave and a white army officer's wife, and their grandparents, especially mean-looking Grandfather James Milliam, a white man who had been barred from marrying his colored sweetheart. Like many other oral histories covering this same period, these stories provided the Delany sisters an understanding of nearly ten decades of the daily life of their African American ancestors. Most of all, their mother's oral history spurred their own efforts in preserving a record of America's black community that stretches back almost to the Declaration of Independence.

"A lot of the girls were just looking for husbands.... I wanted to be taken seriously."

The sisters were now too elderly to take a very active role in the civil rights movement of the 1960s, but they did become involved in issues surrounding neighborhood integration. In 1956, their brother Hap Delany had become the first nonwhite resident of Mount Vernon, New York. After being barred from buying a house there, he had built one, holding his head high when uncouth whites showed their disapproval of his defiance by slashing the tires on his Cadillac. The sisters followed him there a year later. They, too, had a stressful initiation to the neighborhood, when they took some home-grown vegetables to a white neighbor to introduce themselves. Despite a frosty reception, however, they

and several other newly-installed nonwhite neighbors called again on the white couple with fruit and flowers after the tragic loss of their 20-year-old son. In belated proof of acceptance into the neighborhood, each guest received a thank-you note.

Gifts for Tomorrow

Their years of retirement passed quietly until 1991, when journalist Amy Hill Hearth came to interview the sisters on the occasion of Dr. Delany's 100th birthday. In collaboration with Hearth, the sisters published their family chronicles in *Having Our Say,* which remained on the *New York Times* bestseller list for six months and brought them several television interviews. In 1994 *Having Our Say* was followed by a second book called *Delany Sisters' Book of Everyday Wisdom,* also written with Hearth. The sisters' final triumph came in 1995, when *Having Our Say* was produced as a play. Both sisters enjoyed the performances they saw, but 104-year-old Dr. Bessie Delany did not survive to see the end of its run. Her passing in September was marked a funeral service that lasted two-and-a-half hours and the presence of sister Sadie, 106, needle-sharp and brave to the last.

Selected writings

(With Amy Hill Hearth) *Having Our Say,* Kodansha International, 1993.
(With Hearth) *Delany Sisters' Book of Everyday Wisdom,* Kodansha International, 1994.

Sources

Books

Gunther, Lenworth, *Black Image: European Eyewitness Accounts of Afro-American Life,* Port Washington, N.Y., Kennikat Press, 1978.
(With Amy Hill Hearth) *Having Our Say,* Kodansha International, 1993.
(With Hearth) *Delany Sisters' Book of Everyday Wisdom,* Kodansha International, 1994.

Periodicals

New York Amsterdam News, May 27, 1995, p. 23.
New York Times, September 29, 1995, p. A29.
New York Times Biographical Service, September, 1993, p. 1306; September 26, 1995, p. 1408.
Smithsonian, October 1993, p. 144.

—Gillian Wolf

Marilyn Ducksworth

1957—

Publishing company executive

Though she is unquestionably the highest-ranking black woman in publishing, she stays resolutely out of the limelight. But many people who have worked with her name the same three secrets of her success: long hours, hard work, and shrewd marketing of each year's list of new books. Together, they account for her meteoric rise to a coveted vice presidency at the Putnam Publishing Group, one of America's oldest and most highly-respected literary institutions.

When Marilyn Ducksworth graduated from Tufts University in 1979, she seemed to be heading straight for a career in either journalism or teaching. But instead of following these well-worn tracks she found herself a job in the publicity department of Doubleday and Company in New York.

Doubleday

As a new trainee, she found herself learning ... and learning ... and learning. One of the most important things she learned was that the entire organization was serving the same two important masters—the booksellers with shelves full of Doubleday's wares, and the buying public, whose dollars are always the final judge of every book's success. She also discovered that the techniques used for publicity are crucial marketing tools to most publishers, who compete not only against each other, but also against the hundreds of other temptations awaiting a buyer's attention in the marketplace.

By the time Ducksworth came to Doubleday, publishers had been augmenting their advertising with publicity for about 20 years. Credit for this inspiration usually goes to Esther Margolis, formerly of Bantam Books, who was casting about for a fresh way to promote the novels of Jacqueline Susann. Since those early days it has has become such an important speciality that, as a *Publishers Weekly* article in November 1990 noted: "Books are acquired with their publicity potential in mind, and the sums paid for them reflect that potential."

What spurred this huge growth spurt in publicity's importance was the advent of cable TV, which allows the syndication and satellite beaming of talk shows. Since millions of viewers watch these shows every day, publishers are eager to see that their authors are interviewed by influential hosts like Oprah Winfrey and Geraldo Riviera.

Maintaining a foothold in this fast-paced, competitive environment is not easy. But even at the dawn of her career Ducksworth managed not only to keep pace with other publishing contenders, but also to maintain a reputation for the highest integrity. "Her credibility is so intact," Marie Dutton Brown, a former senior editor at Doubleday once remarked. "People know that they are dealing with a professional."

One mark of Ducksworth's professionalism came to the fore in 1983, when a Doubleday book called *Children of the War* by Roger Rosenblatt caught her interest. As Ducksworth later told *Black Enterprise*, her department was frantically busy promoting other titles when the Rosenblatt book appeared, but she felt it was a fine piece of work, and worth far more attention than it was receiving. So she worked around her other duties to create a campaign for *Children of the War*, and even secured an interview for the author on an episode of the "Phil Donahue Show" which subsequently won an Emmy.

A streamlined professional to her fingertips, Marilyn Ducksworth also shows the professional's typical reluctance to stop growing. By 1985, she had spent six years at Doubleday, and felt it was time to move on. Long past her trainee days, she left the company with the title of publicity manager, not only for the flagship publishing house itself, but also for subsidiaries-- Anchor Press, Dolphin Books, and Dial Press.

The Putnam Group

During the summer of 1985 she joined The Putnam Publishing Group. A venerable corporation that dates back to pre-Civil War days, Putnam is now the umbrella company for several equally well-recognized subsidiaries such as Grosset & Dunlap, Inc., Jeremy Tarcher, Howard McCann, and Riverhead Books. Between them, these companies in the Putnam lineup cover a broad range of books for adult and school age readers both in America and in many other countries.

Hired as the publicity manager for the subsidiary G.P. Putnam's, Ducksworth initially headed a staff of three. However, before long there were 13 desks in the publicity department, and she herself had risen to the rank of director for the entire Group. Her new appointment made her the highest-ranking black woman in the publishing field, and one with considerable say over how titles at Putnam and its subsidiaries are presented to the public.

Though her publicity department works alongside a 10-member planning board, which comes to a joint decision about how much publicity each new book should receive, Ducksworth is the final arbiter of a publicity campaign which may cost anywhere from $10,000 to $250,000. Possibilities range from visits to local bookshops for obscure authors to fullblown campaigns for possible bestsellers involving city-to-city tours, newspaper and talk show interviews, and even coaching for an author unaccustomed to the spotlight and the camera.
]
While the main object of any campaign is to sell as many books as possible, the experienced publicist knows that he is also expected to shape the company's public image. Every publisher wants to be known for the prominent authors his house represents, the interesting books it produces, and the integrity of the research that goes into every publication on its list. One way in which the publicist can help to bring all these desirable qualities to the attention of the public is by placing as many new titles as possible where they are most visible—on the *New York Times* bestseller lists.

In March 1989, Marilyn Ducksworth achieved the seemingly-impossible. Due to her efforts, seven Putnam titles appeared on the *New York Times* bestseller list at one time. Among the authors listed: Dick Francis (*The Edge*) Dean Koontz (*Midnight*) Tom Clancy (*The Cardinal of the Kremlin*) and veteran actor George Burns' affectionate memoir of his wife, *Gracie*. Needless to say, all these titles remained bestsellers for months.

While this once-in-a-lifetime event did a great deal to burnish the Putnam image in 1989, a later incident could have brought serious legal consequences. Events centered around an expose-type biography of Senator

Edward Kennedy penned by a former Kennedy aide named Richard E. Burke, who had claimed, in 1981, to have been subjected to frightening death threats. Later, after admitting these had been a hoax, Burke had been forced to resign.

Though Putnam had been very interested in the Burke manuscript, the appearance of this telltale skeleton killed all plans to purchase it. Ducksworth's reticent comment to the *Publisher's Weekly* on August 17, 1992 said what was necessary, but no more. "...we had to make a decision, and we felt we couldn't proceed with the book." The result was exactly as anticipated—a short-term loss for a season's list, but a longterm protection for the Putnam reputation.

Other publicity-related hurdles Ducksworth has faced have stemmed from authors' unwillingness to put their best efforts into their publicity campaigns. One experience came in 1989, when she was working on a fascinating account of a man convicted of killing his wife and two daughters called *Blind Faith*. Despite the major sales and review potential of this title, author Joe McGinniss hesitated to undertake a major tour because of intricate legal issues surrounding the journalistic structure he had chosen to use.

Ducksworth's dilemma: run the risk of losing potential sales because of McGinniss' reluctance, or run the risk of legal repercussions that could tarnish the Putnam image? As always, she took this challenge in stride and opted for no-holds-barred action. Two months and 150 telephone calls later, she was able to persuade McGinniss to do a couple of radio interviews, appear on the influential "Phil Donahue Show", and handle a satellite hookup that connected him with viewers in New York, Los Angeles, San Francisco, and Boston. As a result of this publicity, Putnam sold some 380,000 copies of *Blind Faith,* as opposed to 174,765 copies of a previous McGinniss work publicised in different ways.

Authors may also dig their heels in more subtle ways that carry less risk, but need more patience. Amy Tan, author of the blockbuster novel *The Joy Luck Club*, explained her feelings about the large parties usually given by Putnam during the annual American Booksellers Association convention. Like many other best-selling authors, Tan usually enjoys meeting the retailers who stock her books, but finds the parties themselves a little stressful. "... when I'm standing there and the cameras are all going, I feel like I'm being shot—executed," she confided to the *New York Times* in June, 1991, during a Putnam party at the Four Seasons Hotel in New York. While sympathetic up to a point, Ducksworth put forth sound reasons for this particular gathering. "You get

major booksellers, major media, major authors, and a major celebratory thing—and that all adds up to great press for our books."

One facet of Marilyn Ducksworth's expertise is the ability to cope with the unexpected. This was rigorously tested in 1991, when the Persian Gulf War changed the priorities of several television shows regularly hosting the authors of soon-to-be bestsellers. Carol Hartsough, author of *The Anti-Cellulite Diet* was originally scheduled for a two-week tour, but was cut to one when Ducksworth discovered that television stations preferred not to concentrate on personal topics like dieting at this time.

The 1990s

If there have been any changes in marketing strategy during the 1990s, these have centered around new literary developments. Children's books, for example, have burgeoned. But interesting as their marketing is, it is very different from marketing books intended for adult consumers. "We're a news show and children's books are rarely news," the book editor of the "Today Show" explained to *Publishers Weekly*, in April 1990. "The content just doesn't lend itself to real discussion."

As from 1988 Putnam's solution to the children's book challenge was to merge the children's and adults' publicity departments. Still, this did not mean that both adult and children's books were handled in exactly the same way. As Ducksworth, now a vice-president and executive publicity director, reflected in the April 27, 1990 issue of *Publishers Weekly,* it is important to understand what the interviewer is looking for, and to make sure her office provides it. Another must, she feels, is to ensure that every children's book being promoted is presented with a newsworthy angle. As always, her intuition on this occasion was quite correct. Within two years of the merger, Putnam began to reap a handsome reward, in the form of six to eight major media tours per season for children's book illustrators or writers.

By far the most important development of the 1990s is the new renaissance in black literature and publishing. Though authors such as Maya Angelou and Toni Morrison have been in the vanguard of this movement for many years, the literary trend now is for protagonists whose challenges and lives center around contemporary issues common to middle class black readers of today.

Ducksworth believes that the marketing potential for this type of commercial fiction has always been present, but that up to now insufficient attention has been paid to publicizing the work of black writers in the general media. As long ago as 1989 she noted: "They're just as interested in books by black authors as we are in ones by white authors."

"You get major booksellers, major media, major authors, and a major celebratory thing-- and that all adds up to great press for our books."

Nevertheless, the principal market for works by black authors lies with black readers, and many sources acknowledge that reaching black buyers requires different techniques from those primarily used for their white counterparts. "That review in the *New York Times* is not going to sell books, Vanesse Lloyd-Sgambati, a literary promoter told *Newsweek* in April, 1996: "Forget booking your author on the morning TV talk shows. "At 8.00 in the morning, most African-Americans aren't watching TV. They're on their way to work." Her solution points in different directions: "radio's a better way of getting the message across." Lloyd-Sgambati also advocates using churches, since word of mouth is still the black community's greatest form of publicity. Whichever method proves to be the most efficient, Marilyn Ducksworth is listening, learning, and selling.

Sources

Black Enterprise, August 1989; February 1995.
Newsweek, April 29, 1996, p. 79.
New York Times, February 14, 1981, p. 16; February 19, 1989; March 26, 1989; June 2, 1991, p. 41; February 18, 1991.
Publishers Weekly, February 17, 1989; April 27, 1990; November 16, 1990, August 17, 1992.

—Gillian Wolf

Cesaria Evora

1941—

Singer

Commonly called "the barefoot diva" because she often performs on stage in bare feet, Cesaria Evora of the Cape Verde islands is the world's reigning interpreter of a mournful genre of blues music known as morna. Morna is based on the Portuguese fado and features bluesy vocals set against a background of acoustic guitars, fiddles, accordion, and *cavaquinho,* which is a small, four-string guitar. "For years, the master of the morna has been Cesaria Evora, a Cape Verdean with a rich alto voice who has been accurately described as a cross between Edith Piaf and Billie Holiday," wrote Geoffrey Himes in the *Washington Post.* Evora's repertoire over the years has featured the compositions of top Cape Verdean songwriters such as Nando Da Cruz, Amandio Cabral, and Manuel De Novas.

Largely unknown until she was propelled into international acclaim at the age of 45, Evora has attracted legions of fans with sentimental, intimate songs that are delivered "with a pitch-perfect, full-toned resonance," according to Himes. "My songs basically express feelings about relationships, love relationships, and they sing about the lack of rain in the country," Evora said in *Pulse!.* Singing in a Creole variation of Portuguese known as Criuolo, Evora has won over legions of fans who do not understand a word of her soulful ballads. "Well, now I've been to different countries and the way people respond to me tells me that they really like the music, even though they don't understand the language," Evora told the *San Francisco Bay Guardian.*

Sang About Longing and Loss

Many of Evora's songs are filled with a sense of longing and homesickness that strikes a chord in her homeland, since over half of all Cape Verdeans have emigrated out of the country. "Life in the islands is not easy, because there are very few resources, and you could say that my life and life in the islands are related," she told *Pulse!.* "But in reality, the people are very happy. They enjoy life." Evora's songs offer advice to young people, pay homage to the elderly, lament the loss of a lover, and address other nostalgic themes. Her shoeless performance mode has been said to be her way of symbolizing the plight of poor women and children in her native land, although some accounts indicate that her nickname

At a Glance...

Born 1941 in Mindelo, Cape Verde; married and divorced three times; two children; two grandchildren.

Began singing in bars in Cape Verde, 1950s; was discovered in Europe when tapes of her radio performances were sent to Holland and Portugal, 1960s; did not sing publicly, 1970s–1985; recorded two songs for a Cape Verdean woman's music anthology, 1985; recorded first album, *La Diva aux Pieds Nus*, in Paris, France, 1988; achieved major success with *Miss Perfumado*, 1992; went on world tour, early 1990s; had first major U.S. tour, 1995; performed in Montreal Jazz Festival, 1995.

Addresses: *Home*—Sao Vicente, Cape Verde; Record company—Nonesuch Records, 75 Rockefeller Plaza, New York, NY 10019.

stems from a visit to Paris when she refused to wear shoes. "I got that name because the first record I recorded in France was called 'Barefoot Diva,'" claimed Evora herself in the *New York Times*.

Cesaria Evora was born in the port town of Mindello on the Cape Verde island of Sao Vicente, and lived for many years under Portuguese colonial rule until the country gained its independence in 1975. Life was a struggle for her as a child after her father, a violinist, died at a young age and left her mother to take care of seven children. Most of her siblings emigrated to other countries, but Evora stayed in Cape Verde and has always felt strong ties to her homeland.

Surrounded by music as a child, Evora started singing at an early age. "I started singing in the neighborhood where I lived, just with my friends...It was just to amuse ourselves," she told *Rhythm Music*. She began performing in various bars in Mindello, and took up morna at age 16 after a romantic involvement with a guitarist. After a recording she made on national radio made the rounds, she began to be invited to sing in bars throughout the ten islands that make up the Cape Verde chain. According to Nonesuch Records, "With a voice conveying power, vulnerability and an emotional affinity for this style, Evora quickly found a niche for herself in Mindello's musical life and through committed performances

gained a distinguished reputation as the 'Queen of Morna.'" Evora's frequent accompanist at the time was the well-known clarinetist Luis Morais. "In Cape Verde ...I used to sing for tourists and for the ships when they would come there'" she said in the *San Francisco Bay Guardian*. "That's why I always thought that maybe if I made it, people from different countries would love my music."

By age 20, Evora had achieved a measure of fame at her local radio station. A few tapes of her performances at the station made their way to Holland and Portugal in the 1960s and were recorded into albums. Despite this exposure, Evora never left Cape Verde for many years, and she stopped singing altogether in the 1970s. "There was no real progress," she acknowledged in *Pulse!*. "I wasn't making any money out of it, so I just stopped."

Found Fame in France

Evora came out of retirement in 1985, when she went to Portugal and recorded two songs for a women's music anthology at the request of a Cape Verdean women's organization. Her big break came in the 1980s when she met José da Silva, a Frenchman originally from Cape Verde who became entranced with her singing. Da Silva convinced Evora to go to Paris with him to record some of her music for his Lusafrica label. "Because I couldn't find anyone to help me out in Cape Verde, I had to start recording in France in 1988," she told the *New York Times*. That year she recorded *La Diva aux Pieds Nus*, then followed with *Distino di Belita* in 1990, and *Mar Azul* in 1991. Her 1992 album, *Miss Perfumado*, made her a major star in France and Portugal, and sold over 200,000 copies in France alone. This recording featured two of her most popular songs, "Sodade" and "Angola." "The record shimmers throughout as strings and accordions mingle deliciously around Cesaria's sublimely relaxed voice," noted Banning Eyre in *Rhythm Music*. Evora's reputation across the world soared after this release as she went on tour in Europe, Canada, Africa, and Brazil. At the age of 51, she had suddenly become a major star.

When Evora began her first major U.S. tour in the fall of 1995, she was greeted by sell-out performances across the country. She received thunderous standing ovations at the Montreal Jazz Festival that year. "I know this is my opportunity," she noted in *Pulse!* in discussing the tour. "They're going to feel my message through my presence and my music." Her 1995 release, *Cesaria Evora*, on Nonesuch Records was cited by *New York Times* music critic Neil Strauss as one of the ten best albums of the year. In the *San Francisco Bay Guardian*, Josh Kun called the album "remarkable." The record went double gold in France and reached number seven on the album charts in Portugal according to *Billboard Magazine,* claimed Nonesuch Records publicity materials.

> "Life in the islands is not easy, because there are very few resources, and you could say that my life and life in the islands are related."

Simplicity has been a hallmark of the Evora style, as was emphasized by Jon Pareles in his *New York Times* review of a 1995 performance at the Bottom Line in New York City: "She [Evora] stated melodies almost unadorned, lingering with vibrato at the end of a phrase and sometimes languidly sliding down to a note." Pareles added, "In her tranquil contralto, there were painful memories and unsatisfied longings, a sense of pensive reassurance and of inconsolable loss." Evora also found a very appreciative audience at a performance at Birchmere in Washington, D.C. that year. *Washington Post* reviewer Mike Joyce said, "Evora projected an unusual combination of vocal power and emotional vulnerability." "At times Evora not only sang of heartache, she seemed to personify it, each gesture reflecting the weight of her experience and pain," Joyce also noted.

Personal Setbacks Influenced Music

Much of the emotion of Evora's singing draws on her own experience. Known as a heavy drinker and smoker, she has endured three painful divorces and the blindness of her mother, in addition to her father's untimely death. She vowed never to live with a man again after her third divorce, according to Neil Strauss in the *New York Times.* "I am married to my mother [with whom she still lives], my children [a 35-year-old son and a 27-year-old daughter], and their two children," Evora said in *Rhythm Music.*

Most of Evora's albums have one or more morna songs written by her uncle, the well-known morna composer

Francisco Xavier da Cruz. For a number of years her main performance venue has been The Piano Bar of Mindello on Sao Vicente where she lives. She has performed in numerous world music festivals, and as the opening act for top stars such as Natalie Merchant. Evora is dedicated to her Cape Verdean roots and has not been lured by the trappings of stardom or affected by the globe trotting and international fame of her later years. "I wasn't astonished by Europe and I was never that impressed by the speed and grandeur of modern America," she said in *World Music.* "I only regret my success has taken so long to achieve."

Selected discography

La Diva aux Pieds Nus, Lusafrica, 1988.

Distino di Belita, Lusafrica, 1990.
Mar Azul, Lusafrica, 1991.
Miss Perfumado, Lusafrica, 1992.
Cesaria Evora, Nonesuch, 1995.

Sources

Books

Broughton, Simon, Mark Ellingham, David Muddyman, Richard Trillo, *World Music: The Rough Guides,* The Rough Guides, 1994, pp. 278–279.
Sweeney, Philip, *The Virgin Directory of World Music,* Henry Holt, 1991, p. 30.

Periodicals

Christian Science Monitor, September 29, 1995, p. 12.
New York Times, September 21, 1995; September 23, 1995, p. C13; January 4, 1996.
Pulse!, October 1995, p. 42.
Rhythm Music, September 1995.
Village Voice, October 3, 1995, p. 67.
Washington Post, September 22, 1995, p. D11.
Washington Post Weekend, September 15, 1995, pp. 15–16.

Further information for this profile was obtained from Nonesuch Records publicity materials and the website for the *San Francisco Bay Guardian* on the Internet.

—Ed Decker

Willie E. Gary

1947—

Attorney

Willie E. Gary is one of the most successful and visible personal injury and medical malpractice lawyers in the United States. The multimillion-dollar awards that he regularly wins for his clients frequently make newspaper headlines. Viewers across the country have glimpsed his posh oceanfront house on television's *Lifestyles of the Rich and Famous*. Unlike many others who are equally rich and famous, however, Gary's life has been a true rags-to-riches story. Throughout his career, Gary has continued to use the combination of determination and skill that made possible his rise from abject poverty to a position of wealth and influence.

Gary, the sixth of Turner and Mary Gary's eleven children, was born on July 12, 1947, in Eastman, Georgia. His father was a sharecropper who managed a 200-acre farm. Gary's complicated birth generated steep hospital bills, forcing his father to sign over the farm in 1948. The family then moved to Silver City, Florida, where all 13 members lived in a tiny wooden shack. They became migrant workers, traveling with the seasons between the corn, sugar cane, and bean fields of Florida, Georgia, and the Carolinas. Gary began

working alongside his parents and older siblings at the age of nine, attending school in the morning and hitting the fields in the afternoon.

Used Football as Ticket to College

An eager student, Gary was often frustrated by the long gaps in his education that the family's itinerant lifestyle caused. From an early age, Gary showed a strong aptitude for business. While still in junior high, he started his own lawn-mowing business, eventually saving enough money to buy a truck for his father. When the family moved to Indiantown, Florida, in 1960, Gary and his father started a business together, selling produce from the back of the truck that his lawn-mowing profits had purchased.

In high school, Gary began playing football. Although he was only five feet seven inches tall, he saw that an athletic scholarship was his best hope of attending college. After graduating from high school, Gary tried out for football scholarships at a number of Florida colleges during the summer of 1967. He made it to the final cut at one of them, Bethune-Cookman College in

At a Glance...

Full name, Willie Edward Gary; born July 12, 1947, in Eastman, GA; son of Turner (a share-cropper) and Mary Gary; married Gloria Royal; children (all sons): Kenneth, Sekou, Kobie, Ali. *Education:* Shaw University, B.A., 1971; North Carolina Central University, J.D., 1974. *Politics:* Democrat. *Religion:* Baptist.

Gary, Williams, Parenti, Finney, Lewis & McManus (law firm), Stuart, FL, senior partner, 1975--; Gary Enterprises, president.

Member: American Bar Association; American Board of Trial Advocates; American Trial Lawyers Association; Federal Judicial Nominating Committee; National Bar Association; National Bar Institute, Board of Directors; Sigma Delta Tau Legal Fraternity; NAACP; National Rainbow Coalition, Board of Trustees; Urban League.

Awards: United Negro College Fund, College Alumni of the Year, 1989; Black College Alumni Hall of Fame, 1993; Council of Independent Colleges, Award for Personal Philanthropy & Volunteerism, 1993; United Negro College Fund, National Alumni Council Achievement Award, 1993; NAACP Image Awards Key of Life, 1994; C. Francis Stradford Award, National Bar Association, 1995. Received honorary degrees from North Carolina Central University, 1990, Bethune-Cookman College, 1991, Shaw University, 1991, Florida Memorial College, 1992, Southern University, 1992, and Nova University, 1994.

Addresses: *Office*—Gary, Williams, Parenti, Finney, Lewis & McManus, Waterside Professional Building, 221 W. Osceola St., Stuart, FL 34994.

Daytona Beach, but ultimately failed to catch on with any of those schools. On the advice of his high school coach, Louis Rice, Gary made a final desperate attempt at landing a football scholarship by traveling to Shaw University in Raleigh, North Carolina, a traditionally black school whose football coach was an old friend of Rice's.

Gary arrived in Raleigh with $13 in his pocket and no return ticket. The Shaw football coach immediately informed Gary that there were no more spots open on the football team, especially for such a small man. Lacking money to get home, Gary hung around the university, sleeping in dormitory lounges and surviving on food smuggled out of the cafeteria by members of the football team. He cleaned the locker room and helped out the football program in other ways. The coach was duly impressed with Gary's determination, and when a player was injured, Gary was offered a spot on the roster. His hard work was further rewarded when school officials eased the admission process, waived the enrollment fee, and gave him a scholarship.

Gary's years at Shaw were busy ones. In addition to his role as defensive captain of the football team, he found time to marry his high school sweetheart, Gloria Royal, and have the first of their four children, son Kenneth. He also launched a successful business--lawn care once again--while still a student. By bidding on large landscaping jobs and hiring others to do the work, Gary was bringing in about $25,000 a year by the time he graduated from Shaw. In 1971 he received his degree in business administration. Rather than make a full-time career of lawn care, Gary decided to study law. He enrolled in law school at North Carolina Central University in nearby Durham. Gary's second child, Sekou, was born during his stay in Durham.

Founded County's First Black Law Firm

Gary graduated from law school in 1974, then moved with his growing family back to Florida. The following year, at age 27, he opened Martin County's first black law firm. Gary was the firm's only attorney, and Gloria Gary handled its secretarial and administrative duties on top of her regular job as a junior college instructor in West Palm Beach. Success as a lawyer came quickly for Gary. Two high-profile cases established his reputation as a talented courtroom battler. First, he successfully defended a school bus driver accused of rape in a highly publicized criminal case. Just a few months later, Gary won his first personal injury case, earning a $250,000 settlement for the widow of a truck driver killed trying to avoid a woman who had pulled into his path. Gary's success in those early cases brought a steady flow of new clients to the firm.

Gary's firm quickly began to land eye-popping settlements one after another. In 1976 the firm added two full-time secretaries and opened a second office in Fort Pierce, Florida. By the mid-1980s, the firm was grossing over $100 million a year. Gary received national attention in 1985, when he successfully sued Florida Power & Light Co. over the electrocution death of seven members of a Jupiter, Florida family. Although the precise amount of that settlement was not disclosed, it has been estimated at $100 million, of which the law firm received about 40 percent.

> "I don't take pride in having good cases. Usually, a good case is a tragic situation and nobody likes to see anyone get hurt or lose their lives."

In spite of the huge sums his cases often involve, Gary's acquaintances firmly and unanimously agree that it is concern for others, not money, that motivates his work. In a 1987 *Ebony* article, Gary was quoted as saying, "I don't take pride in having good cases. Usually, a good case is a tragic situation and nobody likes to see anyone get hurt or lose their lives." As his personal wealth grew, Gary became almost as well-known for his generosity as for his courtroom skills. Before the end of the 1980s, he had already contributed hundreds of thousands of dollars to a variety of causes in his old hometown of Indiantown, Florida. In 1992, Gary gave his alma mater Shaw University a gift of $10 million. He has also spoken voluntarily before countless community and school groups over the years.

Lifestyle Featured on TV

By 1993 the law firm of Gary, Williams, Parenti, Finney & Lewis had 70 employees. In addition to the firm, Gary and his wife also operate Gary Enterprises, a company organized to manage their many ventures in real estate-including the buildings that house the law firm's Stuart and Fort Pierce offices--and other areas, with Gloria Gary serving as CEO. Although the people who have known him for a long time swear that money has not changed him, Gary is not bashful about his wealth. He lives in a $5 million oceanfront palace and drives, among many other luxury cars, a Rolls Royce.

Gary's fame has been enhanced by his many television appearances. He was featured in a 1992 episode of *Lifestyles of the Rich and Famous.* Other appearances have included spots on the *Oprah Winfrey Show* and CBS Evening News's *Eye on America* with Dan Rather. He was also featured as "Person of the Week" on *ABC World News Tonight with Peter Jennings.* Gary counts among his personal friends celebrities from the worlds of politics, business, and entertainment. He has served for several years as General Counsel to the Reverend Jesse Jackson, and in 1994 he received the 26th Annual NAACP Image Award "Key of Life."

In August of 1995, Gary was selected from among 25,000 lawyers for the C. Francis Stradford Award, the National Bar Association's highest honor. In choosing Gary for the award, his peers recognized that his contributions to law and to society extend far beyond the multimillion-dollar settlements he wins for his clients. As Gary stated upon accepting his Stradford Award, "I do what I do, not for the money or publicity, but because I love my profession and people. The only way our children will believe that they can attain their goals is for us to encourage them and provide a path for them to follow."

Sources

Black Enterprise, August 1993, p. 68
Columbus Times, September 19, 1995, p. B5.
Ebony, October 1987, p. 127; October 1992, p. 106.
New York Times, February 5, 1992, p. B7.
People Weekly, April 13, 1992, p. 65.

—Robert R. Jacobson

Nelson George

1957—

Writer

Nelson George's writerly ambition is matched only by his versatility. After establishing himself as one of the keenest critics of African-American culture, he ventured into novels and screenwriting; by his mid-30s he had already amassed an impressive body of work. He has traced the histories of musical genres, studied the effects of Hollywood on black people and vice-versa, penned broad cinematic comedies, and engaged in deeply personal ruminations on black masculinity. "I'm trying to expand what I've been doing," George explained in the British periodical *The Weekly Journal*. "Instead of writing about other people's work, I'm trying to create more things that express my point of view."

George grew up in Brooklyn, New York. His parents divorced when he was a young boy, and young Nelson was raised by his mother; his literary ambitions manifested themselves early on. "At the age of three," he wrote in a biographical essay distributed by his publisher, "my mother taught me my ABC's and I was reading before I entered the first grade." He added that his mother later worked as a schoolteacher, introducing other children to the joys of reading over a period of 20 years. In an

Essence magazine roundtable on black masculinity, he credited his mother's post-divorce relationship with helping him develop a healthy perspective. "Fortunately for me, she had a relationship with a guy she went out with for about seven years. He taught me how to shoot a layup, but more important, the interaction between my mother and him was always very affectionate and very warm. I got a lot out of that that was subliminal, a lot to do with respect for women. So much of that respect comes from seeing how your father, or an adult male, deals with women on an individual basis."

Hemingway, College, and Journalism

Layups, however, would not be George's passion—though he would describe them in his elegant prose many years later. He was, as he put it in his press bio, "the biggest bookworm in the Brooklyn projects," devouring everything from comic books to the stories of Ernest Hemingway, which "made me want to be a writer. The master's tales of growing up in Michigan were written in a (deceptively) simple style that, I, like generations of young writers before me, thought could be easily imitated." George's attempts at aping the legendary author led to the emergence of his protagonist Dwayne Robinson who, like Hemingway's Nick Adams, served as an autobiographical double. Dwayne emerged many years later as the hero of George's first novel, *Urban Romance.*

George attended St. John's University in Queens, New York and immediately found his way into some journalism internships. From the very beginning, he covered a wide range of subjects, from film and sports writing for the *Amsterdam News* and music articles for *Record World* and--thanks to a well-connected friend--the recording industry bible, *Billboard.* By 1982 he was the latter publication's black music editor.

Chronicled Decline of Soul Music

He spent seven years at *Billboard,* during which time he

also authored several books, among them a biography of pop megastar Michael Jackson, and *Where Did Our Love Go?: The Rise and Fall of the Motown Sound,* a book about Detroit's soul music label. George's researches into Motown were not welcomed by the company's founder, Berry Gordy, Jr.; the writer told the *Chicago Tribune* after the book's publication that he had experienced "subtle intimidation" from the record company. His unflinching portrayal of the label's history, however, was among the first to examine the contributions of the house musicians who toiled in relative obscurity but helped make countless Motown hits. In writing the 1986 book, George related, "I had two responsibilities: to deal with the history and who recorded what when; and to try to give as many people behind the scenes as much [credit] as possible."

1988 saw George publish a broader examination of soul music's commercial fortunes, *The Death of Rhythm & Blues.* Mark Feeney of the *Boston Globe* gave the tome a typically mixed review, deeming it "ambitious, provocative, disappointing," and asserting that "the passion that often makes his book bracing to read also produces considerable sloppiness" of style, argumentation, and research.

Broadened Range at Voice

In 1989 George began a six-year stint as a columnist at *The Village Voice,* arguably the hippest "alternative" paper in the country. In his press biography he referred to his tenure there--producing a column called "Native Son"--as "the turning point in my creative development." This sort of writing, he noted, differed from his prior journalistic efforts in that it "required creating a mood, painting small pictures with words." He recollected that one specific composition, "To Be a Black Man"--a particularly fervent creed about racism--"generated a strong emotional reaction. This response renewed my confidence in my ability, not just to analyze, but provoke." A number of his *Voice* essays would be collected in his 1993 book *Buppies, B-Boys, Baps and Bohos.*

George pursued a dizzying array of projects during the early 1990s. Dismayed by the increasingly violent and cynical content of much rap music but opposing any kind of external censorship, he helped recruit a number of hip-hop artists--among them KRS-One, Chuck D. and Flavor Flav of Public Enemy, Kool Moe Dee and M. C. Lyte--for "Self-Destruction," a single that counseled against violence and drugs and stood in favor of education and community survival. The record became *Billboard's* top rap single of the year and sold half a million copies. "The idea is unity," George explained in the

Boston Globe. "These were very disparate rappers, but they came together as a community. One of the words rarely used anymore is `brotherhood'--and that's what we're aiming for." George, who has long argued that rap can serve as a tool for communication and education, edited a book to accompany the recording; *Stop the Violence: Overcoming Self-Destruction* put the song's argument into cogent prose.

Worked in Film, Examined Black Archetypes

George also ventured into the film world, serving as co-executive producer on the horror spoof *Def By Temptation* and co-scripting and associate producing the comedy *Strictly Business.* 1992 saw the public television special *Everybody Dance Now*--which boasted George as a co-producer--win a Peabody Award. He was the sole writer and a co-producer on the 1993 rap parody *CB4,* featuring Chris Rock of *Saturday Night Live,* and saw his writing skewered by many of his peers in the press.

In the meantime, he penned a book on basketball, *Elevating the Game,* won a Grammy Award for his liner notes to singer James Brown's CD compilation *Star Time,* and published *Buppies,* which explored four paradigms of African-American identity. The *Chicago Tribune* cited an explanatory passage from the book: "There is the Buppie, ambitious and acquisitive, determined to savor the fruits of integration by any means necessary; the B-Boy, molded by hip hop aesthetics and the tragedies of underclass life; the Black American Princes or Prince a/k/a Bap, who whether by family heritage or personal will, enjoys an expectation of mainstream success and acceptance that borders on arrogance; and the Boho, a thoughtful, self-conscious figure … whose range of interest and taste challenges both black and white stereotypes of African American behavior." George, the *Tribune*'s reviewer observed, seems to fall into the latter category, and this fact "is what makes this collection of columns enthralling." *Entertainment Weekly* disagreed, opining that "As hip-hop, like jazz before it, makes its way into all facets of American life, we could use a thoughtful examination of its meaning. This isn't it."

Novelistic Foray into Romance

George tried his hand at novel-writing with 1994's *Urban Romance,* which examined male-female relations against the backdrop of rap music's development. Dwayne Robinson, the character George developed in

some of his earliest forays into fiction, is the book's protagonist; his B-Boy roots doom his affair with the "Bap" Danielle. "I worked on *Urban Romance* for six years," George told the *Amsterdam News,* "and kept peckin' away because it was something I always wanted to do--write a novel. I wondered sometimes if I'd ever finish the thing." While working on other projects, he produced his narrative sporadically. "Early last year [1993] I got a break-through," he added, "and figured out how to do it. Before I'd been doing reporting, but I learned from making movies how to structure my novel."

He observed in the *Weekly Journal* that he "enjoyed writing the novel because it let me deal with the more emotional side of my life," and expressed satisfaction "that the book got a good reception from women. I've been touring around with it and a lot of women come to the readings. I think it's because I tried to write about folks in a very holistic way: dealing with *every* aspect of the characters, i.e. emotions and family contacts." After the mainstream success of Terry McMillan's *Waiting to Exhale,* a tale of black women's romantic frustrations that later became a smash film, readers were evidently ready for a similar book from a black man; *Urban Romance* sold well, and the HBO cable network saw sufficient merit in the work to buy the film rights for a projected 1996 production.

Once again, critical reaction was mixed. "Though *Urban Romance* is an enjoyable novel it lacks something," ventured Alice Charles in the *Weekly Journal,* "mostly due to the characterization. Often it seems that Danielle and Dwayne are not fully human, but serve only as vehicles for George's posturing on the state of the music industry." The *Philadelphia Inquirer* complained that "the narrative voice of *Urban Romance* fails to recognize the subtle complexities of love in the black community," causing the book's central relationship to seem "superficial." Bryan Thompson of the *Indianapolis Recorder,* on the other hand, deemed the novel "a thought-provoking work of art that delves into the psyche of Black men as it relates to sex, career mobility and machoism."

"Trying to Balance"

In 1995, George published *Blackface: Reflections on African-Americans in the Movies,* which mixes critique and memoir in its exploration of the black screen experience. The *Quarterly Black Review of Books* described the work as "a heterogeneous little book that stuffs autobiography, criticism and How I Made *CB4* into 200 schizophrenic pages" and complained that George "sometimes stretches too far to get a connection between the personal and the cinematic." For Michael E. Ross of *Entertainment Weekly,* however, the work was "insightful as a chatty personal perspective, and comically caustic view of the often dispiriting way in which movies, like so much creative sausage, are made."

George's second novel, *Seduced,* was published in 1996. In his essay accompanying the publisher's publicity materials, he described the book as "basically an accumulation of many life experiences. It is set in the record business, where I worked for many years, and the black middle class sections of Queens, where many of my friends reside. Most importantly, it depicts an artist trying to balance professional ambition with his personal life--a problem I, myself, have experienced." The book's central character this time is an aspiring songwriter-musician named Derek Harper, whose personal and professional odyssey through the music business yields a number of revelations. George wrote not only prose but also lyrics for the narrative.

"There's so much diversity to who we are. But our diversity doesn't get acknowledged within our own descriptions of ourselves."

While still relatively young, Nelson George conquered a startling range of media, from journalism to film to novels. Through it all he has attempted to chart the Black experience through the filter of popular culture, from the largest political developments to the most personal struggles. And he has been at pains all along to record the range of identities that fall under the blanket designation "black." As he noted in *Essence,* "there's so much diversity to who we are. But our diversity doesn't get acknowledged within our own descriptions of ourselves."

Selected writings

Top of the Charts, New Century Books, 1982.
The Michael Jackson Story, Dell, 1984.
Where Did Our Love Go?: The Rise and Fall of the Motown Sound, St. Martin's Press, 1986.
The Death of Rhythm and Blues, Pantheon, 1988.
(Editor) *Overcoming Self-Destruction,* Pantheon, 1990.
Elevating the Game: Black Men and Basketball, HarperCollins, 1992.
Buppies, B-Boys, Baps and Bohos: Notes on Post-Soul Black Culture, HarperCollins, 1993.
Urban Romance, G.P. Putnam's Sons, 1994.
Blackface: Reflections on African-Americans and the Movies, HarperCollins, 1995.
Seduced, G.P. Putnam's Sons, 1996.

Sources

American Visions, April 1993, p. 32.
Amsterdam News (New York), March 25, 1994, p. 23.
Boston Globe, July 17, 1988, Books section, p. 90; May 24, 1990, Arts and Film p. 81.; March 15, 1993, Living, p. 32.
Chicago Tribune, February 20, 1986; September 5, 1988; March 13, 1994.
Commercial Appeal (Memphis), March 14, 1993, p. G3.
Entertainment Weekly, February 26, 1993, p. 53; February 18, 1994, p. 111; January 20, 1995, p. 49.
Essence, November 1995, pp. 97-98, 105, 152-154.
Indianapolis Recorder, June 11, 1994, p. B4.
Philadelphia Inquirer, February 13, 1994, p. HO2.
Quarterly Black Review of Books, February 28, 1994, p. 8; February 28, 1995, p. 20.
Washington Informer, January 26, 1994, p. 12.
Weekly Journal (United Kingdom), October 6, 1994, p. 9; October 27, 1994, p. 9.

Additional information was provided by G. P. Putnam's Sons publicity materials, 1996.

—Simon Glickman

Nathaniel Glover, Jr.

1943—

Law enforcement official

Like most of us, Nathaniel Glover grew up believing that, should danger arise, he could always count on help from the police. But, as Glover found out, growing up black in the 1960s in the American South, reality was a different matter altogether. The police were nowhere to be found.

The year was 1960, the place, Jacksonville, Florida, Glover's hometown. Just 17-years-old at the time, young Nat Glover regarded the hubbub around civil rights and sit-ins at the local Woolworth's with detached interest; it didn't affect him. Then, one day, a mob of rural whites—perhaps 70 or 80 men—rolled into town in their pickups. Those civil rights protestors and sit-in demonstrators were getting out of hand, the good old boys had decided, and they needed to be taught a thing or two. "They all came to town with brand new ax handles and pretty much shut the downtown area down," Glover recalled in a telephone interview with *CBB*. "Even the white folk shopping left town."

But not the young brash Glover. As he usually did, he stayed late at his Morrison's Cafeteria job cleaning up, then left to go home—right down the city's main street, right past the angry white men. "I looked around; I was the only person downtown, certainly the only black face," Glover said. "I did see demonstrators, but I also saw police officers." So he felt safe—and boldly strolled right past the angry crowd.

"There was something in me: I could have walked around the block and avoided that crowd. Of course the mob stopped me and made a few choice comments." Asked where he was going, he replied, hinting at a challenge: "home; where do you think I'm going?" And at that, one of the ax handles came down on his shoulders hard. Dazzed and hurt, he stayed on his feet and hobbled over to the nearest police officer. "I thought he'd be helpful," Glover said, But the officer simply told the youth to get his posterior out of town. Now ``I went home and cried," Glover recalled. "But not because of the blow; I was crying because I thought in my mind that I had done what a coward would do, run away from a fight."

It was one of the formative events of his youth that pointed Glover in the direction that has been his career now for 30 years: law enforcement. At age 56, Glover has reached a zenith of sorts, since his 1995 election as the first African-American sheriff of Jacksonville, the same Deep South metropolis where he was once put down physically and emotionally. Perhaps Glover's ascension can be seen as one of those hopeful signs that, three decades after the Civil Rights Era, the South is trying to heal its racial wounds—and sometimes succeeding.

Growing Up in the Ghetto

Glover was born on March 29, 1943, in Jacksonville to

At a Glance...

Born Nathaniel Glover Jr., in Jacksonville, FL; son of Nathaniel and Arsie (Singletary) Glover. Married Doris Bailey Nov. 22, 1964; children: Clementine Valretha and Michael Eugene.

Education: Edward Waters College, Jacksonville, FL, BS, social science, 1966; University of North Florida-Jacksonville, MA, education, 1987; graduate of the 130th Session of the FBI National Academy.

Career: Jacksonville city police patrolman, 1966-69, investigator, Detective Division, 1969-74, promoted to sergeant, Detective Division, 1974. Head of Police Hostage Negotiation Team, 1975-86. Chief of services, 1986-88. Deputy director of police services, 1988-91. Director of police services, 1991-Feb., 1995. Elected sheriff of Duval County (and Jacksonville) April, 11, 1995, took office July, 1995.

Selected honors: Recipient, Sallye B. Mathis Award for outstanding community service from the Jacksonville branch of the NAACP, 1991; Brotherhood of Police Officers Law Enforcement Officer of the Year Award winner, 1977; state runnerup for the Florida Retail Federation's Law Enforcement Officer of the Year, 1976.

Addresses: Office—c/o Jacksonville Sheriff's Office, 501 East Bay St., Jacksonville, FL, 32202.

Arsie and Nathaniel Glover, a household domestic worker and contract plasterer, who doubled on weekends as a Baptist preacher. There were six children in the home; Nathaniel was the third in line.

Jacksonville, a major East Coast seaport, insurance center and locus for three naval bases, was still very much a small Southern town in those days. The Glovers struggled to get by; the sheriff describes his youth as "somewhat difficult"; by sixth grade he was already working odd jobs. His young years were deprived not just economically, but in other ways too; segregation was the law of the land. "You had to stay in your place," he said. "The feeling then was that you were a second-class citizen. There was that prevailing [idea] that white people were superior and that as long as you stayed in your place you would not have any problem. I think that whole notion was perpetuated by the adults at that time because you didn't see much rebellion."

Furthermore, the area where he grew up was "quintessential ghetto." Yet despite the inevitable gangs, the crime back then was far less violent than today, he

remembers. "I lived in a neighborhood where there were no less than three moonshine houses in a two-block area, and I used to see the police officers come and go and never arrest anybody." As for a police presence, it was barely there, probably because there were no black police officers on the city force until the 1950s. Even then, they were labeled "colored officers" and limited to riding together in black districts. Arresting whites was strictly prohibited.

Despite this rigidity, young Nathaniel was intrigued. Glover remembers listening to police stories on the radio. "I just always wanted to be a detective. This [ax handle] experience did not discourage me. If anything, it strengthened my resolve."

Glover credits a strong parental presence in his life for keeping that resolve solid. "I went to school and most of the guys in my neighborhood were dropouts and having fun, buying cars. But I had to go to school. It was very unusual for me to finish 12th grade. I didn't do it because I was in pursuit of academic excellence or afraid of the truant officer." He laughs. "I was afraid of my mother." That strong parental example also held the family together during an early tragedy: the death of Glover's older sister from heart failure while he was in college.

Law Enforcement Career Takes Off!

In 1966 Glover graduated from Edward Waters College in Jacksonville with a B.S. degree in social science and almost immediately went to work for the police department as a patrol officer. Two years later, the city and county departments consolidated, making the reigning sheriff at the time head of law enforcement for both Jacksonville and surrounding Duval County--an area that encompasses an area of 764 square miles and has a population today of about 700,000.

Only two years into his career, Glover joined the detective ranks, working first in a civilian capacity, then attending a training academy for three months. He was promoted to sergeant in 1974. There were other black cops and detectives on the force by then; but, "racism was certainly present," Glover said. The first black officers in Jacksonville had to accept a precinct office located in the basement under a municipal swimming pool. Glover himself was one of the first patrolmen to integrate a beat.

By the time he became a detective in 1969, Glover was already a father for the second time. He and his high school sweetheart, the former Doris Bailey, married in 1964, then had a son and daughter. In 1975 Glover formed the police hostage team, with which he would remain until 1986. The team unfortunately proved necessary: Glover recalls the hijacking of a Greyhound bus by a man with a gun threatening 32 passengers. Glover and an FBI agent subdued him after four hours.

There were other dangers encountered in those years, like the burning house the young officer entered to save a man caught there. The man was burned over 80 percent of his body. Glover himself was overcome by smoke and had to be hospitalized; but, both men survived. Later, there were the deaths of Glover's fellow officers, including a plainclothes detective shot by a robber in May 1995. The man was a close friend of Glover's.

In 1987 Glover received his master's of education degree from the University of North Florida in Jacksonville and about the same time began the first of several administrative jobs in the Sheriff's Department. Now he was off the street, dealing with—not criminals—but records and patrol cars and the property room. From 1986-88 he was chief of services. Then he became deputy director of police services, adding the sheriff's department building to his list of responsibilities. In 1991 he was appointed director of police services, a job that entailed all the tasks he already had, plus contract negotiations with the labor unions.

It was a heady position to be in, for a man who had grown up in the segregated South. The salary was top-of-the-ladder; the job was one of the top three in the department. He was the man to see about the Jail Division, the Prison Division, and the Human Resources Division. And any time he liked, he could retire to rest on his laurels with a comfortable pension and an excellent career record to look back on. Plus there had been honors: he had been the Florida Retail Federation's "Law Enforcement Officer of the Year" in 1976 and the Brotherhood of Police Officers "Law Enforcement Officer of the Year" in 1977. He was active on several community boards with a slew of awards to show for it, including the Sallye B. Mathis Award for community service from the Jacksonville Branch of the NAACP in 1991. He was president of his church. But Glover wasn't about to retire from law enforcement. Not yet--first he had to reach the top.

Worn Shoe Leather and Community Policing

When the incumbent sheriff, Jim McMillan, announced in 1994 that he would not run again, a citizens group began to pressure Glover to get involved. He agreed and threw his hat in the ring; ambition was part of it, he said, but there was another reason, too: "It doesn't take a genious to figure out that a disproportionate portion of the crime [in urban centers like Jacksonville] is committed by blacks on blacks. The potential to have a black law enforcement officer would be good in that area as well."

Out of the five original candidates, Glover and two other Sheriff's Department staffers were still in the race after the primary; one of those opponents was his counterpart; Glover was then director of police services; the opponent was director of services. And, inevitably, Sheriff McMillan was asked to endorse one of the three. He chose the director of police services. Jacksonville was not yet ready for a black sheriff, he told a reporter. And there was precedent for his statement: Blacks in Jacksonville had been elected for years to the city council. But they had come only from black-majority, single-member districts.

Still, Glover was determined; he set out to prove the sheriff wrong, even though he entered the race late and raised only half the funds of his opponents. But the community, black and white, rallied to his side. One reason may have been that Glover walked each of the city's 93 beats before the election. "I walked the whole city and talked to the people. I told them I wanted to hear what they had to say about what they wanted from their police department. I raised their consciousness level."

His strategy paid off. On Election Day, April 11, 1995, Glover captured 55 percent of the vote from a city that was only 24 percent black. He became Florida's first elected black sheriff since Reconstruction, and he inherited a serious responsibility: a department with 2,400 employees and a $158 million annual budget. The black community was exultant. A state representative, Willye Clayton-Dennis, said at the time: "We are no longer that little country town that people will pass by on their way to other places in Florida. This is a plus this city needed."

As for Glover himself, he took those Election Day numbers as a mandate for his philosophy of "community policing." Glover described this concept as "a police strategy where police officers work with the community in identifying a problem in the community and try to solve those problems in the community." As such, since taking office in July 1995, the new sheriff has moved toward installing 17 citizens' advisory councils and six police substations. With help from local businesses, he is also instituting "stop" stations where officers can use phones and restrooms. These stop stations are particularly important, Glover said, in neighborhoods where officers do not live and where there are no police cars parked in driveways [in Jacksonville, officers take their vehicles home at night, partly for symbolic reasons].

> "I walked the whole city and talked to people. I told them I wanted to hear what they had to say about what they wanted from their police department. I raised their consciousness level."

Whether he will run again in four years remains a question. "If we are making some progress and doing the community some good and the community feels that we are—if our plans for a feeling of safety and security in the community are working—then I will run for re-election," Glover said. In the meantime, he wants to work harder on crime prevention and the area of juvenile crime. And, of course, there are his plans for community policing. "There was a time," he told a local victims' publication, "when police said, `Law enforcement is our job. Let us do it.' And citizens said, `Law enforcement is your job. You do it.'" "But today leaders in law enforcement know the police cannot do it alone."

Sources

Periodicals

"Jacksonville Gets First Black Sheriff," *The Atlanta Journal/Constitution,* June 29, 1995, p. C9.
"Justice," *Jet,* July 17, 1995.

Other

Telephone Interview with Nathaniel Glover, April 21, 1995.

—Joan Oleck

Lawrence Otis Graham

1962—

Lawyer, author, consultant

A corporate lawyer whose work revolves around such issues as the purchase and sale of companies, Lawrence Otis Graham also heads a management company whose mission is to guide corporations bent on hiring workers from a wide variety of ethnic backgrounds. Neither law nor diversity counseling is Graham's first advice-giving venture. An instinctive observer with a talent for finding a market gap, he was a 17-year-old university student when his first book appeared. Since then, he has written nearly 20 other titles and numerous magazine articles that have shown his readers how to get into medical or law school, how to diminish the prejudice that seals glass ceilings in place for women and various other minority groups, and how to bridge the cultural gaps that make an integrated life so difficult to achieve. He is an increasingly familiar guest on television talk shows, and a teacher at Fordham University, where his class on justice for women and other minorities in the corporate setting is popular with Afro-American Studies students.

Lawrence Otis Graham comes from a New York family accustomed to affluence. His grandparents owned a Memphis trucking firm, and his father continued in the business tradition by carving his own niche in real estate. His mother chose a career as a social worker. Despite their position as members of the black upper-middle class, Lawrence Graham's parents had no illusions that their son's entry into a white-dominated world would be easy. So, determined to ensure that he would follow their example and reach his fullest potential, they taught him a creed that would give him the confidence to target high goals and work towards them. "Find your own identity," they always said, "and never let television, the media or anyone else define your role for you."

He has followed this advice assiduously, though he has not always found that such resolute individuality produces comfort. While integrating smoothly with white colleagues in all fields, he feels twinges of unease in the white world; while able to adapt to any black group he enters, he seldom feels completely accepted. As he told *Washington Post* reporter Malcolm Gladwell in 1995: "You are living in a white world but you have to hold on to black culture.... One group says you have sold out and the other never quite accepts you."

At a Glance...

Born December 25, 1962, in Westchester County, NY; son of Richard C. and Betty Graham. *Education:* Princeton University, B.A., 1983; Harvard University, J.D., 1988.

Admitted to Bar, 1989; Weil, Gotshal & Manges (law firm), attorney, New York, NY, 1988; Smith, McDaniel & Donahue (law firm focusing on environmental issues), attorney; adjunct professor at Fordham University; lecturer at Harvard Business School, University of Virginia School of Commerce, and University of Pennsylvania School of Law; legal commentator, WNBC-TV New York; author.

Member: City of New York Bar Association; American Bar Association; National Bar Association.

Awards: Named Young Lawyer of the Year, 1993, National Bar Association.

His first taste of nonacceptance occurred at age 10, when he went with a white friend to a country club pool. He plunged into the water along with everyone else, who promptly scrambled out. Thinking there was something in the pool to be afraid of, he followed and soon found that he himself had unwittingly prompted the flight. Nevertheless, by the time he reached high school, his background made him far more comfortable as the lone black member of the tennis team and the school orchestra (he played the oboe) than he was with the few working-class black students he encountered.

Onward and Upward in the Ivy League

When the time came to decide on a college, Lawrence Graham chose Princeton. His family objected strongly, since the Ivy League school had been known in the past for its anti-minority bias. Reminders of former president Woodrow Wilson's staunch anti-black policy were raised. There were recollections of Princeton's accidental integration in 1944, when four black students had been included in a Navy ROTC program. There were quotations from a 1949 speech made by singer Paul Robeson, a Rutgers graduate, who recalled his bitter childhood in the town of Princeton itself. Still, Lawrence did not let his family's objections sway him. Intent on getting the best

education his intellectual ability deserved, he insisted on attending Princeton because it had been listed by many college reference books as one of America's most competitive and top schools.

Once arrived, he found that the racism of the 1940s had declined. There were now many black students on campus, including such famous Afro-Americans as novelist Toni Morrison. However, the situation was still far from ideal. In an essay called "The Underside of Paradise," which appears in his collection *Member of the Club,* Graham sums up his undergraduate experience: "What I found at Princeton was a campus, a student body, a faculty, and a community that had no tolerance for black students who wanted an integrated experience. Regardless of your views, you were compelled to choose between black and white." Ironically, he found the situation identical in both black and white groups.

NEVER Take No for an Answer

He did not allow this to derail his own ambitions. In fact he wrote one book each year until he graduated. His first, *The Ten Point Plan for College Acceptance,* required visits to 50 schools in six states, but was completed by the time he finished his freshman year. "I decided to write an article about getting into college," he said. "No one would publish it because I was an unknown 17-year-old, so I decided to make it into a book instead. I came to New York by bus with two rolls of dimes and started calling publishers from a call box on Park Avenue." Most publishers' receptionists laughed when he spoke to them, but he was not discouraged. "I take an entrepreneurial approach to everything," he later observed. "I NEVER take no for an answer."

Eventually one publisher suggested he get an agent to help sell his book. Grateful for the advice, Graham flipped the telephone directory from 'P' for publishers to 'L' for literary agents, and opened his second roll of dimes. He had reached "Zeckendorf, Susan," the next to last name on the list, before getting an appointment, which eventually led to the book's publication. The *Ten Point Plan* sold 20,000 copies and earned him guest appearances on the *Phil Donahue Show* as well as on the *Today Show.*

By the time he was a senior at Princeton, both *Jobs in the Real World* and *Conquering College Life* had been completed. Graham had also honed his skills to cover his confusion over his personal social niche. "With my antiapartheid activism," he recalls, in an article called "The Underside of Paradise," "the militant blacks forgave me for rooming with whites. With my published books, talk-show appearances, conservative clothes, the bigoted and not-so-bigoted whites made me an exception to their rule of not socializing with blacks."

From Teen to Twenty at Harvard

Graham graduated from Princeton in 1983 and entered Harvard University Law School. He continued to write a book each year. Characteristically, he also kept an eye out for other stimulating opportunities. In 1984, with the help of his roommate, Lawrence Hamdan, he became aware of the possibilities offered by the hitherto untapped teen-to-twenty market. Graham and Hamdan focused on the $200-million collective spending power this group represented, and even went so far as to hire 135 young testers nationwide to keep them abreast of trends in movie heroes, television shows, and clothing of high-school aged consumers. The two young entrepreneurs gave their teenage targets the name "flyers" (Fun Loving Youth en Route to Success) and established F.L.Y.E.R.S. Services Inc., to counsel corporate marketers on ways to reach them. Soon, the two Harvard students boasted such clients as Nestle and Benetton, and by 1987 had sold $250,000 worth of advice. In addition, they had produced two books--the lighthearted *F.L.Y.E.R.S.: Fun-Loving Youth En Route to Success* (published in 1985 by Simon & Schuster), and *Youth Trends,* a more serious look at methods of marketing to teenagers, which was published in 1987 by St. Martin's Press. Seeing the success of this venture, they also began to sell a line of F.L.Y.E.R.S. tote bags, tee shirts, notebooks, windbreakers, and other products in stores.

Into the Real World

Graham did not let the success of F.L.Y.E.R.S. distract him from his longterm goal of becoming a successful lawyer. He began to interview for jobs in 1986, lining up many appointments with New York law firms to make sure he would make the right choice after graduation. A meeting in one Wall Street office affected Graham deeply. Graham was interviewed by one of the firm's 250 lawyers, who made two remarks he found anti-Semitic. When invited to ask questions, Graham asked the interviewer how many of the firms attorneys were black. "Why should that matter?" was the disturbing answer. Immediately he started thinking about another book, which eventually appeared in 1993 as *The Best Companies for Minorities.*

Covering the largest industries in the U.S. economy, including the automotive industry, food, publishing, insurance, and accounting, Graham planned to investigate 625 Fortune 1000 companies offering the best hiring practices, support and mentoring systems, and opportunities for advancement to the most diverse population. Of these, Graham intended to choose the top 100 companies. However, in the end only 85 businesses were able to meet his stringent criteria. Among them were longtime activists in the minority arena, such as McDonalds, Avis, and General Motors.

Sparks Controversy With Books on Racism

In 1992, Graham followed up on some remarks that had prompted him to start his research for *The Best Companies for Minorities.* After interviewing more than 600 black professional people in top corporations, he learned that they felt like outsiders, because they were excluded from membership in places such as the exclusive country clubs where their white colleagues went to strengthen their networking relationships. The discovery prompted him to choose the country-club environment as the subject for an article called "The Invisible Man," which originally appeared in the *New Yorker,* and was later reprinted in *Member of the Club.*

In his essay Lawrence explains how he prepared himself for the assignment, first by rewriting his resume to omit both Harvard and Princeton from his academic record, then by buying himself an unassuming wardrobe. Graham set out to find himself a waiter's post by calling eight country clubs. The results of just these telephone calls were enough to show him that racism is alive and well in America. Of the eight clubs, five invited him to apply, but promptly rescinded their offers when he appeared in person to interview. In the end, two job opportunities came of this research. Graham chose a busboy position offered by the elite Greenwich Country Club in Connecticut. He stayed there for a month, though he found the atmosphere as genteelly racist as he had feared it would be, and the hours far too long for the meager paycheck he received.

A stream of letters to the magazine's editor followed publication of "The Invisible Man" in the *New Yorker* of August 17, 1992. One Greenwich Country Club member, concerned enough to want to excuse himself from the bias of his colleagues, showed himself to have missed the point entirely by suggesting that Graham would have advanced his own cause more successfully had he chosen to talk to the membership committee instead of writing about the club's deficiencies. A resident of Greenwich who did not belong to the Country Club chortled with glee at the unwelcome scrutiny the biased and boring members had received. A couple of black letter-writers mistakenly accused him of scoffing at the skimpy paycheck many families live on. Graham found the controversy stimulating, since it gave him a way to reach an even wider audience. Its message of racism was strong enough to catch the eye of Warner Brothers Studios, who contracted with him for a movie.

> "You are living in a white world but you have to hold on to black culture.... One group says you have sold out and other never quite accepts you.

Graham continued to explore the awkwardness of American integration. "My Dinner with Mr. Charlie," also included in the *Member of the Club* collection, detailed his dining experiences in 10 of New York City's top restaurants. His agenda this time was twofold: to find out how many minority employees worked in each place, and to discover whether or not black clients would be welcomed. His results were discouraging. Several of the restaurants such as Lutece, Mortimer's, Le Cirque, and the 21 Club--culinary legends nationwide--confirmed his suspicions. Most tables he was offered were too close to the kitchen or the bathroom, and he was mistaken for a staff member far too many times for comfort. All this led to one lasting conclusion--that fine dining experience differs markedly according to one's skin color.

Kaleidoscopic Life: Lawyer, Teacher, Entrepreneur

While Graham' articles and books on integration continue to appear, he does not neglect either his legal duties or his responsibilities as president of the White Plains, New York-based Progressive Management Associates. Here, he counsels minority graduates heading for the workplace. "Spend more time finding role models in the fields of business, politics and education," he urges. "Prepare yourself with as much education as possible--we can no longer rely on the glamour professions like the entertainment or sports world."

Selected writings

Ten-Point Plan for College Acceptance, Quick Fox, 1981.
Conquering College Life: How to Be a Winner at College, Washington Square Press, 1983.
Your Ticket To Business School, Bantam, 1985.
Your Ticket To Law School, Bantam, 1985.
Your Ticket to Medical or Dental School, Bantam, 1985.
(With Betty Graham) *Teenager's Ask and Answer Book,* Messner, 1986.
The Best Companies for Minorities, Plume, 1994.
Member of the Club, HarperCollins, 1995.

Sources

Chicago Tribune, January 30, 1994.
Inc., October 1987, p. 10.
People Weekly, January 25, 1982, p. 97.

—Gillian Wolf

Ken Griffey, Jr.

1969—

Professional baseball player

His teammates like to call him "Junior," but Ken Griffey Jr.'s talents are anything but minor. A hard-hitting center fielder for the Seattle Mariners, Griffey has been a significant force behind that team's emergence as an American League division champion in recent years. He can dominate on offense or defense, and his engaging personality has brought him widespread fan approval in a time when most major league baseball players are perceived as spoiled and arrogant. *Atlanta Journal and Constitution* reporter Terence Moore has called Griffey "the Hank Aaron, Willie Mays and Roberto Clemente of our time," and *Sports Illustrated* correspondent E. M. Swift described Griffey as "the kind of player after whom babies and candy bars are named."

Tagged as a top-level prospect when he was only 17 years old, Griffey joined the major leagues in 1989 at the tender age of 19. Baseball was in his genes: his father, Ken Griffey Sr., was a baseball superstar in his own right and was still an active player when his son joined the American League. The Griffeys have made history as the first father-son tandem to play major league baseball simultaneously. Their fame in this re-

gard reached a peak in the 1990 season, when they both worked for the Mariners. As if that publicity weren't enough, Griffey Jr. has taken his place in the game's upper echelon by virtue of his personal accomplishments. Swift, for one, praised "Junior" for "his great arm, his fluid stride, his viperlike uppercut swing," as well as "the pure joy that the kid derives from playing, which, on a good day, can be felt in the corners of the stands." The reporter concluded that Griffey draws attention for "the way he turns this big-buck, high-pressure business called baseball back into a playground game."

The Apple Fell Close to the Tree

The same year George Kenneth Griffey Jr. was born, his father signed to play baseball with the Cincinnati Reds organization. In fact, Ken Jr. was born during the autumn after his father's first season of play in the Reds' minor league system. The family then lived in the Griffey home town of Donora, Pennsylvania, but as Ken Sr.'s career took off, "Junior" and his brother moved with their parents through a series of minor league towns.

At a Glance...

Full name George Kenneth Griffey, Jr.; born November 21, 1969 in Donora, PA; son of Ken (a baseball player) and Alberta Griffey; married, wife's name Melissa. *Education:* Graduated from Moeller High School, Cincinnati, OH, 1987.

Professional baseball player, 1987--. Signed with Seattle Mariners as first choice in first round of 1987 amateur draft; minor leaguer in Mariners' system, 1987-89, reached parent club as non-roster player, 1989; starting outfielder for Mariners, 1989--.

Selected awards: Finished third in balloting for 1989 Rookie of the Year; member of American League All-Star Team, 1990-94, named All-Star Game Most Valuable Player, 1992; Golden Glove awards, 1990, 1991, 1992.

Addresses: *Home*—Renton, WA. *Office*—c/o Seattle Mariners, P.O. Box 4100, 411 1st Ave. South, Seattle, WA 98140.

Their travels came to an end in 1973 when Griffey Sr. made the parent club, which happened to be one of the best major league baseball has ever seen--the famed Cincinnati "Big Red Machine."

The demands of major league baseball are not necessarily compatible with fatherhood. Baseball players travel frequently and pursue their trade at odd hours. They work weekends and evenings. Nevertheless, Griffey recalled in the *Chicago Tribune:* "My dad was a dad first and a baseball player second." The elder Griffey taught his sons to hit a baseball as soon as they could hold a bat. He took them to Reds batting practice, where they hobnobbed with the likes of Pete Rose, Johnny Bench, and Tony Perez. When the Reds played in the World Series in 1975 and 1976, young Griffey looked on from the best seats in the stadium. "I watched my dad play for years," he told *People.* "I talked to him every day about the game. There isn't one thing I've seen so far that he hasn't told me about beforehand."

When Ken Griffey Sr. was traded to the New York Yankees in 1981, his wife and sons stayed behind in Cincinnati. The separations were even more prolonged and difficult than they had been before, and in the odd moments when Griffey Sr. could catch one of his son's

Little League or school games, he was mobbed for autographs and pictures. Father and son never let the circumstances alter their relationship, however. Griffey Jr. told *Ebony:* "If I needed to talk to [my father], I would call him after the game, and we'd talk. If I did something wrong [on the field], he'd fly me to New York and say, 'You can't do that!' Then he would send me home the next day, and I'd play baseball." Interestingly enough, the younger Griffey recalled in the *Chicago Tribune* that he often played at his worst when his father was in the stands. "I was always trying to impress him by hitting the ball 600 feet," he said.

It was talent, and not family connections, that enabled Griffey to join Cincinnati's competitive Connie Mack League, a summer amateur program composed mostly of high school graduates. Even though at 16 he was among the very youngest of the players, Griffey was such a success in the league that his team advanced to the Connie Mack World Series--and he hit three home runs in the championship match. He also played high school baseball and was such a good running back with the Moeller High School football team that he was offered a football scholarship to the University of Oklahoma. He turned the scholarship down and made himself available for the 1987 baseball draft. Defending his decision, he told the *Chicago Tribune* that baseball "is a lot safer and you last longer."

Fast Track to the Majors

Griffey was the number-one pick in major league baseball's 1987 amateur draft. He was chosen by the Seattle Mariners' organization and signed with a $160,000 bonus. In a show of youthful bravado, the 17-year-old player announced that he would make the major leagues within two or three years. No one expected him to live up to that boast--even his father had spent four-and-a-half years on farm teams. Nevertheless, the exuberant Griffey Jr. began his professional career in Bellingham, Washington, batting .320, hitting 14 home runs, and completing 13 steals.

The sailing was not completely smooth, however. Griffey experienced adjustment problems when faced with the pressures of professional baseball. He was far from home, and his father was busy with his own career. Years later Griffey revealed that he attempted suicide by swallowing more than 270 aspirin tablets one night during that rookie season. "I got depressed, I got angry. I didn't want to live," he explained in *Jet* magazine. "The aspirin thing was the only time I acted. It was such a dumb thing."

Griffey found his stride during his second minor league season when, despite injuries, he was voted the top major league prospect in the California League. As the 1989 spring training season began, Griffey was determined to find a spot on the Seattle Mariners' roster. Serious and determined, he studied the opposing pitchers, practiced his fielding diligently, and wound up batting .359 with two home runs and 21 runs batted in during spring training games. Sure enough, he earned a place on the team. When he took the field for his first major league game, he was 19--one of the youngest men ever to make the majors.

Newspapers and magazines seized upon the Griffey family story. While Ken Jr. was making his debut with the Mariners in Seattle, his father was returning to the Reds and marking his twentieth anniversary in professional sports. It was a historic moment for baseball, surpassed only in 1990 when the two men both played for the Mariners simultaneously. The extra attention might have proven difficult for some rookie players, but "Junior" took it all in stride. "Once he stepped onto the field," Swift wrote, "the kid seemed to relate best to destiny. From the start he showed an almost preposterous flair for the dramatic. He doubled in his first official big-league at-bat. He hit an opposite-field homer on his first swing before the hometown fans in the Kingdome. He hit a game-winning two-run homer in his first pinch-hitting appearance in May [1989]." The correspondent added: "One Seattle columnist suggested that the Ken Griffey Jr. candy bar, of which some 800,000 were sold last year, was hardly enough for the lad. Boeing, he wrote, should name a plane after him." Only a late-season injury robbed Griffey of the statistics necessary to earn Rookie of the Year honors. He finished third in the balloting.

Centerpiece of a Franchise

Griffey put the Mariners on the baseball map in 1990, batting .300 and earning his first of three consecutive Gold Glove awards. He also became the second youngest player ever to start an All-Star Game. That same season saw both Griffeys playing for the Mariners--an historic first for baseball that may never be repeated. Griffey Sr. joined the Mariners late in the season after being released by the Reds. Jim Lefebvre, the Mariners' manager at the time, told the *Los Angeles Times* that the teaming-up of the two Griffey stars was "a great day for baseball." Lefebvre commented: "Here he is a father, a veteran player ending his career, and the son is a brilliant young talent, just like his father was when he was first starting his career, and they're both going to be out there together."

By 1992 the days of father and son playing for the same team were over, and the era of Ken Griffey Jr. had begun. In 1992 Griffey batted .308, hit 27 home runs, and was named Most Valuable Player at the All-Star Game after turning in a three-for-four evening with a home run. He also charmed fans and the media alike with his willingness to grant interviews and his obvious love for baseball. Not surprisingly, observers began to predict a Hall of Fame career for the young star. Griffey made light of these predictions, telling *Sport* magazine: "I just want to go out there and contribute. No matter what happens, you got to be lucky to get in the Hall of Fame. You got to have a long, healthy career."

Hall of Fame prospects are also boosted by post-season play. During the early years of Griffey's major league career, his talents seemed wasted on a struggling team like the Seattle Mariners. That is no longer the case. The Mariners have become contenders, with the perennially strong Griffey leading the way. The team took off in the spring of 1995, showing playoff possibilities under the new divisional rankings. Ironically, Griffey almost missed the post-season show. On May 26, 1995 he broke both bones in his wrist when he crashed into the Kingdome wall while chasing down a fly ball. The injury required the installation of seven screws and a 4-inch metal plate in his left wrist, and he was expected to miss at least three months of play. Nevertheless, he returned to the lineup August 15 and, after struggling through the season's later weeks, found his stride again in time for the divisional and league playoffs.

> "I just want to go out there and contribute. No matter what happens, you got to be lucky to get in the Hall of Fame. You got to have a long, healthy career."

The 1995 American League Divisional Playoffs--the first of their kind--pitted the Mariners against the Yankees in a best-of-five series. It was during the fifth and deciding game that Griffey had his defining moment as a potential baseball immortal. The game went into extra innings, and the Yankees took a five-to-four lead in the top of the 11th inning. When the Mariners came to bat, Griffey hit a single with a man on base to place runners at first and third. Then Edgar Martinez hit a hard shot into the left field corner. The man on third scored easily to tie the game, but Griffey was not to be denied.

Turning on the base-running speed for which he is known, he streaked around the diamond and slid across home plate just in front of the outfielder's throw. Griffey's feat brought the Mariners their first divisional title and the right to meet the Cleveland Indians in the 1995 American League Playoffs.

"It's Never Work"

Griffey signed to play for the Mariners through the 1996 season, and he has expressed little interest in leaving Seattle. He and his wife live there all year around, and they are frequently visited by other members of the Griffey family. Many major league players are obsessed with their statistics and their salaries, but Griffey is the exception to that rule. He wants to do well, but he also intends to enjoy himself while pursuing that Hall of Fame display. Baseball, Griffey told the *Chicago Tribune,* "is never work. Work is something you have to go do and you don't want to. If you do something that's fun, you can't call it work." The superstar added that his career

is "sometimes like a dream, one of those dreams that are real good and you're in a deep sleep and you never really want to wake up."

e most I've done to handle the attention is change my name on the road at our team hotel." He concluded, "Hey, it's not like I'm a rock star or something. They have it much worse. Me? I'm just out there having fun."

Sources

Atlanta Journal and Constitution, July 13, 1994, p. E2.

Boston Globe, October 13, 1995, p. 93.

Chicago Tribune, April 17, 1992, p. C1.

Ebony, September 1989, pp. 78-82.

Jet, April 6, 1992.

Los Angeles Times, September 1, 1990, p. C1.

People, July 17, 1989, pp. 77-78.

Sport, March 1991, pp. 38-45.

Sports Illustrated, May 16, 1988, pp. 64-68; May 7, 1990, pp. 38-42; August 8, 1994, pp. 24-31.

—Mark Kram

Anthony P. Griffin

1954—

Lawyer

Anthony Griffin is a Galveston-based civil rights lawyer with a difference. Remembering his own humble roots, he has chosen to invest more than $2 million to finance an office-block and shopping complex in the city's poorest neighborhood. In this way, he hopes to encourage government investment in sidewalks, garbage collection, and beautification, which he feels are sorely neglected. He also has a well-earned reputation as a fierce defender of First Amendment rights for all American citizens, whether their message is popular or not.

All this is enough to bring prominence to any civil rights activist. Yet Anthony Griffin insists on keeping a low profile in all matters unrelated directly to his legal practice. "I don't give up information surrounding myself because a lot of times the first line of attack is your loved ones. I don't take risks that others are willing to take simply because of what I do for a living," is his uncompromising statement on this matter.

Griffin was born in 1954, in Baytown, Texas. He is reticent even on the matter of his youth, noting merely that he was one of seven children. He chose to stay in-

state after graduating from the University of Texas Law Center, and went into practice on his own, in Galveston.

While he practices within several legal specialities, he is particularly sought after for matters dealing with civil rights issues. He keeps his name on a panel of lawyers who volunteer their services pro bono for the American Civil Liberties Union, and did the same for the National Association for the Advancement of Colored Peoples until October 1993, when their association came to an abrupt end.

This drama involved several major players. The kingpin was Anthony Griffin himself, who was representing a member of the sinister Ku Klux Klan in a matter involving freedom of speech. Appearing at the request of the ACLU, Griffin was cool, sure of his legal stance, and determined to stand stoutly behind the First Amendment, which guarantees free speech to all citizens in a democratic country like America. Just as determined in their opposition to his appearance was the National Association for the Advancement of Colored Peoples, a longtime friend for whom Griffin had also appeared without fee.

Desegregation in Vidor

The roots of the problem went back to the beginning of 1993, when Vidor, an all-white town Texan town near the Louisiana border, began to carry out a court order to integrate its public housing complex. During the year Vidor's 11,000-strong population increased, but the town's first black residents in 70 years, were not permitted to live in peace. The Ku Klux Klan saw to that.

By the time the events of Vidor came up, the Ku Klux Klan had had almost 130 years to hone their racism. Much given to harassment, lynching, and even murder to make their presence known, from their earliest days they had sallied forth dressed in hooded white shrouds and bearing burning crosses, bent on bringing misery and destruction to anyone in their path who happened to be Jewish, Catholic, or black. While neither hoods nor robes appeared at the Vidor housing complex, the bullying and the intimidation were so virulent that the Texas Human Rights Commission issued a restraining order against the two Klan groups responsible for most of the action. In addition, there were were several cameras on-site, to record the presence of placards bearing such messages as "I Will Work to Keep Vidor White, Will You?" Also noted were the actions of Michael Lowe, grand dragon of one of the Klan groups, who was shown knocking on the door of a new black resident and taunting him.

This protracted harassment spurred the Texas Human Rights Commission to demand membership lists and accompanying financial information first from Charles Lee, leader of the White Camelia Klan based in Cleve-land, Texas, then from Michael Lowe, whose Knights of the Ku Klux Klan is affiliated with the Arkansas-based group behind grand dragon-turned state legislator David Duke. Both Lee and Lowe balked at this government demand. Eventually Lee complied, after a contempt of court charge landed him in jail for 12 days. Lowe, however, was made of sterner stuff. He refused to hand over his documents, choosing instead to call the American Civil Liberties Union (ACLU) and ask for representation.

The American Civil Liberties Union

An organization formed in 1920 especially to preserve the constitutional rights of Americans to freedom of speech, religion, and expression, the ACLU has long been accustomed to such requests from unpopular groups who want protection from government interference. In just one instance, its exercise of the First Amendment's mandate to allow free speech and assembly guaranteed a Nazi group the right to march in Skokie, Illinois in 1978, despite the anguished protests of the Holocaust survivors who lived there. This may seem unfair, but as constitutional lawyer Linda Monk reminds us, in her book *The Bill of Rights: A User's Guide,* the ACLU follows the reasoning of Justice Oliver Wendell Holmes, who specified that the First Amendment is not designed to protect "free thought for those who agree with us but freedom for the thought that we hate."

It was this Holmesian directive that made the ACLU grant the request of Ku Klux Klan grand dragon Michael Lowe. They consulted their list of lawyer volunteers, and without making any distinction between blacks and whites, picked a name—Anthony Griffin of Galveston.

For any lawyer, a pro bono appearance is an undertaking that requires a careful decision. Not only does he forego any fees for his work and his preparation—he also loses the opportunity to earn money by spending his time in ways which will earn him a reward. As an experienced lawyer, Griffin understood all this. He was also quite aware of the strange quirk of fate requiring him, an African American lawyer with an impeccable civil rights record, to defend the free speech rights of the group symbolizing the ugliest racism in America.

Still, Griffin accepted the case immediately. "I considered it an honor," he said to the *Chicago Defender,* in September 1993. "It is anytime you have the opportunity to defend the Bill of Rights." But this was not his only reason for accepting the challenge. He had a very distinct memory of a 1958 case known as NAACP v Alabama, in which the NAACP had been ordered to produce its membership lists for state inspection. When their refusal landed them in court, First Amendment protection had granted the NAACP the power to keep their membership lists private, on the grounds that public disclosure might subject their members to reprisals. Now, that First Amendment protection had to be extended to a far less worthy organization. "Lord knows, don't hear me say I'm an apologist for the Klan," he told the *Washington Post,* on September 29th, 1993, the day the legal proceedings began. "But it's very easy to give the First Amendment to groups we like ... It's very difficult to apply those principles to people who anger us."

A Study in Contrasts: Griffin and the Grand Dragon

As every single newspaper covering the ensuing legal proceedings remarked, Griffin and Lowe made an odd couple. Griffin was 38 years old, poised, and highly educated. His client, on the other hand, was a carpenter with a high school education, who admitted to having spent six years in jail for burglary. At 44 years of age, Lowe was still living with his "mama" and his "daddy" in Waco, where his Klan robe hung behind his bedroom door. He was still boasting of the huge tattoo on his back which showed a robed Klansman, and, even after being caught bullying the residents of the Vidor housing complex, he was still claiming to be a separatist rather than a white supremacist.

He was also still eager to tell the *New York Times* all about his first meeting with the lawyer assigned to him by the ACLU. "I saw this NAACP pin on the wall," he said." Then I started looking at the shelves, and there were these books on African and African American history." Then, Lowe continued, realization dawned. "Holy moly!" he told his girlfriend, "I think this guy's black!" Griffin, well-acquainted with the Klan and its position in the community, felt no such amazement. All accounts of the meeting agree that he took brisk control of the situation, and curtly gave Lowe to understand that this case was not about relationships between African Americans and the Ku Klux Klan—it concerned only the First Amendment rights of free speech.

As he had expected, Griffin won his case. In applause the *Galveston County Observer News/An African American* Monthly Newspaper, which remarked: "For those who do not want the Ku Klux Klan to have their rights protected, you should consider which of your rights you are willing to give up because the Klan has to give up

theirs. It may be you giving up yours tomorrow."

> "I don't like the Klan, but if I don't stand up and defend the Klan's right to free speech, my right to free speech will be gone."

Nevertheless, it was a Pyrrhic victory at best. Having worked against vicious Klan discrimination since its establishment in 1909, the NAACP felt bitterly betrayed. Unable to see that their opposition to giving First Amendment rights to the Klan was also a form of discrimination, they chose to fire Griffin from their roster of lawyer-volunteers. "When he represented the Klansman in court ... he voluntarily relinquished his post," Gary Bledsoe, president of the Texas NAACP informed the *Chicago Tribune.* "By representing the Klan, he is in direct conflict with the mission of the NAACP." They were not alone in this view. "We can only wonder," came a caustic comment from the *New York Amsterdam News,* "what the thousands of people lynched, burned, beaten, and maimed by the Klan since the end of the Civil War would feel about Griffin's *noblesse oblige.*"

Griffin himself was mystified by all the enmity. I had no idea it would be like this," he remarked to Starita Smith of *Emerge* magazine. "I thought that we could fight the fight and get it over with." Instead, he found himself reluctantly accepting invitations for radio and television interviews, in order to emphasize the significance of the First Amendment and its importance for all Americans, whether they hold popular views or not. "I don't like the Klan, but if I don't stand up and defend the Klan's right to free speech, my right to free speech will be gone," was the essence of his message.

In 1995 he took the matter further, and chose to add a chapter to a multi-author book called *Speaking of Race, Speaking of Sex: Hate Speech, Civil Rights, and Civil Liberties.* Griffin's section consisted of three fables, each one illustrating one of his major points about the First Amendment. He made his point, though the book received lukewarm reviews at best.

The Klan and the Adopt-a-Highway Program

Before the book was off the press the Klan came to him

with another problem. This time, they wanted to join the state's eight-year-old Adopt-A-Highway Program, which promised a sign with their name on it in exchange for regular litter removal in their designated area. The stretch of highway concerned was in Vidor, not far from the housing complex that had felt their influence a year before. As *Houston Chronicle* staff reporter Wendy Benjaminson noted, several groups of prisoners, pit-bull fanciers, and nudists were given the opportunity to become blacktop parents for the purpose of trash control, but the courts denied the Klan this right.

There was no evasion about why the group had been turned down. "It is the opinion of this court that the Ku Klux Klan has applied to adopt a highway as subterfuge to intimidate those minority residents already living in the Vidor housing complex, and to discourage further desegregation," wrote U.S. District Judge Joe Fisher. Even Griffin agreed that the Klan was more interested in making a point about free expression than in picking up trash. But, ever the realist, he had to note that barring them from this activity was unlikely to prevent people from uttering racist epithets while walking past this or any other housing complex. Alas, life does not work that way.

Sources

Monk, Linda R, *The Bill of Rights:* A User's Guide, Close-Up Publishing, 1991, p. 72.

Periodicals

Chicago Defender, September 20, 1993, p. 12.
Chicago Tribune, October 3, 1993, p. 21.
Emerge, March 31, 1995, p. 55.
Houston Chronicle, September 30, 1993, May 8, 1994; July 27, 1995, p. 36.
Houston Post, October 3, 1993, p. 31; October 22, 1993, p. A19; November 30, 1993, p. 12; December 4, 1994, p. A1.
New Amsterdam News, September 11, 1993, p. 26.
Washington Post; September 4, 1993, p. A27; September 4, 1994, p.A47; September 29, 1993, p.A3; October 6, 1993, p. A18; June 25, 1994, P. A1: January 27, 1995, p. C2.

—Gillian Wolf

Bethann Hardison

19(?)(?)—

Modeling agency owner

"Tall, lithe, and lively, Bethann [Hardison] is regal without being self-righteous, maternal without being matriarchal, meticulous without being anal retentive," asserted Greg Tate in *Vibe* magazine. "She's the Woman, and a warrior-woman to boot." Hardison, founder of the respected modeling agency that bears her name, has long been a ground-breaker in the world of fashion, as both a model and a businessperson. Especially since going into business for herself in 1984, she has helped guide the careers of some of the most prominent African American faces in recent times, and she is the founder of a watchdog/charity/networking group of positive image-makers called the Black Girls Coalition. By her agency's promotion of women of color, "Hardison has greatly expanded racial diversity" in the fashion industry, noted a reporter in an *American Photo* magazine special issue on "The 100 Most Important People in Photography." The reporter concluded: "[Hardison] has challenged, and helped change, common notions of beauty."

Hardison grew up in Brooklyn, New York in a family of devout Muslims. From an early age she was busy attempting to shatter the status quo: she was her high school's first African American cheerleader, and, upon entering New York City's garment district in search of a job in the fashion industry, was the first African American salesperson in a showroom. Sometime around the late 1960s, a young African American designer named Willi Smith encountered Hardison in an elevator. He imme-

diately asked her to model for him, and Hardison's start as his fitting model soon led to runway and print work for other designers.

Hardison became one of a handful of African American models in the early 1970s whose frames showed off the clothes of top designers in the European and New York collections, appeared in fashion spreads for the likes of *Vogue* and *Harper's Bazaar,* and broke new ground for African American women in the industry. Iman, Beverly Johnson, and Pat Cleveland were all Hardison's contemporaries. Eventually she went into partnership with Smith, and in 1980 joined a start-up modeling agency as a booker. The agency was called Click, and with its unusual roster of models "became known for a more exotic, less traditional kind of beauty," noted a *Mirabella* correspondent. Hardison's job as a booker involved teaming members of Click's talent roster with clients—designers, magazines, ad agencies—looking for models. By 1981 she was head of Click's women's division, in any agency its most powerful and lucrative department.

Opened Doors With Own Agency

A friend who was then in law school helped convince Hardison of her own potential to make a much larger impact on the fashion industry. Urging her to start her own agency, he put up the money, and Hardison negotiated with the young women who were interested in jumping ship from the bigger agencies; the models agreed to wait for payment until the clients paid the new agency, in lieu of obtaining the usual agency advance. With that spirit of goodwill, Bethann Management was born in 1984. Its initial roster included 16 models, nearly half African American. Yet Hardison has reiterated that it was never her intention to run an exclusively "people of color" agency, but it has been her aim to bring more diversity into the business.

Hardison will interview a potential signee on two or three occasions. "I'm looking for something beyond just a face," she told Stephanie Dolgoff in *American Photo.* "The more intelligent they are, the more open and well rounded they are, the more they convey in photographs." One of Bethann Management's early successes was Veronica Webb, a teenager from Detroit who went on to work the runways of top designers such as Chanel in the mid-1980s, eventually joining the ranks of the top-earning supermodels. Webb later won a coveted contract with Revlon in the type of multimillion-dollar deal that is the holy grail of the modeling game—and one that is often hard to achieve for African American models.

Lent Novices Guidance and Encouragement

With a roster that sometimes numbers almost 30 models, Hardison takes an involved role in helping to keep

the young men and women focused on the hard work of modeling. In addition to taking scrupulous care of their personal appearances and physical health, Hardison also instructs them to "educate yourself constantly about the business you have stepped into," she explained in *Essence.* "Learn about finances, learn how to be professional, learn personal public relations. Work hard to get and keep a healthy attitude. It's important to remember where you come from, so you will always know where you are going."

Since its inception Bethann Management has striven to increase African American visibility in the fashion world and the corresponding onslaught of media images the industry generates annually. In *Essence* Hardison admitted that she has fought an uphill battle. "The industry is looking for Black images that are compatible with their white counterparts, but always with the white images first and Black images—if at all—second," she said. In 1988 Hardison—with her friend Iman—co-founded the Black Girls Coalition, a loose group of industry insiders working to change the status quo. "Racism is practiced every day in the industry, but they don't realize it," Hardison pointed out in *Interview* magazine.

One of the press conferences held by Hardison and other members of the Black Girls Coalition in the early 1990s excoriated the top players in fashion—the designers, the magazines—for subtle racism; a few months later Naomi Campbell became the first woman of African descent to grace the cover of *Allure.*

> "I want to do more than just run an agency. I'm here to give other young women an opportunity. I want them to know there's someone who will take time to communicate with them."

"I want to do more than just run an agency," Hardison admitted in *American Photo.* "I'm here to give other young women an opportunity. I want them to know there's someone who will take time to communicate with them." That helping hand continues to extend to members of both genders in Bethann Management's talent roster, as witnessed in the rising career of Harlem's own Tyson Beckford. The young man broke new ground as one of the most sought-after—and highest paid—African American models in the industry. Discovered by the hip-hop culture magazine *The Source,* Beckford learned about Bethann Management when Hardison's son, actor Kadeem Hardison—formerly of *A Different World*—was a guest on Arsenio Hall's late-night talk show and spoke of his mother's business. By 1996, under Hardison's watchful *eye,* Beckford had become the first African American male to appear in Ralph Lauren clothing in the American designer's lavish print advertising campaigns. Beckford then signed a lucrative contract with Lauren, also a significant achievement for an African American model of either gender. "I've gone out with him and seen that folks really are proud because he is like them," Hardison told *Vibe.* "He's not some polished-up boy from college who's light enough and keen enough to get away with something."

Joined Energies to Combat Racism, Indifference

Hardison and other members of the Black Girls Coalition work to help clear the path for other African Americans interested in the fashion industry, both behind the scenes as well as in front of the cameras. The group also tackles more weighty issues such as home-lessness. "I'd like to think I'm here to make a difference," Hardison asserted in *Vibe.* "I never expected to make big money at what I do. But in terms of respect and longevity, I can make a difference for a Tyson, a Veronica Webb, a Roshumba, or the next young person who comes along." Yet Hardison did once divulge dreams of another world far removed from the glamorous, high-stakes fashion scene. "I'd like to own a bar in Anguilla," she once confessed in *Mirabella.* "And then maybe I'd sell collectibles, things picked up from my travels."

Sources

American Photo, May/June 1993; January/February 1994.
Essence, January 1987, p. 42; July 1994, p. 79.
Interview, October 1993, p. 78.
Mirabella, July 1990.
Vibe, May 1995, p. 34.

Additional information provided by Bethann Management, Inc., 1996.

—Carol Brennan

Rt. Rev. Barbara Harris

1930—

Cleric

"Our church is notorious for its short lived love affairs with one cause or another. Today it's the homeless. Tomorrow they'll be all but forgotten." The Reverend Barbara Harris preached these words in the Washington, DC Cathedral a year after her elevation as the first black woman—and the first woman—ever to reach the level of bishop in the Episcopal Church. Harris has built a religious career based on the social aspects of the Gospel, her words reflecting the life of one who has not been afraid to heed Jesus Christ's call to "deny yourself, take your cross and follow me."

Early Spiritual Life

From a young age Harris felt a call to a life of service to Christ lived out through the established church. As a teenager she founded a youth group at St. Barnabas Church in the Germantown section of Philadelphia, a group that would go on to become the largest such organization in the city. She also found time to accompany the church choir on the piano. When she finished high school, she took some training in advertising and went to work in public relations, well aware that the

Episcopalian priesthood was closed to women at that time.

Harris's commitment to active ministry found an outlet with the St. Dismas Society of her area. St. Dismas is the legendary name given to the thief crucified next to Jesus who begged for forgiveness. He is often referred to as "The Good Thief." The St. Dismas Society is an organization that visits and ministers to prisoners. Harris dedicated more and more of her time to this activity, becoming a board member of the Pennsylvania Prison Society and remaining in that grueling position for 15 years. Her colleague, the Reverend Paul Washington, has estimated that Harris was so zealous in this work that she spent enough time in the prisons over that period to have served two years of captivity herself. In the early 1960s she also spent a good deal of time working in the civil rights movement, spending her vacations registering voters in the South and marching with Dr. Martin Luther King, Jr.

The First Women Priests

About the time that Harris was looking for new oppor-

At a Glance...

Born in 1930 in Philadelphia, PA; daughter of Walter and Beatrice (maiden name, Price) Harris. *Education:* Attended Charles Morris Price School of Advertising and Journalism, Villanova University, Urban Theology School of Sheffield, England; Hobart and William Smith College, STD, 1981.

Worked in community relations department of Sun Oil Company; served as president of Josephine Baker Associates; ordained priest in the Episcopal Church, 1980; St. Augustine of Hippo Parish, Norristown, PA, priest-in-charge, 1980-84; Church of Advocate, interim rector, 1984-88; Episcopal Church Publishing Company, executive director, 1984-89; Episcopalian Diocese of Massachusetts, suffragan bishop, 1989—. Former board member of Pennsylvania Prison Society.

Selected awards: Honorary degrees from General Theological Seminary, Episcopal Divinity School, and Amherst College, all 1989.

Addresses: *Office*—Suffragan Bishop, Episcopal Diocese of Massachusetts, 138 Tremont St., Boston, MA 02111.

were the successors of the original apostles, and that their authority was handed down in an unbroken chain of succession from those first followers of Christ. According to these traditionalists, since none of the original apostles were women, neither should any successive bishop be female. The protest over that point was rather mute at first, only becoming a firestorm later when Harris stood prepared to ascend to that rank.

Her days of controversy in the future, Harris was overjoyed at the opening of the Episcopal clerical ranks to women. She went back to school to study theology and to prepare to enter the priesthood. Her studies took her to several well-respected institutions, including Villanova University and Hobart and William Smith College in America, and the Urban Theological School of Sheffield, England. When she came back to the United States, she received her Doctor of Divinity degree and pursued additional studies at Amherst College.

Harris has striven to be a bishop for the whole church, avoiding a concentration on just issues of gender and race.

Harris became a deacon in 1979 and was ordained to the priesthood in 1980. Almost immediately upon her ordination, she made a name for herself as a social activist. Besides parish work, she also took on the position of Executive Director of the Episcopal Church Publishing Company (ECPC), a liberal organization that published the controversial magazine *The Witness.* In her regular column in that publication, Harris took on such issues as bombers who targeted abortion clinics— whom she regarded as terrorists—and the politics of AIDS.

Became First Female Bishop

According to the rules of the American Episcopalian Church, after a person is elected bishop in her local diocese, she must be confirmed by more than half of the nation's other bishops before being elevated to the chair. As soon as Harris was nominated in her diocese, traditionalists and other opponents launched an intense campaign to discredit her. The issue of her gender could not be held against her, since the denomination had opened the bishop's position to women. However, Harris's detractors attacked her non-traditional training

tunities to serve the church, support in the Episcopal denomination was swelling for the ordination of women as priests. In 1974, without the permission of the Episcopal hierarchy, 11 women accepted ordination from several retired bishops. The women were quickly dubbed the "Philadelphia 11." Barbara Harris was not among the women, but she did take part in the ordination ceremony, carrying the crucifix that led the opening procession. In a hastily-convened session, the American bishops declared the ordinations invalid. Despite the hierarchy's condemnation, four more women accepted ordination the next year in a Washington, DC church.

At the regularly scheduled Episcopal convention in 1976, the bishops decided to accept all the ordinations as valid and to allow women to be ordained from that time forward. At the same time they decided to open all ministries to women, including the seat of bishop. This was a momentous step, since in the 450-year history of the Episcopal Church no woman had ever served in that capacity. In fact, traditionalists believed that bishops and even her personal life despite the fact that she had demonstrated a deep commitment to her faith. The issue of her race was not raised, but it probably played some part in fomenting opposition to her sitting in the bishop's chair.

Harris's liberal social views were perhaps the strongest cause of the opposition she faced, but they also had proven popular with a large segment of the Episcopal church membership. Her supporters carried the day with force, and she immediately reached out to take a conciliatory position as she was confirmed as suffragan, or assisting, bishop of Massachusetts. Despite a few lingering protests outside the church when she was installed, rejoicing was widespread at her consecration as bishop. The celebration even exceeded the boundaries of the Episcopal Church: other denominations sent supporters to witness the occasion, and among the musicians was the Choir of the African Methodist Church which broke into the hymn, "Ride on King Jesus," upon seeing Harris enter the church.

Since her election, Harris has striven to be a bishop for the whole church, avoiding a concentration on just issues of gender or race. An *Ebony* magazine reporter pointed out, however, that she remains an "international Symbol of the struggle for gender equality in the Church." Her attitude remains remarkably free and open. Recently when a loyal church member bent over to kiss her ring, symbol of her authority as bishop, she pulled her hand back, saying "Forget the ring, Sweetie, kiss the bishop."

Sources

Ebony, November 1995, p. 122.
Philadelphia Tribune, April 29, 1984, p. D6.
Washington Post, January 26, 1989, p. A4; September 11, 1989, p. E1.

—Jim McDermott

E. Lynn Harris

1957—

Author

E. Lynn Harris had a secret he kept from his co-workers for a long time. The first person he spoke to about his secret was well-known author Maya Angelou. In 1983 she was speaking at a corporate conference in the company where Harris worked. It was there he confessed his secret to her. He wanted to become a writer. "She told me I should write something every day," he said in *People* magazine, "even if it was just one word." This dedication to his dream has made Harris an extremely popular author today.

Popular, But No Friends

E. Lynn Harris was born in Flint, Michigan in the late 1950's. His mother was a single parent who raised him and his three sisters on her salary from factory jobs. "My mother was a single parent who always worked two jobs," Harris told the *Chicago Tribune*. "We have never been a sit-down-at-the-table-and-discuss-our-lives-type. But there has always been a lot of love there." Harris recalls watching white families on television and wondering why his family did not act the way they did. "I realize now that we, black families, respond to things different-

ly," he added in the *Tribune*.

When Harris was four years old his mother moved to Little Rock, Arkansas, where Harris spent the remaining time of his growing up years. His mother had a small four room house. *The Houston Chronicle* said that as a teenager Harris "used to lie about his modest, single-parent background and pretend to be the scion of a well-off family." "I started working odd jobs at age 12 to help support the family," said Harris in *The Atlanta Constitution*. Even though life wasn't easy he managed to do right. "My mother is my greatest inspiration because she worked so hard to bring us up right. She leads by example." According to *The New York Times*, Harris was 14 when he first met his father, who was killed a year later.

Harris attended high school several miles away from his home and commuted the distance daily. The school was a predominately white school. Harris says he attended the school because students received a better education at that school than the schools closer to his home. When he graduated, E. Lynn Harris went on to attend the University of Arkansas in Fayetteville. It was there that he decided he was going to become a writer. He majored

At a Glance...

Born 1957 in Flint, Michigan, son of Etta Harris an assembly worker and single parent. 3 younger sisters. Single, no children. *Education:* University of Arkansas at Fayetteville, B.A. in Journalism, 1977; further classes in business at Southern Methodist University.

Corporate Sales Staff, IBM, AT & T, and Hewlett-Packard, 1977-90; Author, 1990-present.
Author: *Invisible Life,* self published, 1992; Anchor Books, 1994. *Just As I Am,* Doubleday, 1994; *And This Too Shall Pass,* Doubleday, 1996.

Addresses: *Agent*—Doubleday Books, 1540 Broadway, New York, New York 10036.

in journalism and received his degree in 1977. While at Arkansas Harris was the first black male cheerleader, the first black yearbook editor, and president of his fraternity. He told *The Houston Chronicle* that he was in that workaholic mode, being the most popular, but not having any friends.

To this day Harris remains an Arkansas Razorback fan. He seems more devoted than their other big fan Bill Clinton. "I get upset and depressed for a day when Arkansas loses. I don't even read the sports pages. It's just my passion," he told *USA Today.* He went on to tell the story of how he rushed through a book signing and interviews one night a couple of years ago during the NCAA basketball tournament, "it was the one time that I prayed no one would show up," he said.

Harris Discovers His Sexuality

"I was miserable because I was living a lie," he told *The New York Times.* "Mr. Harris said he fretted over his looks and lied about his sexuality for years," the paper continued. "He drank too much. He was lonely." Mr. Harris relates one story where he called his mother crying because he had broken off a relationship with a lover. He said in *The Commercial Appeal (Memphis),* that his mother told him "You're my baby and I love you no matter what" "And I said, "I know mom, but sometimes you need somebody more than your mother to love you." She didn't know at the time that Harris was gay. When asked about his sexuality Mr. Harris has given

different answers. To some reporters he has said he is gay and has known this for many years. At other times he has said that he relates to one of the characters from his first two novels, Raymond Tyler, Jr., "I see myself as a gay man, but when I see an attractive woman," he said in *The Dallas Morning News,* "or think about settling down and making a home for myself, I still feel that ambivalence. I think it's an issue that troubles a lot of men."

After college Harris was hired immediately by IBM. He spent approximately the next thirteen years selling mainframe computers for IBM as well as AT&T and Hewlett-Packard. He lived in Dallas, Houston, and New York City before moving to Atlanta. Harris has said he was earning $90,000 a year at his sales job before he left. *The Houston Chronicle* called him, "successful but not happy." They also added " ... he turned to writing as a form of therapy to help alleviate feelings of depression." "Part of the depression was that being black and gay had caused me so much pain," he said in *The Houston Chronicle,* If someone understood the pain that living this life could cause, maybe they would see that nobody would go out willy-nilly and choose it, and they would show more empathy." As with many gay men it took some time before Mr. Harris could feel comfortable with his sexuality.

> "I had over 5,000 copies in rented office space. At the first book party we sold only 42, and I felt sick."

After leaving his high powered sales job, Harris began writing. When he completed his first book he sent it to several publishers. Not a single publisher would agree to publish the manuscript. Some even went so far to say that black people didn't want to read about the things he was writing. Even a national publisher of gay books rejected the manuscript. After some soul searching and getting over the pain of all the rejection letters, Harris decided he would publish his own book. According to *Publishers Weekly* he contacted AIDS agencies and they were able to provide the money he needed in exchange for a portion of the proceeds in return for helping him promote the book. He was also able to find a printer that would work with him to arrange payment for their work. "I got the book printed right before the Christmas of 1991, and that's when the horror started," he said to the magazine. "I had over 5,000 copies in rented office space. At the first book party we sold only 42, and I felt sick."

He began carrying around boxes of the book in the trunk of his car. He left copies at beauty salons, women's groups, black-owned bookstores and even went door-to-door in an effort to sell the book. Bookstores began calling him when customers began requesting the book they had seen in beauty salons. It wasn't long before *Essence* magazine named his book one of their ten best of the year. He worked hard enough that eventually he had sold 10,000 copies of the book that he published. For many first books, published by major publishers, this is considered to be a successful book. All Harris' work finally netted him a contract with a publisher. Doubleday signed him to a writing deal, after reading an article about him in *The Atlanta Constitution*. They re-issued the first book *Invisible Life* in paperback, and published in hard-cover his second book *Just As I Am.*

Finally, Success Arrived

Harris became well-known. He is greeted by hundreds of fans when he arrives for book signings at stores around the country. His third book spent several weeks on *The New York Times* bestseller list. "Slowly I'm seeing more men, slowly I'm seeing more whites," Harris said recently in *The Houston Chronicle*. "But the majority are Black women. They are very fervent in their support." Being a former salesman, he knows that his fan base has grown because the amount of time his latest book has spent on the bestseller lists. On why his books are popular Harris told the *Chicago Tribune,* "The characters and situations are so real that people learn something about themselves and about other people." He also feels that the books touch everyone in the black community, both gay and straight. "Most of the black community believe that certain people like up-standing or popular black people can't be (gay or bisexual)," he told the Chicago paper. The *Tribune* also added that "the popularity of his novels have forced the African American community to examine this once hidden side of the black culture."

Harris now splits his time between homes in New York City and Atlanta. He is working on his memoirs which are scheduled to be published next year. They are tentatively entitled, For Colored Boys Who Have Considered Suicide When Being Gay Was Too Tough, a word play on the title of Ntozake Shange's play *For Colored Girls Who Have Considered Suicide/When The Rainbow Is Enuf.* He is also working on the sale of the screen rights of his books, so that they can be made into movies, as well as two other novels.

Harris is still single, though *The New York Times* says he "prays for a partner. Someone who loves basketball and ballet. Someone who's willing to tell the truth. Someone who's willing to accept love." These thoughts are a long way from the young boy that dreamed of a middle class life. "I know now it's okay to have dreams—just make sure they're your own."

Sources

The Atlanta Constitution, June 9, 1992, p. D1.
Chicago Tribune, December 5, 1994, p. C1.
The Commercial Appeal (Memphis), April 4, 1996, p. 1C.
The Dallas Morning News, April 3, 1996, p. 1C.
Emerge, July/August 1996, p 77.
Essence, April 1996, p. 88.
The Houston Chronicle, April 14, 1996, p. 20.
The New York Times, March 17, 1996, p. A43.
People, April 15, 1995, p. 115.
Publishers Weekly, December 6, 1993, pp. 29, 32.
USA Today, August 17, 1994, p. 7D.

—Stephen Stratton

Robert Hayden

1913–1980

Poet, educator

Robert Hayden preferred to think of himself not as a black poet, but rather as an American poet whose work spoke to the universal in the human condition. Although many of his best-known works explore the African American experience, Hayden avoided politics and polemic, opting instead for an artistic body of work in the grand tradition of English literature. He labored in near obscurity for much of his life, only becoming recognized as a preeminent poet in the 1960s and 1970s. Only now is his work being given the critical evaluation it deserves by a new generation of scholars.

Hayden believed that literature written by blacks should be judged by the same critical standards used to judge any work in English. This stance proved distinctly unpopular with younger black poets, who sought to create and define a wholly black literature. While serving as a professor of English at Fisk University in the late 1960s, Hayden came under attack by some of these younger poets, but he never wavered in his defense of critical standards and the aims of great art. As his own relatively slender body of work attracted more attention, he found support from other poets of all races and creeds who shared his views. In 1976 he was named Poetry Consultant at the Library of Congress—an honor equivalent to England's Poet Laureate.

A Youth Devoted to Books

Hayden was born Asa Bundy Sheffey in 1913. His young, poverty-stricken parents separated soon after he was born, and he was adopted by William and Sue Ellen Hayden, who were also poor but who worked hard and held their children to high standards. The family lived in a Detroit ghetto with the ironic nickname Paradise Valley. Life was hard there, and Hayden's parents often quarreled. Nevertheless, both of them were deeply interested in their adopted son's achievements.

A severe case of myopia hampered Hayden's ability to play active games. His mother fought for his right to attend classes for the partially sighted, and he learned to read by holding the book six inches from his face—a practice he had to continue throughout his life. He also learned how to play the violin, but as the music became more complicated he had more and more trouble seeing

At a Glance...

Full name Robert Earl Hayden; born Asa Bundy Sheffey, August 4, 1913, in Detroit, MI; died of heart failure February 25, 1980, in Ann Arbor, MI; son of Asa and Gladys Ruth (Finn) Sheffey; foster son of William and Sue Ellen (Westerfield) Hayden; married Erma I. Morris (a pianist and composer), June 15, 1940; children: Maia. *Education:* Detroit City College (now Wayne State University), B.A., 1936; University of Michigan, M.A., 1944. *Religion:* Baha'i.

Federal Writers' Project, Detroit, MI, researcher, 1936-40; University of Michigan, Ann Arbor, teaching fellow, 1944-46; Fisk University, Nashville, TN, 1946-69, began as assistant professor, became professor of English; University of Michigan, professor of English, 1969-80. Consultant in Poetry, Library of Congress, 1976-78. Visiting poet and lecturer at numerous American universities.

Member: American Academy and Institute of Arts and Letters, Academy of American Poets, PEN, American Poetry Society, Phi Kappa Phi.

Selected awards: Jules and Avery Hopwood Poetry Award from University of Michigan, 1942 and 1944; Julius Rosenwald fellow, 1947; Ford Foundation fellow in Mexico, 1954-55; World Festival of Negro Arts grand prize, 1966, for *A Ballad of Remembrance;* Russell Loines Award, National Institute of Arts and Letters, 1970; National Book Award nomination, 1971, for *Words in Mourning Time;* Academy of American Poets fellow, 1977; Michigan Arts Foundation Award, 1977; National Book Award nomination, 1979, for *American Journal.*

it. He had to drop out of the Sunday school orchestra at his local Baptist church, but the loss did not trouble him deeply—he still had his books and his writing.

Hayden began writing poems, stories, and plays while still in elementary school. By the time he reached high school he was sure he wanted to be a poet. He spent much of his spare time reading novels and poetry, drawing solace from literature in the face of his troubled family life. When Hayden was a teenager, his natural mother returned to Detroit and sought a relationship

with him. He welcomed contact with her, but her presence only increased the tensions in his adoptive household. Relief came in the form of the books he read and pondered, including George Eliot's *Romola,* Nathaniel Hawthorne's *The Marble Faun,* and Edward George Bulwer-Lytton's *The Last Days of Pompeii.* In the *Dictionary of Literary Biography,* Hayden is quoted as saying: "I loved those books, partly because they took me completely out of the environment I lived in, and they were full of strange and wonderful things that I'd had no direct experience with."

In 1932 Hayden earned a scholarship to attend Detroit City College (now Wayne State University). There he majored in Spanish and minored in English, assuming that he would teach school when he graduated. After earning his bachelor's degree in 1936 he found a Depression-era job as a folklore researcher with the Federal Writers' Project in Detroit. He supplemented the meager federal income by serving as a theater, movie, and music critic for the *Michigan Chronicle,* a black weekly newspaper. In his spare time he continued to produce poetry, and his first volume, *Heart-Shape in the Dust,* was published by Detroit's Falcon Press in 1940. That same year he married pianist Erma Morris.

The Apprentice Poet

In 1941 Robert and Erma Hayden spent a brief period in New York City, where Mrs. Hayden studied music at Juilliard. While there the Haydens were invited to dinner by renowned Harlem Renaissance poet Countee Cullen, who had read Hayden's first book and liked it. The opportunity to meet and talk to one of his favorite poets had a profound effect on Hayden. He was inspired to pursue his own literary ambitions quite seriously. When the couple returned to Michigan, Hayden enrolled in graduate courses at the University of Michigan in Ann Arbor. By 1942 he was a full-time student, taking courses in playwrighting, poetry, and literature.

One of Hayden's teachers in Ann Arbor was the renowned American poet W. H. Auden. Hayden later described his professor as "awe-inspiring" and "absolutely brilliant," the perfect mentor for an apprentice artist struggling to learn both the craft of writing and the necessary self-awareness that poetry demands. Some critics feel that it was Auden who most strongly influenced the critical and creative principles that would form the basis for Hayden's poetry. Whatever the case, Hayden began to get recognition for his work while at the University of Michigan. He twice won the prestigious Jules and Avery Hopwood Award for poetry while at the school, and after earning his bachelor's degree he became the first black teaching fellow in the university's English department.

During his student days at Michigan Hayden also embarked upon a lifelong affiliation with the Baha'i faith, a Middle Eastern religion that emphasizes racial harmony, unity of religious faiths, and a coming world peace. The Baha'i world view informed many of Hayden's mature works and influenced his personal philosophy of poetry, as James Mann noted in the *Dictionary of Literary Biography.* Mann wrote that Baha'i "teaches that the work of the artist is considered a form of worship, a service to mankind that has spiritual significance. Hayden was sustained in his life as a poet by the assurance of his faith that his work is of spiritual value."

Poet, Professor at Fisk

By 1946 Hayden had published two of his best-known poems, "Middle Passage" and "Frederick Douglass." The 177-line "Middle Passage" is a modernist poem treating upon various aspects of the slave trade to colonial America, including the thoughts of slave traders and a narrative of a slave rebellion aboard a Cuban vessel. The poet also includes passages on the names of slave ships, the yarns of old sailors, and even bits of hymns the slave traders sang. "Frederick Douglass" is a shorter, unrhymed sonnet about the famous black orator who began his life as an abused and runaway slave. The first draft of "Middle Passage" appeared in the 1946 edition of *Cross Section,* an annual poetry anthology. "Frederick Douglass" was published in the *Atlantic Monthly* magazine.

On the strength of his scholarship and his published poetry, Hayden was offered an assistant professorship at Fisk University, a predominantly black school in Nashville, Tennessee. Not surprisingly, he had a great deal of difficulty adjusting to life in the South, where institutionalized segregation affected everything from seating on buses to use of restrooms, restaurants, and movie houses. Mann wrote: "By necessity the Haydens taught themselves to live with segregation, though never to adjust to it, and they formed relationships with unprejudiced people of goodwill who had similar interests in the arts. Hayden's concern for the art of poetry prevented him from writing in a polemic way about his experiences during these two decades, although he did employ it as subject matter."

Hayden stayed at Fisk from 1946 until 1969, often teaching as many as five college courses per semester. He also served as an advisor to the student newspaper. The responsibilities left little time for creative writing,

and in the 1950s he produced only 11 new published poems, all of which appeared in the slender volume *Figure of Time.*

> "There's no such thing as black literature. There's good literature and there's bad. And that's all!"

The 1960s brought new recognition and new challenges to the poet. In 1962 Hayden published *A Ballad of Remembrance* (published to a wider American audience as *Selected Poems* in 1966). The poems in this volume cover a variety of experiences and themes, including the quest for meaning in life, racism, the poet's past, and spiritual redemption through suffering. *A Ballad of Remembrance* put Hayden on the international literary map when it won the first-ever World Festival of Negro Arts grand prize for poetry in 1966. American critics responded favorably to *Selected Poems* as well.

The Artist Defends His Views

Just as Hayden's work was beginning to receive the critical recognition that had long eluded him, he drew the fire of a new generation of black poets who were working from an entirely different perspective. At a black writers' conference held at Fisk in 1966, some of the younger poets attacked Hayden for his refusal to be categorized as a "black poet" and his insistence that his work be judged by all the critical and historical standards brought to bear upon any other English-language poetry. The young militant poets were seeking to create a "black aesthetic" based on the notion that black literature owed no debt to "white" standards and should serve a political purpose as part of a black revolution. As both an artist and a Baha'i Hayden objected to these views, and he did not back down even though the criticism leveled at him stung him deeply. His response, as quoted in the *Dictionary of Literary Biography,* was simple and succinct: "There is no such thing as black literature. There's good literature and there's bad. And that's all!"

Mann wrote: "Nothing impresses one about Hayden so much as his qualities as a man, the nobility with which he confronted his life as it came to him: the terrible pain of racial discrimination; the long period of virtually total obscurity as a writer; the excessively burdensome long hours of teaching; thoughtless and unfair criticism by members of his own race; and finally, the years of honors and fame, borne with humility and grace. Having experienced extremes of fortune, he endured with dignity and with the highest principles."

Years of Honors and Fame

In 1969 Hayden returned home to the University of Michigan as a professor of English. While there he published three volumes of verse, two of which—*Words in the Mourning Time* and *American Journal*—were nominated for the National Book Award. In 1976 Hayden was named Consultant in Poetry to the Library of Congress, an honored position that brought him to the nation's capital for two years. He also undertook a greater number of poetry readings and visiting professorships at numerous American colleges and universities. One of his students, Michael R. Brown, recalled a Hayden reading in a *Commentary* essay: "At his reading he took a back seat to the young poets and his friends. His reading was shorter, but balanced ... art, people, and the iron lessons of history. Without teaching, he put the young poets to school, and they noticed."

Hayden's health began to fail as the 1970s progressed. He died of heart failure in the University of Michigan's hospital early in 1980. Two volumes of his work were published posthumously: a prose collection from the University of Michigan Press, and *Robert Hayden: Collected Poems* by Liveright. Some observers have claimed that Hayden might have published more poetry had he been less burdened by his duties as a teacher, but in fact the poet was a perfectionist who spent long hours revising and re-working poems, even those that had already been published.

Hayden once described himself as "a romantic who has been forced to be realistic," and indeed his work never shied from the realities of racism and cruelty. Nevertheless, his Baha'i faith provided him with an essentially optimistic outlook. According to Norma R. Jones in the *Dictionary of Literary Biography,* the writer's work "deals with the awful realities of American history; yet, because he sees the future of the nation as a passage from death to life, he is more a poet of hope than of despair. His chosen role as an American poet, yet aware of the injustices perpetuated against his race, gives him a unique perspective in American letters." Jones concludes that Robert Hayden "has demonstrated that in one man the black poet and the American poet can be the same."

Selected writings

Heart-Shape in the Dust, Falcon Press (Detroit), 1940.

(With Myron O'Higgins) *The Lion and the Archer,* Hemphill Press (Nashville), 1948.
Figure of Time: Poems, Hemphill Press, 1955.
A Ballad of Remembrance, Breman (London), 1962, revised as *Selected Poems,* October House (New York), 1966.
Words in Mourning Time, October House, 1970.
The Night-Blooming Cereus, Breman, 1972.
Angle of Ascent: New and Selected Poems, Liveright, 1975.
American Journal, Effendi Press (Taunton, MA), 1978, revised and enlarged edition, Liveright, 1982.
Collected Prose: Robert Hayden, University of Michigan Press (Ann Arbor), 1984.
Robert Hayden: Collected Poems, Liveright, 1985.

Also editor of volumes such as *Afro-American Literature: An Introduction,* 1971; *The Human Condition: Literature Written in the English Language,* 1974; and *The United States in Literature,* 1979. Contributor of poetry to magazines and anthologies.

Sources

Books

Dictionary of Literary Biography, Volume 5: *American Poets since World War II,* Gale, 1980, pp. 310-18.
Dictionary of Literary Biography, Volume 76: *Afro-American Writers, 1940-1955,* Gale, 1988, pp. 75-88.
Fetrow, Fred M., *Robert Hayden,* Twayne, 1984.
Greenbert, Robert M., *American Writers: A Collection of Literary Biographies,* Scribner, 1981.
Hatcher, John, *From the Auroral Darkness: The Life and Poetry of Robert Hayden,* George Ronald, 1984.
Miller, R. Baxter, editor, *Black American Poets Between Wrolds, 1940-1960,* University of Tennessee Press, 1986, pp. 43-76.
Williams, Pontheolla Taylor, *Robert Hayden: A Critical Analysis of His Poetry,* University of Illinois Press, 1987.

Periodicals

Commentary, September 1980, pp. 66-69.
Negro Digest, June 1966, pp. 164-75.
New York Times, February 27, 1980, p. B5.
Obsidian, spring 1981, special issue on Hayden.
World Order, fall 1981, special issue on Hayden.

—Anne Janette Johnson

Larry Irving, Jr.

1955—

Government official

Larry Irving is the Assistant Secretary for Communications and Information of the U.S. Department of Commerce, and director of the National Telecommunications and Information Administration (NTIA). He was appointed to the posts in 1993 by President Bill Clinton to help develop the country's telecommunications policies. He is also an energetic promoter of online access and its entrepreneurial opportunities for minorities and women, a concern for which *Newsweek* magazine dubbed him "the Net's conscience."

Irving has an almost palpable zeal for all things high-tech that extends beyond the confines of his job. He spends about 15 hours a week just randomly browsing the Internet, in addition to the four or five online hours he puts in daily for work. His enthusiasm for the possibilities this technology presents is unbridled: "I mean, is this cool, or what?" he asked in a *USA Today* profile.

Born in Brooklyn, New York, Irving grew up in a working-class family with a love of learning that he nourished with trips to the public library. He was awarded a baccalaureate from Northwestern University in 1976 and went on to law school at Stanford University, where he was elected class president in 1979. That same year he earned his J.D. degree, and after graduation he became an associate at the Washington, DC law firm of Hogan and Hartson. His political career, however, began in 1983 when he left the firm to join Congressman Mickey Leland's staff as legislative director and counsel.

In 1987 Irving became senior counsel to Congressman Edward Markey, a ranking member of the House Telecommunications and Finance Subcommittee. During the four years he spent in this position, Irving played a major role in the passage of several key pieces of telecommunications legislation: the Children's Television Act of 1990, the Television Decoder Circuitry Act of 1990, and the Cable Television Consumer Protection Act of 1992. In 1993 he was tapped to fill the NTIA position he now holds, where he has become an ardent and optimistic proponent of online communications and the Internet. Regarding the Internet, he told *USA Today:* "It's going to be where our children work, how our children are educated, how our children are provided health care. But it also will be how we're educated, where a lot of us will work, and how a lot of us will get health care.... I don't care what your business is, a person who understands and uses technology is going to reap economic rewards."

Encouraged Investment in Cyberspace

His own enthusiasm notwithstanding, Irving points out that not everyone is being swept up in the information revolution. He is concerned that minorities are being left behind, and the statistics bear him out: In 1989 the Census Bureau reported that home computer use by

At a Glance...

Born July 7, 1955, in Brooklyn, NY; married Leslie Wiley, 1987. *Education:* Northwestern University, B.A., 1976; Stanford University Law School, J.D., 1979.

Hogan and Hartson (law firm), Washington, DC, attorney, 1979-83; legislative director and counsel to Congressman Mickey Leland, 1983-87; staff chair of the House Fair Employment Practices Commission, 1985-87; senior counsel to the Subcommittee for Telecommunications and Finance of the House Committee on Energy and Commerce, 1987-92; assistant secretary of commerce and director of the National Telecommunications and Information Administration, 1993—. Member of board of directors, House of Representatives child-care center.

Member: American Bar Association, National Conference of Black Lawyers, District of Columbia Bar Association, Stanford Law School board of visitors.

Addresses: *Office*—U.S. Department of Commerce, National Telecommunications and Information Administration, 14th Street and Constitution Ave. N.W., Washington, DC 20230.

African Americans was less than half that of whites, and black children used home computers two-and-a-half times less than their white counterparts. When it comes to the "Information Superhighway," Irving told *Emerge* magazine, "African Americans do not have to be road kill, but it is going to require a concerted effort. We either have to get on it or be left behind."

To this end, Irving has actively encouraged minority investment and participation in the telecommunications industry. In a 1994 issue of *Emerge* magazine he advised minority business owners that to "become a player" in telecommunications "is going to take tens of millions of dollars." To raise the necessary funds, he suggested, minorities "are going to have to consolidate with nonminorities." Fortunately, he pointed out in a *Chicago Tribune* article, the interactive nature of the field itself "can serve as an integrator." He added: "I don't know if it will. It will take a lot of people working hard. It only has possibilities if more African Americans and Latinos get involved."

In April of 1995 Irving and the Minority Telecommunications Development Program (MTDP), a branch of the NTIA, sponsored a conference on capital formation for minority telecommunications businesses. The meeting highlighted individual success stories, helped participants find financial help and federal assistance, and outlined the many entrepreneurial opportunities available in the field.

Proposed Regulations to Protect Minorities

Irving has worked hard to ensure that legislation like the landmark telecommunications bill passed in 1996, which lifted many of the restrictions on media ownership, does not shut out minorities and small businesses. He remains concerned that as regulations fall, television and radio station prices will jump, making it impossible for all but the wealthiest contenders to compete. Irving wants to make certain that the federal government does its part to encourage minority representation in telecommunications businesses. "When we get to that new world, let's start regulating the new world," he suggested in the *Boston Globe*.

> "I don't care what your business is, a person who understands and uses technology is going to reap economic rewards."

The prospect of regulated cyberspace as foreseen by Irving does not please everyone. Thomas Donlan, writing in *Barron's* magazine, complained that "the government mandate for universal access" Irving proposes is the equivalent of "rent control in cyberspace." This concept, he says, led to the massive AT&T monopoly that existed until 1984 and actually delayed technological advances because implementing them would have raised user rates. "Irving," Donlan stated, "wants to extend that handicap into the 21st century."

Determined to Ensure Access

Despite criticism, Irving clearly believes that minorities must not leave the rapidly-developing field of telecommunications to others. "Monopolization of the marketplace of ideas should concern each of us," he said in a

Washington Post article. "It is fair to say that if one person controls ... [many] media sources, that person will have a strong influence on how ... [a] community thinks." Irving elaborated in *Emerge:* "We have to get the technologies deployed in minority communities, make sure our children are technologically literate, and seize the entrepreneurial opportunities."

While Irving is determined to secure minority representation on the information infrastructure and is optimistic about the future, he is also realistic. "I don't believe every household in America is going to have online services available at home any time in the near future," he told *USA Today.* He believes that government can bridge the gap, however, by putting computers and leading-edge technology into schools and other public facilities. His department will spend $86 million in 1996 and 1997 to fund experimental programs that further this goal. This, to put it plainly, is Larry Irving's mission.

"I just want every kid to have access to this stuff," he told *USA Today.* "If the only thing I contribute in life is to make this kind of technology available in schools and libraries around this country, then I've done a pretty good thing."

Sources

Barron's, January 31, 1994, p. 10.
Boston Globe, June 26, 1995, p. 1.
Chicago Tribune, May 28, 1995.
Emerge, Volume 6, no. 2, 1994, p. 60.
Newsweek, December 25, 1995/January 1, 1996, p. 44.
New York Beacon, Volume 2, number 63, 1995, p. 2.
New York Voice Inc./Harlem USA, August 24, 1994, p. 24.
USA Today, January 17, 1995, p. D3.
Wall Street Journal, February 16, 1993, p. B11.
Washington Post, June 24, 1995, p. H1.

—Amy Strumolo

Shirley Ann Jackson

1946—

Physicist, government official

"Shirley the Great." That's what Shirley Ann Jackson, age 4, declared to her mother she would someday be called. But, as Vice President Al Gore described in May of 1995 at Jackson's swearing-in ceremony for chairman of the nation's Nuclear Regulatory Commission, little Shirley was too young in 1950 to know the obstacles that could hinder even a smart and ambitious little black girl. "D.C. schools were still segregated," Gore said of the scenario for the Washington native in those years. "There's a wonderful school a few blocks away, but Shirley isn't allowed to walk through the doors. "And even at the high school level in Washington, the schools lack the small classes and modern labs that a budding scientist needs...to become Shirley the Great."

Fortunately, two historic events intervened to help Jackson rise to the top of her field and become the first African American woman to receive a doctoral degree at the Massachusetts Institute of Technology and to be named a commissioner of the NRC. One was the U.S. Supreme Court decision, Brown v. Board of Education, of 1954, which mandated the integration of schools.

The second was the Soviet launch of Sputnik—a wakeup call to the U.S. government to start helping American scientists catch up.

Suddenly, "Shirley the Great" seemed more than possible. Suddenly, the outlook was dramatically improved for young Americans interested in and talented in science, whether male or female, white or black. And Jackson had the drive to succeed. It's not every American, after all, who's smart enough to figure out what makes a nuclear power plant tick and then deal with the complicated politics of "selling" that energy source to a frightened public.

Bumblebees, Go-Karts, and Particle Physics

She was born in Washington, D. C., on August 5, 1946, and grew up in the city's northwest district. The second daughter of Beatrice and George Jackson; her mother was a social worker, her father a postal worker. Early on, she showed a gift for science and was encouraged by her father, who got involved with her science projects,

At a Glance...

Born Shirley Ann Jackson, August 5, 1946, in Washington, DC; daughter of Beatrice and George Jackson; married to Dr. Morris A. Washington; one son, Alan. *Education:* B.S. in physics, Massachusetts Institute of Technology, 1968, Ph.D. in physics, MIT, 1973; postdoctoral education at the Fermi National Accelerator Laboratory, Batavia, IL. and European Center for Nuclear Research, Geneva, Switzerland.

Career: Condensed matter theorist and other positions, AT&T Bell Laboratories, Murray Hill, NJ, 1976-91; consultant, semiconductor theory, Bell Labs, 1991-95; physics professor, Rutgers University, New Brunswick, NJ, 1991-95; commissioner and chairman, U.S. Nuclear Regulatory Commission, May 1995—.

Directorships: N.J. Resources Corp., Public Service Enterprise Group, Sealed Air Corp. Corestates New Jersey National Bank, CoreStates Financial Corp.

Selected honors: First African American woman awarded the Ph.D. in any subject from MIT; first African-American to become a commissioner of the NRC; fellow of the American Academy of Arts and Sciences; fellow of the American Physical Society; life member of the MIT Board of Trustees 1992—; former member of an advisory council to the secretary of energy; former member of research councils of the National Academy of Sciences and Advisory Council of the Institute of Nuclear Power Operations; recipient, Governor's Award (Thomas Alva Edison Science Award) of the State of New Jersey, 1993; Honorary Doctor of Science, Fairleigh Dickinson, NJ, 1993; recipient of scholarships and fellowships from Ford Foundation, Martin Marietta Corp., National Science Foundation, and others.

Addresses: *Office*—c/o U.S. Nuclear Regulatory Commission, Washington, D.C. 20555.

Post of her recollection of building soapbox go-karts with her sister, Gloria, and how this fed into her lifelong interest in "how things work." She also described how both her parents believed strongly in education and how this factor—together with an accelerated program in mathematics and science at Roosevelt High School—helped prepare her for the intellectual rigors ahead.

There were emotional rigors, as well, considering the proximity of Barnard, the excellent school to which Vice President Gore referred, just three blocks from Jackson's childhood home in the then-predominantly white Petworth area. But Shirley was black, so she and Gloria had to be driven miles across town to a black school. Despite this discrimination, "I had a good educational experience" in Washington, Jackson told *The Post.* "I had a supportive community and family." She was also a straight-A student at Roosevelt and valedictorian of her Class of 1964. Then, she left for college at MIT, still a rare destination for a black woman at that point, the height of the civil rights struggle. As Jackson said, "The biggest challenges were more after I left Washington."

In 1964 she was one of 45 women and a handful of African Americans in her 900-member freshman class. Jackson was unprepared for the loneliness, she told *Science* magazine. "The irony is that the white girls weren't particularly working with me, either," she said. The white women even refused to sit at the same cafeteria table with her and made it clear they didn't want her in their study groups. "I had to work alone," Jackson said. "I went through a down period, but at some level you have to decide you will persist in what you're doing and that you won't let people beat you down."

Rising above the social isolation, Jackson delved more and more into the scientific world she loved, discovering a particular niche in materials science. She thrived academically and upon her graduation in 1968, she was offered fellowship support to stay on for her Ph.D. in physics. Her specialization was theoretical elementary particle physics, and her graduate work was directed by James Young, the first full-time tenured black professor in the Physics department. She received her advanced degree in 1973, the first black woman at MIT to realize that goal in any academic category. But science was hardly Jackson's only interest, keenly aware of her own position as an African American, she lobbied MIT to admit more minorities and tutored at the YMCA in Boston's black neighborhood of Roxbury.

Became "Shirley the Great"

From graduate school, she moved on to the Fermi National Accelerator Laboratory in Batavia, Illinois, and the European Center for Nuclear Research in Geneva,

even the one involving live bumblebees that Shirley fed with sugar and collected in 30 jars jammed into the basement crawl space. Jackson told *The Washington*

Switzerland, for postdoctoral stints, working on theories of strongly interacting elementary particles. As she told *Science* about this time in her life, she simply got used to being one of the few women and blacks at meetings. "If you give a physics paper, it had better be good—because people will remember," she said.

In 1976 she accepted a job at AT&T Bell Laboratories in Murray Hill, N.J., where she combined her interest in theoretical particle physics with her employer's interest: gas, films, and semiconductors. She has admitted to *Science* that she was pretty much of a loner in the research world. But despite this aura, she still attracted the notice of another young physicist, Morris A. Washington, whom she later married. The couple have a son, Alan.

> "I went through a down period, but at some level you have to decide you will persist in what you're doing and that you won't let people beat you down."

Jackson stayed at Bell Labs until 1991, when she re-entered the academic world as a professor of physics at Rutgers University in New Jersey. "I wanted to have graduate students, to build my own research groups," she told *Science*. Her career star was already rising: From the mid-1960s to through the late-1970s, she received no less than ten scholarships, fellowships, and grants from sources such as Martin Marietta Co., the National Science Foundation, and the Ford Foundation. She also studied at the International School of Subnuclear Physics in Erice, Sicily, and the Ecole d'ete de Physique Theorique in Les Houches, France.

In 1985, Jackson entered the public affairs realm with her appointment by then-governor of New Jersey Thomas Kean to the N.J. Commission on Science and Technology. She was re-appointed and confirmed for a five-year term in 1989. She also served on committees of the National Academy of Sciences, the American Association for the Advancement of Science, and the National Science Foundation. And she published over a hundred scientific articles and abstracts. At each step, she promoted not just science, but the advancement of women in the field.

Corporate participation followed in the 1980s. She was invited onto the boards of the Public Service Enterprise

Group in New Jersey, the N.J. Resources Corp., and Core States/New Jersey National Bank. She also served on an advisory panel to the Secretary of Energy examining the future of Department of Energy national laboratories and on a variety of research councils of the National Academy of Sciences and the Advisory Council of the Institute of Nuclear Power Operations.

All of these appointments, of course, served Jackson well for the high honor to come. But the honor she has said gave her particular satisfaction was her election in June 1991—after 15 years as a term member—to life membership on the board of trustees of MIT. Thus, she became the ultimate insider at the same institution where once she had been a lonely female minority student on the outside looking in.

The Politics of Nuclear Power

When President Bill Clinton nominated Jackson to the chairmanship of the Nuclear Regulatory Commission in 1995, she inherited far more than just an agency (located in Rockville, MD) with 3,000 employees and a $500 million annual budget; she also took on the job of regulating the safety of the United States' aging 110 nuclear power plants and of tackling the touchy politics of extending those plant licenses. In her lap was laid the twin dilemmas of mounting nuclear waste and the plants' dwindling storage space.

And all of this was occurring in 1995—the year of her appointment—just nine years after the Chernobyl nuclear power disaster in Russia that had ended or damaged thousands of lives and threatened, via the long-term effects of radiation poisoning, to claim many more. In fact, The World Health Organization reported in 1995 that thyroid cancer among children had increased 100 percent in areas exposed to Chernobyl's fallout.

What's more, Chernobyl, so far away, was hardly the only concern. Americans were not about to forget the near-miss at Three Mile Island in 1979. And there were other, nuclear-related events in 1995: Environmental "guerillas" set up camp in the Mojave Desert at the site of a proposed nuclear waste dump saying it threatened Southern California's water. Joseph Rotblat, the British antinuclear activist, accepted the Nobel Prize, warning the world's scientists that they were responsible for spurning doomsday programs and exposing plans for weaponry. The NRC ordered Maine's Yankee power plant to reduce its power because it wasn't clear whether the plant could withstand even a small water leak in its cooling system. Federal regulators began investigating an incident at the Hope Creek power plant, where cooling water was misdirected for 19 hours before anyone noticed. And South Carolina Governor David Beasley reopened the Barnwell County, S.C., nuclear dump, underscoring the failed efforts of 15 years to make the Southern states join a federal compact for disposal of their nuclear waste.

This was the "hot" political environment Jackson entered in 1995. She responded with her usual directness and zeal. Days after taking office, *The Energy Daily* newsletter reported, she set off for the Tennessee Valley Authority to spend three days climbing ladders and exploring the internal workings of TVA's units. "I did climb around, looking at reactor cores really close up," Jackson told the newsletter. Her conclusion? "Hal is not running the plants," she said mischievously—referring to the evil computer in 2001: A Space Odyssey—"It's humans.

"That was the virtue of [the tour]. It helped put things into context--up close and personal." Jackson planned to visit every operating reactor during her five-year tenure, Energy Daily reported. "One should visit one's licensees," Jackson said. "I think when you go into the plants, one gets a sense of...the culture...what we used to call, when I was a student, the 'vibes.'" The newsletter continued: "Jackson, 48, comes across as tough, smart and nonsense."

And these were perhaps just the qualities she needed to deal with the controversy that erupted anew over nuclear power from the *Time* magazine cover story of March 4, 1996. The headline was "Blowing the Whistle on Nuclear Safety: How a showdown at a power plant exposed the federal government's failure to enforce its own rules." The story concerned Northeast Utilities' five power plants in New England, particularly Millstone Unit 1 in Waterford, CT. Engineers George Galatis and George Betancourt, blew the whistle to the NRC after two years of internal lobbying, with no success, against a major safety problem: Millstone was off-loading its full core. This meant that every 18 months when the reactor was shut down so fuel rods could be replaced, the old rods, still radioactive, were improperly placed in the requisite cooling pool all at once. In fact, federal guidelines require older plants like Millstone to move only one third of the rods into the pool. But Millstone's administrators wanted to save time and money.

Time's investigation and a report of the NRC's inspector general found that not only had the agency known of this violation and dangerous practice but that it had been going on for 20 years and that Millstone I had been issued waiver after waiver by the NRC. "The agency completely failed," NRC acting Inspector General Leo Norton told *Time*. "We did shoddy work. And we're concerned that similar lapses might be occurring at other plants around the country."

Jackson, as NRC chairman, went into overdrive to protect her agency. She ordered the agency's second whistle-blower study in two years and a nationwide review of all 110 plants to discover how many had been moving fuel in violation of standards. At a press conference on March 8, 1996, she told reporters: "For whatever else may be said about the article, it pointed to areas for improvement—technical, managerial, and legal—on the part of both the utility involved and the NRC. The fact that we already knew about the problems and were dealing with them is not a sufficient answer; they should not have occurred in the first place." In a letter to *Time*, however, she dismissed "any suggestion that the Millstone situation borders on an impending Chernobyl-type disaster."

Nonetheless, the NRC, under Jackson's direction, shut down all three Millstone plants. And the public waited for the NRC report. It was a moment both positive and negative for Jackson: negative because she faced a major crisis for the agency she headed, but also positive because during all the hubbub, no one seemed to be noticing any more that she was black or female or anything else besides a highly respected scientist with a big political football in her hands.

Sources

Periodicals

"Nuclear Warriors," *Time* magazine, March 4, 1996, p. 46.
"New NRC Chairman Targes License Extension As Top Priority," *The Energy Daily,* August 22, 1995.
"Women in Science '93—Gaining Standing—by Standing Out," *Science,* April 16, 1993, p. 392.
"Equation for Success," *The Washington Post,* p. B13.

Other

Transcript of Shirley Ann Jackson press conference at Nuclear Regulatory Commission, April 9, 1996.

Biographical materials and resume supplied by Nuclear Regulatory Commission.

Transcript of Vice President Al Gore's Remarks at Swearing-in of Shirley Ann Jackson, White House Press Office, May 26, 1995.

—Joan Oleck

Charles S. Johnson

1893–1956

Sociologist, writer, educator, editor

A leading sociologist of his generation, Charles S. Johnson spent his career as a researcher, writer, critic, editor, and administrator. Rising in his career at a time when sociology was making new inroads into American universities, Johnson looked to his academic profession and the emergence of the African-American arts as means for dismantling the barriers of racism. A major figure behind the vibrant African-American art movement of the 1920s, Johnson has been recognized as one of the godfathers of the Harlem Renaissance--a period much indebted to his editorship of the Urban League's *Opportunity* magazine. His subsequent sociological studies of the 1930s and 1940s as well as his participation in countless academic and government-sponsored committees have earned him praise as an inveterate champion of race relations.

Born on July 24, 1893, in Bristol, Virginia, Charles Spurgeon Johnson received a broad classical background from his father, Reverend Charles Henry Johnson, an emancipated slave whose former master tutored him in learning Greek, Latin, and Hebrew. As a child, Johnson read avidly and worked in a barbershop. Because Bristol did not have a high school that accepted

blacks, he attended Wayland Academy in Richmond. He then attended Virginia Union University and funded his tuition by working summers aboard steamships sailing between North Folk and New York City. In addition to playing on the university's football team, he served as student council president and editor of the school's newspaper.

After earning a B.A. and graduating with honors from Virginia Union University in 1916, he attended the University of Chicago, but briefly left his studies to volunteer for the army. One of four hundred thousand African-Americans to serve in the military during World War I, he went to France with the 103rd Pioneer Infantry Division and rose to the rank of sergeant-major. Returning to America, he resumed his studies at the University of Chicago under several prominent scholars, including the renowned sociologist Robert E. Park. Despite Park's belief in the peculiar racial endowments of blacks, he exposed Johnson to a cyclical theory that posited that contact and interaction between different racial groups was requisite to breaking the barriers of segregation and discrimination. "The Chicago group demonstrated to Johnson," wrote Richard Robbins in *Black Sociologists,* "the value of the synthesis of sociological theory--especially the theory of cycles--and comprehensive research combining the statistical survey and the personal document."

"Red Summer" 1919

After graduating from the University of Chicago with a Ph.B (Bachelor of Philosophy), Johnson worked as a researcher for the Chicago Urban League. A year later, beginning in May 1919, a wave of race riots erupted in twenty-six Northern and Southern cities. On July 27, Chicago witnessed the outbreak of a seven-day citywide race riot which claimed the lives of 23 African-Americans and 15 whites. Through the recommendation of Chicago Urban League president Robert Park, he

gained an appointment to the Illinois Governor Frank Lowden's Committee to Investigate the Chicago Riot. Among the panel's six black and six white members, Johnson served as "associated executive secretary" under white executive secretary Graham Romeyn Taylor, with whom he co-authored the committee's seven-hundred-page report, published in 1922 as *The Negro in Chicago: A Study of Race Relations and a Race Riot.* Though it minimized the responsibility of white oppression for the violence and offered little for the formation of public policy, the study--acclaimed in scholarly journals and newspapers--is considered a landmark work of scholarship.

The Urban League and the Harlem Renaissance

In 1921 Johnson became the Urban League's first national director of its newly established office of research and investigation in New York City. He accepted the position at a yearly salary of $3600. During his first year with the national office, he edited the league's tabloid-style periodical *Urban League Bulletin.* In an effort to upgrade the organization's publication, the league launched a new monthly publication called *Opportunity: Journal of Negro Life* in 1923 and selected Johnson as chief editor. "Under Johnson's leadership," wrote Nancy J. Weiss in *The National Urban League,* "*Opportunity* presented a reasonably balanced overview of Negro life in the 1920s." For Johnson this balance included a combination of academic scholarship and African-American arts, both of which he foresaw as equally powerful in advancing the cause of racial assimilation in American society. As David Levering Lewis noted in *When Harlem Was in Vogue,* Johnson looked upon the African-American arts as providing "a small crack in the wall of racism that was worth trying to widen." Lewis added, "If the road to the ballot box and jobs was blocked, Johnson saw that the door to Carnegie Hall and New York publishers was ajar." Years later, as quoted in *Harlem Renaissance Reader,* Johnson expressed the purpose of the *Opportunity,* as "that of providing an outlet for young Negro writers and scholars whose work was not acceptable to other established media," and that its goal was to "disturb the age-old customary cynicisms" of the white publishing industry.

The New Negro Movement

In 1925 Johnson's essay, "The New Frontage on American Life," appeared in Alain Locke's famous anthology *The New Negro.* As editor and contributor, Locke announced a new dawning of the Negro, one that in the wake of his aesthetic and intellectual achievements would bring about a "New America." One of over thirty contributions, Johnson's essay revealed--consistent with the cyclical theories of the Chicago School--the conflicts and struggles of African-American migration from rural to urban life. Aware of the economic strife, lack of union representation, and violence, he foresaw such manifestations of conflict as stages in the ultimate assimilation of African-Americans. He believed that conflict would, over time, give way to racial cooperation, concluding in his essay, "where there is conflict there is change."

1925 Johnson, in cooperation with the Department of Industrial Relations, directed a study of negroes and unions. He made an important contribution to the Harlem Renaissance by organizing the *Opportunity*'s annual prize awards for literature and its elegant banquet award dinner held at the Fifth Avenue Restaurant. In the following year an *Opportunity* prizewinner, poet Countee Cullen, became the magazine's assistant editor and author of the periodical's column "Dark Tower"--an acclaimed piece featuring works by African-American poets and writers.

At the end of 1927, the *Opportunity*'s benefactor, the Carnegie Corporation cancelled the organization's annual eight-thousand-dollar grant. Even during its peak year the *Opportunity,* a publication circulated to an interracial audience, sold only eleven thousand copies. In need of funding, Johnson then turned to his friend, Sears Roebuck president Julius Rosenwald. Learning that Rosenwald would not provide monetary support for the magazine, Johnson contemplated returning to academia. That same year, he edited an anthology published by the Urban League, *Ebony and Topaz,* a work combining the contributions of sociologists like E. Franklin Frazier and Ellsworth Faris, along with numerous literary figures such as Claude McKay, Countee Cullen, and James Weldon Johnson.

Department Head at Fisk University

Without major funding for the *Opportunity,* Johnson decided to return to academic pursuits. "Although the years with the *Opportunity* were a valuable experience for Johnson," noted Richard Robbins in *Black Sociologists,* "social science was to prove a stronger force than involvement in the Harlem Renaissance." Although he left the magazine, Johnson viewed art and social science as equally effective forces for evoking social change. In his introduction to Jean Toomer's classic *Cane,* Arna Bontemps quoted Johnson, who stated: "A brief ten years have developed more confident self-expression, more widespread efforts in the direction of art than the

long, dreary two centuries before." Decades later Johnson expressed, as quoted in *Harlem Renaissance Reader,* an undaunted faith in the contributions of the movement by describing it as "the comet's tail of a great cultural ferment in the nation, the 'melting pot era,' a period of ascendancy of unbridled free enterprise."

Having made vital contributions in promoting the African-American arts, Johnson returned to the study and instruction of social science. In 1928 he became chairman of Fisk University's sociology department in Nashville, Tennessee, where he helped the institution become a leading a center for the training of blacks in the field of sociological research. In 1930 he served on a three-member League of Nations team that investigated forced labor practices in Liberia. On his way to Liberia, Johnson and his private secretary, John F. Matheus--another contributor to the *New Negro* anthology--traveled to Paris where they visited Countee Cullen and Paul Robeson, and attended parties at several of the city's fashionable salons. Despite his feted reception in Paris, Johnson became outraged over the labor conditions in Liberia, and recorded his impressions in *Bitter Canaan: The Story of the Negro Republic,* which was published after his death.

In the early 1930s Johnson conducted research on six hundred black families in Macon County--findings which were published his 1934 work *Shadow of the Plantation*--a significant study that, as Robbins pointed out in *Black Sociologists,* "took on a racial myth, the conception of the easygoing plantation life and the happy Negro, and replaced the myth with the objective truth: Macon County was a twentieth century form of feudalism based on cotton cultivation." Johnson's 1935 publication *The Collapse of the Cotton Tenancy: 1933-1935* emerged as another landmark study. Outside the influence Marxist thought, Johnson's Southern studies, as Robbins observed, "arrived pragmatically at a very close understanding of the way powerful agrarian and industrial interests shaped the 'human relations' of race and racism."

Academic Advisor During the Great Depression

During the Depression Johnson became an advisor to a number of committees and governmental agencies. In 1931 he became a consultant to a branch of President Herbert Hoover's Conference on Home Building, the Negro Housing Committee. Three years later, he served on President Franklin D. Roosevelt's New Deal agency, the Tennessee Valley Authority, and on an advisory board for the National Youth Administration. In 1936-

37 he became a consultant to the U.S. Department of Agriculture regarding farm tenancy.

"Where there is conflict there is change."

Johnson's 1938 publication, *The Negro College Graduate,* dealt with the struggle of African-Americans to attain higher education. In the following year, he contributed to the planning of Swedish sociologist Gunnar Mydral's famed study *An American Dilemma.* From research prepared for the Southern Rural Division, Negro Youth Study, for the American Council Youth Commission and the Council of Education, Johnson compiled his work *Growing Up in the Black Belt* in 1941. An in-depth study of blacks who resided in eight southern counties, the book's methodical research incorporated the use of questionnaires, open-ended interviews, and personality profiles. Two years later saw the publication of Johnson's work *Patterns of Segregation* and his appointment to a program on race-related problems for the American Missionary Association of the Congregational Christian Church. That same year, he also served as director of the Julius Rosenwald Fund's interracial relations program.

African-American Sociologist in Postwar America

Johnson's involvement in governmental agencies continued after World War II. In 1946 he served as a member of the United Nations Educational, Scientific, and Cultural Organization (UNESCO) delegation in Paris. In cooperation with the United States Education for Japan Commission, he assisted in the investigation and reorganization of the country's educational system. That same year, he succeeded Fisk University President Thomas Elsa Jones, becoming the institution's first black president. In 1947 Johnson and Herman H. Long produced their study *People v. Property: Race Restrictive Covenants in Housing.* Compiled from three years of research, the book addressed itself to inadequate housing conditions and discrimination among minority groups. Johnson remained President of Fisk until his death on October 27, 1956.

Throughout his career Johnson fought to usher in a new era of desegregation and racial assimilation. Echoing the accomodationist views of Booker T. Washington, he looked upon the African-American struggle to attain proper education and employment as an imminent conflict that, over time, would yield to a period of racial equality. Like activist and writer W. E. B. Du Bois, he promoted higher learning and the arts, and looked to them as a means of accelerating the cycles of social and cultural assimilation. "Johnson made his appeal to experience," wrote S. P. Fullinwinder in *The Mind and Mood of Black America.* "It is out of experience, he said, that we must forge our values and bring meaning to life." In life Johnson proved himself as an individual of vast experience. A tireless and inveterate scholar and administrator, his participation as advisor on numerous committees and governmental agencies brought him high regard among his colleagues; his genuine concern for the advancement of his race relations and the cultivation of African-American arts have earned him respected place in the history of American social thought and culture.

Selected writings

The Negro in Chicago: A Study of Race Relations, Urban League, 1922.

(Editor) *Ebony and Topaz: A Collection,* National Urban League, 1927.

The Negro in Civilization: A Study of Negro Life and Race Relations in the Light of Social Research, Holt, 1930.

(With Edwin R. Embree and W. W. Alexander) *Shadow of the Plantation,* University of Chicago Press, 1934.

The Collapse of Cotton Tenancy, University of North Carolina Press, 1935.

A Preface to Understanding, New York Fellowship Press, 1936.

The Negro College Graduate, McGrath, 1938.

Growing Up in the Black Belt: Negro Youth in the Rural South, American Council on Education, 1941.

Backgrounds to Patterns in Negro Segregation, Crowell, 1943.

Patterns of Negro Segregation, Harper & Brothers, 1943.

Into the Mainstream: A Study of the Practices of Race Relations in the South, University of North Carolina Press, 1947.

(With Herman H. Long) *People Versus Property: Race Restrictive Covenants in Housing,* Fisk University Press, 1947.

Education and the Cultural Crisis, Macmillan, 1951.

Bitter Canaan: The Story of the Negro Republic, Transaction Books, 1987.

Sources

Books

Black Sociologists: Historical and Contemporary Per-

spectives, edited by James E. Blackwell and Morris Janowitz, University of Chicago Press, 1974.

Fabre, Michel, *Black American Writers in France, 1840-1980,* University of Illinois Press, 1991.

Fullinwinder, S. P., *The Mind and Mood of Black America,* Dorsey Press, 1969.

Harlem Renaissance Reader, edited by David Levering Lewis, Penguin, 1994.

Lewis, David Levering, *When Harlem Was in Vogue,* Oxford University Press, 1989.

Mydral, Gunnar, *An American Dilemma: The Negro Problem and Modern Democracy,* Harper & Row, 1944.

The New Negro: An Interpretation, edited by Alain Locke, Arno Press, 1925.

Toomer, Jean, *Cane,* Harper & Row, 1923.

Weiss, Nancy J., *The National Urban League,* Oxford University Press, 1974.

—John Cohassey

Amalya Lyle Kearse

1937—

Lawyer, federal judge

Appointed to the U.S. Court of Appeals, Second Circuit, by President Carter in 1979, Amalya Lyle Kearse is distinguished as the first woman and only the second black to sit on that court. Kearse has been considered for a possible Supreme Court appointment by the Reagan, Bush, and Clinton administrations, and she was also considered as a possible nominee to the post of U.S. Attorney General in 1992. Although she remains on the U.S. Appeals Court bench, she has won the approval of both liberal and conservative law professors. She was the first choice for a seat on the high court by 50 top lawyers in a 1993 poll conducted by the *Los Angeles Daily Journal,* a legal newspaper. In addition to her legal career, Kearse is a world class bridge player and has been a five-time national bridge champion. She has written, translated, and edited several books on bridge.

Called "enigmatic" and "fiercely private" by a *Wall Street Journal* reporter in 1993, Amalya Kearse has kept most details of her family and childhood to herself. She was born on June 11, 1937 in Vauxhall, New Jersey. Her father, Robert Freeman Kearse, was Vauxhall's postmaster. He was supportive of his daughter's career choice. "My father always wanted to be a lawyer," Kearse told the *New York Times* in 1979. "The Depression had a lot to do with why he didn't. I got a lot of encouragement." Profiled in *Ebony* in 1966 as an up-and-coming corporate law attorney, Kearse revealed

that her legal aspirations began in childhood. "I became an attorney," she stated, "because I once wanted [as a child] to be an FBI agent." Kearse's mother, Myra Lyle (Smith) Kearse, was a medical doctor in Vauxhall—although later she served as the anti-poverty director of Union County—and hoped her daughter would pursue a career in medicine. "But I couldn't," Kearse explained in the *New York Times.* "I was too squeamish. Besides, I liked going through old law books."

Kearse attended elite Wellesley College, where she took a course in international law, reinforcing her desire to be a lawyer and sparking her interest in litigation. "I decided I wanted to be a litigator," she recalled in the *New York Times.* "There was a moot court and I found that very enjoyable." She earned her bachelor of arts degree in philosophy in 1959. Against the advice of counselors at Wellesley, Kearse went on to enroll in law school at the University of Michigan in Ann Arbor. One of only eight women in her class, she graduated *cum laude* in 1962. While at Michigan she was editor of the law review and won the Jason L. Honigman Award for her outstanding contributions. According to a *New York Times* correspondent, "even before she received her degree, she received job offers from several Wall Street firms." Kearse ultimately chose to join the corporate law firm of Hughes, Hubbard, and Reed in 1962 as an

At a Glance...

Born June 11, 1937, in Vauxhall, NJ; daughter of Robert Freeman (a postmaster) and Myra Lyle (a doctor; maiden name, Smith) Kearse. *Education:* Wellesley College, B.A., 1959; University of Michigan Law School, J.D., 1962.

Lawyer, federal judge, author. Hughes, Hubbard, and Reed, New York, NY, associate, 1962-69, partner, 1969-79; U.S. Court of Appeals, Second Circuit, judge, 1979—. Adjunct lecturer, New York University Law School, 1968-69; member of editorial board, Charles Goren (bridge expert), 1974—. Member, American Law Institute, 1977—; fellow, American College of Trial Lawyers, 1979—.

Selected awards: Order of the Coif; Jason L. Honigman Award for Outstanding Contribution to Law Review Editorial Board, University of Michigan; "Bridge Personality of the Year" from International Bridge Press Association, 1980; Outstanding Achievement Award from University of Michigan, 1982; Golden Plate Award from American Academy of Achievement, 1984; women's pairs bridge champion, national division, 1971, 1972, world division, 1986; national women's teams bridge champion, 1987, 1990, 1991.

Member: American Bar Association, New York Bar Association, National Association of Women Judges.

Addresses: *Office*—U.S. Court of Appeals, U.S. Courthouse, Foley Square, New York, NY 10007-1501.

associate trial lawyer. In addition to her work with the firm, she was also an adjunct lecturer in evidence at New York University Law School for two years. She also served on the board of Big Sisters, which assisted Family Court. In 1969 she was invited to become a partner at Hughes Hubbard.

Kearse was one of three women profiled by the *New York Times* in a 1970 article applauding their status as the only female partners in Wall Street firms. Kearse herself was the first female black partner in a Wall Street

firm. Orville Schell, a senior partner at Hughes Hubbard, offered high praise for his pioneering colleague in 1979. "She became a partner here not because she is a woman, not because she is black, but because she is just so damned good—no question about it," he told the *New York Times.* Kearse was certified to appear before the benches of New York's Federal District Courts, the U.S. Court of Appeals (Second and Fourth Circuits), and the U.S. Supreme Court. A *Wall Street Journal* reporter noted in 1993 that while at Hughes Hubbard, "Kearse built her reputation on antitrust and other business litigation. In one of her biggest victories, she represented Broadcast Music, Inc., the music licensing organization, before the U.S. Supreme Court in the late 1970s. In the decision, the court backed away from the use of strict statistical standards, such as similarity of prices, in determining whether a business has a monopoly."

Appointed to Appeals Bench

In June 1979, Democratic President Jimmy Carter named Kearse, a Republican at the time, to the Second U.S. Circuit Court of Appeals, which serves New York, Connecticut, and Vermont. A *New York Times* correspondent observed at the time that she was "the first woman ever to sit on the Federal appeals court in Manhattan and only the second black in the court's history." Thurgood Marshall was the first, appointed in 1961. And at the age of 42, Kearse was also one of the youngest judges in the history of that court, which the *New York Times* further noted, "is considered by many lawyers to be the most important court in the country, after the United States Supreme Court."

As a federal judge, Kearse has impressed liberals and conservatives alike, partly because of her command of the law, and partly because her decisions do not allow her to be predictably categorized. In a *Washington Post* profile in 1994, a reporter observed that Kearse "has a reputation for a sharp intellect, even on complicated business issues that confound some other judges. Her votes on social issues please the liberal-leaning groups." On the other hand, conservatives were pleased in 1984 when Kearse rendered an opinion that restricted circumstances under which private plaintiffs can seek triple damages in lawsuits brought under the RICO act. A decision in 1990 "approved a stricter statute of limitations for bringing securities-fraud suits. The standard was adopted by the Supreme Court in another case," wrote Jonathan Moses in the *Wall Street Journal* in 1993.

"A *Wall Street Journal* reporter observed" Judge Kearse's towering intellect is recognized by her colleagues, who call her 'our resident genius.'"

Kearse's positions on social issues are illustrated by her dissenting opinion in the 1989 case *Rust v. Sullivan,* which upheld President Bush's gag order prohibiting federally funded clinics from dispensing abortion information. The *Los Angeles Times* quoted her opinion, which stated in part: "The present regulations deny a woman her constitutionally protected right to choose. She cannot make an informed choice between two options when she cannot obtain information as to one of them." In a 1984 majority opinion Kearse wrote that prosecutors should not be allowed to exclude minorities from juries with peremptory challenges.

Considered for Supreme Court

Kearse has been considered several times for possible appointment to the U.S. Supreme Court. In the early 1980s she was one of eight candidates put forward by the National Women's Political Caucus for consideration by President Reagan for possible replacement of Justice Potter Stewart. In 1991 the Bush administration appraised Kearse, along with Clarence Thomas and others, for high court appointment. Her name appeared on a 1992 list of possible nominees being considered by the Clinton administration for the position of U.S. Attorney General, but she was passed over in favor of Janet Reno. Kearse's record was reviewed in 1993 as President Clinton looked for a replacement for Supreme Court Justice Byron White, and again in 1994 when Justice Harry Blackmun announced his retirement. Insiders speculated that, although considered a moderate with centrist views, Kearse was likely viewed as too liberal in her leanings by the Republicans, and considered too conservative by the Clinton administration.

A *Wall Street Journal* reporter wrote in 1993 that "by all accounts Judge Kearse is brilliant," noting further that she is described by colleagues as "demanding and

precise." In another article, a *Wall Street Journal* staff member observed: "Judge Kearse's towering intellect is recognized by her colleagues, who call her 'our resident genius.'" She is much admired as well by fellow judges, who hold her exacting constructions of legal precedent in high regard.

Kearse is also highly respected in the world of tournament bridge. She is a top national and world class player who won the Women's Pairs Bridge Championships National Division twice, its World Division once, and was the National Women's Teams Bridge Champion in 1987, 1990, and 1991. She was named Bridge Personality of the Year by the International Bridge Press Association in 1980. Kearse has authored *Bridge Conventions Complete* (1975) and *Bridge at Your Fingertips* (1980) and has translated two other books on bridge from French to English. She is also a member of the editorial board of Charles Goren, the recognized bridge authority.

Selected writings

Books

Translator and editor, with Alan Truscott) *Championship Bridge,* 1974.
Bridge Conventions Complete, 1975, 3rd edition, 1990.
(Editor) *Official Encyclopedia of Bridge,* 1976.
(Translator and editor) *Bridge Analysis,* 1979.
Bridge at Your Fingertips, 1980.

Other

Federal Minimum Wage Standards, October 1973.
Employers and Social Security, November 1973.

Sources

Books

African-American Almanac, 6th edition, Gale (Detroit, MI), 1994.
African American Encyclopedia, Volume 4, Marshall Cavendish (New York), 1993.

Periodicals

Ebony, September 1966, p. 6.
Essence, May 1995, p. 146.
Jet, March 27, 1980, p. 9; July 9, 1981, p. 7.
Los Angeles Times, June 29, 1991, p. A18.
New York Times, June 22, 1970; June 25, 1979;

September 10, 1981; December 9, 1992; May 5, 1994.
Scholastic Update, November 30, 1984, p. 2.

Wall Street Journal, May 19, 1993, p. A15; June 14, 1993, p. B5.
Washington Post, April 13, 1994, p. A10.

—Ellen Dennis French

Flo Kennedy

1916—

Lawyer, political activist, lecturer

Flo Kennedy has had a remarkably long and visible career as a lawyer, militant activist, and feminist. Since the 1950s, when as an attorney she fought for royalty rights due the estates of musical legends Billie Holiday and Charlie Parker, Kennedy has unflinchingly attacked racism, inequity, and hypocrisy wherever she has found it. An original member of the National Organization for Women (NOW) and the founder of the Feminist Party, Kennedy has been a vocal spokesperson for women, blacks, homosexuals, and other minorities, and a staunch defender of civil rights. Variously called outspoken, outrageous, profane, and a woman of "immeasurable spirit," Kennedy was once described in *People* as "the biggest, loudest, and indisputably, the rudest mouth on the battleground where feminist activists and radical politics join in mostly common cause." Fellow feminist and friend Gloria Steinem has said that for those in the black movement, the women's movement, the peace movement, and the consumer movement, "Flo was a political touchstone—a catalyst."

Born Florynce Rae Kennedy on February 11, 1916 in Kansas City, Missouri, she was the second of Wiley and Zella Kennedy's five daughters. Wiley was first a Pullman porter with the railroad and later owned a taxi business. Zella worked outside the home only during the Depression. Neither parent was very strict, and Kennedy wrote in her autobiography, *Color Me Flo: My Hard Life and Good Times,* that her parents' protective attitudes combined to make her and her sisters feel very special. "All of us had such a sense of security because we were almost never criticized," she recalled. She has suggested that her upbringing contributed significantly to her anti-Establishment outlook. "I suspect that that's why I don't have the right attitude toward authority today, because we were taught very early in the game that we didn't have to respect the teachers, and if they threatened to hit us we could just act as if they weren't anybody we had to pay any attention to," she wrote.

Kennedy's childhood, while not always prosperous, was a happy time. Zella instilled both tenacity and optimism in her daughter. "Zella never accepted poverty, and yet she didn't resent it either, and we laughed a lot when we were really desperately poor," Kennedy wrote of her mother in *Color Me Flo.* "She always made an effort to

At a Glance...

Born Florynce Rae Kennedy on February 11, 1916, in Kansas City, MO; daughter of Wiley (a Pullman porter and taxi owner) and Zella Kennedy; married Charles Dudley Dye (a writer), 1957 (deceased). *Education:* Columbia University, B.A., 1948, J.D., 1951.

Lawyer, political activist, lecturer, author. Lawyer in private practice in New York, NY, 1954-66; founder and director of Media Workshop and Consumer Information Service, 1966; founder and director of Feminist Party, 1970; national director, Voters, Artists, Anti-Nuclear Activist and Consumers for Political Action and Communication Coalition (VAC-PAC); national director, Ladies Aid and Trade Crusade.

Member: National Organization for Women (1966-70), New York Bar Association.

Addresses: *Home*—San Francisco, CA.

maintain some kind of esthetic surroundings.... She was determined to have rose bushes, although our yard had too much shade.... But every year Zella decided she was going to have grass and roses.... We never had a single rose from any of those bushes, yet she persisted in going out and buying them. It was Zella who epitomized hope for us—she never gave up."

Aimed for Law School

Kennedy graduated from Lincoln High School in Kansas City at the top of her class, but she did not immediately go on to college. Although she felt that one day she probably would attend college, opportunities for higher education for blacks were limited "really kind of un-heard-of," she stated. Instead, Kennedy opened a hat shop in Kansas City with her sisters, an enterprise that was fun, if not exceptionally prosperous. While Kennedy admitted she may have been "a little more outspoken, a little crazier than the rest" in high school, she was more interested in boys than politics. Within a few years of graduation, however, she was involved in her first political action. She helped organize a boycott when the local Coca Cola bottler refused to hire black truck drivers.

Following her mother's death from cancer, Kennedy and her sister Grayce moved to New York in 1942. Ignoring those who advised her to become a teacher or a nurse at City College, Kennedy enrolled at Columbia University in 1944 as a pre-law student. She supported herself working at various part-time jobs. She explained her decision in 1976: "I thought anybody with the brains and energy to become a teacher ought to want to become something better." She elaborated, "I find that the higher you aim the better you shoot, and even if it seems you're way beyond yourself ... it always turns out that you can do a lot more than you thought you could." When in her senior year she again aimed high, attempting a concurrent enrollment at Columbia Law School, she was refused admission. Told she had been rejected not because she was black but because she was a woman, Kennedy was no less incensed. She promptly wrote the dean a letter suggesting the move was racially motivated and hinting that a lawsuit might follow. In 1948 she was admitted to the law school, one of eight women and the only black member of her class. She received her B.A. in 1948 and was awarded her law degree in 1951.

After law school Kennedy clerked with the law firm of Hartman, Sheridan, and Tekulsky, and she was admitted to the bar in 1952. By 1954 she had opened an office on Madison Avenue. It was rough going at times, and she had to take a job at Bloomingdale's one Christmas in order to pay the rent.

The late 1950s brought Don Wilkes, a law partner, and Charles "Charlie" Dye, a Welsh writer ten years her junior whom she married in 1957. Neither relationship was to last long. After several disappointing legal defeats, Wilkes ran off with most of the firm's assets, leaving Kennedy over $50,000 in debt. Although Dye was very supportive during this crisis, the marriage was rocky due to his alcoholism, and he died soon after.

Activism Began With Media Workshop

Before Wilkes left, the firm had taken on a case for blues singer Billie Holiday. When Holiday died, Kennedy continued to represent the estate, and later she represented the estate of jazz great Charlie Parker as well. In both situations Kennedy successfully fought the record companies to recover money from royalties and sales due the estates. Kennedy's experience with this estate work signaled the beginning of her disillusionment with law. "Handling the Holiday and Parker estates taught me more than I was really ready for about government and business delinquency and the hostility and helplessness of the courts," she wrote in her memoir. She

continued: "Not only was I not earning a decent living, there began to be a serious question in my mind whether practicing law could ever be an effective means of changing society or even of simple resistance to oppression."
"

As a result of these experiences, as well as her conviction that a government conspiracy shrouded the assassination of President Kennedy, the enterprising attorney began to reassess her ability to effect social change through the judicial system. In 1966 Kennedy set up the Media Workshop in order to fight racism in media and advertising. When Benton and Bowles, a large ad agency, refused to provide the Workshop with requested hiring and programming information, the group picketed the Fifth Avenue office. "After that they invited us upstairs," Kennedy recalled, "and ever since I've been able to say, 'When you want to get to the suites, start in the streets.'"

Thus began Kennedy's career as an activist. She was highly visible in this role during the 1960s, picketing the Colgate-Palmolive building with members of NOW, and also protesting at WNEW-TV. The group's media protest led them to CBS, where they were arrested for refusing to leave the building. Eventually CBS withdrew the complaint.

In 1966 Kennedy represented activist H. Rap Brown and was present at the four Black Power Conferences, and at the Black political caucuses as well. She also attended the first meeting of the fledgling National Association for Women, but she was soon disappointed by NOW's reluctance to go head-to-head with the issues of the day. "I saw the importance of a feminist movement, and stayed in there because I wanted to do anything I could to keep it alive, but when I saw how retarded NOW was, I thought, 'My God, who needs this?'" In November of 1971 Kennedy founded the Feminist Party. Its first action was to support Shirley Chisholm's presidential candidacy.

Launched a Speaking Career

The speaking career that would take Kennedy through the next two decades began in 1967 at an anti-war convention in Montreal. She became incensed when Black Panther Bobby Seale was not allowed to speak. She wrote in her memoir: "I went berserk. I took the platform and started yelling and hollering." An invitation to speak in Washington followed, and her lecturing career was born. Kennedy's activist and speaking careers continued throughout the 1970s and 1980s, and included the Coat Hanger Farewell Protest on the

abortion issue, anti-Nixon demonstrations, picketing Avon International for support for the three-hour *Celebrate Women* TV program, the MAMA March—the March Against Media Arrogance—and the organization of a demonstration at Harvard University protesting the lack of women's restrooms. In 1971 Kennedy co-authored *Abortion Rap* with Diane Schulder, and in 1981 she wrote *Sex Discrimination in Employment: An Analysis and Guide for Practitioner and Student,* with William F. Pepper. She was national director of Voters, Artists, Anti-Nuclear Activists and Consumers for Political Action and Communications Coalition (VAC-PAC) and also national director of the Ladies Aid and Trade Crusade. According to a *Jet* magazine article published in 1986, these organizations' "commandments" include "Thou Shall Not Use Our Dollars to Finance Racism and Sexism on Network Television."

> "I saw the importance of a feminist movement, and stayed in there because I wanted to do anything I could to keep it alive."

In 1986 Kennedy was "roasted" by friends and colleagues at a 70th birthday party in New York City. Among those honoring her at the event were activist Dick Gregory and civil rights attorney William Kunstler. That Flo Kennedy's career has lengthened to four decades is no surprise when one considers her approach to activism. She described her philosophy about her struggles and victories in her autobiography as being "like a successful bath; you don't expect not to take another bath.... Countermovements among racists and sexists and nazifiers are just as relentless as dirt on a coffee table.... Every housewife knows that if you don't sooner or later dust ... the whole place will be dirty again."

Selected writings

(With Diane Schulder) *Abortion Rap,* McGraw Hill, 1971.
Color Me Flo: My Hard Life and Good Times, Prentice-Hall, 1976.
(With William F. Pepper) *Sex Discrimination in Employment: An Analysis and Guide for Practitioner and Student,* Michie Co. (Charlottesville, VA), 1981.

Sources

Books

Kennedy, Flo, *Color Me Flo: My Hard Life and Good Times,* Prentice-Hall, 1976.
Notable Black American Women, Gale, 1992.

Periodicals

Essence, May 1995, p. 140.
Jet, March 31, 1986, p. 6.
People, April 14, 1974, p. 54.

—Ellen Dennis French

Chaka Khan

1953—

Vocalist

Chaka Khan has enjoyed a long and fruitful recording career that spans over two decades, but her soaring voice has failed to put her in the same superstar strata as other African American divas of her generation like Patti La-Belle or Tina Turner. Khan's career came of age as disco dawned in the early 1970s, and with her first hit as a member of Rufus the singer became a dynamic presence on the scene. "She was funkier, more contemporary than Aretha Franklin, as she could be just as diverse. Within a mere six years, she would have her own cult of singers who would try to emulate her sound," wrote Curtis Bagley in *Essence*. An even more successful solo career followed, as well as more Grammy Awards, but her presence on the pop/R&B scene by the mid-1990s had become a lightweight one. The London-based singer was remedying that by 1996, however, with her contributions to the soundtracks of several successful films and plans for a new record as well as a tell-all autobiography.

Khan was born Yvette Stevens, the oldest of four children, on the South Side of Chicago. Both parents worked for the University of Chicago, one as a photographer, the other as a research supervisor. Unlike other

future R&B stars who cut their musical teeth in church gospel choirs, Khan was raised Roman Catholic--but was exposed to jazz. The singer recalled for *Essence* writer Isabel Wilkerson that she was first exposed to Billie Holiday through her grandmother's record collection. "She's one of my mentors," Khan said of Holiday. "She's one of the first jazz players I ever heard.... The naivete, the suffering, the pain and all the things that come along with the suffering and the pain. She was victimized, and that led to excesses I can relate to and understand. She's a Black woman who went through a lot."

Began Performing At An Early Age

Khan formed her first ensemble with a group of her preteen friends who called themselves the Crystalettes. Their name came from her observation of how the street lights sparkled against the new snow below their Hyde Park high-rise. Big fans of Gladys Knight, Khan and the Crystalettes sang in talent shows where local fans dubbed her "Little Aretha." The official name change to "Chaka" came when she was thirteen and joined an African

At a Glance...

Born Yvette Stevens, March 23, 1953, in Chicago, IL; daughter of a photographer and a research supervisor; married Assan Khan, c. 1970 (marriage ended); married again briefly in the mid-1970s; children: Milini, Damien.

Singer. Joined musical group Rufus in 1972; released first two albums *Rufus* and *From Rags to Rufus*, both 1973, for ABC-Dunhill Records; had gold record with single "Tell Me Something Good" from *From Rags to Rufus*, 1974; left group to pursue solo career, 1978; signed with Warner Brothers Records, 1978; released first solo LP, *Chaka,* in 1979; released several solo LPs, but scored hit with the song "I Feel for You," written by Prince, 1984; recorded several other albums and songs for movie soundtracks throughout the 1980s and 1990s.

Awards: Grammy Awards, National Academy of Recording Arts and Sciences, for best group vocal and vocal arrangements, 1983, and for best rhythm and blues female vocal performance, 1983 and 1984.

Addresses: *Home*—London, England. *Office*—c/o Geffen Records, 9130 Sunset Blvd., Los Angeles, CA 90069.

music group called Shades of Black; it was the onset of the Black Power movement in the mid-1960s and its leader rechristened her Chaka Adunne Aduffe Hodarhi Karifi. Her teen years were spent singing in a number of bands, but Khan also pushed her luck in more potentially self-destructive ways. She told *Essence* that she used to carry a gun, and even practiced with it once a week: "When I did think about killing people with it, I developed ulcers, and I just threw the gun in the lake."

After dropping out of high school, Chaka moved out of her parents' house when she entered into a common-law marriage with Assan Khan, a bass player from East India. Both wore matching bleached blond coifs, and she was now singing in a group called Lock and Chain. Khan then jumped ship to an act called Lyfe before joining up with another ensemble called Rufus, which had attracted a large Chicago-area following. Working as a file clerk by day, she began hanging around Rufus by night and befriended their frontperson, a woman named Paulette McWilliams. At the time, Rufus was doing dance songs and Sly and the Family Stone covers; when McWilliams quit in 1972, Khan took her place. She was eighteen.

Enters the Majors with Rufus

Rufus won a record deal with ABC-Dunhill, and Khan followed them out to California. Their debut LP, *Rufus,* was released in 1973 to scant notice and little commercial success. During the recording of a second release, recent Grammy Award-winner Stevie Wonder showed up one day at the Torrance studio, much to the astonishment of the band. The visit would spark Rufus's first hit, the Grammy-winning "Tell Me Something Good." Khan recalled the event in a 1974 interview with Jay Grossman of *Rolling Stone.* "He sat down at the clavinet, y'know, and just wrote the song," she related about Wonder. "The first tune that he laid down, y'know, the first rhythm track, I said, `I don't like that one so much.' And it seemed as though he was a little upset over that, and I thought, `Well, a lot of people must not say that to him!' So he said, `What's your birth sign?' I said `Aries-Pisces,' and he said, `Oh, well here's a song for you.'"

After members of Rufus wrote lyrics for the track, Khan began to sing the "Tell Me Something Good" in her own style, but Wonder, still at the studio, interrupted. "NO NO NO!" Khan recalled him protesting in the interview with Grossman. "`Sing it like this!' And it turned out for the better," she said in the *Rolling Stone* interview with Grossman. "I don't know what would have happened if I'd done it myself, but just him being there--I'd been loving this guy for like 10 years." Khan was nine months pregnant when she recorded the LP; they exited the studio on December 17, 1973, and she gave birth to daughter Milini four days later.

"Tell Me Something Good" catapulted Khan and Rufus to instant stardom, complete with gold records on their living-room walls, a Grammy, sold-out tours--and the accompanying heady lifestyle. Khan soon gained a reputation as a wild child of the 1970s. To *Essence's* Wilkerson, Khan described those drug-fueled days of her life as a "runaway carriage, the reins flying." Much of it she only knows through others' accounts of her behavior. Discussing the possibility of an autobiography, the singer told Wilkerson that "I need to get a hypnotist, okay? I'm trying to write my life story, and it's like we're going to have to call in a professional at some point and put me in a trance because it's deep."

Despite the substance abuse problems, Khan still went on to record several hit albums with Rufus during the

1970s, such as *Rufus Featuring Chaka Khan.* Her career was her saving grace, she told Bagley in *Essence.* "Throughout all my whimsical flights, I have never let anything get completely away from me," Khan said. "Music has always been a grounding factor for me. It has been my one reality check. Even when my head was in the clouds, I always had at least one foot on the ground. That's why I'm alive today."

Solo Efforts met with Further Acclaim

In 1978 Khan made a successful transition to a solo recording career when she signed with Warner Brothers. Her solo debut came later that year with *Chaka Khan,* an overwhelming hit buoyed by its first single, "I'm Every Woman." She continued to record several solo efforts, achieving a minor hit in 1981 with *Whatcha Gonna Do for Me?* However, Khan preferred to make scat and jazz-influenced records instead of straightforward, commercial R&B, until Warner Brothers insisted on a more mainstream sound in 1984 when it came time for her to record her sixth solo effort. Khan remembered a song called "I Feel for You" by Prince that appeared on his second album in 1979. Her producer modernized it a bit for her, bringing in Stevie Wonder to blow harp and Grandmaster Melle Mel, then one of the biggest names in the breaking rap scene, to add his own distinctive voice to the mix.

> "She was funkier, more contemporary than Aretha Franklin, as she could be just as diverse. Within a mere six years, she would have her own cult singers who would try to emulate her sound."

"I Feel For You" was an overwhelming success upon release, charting in the Top Five, and perhaps best remembered for Melle Mel's distinctive triple-fast "Chaka Khan" rap. Khan recalled the moment she first heard it in an interview with *Rolling Stone*'s Debby Bull. After laying down her own vocals, Khan went into the studio the next day and listened to the new version. "I thought 'Oh, God.' It was great, yes, except for how am I going to live this down? Every time a guy walks up to me on the street, I think he's going to break into that rap. And most of them do." The album, also entitled *I Feel For You,* won Khan her third Grammy and was her biggest success

to date.

By this time Khan was living in New York City with Milini and son Damien, born in 1979. She was married a second time briefly in the 1970s but during the mid-1980s was romantically involved with a Harlem schoolteacher who had originally tutored her daughter: "His salary is nowhere near mine, but he still brings his money in. He didn't give up his job like my other two husbands did--immediately stop work and groove and say, 'My work is now you,'" Khan told Bull in *Rolling Stone.* "No woman wants to hear that. A woman wants to wake up in the morning to the smell of aftershave lotion and not see anybody there."

Khan Found Peace Abroad

Still single, Khan relocated her family to London at the onset of the 1990s after stopping briefly there on a tour and falling in love with the city. She also thought it would be a better environment in which to bring up her teenage son. "Right now in America there's a bounty on young Black boys," Khan told Wilkerson in *Essence.* "And I want him to get some kind of quality education, to speak other languages and live until he's 20 at least." Other members of her family stay for extended periods, including Milini with Khan's granddaughter Raeven, Khan's father from Chicago and sister Yvonne, who followed her older sister into the music business in the 1970s as Taka Boom.

Khan continues to record, and has done a number of works for the soundtracks of popular movies. For the Wesley Snipes/Patrick Swayze film *To Wong Foo: Thanks for Everything, Julie Newmar,* Khan contributed "Free Yourself." She also sang "Love Me Still," the theme song for the 1995 Spike Lee film *Clockers.* The singer also considers making a transition from singer to actress via a television sitcom, perhaps inspired by seeing her contemporary Patti LaBelle excel in the medium. In early 1995 Khan did a stint on the London stage as Sister Carrie in the gospel musical *Mama, I Want to Sing.* She hobnobs in aristocratic circles and enjoys a cult-like following in Europe, where she tours occasionally to great success. Khan seems happy to have grown up, settled down, cleaned up, and found an inner peace. Of that last personal achievement, the singer explained to Wilkerson that "it's a place you evolve to, not a place you go to consciously, you dig? You wake up better and better. Sometimes you slip. Basically, you just live."

Selected discography

(With Rufus) *Rufus,* 1973.
(With Rufus) *From Rags to Rufus,* 1973.
(With Rufus) *Rufus Featuring Chaka Khan,* mid-1970s.
Chaka Khan, 1979.

Whatcha Gonna Do for Me?, 1981.
I Feel for You, mid-1980s.

Sources

Essence, January 1986, p. 69; October 1995, p. 84.
Rolling Stone, October 24, 1974, p. 17; February 14, 1985, p. 11.

—Carol Brennan

Eriq La Salle

1962—

Actor

Becoming an overnight sensation as part of the ensemble of actors on television's top-rated *ER* series, which premiered in the fall of 1994, Eriq La Salle has received high praise for his portrayal of a driven, uncompromising surgical resident. He earned an Emmy nomination for his role during the first season, and has attracted legions of fans in his role as Dr. Peter Benton. "Much more than a pretty face, he [La Salle] is helping to redefine the face of prime time television and is determined to create more opportunities for African Americans in film," noted Rochelle Watson in *about...time* magazine. La Salle has admitted to sharing some traits with his character, notably the attitude of an overachiever. "We are a society of underachievers, so I think it's necessary to be an overachiever," he told *USA Weekend.*

Being black has had a major effect on La Salle's life and career. He grew up in an area of Hartford, Connecticut, that he said was "99.99 percent minority," according to the *New York Times.* La Salle was raised by Ada Haynes, a foster mother who had to work several jobs to support her brood. Haynes made it clear to her foster son that he would have to work harder than whites just

to be considered equal. "What my mother said empowered me; it didn't victimize me," La Salle confided in *USA Weekend.* "That advice instills in you that life ain't fair—get over it and get on with it. I'm not a cynic. I just say, 'OK, I can't sit on my a— and do ABC. I have to do XYZ to get noticed for ABC.''

Liked Attention Given to Performers

As a child watching his cousin perform at a dance at his school, La Salle was very impressed by the attention that his fellow schoolmates gave his cousin. "There was something about that experience I wanted to know more about," he told NBC. He decided that acting would be his career after joining a local youth theater group at age 14.

La Salle earned acceptance into the prestigious Juilliard school in New York City. While there he and other black students pressured the school to hire a black stage director. In the *New York Times* La Salle claimed that the director hired by the school was incompetent and had to be let go. When another group of black students later tried to get another black director into the school,

At a Glance...

Born July 23, 1962, in Hartford, CT, one of four children. *Education:* Juilliard; New York University, B.F.A., 1984.

Joined local youth theater group at age 14; entered the Juilliard school, New York, NY, 1982; appeared in numerous plays, New York, NY, 1980s; landed role in daytime soap opera (*One Life to Live*); moved to Los Angeles, CA, 1991; cast in prime-time dramatic series (*The Human Factor*), 1992; appeared as guest star on various television series, 1990s; received star billing for role in a feature film (*D.R.O.P. Squad*), 1994; wrote, directed, and starred in a short film (*Psalms from the Underground*); cast in top-rated television series (*ER*), 1994; earned an Emmy nomination for his role on *ER*, 1995; directed a movie for HBO on cable television (*Angel of Harlem*).

Addresses: *Home*—Los Angeles, CA.

the administration claimed that they had tried that already, and it had not worked out. "I'm not the kind of person to blame everything on racism," La Salle noted in the *New York Times.* "But I think it's so intertwined in our society that it's a factor intentionally or unintentionally."

Although La Salle had entered Juilliard for a four-year program, he was asked to leave after two years because his instructors did not think he would be able to suppress his inner city speech patterns. "I didn't see it coming," said La Salle in the *New York Times.* "I was training privately with speech teachers, and the word I was getting back was that I was improving. And then at my evaluation, they told me of their decision." Training after Juilliard continued for the actor in New York University's graduate theater program. After graduating he found steady work in several productions for Joseph Papp's Shakespeare in the Park Theater company in New York City. A few weeks later he was cast in a low-budget Italian feature, and from there he landed a series of roles in plays in New York City.

Landed Role in Soap Opera

Entry into television came for La Salle in the role of reporter Mike Rivers on the daytime soap opera, *One Life to Live.* After moving to Los Angeles in 1991, he then played a doctor on the series *The Human Factor,* but the series was canceled after less than a full season. He also made frequent guest appearances on shows such as *L.A. Law, Quantum Leap,* and *A Different World,* and on cable television he appeared in HBO's *Vietnam War Stories.* His made-for-television movie credits include *Empty Cradle, Circumstantial Evidence, What Price Victory,* and *Leg Work.* On the big screen La Salle was seen in the feature films *Coming to America, Five Corners, Jacob's Ladder,* and *The Color of Night,* and he received star billing in 1994 for his role as a high-powered advertising executive in *D.R.O.P. Squad.*

Before landing his role in ER, La Salle wrote a screenplay about a female black militant called *Psalms from the Underground.* When he couldn't find anyone to produce it, he spent $140,000 of his own money to make it into a 35-minute film. La Salle both directed and starred in the film, whose rights were later bought by actor/director Mel Gibson. The film is planned to be developed into a full-length feature.

ER's producers had still not cast the role of Dr. Peter Benton two days into the filming of the show. "When casting waits that long, they're basically waiting for someone to come in and *take* the role," La Salle was quoted as saying in *Essence.* "So I came into the office with a stethoscope and surgical greens I had left over from another series I did, *The Human Factor.*" Three days later La Salle received the news that he had won the role. "We looked at a lot of people for the Benton role," said *ER* executive producer John Wells in the *New York Times.* "The others either played him as totally arrogant, or they shied away from playing his arrogance. Eriq walks the high wire."

Drew on Own Background for Role

La Salle claims that he draws considerably on his own experience to play the role of Dr. Benton. "Where I grew up, the philosophy in my community was that you can't be as good as your white counterparts; you have to be *better,*" said La Salle according to the *New York Times.* "And Benton, my character, I think, embodies what I've learned. He's not out to win a popularity contest." "He's confident and competent," he told NBC about his character. "He's a tough guy on the surface, but underneath, there's something else going on." He added in the *Detroit Free Press,* "My character is not just an overachiever, he's got that God complex that surgeons have—that feeling that they're the highest of the high. Dr. Benton is strong, arrogant, intelligent, stubborn. But most of all he's a black man on TV who has the guts to be offensive."

On the *ER* set, fellow actors have noted similarities between La Salle and his character. He has been very adamant about what his character would and would not do, and he has balked at scenes where Dr. Benton submits to others. As he told *Entertainment Weekly,* "Benton does not acquiesce." His fellow actors have commented on his mischievous sense of humor, according to *Ebony,* and they've also acknowledged a sensitive side in the actor. "He comes off as this macho, good-looking man, but he's like honey," confided co-star Julianna Margulies to *Entertainment Weekly.*

"We are a society of underachievers, so I think it's necessary to be an overachiever.

The significance of race to his role in *ER* has been emphasized by La Salle. As he stated in *about...time* magazine, "I am an African American who gives orders. I'm sure there are [some] who do have problems seeing me telling others what to do and doing it with the type of arrogance and confidence that I portray." He considers *ER* a breakthrough show in its serious treatment of black characters, who have mostly been relegated to situation comedies. "As long as America is laughing with us, they're comfortable," he continued in *about...time.* "Sitcoms are silly situations, so it's not so much that [the situations] are true or even possible. [They are] palatable and digestible for white America...and not threatening."

La Salle has given a lot of credit for his and the show's success to the producer, John Wells, and pilot director, Rod Holcomb, as well as to series creator Michael Crichton's overall vision and the quality of the scripts. "What is not known is that Michael Crichton wrote the script [for *ER*] 20 years ago, and even 20 years ago, he had an African American in mind [for the role of Dr. Benton]," La Salle told *about...time.* "It's unbelievable that [even back then] he tapped into the intensity of being a doctor who happens to be African American, who happens to be female, who happens to be Jewish, who happens to be whatever."

Directed Award-Winning Films

La Salle has written, directed, and produced two short films that won awards at the Worldfest Houston Film Competition and the USA Film Festival. During a break from his *ER* work, he directed a movie for HBO called *Angel of Harlem.* His goal is to direct a feature film, and use that opportunity "to help break down some of the barriers in the business that minorities face," according to *about...time.* The actor is passionate about billiards, table tennis, and weightlifting, and is highly skilled in the martial arts. He also has a deep religious faith that he credits with helping him through the rough times in his life. In *USA Weekend,* he offered the following advice for doctors who have God complexes like his character on *ER*: "Yes, you're doing amazing things. But know that all amazing things come from God."

Sources

about...time, April 30, 1995, p. 10.
Detroit Free Press, October 15, 1995, p. 4E.
Ebony, April 1995, p. 50.
Essence, July 1995, p. 54.
New York Times, November 6, 1994, p. C30.
USA Weekend, October 27–29, 1995, p. 14.

Further information for this profile was obtained from websites for the National Broadcasting Company Inc., *Entertainment Weekly,* and *People Magazine* on the Internet.

—Ed Decker

Maria Liberia-Peters

1941—

Politician, author

Maria Philomena Peters was born in the midst of World War II on Curacao, in the Netherlands Antilles. She is the middle child of five, having an older brother and sister and two younger sisters. Her father, James, was born on Sint Maarten, and her mother, Mabel, was born on the island of Saba, both islands are part of the Dutch colony.

Spiritual Values

Due to the strategic and industrial importance of the islands, U.S. Army troops were stationed there for seven years during World War II. German submarines had tried to sink tankers that carried crude petroleum to the large oil refineries located on Curacao. The Netherlands Antilles were also important to the Dutch because the homeland was occupied by Germany. Many companies established offshore offices in the Antilles to enable their continued existence. In 1954 the Antilles became autonomous, meaning they are self-governing except for their defense and foreign affairs being handled by The Netherlands. The Netherlands Antilles are a group of five main islands and several smaller ones, spread out in the Caribbean. Two of the islands, Bonaire and Curacao, lie just north of the coast of Venezuela. The other three

main islands, Saba, St. Eustatius (or Statia), and Sint Maartin the Dutch half of the island, the other half is Saint Martin, a French colony), are located in the Central Caribbean. Aruba was part of the colony at one time, but was separated from the other islands in 1986.

Maria remembers growing up in Curacao quite vividly. "We grew up in a rather poor neighborhood", she said in a press release. "But my father being a real family man teamed up with my mother. Daddy was out at work and brought every penny of his earnings to my mother, and mommy ran the household and insisted that we work hard and do our homework." Her mother opened a small neighborhood grocery store to try and help make ends meet for the family. Mrs. Liberia-Peters remembers working in the store after homework in the press release, "I can still remember clients asking for … two onions, a can of sweetoil, half a pound of pig-tail, etc …," she said. "My parents taught us about hard work," she told *CBB*, "My mother was up every day at 4:30 in the morning and always on the go. Mommy and daddy instilled in us high spiritual values."

When she was 14, Liberia-Peters recalls that she began

At a Glance...

Born Maria Philomena Peters, May 20, 1941 in Willemsted, Curacao, Netherlands Antilles; daughter of James Louis Peters (a construction foreman) and Mabel Albertina (Hassell) Peters (a homemaker and shopkeeper); married Niels Francisco Liberia on December 19, 1972; two children, Crystal Mary-Jo and Niels Maurice. *Education:* Bachelor's degree, 1962, in teaching and administration, the Normal Training School for the Teaching of Children, Emmen, The Netherlands; Degree in Pedagogics, 1972, University of the Netherlands; continuing classes at Ohio State University.

Head teacher of Kindergarten schools, Maria Goretti school, 1962-64, and John Marrits School, 1964-67, both on Curacao; Supervisor of public schools for early childhood, 1967-72; Instructor, methodology and didactics, Pedagogic Academy, Willemsted; and Supervisor of Roman Catholic Schools for Early Childhood Education, 1972-75; Commissioner in the Executive Council of the Local Government of Cura(ao, 1975-80, 1983-84; Inspector for Early Childhood at the Ministry of Education, 1981-; Member of the Staten (legislature) of Netherlands Antilles, 1982-; Minister of Economic Affairs, 1982-83; Prime Minister of Netherlands Antilles, 1984-86, 1988-94; opposition leader, 1986-88, 1994-; Chair of the Board, Regional Conference for the Integration of Women in the development of Latin America and the Caribbean, 1991-94.

Awards: Grootofficier in de Orde van Oranje Nassau, Kingdom of The Netherlands; Gran-Cruz del Orden de Boyaca, Republic of Colombia; Gran Corden en el Orden del Libertador, Republic of Venezuela

Addresses: *Office*—Parliament Building, Wilhelmina Plein #4, Willemstad, Curacao, Netherlands Antilles.

taught her "'In order to make progress in life you have to work. Don't be afraid nor ashamed of any work, as long as your conscience can bear it.'"

The people of the Netherlands Antilles are a very educated populace. Their illiteracy rates are among the lowest in the Western Hemisphere. Like many people in the country Maria speaks four languages; English, Dutch, Spanish, and Papiamento, the common language of the Netherlands Antilles, which is a mixture of Spanish, Dutch, English, and Portuguese, with additions from Arawak and African languages. She attended the Wilhelmina school on Curacao when she was a teenager, and she played on the women's basketball team, where she met Niels Liberia, a well-known basketball player in the Antilles, who was assisting the coach. When the *New York Times* asked her what impressed her about Mr. Liberia, she replied, "His hook shot!" Shortly after finishing her regular schooling, Maria left for Holland to continue her schooling in Emmen at the Training College for Early Childhood Education. When she completed her degree she returned to The Antilles to become a kindergarten teacher. After a few years she "felt the necessity to go back to school," she said in her press release.

Changing Careers

After receiving her degree in Pedagogics (the study of teaching) Maria again returned to Curacao. She returned to her position as Supervisor of Government Schools for Early Childhood Education, as well as teaching at the Training College for Teachers there on the island. Meanwhile, her friendship with Niels Liberia had bloomed into romance. Fifteen years after she first met Niels Liberia they were wed on December 19, 1972. Mr. Liberia is a civil servant for the islands government.

While teaching Mrs. Liberia-Peters learned first hand about organizing parent groups and social issues affecting the population. She joined the National People's Party, a political party of the islands. She was asked to run for a seat on the Curacao island council in 1975 an she won. Some of her notoriety before the election came from forming the Steering Committee for Women's Organizations in 1974, which worked for programs on the island in conjunction with the International Women's Year in 1975. From this position she was named to the Executive Council of the island government. This body met regularly with the representative from Queen Beatrix of The Netherlands.

During this time Mrs. Liberia-Peters was informed by her doctors that she would be unable to conceive. She and her husband made the decision to adopt children.

selling homemade bread and cupcakes in the neighborhood. Her mother would bake the items in the family kitchen and Maria and her oldest sister Iris would go door-to-door selling the freshly baked items. She credits her mother and father with instilling the family with good spiritual values. In the press release she notes that they

She said in her press release that, "There are so many children in this world who need help. We hope that more couples would open up to children who for one reason or the other cannot be raised by their biological parents." The Liberia's two children are now teenagers. They were both born in the United States and were adopted through the Roman Catholic Archdiocese of New York. Mrs. Liberia-Peters says that "adopting a child brings triple happiness: 1) there is no difference in the love you share with an adopted child versus the love you would share with a child you bore; 2) you fill the life of the child with all he or she needs as a human being; 3) someday you may be able to meet the biological parents and say thanks to them for granting you the opportunity to fulfill a dream and the undoubtedly anguished feeling that has haunted them for long years will be taken away."

In 1982 Maria Liberia-Peters was elected to the Staten, or legislature, of the Netherlands Antilles. She quickly was appointed to be Minister of Economic Affairs by the coalition government in power. This government lasted only a short while before collapsing in 1984. In September of that year Maria was asked to form a new coalition government, and she was sworn in as Prime Minister. She was soon demonstrating her independence as she chose to dance and participate in the annual Carnival parade instead of sitting in the traditional, reserved seat of the Prime Minister. She told the *New York Times* that "she would not feel happy as a spectator ... knowing that I am standing at the side." Liberia-Peters went on to explain that "some people just feel it's not appropriate for the prime minister. But she added, "In the first place I'm Maria and in the second place I'm the prime minister. So I'm going." So participants in the parade could see her tall figure dressed in a green and pink lame dress dancing in the streets.

Maria Liberia-Peters served as Prime Minister of the Netherlands Antilles on two different occasions. The first time was brief, from 1984-86. The second time was from 1988-94. She states that her biggest challenge was during the period when Shell and Lago Standard Oil had announced the intended closure of their huge oil refineries on Curacao and Aruba. Liberia-Peters was able to work out an agreement with the Venezuelan state owned oil company, PDVSA, to manage the refinery. The closure of these refineries would have meant the loss of over 20% of the jobs in the Netherlands Antilles. Although the refinery on Aruba did close, it later reopened under different company management. One of the decisions Maria had to make during this time was the introduction of a 10% income tax on all wages. This was "to form a national fund to serve as a bumper" against economic hard times, she said in her press

release. Although her party won more seats in the election three months following this decision, her opponents quickly formed a coalition government which was the reason behind Liberia-Peters temporarily leaving office in 1986.

Leadership Style

To many people the transition from kindergarten teacher to prime minister may seem very unusual, but not to Liberia-Peters. In *Women World Leaders,* Liberia-Peters states, "... at a certain moment, from your position as teacher and educator, you start to become the ears and eyes, and the feet of those who cannot walk, hear, and see ... that's the way I walked right into politics." "You govern with psychology and keep meeting," Liberia-Peters said in *Women World Leaders,* there is basically no difference in the behaviour of a four, five, six year old, or a forty, fifty or sixty year old, there's basically no difference. And I keep telling them that in the meeting of the Council of Ministers." According to Olga Opfell in *Women Prime Ministers and Presidents,* "Liberia-Peters was complimented for her ability to reach consensus among the ministers."

> "My father told me everyone has power, the power to serve, and that is what I have done."

Maria in an interview with *CBB* stated that "my father told me everyone has power, the power to serve, and that is what I have done." "Politics is a real power play, you must explain these events to the people." The opinion people have of politicians in the United States is no different than the one they hold in the Netherlands Antilles according to Liberia-Peters. "It's a hard knock game," she told *CBB*, "There is a lot that can lead you to do bad. You must remember your mission and comply with it or you can get lost and astray. You need strong legs to stand on and you need to stand before your decisions." Not all of Liberia-Peters' decisions have been popular. "Yes," she chuckled while acknowledging this to *CBB,* someone else said, "Victories have many fathers, but defeat is an orphan."

Since 1994 Maria has been the opposition leader in parliament. She said in her interview with *CBB* that "My schedule has slowed down a lot because I don't have as many responsibilities currently." One of the projects that she views as important is the establishment of a Caribbean policy studies center or regional think tank. Maria sees that the larger nations are forming blocks to advance their goals, such as the North American Free Trade Agreement, and she feels that the Caribbean needs to do the same to protect their interests. "If everyone bundles up together maybe something good will happen." Liberia-Peters has been a driving force in the Caribbean Council for Europe's recent feasibility study of this idea.

As for the future, she will remain in politics for the time being. She does recognize that she will leave the hectic life in the public eye eventually. She would like to return to teaching. Not to a classroom, perhaps, but to consultancy work. She would like to teach politics at the grass roots level. "The art of politics," she told *CBB*. "What goes on with politicians." This would allow her to continue in the roll she believes she was put here for, the role of dedicated public servant.

Sources

Books

Liswood, Laura, *Women World Leaders,* HarperCollins, 1994.
Opfell, Olga S. *Women Prime Ministers and Presidents,* McFarland and Company, 1993, pp. 121-127.

Periodicals

New York Times, August 19, 1985, sec. C, p. 12.
Inter Press Service, June 21, 1993.

Additional information for this profile was obtained from a press release and curriculum vitae provided by Mrs. Liberia-Peters and a *CBB* interview with Liberia-Peters on April 14, 1996.

—Stephen Stratton

Ken Lofton

1967—

Professional baseball player

During Game Six of the 1995 American League Championship Series, Kenny Lofton had to hit the dirt to stay out of the way of a 99 mile-per-hour fastball thrown by Randy Johnson, one of the most feared pitchers in baseball. A few innings later, Lofton got the base hit that beat Johnson and clinched the pennant for the Cleveland Indians. In many respects, the drama of that game is symbolic of Lofton's own life story. By constantly refusing to be intimidated, whether by the harsh circumstances of his youth or by early career setbacks, Lofton has emerged as an exciting baseball superstar.

Born on May 31, 1967, in East Chicago, Indiana, Lofton spent his entire childhood in a state of desperate poverty. His mother, Annie, was a teenager when he was born. His father did not take part in his upbringing, and neither Lofton nor other family members ever mention the man. Lofton weighed three pounds at birth and was so small his mother was afraid to hold him. Instead, she carried him around on a pillow made by his grandmother, Rosie Person.

Raised by Grandmother

Shortly after giving birth to Lofton, his mother returned to high school, leaving the baby in the care of Person. Person's husband had died in 1960, and since she herself was going blind from glaucoma, Social Security was the family's only source of income. Person, Lofton, and other family members lived in a cramped apartment in a rough East Chicago neighborhood. Although they were extremely poor, Person somehow always managed to provide enough food for the family. The sad experience of seeing other children with toys and clothes that his family could not afford has had a profound effect on Lofton as an adult. He is very protective of his privacy, but is also generous with charitable organizations—two characteristics that can be traced to the hardship of his youth.

In high school Lofton excelled in both baseball and basketball. It was basketball that provided his escape from the slums. Courted by a number of colleges, Lofton accepted a basketball scholarship to the University of Arizona. At Arizona, he was sixth man on a team that made it to the Final Four of the 1988 National Collegiate Athletic Association (NCAA) tournament, and he set season and career school records for steals. On a whim, Lofton decided to try out for the baseball team during his

At a Glance...

Born Kenneth Lofton, May 31, 1967, in East Chicago, IN; grandson of Annie Person. *Education:* Attended University of Arizona.

University of Arizona basketball team, point guard, reaching the Final Four in the 1988 NCAA tournament; drafted by Houston Astros in 17th round of 1988 amateur draft; minor league player in Astros farm system, 1988-91, member of Houston Astros, 1991; traded to Cleveland Indians, December, 1991, member of Indians, 1992—.

Selected awards: Gold Glove Award, 1993, 1994, 1995; named to American League All-Star Team, 1994, 1995.

Addresses: *Home*—Tucson, AZ. *Office*—Cleveland Indians, 2401 Ontario St., Cleveland, OH 44115-4003. *Agent*—Steven Zucker, 33 N. Dearborn, 19th Floor, Chicago, IL 60602.

junior year. Although he saw limited action on the baseball team, his speed caught the eye of scouts, and he was chosen by the Houston Astros in the 17th round of baseball's amateur draft that June. He began playing minor league baseball part-time, while still finishing out his college basketball career.

Honed Skills in Minors

Because he played so little baseball in college, Lofton required several years of training to develop his skills to the major league level. The one area in which he excelled from the start was base stealing, since his pure speed could compensate for any lack of experience or technique. In his first year as a professional baseball player, Lofton batted only .214 for the Class A Auburn team, but he stole 26 bases in just 48 games. After stealing another 26 bases in his first 34 games at Auburn in 1989, Lofton was promoted to Asheville of the South Atlantic League. At Asheville his batting average improved to .329, and he remained a terror on the base paths, stealing 14 bases in 22 games.

When his college basketball career was over, Lofton was able to concentrate on baseball full-time. He spent the entire 1990 season, his first full season as a pro, at Class

A Osceola of the Florida State League. His .331 batting average was second highest in the league that year. From Osceola, Lofton made the jump to AAA, the highest level of minor league play. He spent most of the 1991 season at Tucson, where he led his team to the Pacific Coast League championship and made the league's All-Star squad. In September of 1991, the Astros promoted Lofton to the majors. In his very first major league game he had three hits and scored three runs against the Cincinnati Reds.

Gained Stardom in Cleveland

During the 20 games he played with Houston that year, however, Lofton batted only .203. In addition, the Astros already had a young centerfielder, Steve Finley, with whom they were happy. Unwilling to wait for Lofton to develop his skills further, Houston more or less gave up on him. He was traded to the Cleveland Indians in December of 1991.

Lofton is now generally considered one of the two or three best center-fielders in baseball and probably the game's single best lead-off hitter.

The trade to Cleveland turned out to be the best thing that could have happened to Lofton's career. Under the guidance of Indians first base coach Dave Nelson, Lofton was given intensive training in the finer points of base-running, bunting, hitting to the opposite field, and fielding. Improving steadily as the 1992 season progressed, Lofton posted a .285 batting average, and his 66 stolen bases were the most ever recorded by an American League rookie. He came in second in the race for American League rookie of the year. Prior to the 1993 season, Lofton signed a new four-year contract with the Indians worth $6.3 million.

Lofton's career truly blossomed in 1993. In addition to hitting .325 and leading the majors with 70 stolen bases, he became a defensive star as well, winning the Gold Glove Award as the league's best defensive centerfielder. As the 1990s continued, the Indians emerged as one of the strongest teams in the American League. Lofton was the catalyst among a talented nucleus of young players that included power-hitting outfielder Albert Belle and second baseman Carlos Baerga. Lofton put up amazing numbers in the strike-shortened 1994 season, batting .349, stealing 60 bases, and capturing another Gold Glove. He also made the American League All-Star Team for the first time during the 1994 season.

Appeared in World Series With Indians

Injuries hampered Lofton's play for much of the 1995 season. He nevertheless managed to lead the league in steals for the fourth straight year, win his third straight Gold Glove, and make his second straight All-Star Game appearance. Most importantly, he helped take the Indians to the World Series for the first time in decades. Although they lost the Series to the Atlanta Braves, Cleveland's appearance in the postseason brought the talents of Lofton and company to the attention of a much wider audience than ever before. Given the way he guards his personal privacy, this attention was not entirely welcome in Lofton's case.

Lofton is now generally considered one of the two or three best centerfielders in baseball, and probably the game's single best lead-off hitter. Some baseball insiders consider him one of the best active players in either league. Regardless of these speculative rankings, Lofton is unquestionably one of baseball's most entertaining players. As Toronto second baseman Roberto Alomar told the *Boston Globe*, "He's one of those players you just sit back and enjoy watching."

Sources

Boston Globe, October 15, 1995, p. 89.
Los Angeles Times, October 19, 1995, p. C1.
New York Times, March 21, 1993, p. S7.
Sporting News, October 30, 1995, p. 11.
Sports Illustrated, May 1, 1995, p. 96.

—Robert R. Jacobson

Kenny Lofton on baseball field.

Henry Lyons

1942(?)—

Religious leader

In 1994 Henry J. Lyons was elected president of the National Baptist Convention USA, the largest African American religious organization in the country. As head of its 8.2 million members, Lyons oversees what is perhaps the most powerful and influential institution in the African American community. To Lyons, who saw his new leadership role as a calling, it was time to harness the spirituality of that community to redress some of its setbacks. "We've got to lift the name of Jesus; yes, that's No. 1," Lyons told *Ebony* writer Lisa C. Jones. "But it's also got to be shown that we're about the business of turning our communities around. We're going to have to take back our streets and our neighborhoods."

Destined to Lead

Lyons was born in the early 1940s in Gainesville, Florida. An only child, he lived behind a small Baptist church and his baptism took place in a nearby pond. When he was twelve-years-old, his pastor prophesied that he would one day lead the Baptists. "I had no idea what he was talking about," he recalled in *Ebony*. But

later, while he was a divinity student at Morehouse College in Atlanta, he received what he felt was a direct sign from God, an echo of his pastor's earlier prediction, and was guided to a particular passage in the Bible. Toward the end of his undergraduate studies, Lyons obtained his first post as head of a religious community at Abyssinia Baptist Church in Brunswick, Georgia. He later headed Macedonia Baptist Church in Atlanta, then moved to Ohio for further study. There, at the Cincinnati Baptist College, he served as an academic dean while working on his doctorate in divinity. By the early 1970s he had further supplemented his education with yet another advanced degree, a Ph.D. in sacred theology from Jerusalem's Hebrew Union University.

Near this time Lyons also wed his wife Deborah; together they would raise three children--Derrick, a Marine Corps sergeant, Stephanie, a teacher, and Vonda, a college student majoring in communications. For the large part of his career Lyons served as head of Bethel Metropolitan Baptist Church, in St. Petersburg, Florida. He also became active in the Florida General Baptist Convention, rising to hold its presidency in 1981, and

At a Glance...

Born c. 1942, in Gainesville, FL; married, c. 1972; wife's name, Deborah; children: Derrick, Stephanie, Vonda. *Education:* Received undergraduate degree from Morehouse College; received D.Div. from Cincinnati Baptist College; Hebrew Union University, Ph.D. in sacred theology, 1972. *Religion:* Baptist.

Career: Abyssinia Baptist Church, Brunswick, GA, pastor, mid-1960s; Macedonia Baptist Church, Atlanta, GA, pastor, late 1960s; Cincinnati Baptist College, Cincinnati, OH, academic dean, late 1960s; Bethel Metropolitan Baptist Church, St. Petersburg, FL, pastor; Florida General Baptist Convention, St. Petersburg, president, 1981--; National Baptist Convention USA, Nashville, TN, president, 1994--.

Addresses: *Office*—National Baptist Convention USA, 1700 Baptist World Center Dr., Nashville, TN 37207.

also in the parent organization, the National Baptist Convention USA (NBCUSA) headquartered in Nashville, Tennessee. Eventually Lyons's work as president of the Florida organization, which raised funds and constructed low-income housing units, garnered him a vice-presidency of the national organization. In 1994, the longtime president of the NBCUSA, Dr. T. J. Jemison, announced his retirement after two six-year terms, according to the limit imposed under the organization's by-laws. Jemison had been only one of a handful of presidents of the Convention in its six decades of existence, and Lyons decided to run in the election to succeed him. He stressed a reform agenda in his bid for the presidency. "It was well-known that President Jemison held a tight rein on the financial purse of the multibillion dollar organization," noted the *Sacramento Observer.* "During his campaign candidate Lyons insisted that the organizational delegates investigate the status of NBCUSA monies."

Election Made Headlines

At their national convention in New Orleans in early September of 1994, Lyons won 3,545 votes, just a few hundred more than his nearest opponent. A month later, a faction of Alabama pastors--supporters of another candidate--filed a lawsuit that charged election

fraud. The court injunction prevented Lyons from taking office and put a freeze on all church business at the national level. Detractors charged that some voting delegates had been prevented from casting their vote in the presidential balloting in New Orleans, and then presented 44 affidavits to Washington, DC's Superior Court--where the NBCUSA is chartered--claiming election fraud. Later, some of those NBCUSA delegates told Judge Zenora Mitchell-Rankin that they had not signed the affidavits, and others admitted they were either ineligible to vote or were not even present in New Orleans. The judge ruled in favor of Lyons, lifted the injunction against church business, and ordered the Alabama faction to pay Lyons $150,000 in addition to his attorneys' fees and court costs.

> "I see this as an opportunity, as a window to do something positive and to turn this whole business around for our people.

When Lyons finally took office with the court's help, it fulfilled the prediction his pastor had made and his later prophetic experience when he was a student at Morehouse. "I received a clear mandate, orders, from God himself," Lyons told *Ebony* writer Lisa C. Jones of that day. "He let me know I was to lead this organization. He led me to *Isaiah 62:10,* 'Go through the gates...gather out the stones...lift up standard for the people.' Those words burned in my heart. And then it all came into focus."

Began Era of Reform

Upon assuming the reins of the NBCUSA, Lyons tackled a number of pressing financial problems, including a huge debt on the six-year-old Nashville headquarters. A large mortgage payment was immediately due, plus late fees and interest charges that had been accruing. Tradition in the organization dictated that the proceeds from his inaugural banquet--which could have hosted as many as 1,900 people--would go to Lyons; instead he declared that the monies raised would go directly back into the NBCUSA. He also flew coach class, a first for the president and a shock to his staff. In response, he asked them, "How in the world can you fly first class when the organization you represent is dead broke? We need some money, we need to realign ourselves financially, get on the good foot, then fly first class. Right now the ox is in the ditch," the *Philadelphia Tribune* reported.

The NBCUSA's new era of reform was matched by Lyons's commitment to its more basic focus: addressing members' spiritual welfare, and helping others in need. It sent several thousand dollars to help Rwandans in that country's 1995 civil strife, and provided aid to several other impoverished African and Caribbean nations. Lyons also sought to improve conditions at home as well. He planned to open an NBCUSA office in Washington, DC, in order to focus on solving problems within the African American community; working on a national level on behalf of the 8.2 million African American members--over a fourth of the U.S. African American population--was of primary importance. Drug abuse, gang violence, and education were especial targets, and Lyons even announced a willingness to meet with gang leaders if necessary. "The gangs have become an entity in our community to be reckoned with," Lyons told *Ebony.* "We have to talk to them and let [them] know that, unless things improve, our whole race is at stake."

Hoped to Engender Great Change

Lyons also made a point of speaking out against affirmative action setbacks in Congress and the Supreme Court in 1995, and called for NBCUSA members to take part in a civil rights march in Birmingham, Alabama in September of that year. The action would be held in conjunction with the organization's annual meeting there.

He also voiced criticism over the handling of President Bill Clinton's nomination of Dr. Henry Foster as Surgeon General, suggesting that race--not the physician's pro-choice stance--was the real issue. Lyons also took on the formidable Reverend Jesse Jackson in the media after Jackson asserted that Lyons had endorsed the Million Man March on Washington, DC scheduled for October of 1995. Lyons and another prominent Baptist leader decried Jackson's use of their names, and asserted that they would not lend support to the march called for by Nation of Islam leader Louis Farrakhan. Such a prominent national profile has gained Lyons access to the White House, and First Lady Hilary Rodham Clinton was even photographed attending one of Lyons's services at the Bethel Metropolitan Baptist Church, where he continues to preach. The national spotlight fails to distract Lyons from the goals he has set for the NBCUSA, however. "I see this as an opportunity, as a window to do something positive and to turn this whole business around for our people," he told *Ebony.*

Sources

Christian Century, October 12, 1994, p. 921.
Ebony, January 1995, p. 86.
Michigan Citizen, August 19, 1995, p. B4.
Philadelphia Tribune, September 13, 1994, p. 1A; December 23, 1994, p. 1D.
Sacramento Observer, November 9, 1994, p. A1.
Washington Informer, September 7, 1994, p. 20; July 19, 1995, p. 22.

—Carol Brennan

Ali Mazrui

1933—

African scholar, political scientist, author

Ali Mazrui is one of the world's most prolific and controversial writers on Africa. The author of more than 20 books and hundreds of essays, Mazrui has profoundly influenced ideas about Africa among scholars and members of the general public alike. Although his views do not always sit well with American audiences, Mazrui's powerful writing style has made it impossible for even his harshest critics to ignore the unique perspective he brings to a huge variety of African issues. His soft-spoken charm and eloquence as a lecturer have also made him a favorite among students at every university he has served.

Mazrui was born on February 24, 1933, in Mombasa, Kenya. An old and prominent Muslim clan, the Mazruis had ruled the city-state of Mombasa during the 18th century. Mazrui's father, Al'Amin Ali Mazrui, was Chief Kadhi of Kenya, the country's top judge of Islamic law. As the son of an eminent Muslim scholar, Mazrui was expected to follow in his father's footsteps. British colonialism changed the direction of his education, however, and after attending local schools as a child, Mazrui continued his studies in England. He graduated from the University of Manchester in 1960.

After receiving his B.A. from Manchester, Mazrui received a Rockefeller Foundation fellowship to attend Columbia University in New York, where he received his M.A. in 1961. From there, he returned to England to begin working on his doctorate at Oxford University. In 1962 he took a job as a political analyst for the British Broadcasting Corporation (BBC). He also married a teacher named Molly Vickerman that same year. Mazrui moved back to Africa in 1963, but continued working for the BBC on a part-time basis until 1965.

Taught in Uganda

In 1963 Mazrui moved to Kampala, Uganda to teach political science at Makerere University. In addition to his work for the BBC, he did some writing and broadcasting for Radio Uganda and Radio Tanzania over the next couple of years. In 1965 Mazrui was named head of Makerere's political science department. After completing his doctorate at Oxford the following year, he also began taking on visiting professor assignments at overseas universities, including stints in the United States at the University of Chicago, Northwestern University, UCLA, and Harvard University.

Mazrui's first three books were all published in 1967.

One of them, *Towards a Pax Africana,* was a published version of his Oxford dissertation. The Pan-African, anti-colonialist views expressed by that book became ongoing themes in Mazrui's writings over the years. The other two books were *The Anglo-African Commonwealth* and *On Heroes and Uhuru-Worship.* The simultaneous publication of those three influential books made Mazrui a rising star among African scholars, and he was chosen as dean of the Faculty of Social Sciences at Makerere soon thereafter. He was also elected to various offices in the International Political Science Association, the International Congress of Africanists, and the International Sociology Association during the period that followed.

Throughout the remainder of the 1960s, Mazrui's reputation as one of Africa's leading scholars continued to grow. In 1971, a military coup brought Idi Amin to power in Uganda. For a while, Mazrui was one of Amin's favorite intellectuals. Within a year, however, the notoriously unpredictable dictator had changed his opinion, and Mazrui prudently opted to leave the country. In spite of this turmoil, Mazrui remained very productive during this period, publishing three books between 1970 and 1972, including his only novel, *The Trial of Christopher Okigbo. The Trial of Christopher Okigbo,* published in 1971, is a utopian tale taking place in heaven that addresses the question of the artist's role in politics.

In 1973 Mazrui accepted a position at the University of Michigan. He remained there for the next 18 years, serving as director of the university's Center for Afroamerican and African Studies from 1978 to 1981. At Michigan, Mazrui solidified his position as one of the most important writers on African politics in the world. He continued to write prolifically, and in 1979 he was selected to give the prestigious Reith Lectures, delivered annually in England over the BBC. The lectures were subsequently published in book form as *The African Condition.*

Sparked Controversy with *The Africans*

Mazrui became a well-known figure outside of academia in 1986, when he wrote and hosted the nine-part television series *The Africans: A Triple Heritage,* broadcast in England on the BBC and in the United States on PBS. The show's subtitle refers to the three legacies—Islamic, indigenous, and Western—that have been most apparent in the formation of modern African identity. The controversy that surrounded the series brought Mazrui a degree of fame far beyond what his appearance on the screen could have accomplished alone. Conservatives, led by National Endowment for the Humanities (NEH) chairperson Lynne Cheney, con-

Western bias. Among their complaints were that Mazrui spoke favorably of Libyan leader Moammar Qaddafi. The NEH went so far as to demand that its name be removed from the show's credits.

> In writing, Mazrui has frequently referred to his own background— a combination of Islamic law, Kenyan culture, and a Western education—as reflection of the triple heritage that has shaped modern Africa

In reality, colonialization and the West shared the blame for Africa's ills with a number of other culprits in Mazrui's analysis. Rather than presenting an unbalanced view of African issues, Mazrui insisted that part of the intent of *The Africans* was to restore balance to the overwhelmingly pro-Western coverage of African matters generally seen in America, by presenting a purely African perspective. In spite of the wrath it incurred, the series was widely acclaimed in many other circles, and the accompanying book of the same title was a best-seller in England.

Left Michigan for SUNY

The criticism that Mazrui received from conservatives as a result of *The Africans* did not hurt is career a bit. While the controversy was still raging, Mazrui was named Andrew D. White Professor-at-Large at Cornell University. In 1989 he was lured away from Michigan by the State University of New York, Binghamton, after receiving a call from New York Governor Mario Cuomo. Having divorced his first wife in 1982, after 20 years of marriage, Mazrui married Pauline Uti, a teacher from Nigeria, in 1991. That year, he was named director of Binghamton's Institute of Global Cultural Studies. During his time at Binghamton, Mazrui has continued to serve in an advisory capacity on numerous issues to numerous organizations, including the United Nations, and has served on the editorial boards of several academic journals.

In his writing, Mazrui has frequently referred to his own background—a combination of Islamic law, Kenyan culture, and a Western education—as a reflection of the triple heritage that has shaped modern Africa. Like the range of influences that produced his thinking, the range of subject areas that Mazrui has chosen to study over the course of his career is also extremely broad. In fact,

some critics believe that Mazrui writes about so many different topics that none of them ever receive the thorough treatment that they deserve. That criticism does not bother Mazrui. His role, as he sees it, is to provoke debate. There is no doubt that he has succeeded in achieving that goal.

Selected writings

Books

The Anglo-African Commonwealth, Pergamon, 1967.
On Heroes and Uhuru-Worship, Longmans, 1967.
Towards a Pax Africana, Weidenfeld & Nicolson, 1967; University of Chicago Press, 1967.
Violence and Thought, Longmans, 1969; Humanities, 1969.
(Co-editor, with Robert I. Rotberg) *Protest and Power in Black Africa,* Oxford University Press, 1970.
The Trial of Christopher Okigbo, Heinemann, 1971; Third Press, 1972.
Cultural Engineering and Nation-Building in East Africa, Northwestern University Press, 1972.
(Co-editor, with Hasu H. Patel) *Africa in World Affairs: The Next Thirty Years,* Third Press, 1973.
World Culture and the Black Experience, University of Washington Press, 1974.
Soldiers and Kinsmen in Uganda: The Making of a Military Ethnocracy, Sage, 1975.
The Political Sociology of the English Language: An African Perspective, Mouton, 1975.
A World Federation of Cultures: An African Perspective, Free Press, 1976.
Africa's International Relations: The Diplomacy of Dependency and Change, Westview, 1977.
(Editor) *The Warrior Tradition in Modern Africa,* Brill, 1977.
Political Values and the Educated Class in Africa, Heinemann, 1978; University of California Press, 1978.
The African Condition: A Political Diagnosis, Heinemann, 1980; Cambridge University Press, 1980.
(With Michael Tidy) *Nationalism and New States in Africa,* Heinemann, 1984.
The Africans: A Triple Heritage, Little, Brown, 1986; BBC, 1986.
(Co-editor, with T. K. Levine) *The Africans: A Reader,* Praeger, 1986.
Cultural Forces in World Politics, Heinemann, 1990.
(Editor) *Africa Since 1935,* Volume VIII of the UNESCO General History of Africa, 1993.

Television

(Writer and host) *The Africans: A Triple Heritage,*

BBC and PBS, 1986

Contributor to numerous scholarly journals.

Sources

Monograph

Nyang, Sulayman S., *Ali A. Mazrui: The Man and His Works,* Brunswick Publishing Company, 1981.

Periodicals

International Social Science Journal, no. 1-2, 1973, p. 101.
New York Times, October 5, 1986, sec. 2, p. 27.
People Weekly, November 24, 1986, p. 145.
Philadelphia Tribune, November 1, 1994, p. 3D.
Washington Post, October 5, 1986, p. Y7.

—*Robert R. Jacobson*

Kaire Mbuende

1953—

Statesman, diplomat

As executive secretary of the Southern African Development Community (SADC) since January, 1994, Dr. Kaire Mbuende managed the regional transitions from war to peace, from hostility to cooperation and investment, among nations in Southern Africa. Not so long ago Dr. Mbuende played a far different role: until 1989, he helped organize the revolution for independence in Namibia, a South West African country previously a colony of South Africa and the last colony in Africa. In that struggle Dr. Mbuende had been imprisoned, tortured, and interrogated by the former South African authorities in Namibia. Now that Namibia is politically free and South Africa has overcome apartheid, the former South African system of segregation and disenfranchisement of people of color, Dr. Mbuende has played a leading role in building reconciliation and developing new trade across the region. "My dream is to see a Southern Africa free of conflicts devoting its human and natural resources in pursuit of economic development, social progress, and cultural advancement," Dr. Mbuende wrote in an interview with *Contemporary Black Biography*.

Yearned for Justice as Youth

Kaire Munionganda Mbuende was born on November 28, 1953, in the city of Windhoek, Namibia, to Lydia and Gabriel Mbuende, a devoted and nationally known primary school teacher. Mbuende was influenced by the leadership qualities of his grandfather at a young age. "My grandfather's political involvement and his teaching based on a deep religious conviction created a yearning for justice in me at an early age," Dr. Mbuende recalled in a faxed interview with *CBB*. Mbuende's grandfather, Gotthard Mbuende, was a member of the Herero Chief Council under the leadership of Chief Hosea Kutako.

Mbuende did not involve himself in politics until he was 18. He participated in a student strike at Augusteun High School in 1970 and subsequently joined the South West African People's Organization (SWAPO), the organization leading the struggle for independence. With other prominent Namibians such as Ndali Kamati, Martin Kapewasha, Jerry Ekandjo, and Festus Naholo, Mbuende founded the SWAPO Youth League in 1971. Mbuende began to help lead democratic protests and civil disobedience against the ruling South African apartheid regime in Namibia.

African Liberation Revolutionary

Throughout the 1970s Mbuende lived the struggle for freedom in Namibia. From 1972 to 1974 he served on the Executive Committee of SWAPO in Namibia and was vice-chairman of the Windhoek Branch, deputizing the late Benjamin Namalambo. During that time Mbuende

At a Glance...

Born Kaire Munionganda Mbuende, November 28, 1953, in Windhoek, Namibia; son of Lydia and Gabriel Mbuende, schoolteacher; married Claudia Karangere Mbuende; three children. *Education:* Lutheran College, Makumira, Tanzania, B.D., 1978; University of Lund, Sweden, B.A. (with honors), 1980; University of Lund, Sweden, Ph.D., 1986.

Member of SWAPO Executive Committee, Namibia, 1972-74; SWAPO External Headquarters, Lusaka, Zambia, information officer, 1974-75; University of Aarhus, Denmark, assistant lecturer, 1981; University of Lund, Sweden, assistant lecturer, 1984-86, lecturer, 1986-87; Institute for Future Studies, Stockholm, Sweden, reader, 1987-89; government of Namibia, member of Constituent Assembly, 1990, member of Parliament, 1990-93, deputy minister of agriculture, water, and rural development, 1990-93; Southern African Development Community (SADC), Botswana, executive secretary, 1994-.

Member: Central Committee, SWAPO, 1991--.

Addresses: *Office*—Southern African Development Community, Private Bag 0095, Gaborone, Botswana.

Scholar-in-Exile Until Independence

Earning a B.D. degree in 1978 from Lutheran College in Makumira, Arusha, Tanzania, and a B.A. in economic history and sociology in 1980 from the University of Lund, Sweden, Mbuende embarked on a career as a social scientist in unofficial exile until free elections were held in Namibia in 1989. Mbuende published numerous articles on sociological theory and development studies and worked as a lecturer, then reader, in universities in Denmark and Sweden until 1989. In 1986 Mbuende attained his Ph.D. in economic sociology from the University of Lund, Sweden. After Mbuende returned to his native country, working after the electoral victory as a minister in the new government, he continued publishing original commentary, then on the practice of economic integration in Southern Africa. When the United Nations-supervised elections provided the opportunity for a new government and political independence, however, Mbuende's focus shifted from the academy back to the struggle for state power.

Mbuende returned to Namibia for the UN-supervised elections in 1989. He rose swiftly with his party, SWAPO. Appointed first the Head of SWAPO Election Directorate in the Gobabis Region (now Omaheke Region), after SWAPO won the historic election Mbuende became a Member of the Constituent Assembly. The Constituent Assembly was charged with the task of writing and adopting the Constitution of the Republic of Namibia in 1989. In 1990, when the Constituent Assembly was transformed into the National Assembly, Mbuende became a Member of Parliament.

Became Deputy Minister of Agriculture

Also in 1990 Dr. Mbuende began serving his first appointment, as Deputy Minister of Agriculture, Water, and Rural Development for the newly-independent Namibia. This post lasted until 1993, just before Mbuende began his tenure as executive secretary of the Southern African Development Community (SADC), in Botswana. As deputy minister of agriculture, Mbuende faced three challenges. First, he had to change the culture of the civil service from the days of colonialism. Now, priority was to go to "the development of small-scale Africa farmers who constitute the majority of the people of Namibia," he wrote in an interview with *CBB*. Second, Mbuende was charged with boosting crop production that had previously been neglected under colonial rule to render Namibia then "a dumping ground for South African products," Mbuende wrote in the *CBB* interview. Finally, Mbuende had to restructure agricultural production to meet local needs rather than only those of South Africa

addressed political rallies and organized and participated in civil disobedience. The South African government in Namibia imprisoned, interrogated, and tortured Mbuende for his political activities.

In July of 1974 Mbuende left Namibia to join the armed revolution against South African apartheid rule in Namibia. After rising to the position of platoon commander in the training program of the People's Liberation Army of Namibia (PLAN), the military wing of SWAPO, Mbuende was appointed to service as an Information Officer with the SWAPO External Headquarters in Lusaka, Zambia. In that post Mbuende produced broadcasts on the political, social, economic, and military situation in Namibia. Soon after Mbuende returned to his studies-- first in Tanzania and then in Sweden. While a student Mbuende participated in the campaign to mobilize political, material, and financial support in the Nordic countries for the struggle for independence in Namibia.

and international markets.

Mbuende's achievements were numerous. First, he averted a major catastrophe by managing Namibia's food resources effectively during a major drought. Mbuende oversaw the drought relief programme in Namibia. Starvation resulted in the Horn of Africa during the drought, but in Namibia not a single life was lost. Mbuende successfully met the routine challenges presented him in his post as well. He made the small-scale African farmer the focus of government programs. He helped move technology into rural areas by establishing Rural Development Centres. He launched a campaign that resulted in a 50 percent increase in maize production and a 75 percent increase in millet production during the 1990-91 growing season. Finally, Mbuende started the slow process of land redistribution with the introduction of affirmative action loans by the Agricultural Bank of Namibia for African farmers in their efforts to acquire commercial farms.

Namibia has also faced the challenge of meeting the rights of minority ethnic peoples. While deputy minister of agriculture, Dr. Mbuende contributed to a general improvement in the human rights situation of these minority peoples, particularly for the San in Namibia. Unlike the policy before independence, communal land rights were respected in practice, if not in explicit legislation. President Sam Nujoma set a precedent in Nyae Nyae, formerly Eastern Bushmanland. Nujoma said during a visit to the area that anyone wishing to settle in a communal land must receive the permission of the traditional leaders in the area, in addition to the Ministry of Lands, Resettlement and Rehabilitation. When settlers from the nearby Hereroland attempted to water their cattle from community boreholes without permission in late 1991, the Nyae Nyae Farmer's Cooperative escorted the settlers peacefully back to the Herero border with the promised, although not necessary, backing of the local police and the Regional Commissioner. All this occurred during Mbuende's tenure as Deputy Minister. Mbuende had written in a pre-Independence SWAPO position paper that the San societies were particularly disadvantaged by the violence they were subjected to under apartheid. Now the San's communal land rights were being upheld in practice.

Fostered Investment in Southern Africa

In January of 1994, Mbuende assumed the top position, executive secretary, of the Southern African Development Community (SADC), a leading institution for regional development in Southern Africa. Mbuende brought

visionary goals to this historic organization. "My long term goal for SADC is to ensure the political, economic, social, and cultural integration of the countries of Southern Africa," Mbuende wrote in an interview with *CBB*. Politically, integration meant a common commitment to democracy, transparency and open government, accountability, and respect for human rights. In addition, member states would work through SADC to achieve peaceful and diplomatic conflict resolution.

Mbuende hopes that the peaceful political climate will form, in turn, the proper environment for renewed investment in the region. "The promotion of private domestic and foreign investment is high on the agenda," Mbuende wrote in an interview with *CBB*. Mbuende envisions that investment targeted toward the manufacturing and service sectors will transform the region from primary to industry-based economies. His goal is that such investment will take place within a larger economic infrastructure of unity across the region. Eventually, Mbuende hopes that unity will be realized in a Southern African Free Trade Area, to be achieved within the next five years and in turn lead to the establishment of a Customs Union and then a Common Market.

SADC is the successor to SADCC, the Southern African Development Coordination Conference, an organization of regional integration for the states that bordered South Africa while South African was still under apartheid rule. The difference between the organizations, after South Africa was freed, was marked. Mbuende explained to Margaret Novicki of *Africa Report* just how the two organizations differed: "Basically what we are talking about in terms of integration is not really market integration--that we are selling or trading more--but political cooperation, cooperation in the field of the military, security, cultural exchange, and information, as well as development cooperation, in infrastructure development and investment. So it is much more comprehensive."

SADC itself was formed by a treaty following two meetings to discuss the role of SADCC in a post-apartheid Southern Africa. SADCC was formed to assist the frontline states in their effort to support the struggle to liberate Namibia and free South Africa. Bordering South Africa to the North and Namibia to the East, these states were economically dependent on South Africa's ports for imports and exports. In order to gain some modicum of economic independence, these states joined together to find alternate ports for their imports and exports. That economic freedom afforded the frontline states more leverage in pressuring South Africa to abandon apartheid. When South Africa was securely on the road to freedom, a new purpose had to be discovered for the economic and political union. The states met in Maputo in 1992, where they decided that there had been too much advantage gained by their mutual cooperation to abandon the organization. Member states decided to deepen their level of cooperation now that South Africa was being freed. In Windhoek, Namibia, in 1992, the member states adopted the treaty founding the Development Community (SADC) out of the Development Coordination Conference (SADCC).

> "My dream is to see a Southern Africa free of conflicts devoting its human and natural resources in pursuit of economic development."

In an interview with *CBB* Mbuende highlighted four areas of achievement since taking the helm of the new SADC in January of 1994. First Mbuende pointed to the implementation of the conflict resolution mechanism between member states. Mbuende cited in particular the use of diplomacy in resolving the conflicts in Lesotho, in the impending crisis in the run up to the elections in Mozambique, and in support of the peace process in Angola. Next Mbuende identified the democratization of South Africa and its subsequent membership in SADC in August of 1994 as a major victory. "It was an honour and privilege to have facilitated the entry of South Africa in SADC," Mbuende wrote.

Third, SADC achieved a high level of cooperation between the public sector and the private sector in developing Southern Africa. The Southern African Economic Summit, held in Johannesburg, South Africa, in May 1995, and jointly organized by SADC and the World Economic Forum testified to that increased cooperation. Mbuende predicted that Summit would become an annual event. Finally, Mbuende cited international relations as an area of achievement. "A qualitatively new relationship was entered into between SADC and

European Union through what came to be known as the 'Berlin Initiative' following the convening of a Joint Meeting of Ministers of Foreign Affairs of SADC and the European Union in Berlin in September 1994," Mbuende wrote in an interview with *CBB*. In addition, SADC pursued close relations and an active dialogue with Japan and the United States.

Selected writings

Books

Namibia the Broken Shield: Anatomy of Imperialism and Revolution, Liber, 1986.
Church and Liberation in Namibia, Pluto Press, 1989.
Social Movements and the Demise of Apartheid Colonialism in Namibia, CODESRIA, forthcoming.

Periodicals

"The April Massacre: Conspiracy or South African Intransigence in Namibia," *Southern Africa Political and Economic Monthly,* Vol. 2, No. 11, 1989.
"Constitutionalism and the Problem of Transformation in Namibia," *Southern Africa Political and Economic Monthly,* Vol. 3, No. 5, 1990.
"Living in the Shadow of Drought," *Namibia Review,* Vol. 1, No. 5, 1992.

Also author of articles published in numerous other journals and books in Europe and Africa.

Sources

Periodicals

Africa Report, July/August 1994, pp. 45-7.
Namibia Brief, No. 16, March 1992, pp. 33-8.

Other

Written interview, June 2, 1995.

—Nicholas Patti

Lonette McKee

1952—

Actress

In the age of PCs, MTV, and MS-DOS it's superficially easy to see *Show Boat* as a dated cultural artifact. "Those who succumb to this trendy temptation deserve to be digitized," said Jack Kroll in *Newsweek*. Cynics and youth-cult types may yawn at the idea of reviving a nearly 70-year-old musical, but others rejoice. When a $10 million, Canadian-produced revival of the 1927 Jerome Kern-Oscar Hammerstein musical steamed into Broadway's huge Gershwin Theatre in the fall of 1994 it attracted 14,689 paying customers in its first full week of performances, the second highest weekly total ticket sales in Broadway history. The sumptuous production drew high praise, much of it for costar Lonette McKee. "Without question the most magnetic performer is the stunning Lonette McKee.... Ms. McKee sings only two songs, "Can't Help Lovin' Dat Man" and "Bill', and her languid, throaty "Bill" is, in this sweeping show, the only truly intimate moment. One friend of mine cried during the song because she found it so moving, and another cried because he realized that was the last he was going to hear from Lonette McKee for the rest of the evening," said Nancy Franklin of the *New Yorker*. Nelson Pressley of the *Washington Times* noted, "Miss McKee's emotional, unglitzy blues nearly stops the show."

When the revival of *Show Boat* premiered in Toronto in the autumn of 1993, black groups protested. They felt the classic musical perpetuated negative stereotypes of people of African ancestry. The proudly African American Lonette McKee disagrees. "It's crazy. It's not true," she told the *Orlando Sentinel*. "They might be thinking of the original book [by Edna Ferber], but they haven't seen our show. They think that black people are being portrayed in a less than favorable light, and I don't know what they're basing it on." McKee should know. This is the second time she has taken on the role of Julie LaVerne, a light-skinned black woman who passes for white in order to work as a singer on a turn-of-the-century Mississippi River showboat. In 1983 McKee played Julie in a well-received Houston Grand Opera production that ran on Broadway for several months. She was the first black woman to play the part of Julie in a major production (legendary singer Helen Morgan originated the role in 1927 and appeared in the 1936 film version; Ava Gardner took the role in the 1951 film). Comparing her later portrayal of Julie to her earlier work, McKee told John Istel of *American Theatre*, "I wanted to make her a little blacker. I wanted to play her more realistically. Not as Julie trying to pass as white but just plain Julie--as she is."

Mckee Defines her Race

Similar to her on-stage character, McKee has had trouble with people not accepting her as she is. Born in Detroit, the second of three daughters of an African American father and a Swedish American mother, the race issue has plagued McKee all her life. "In the Detroit ghetto where I grew up, I wasn't accepted by white kids

or black. I just didn't fit in.... Now I consider myself black, because I've never been given the same treatment, respect, or opportunities that blond, blue-eyed, white girls have gotten," she told *People* in 1986. As a toddler, McKee sat down at an upright piano and began singing and composing her own songs to the astonishment of her unmusical family. By the time she was eight, McKee was singing professionally--and at age 14, her recording of the Motown style song "Stop, Don't Worry About It," with Dennis Coffey and the Detroit Guitar Band, was a local Detroit hit. McKee, whose parents were divorced, began hanging around with a lot of older musicians and seemed headed for trouble. With her mother's blessing, she dropped out of high school at age 16 and moved to Los Angeles to live with her older sister.

On the West Coast, the statuesque McKee worked at various jobs (including a stint as a secretary to Bill Cosby) while pursuing an acting and singing career. In 1972 she landed role as one of "The Soul Sisters" on television's *The Wacky World of Jonathan Winters* and two years later recorded a gospel-tinged pop album for a small Los Angeles record label that later went bankrupt. McKee's big break came when she was cast in the 1976 movie *Sparkle*, the story of a "girl group" similar to The Supremes. She beat out five hundred other aspirants for the part of the group's lead singer. *Sparkle*, which costarred Irene Cara and Philip Michael Thomas, was not a hit when first released, though it has since become something of a cult film.

McKee's performance as a doomed, drug-addicted singer garnered many favorable reviews. Pauline Kael of the *New Yorker* said McKee "lays waste to the movie, which makes the mistake of killing her off in the first half ... she has the sexual brazenness that screen stars such as Susan Hayward and Ava Gardner had in their youth." Stardom for McKee seemed immanent. "I think I've always known that I'm pretty, and I've played against it," a youthful McKee told *Mademoiselle* a few months after *Sparkle* was released. "People take one look at me and say `she just couldn't be talented, she just couldn't be bright.' But I'll tell you, I don't let nothin' happen. I make things happen."

Difficulty Finding Roles

At this time McKee considered her mixed race heritage an advantage since she assumed it would allow her to play both black and white roles. She eventually realized the opposite was true. For white roles she was too black, for black roles too white. An older and wiser McKee told the New York *Times* in 1987, "I had little knowledge at that time of how difficult it would be to find roles for somebody like me. I came in on a high like *Sparkle* and then turned around and had years of no work after that." McKee's private life also went through a difficult period after *Sparkle.* She dated Warren Beatty and screen-writer Robert Towne but was more seriously involved with abusive boyfriends and experimented with cocaine. McKee became a health-conscious vegetarian, though she has not kicked a cigarette habit. "I'm compulsive, so I have to do something slightly self-destructive or I'm not happy," she explained to Charisse Jones of the *New York Times.*

The word that best describes McKee's film career is "underutilized." Elvis Mitchell wrote in *Film Comment,* "Hollywood is guilty of a shameful neglect of an engagingly friendly, but lusty presence ... McKee is better than so much of what she gets. Not girlish and insubstantial, she's dynamic and indestructible." McKee played Richard Pryor's love interest in *Which Way is Up?* (1977) and his accountant in *Brewster's Millions* (1985). In *Cuba* (1979), directed by Richard Lester and costarring Sean Connery, McKee had a supporting role as a cigar factory worker who aspires to a better life. It seemed that McKee's had a second chance at stardom with *The Cotton Club* (1984), Francis Ford Coppola's $50 million saga of the legendary Harlem nightclub of the 1920s and 1930s. McKee played Lila Rose Oliver, a light-skinned torch singer who passes for white trying to get a job on Broadway. Expense and production troubles made *The Cotton Club* one of the most talked about films of the early 1980s, but when it finally reached theaters it got unenthusiastic reviews and audiences stayed away.

"After *The Cotton Club* everyone said that this was it, that I was going to be a big star. And it didn't happen," McKee told the *New York Times.* McKee again played a singer in *Round Midnight* (1986), based on the life of jazz saxophonist Dexter Gordon. Written and directed by Frenchman Bertrand Tavernier, this tale of the Paris jazz scene in 1950s was well-received. McKee worked a second time for Coppola in *Gardens of Stone* (1987), a story of the army unit assigned to Arlington National Cemetery during the Vietnam War (she played an aide to a senator). McKee has also been in two Spike Lee films--*Jungle Fever* (1991), in which she was Wesley Snipes' betrayed wife, and *Malcolm X* (1992). "She's a great actress. It amazed me that she wasn't working more," Lee told *People.*

Big Broadway Debut

McKee's Broadway debut came in *The First,* a musical version of the life of Jackie Robinson, the first black man

to play major league baseball. She played Robinson's wife Rachel. *The First,* with music by Bob Brush and lyrics by Martin Charnin, opened at the Martin Beck Theatre in November of 1981. "Though the role of Rachel Robinson hardly exists in the script, the striking Lonette McKee manages to fill her with vitality and warmth," wrote Frank Rich in the *New York Times.* McKee got good notice, but the show closed after a month. "I think it's racism by the critics," McKee told *Jet.* "I don't think they want to see a good Black piece prevail, especially not anything with this much depth ... there's a heavy, heavy story behind Jackie's life and I think they don't want to deal with that."

McKee was soon back on Broadway in the Houston Grand Opera production of *Showboat,* which opened at the Uris (now Gershwin) Theatre in April 1983. "The lovely Julie of Lonette McKee is simply terrific," said Clive Barnes in the *New York Post.* When *Showboat* played a pre-Broadway run in San Francisco, McKee met Leo Compton, a youth counselor working part-time as the Theatre's doorman. A week after the meeting, Compton proposed marriage and they wed in February, 1983. The union lasted seven years.

> "I would much rather be alone, writing at home, than on stage with a bunch of makeup on and a heavy costume."

In *Lady Day at Emerson's Bar and Grill,* a one-woman show about singer Billie Holiday, McKee tackled the most challenging role to date in her career. The play, by Lanie Robertson, took place at a seedy Philadelphia saloon a few months before heroin-addicted Holiday's death in 1959. "Every day was therapy, and I thank God that Andre [director Andre Ernotte] was so sensitive and so gentle with me and with her, the whole subject," McKee told E. R. Shipp of the *New York Times. Lady Day at Emerson's Bar and Grill* had a four-week run at off-Broadway's tiny Vineyard Theatre in June 1986. Enthusiastic response brought about a reopening at the larger Westside Arts Theatre in September 1986 where it stayed for several months.

A long-time Holiday fan, McKee was intimidated at first by the thought of portraying the great singer. To prepare for the role McKee surrounded her herself with photos of Holiday and with gardenias, the singer's trademark flower. There was no attempt at imitation.

"Miss McKee is as engaging a performer as everyone has said she is, but, as far as I could tell, she bears little resemblance--physical, temperamental, or vocal--to Billie Holiday, and perhaps the best thing to do is to forget Miss Holiday and her glorious recordings and just enjoy the show for what it is," wrote Edith Oliver in the *New Yorker.*

McKee left *Lady Day at Emerson's Bar and Grill* a few weeks before her contract expired because the demanding role had taken such a toll on her vocal chords she could no longer sing. After recuperating, McKee mounted a cabaret act at Manhattan's Ballroom club in September of 1987. She was brought back by popular demand the following month. "The movies and the theater have only skimmed the surface of her protean talents," wrote Stephen Holden of McKee's cabaret performance in the *New York Times.* "Equally at ease performing pop-soul, swing and classic theater songs--all with a sense of dramatic command that is decisive but never overblown."

The Theater Can Wait!

McKee's television work includes the mini-series, *The Women of Brewster Place,* produced and costarring Oprah Winfrey, and the Alex Haley family saga *Queen.* She has also made appearances on *Spenser: For Hire* and *The Equalizer.* Recalling a guest shot on *Miami Vice,* McKee told *People,* "Don Johnson kissed me goodbye on the mouth and gave me the flu, but who can complain."

Since 1991 McKee has been in a relationship with musician Bryant McNeil who is in the rock band Jim Crow. They share a Manhattan brownstone decorated with antiques and African art. She and McNeil have started their own recording company, Flat Daddy Records. "We want to put music out there that goes beyond cheap sex and idiotic violence," McKee told Raoul Dennis of the *New York Times.* An animal rights advocate who has several pet birds, McKee has determined that a portion of the company's profits will go towards establishing wildlife sanctuaries in urban areas. Physically challenged people are another of McKee's concerns (her younger sister, Carol, has cerebral palsy).

The success of *Showboat* has put McKee yet again on the brink of major stardom. Film, television, and theater offers are pouring in. McKee is not in a hurry to dive into a new project. "I would much rather be alone, writing at home, than on stage with a bunch of makeup on and a heavy costume," she explained to Charisse Jones of the *New York Times.* McKee is writing scripts featuring parts for African American actors. She is also at work on a novel, *Queen of the Birds* (the title comes from McKee's passion for nursing sick or injured birds, then releasing them back into nature). "It's kind of the story of my life," McKee told *People.* "I've struggled. But these hardships have made me stronger and more spiritual ... I know it will be all right."

Sources

American Theatre, February 1995, pp. 40-41.
Film Comment, March/April 1985, pp. 40-41.
Jet, December 10, 1981, p. 61; December 24, 1984, pp. 58-62; June 30, 1986, p. 55; October 13, 1986, pp. 52-54; March 20, 1989, pp. 58-60; July 1, 1991, p. 65; October 31, 1994, pp. 36-39.
Mademoiselle, April 1977, pp. 199-200, 230, 233.
Ms., December 1986, p. 18.
New Republic, July 29, 1991, pp. 28-29.
Newsweek, October 20, 1986, pp. 79, 81; October 10, 1994, p. 77.
New York, June 23, 1986, p. 59; June 17, 1991, pp. 76-78; October 17, 1994, pp. 68-69.
New Yorker, September 27, 1976, pp. 127-129; September 29, 1986, p. 129; May 18, 1987, pp. 84-85; October 17, 1994, pp. 111-112.
New York Post, April 25, 1983, p. 17.
New York Times, November 18, 1981, p. C25; February 21, 1987, p. A10; February 22, 1987, p. C6; September 24, 1987, p. C16; October 23, 1987, p. C27; February 7, 1993, Section 3, p. 11; December 29, 1994, pp. C1, C8.
Orlando Sentinel, October 17, 1993, p. D4; November 27, 1994, p. F1.
People, November 3, 1986, pp. 53-57; November 28, 1994, pp. 159-160.
Time, October 6, 1986, p. 94; October 10, 1994, p. 80.
Variety, July 8, 1987, p. 74.
Washington Times, October 4, 1994, p. C14.

—Mary C. Kalfatovic

Gilbert Moses

1942–1995

Theater, film, and television director

Gilbert Moses had about as varied a career as a director can have. From his early work in the 1960s as founder and artistic director of the pioneering Free Southern Theater company, Moses went on to direct in just about every dramatic context imaginable, including Broadway, Hollywood, television, and opera. He found time to play some rock and roll along the way as well. In his earlier, more provocative work, Moses called for a more thorough examination of the lives and identity of African Americans. Although the material he chose to direct became increasingly mainstream over the course of his career, his work never ceased to reflect that overriding artistic aim.

Moses was born and raised in Cleveland, Ohio, one of seven children. Although his elementary school had both black and white students, Moses was one of only a few black children to be placed in the school's special classes for bright children. This isolation created in Moses a sense of inferiority. As he told Charlayne Hunter of the *New York Times* in a 1972 interview, he often felt "caught between two worlds" in school, where the subtle forms of exclusion made him feel like "a dim space in the room."

At the age of nine, Moses began acting with Cleveland's Karamu Theater, a celebrated community theater group. He found that the theater provided an escape from the insecurity he experienced in school, and Karamu became the one place in which he felt totally comfortable. Moses continued to act with Karamu through his high school years. After graduating from John Adams High School, he received a scholarship to attend Oberlin College in Ohio, where he studied French and German.

Founded Free Southern Theater

Moses spent one of his college years studying at the Sorbonne in Paris. While in France, Moses was inspired by the work of Jean Vilar and his Theatre National Populaire. Upon his return to the United States, Moses set out to create the kind of socially relevant theater that Vilar was doing. After graduating from Oberlin, Moses headed to the South in 1963 to take part in the civil rights movement. Settling in Jackson, Mississippi, Moses went to work as a journalist for the Jackson Free Press newspaper. Around the same time, he and a college of first-time theater-goers. In addition to addressing segregation and other important issues of the day, the company was interested in creating a black audience for theater in general. Though very successful by most measures, the Free Southern Theater was not without its problems. The combination of internal political squabbles, threats from Southern racists, arrests of company members, and, finally, the breakup of his own marriage to company member Denise Nicholas, was eventually too much for Moses to handle. He left the group in 1967.

During the period following his departure from the Free Southern Theater, Moses focused on playing music. A skilled rock guitarist, he played with such well-known musicians as Steve Miller and Michael Bloomfield, and was a member of a group called The Street Choir. By 1969, Moses was ready to return to theater. That year, he directed an off-Broadway production of Amiri Baraka's *Slaveship,* for which he also wrote original music. Moses won an Obie award for his innovative direction of *Slaveship,* securing him a spot on the New York theatrical world's map.

Made Broadway Debut with Musical

After his success with *Slaveship,* Moses spent the next couple of years directing regional theater, working in, among other places, Washington, D.C., Boston, and San Francisco. He returned to New York in 1971 to make his Broadway directorial debut with *Ain't Supposed to Die a Natural Death,* a musical by Melvin Van Peebles, which ran on Broadway for two years. Moses won a Drama Desk award and was nominated for a Tony. His next big theatrical success came in 1975, when he directed *The Taking of Miss Janie,* by Ed Bullins. Moses won several awards, including an Obie, for his direction of *Miss Janie,* and the play was named best new American play of the season by the New York Drama Critics Circle.

> We as blacks are starved for images of ourselves all over this country."

Meanwhile, Moses was making his initial forays into film direction around this time. In 1973 he directed and composed the musical score for *Willie Dynamite.* His other feature film was *The Fish That Saved Pittsburgh*

friend, John O'Neal, founded the Free Southern Theater, a racially-integrated troupe committed to performing cutting edge theater with a social conscience.

Through the mid-1960s, Moses toured the South with Free Southern Theater, performing in churches and other low-cost venues for an audience consisting largely

(1979), starring basketball legend Julius Irving. Back on Broadway, Moses directed and helped create *The Wiz,* the all-black version of the classic *The Wizard of Oz. The Wiz* won a Tony Award for singer Dee Dee Bridgewater, who by this time was also Moses's wife.

Shifted Focus to TV

Moses also launched his television directing career in the 1970s. In 1977 he directed two episodes of the groundbreaking *Roots* miniseries, for which he earned an Emmy Award nomination. Subsequent television directing credits have included episodes of *Benson, Paper Chase,* and *Law and Order,* as well as a number of made-for-TV movies and "After-School Specials." For a period in the early 1980s, Moses went to work for evangelist Pat Robertson's Christian Broadcasting Network, where he produced and/or directed both the popular *700 Club* and the Christian soap opera *Another Life.*

During the 1980s, Moses returned to teaching, a job he had first tried his hand at in the early 1970s at New York University. These educational forays included stints as visiting professor at Cornell University in 1981, California Institute of the Arts in 1982, and Carnegie-Mellon University in 1985. As the decade continued, he remained active both on the stage and on the TV studio. In 1987 Moses directed *Dreaming Emmett,* a play by acclaimed author Toni Morrison, at the Brooklyn Academy of Music. He also directed the television movie *A Fight for Jenny* for NBC that year. Moses continued to direct for television periodically until his 1995 death

from multiple myeloma, a form of bone marrow cancer.

Although Moses took his work in many different directions over the course of his career, certain themes remained constant. In a 1987 *Essence* article, Don Armstrong pointed out that Moses's directorial work "is best characterized not by its diversity of political, historical, and sociological interests, but by the innovative techniques he brings to a production." He also never stopped presenting the black experience to American audiences, whether through the writing of Amiri Baraka in the 1960s or of Toni Morrison in the 1980s. In a 1972 *New York Times* interview, Moses stated that "we as blacks are starved for images of ourselves all over this country." On film, stage, and videotape, Moses helped to fill that void.

Selected writings

"Roots" (an absurdist one-act play, 1966), published in *The Free Southern Theater by the Free Southern Theater,* Dent, Schechner, and Moses, 1969.

Sources

Cleveland Plain Dealer, April 18, 1995, p. 9B.
Essence, December 1974, p. 26; January 1987, p. 26.
New York Amsterdam News, April 22, 1995, p. 25.
New York Times, April 18, 1995, p. B8.
New York Times Biographical Edition, March 1972, p. 594.
Washington Post, April 25, 1983, p. D7.

—Robert R. Jacobson

Cecil Murray

1929—

Cleric

The Rev. Cecil (Chip) Murray is the religious leader every spiritually-conscious person would like to follow. A man of exceptional integrity, he heads a church whose 8,500 congregants include Dionne Warwick and Arsenio Hall, a church supported by an annual budget of $5 million, which is nevertheless a church that takes loving care of the less fortunate in Los Angeles' inner-city black community. He is a tireless campaigner for jobs and training programs, never turns anyone in need away from his door, and somehow has also found the time to spearhead the construction of low-income housing projects, start drug rehabilitation programs, and organize funds for college scholarships. He is a truly focused man, whose life is his work, and whose work is his life.

Chip Murray's Mentor

Chip Murray grew up in a middle-class black neighborhood in West Palm Beach, Florida, the second of three children. The family lost their mother when they were very young and were sent to stay with relatives for a short time. But their father remarried and brought them back to their home, where their stepmother gave them the loving support they needed to ease their way to adulthood.

The principal of the school his son Chip attended, Edward Murray was commonly known as "Prof." He was a powerful influence upon his children, teaching them by personal example to practice what they preached. What Prof Murray preached was never to knuckle down to racism, a lesson that was painfully slammed home one night when he and his two sons confronted three white bigots who had been bullying indigent blacks on their way to collect government-issue food. Edward Murray tried to reason with the whites, but met only flying fists and curses. After the fight was over, he took some blood from one of his cuts and sealed a blood oath with each of his two sons, to make them swear to love and protect their fellow-blacks.

"I guess my dad was about the most fearless person I knew," Reverend Murray told the *Los Angeles Times* in August, 1992: "I'm sure he must have felt the fear, so he must have gone on in spite of it. " Go on Prof Murray did, but the pain and fear of that night were so overwhelming that he began to turn to alcohol in order to dull

At a Glance...

Born September 26, 1929, in Lakeland, FL; Edward and Minnie Lee Murray; married Bernadine Cousin, June 25, 1958; one son. *Education:* Florida A & M University, BA 1951; School of Theology at Claremont, Doctor of Religion, 1964.

US Air Force, captain, Jet Raider interceptor and navigator; US Air Force Reserves, 1951-61; First African Methodist Episcopal Church, minister; religious posts in Los Angeles, Seattle, Kansas City and Pomona.

Member: African Methodist Episcopal Church, general board, 1972-; National Council of Churches, general board, 1972-; NAACP; SCLC; Urban League; United Nations Association of the USA; National Council on Aging, general board, 1990-;

Awards: Soldiers' Medal for Heroism, 1958; William Nelson Cromwell Award, 1977; Ralph Bunche Peace Prize, 1992; AME Church Daniel Alexander Payne Award, 1992; NAACP, Los Angeles Community Achievement Award, 1986; National Association of University Women, Outstanding Role Model, 1992.

them. Insidiously the bottle began to claim him, until it finally broke up his second marriage. Alcohol-sodden, he died in 1952 at just 52-years-old, leaving behind nothing for his son Chip but the memory of the oath to protect black people from racism and help them in any way possible.

An Award for Valor

For seven years, this promise lay fallow in Cecil Murray's mind. He had chosen to enter the Air Force after his 1951 graduation from Florida A&M University, and the demands of his first post as a jet radar intercept officer in the Air Force's Air Defense Command left him little time for public service of any kind. He was just as busy after he moved on to the post of navigator in the Air Transport Service, but the essence of his father's blood oath was brought forcibly back into his memory when tragedy stalked into his life for the second time.

Catastrophe announced itself with an explosion in the

nose tank of a jet in which he was flying, just as it was lifting up from a runway. Within moments, escaping jet fuel covered the plane in a seething mass of flames. Moving swiftly, Murray managed to hurl himself free. Then, when his own danger had passed, he saw to his horror that the pilot had not been as lucky. He had managed to climb out of the cockpit, but he had then slipped in the burning oil pouring along the wing, and his body was being consumed by the blaze. Murray ran to help, smothering the blaze as best he could. Nevertheless the flames burned 90% of the pilot's body, leaving injuries too great for him to overcome. The pilot died a few weeks later, leaving a legacy that Murray treasured far more than the medal he won for his valor. According to the *Los Angeles Times*, "I love you," were his last words to his brave fellow crew-member—an accolade indeed from a white man born in South Carolina.

Fulfilling at least the "help your fellows" part of Murray's father's request, this incident proved to be a turning point. He continued to enjoy flying for a further three years, but his sights were no longer set on the Air Force as a longterm career. Recognizing that his true mission in life was to help his fellow-blacks, and that the most powerful way of doing this was via the pulpit, he began to think of entering the ministry serving the First African Methodist Episcopal Church.

A Church with a Long History

The First African Methodist Episcopal Church (FAME) was originally part of the Methodist Episcopal Church founded in 1784 in Philadelphia. Its own history as an institution began to crystallize shortly after the supposedly multiracial St George's Church built a gallery, to which black worshippers were banished. They resented being sidelined, but made no official protest until one Sunday in November 1787, when a group of white congregants tried to pull several of them away from the altar rail. The furious group of black worshippers was led from the church by a former slave named Richard Allen, who happened also to be a licensed Methodist preacher. Allen, a prosperous business man, immediately started an African American-oriented church, and bought an abandoned blacksmith's shop in which to base it.

Despite their separation by 150 years, there was no denying that FAME's origins and Prof. Murray's blood oath had sprung from the same struggle against racism. Chip Murray felt strongly that destiny was beckoning. Without further delay he entered the School of Theology at Claremont and found himself a part-time janitor's job in order to support himself while his wife added to this slender income by working as a clerk at the school.

In 1964 Murray graduated with a doctorate in religion. His first post was in Pomona, in a church too tiny even to boast plumbing. Next came a transfer to a larger church in Kansas City, after which Murray was transferred to Seattle, Washington, where he settled for a six-year stay that saw his congregation soar to reach 2,000 members.

In 1977 Reverend Murray was transferred again, this time to Los Angeles. On the surface this seemed an extremely challenging assignment, since it involved a debt-ridden church with only 300 elderly congregants, but it was not long before the Herculean task of giving the church an inviting, black-oriented identity was well under way.

As a first step Murray added a liberal helping of gospel flavor to the music, which now featured drums, cymbals, and other percussion to give it a throbbing beat. Next, in order to attract young black men who could go out into the poverty-stricken inner-city community, he honored the church's founding father by starting the Richard Allen Men's Society. Today this association is involved in the nationwide fight against drugs, and is also active in mentoring fatherless children.

By 1990 a wide variety of activities to improve the lives of poor black Americans was making Reverend Cecil Murray's name a familiar one outside the world of the church. His style was forthright, his candid comments frequently discomforting. Unperturbed by the embarrassed sniggers of self-righteous congregants, he did not hesitate to hand out AIDS-awareness kits containing condoms whenever he found it necessary. With blistering scorn he criticized the "Just Say No, " slogan suggested by the Reagan White House as an antidote to drug use; he even took great care, in a *Los Angeles Times* article in March, 1990, to list some of the tragic social and economic consequences of such ineffectual White House equivocation.

In August 1990 *Los Angeles Times* readers felt the lash of Murray's uncompromising honesty again. His subject this time was the bitter relationship between black Californians and the 267,000-strong Korean community—a subject that was common knowledge. But the problem had seldom been treated to the media spotlight, and Murray now felt it was time to correct this deficiency. He chose to do so in an article called "Body Language Stokes the Anger," using as a painful example the contempt he found in Korean retailers in their day-to-day dealings with black customers.

As always, he did not content himself with a mere outline

of the situation. Instead, he proposed a crisply-worded three-point plan for improving this obviously acrimonious relationship. First, he noted, it was vital that the two communities get together and talk, so they could understand each other's viewpoints. His next suggestion was that the Korean merchants hire some black workers, so that potential customers from the black community would be comfortable shopping in their stores. His third recommendation, the most daring one of all, proposed that the Koreans sponsor some scholarships for black youth and some workshops for budding black entrepreneurs. Murray's article was thoughtful and boldly forthright, but it did not bring a break in the cloud of bigotry. Sadly, it proved to be prophetic of further suffering to come.

1991—The Year the Storm Broke

The storm broke in early 1991, when a high school student named Latasha Harlins was shot in the back of the head by a Korean storekeeper after an argument involving a carton of orange juice. This tragic, needless death was neither the first nor the last in the blood-spattered list that would claim the lives of 13 Korean storekeepers before another year had passed. But for inner-city Los Angeles blacks, the teenager's murder was a special symbol; the epitome of an unconcerned government, an ever-dwindling supply of jobs and a powerlessness that they were no longer prepared to endure. Latasha Harlins' death was the tinder of a long-smoldering black rage that would shortly burst forth across Los Angeles.

The detonator to the definitive explosion was set just after midnight on March 3, 1991, when four white police officers forced a speeding Hyundai to a stop on the Los Angeles freeway. They handcuffed and arrested two of the three black men traveling in the car, but found the driver, Rodney King, much more intimidating because of his hefty build and 6 feet 3-inch stature. So they hit King with two Taser darts, each carrying 50,000 volts of electricity, and followed up with 56 blows to his body. Then, as far as they were concerned, the literally long arm of the law had triumphed again.

At the time the case seemed a simple one. However, the following day it took a complicated turn after amateur photographer George Holliday produced a videotape he had made of King's brutal beating. Disciplinary Police Department action was taken against the police officers, but a horrified America demanded some public legal action. On March 3, 1992, this demand was met. After the proceedings were moved from seething Los Angeles to a county more friendly to the police, the closely-televised trial of the four white officers began. It came to an end on April 29, 1992 with a verdict of "not guilty."

The Los Angeles Riot

If the Los Angeles Police Department had imagined that their troubles were now over, they were destined for disappointment. About two hours after the verdict was announced, a liquor store in South Central Los Angeles called for police help in settling a disturbance. Four patrol cars arrived to find a swelling crowd of bystanders, who soon started throwing rocks and shouting at the police. It took just one hour for Los Angeles to start writhing in the grip of a full-blown race riot; within a day, television newscasts showed gut-wrenching footage of beatings, showers of broken glass, and laden looters staggering triumphantly through the charred wreckage of once-flourishing businesses.

On the first night of the disturbance, Rev. Murray and 5,000 of his 8,500 parishioners were praying together for peace. One-half a block away, a fire was burning, as he later said, "like Dante's Inferno," yet the firemen would not come to help unless they were guaranteed protection. Rev. Murray did not hesitate. For three hours, he and 100 other men stood between the rioters and the firemen, acting as a human shield.

An uncompromising realist, he had anticipated trouble on the very night the King verdict was announced. As reported by the *Los Angeles Times* of May 3, 1992, his message now to his flock must have come over loud and clear: "Under no circumstances will we pretend that the looting, the burning, and the arson are excusable. And in the same breath that we say that, we must say that this miscegenation of justice in the courtroom ... was injurious to us all." (The entire country agreed with him. Such vociferous protests resulted from this verdict that the four policemen were retried in a Federal courtroom, and two of them were found guilty and punished for their brutal beating of Rodney King.)

The Federal trial, however, was still in the future. The immediate problem now was to stem the fury that was destroying Los Angeles. Meeting the crisis took about a week, plus 2,000 National Guardsmen, 1,000 federal officers, and 4,500 military troops mobilized by President George Bush. When the city lay in an uneasy calm again, there was time to count the unnecessary injuries, the wasted opportunities, and the ruined businesses. For everyone, the toll for the long-simmering lack of communication between the black and white citizens of Los Angeles was high—Police Department figures showed 52 dead, 20,000 jobs lost, and $735 million in property damage.

The Church Threatened by White Supremacists

While a mere seven days saw the end of the violence, the entire country understood that years would pass before Los Angeles' deeply-rooted scars truly began to heal. For Reverend Murray, the message of difficult recuperation came as an ominous personal warning, delivered to him while the city was still in flames. It happened on the second night of the riot, just after television journalist Ted Koppel had finished taping his show at the First African Methodist Episcopal Church. Murray and a couple of companions were walking through the parking lot when several gang members suddenly stepped into their path. Menacing shouts of "You sellout!" followed Murray to his car, but he was unconcerned about the threat to his personal safety. His companions, however, viewed the incident quite differently.

> "Soul force is greater than sword force. In this lovely city we have 146 different nations. We've got to learn how to love together. There's enough room for everybody."

Their anxiety was quite justified, for this was not the first alarming episode Murray had experienced. For two years before the riots both he himself and the church had been the targets of a steady stream of hate mail, which had swelled to a river in mid-1991 after church members had launched a petition calling for the resignation of Los Angeles Police Chief Darryl Gates. Now the city's turmoil had brought out the true intention of these vicious attacks — to assassinate Rev. Murray and burn down the church, in order to start a full-blown race war between America's black and white citizens.

On June 20, 1993 Rev. Murray received a call from Special Agent Parsons of the FBI. Parsons warned him that his life was in danger, and told him that there were hate groups bent on destroying his church. Parsons also asked him to keep their conversation private, since the FBI was currently wrapping up an investigation of a number of white supremacist groups, and was expecting to make several arrests. As promised, the FBI pounced on July 15, arresting members of the White Aryan

Resistence, the Fourth Reich, and a relatively new group of Nazi sympathizers called the Fourth Reich Skinheads, whose ranks included a Continental Airlines flight engineer named Christian Nadal and his wife Doris.

The Sunday following the arrests found the First African Methodist Episcopal Church buzzing with more than 2,000 congregants at each of its three morning services. Each group found its pastor calm, unshaken, and secure in his long-time philosophy of conciliation and universal redemption. In its issue of August 2, 1993, widely-read *People* magazine quoted from the sermon Rev. Murray gave on that fateful Sunday: "Soul force is greater than sword force. In this lovely city we have 146 different nations. We've got to learn how to love together. There's enough room for everybody." Amen.

Sources

Cohen, Jerry and William S. Murphy, *Burn, Baby, Burn! The Los Angeles Race Riot,* August 1965, E.P. Dutton & Co. 1966.

Gooding-WilliAms, Robert, ed., *Reading Urban Uprising,* Routledge, 1993. Melton, J. Gordon, ed., *Encyclopedia of American Religions,* Volume I, McGrath, 1978.

Wall, Brenda, *The Rodney King Rebellion,* African-American Images, 1992.

Periodicals

Essence, November 1992, p. 56.
Humanist, November/December 1992, p. 11.
Los Angeles Sentinel, July 22, 1993.
Los Angeles Times, March 21, 1990; Magazine, August 29, 1991; October 14, 1991, Sec. B. p. 1; May 3, 1992, Sec. M., p. 3; August 16, 1992, p. 12.
New York Times, September 13, 1992, Sec. 4, p. 7.
People, August 2, 1993, p. 82.
Time, July 26, 1993, p. 49.
U.S. News & World Report, May 18, 1993, p. 34.

—Gillian Wolf

Eddie Murray

1956—

Professional baseball player

Eddie Murray's career is one of the most remarkable in major league baseball. Without ever calling attention to himself or his spectacular feats, he has claimed a place amongst the greatest hitters of all time. On June 30, 1995 Murray slugged his 3,000th hit, becoming one of the 20 most productive batters ever to play the game. He is also one of the most consistent performers in the major leagues, having played 150 or more games in a season 15 times while visiting the disabled list only once since 1973. Today, in the twilight of his career, Murray continues to draw respect for his hitting—especially in clutch situations—and for his leadership abilities as well. *Sporting News* correspondent Michael P. Geffner wrote: "To think of Murray as anything other than a great player these days is not to have a dissenting opinion anymore but to be dead wrong, blind not only to the inner game but to an understanding of what truly raises baseball to something classic and beautiful—when the game is executed purely and seamlessly. Which is Eddie Murray to a T."

Murray is well on his way to hitting 500 home runs, an achievement that would make him only the third player in history to get 3,000 hits and 500 homers. The other two players who have reached that goal are Hank Aaron and another Murray-type switch-hitter, Willie Mays. Murray has already compiled more runs batted in than immortals such as Mickey Mantle, Joe DiMaggio, and Reggie Jackson. He has more doubles than Babe Ruth and ranks second all-time for home runs by a switch hitter. And yet Murray has never won a Most Valuable Player award or one of those sneaker contracts that make athletes immeasurably wealthy. "Murray rarely inspires you to breathlessness," noted Geffner. "His game never has been one of knock-'em-dead showmanship, but of delicious subtlety and nuance.... It is a game so blatantly understated, so incredibly unpretentious, that it has made Eddie Murray the most underrated and misunderstood player of his generation."

Recent seasons with the Cleveland Indians have helped to revive interest in Murray and his career. As the Indians advanced to the 1995 World Series—the team's first fall classic appearance since 1954—Murray was seen as one of the driving forces behind the Indians' season, a veteran who could impart his wisdom to younger players

At a Glance...

Born February 24, 1956, in Los Angeles, CA; son of Charles (a mechanic) and Carrie Murray. *Education:* Attended California State University at Los Angeles.

Professional baseball player, 1973—. Selected by Baltimore Orioles in third round of June 5, 1973 free agent draft; minor league player in Orioles organization, 1973-77; member of Baltimore Orioles, 1977-88; traded to Los Angeles Dodgers December 4, 1988; member of Dodgers, 1988-91; signed as a free agent by New York Mets, November 27, 1991; member of Mets, 1991-93; signed as a free agent by Cleveland Indians, December 2, 1993; member of Indians, 1993—.

Selected honors: Named Appalachian League Player of the Year, 1973; named American League Rookie of the Year, by Baseball Writers' Association of America, 1977; Gold Glove first baseman, 1982, 1983, 1984; member of American League All-Star Team, 1978, 1981-86; member of National League All-Star Team, 1991. Compiled 3,000th career hit June 30, 1995, while with Indians.

Addresses: *Office*—Cleveland Indians, Jacobs Field, 2401 Ontario St., Cleveland, OH 44115.

the garage and try to hit the ball out through a doorway 10 feet high and 12 feet wide—a tailor-made training ground for a line-drive hitter. The Murray brothers even played baseball when they didn't have a ball. "We'd hit anything—bottle caps, the plastic lids off Crisco cans," Murray told *Sports Illustrated.* "We'd be standing around in the yard with bats in our hand and see something on the ground. We'd say, `I wonder if we can hit this?'" Laughing, he added: "Once you've hit a Crisco lid, baseballs seem easy."

Murray was a star baseball and basketball player at Locke High School in Los Angeles. He dreamed of playing baseball professionally, and his ambitions hardly seemed out of reach. Three of his brothers, Leon, Venice, and Rich, all signed with the Giants and played in the minor leagues. Eddie himself was scouted by a number of major league franchises. Interestingly enough, many scouts thought the laconic Murray lacked the necessary intensity to play professional ball. Naturally nonchalant, he was perceived as lazy and unmotivated by some. The Baltimore Orioles felt otherwise. They gave Murray a 190-question psychological exam measuring such traits as desire and composure. He scored especially high in self-control and ambition. After protracted negotiations with the Murray family, Baltimore signed Murray in the summer of 1973 and gave him a $25,500 bonus. He was 17-years-old.

Murray spent the next four seasons progressing through Baltimore's farm system. In his first year as a professional he batted .287 in the Appalachian League, but rather than hurry him on to higher levels, the club officials moved him up just one step each year. By 1975 he had landed on a double-A team in Asheville, North Carolina, and it was there that he began to experiment with left-handed hitting. Once again he called on his childhood lessons to help him as a switch-hitter. "In the yard, we'd pretend to be different players in major league lineups and bat righty or lefty, depending on who they were," Murray explained in *Sports Illustrated.* Whatever the case, he made the transition smoothly, hitting a double in his first left-handed at-bat.

while still producing results himself. In *Sports Illustrated,* Tom Verducci called Murray "an intelligent hitter whose knack for getting hits is heightened in clutch situations." More to the point, the reporter added: "This is Murray too: a beloved teammate, a quiet leader, and a charitable and intensely private person."

A Baseball Family

Few people have ever had a childhood more perfectly suited to the sporting life than Eddie Murray. He was born in 1956, the eighth of twelve children of Charles and Carrie Murray. All of Murray's siblings—four boys, seven girls—loved to play baseball. Their back yard in East Los Angeles was a baseball diamond, the garage a most demanding batting cage. A favorite game was "Strikeouts." The batter would stand at the back wall of

Expectations Fulfilled

After a strong showing in spring training, Murray made the Baltimore Orioles in 1977. He broke into the lineup as a designated hitter, because the team already had a solid first baseman in veteran Lee May. Murray lost little time establishing himself as the big leaguer the Orioles had predicted he would become. In his rookie year he batted .283 with 27 home runs and 88 runs batted in, good enough to win him Rookie of the Year honors from the Baseball Writers' Association of America. The following season he took over duties at first base, and a superstar was born.

Over twelve seasons in Baltimore, Murray topped the team in home runs seven times, was the r.b.i. leader nine times, and was named team Most Valuable Player seven times. He was a driving force behind the Orioles' 1979 American League Championship and was the acknowledged team leader when Baltimore won the 1983 World Series. In that Series, Murray hit two home runs in the decisive fifth game against Philadelphia, helping the Orioles to take the Series crown. He was so popular in Baltimore that crowd chants of "Ed-die! Ed-die!" echoed for blocks around the stadium whenever he came to bat.

Off the field Murray was renowned for his refusal to speak to the press. His personal avoidance of the media began in 1979 when a New York columnist wrote a disparaging article about Murray's family, right during the World Series. Murray was so upset by the piece that it seemed to affect his play as the Orioles were defeated by the Pittsburgh Pirates in seven games. After that the mercurial Murray declined almost every interview opportunity. "I don't need to see my name in the paper every day," he explained in a rare *Sports Illustrated* profile. "I only care what the other players know of me. I let my baseball do the talking."

His baseball proved to be one terrific talker. Not only was Murray a consistent threat at the plate, he won Gold Glove honors at first base in 1982, 1983, and 1984. He was also meticulous in his preparation for each competition, stretching carefully so as to avoid injuries. Through his 12 seasons with the Orioles, he visited the disabled list only once, for 24 days, in 1986. Otherwise he rarely missed more than 10 or 11 games each season. While visiting teams despised him for his intelligent hitting and fierce competition, his Oriole teammates found him accessible and helpful, both on and off the field. Cal Ripken, for instance, told the *New York Times* he missed Murray in the Oriole lineup "a lot ... like when you're really struggling and need someone of his prominence to lean on a little bit."

Unfortunately, the Orioles' fortunes declined in the mid-1980s, and both the fans and the front office began to question Murray's level of contribution to the team. In 1986, just a year after Murray's mother and sister both died suddenly, Baltimore owner Edward Bennett Williams publicly scolded the player for "doing nothing." In response, Murray asked to be traded. Eventually the matter was smoothed over, but Murray continued to be disappointed with an Orioles system that he felt was not

what it had once been. After the 1988 season, he was traded to the Los Angeles Dodgers for pitchers Brian Holton and Ken Howell and shortstop Juan Bell.

Of Murray's three seasons in Los Angeles, the most memorable was 1990, when he hit .330 with 26 home runs and 95 r.b.i. In 1991 he achieved free agent status and signed with the struggling New York Mets. Over two seasons with that team he batted in 193 runs, but his presence did little to improve New York's fortunes. Murray was once again a free agent in 1993 when he signed a one-year, $3 million deal with the Cleveland Indians. The man who signed him, Indians general manager John Hart, well remembered Murray. Hart had been a third base coach for the Orioles. "I was tickled that no one else wanted him," Hart explained in the *Sporting News.* "Because I knew what he could do for us.... I wanted him around my young players. If there's anybody a young player should watch, I thought, it's Eddie Murray. He's a great model of baseball behavior."

3,000 Hits and Counting

Murray quickly proved that he could do more than just provide leadership to the younger Cleveland Indians. He helped the Indians to dominate during the strike-shortened 1994 season, and through the first 16 games of the 1995 season he batted at a .422 clip with 27 hits in 64 at-bats. Murray's strength has always been hitting in clutch situations, when that trademark nonchalance masks a cunning ability to stay cool and manipulate a pitcher. New York Yankees third baseman Wade Boggs told the *Sporting News:* "Eddie has just always been one of those 'lay in the weeds' guys. He comes out just long enough to really hurt you, then goes back into hiding again."

The 1995 baseball season held many highlights for Murray. First, on June 30, he stroked his 3,000th hit, a single off Minnesota Twins pitcher Mike Trombley. With that hit Murray joined an elite club that includes the likes of Pete Rose, Ty Cobb, Hank Aaron, Willie Mays, and Dave Winfield. Characteristically, Murray underplayed the achievement—although he did on this occasion speak to the press. "My approach has never been to reach any goals like a No. 3,000," he said in the *New York Times.* "Never looked at it that way.... Records are not what I've focused on."

Just a few weeks later, the whole nation watched while Cal Ripken of the Baltimore Orioles broke one of baseball's longest-standing records—the one for most consecutive games played held by Lou Gehrig. Ripken made an emotional speech after breaking the record, thanking his parents and just one colleague: Eddie Murray. "I get all the credit for my game streak, but a lot of how I approach the game was influenced by Eddie, ... because when I came along, he kind of took me under his wing," Ripken told the *New York Times.* "That's always been important to him, to be in the lineup every day because in a long season you're going to need the wins."

> "I don't need to see my name in the paper every day."

Winning has always been paramount to Murray, so he was most pleased in 1995 about the Cleveland Indians' successful drive to the World Series. The Indians had not appeared in a World Series since 1954, but with a combination of young talent and strong veterans such as Murray, they skimmed over all the opposition in the American League. As opponents in the World Series they drew the Atlanta Braves, a team that had vast experience in post-season play. Atlanta pulled to a two-game lead in the best-of-seven series and held the Indians to a tie through nine innings in Game Three at Cleveland. Enter Eddie Murray. After going 0-for-5 in his previous plate appearances, he strode up to bat in an 11th inning clutch situation—and delivered in his usual workmanlike manner. His single brought in the winning run in the 7-6 Indians victory and kept the team from falling into an embarrassing deficit. Although Atlanta went on to win the Series, the Indians did not get swept.

Murray's next goal-that-is-not-a-goal is 500 career home runs. With his usual number of at-bats, he could accomplish that feat in 1997 or 1998. If he does, he will join only two other players—Aaron and Mays—in the category of 3,000 hits and 500 homers. Murray has no plans to retire, and thanks to his years of careful conditioning, he is still playing relatively injury-free. His final destination will be the Baseball Hall of Fame in Cooperstown, New York, but he is not in a hurry to get there. He would rather continue to play. Murray told the *Sporting News* that he has never chased the numbers or the prestige of induction into the Hall of Fame. "I think, like any kid, my goal was to get to the major leagues," he said. "... I don't like setting numbers. Numbers, I think, add pressure to the situation." He concluded: "I like to attack the season as a whole. You try to do better than you did the year before. If you do, so be it. If you don't, so be it. I can live with myself knowing I've done the best job I could possibly do." His job isn't finished yet.

Sources

Books

Professional Sports Team Histories, Volume 1: *Baseball,* Gale, 1994, pp. 123-43.
The Sporting News Official Baseball Register, 1995 edition, Sporting News, 1995.

Periodicals

New York Times, May 10, 1992, p. L5; May 15, 1995, p. C11; July 1, 1995, pp. A27, 29; October 25, 1995, pp. B11-12.
Sporting News, July 3, 1995, pp. 10-13.
Sports Illustrated, June 21, 1982, pp. 34-40; March 14, 1988, pp. 30-37; May 22, 1995, pp. 56-58, 60.

—Mark Kram

Maria Mutola

1972—

Track and field athlete

Dominating her fellow runners in the middle distance events, Maria Mutola became one of the world's most consistent winners on the women's track and field circuit in the 1990s. She was undefeated against top international competition while maintaining an active performance schedule in her premier event, the 800-meter run, from the fall of 1992 until her fluke disqualification in the World Track and Field Championships in August of 1995. Her personal best of 1:55.19 in the 800 meters was the seventh fastest in history as of April of 1996.

One of seven children, Mutola grew up in a poor area of Maputo, the capital of Mozambique. Her first athletic passion was soccer, and by age 13 she was the best female player in her country. "She had the right stuff to handle herself," said Craig T. Greenlee in *Upscale*--"Speed, nifty footwork, tough mindedness and a refusal to back down from the dudes." Mutola played on a boys' team because there were no female soccer teams in Mozambique, but her scoring of a tying goal in the city championship led to protests by the opposing team. "They said it was a big problem to play a girl with the boys," claimed Mutola according to Reebok, her spon-

sor in track and field.

While on the soccer field, Mutola's speed and endurance were noted by José Craverinhas, Mozambique's most renowned poet. He mentioned the athlete's talent to his son Stelio Craverinhas, who coached the country's top track club. When Mutola was approached to join the club, she was at first reluctant to make the shift into running--especially after her initial workouts with the team. "In soccer we used to practice four days a week," she told Reebok. "Today practice, tomorrow a rest day. Track and field every day. I said, 'Oh my God!'" Mutola went back to the soccer field, but Craverinhas pursued her and enticed her to return to the track. Her conversion soon paid off, as Mutola won national titles in the 400-meter and 800-meter runs and became part of the national team after just a few months of training. Two years later she won the African championships in the events.

National Hero at Fifteen

Developing rapidly, Mutola earned a spot on Mozambique's contingent for the 1998 Olympics in Seoul, South Korea. She was also selected to carry her nation's flag in the opening ceremonies. Just 15 years old, Mutola managed a highly respectable 2:04.36 time in the 800-meter heats at the Olympics, but did not make it past the opening round. By this time she was famous in her home country, and the subject of frequent articles and magazines in Mozambique and bordering South Africa.

After the Olympics Mutola went into a holding pattern for the next few years, with her yearly bests actually declining in 1989 (2:05.70) and 1990 (2:13.54). Rumors spread about her moving to Portugal to train, but instead she moved to the United States on a scholarship set up by the International Olympic Solidarity program. This program made it possible for athletes from poor countries to live in settings with better training opportunities. In May of 1991 Mutola arrived in Oregon and became a student in Springfield High School because one its teachers spoke Portuguese, her native language. Her new school was also near Eugene, site of the University of Oregon and a renowned haven for runners.

Moving to the United States proved to be a boon for Mutola's running. During the summer of 1991 she broke every Mozambique record in distances from 400 through 3,000 meters. Since her arrangement with Olympic Solidarity banned her from prep competition, Mutola competed in meets around the United States against top international competitors. She shone in her first 800-meter race against the world's best when she staged a come-from-behind victory in the New York Track and Field Games at Columbia University's Wein Stadium in July, in a time of 2:00.22. A stress fracture hindered her in the 1991 World Track and Field Championships, but she still managed to finish fourth in a junior world-record time of 1:57.63.

Became Dominant Middle-Distance Runner

At the 1992 Olympic Games in Barcelona, Spain, Mutola turned in solid fifth-place and ninth-place finishes in the finals of the 800-meter run and 1500-meter run, respectively. Nineteen years old at the time, she was the youngest finalist in both events. After a loss in a meet in September in Berlin to Olympic champion Ellen van Langen, she began her incredible streak of victories in the 800 meters that spanned over 40 races in almost three years. Many high points marked her 1993 season, both indoors and out. She placed first in the 800 meters in the World Indoor Track and Field Championships that year in a time of 1:57.55, then ran the fastest 800-meter time ever in the United States outdoors (1:56.56) in her return to the Reebok New York Games. She confirmed her domination by beating the world's best with a blazing 1:55.43 in the 1993 World Outdoor Track and Field Championships in Stuttgart, Germany. The second place finisher clocked in at 1.67 seconds behind, making Mutola's margin of victory the largest in any world championship or Olympic final. For the year she broke the 1:57 barrier five times, more than twice as often as any other female runner.

When *Track & Field News* named Mutola as the top women's 800-meter runner for 1993, the 21-year-old athlete became the second-youngest ever to be so honored in the event. Mutola stayed in the fast lane the next year, hitting another high point in the Weltklasse meet in Zurich, Switzerland, with a victory time of 1:55.19. Her mark in the race was the fastest for that distance in five years, and the seventh fastest of all time. Once again in 1994 she was designated the world's top runner in the 800 meters by *Track & Field News.* The magazine also rated her as the number two female track athlete overall for the year.

> "Today practice, tomorrow a rest day. Track and field every day. I said, 'Oh my God!'"

Continuing to build on her unbeaten string in 1995, Mutola won by a margin of over two seconds in the World Indoor Track and Field Championships at Barcelona. She also produced the world's fastest time for a woman at 1500 meters (4:01.6) in her only attempt at the distance for the year. Her winning streak came to an unexpected end in the World Outdoor Track and Field Championships in Göteborg, Sweden, when she ran outside her lane in a semifinal heat and was disqualified. The eventual victor, Ana Quirot of Cuba, had lost to Mutola in a race in Monaco two weeks before the championships. Despite this setback, Mutola's domination during the year earned her a third consecutive number-one ranking in her event.

Broke Long-Standing Record

Continuing to show that she was equally invincible indoors and out, Mutola set a new world's record in the 1000-meter run in Birmingham, England, in February of 1996. Her time of 2:32.08 took nearly two seconds off the previous best mark, which had been set 18 years earlier. "I think I can break it again," said Mutola after the race, according to *Track & Field News.* Eight days later in a meet in Liévin, France, she followed up this performance with the second fastest 800 meters ever run indoors (1:57.13). Around this time she also announced her intention to run both the 800 meters and 1500 meters in the upcoming Olympic Games to be held in Atlanta, Georgia. "It will be hard, but I've been doing longer distances this winter in preparation," she told *Track & Field News* about her plan in the April 1996 issue. At just 23 years old, Maria Mutola has already secured a spot for herself in the Track and Field Hall of Fame.

Sources

Everybody's: The Caribbean-American Magazine, July 31, 1993, p. 26.
New York Times, February 27, 1993, p. 32; February 11, 1996, p. S10.
Track & Field News, February 1994, pp. 8, 21; May 1995, p. 33; October 1995, p. 31; December 1995, p. 38; January 1996, p. 10, 44; April 1996, p. 25.
Upscale, December/January 1995, pp. 104, 125.
Weekly Journal, August 5, 1993, p. 16.

Other information for this profile was obtained from Reebok International Limited publicity materials.

—Ed Decker

Zena Oglesby

1947—

Adoption rights activist

In Losing Isaiah, the 1995 film about transracial adoption starring Jessica Lange and Halle Berry, a key courtroom scene zeroes in on the legal question to be decided—Who will have custody, the black biological mother or the white adoptive mother? But also at issue is the deep abiding anger many African Americans feel toward this controversial issue. "Wouldn't you say," a lawyer for the white adoptive mother notes, [questioning a black social worker on the stand], "that you're putting political policy above the emotional health of these children?"

"No," the social worker replies. "All things being equal, the black child is better off with black parents." The lawyer: "'All things being equal.' What if all things are not equal?" The social worker: "Ms. Jones, I am sick and tired of the attitude that says that taking poor black children out of their environment and placing them in an affluent household is better for the child. What kind of values does that suggest?"

Rich Families Versus Poor Families

Zena Oglesby, a Los Angeles-based adoption rights activist for the African American community, would second that notion. As the founder and executive director of the Institute for Black Parenting, Oglesby has dedicated his career to ending what he characterizes as the nationwide buying and selling of black and interracial babies and the frequent preference adoption agencies

give white couples because they have ready cash and affluent homes and because adoption workers simply assume black adoptive parents can not be found.

"Go to any white adoption agency and ask them how many black people do they have who will pay $25,000 for a baby," Oglesby said in a telephone interview with CBB. "What you will get is 'virtually none,' and that's why they place them transracially with anyone who has the money. That has always been the practice in America, and nobody is challenging that practice. "But if you're talking about a baby, there is no shortage of black families to adopt a baby. Period. Exclamation point. I've got 50 [black] families right now waiting for an infant. And I can give you the names of ten other adoption agencies that have way too many people waiting for babies."

"The problem," said the 49-year-old Oglesby, "is assumptions manipulated by ill-informed media. The problem is untrained black parents who often lose out to white parents for just that reason. The problem is the failure by the white community to consider that stiff adoption "fees" to acquire a baby feel an awful lot like slavery transactions to even high-income black couples. The problem is legislation like the 1994 Multiethnic Placement Act, the first of several legislative efforts to remove traditional barriers for whites to adopt transracially. And the result? Black and transracial children who could have gone to African American families going,

At a Glance...

Born Zena Oglesby on May 2, 1947, in Milwaukee, Wis.; son of Zena Sr. (a steelworker) and Eddie Mae (Owens) Oglesby (a county employee); married three times, to: Carolyn Tuggle, Mae Harris, and (since 1988) Renee Dixon. Children: Lisa (by Carolyn Tuggle), Jamal (by Renee Dixon) and (her two children from an earlier union), Christien and Brandon. *Education:* attended University of Wisconsin-Whitewater, University of Wisconsin-Milwaukee, B.A. 1973, M.A. 1975, incomplete work for Ph.D., University of Texas-Austin, 1980-83.

Career: Activist for African American adoption. Social worker for Milwaukee schools; social worker in adoptions for San Bernadino County; training administrator for federal Adoption Resource Center, Region Nine; supervisor for Child Protective Services, Riverside County; case manager for South Central Regional Center for disabled children, Los Angeles; founder/exec. dir., Institute for Black Parenting, 1988—.

Addresses: *Office*—c/o The Institute for Black Parenting, 9920 La Cienga Blvd., Suite 806, Inglewood, CA 90301.

instead, to white families. There, they will almost certainly be loved, but they also almost certainly will struggle with questions of identity for the rest of their lives."

"The real issue is the American conscience," Oglesby said. "Is America interested in fairness or not? The law that was just passed demonstrates that they are not. The African American community in this country does not know what has happened. When they find out, they're going to be very, very upset."

Oglesby Early Years

Oglesby himself, fortunately, did not suffer the kinds of identity trauma he speaks of among black adoptive children. Instead, he was born on May 2, 1947, into an intact household headed by his father, Zena Sr., and his mother, Eddie Mae. His father was a steelworker, his mother a county employee in corrections and mental health. There were two younger brothers and a sister in the household, and home was north Milwaukee, the

inner city. Was the youthful Oglesby surrounded by the drugs and crime that this scenario suggests? Yes, he can say now, but he considered his childhood normal and calm. "Most people living in the inner city don't notice they have problems."

> "What I'm afraid of is black babies being sent to northern Idaho where they will never see another black person. It's not enough in America just to have love; there's still institutional racism.

Schooling was local, at Rufus King High School, followed by a year of college at the University of Wisconsin-Whitewater. The Vietnam war was raging at the time, and Oglesby was determined to stay out of it; the college deferment was one route, but the deferment ended; so he returned home, where he attended Milwaukee Area Technical College. Still managing to avoid the draft, Oglesby married his first wife, Carolyn Tuggle, and became a young father, to daughter Lisa, in 1970. But the marriage was short-lived. Oglesby, nevertheless, stayed in school, transferring to the University of Wisconsin-Milwaukee, where he received his undergraduate degree in criminology in 1973 and his master's degree in social work in 1975.

Fresh out of school, he went to work for the Milwaukee school board, where he was part of the city's desegregation team in those turbulent times. In 1976 he married again; his second wife was Mae Harris. As part of this new start, the couple relocated to San Bernadino, CA, following a vacation there. And it was in San Bernadino that Oglesby really began to feel at home and to carve out the area of social work that would be his vocation--adoption.

Arriving at Adoption as the Central Issue

"I was the first black social worker ever hired in adoptions in the county," he recalled. But he was working strictly on linking black babies to black families. "Interracial adoption was not an issue in the public sector because people adopting transracially were doing it through the private agencies and paying for them, which had nothing to do with the business I was in. There was nobody at that time interested in adopting black children, period. That adoption application at that time said 'anything but black,' as a matter of fact."

Oglesby worked for San Bernadino for three years before taking his next job, in a federal program, the Adoption Resource Center, for Region Nine, where he administered training resources for California, Nevada, Arizona, Hawaii, and the Pacific Trust islands. This job was a real eye-opener, Oglesby remembered. "I was working in adoption doing recruitment because there were no African American families around, and conventional wisdom had it that African Americans 'didn't adopt' and that didn't seem right to me since the black extended family seemed so incredibly strong. So I started doing recruitment, and it was obvious that [that impression] was not true ... we ended up with almost 100 families in six months."

Why this information gap? Adoption, Oglesby said, was and is "an extremely well-kept secret" for blacks, and when African Americans did come forward they were often screened out "due to cultural incompetence." Adoption personnel, he said, didn't know what they were looking at,"and they were looking for Donna Reed." To better prepare himself for dealing with this problem on an even broader basis, Oglesby enrolled as a Ph.D. student at the University of Texas in Austin in 1980. But he dropped out of the program after his second marriage broke up, and returned to California. In 1983, he went to work supervising child protective services for Riverside County. There, he saw still more evidence of the problem—kids going into the system and not coming out, no emphasis on preserving families, a singleminded emphasis on taking kids away from parents and relegating them to foster care, where caseloads have skyrocketed, along with foster-family child abuse.

A big problem, Oglesby explained, was and is "untrained" parents: "Eighty percent of the children removed are removed for neglect, not abuse, and when I say 'neglect,' I mean very simplistic things that can be corrected very easily." Welfare mothers are a case in point, he said. They can be taught to parent, taught not to leave their children while they run to the store—the types of things children get removed from their families for.

New Job, Wife, and Child

By the mid-1980s, Oglesby was ready to change jobs again; this time, he went to work for the quasi-public South Central Regional Center for disabled children in Los Angeles, first as a case manager, then a transportation specialist. Through a coworker at the center, he

met his third wife, Renee, who he married in 1988; the couple had a biological child, Jamal, 4-years-old. Oglesby's wife is also the mother of Christien, 17-years-old, and Brandon, 14-years-old. With Oglesby's own first biological child, Lisa, now 26-years-old, the household is a large one.

And it has given Oglesby plenty of practice in parenting himself. It has also strengthened the ideas he has put together over the years for a center on black parenting, which he designed while at the Los Angeles center and then left to found in Los Angeles in 1988 (the center has since relocated to nearby Inglewood). Why adoption as an issue? "Kids are trapped and I don't know how anyone who works with them can ever move away from it," Oglesby said in the interview. "You try, but you can't. I went from a paid position to always working free of charge," to recruit black adoptive parents and to train other recruiters in the African American community. En route, "It became clear to me that no amount of work was going to change the public sector. That it was important that private agencies be created that were run by African Americans, that were going to be culturally competent in the first place, and, secondly, fully licensed by the government to do what public agencies could do."

Keeping Black Families Together

Today, the Institute for Black Parenting is a licensed adoption and foster care agency that makes about 50 placements a year, primarily to hard-to-place children; it also has about 220 children in foster care. Celebrities like actor Blair Underwood and basketball great Kareem Abdul-Jabbar help recruit families. The staff consists of 40 full-time and 20 part-time employees. Funding is from federal and state sources, not "adoption fees"; the Institute is one of three minority agencies in Los Angeles created out of special funding to place black children with black families.

But Oglesby said he sees the Institute in jeopardy as the result of the Democratic-sponsored Multiethnic Placement Act passed in 1994. "I'm in danger of being investigated by the [Justice Department's] Office of Civil Rights for doing what I was created to do," he said. Already, the law—which was aimed at blocking race from becoming a factor in public-sector adoptions—has spawned similar moves at the state level, Oglesby said. Two Hispanic adoption agencies in California have been de-funded before opening, and a law in Texas has been passed forbidding social workers there from mentioning race with clients, he said.

A second potential law has also appeared on the

horizon. In May 1996, President Bill Clinton expressed "strong support" for a Republican-sponsored bill to move further to block race from being an issue in adoptions. In an interview an aide to the bill's sponsor, U.S. Representative Susan Molinari, a Republican from New York, the aide said that Clinton's own Health and Human Services agency had watered down the 1994 bill so much that Molinari had seen the need to file another. The Molinari measure, if passed, would fine states that delay interracial adoptions so as to await the possibility of a same-race placement.

The bill not only had Clinton's support, but in a *New York Times* report, the National Association of Black Social Workers task—which is generally opposed to interracial adoptions—said that the group "could live" with the bill, because of compromise language allowing race to be considered if more than one qualified family sought to adopt the same child.

Viewing these developments, Oglesby, however, said he has to redouble his efforts to get the word out to the black community about what is happening to its parentless children. "The more infertile America becomes, the more thirsty it is for other children—just to have babies to raise them," he said. While philosophically opposed to transracial adoption, he also opposes ripping children from families—even white families—once they have been placed. "What I am afraid of is black babies being sent to northern Idaho where they will never see another black person. It's not enough in America just to have love; there's still institutional racism."

So, one of the main things Oglesby advocates is action to acculturate black children—and here he includes biracial children, as well. Another thing is keeping black families together, through adoption assistance funds (which he says the Republicans' Contract for America is trying to eliminate) and through parental training. He also wants to end "the classical mistake media make"— assuming there are too few African American parents

for African American babies. This is true for older, hard-to-place children. It is not true for infants, he insists. "The real issue is that every single transracial adoption case adjudicated in America is children under three," he said.

Last, and perhaps most important, is the practice of buying babies in America and all the bizarre policy and practices it fosters. Oglesby likes to mention an ad he saw for a San Antonio agency which advertised African American babies at $7,500, biracial babies at $10,000 and Hispanic babies at $12,000, "based on the color of the baby."

"In our profession, we are taught to go out and find children for families, not families for children," Oglesby said. "And the government has passed a law that provides children for infertile families. My profession— what I've dedicated 20 years to—is finding families for children. "I don't owe the families anything because I haven't taken any money from them. If I can find a family that fits the children's needs, fine. If the family doesn't fit what that child needs, I tell the family goodbye. Because I'm not in this business to find you a baby. Private adoption agencies across this country— that's exactly the business they're in."

Sources

Periodicals

Los Angeles Times, August 8, 1993, p. J1.
New York Times, May 7, 1996.

Other

Telephone Interview with Zena Oglesby, April 12, 1996.
Telephone Interview with James Mazzarella, aide to U.S. Rep. Susan Molinari, May 7, 1996.

—Joan Oleck

Charles Ogletree, Jr.

1933—

Lawyer

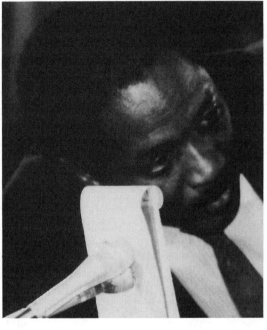

Charles Ogletree, Jr. is considered one of the most tenacious and successful trial lawyers in the United States. The Harvard University professor is a passionate advocate of a defendant's right to a fair trial within the American justice system--a Constitutional right one might find it difficult to receive if a member of a minority group. For several years Ogletree worked in Washington, DC's public defender's office, a difficult area of law which generally attracts only the most ideologically dedicated and stamina-imbued law school graduates. Those experiences were carried over to the Ivy League halls of Harvard Law School, where Ogletree has single-handedly made significant inroads into how students at the country's most prestigious legal training ground view both the African American community and the criminal justice system.

Ogletree was born December 31, 1952, to Charles Sr. and Willie Mae Ogletree, the first of their five children. He grew up in a rural northern California community called Merced, which had a small African American population that lived south of its railroad tracks. His maternal grandparents, known as Big Daddy and Big Mama, were an important influence on the young

Ogletree. With his grandfather he would fish for hours, and from Big Mama he learned how to cook and thus, learning self-sufficiency. Both grandparents he would later credit as having a profound influence on his demeanor and tactics as a trial lawyer. The marriage of Ogletree's parents, however, was plagued by periodic violence, and they eventually divorced, although they remained on good terms. A bright child who spent free hours in the public library and brought home good grades from school, his first brushes with the law--especially watching his father being taken away in cuffs after incidents of domestic violence at the Ogletree house--instilled in him a deep distrust of and feelings of powerlessness toward the law enforcement community.

Drew Strength From Humble Origins

The Ogletree family was part of the migrant worker community around Merced, and when Charles, Jr. became old enough he also began working in the fields, picking figs and other fruit. From this he learned a certain inner competitiveness--every day he would strive

At a Glance...

Born December 31, 1952, in Merced, CA; son of Charles Sr. and Willie Mae (Reed) Ogletree; married Pamela Barnes, August 9, 1975; children: Charles J. III, Rashida Jamila. *Education:* Stanford University, B.A., 1974, M.A., 1975; Harvard Law School, M.A., J.D., 1978.

Career: District of Columbia Public Defender Service, Washington, DC, staff attorney, 1978-82, director of staff and training, 1982-83; American University, Washington, adjunct professor, 1982-84, deputy director, 1984-85; Antioch Law School, Washington, adjunct professor, 1983-84; Jessamy, Fort & Ogletree (law firm), Washington, partner, 1985-89, Jessamy, Fort & Botts, of counsel, 1989--; Harvard Law School, Cambridge, MA, visiting professor, 1985-89, director, introduction to trial advocacy workshop, 1986, assistant professor, 1989, director, Criminal Justice Institute, 1990-.

Member: American Bar Association, National Conference of Black Lawyers, National Bar Association, American Civil Liberties Union, Bar Association of DC, Washington Bar Association, National Legal Aid and Defender Association (defender committee member), Southern Prisoners Defense Committee (chair, board of directors), Society of American Law Teachers (board member), National Mentor Program (member, advisory committee), Stanford University Board of Trustees.

Awards: Hall of Fame, California School Boards Association, 1990; Richard S. Jacobsen Certificate of Excellence in Teaching Trial Advocacy, 1990; honoree, Charles Hamilton Houston Institute, 1990; Award of Merit, Public Defender Service Association, 1990; Personal Achievement Award, National Association for the Advancement of Colored People and the Black Network, 1990; Nelson Mandela Service Award, National Black Law Students Association, 1991.

Addresses: *Office*—Harvard Law School, Hauser Hall, Room 320, 1575 Massachusetts Ave., Cambridge, MA 02138.

I've Known Rivers: Lives of Loss and Liberation. "Before I got to college I had never met any of these kinds of people." Another incident that occurred in his teens severely impacted Ogletree's views on law, order, and justice, especially for members of the African American community. In high school he was part of a tight-knit group of young African American males that were determined to stay out of trouble. All earned good grades, were involved in athletics, and respected Eugene Allen, considered the brightest of the clique. After Allen's run-in with Merced's high school football coach--and incurring the wrath of the town's white community by dating the daughter of a white judge--Allen was accused of setting fire to the coach's residence. He was convicted and sent to a youth camp, where he was involved in a race riot and charged with the death of a white inmate. Sent to San Quentin for the crime, he was co-charged with killing a prison guard, although the decision was overturned and Allen was removed from Death Row. The sad story of one of his closest friends, so similar to Ogletree himself at the age of 17, made it painfully aware of how difficult it was for young African American males to receive fair treatment once inside the criminal justice system, and how easily it can take down a young life so full of promise.

In 1970, after high school, Ogletree enrolled in Stanford University outside San Francisco. His dormitory marked the first time he had ever had his own room, but yet he was also dismayed by the elitism of the institution. Fortunately, he was also quite near the epicenter of the Black Power movement that had coalesced around San Francisco, the city of Oakland, and the University of California at Berkeley at that point in history. Ogletree became a campus radical, organizing an Afrocentric (though still integrated) dormitory, where he met his future wife, Pamela Barnes. He edited a campus Black Panther newspaper called *The Real News,* traveled to Africa and Cuba as part of student activist groups, and attended the nearby trial of Black Power activist and Communist Angela Davis nearly every day. It was his first intensive experience in the courtroom, and one that sparked an intent to possibly pursue trial law as a career. Some of parts of the Davis trial were tedious, Ogletree recalled in *I've Known Rivers,* but "the process and strategies were fascinating. I sat there wondering how they were going to tie all this together."

Difficulty in Adjusting to Harvard's Climate

After graduating with a B.A. from Stanford in 1974, Ogletree stayed on a year to earn a master's degree in international relations. At the urging of his soon-to-be

to pick more than he had the day before. As an adult, Ogletree compared his humble upbringing with that of his own children, raised in relatively affluent African American middle-class surroundings: "In the normal course of their lives they meet professors, lawyers, doctors," he recalled for Sara Lawrence-Lightfoot in wife, he applied to Harvard Law School; the newlyweds moved to the Boston area upon his acceptance and enrollment in the fall of 1975. From the start, Ogletree recalled, he felt unease in the markedly different, monied East-Coast enclave. Furthermore, the city was then in the middle of a vicious battle over busing that pitted its ethnic-American communities against the African American populace. Academia itself was also especially tedious, and at one point he nearly quit the prestigious School of Law. "At Harvard the pressure was on, participation was mandatory, there was always a lot of competition and tension in the air," Ogletree recalled in *I've Known Rivers*. He survived by closely allying himself with other African American students and continued his political activism, even becoming national president of the Black Law Students Association.

After receiving a juris doctor degree from Harvard in 1978, Ogletree was hired by the District of Columbia's Public Defender's Service, which provided free legal counsel to those accused of a crime who were unable to afford an attorney guaranteed them by the U.S. Constitution. With wife Pamela and son Charles III (a family made complete with the arrival of daughter Rashida in 1979), Ogletree moved to the nation's capital, also home to some of the most blighted and crime-ridden urban pockets in the country. He had originally thought that perhaps he had not gained very much from his experiences at Harvard, but later asserted that everything he learned came back in surprising ways as he began to argue cases before the bench--and win. Soon Ogletree had gained a reputation as a formidable courtroom presence, although it took him a while to understand that himself. Initially, he would attribute most victories to luck, but then, as he told Lawrence-Lightfoot in *I've Known Rivers,* "it was only after I kept on winning and began to gain a strong reputation among my peers ... that I began to admit to myself that I had a special talent for this work."

Gained A Reputation For Success

Ogletree became known for a cool, collected courtroom demeanor, which he has said was inherited from his grandfather and their fishing expeditions together, during which the elder man would sit impassively for long stretches of time. Ogletree himself took up fishing in his thirties as a means of relaxation from his hectic schedule that not only included his grueling hours in the Public Defender's Service--where he was named director of staff training in 1982--but his teaching position at American University and later Antioch Law School, rounded out by his involvements in numerous professional organizations. After a time Ogletree left the Public

Defender's Service, and between 1985 and 1989 Ogletree was a partner in the Washington law firm of Jessamy, Fort, & Ogletree while concurrently serving as a visiting professor at Harvard Law School.

> "It was only after I kept on winning and began to gain a strong reputation among my peers ... that I began to admit to myself that I had a special talent for this work."

In 1986 Ogletree became director of Harvard's introduction to trial advocacy workshops, a program he founded to inject a more clinical, hands-on approach into a curriculum known to be a bit too focused on the theoretics of law. Through the intensive workshops, students--even if they are not planning a career in trial law--will walk away with a sense that the law can be "an instrument for social and political change ... a tool to empower the dispossessed and disenfranchised ... and a means to make the privileged more respectful of differences," as Ogletree explained in *I've Known Rivers*. He also founded the School's Criminal Justice Institute in 1990, a broad program heavily involved with the poorer communities in Boston, and began a Saturday School so African American students could learn from other professionals of their own heritage. The conferences are often sold out and well integrated.

Served as Counsel in Senate Confirmation Hearings

Ogletree also gained prominence in 1991 when he was asked by the National Association for the Advancement of Colored People to write up an investigation into the legal career of a former Equal Employment Opportunity Commission chief and African American judge Clarence Thomas, a staunch Republican. The group thought they should cast their support of the presidential nominee for the Supreme Court on the basis of race, even though Thomas's legal rulings and writings consistently seemed to work against the civil rights principles upon which the NAACP had been founded. Ogletree drafted a thirty-page report on Thomas that was instrumental in the NAACP's vote of no confidence for the nominee. He later became further embroiled in the battle against Thomas when charges of sexual harassment were leveled against the judge by a law professor and former

EEOC subordinate named Anita Hill; Ogletree served as her attorney during the contentious Senate confirmation hearings in the fall of 1991.

The following year, Ogletree's career at Harvard--whose decision-makers had named him assistant professor in 1989--became the subject of controversy when a paper he had submitted to the school's Law Review Journal was called into question by some of the publication's staff. However, the prestigious university's dearth of tenured African American professors as well as vicious rivalry between political camps among the student body seemed to be behind much of the flap. The *Wall Street Journal* as well as the *New Republic* covered the incident, but Ogletree was granted tenure and the Law Review editor censured. The fractious atmosphere that has replaced the elitism of Ogletree's student days at the school make him question his own reasons for staying on. "Am I doing right by my people working here at the university?" he wondered in *I've Known Rivers.* "This remains an open question."

Sources

Books

Lawrence-Lightfoot, Sara. *I've Known Rivers: Lives of Loss and Liberation,* Addison-Wesley, 1994.

Periodicals

Bay State Banner, April 28, 1994, p. 17.
Jet, June 28, 1993, p. 10.
New Republic, June 7, 1993, p. 11.
Wall Street Journal, December 4, 1992.

—Carol Brennan

Deval Patrick

1956—

Government official

Deval Patrick is the Justice Department's assistant attorney general for civil rights. He is an eloquent and impassioned champion of affirmative action and an outspoken advocate for the nation's minority and disabled citizens. His zealous enforcement of civil rights laws stems from his conviction, voiced in a Los Angeles Town Hall speech, that "legions of racial and ethnic minorities feel less of a sense of opportunity, less assured of our equality, and less confident of fair treatment today than we have in many, many years."

Deval Laurdine Patrick was born on Chicago's gritty South Side in 1956. When he was four years old his father abandoned the family to pursue a musical career, leaving Deval, his mother, and sister impoverished. The family, which spent several months on welfare, was at one point so destitute that they could afford only two beds for their basement apartment, a problem that required one of them sleep on the floor every third night.

As a child, Patrick went to the Mary C. Terrell elementary school, a building that bordered the Robert Taylor Homes, a large and notoriously dangerous housing project. So great was the threat of violence that students had to slide a pass under the school door to get inside. Young Deval worried that the rest of his academic career would be equally bleak. The Woodlawn riots, which tore Chicago apart in 1968 did little to ease his fears.

Poverty and grim surroundings notwithstanding, Deval was an outstanding student. One of his teachers recalled that even in the sixth grade his studiousness and leadership was obvious. Apparently, so was his ability to persuade an audience; when a school essay contest invited entries on "Why My Father Should Be Father of the Year," Deval won the competition with a paper entitled "Why My Grandmother Should be Father of the Year."

Admitted to Elite Prep School

By eighth grade he was first in his class. A teacher encouraged him to apply to A Better Chance, a scholarship program that sent children of limited means to college preparatory schools. He applied to Milton Academy and was accepted. As he recalled for the *Boston Globe*, "I just got a letter one day from Milton . . . [that]

At a Glance...

Born on July 31, 1956, in Chicago, IL; son of Laurdine Kenneth "Pat" (a jazz musician) and Emily Mae (Wintersmith) Patrick; married Diane Bemus, 1984; children: Sarah and Katherine. *Education:* attended Milton Academy preparatory school; Havard College, A.B. (cum laude), 1978; Harvard Law School, J.D. (with honors), 1982.

Law clerk to Judge Stephen Reinhardt, US Court of Appeals, Ninth Circuit, 1982-83. Assistant counsel for the NAACP Legal Defense and Education Fund, 1983-86. Partner at Hill and Barlow law firm, 1986-94. Assistant Attorney General, Civil Rights Division, U.S. Department of Justice, 1994—.

Awards: Michael Clark Rockefeller Traveling Fellowship, 1979; Harvard Law School George Leisure award, 1981.

Member: California bar, 1983; District of Columbia bar, 1985; Massachusetts bar, 1987. Director, member of the executive committee, and chairman of the New England steering committe of the NAACP Legal Defense and Education Fund, Inc., 1991-93; Trustee and executive committee member for the Milton Academy preparatory school, 1985—; overseer for public television station WGBH Boston, 1993-94; corporator for Milton Hospital, 1991-94; American Bar Association; Massachusetts Bar Association; Massachusetts Black Lawyers Association; Boston Bar Association (counsel member, 1993); Harvard Club of Boston; Harvard Alumni Association (director, 1993).

Addresses: *Office*—U.S. Department of Justice, Tenth and Constitution Ave. NW, Washington, D.C. 20530.

said you are admitted to Class 4. I wasn't sure it wasn't a military academy until I got there. The whole letter was in a language I didn't quite understand."

This language barrier became even more apparent several months later, when Deval arrived for the first day of school. In a story he has repeated often, Patrick says that the list of required clothing sent by the school called

for a jacket, and his proud family splurged on one. Only as his classmates were dressing for dinner that evening did Deval realize his error--the school wanted its students in blazers, not the windbreaker he was wearing.

The Milton Academy campus was far removed from the harsh reality of urban life, and Deval was awed by its beauty and tranquillity. He was also terrified by the enormous changes he experienced. His fear gradually subsided, however, as he began to enjoy life there. He finally had a room of his own, and could learn without the omnipresent menace of danger he had endured in Chicago. He had a paper route to earn money. And he had his family's unwavering love and support--even if they were hundreds of miles away.

As Deval settled into his new academic life his natural ability once again began to emerge. He recited Kipling's poem "If" during an assembly, giving a performance so stirring that it moved his Latin teacher, Francis Millet, ("a very dry and formal sort of person with this incredible heart and soul," Patrick later recalled in the *Boston Globe*) to tears. "That's the kind of thing that makes a kid like me--or a kid from Nepal--believe that things are going to work out."

"Milton Academy was kind of watershed for him," said Judge Reginald Lindsay, a former colleague who is now a federal district judge in Boston, in a *New York Times* article. Patrick himself said in a speech later reprinted in the *Chicago Tribune* that during his time at Milton "I learned to appreciate education as more than accumulated information and prestige, but instead, to borrow from Robert Frost, as "learning to listen to anything, without losing your temper or your self-confidence."

At Milton, Deval struck up a friendship with A. O. Smith, an English teacher who had taught at the school for 40 years, and his wife Aubrey. "He was so at ease with who he was," Patrick told the *Boston Globe,* "and that made it possible for him to open up to a whole group of people." The couple befriended him, taking him to Cape Cod during vacations where, as Aubrey Smith remembered, they would "chop wood, drink hot chocolate, and talk about the world."

His life and friendships at school began to have a noticeable effect on him, he told the *Boston Globe*. During one visit back home, his sister exclaimed, "He talks like a white boy." The remark triggered an uncomfortable silence. "He speaks like an educated boy," his grandmother corrected her.

But there were still a few shadows in Deval's life. One night when he was 15-years-old, he recounted in the

Washington Post, during a trip to McDonald's with his housemaster, "I remember...this incredible scene where the kids in the parking lot started banging on the window and shouting and chanting, "N-----! N-----! Get out of here!"... The housemaster was nervous and was trying to hustle us out of there....We got in the car and of course he didn't know what to say." But Patrick recalled his own reaction vividly: "I mean it's a lot that you feel: angry, you feel terrified, you feel helpless. The worst that happened was that someone, a couple people, threw their cigarette butts at me. Nobody actually hit me, but you still feel wounded. And if you're not real careful, you can feel ashamed too ... of who you are--and what you are--which is a disaster."

Literature, Africa, and Law School

Patrick's success at Milton paved the way for an equally impressive college career. He applied to five Ivy League universities: Yale, Princeton, Georgetown, Trinity, and Harvard, the one he wanted most because it was his mentor A. O. Smith's alma mater. He was admitted to all of them, and was particularly thrilled by the beautiful calligraphy of Harvard's acceptance letter. He told the story in his Los Angeles Town Hall speech.

"Now, while everyone at Milton is of course expected to go to college, you must understand that no one in my family had ever been. I had applied to five colleges, but there was only one I really wanted. When the letter came on April 15 that I was admitted to that one, I called home and my grandmother picked up the phone. I told her my news, that I was going to Harvard. She told me how proud she was of me, so pleased, so excited, then she paused and said, "Where is that anyway?" His grandmother's words, he said, gave him an important perspective on success: "And I never forgot. Not at Harvard. Not at Harvard Law School. Not through any of the extraordinary experiences or associations I have had since that day."

In his undergraduate studies Patrick majored in English and American literature, where he discovered a particular fondness for the works of Mark Twain. His scholastic ability — he graduated cum laude--helped him win a $5,000 Rockefeller Fellowship, which he used to study and travel--albeit on a shoestring--in Africa. During his year-long journey, he kept an application to Harvard Law School in his backpack. One night, in the desert, he wrote the required essay and filled out the form by flashlight. The school informed him of his acceptance via telegram sent to Khartoum.

Legal studies further honed Patrick's skills as a speaker

and a leader. His team won a spot in the school's Ames Moot Court finals, a competition in which law students prove their skills by arguing actual cases before a Supreme Court justice. Patrick's team asked him to present the oral argument; he was named best speaker in the competition. He was also chosen to head Harvard's Legal Aid Bureau, an organization that gives legal services to the needy. In what would become a familiar type of case for him, Patrick defended a fellow Harvard student, also black, after he was arrested while driving with his white girlfriend.

A Civil Rights Lawyer

After graduating with honors from Harvard Law School, he won a coveted clerkship with a federal judge in California, Stephen Reinhardt of the US Court of Appeals, Ninth Circuit. In 1983 he began to practice law in earnest when he joined the NAACP Legal Defense and Education Fund, challenging racially biased death-penalty convictions and voting-rights cases.

In 1985 Patrick and other NAACP lawyers successfully defended three Alabama civil rights advocates who had been accused of fraud by the Justice Department in a voter-registration drive. In another case, Patrick prevailed against the state of Arkansas and its then-governor Bill Clinton for registration violations in conflict with the Voting Rights Act. "The right to vote is at the heart of a meaningful democracy," he later declared in a speech to the Organization of Chinese Americans. In his Los Angeles Town Hall speech he elaborated, "A person who is denied an effective voice in the governance of his nation simply cannot feel the same sense of investment in the affairs of that nation."

One of Patrick's biggest cases for the NAACP was *McCleskey v. Kemp,* the 1987 Supreme Court death-penalty appeal of Warren McCleskey, a black man who had murdered a white policeman. Patrick argued that his client's sentence should be overturned because capital punishment was unconstitutional. He based his defense on a study of 2,000 Georgia murder convictions which found that those who killed whites were sentenced to death 11 percent of the time, while only one percent of those who killed a black victim were similarly convicted. The study also revealed that blacks convicted of murder received the death penalty more often than whites, a bias that Patrick argued confirmed the illegality of capital punishment. The court disagreed, and McCleskey's sentence stood.

In 1986 Patrick left the NAACP to become a partner at Hill and Barlow, the respected Boston law firm that had once employed governors William Weld and Michael Dukakis. There Patrick continued to devote much of his time to pro bono social and political causes. In one case whose outcome he found particularly satisfying, he defended a group of low-income homeowners, most of them elderly black women, who said they had been illegally pressured into high-interest home-improvement loans by BayBanks, a local financial institution. In the settlement Patrick negotiated, BayBanks set aside $11 million to be used for low-income, low-interest housing loans. In another high-profile case Patrick represented beauty contestant Desiree Washington in her civil suit against boxer Mike Tyson.

Assistant Attorney General

On February 1, 1994, Patrick was nominated by President Bill Clinton to the post of assistant attorney general for civil rights. His nomination followed the unsuccessful bids of Lani Guinier, a law professor at the University of Pennsylvania (and Patrick's cocounsel during his years at the NAACP), and John Payton, the District of Columbia corporation counsel, for the same position. Guinier had been faulted for what critics contended were her undemocratic proposals to increase minority representation and political clout. Payton withdrew after detractors denounced both his spotty voting record and his reluctance to use legal challenges to construct black-majority voting districts. Patrick's nomination was successful despite the similarity of his views to Guinier's, because unlike her, he lacked a paper trail of academic writings for opponents to seize upon. His solid experience as a civil rights lawyer also weighed heavily in his favor.

During his Senate confirmation hearings Patrick announced his intention, reported in the *New York Times,* to use the civil rights post as a "bully pulpit," and said that he would "move firmly, fearlessly, and unambiguously to enforce the antidiscrimination laws." He added that he believed it was Justice Department's responsibility to take the lead, "shaping policies and [filing] lawsuits that promote the notion of an inclusive democracy." His admirers said that Patrick's bold and direct approach would be a sea change from past years, reflecting the Clinton administration's more aggressive civil rights policies. Patrick's nomination was confirmed by the Senate on March 17, 1994.

Once in office, Patrick moved vigorously to reorganize the Justice Department's priorities. He assembled a team of government lawyers to defend legal challenges to voting districts that had been drawn to concentrate black and minority voters. His department also settled the Denny's restaurant public accommodations

lawsuit--the largest in American history--by convincing the chain to pay $45 million for alleged racial discrimination.

In another case that recalled the BayBanks settlement, Justice Department lawyers were able to force a Maryland bank, Chevy Chase Federal Savings, to serve black neighborhoods and provide low-interest loans to their residents. Even though the bank had not discriminated against anyone, Patrick and Attorney General Janet Reno criticized the financial institution because it avoided serving certain minority districts. The bank reluctantly agreed to a settlement in which it would designate $11 million to build new branches and provide below-market-rate loans and mortgages to minorities. This greatly worried members of the financial community, who protested that the Justice Department had exceeded its authority.

Criticism and Conscience

Others voiced similar complaints. A particular nemesis, Clint Bolick, a *Wall Street Journal* columnist and litigation director for the nonprofit law firm Institute of Justice, charged that Patrick used the threat of government litigation to force companies into settlements. "Mr. Patrick," he wrote, "seems determined to pursue high-profile cases that less resemble objective law enforcement than naked extortion." Nor is friction confined to the press: Patrick has felt antagonism from members of Congress as well.

Patrick acknowledges the criticism as part of his job, but it still makes him uncomfortable. "Being a lightning rod takes getting used to," he told *Business Week.* "If I walked on water, certain of my critics would still say that Patrick can't swim." He commented in the *Washington Post* that "[t]he job brings...difficult choices...because they're not always obvious choices under the law."

> "To understand civil rights, you must understand how it feels. How it feels to be hounded by uncertainty and fear about whether you will be fairly treated. How it feels to be trapped in someone else's stereotype."

Patrick stands by his decisions, however difficult reaching them may be, because he is convinced that racism and discrimination can only be addressed by vigilant federal enforcement of civil rights laws. He cites statistics on hate crimes and the many accusations of police brutality brought by minorities to further his claim, and recalls his own bruises from the slings and arrows of discrimination. "To understand civil rights," he said in his swearing-in speech, which was quoted in the *Washington Post,* "you must understand how it feels. How it feels to be hounded by uncertainty and fear about whether you will be fairly treated. How it feels to be trapped in someone else's stereotype."

His mission, as he articulated it to the Organization of Chinese Americans, "is to reclaim the American conscience....to restore the great moral imperative that civil rights is finally all about; to recreate the shared national consensus that discrimination is wrong; and to return the language of civil rights to its essence, back to concepts of equality, opportunity, and fair play....We are a great nation, it seems to me, not just because of what we have accomplished, but because of what we have committed ourselves to become. And it is that sense of hope, that sense of looking forward, that I believe has made not only our civil
rights movement, but ourselves as a nation, an inspiration to the world."

Sources

Periodicals

Boston Globe, April 23, 1987, National/Foreign section, p. 1.; April 25, 1987, Metro section, p. 17.; September 23, 1993, Living section, p.63.; February 2, 1994, National/Foreign section, p. 10; May 8, 1994, Focus section, p. 67; March 25, 1995, National/Foreign section, p. 1.; July 22, 1995, National/Foreign section, p. 8. October 26, 1994, p. A1.; October 21, 1995, National/Foreign section, p. 4.

Business Week, Legal Affairs section, December 12, 1994.

Chicago Tribune, June 22, 1994, section 1, p. 23.

New York Times, February 2, 1994, p. A13.; March 11, 1994, section A, p. 24.

Newsweek, February 13, 1995, p. 34.

Wall Street Journal, October 26, 1994, p. A1; March 14, 1995, section A, p. 18; April 5, 1995, section A, p. 11; April 24, 1995, Letters to the Editor, section A, p. 15.

Washington Post, September 23, 1993, Living section, p.63; February 2, 1994, p. A1; February 14, 1994, p. A13; May 8, 1994, Focus section, p. 67; March 25, 1995, National/Foreign section, p. 1.; July 22, 1995, National/Foreign section, p. 8.; August 9, 1995. Op-ed section; August 20, 1995, section C, p. 6.

Other

Patrick, Deval Laurdine. "The Rise in Hate Crime." Speech delivered at the Organization of Chinese Americans, Los Angeles, July 8, 1994. *Vital Speeches* LXI, no. 1, October 15, 1994, pp. 13-15.
"Struggling for Civil Rights Now: Let Us Recapture Our Perspective." Speech delivered at the Town Hall Los Angeles Luncheon, Los Angeles, October 4, 1994. *Vital Speeches* LXI, no. 3, November 15, 1994, pp. 91-96.

—Amy Loerch Strumolo

Frederick D. Patterson

1901–1988

Association executive

Frederick Douglass Patterson was born October 10, 1901 in the Anacostia section of Washington, D.C. to Mamie and William Patterson. The couple had moved to the nation's capital two or three years previously with their other five children from Texas. Mr. Patterson thought he would be able to find better work in Washington due to the lesser amount of racial problems there than in Texas. He named his youngest son after educator and abolitionist Frederick Douglass, whose onetime home was a couple of blocks away from where they lived.

Moved Around as a Youth.

Frederick's mother was a music teacher and his father was a school principal. They had both received their college degrees from Prairie View College in Texas. Once they arrived in Washington, his father returned to school at Howard University to study law. Mr. Patterson passed the D.C. bar shortly after Frederick was born. Despite all the hard work his parents did to improve the life of the family, nothing could stop them both from dying of tuberculosis before Frederick was two years old.

The same illness would also claim one of Frederick''s brothers a few years later.

Frederick initially went to live with a friend of the family, "Aunt" Julia Dorsey. His siblings all went to live with different family friends except his oldest sister, Wilhelmina Bessie, who was old enough to support herself and attend the Washington Conservatory of Music. In his autobiography Patterson says, "I called Aunt Julia my Civil War aunt, because she was born during slavery." They continued living in the house of his parents when Frederick was still young, and he also started school there.

When Frederick was about seven-years-old his sister Bessie assumed his guardianship. She had finished school and was looking for work. She knew some of the family relatives and decided to go to live in Texas where she thought she would have the most assistance in finding work. Over the next few years Frederick and Bessie were often living in different cities. She was often unable to find teaching work where Frederick could live with her. So Frederick lived with different members of the family while attending school . From the fourth through the eighth grades Frederick attended Sam

At a Glance...

Born Frederick Douglass Patterson, October 10, 1901 in northeast Washington, D.C.; son of Mamie Brooks Patterson, a music teacher and homemaker, and William Ross Patterson, school principal and lawyer; married Catherine Elizabeth Moton in June 1935; 1 son, Frederick Douglass, Jr.; Education: attended Prarie View State College, 1915-1919; Doctorate in Veterinary Medicine, 1923, Iowa State University; Masters in Science, 1927, Iowa State University; PhD in Bacteriology, 1932, Cornell University.

Instructor, Veterinary Medicine and Chemistry, Virginia State University, Petersburg, Virginia, 1923-27; Director, School of Agriculture, Virginia State University, 1927-28; Director of Veterinary Medicine and Instructor of Bacteriology, Tuskegee Institute (now Tuskegee University), 1928-31, 1933-34; Director, Department of Agriculture, Tuskegee Institute, 1934-35; President, Tuskegee Institute, 1935-53; President, Phelps-Stokes Fund, 1953-70.

Author: *Chronicles of Faith: The Autobiography of Frederick Douglass Patterson,* University of Alabama Press, 1991; *The College Endowment Funding Plan,* American Council on Education, 1976; *Robert Russa Moton of Tuskegee and Hampton,* University of North Carolina Press, 1956.

Awards: Honorary Doctorates from Lincoln University, Virginia State University, and Wilberforce University; Presidential Medal of Freedom, 1987; Spingarn Medal, 1988.

Houston College. Although called a college, Sam Houston also had primary and high school divisions too. "I didn't object to school, but I didn't do much with I, Patterson said in *Chronicles of Faith.* "At the time I didn't take my studies seriously. I finished the eighth grade many whippings later." His classmates that year voted Frederick least likely to succeed.

From the eighth grade through the end of High School Patterson attended another boarding school at a college. This one was at Prairie View College, where his parents had attended. Bessie had secured a job teaching

and directing the choir at the school, so the two of them lived together there in Prairie View, Texas. During the summers, he took odd jobs to earn money. One of these was as a driver for a wealthy family. Although Frederick had never driven before applying for the position, he got the job and taught himself to drive. He also taught himself how to play tennis, which became a lifelong hobby. Patterson says he became interested in school when he had to do his work study in the Agriculture Department of the school. He worked for two veterinarians his last couple years of high school. It motivated him so much, spending time with the animals, that he decided he would go to college to become a veterinarian.

College Years

Because the veterinarians he worked with at Prairie View had attended Iowa State University in Ames, Iowa, Patterson decided that he too would go to Iowa for schooling. Since being an out-of-state student is more expensive than being a commuter, Patterson moved to Ames and lived there awhile before he registered for school. Frederick Patterson worked many different jobs while putting himself through veterinary school. He worked at a hotel, washing and ironing clothes, cooking, being a janitor, and running a rug cleaning business. Anything to make ends meet. He lived with six other people on the second floor of a business. He was one of very few black students at Iowa State at that time, and for a while, the only black student in the veterinary program. Patterson said in *Chronicles of Faith* that the only time he had problems with discrimination was when he had to go to military camp one summer in college. Part of his schooling was paid for by the Student Army Corps. He spent the summer training with the Army and was a reserve when he finished school in exchange for the Army paying for some school. At this camp students were segregated by race for dinner. He and one other black student ate at a separate table from all the other white students. Dr. Patterson says that after he returned to Iowa State the other students that had also been at the military camp treated him differently than they had before they went, "they treated me as a pariah," said Patterson. "I learned a lesson with regard to race that I never forgot: how people feel about you reflects the way you permit yourself to be treated. If you permit yourself to be treated differently, you are condemned to an unequal relationship."

Frederick graduated with a veterinary medicine degree in 1923. He moved to Columbus, Ohio to live with his brother John. He only stayed a short time in Ohio, but did manage to pass the examination for licensure of veterinarians in that state. It was shortly after that Patterson was offered a job as professor of veterinary medicine and chemistry at Virginia State University in Petersburg, Virginia. Patterson worked for three years teaching at Virginia State and decided he would return to Iowa State for his master's degree. Once he completed his master's, he was promoted to Director of the Agriculture program at Virginia State. After being on the job for only a year, Patterson accepted a job with Tuskegee Institute (now Tuskegee University) in Tuskegee, Alabama. It was a more important place to research and teach Patterson explained in his book.

Patterson taught bacteriology and was head of the Veterinary Department at Tuskegee. In 1932 he took a leave from his job to earn his doctoral degree from Cornell University in Ithaca, New York. After being back a year at Tuskegee, Dr. Patterson was made head of the Agriculture Department there. He only remained on that job for a year before he was named President of Tuskegee. That same year he married Catherine Moton, daughter of Robert Russa Moton, the former President of Tuskegee. Many people at first were not happy with Patterson as President. They thought he had gotten the job because he married Mr. Moton's daughter. Dr. Patterson however managed to quell the talk when he took the school from the brink of bankruptcy and stabilized Tuskegee's money flow within a few years of becoming President.

Among changes at Tuskegee brought about by Frederick Patterson was the new division of domestic service, with a four year program in nutrition and personal services. He also began a program which changed how sharecroppers and poor farmers lived. Wood for houses had become expensive, so with the help of the School of Mechanical Industries, Patterson designed a house of concrete block. The materials for this house could be found on most farms as the concrete was made with the local clay soil and a little concrete. Soon such houses were appearing all over the south. Patterson also started the George Washington Carver Foundation in 1940. This fund was used to encourage and fund scientific research by African Americans.

One of the more well-known feats of Patterson's administration was the start of the black Army Air Corps at Tuskegee. The school initially used a former cow pasture as the runway. Several pilots were recruited and instruction began. This program led to the group of pilots known as the Tuskegee Airmen, well-known for their bravery in World War II. Although Dr. Patterson drew some flack for the program because of the discriminatory policies of the military, the program was a commercial success with extensive training for black pilots in military and commercial fields.

According to *The New York Times,* "Dr. Patterson soon learned that the school's continuing leadership role brought letters from other schools asking for advice on how to raise money. In 1943 he wrote a column in *The Pittsburgh Courier* proposing the creation of a consortium of black colleges that would raise money for their mutual benefit." about one year later in 1944, 27 schools came together to form the United Negro College Fund. The first year the UNCF raised over 750,000 dollars for its member colleges. These days a yearly telethon hosted by entertainer Lou Rawls raises millions for the organization and is its most prominent fundraiser. This act by Dr. Patterson is viewed my many as his most important act during his life. He served as President of the UNCF from 1964-66.

> "I learned a lesson with regard to race that I never forgot: how people feel about you reflects the way you permit yourself to be treated. If you permit yourself to be treated differently, you are condemned to unequal relationship."

In 1953 Frederick Patterson retired from Tuskegee. He became president of the Phelps Stokes Fund. Phelps Stokes was started in 1901 and funds the education of African students as well as African American and Native American students in the United States. Dr. Patterson was president of the fund from 1953-70. It was during this work that he organized the Cooperative College Development Program to assign federal money to pay for the improvement and maintenance of the black college's physical plant.

In 1970 Dr. Patterson left Phelps Stokes to head up the Robert R. Moton Institute. This institute was established to boost the endowments of black colleges. It has served as a stabilizing influence for several schools because of cutbacks in federal funding in the last several years. In 1987 Patterson was awarded the Presidential Medal of Freedom by Ronald Reagan. In 1988 he was awarded the NAACP Spingarn Medal for "his belief that human productivity and well-being in a free society are the end products of determination and self-preparation."

On April 26, 1988, Frederick Douglass Patterson died

in New Rochelle, New York. Donald Stewart former president of the College Board of the National Association of Schools and Colleges called Dr. Frederick Patterson "a visionary and pioneer in American higher education and in Black American higher education," in *The New York Times.* "He broke new ground for minority students and was always looking ahead into the next decade for new ways to finance education." In memory of his many years of service and dedication to his job the UNCF in 1996 announced the founding of the Frederick D. Patterson Research Institute. It will be the first major research center devoted to black educational data and policy.

Sources

Books

Patterson, Frederick D., *Chronicles of Faith: the Autobiography of Frederick Douglass Patterson,* University of Alabama Press, 1991.

Salzman, Jack, David Lionel Smith and Cornel West, eds. *Encyclopedia of African-American Culture and History,* Simon & Schuster, 1996

Periodicals

Current Biography Yearbook, 1947.
Jet, July 27, 1987, p. 22; May 16, 1988, p. 8
Newsday (Long Island, NY), April 28, 1988, p. 49.
The New York Times, April 27, 1988, p. B8.

Other

Frederick D. Patterson Research Institute, Press Release, February 22, 1996.

—Stephen Stratton

Dennis Rodman

1961—

Professional basketball player

Dennis Rodman is one of the greatest rebounders ever to play professional basketball. Superbly conditioned and a dedicated analyst of the game, Rodman has led the National Basketball Association (NBA) in rebounding for four consecutive years. His rebounding exploits have drawn comparisons with such legends as Wilt Chamberlain, Moses Malone, and Bill Russell, all of whom were taller and heavier. In recent years the eccentric Rodman has achieved fame as much for his off-court antics as for his playing skills. His rainbow-colored hair and multiple tattoos, penchant for conducting interviews in gay bars, and brief romantic interlude with the singer Madonna landed him in headlines far outside the sports pages.

Rodman revels in the outsider image. The hair, the tattoos, the numerous body piercings, and the episodes of cross-dressing are all the product of a man who is as much entertainer as athlete. "I tried something bold," Rodman explained in *Playboy*. "I created something that everyone has been afraid of ... the Dennis Rodman I was born to be." However flamboyant his behavior might be, the Chicago Bulls forward offers no apologies. He feels that he is fulfilling his mission in the NBA as well-

-or better--than anyone. "I don't like people to get inside Dennis Rodman," he admitted in the *Atlanta Journal*. "But once I get on the court, I'm just taking the 22,000 fans that are in the stands and putting them inside me. I like to see people excited and happy, and when they leave the arena they say, `God, that was a great game.'"

Not a Conventional Athlete

No one is more surprised by Rodman's success than Rodman himself. "I'm something I shouldn't have been," he told the *St. Louis Post-Dispatch*. "I should be an average Joe Blow, nine to five." Rodman says this because as a child he was frail and shy, often taking the brunt of beatings by his bigger, more aggressive schoolmates. He was born in New Jersey in 1961, the son of Philander and Shirley Rodman. When he was just three years old, his father--an Air Force enlistee--deserted the family, leaving Dennis and his two younger sisters without a father figure. Despite his success in the NBA, Rodman has not seen his father in 25 years.

Rodman was only five-foot-eleven during high school.

At a Glance...

Full name, Dennis Keith Rodman; Born May 13, 1961, in Trenton, NJ; son of Philander and Shirley Rodman; married Annie Bakes (a model), 1993 (divorced); children: Alexis. *Education:* Attended Cooke County Junior College, 1982-83, and Southeastern Oklahoma State University, 1983-86.

Professional basketball player, 1986--. Selected by Detroit Pistons in second round (27th pick overall) of 1986 National Basketball Association (NBA) draft; member of Pistons, 1986-93; traded to San Antonio Spurs, 1993; member of Spurs, 1993-95; traded to Chicago Bulls, 1995; member of Bulls, 1995--.

Selected awards: Named NBA defensive player of the year, 1990 and 1991; made NBA All-Star team, 1990 and 1992; IBM Award for all-around contributions to team's success, 1992; named to NBA All-Defensive first team, 1989, 1990, 1991, 1992, 1993, 1995.

Addresses: *Office*—Chicago Bulls, 1901 W. Madison St, Chicago, IL 60612-2459.

He did not even make the varsity basketball team at the Dallas, Texas high school he attended. After graduating from high school he drifted through a series of jobs, including serving as a janitor at the Dallas-Fort Worth Airport. According to Mark Seal in *Playboy,* the part-time airport job led Rodman into trouble: "On a dare, he stuck his broom handle through a gift shop grate and stole 15 watches. He was arrested, jailed for a night and released after he told the cops where the watches were." No charges were ever filed in the incident, but it added to the growing strain between Rodman and his mother.

Shortly after the incident with the watches, Rodman's mother issued him an ultimatum: he was to go to college, enlist in the armed services, or get another job. Rodman ignored her. Exasperated, she packed his bags and kicked him out. Their relationship has been cordial but distant ever since. "I'll just say this," Rodman told the *St. Louis Post-Dispatch.* "It left a hole in my life I can't fill up."

Rescue came in the form of a phenomenal growth spurt. Rodman grew almost a foot in a single year, topping out at six-foot-eight. After a year at Cooke County Junior

College in Dallas, he won a basketball scholarship to Southeastern Oklahoma State University. He arrived there, shy and uncertain about his skills, in 1983.

At a basketball camp that Rodman helped to coach, he met a young boy named Bryne Rich. Bryne was suffering deeply from the consequences of an accident that had occurred while he was hunting--his gun had discharged while he was reloading, killing his best friend. Rodman helped Bryne talk through his pain, and in return Bryne introduced Rodman to the Rich family, who practically adopted the soft-spoken college player. Rodman moved in with the Rich family, who offered emotional support and encouragement as his basketball career caught fire.

"Bad Boy" with the Pistons

As a college junior and senior Rodman led the National Association of Intercollegiate Athletics (NAIA) in rebounding, with 16.1 per game in 1985 and 17.8 in 1986. He was named an All-American as a senior and was chosen in the second round of the 1986 NBA draft by the Detroit Pistons. Rodman joined the Pistons for the 1986-87 season as a forward, finding a congenial atmosphere with coach Chuck Daly and a no-holds-barred group of fellow players who would come to be known as the "Bad Boys." A brief marriage during the period to model Annie Bakes ended in divorce after only 82 days, but it produced Rodman's only child to date, a daughter named Alexis. Bakes's only lasting influence on Rodman's life was her influence toward getting tattoos--Rodman has since covered much of his body with them.

Professionally, Rodman became a force to be reckoned with. The Pistons won back-to-back national championships in 1989 and 1990, taking their "Bad Boy" image to a worldwide audience. Rodman established himself as a solid rebounder and important defensive cog in the Pistons lineup, earning NBA Defensive Player of the Year honors in both 1990 and 1991. He had a good relationship with his teammates and coach Daly, and by all reports he was infuriated when some of his friends got traded and Daly left the team. "Dennis kind of grew up with us," Daly explained in *USA Today.* "The Pistons were Dennis's first professional family, and he really liked what the team stood for…. It was a family to him, and when it disintegrated around him, it was tough for him to deal with."

It was during this time that Rodman developed his philosophy on the NBA--that professional basketball exploits its players, forcing them to play more for money than for a sense of team, and expecting them to adhere to a squeaky-clean image at odds with the demands of the game. Asked why he had become so uncommunicative with his coaches and fellow players in the *St. Louis Post-Dispatch,* Rodman had a simple answer: "This business is rotten."

About That Hair ...

In 1993 Rodman signed a three-year contract with the San Antonio Spurs, bringing him home to Texas. There he helped the Spurs to advance to the playoffs by leading the league in rebounding in 1993, 1994, and 1995 (he had been top rebounder with the Pistons in 1992 as well). It was also in San Antonio that Rodman began coloring his hair the many shades that have made him a star beyond the bounds of basketball. Rodman put himself in the hands of hairdresser David Chapa, who created the classic Rodman look by first applying peroxide until the player's hair turned white, then coloring it with bright hair color in shades of Rodman's choosing. On occasion Rodman and Chapa have even collaborated on designs that are colored onto the crown of Rodman's head. The process takes up to three hours and can be painful. It also carries the threat of future baldness. Rodman has suggested that if his hair falls out, he will just tattoo his head.

> "I like to see people excited happy, and when they leave the arena they say, 'God that was a great game.'"

With the Spurs Rodman established himself as a rebounding specialist on a par with the likes of Russell and Chamberlain--both of whom were centers, far taller and heavier than Rodman. In fact, at six-foot-eight and 215 pounds, Rodman is definitely short and slight for his specialty. "I'm surprised that I can even get to the ball compared to most guys who are 6-10 and 7 feet tall," he told the *Chicago Tribune.* "Especially when I've got guys grabbing me and holding me and doing all kinds of things to keep me away from the ball. They don't even know me well enough to be doing some of the things they do." Rodman has compensated for his relative lack of stature by analyzing the behavior of the basketball as it arches toward the hoop and then caroms off in various directions. He can often anticipate how a ball will behave when it fails to fall through the basket--and he responds accordingly. "People think I just go get the damn ball,

because they don't take the time to really look at what I do," he said in *Sports Illustrated.* "Rebounding isn't brain surgery, but there's more to it than being able to jump higher than the next guy. A lot of work is done before you ever even jump."

It was during his tenure with the Spurs that Rodman met singer-actress Madonna on a photo shoot. They began a highly-publicized courtship that added spice to the tabloids for months. While Rodman has refused to comment on the relationship, his Spurs teammate Jack Haley--one of his few close friends--has said that Madonna was very serious about Rodman. "I went out with Dennis and Madonna several times," Haley told the *Detroit News.* "It's not rumor. It's true. I was there. She was dead serious. She wanted Dennis Rodman to marry her. She asked Dennis several times to marry her. I was there, I heard it with my own ears. She wanted to have a baby." Haley added that Rodman was more cautious and unwilling to enter into a serious commitment after such a short courtship. After several months, the pair split up.

Joining the Bulls

When the Spurs failed to make the championship finals in the 1994-95 season, Rodman's image as a nonconformist became an issue. During contract renegotiations, Rodman was traded to the Chicago Bulls--a move that he welcomed, since the Bulls are a perennially talented team. "My sole aim ... will be to help bring the NBA championship back home to Chicago," he told the Associated Press. Rodman appeared at Bulls games with green hair, red hair surrounding a black Bulls emblem, and canary yellow hair. He continued improving as a rebounder, learning the shooting styles of Michael Jordan and Scottie Pippen so he could better react to their missed shots--and he enhanced his image as an eccentric wild man by drawing a two-week suspension after an altercation with a referee. The suspension may destroy his chances of taking a fifth consecutive rebounding crown.

Rodman admits that he is high-strung and that he does not care to build personal relationships with his coaches or teammates. He is also well aware of the entertainment value offered by his outlandish persona. "Show business is what I do on the court," he told *Playboy.* "So that'll be my next career." Rodman added that he relishes the idea of playing a villain in an action-adventure movie. In the meantime, he continues to bring a certain exotic flair to the NBA, defying the squeaky-clean image-makers with every tattoo and hair dye he can muster. "I feel great," he told the *St. Louis Post-Dispatch.* "I can't love life any more. I'm a free, wild, exotic animal loving life, such as it is in the confines of the rules and laws of the universe."

Sources

Books

Steinberg, Alan, *Rebound: The Dennis Rodman Story,* Crown Publishers, 1995.

The Sporting News Official NBA Register: The NBA from A to Z, 1995-96 edition, *The Sporting News,* 1995, p. 188.

Periodicals

Associated Press, March 19, 1996.

Atlanta Journal and Constitution, February 22, 1996, p. sports 1.

Chicago Sun-Times, October 4, 1995, p. 122.

Chicago Tribune, February 29, 1996, p. 1.

Detroit News, May 18, 1995, p. D1.

Philadelphia Daily News, January 11, 1996, p. S6.

Playboy, January 1996, p. 98.

St. Louis Post-Dispatch, March 12, 1995, p. F3.

Sports Illustrated, March 4, 1996, p. 30.

USA Today, May 26, 1995, p. A1.

—Mark Kram

Al Roker

1954(?)—

Television meteorologist

Al Roker may describe himself as "goofy-looking" and "nothing special," but his combination of accurate forecasting and warm, relaxed delivery have won him possibly the most visible weather anchor position on television. Roker is the weekday weatherman for the National Broadcasting Company's *Today* show, a morning news-and-information program watched by millions and millions of Americans. Roker inherited his position on *Today* from the equally affable Willard Scott in 1995, adding a new laurel to a two-decade career in the television weather forecasting business. He is also host of his own cable channel weekend talk show, *The Al Roker Show.* Success has done little to alter Roker's working methods—or his opinion of himself. "We know weather is one of the main reasons people tune in to the news," he said in the *New York Times.* "So I try to do my best to be accurate. Then I hope for the best."

Roker comes from a blue-collar background where his hard-working parents stressed education and achievement. His father, Albert Lincoln Roker, was a bus driver who also served as a labor relations negotiator for New York City's Transit Authority. His mother was a home-

maker who raised the six Roker children in a home in the St. Albans section of Queens, New York. Al Jr., the oldest in the family, graduated from Manhattan's Xavier High School, where he spent four years developing his comic skills and indulging his interests in graphic art.

College Courses Lead to a Job

The cost of tuition at a private college was out of reach for the Roker family, so Al attended the State University of New York at Oswego. There he majored in graphic communications, but he took classes in meteorology to satisfy the university's science requirements. Roker found he had a talent for meteorology, and his interest in the science grew as his studies progressed. While still a sophomore in college, he landed a part-time job as weekend weather forecaster at nearby WTVH-TV in Syracuse. By the time he earned his bachelor's degree in 1976, he had been promoted to weekday weatherman at the station.

Roker did not earn a degree in meteorology, but few television weather forecasters do. In fact, his background contains more science than that of many of his

At a Glance...

Full name Albert Lincoln Roker Jr; born ca. 1954 in New York, NY; son of Albert Lincoln (a bus driver and union negotiator); married third wife, Deborah Roberts (a television journalist), September 16, 1995; children: (second marriage) Courtney (daughter). *Education:* State University of New York at Oswego, B.A., 1976.

WTVH-TV, Syracuse, NY, weekend weather anchor, 1974-75, weekly weather anchor, 1975-76; WTTG-TV, Washington, DC, weather anchor, 1976-78; WKYC-TV, Cleveland, OH, weather anchor, 1978-83; WNBC-TV, New York City, 1983-, began as weekend weather anchor, worked as local weekly weathercaster, currently weather anchor for *Today* show; CNBC-TV, New York City, host of weekend talk show *The Al Roker Show*, 1995-.

Selected awards: Recipient of two Emmy Awards for weather forecasting; twice named Best Weatherman by *New York* magazine; holder of American Meteorological Society's Seal of Approval.

Addresses: *Office*—NBC-TV, 30 Rockefeller Plaza, New York, NY 10112.

colleagues, and he became known for writing his own forecasts and using NBC's radar—rather than the National Weather Service—to keep him up-to-date on local and national weather.

Soon after graduating from college, Roker took a job as weatherman for WTTG-TV in Washington, DC. WTTG is a local independent station, and while there the young Roker had ample opportunity to study other weather anchors' techniques. One local hero Roker studied was the chubby and avuncular Willard Scott, who was then forecasting weather at the NBC affiliate in the nation's capital. Today Roker credits Scott with teaching him the secret to a long career on the air. "I used to be crazy, do all kinds of gimmicky things," Roker admitted in the *New York Times.* "Willard took me aside one day and said, 'Just be yourself. It'll last a lot longer.'"

The Nation's Weatherman

From WTTG Roker moved on to WKYC-TV in Cleve-

land, Ohio. The job in the Midwest was Roker's first with an NBC affiliate, and—as an avid weather-watcher—he admits that he misses the assignment in Cleveland. After five years at WKYC, Roker moved on in 1983 to WNBC-TV in New York City. His parents, who were still living in Queens, were thrilled to welcome him home.

> "We know weather is one of the main reasons people tune in to the news."

Roker's first position with WNBC was weekend weather anchor. By 1985 he had worked his way up to weekly weather forecaster, earning *New York* magazine's "Best Weatherman" award. Roker had the same easygoing, ordinary-guy delivery that characterizes his weather spots now, but he also exhibited a keen understanding of meteorology on both a local and national level. He seemed at ease urging New Yorkers to play hooky from work on sunny spring days, and deeply committed and serious when tracking Atlantic hurricanes and other dangerous weather. With an 80 percent accuracy rate, he quickly earned the American Meteorological Society's prestigious Seal of Approval.

Asked in a 1987 *New York* magazine profile if he would like to replace Willard Scott on the *Today* show at some point, Roker disclaimed any ambitions. "Willard is my idol. The idea of stepping into his shoes terrifies me," he said. Over the next decade, Roker had ample opportunity to shed his fears and prepare to be Scott's replacement. In addition to his duties with the weekly local NBC newscast, he became weatherman for the weekend edition of *Today* and a substitute for Scott on weekdays. By the time Scott retired in 1995, Roker had firmly established himself as the heir apparent.

An Ordinary Guy

A yo-yo dieter with thick glasses who stands about five-feet-eight, Roker thinks a great deal of his appeal lies in his "ordinary Joe" persona. "It's part of my stock in trade," he explained in the *New York Times.* "People look at me and feel superior." Whatever the secret of his success, Roker has achieved what many would consider the pinnacle of television weather forecasting success as the national weather correspondent for the highly-rated *Today* show. Unlike his predecessor, however, Roker has not just settled into the staff of *Today* with no further ambitions. Late in 1995 he inaugurated *The Al Roker Show,* a weekend talk show run on the cable channel CNBC. He also served as narrator for a Public Broadcasting System documentary on weather entitled *Savage Skies.*

Roker's fans are many and diverse. *Entertainment Weekly* once dubbed him a "Cool Ordinary Guy." MTV did a feature on him called *What It's Like To Be Al.* And everyone from New York's mayor Rudolph Giuliani to reporter Barbara Walters turned up at his 1995 wedding to television journalist Deborah Roberts. Roker, who lives in New York, seems truly content with his celebrity status and his high-profile job at NBC. "Our problem is that sometimes we have too much fun," he said of himself and his *Today* co-hosts in the *New York Times.* "We forget we're on television."

Sources

Entertainment Weekly, February 11, 1994, p. 42.
New York, August 17, 1987, p. 20.
New York Times, September 2, 1992, pp. C1, C10.
People, January 23, 1995, p. 73; October 2, 1995, p. 72.

Additional information supplied by NBC News, Inc.

—Anne Janette Johnson

Patrice Rushen

1954—

Musician, composer, vocalist, arranger

Black Radio Exclusive dubbed Patrice Rushen "one of the most talented songwriters in black music." She has garnered similar plaudits for her work as a session musician, producer, arranger, film composer, and musical director for a bevy of awards shows and other ceremonies; her prodigious skills have earned her the nickname "Ms. All That." A musical marvel at a young age, she became a recording star in the 1970s and 1980s with a series of albums that mixed jazz, soul, and funk. After a disappointing period, she switched her emphasis to session playing and composition for both the large and small screens. Even so, she has never lost her enthusiasm for the recording process. "I love making records," she told *Mix* magazine's Robin Tolleson. "I could go in the studio anytime with anybody any day and have a great time." Despite her success behind the recording console, however, she ultimately returned to her own work.

She was born in Los Angeles in the early 1950s, and displayed an aptitude for music early on. "I was enrolled in a special program at USC [University of Southern California] when I was three," she informed Lorenz Rychner of *Home & Studio Recording* magazine.

There she undertook an intensive regimen of music training and began piano lessons by the time she was five. She continued studying, but despite her obvious talents harbored no dreams of studying at a conservatory. "In high school, when I already had been playing for some eight years," she told Rychner, "I realized that I didn't have the desire or discipline to become a concert pianist. All during junior high and high school I was the one who could beat out the tunes of the day on the piano, by ear, which was my way to have fun and be popular." She was still in high school when she began doing paid session work, which helped pay for her college education. 1972 saw her winning a competition at the Monterey Jazz Festival, which helped earn her a recording contract with the Prestige label.

From Jazz Phenom to Pop Star

When the time came, USC was the obvious choice for Rushen's higher education, and she took a double major there in music education and piano performance. She released her first record for Prestige, *Preclusion,* when she was a mere 19 years old; her Prestige recordings--

At a Glance...

Born September 30, 1954, Los Angeles, CA. *Education:* University of Southern California, bachelor's degree in music education and piano performance, 1976.

Keyboardist, songwriter, producer, arranger, c. 1970s—. Won competition at Monterey Jazz Festival, 1972; signed with Prestige Records and released debut *Preclusion,* 1973; signed with Elektra Records and released *Patrice,* 1978; teacher of music at USC summer sessions and instructor at Yamaha Music Clinics in USA and Japan, c. 1980s; signed with Arista and released *Watch Out!,* 1986; musical director of *NAACP Image Awards Special,* 1989, 1990, and 1991, and of Emmy Awards broadcasts, 1991 and 1992; co-founder of group the Meeting, c. 1990s; musical director and composer, *Comic Relief V Benefit Concert* program, 1992; musical director, *People's Choice Awards,* 1993; signed with Hollywood Records, recording *Anything But Ordinary,* c. 1993; released album through Sin-Drome label, 1994; produced and arranged material for film *Indecent Material,* 1994; produced album *No Strings* for singer Sheena Easton, 1994; musical director for Janet Jackson's *janet.* tour, 1994; has composed scores for numerous television programs, including *The Women of Brewster Place, Robert Townsend and His Partners in Crime, Story of a People,* and *Jack's Place,* and for films *Hollywood Shuffle* and *Without You I'm Nothing;* recorded with numerous artists, including Prince, Jean-Luc Ponty, the Temptations, Lee Ritenour, Eddie Murphy, Vanessa Williams, Kenny Burrell, Wayne Shorter, and Sheena Easton.

Awards: Grammy Award nominations, best R&B vocal performance, for "Forget-Me-Nots" and best R&B instrumental for "Number One," 1982; ASCAP Songwriter's Award, 1988; Legacy of Excellence Award, USC Black Student Assembly, 1992; Crystal Award, American Women in Film, 1994.

Addresses: *Home*—Los Angeles, CA. *Record Company*—Sin-Drome Records, 21520 Strathern, Canoga Park, CA 91304. *Publicist*—Shelley Jeffrey & Associates, 433 N. Camden Drive. 6th Floor, Beverly Hills, CA 90210.

Stanley Turrentine, electric violin virtuoso Jean-Luc Ponty, and such leading jazz guitarists as John McLaughlin and Lee Ritenour.

After leaving Prestige for the Elektra label, Rushen began pursuing the R&B side of her sound and developing her chops as a singer-songwriter. While on Elektra, as Tolleson of *Mix* observed, "her style continued to streamline into a pop-funk groove." Such streamlining led to resounding commercial success; among her hits were the singles "When I Found You," "Haven't You Heard," "Never Gonna Give You Up," "Number One," and "Forget-Me-Nots." The latter two tracks earned Grammy nominations for Best R&B Instrumental Performance and Best R&B Vocal Performance, respectively. She continued to do session work for a wide range of artists, including rock guitarist Carlos Santana and legendary soul vocal group the Temptations.

Thwarted by "Business Aspect"

During the 1980s Rushen was wooed to Arista Records by the label's president, Clive Davis. The only fruit of this deal was the 1986 release *Watch Out!,* which yielded a number of successful singles but did not temper her growing disillusionment with the record industry. "The business aspect of things gradually led to a situation where for me, some of the fun was taken out of making albums," she explained in *Keyboard* magazine. "Before you even set foot in the studio, there's a committee that's concerned about what you're gonna do and how you're gonna do it. You're always proving yourself, and that's okay. But at some point you hope that a track record like I have, which means at the very least that I know how to make records, would count for something."

Pop performers who depended on the good graces of the industry for their survival might have capitulated to the process, but Rushen's versatility and outstanding reputation as both player and composer stood her in good stead. Rather than defer to recording-by-committee, she proceeded to change direction, continuing her session playing and branching out into arranging, film scoring, production, music direction, and teaching. Rushen first served as Musical Director for the *NAACP Image Awards Special* in 1989, and continued in that capacity for the next two broadcasts. She took the same role for the 1991 and 1992 Emmy Awards. "People aren't aware of the demands and the artistic and commercial elements that go into those shows," she commented in *Mix.* "If somebody's in there that doesn't know what they're doing, it doesn't happen."

Showed Range as Composer, Producer, Arranger

Rushen's talents as a composer soon made her a name

with the exception of the more R&B-flavored outtakes collection *Let There Be Funk*--predominantly featured earthy instrumental jazz. She also continued doing session work, albeit for an increasingly prestigious circle of musicians that included saxophonists Sonny Rollins and to be reckoned with in the television world, where she scored the series *Brewster Place, Jack's Place,* and *Story of a People,* and comedian Robert Townsend's series of comedy specials for HBO. She also branched out into film composing, providing music for *Townsend's Hollywood Shuffle* and Sandra Bernhard's one-woman feature *Without You I'm Nothing.* And though she also served as music director, conductor, and/or arranger on several other projects, Rushen also found time to conduct music clinics for Yamaha in the United States and Japan. As she told *Home & Studio Recording,* "there are so many young people who don't know where to take their talents to, and I like being in a position to give them some guidance. I have the advantage of a broad musical background to share, from pianist to synthesist to other activities."

She started a production company, Baby Fingers productions, with her partner Charles Mims Jr., and co-founded the jazz-fusion "supergroup" the Meeting, which released its debut in 1991. She took on further challenges by accepting the post of musical director for Janet Jackson's *janet.* tour. Rushen's reputation as a producer, meanwhile, was assured by her collaboration with singer Sheena Easton. The pop diva was given a last-minute assignment to perform a jazz standard onscreen for the film *Indecent Proposal* and phoned Rushen for help. "It was kind of a happy accident," Rushen noted in *Mix,* adding that she brought the singer and a small acoustic combo into the studio and laid the track down live. "She was there. Hit it ... boom! Her record company was knocked out, because they hadn't heard her do this type of thing. And I think she kind of surprised herself, like, 'I can do this!'"

"Three Hats" and More Headaches

The label was so enthusiastic, in fact, that Easton and Rushen were sent back into the studio to do more. "So we said, 'let's hurry up and do it before they change their minds,'" Rushen recalled. Four more demos got them the green light to do an entire album of standards. The company's "only stipulation was they didn't want to spend a lot of money, so no strings. So there was the title of the album." Working on *No Strings* was especially challenging, she added, because "I wore three hats on the session. I don't know if I'd like to do that again soon. Since I was producer, the whole shootin' match became my responsibility. I was also the arranger, thinking of the sound of things and working with [Easton]. And then I played piano also." She praised the enthusiasm and skill of the other musicians, who helped "create an environment where Sheena would feel supported, since it was something new and different for her, and where I would

feel supported because of the level of responsibility that I had in trying to help it happen." Rushen helped Easton take the material on the road in 1994, serving as musical director. The tour began in Canada with shows featuring the Calgary Philharmonic Orchestra; this time, strings were included.

Rushen's solo career continued to suffer, however, even after she signed with Hollywood Records in 1993. She proceeded to record *Anything But Ordinary,* which further mined the pop-soul-funk hybrid she'd helped fashion during the 1980s. Unfortunately, the label was unimpressed and decided not to release the album. "I handed in the tapes, and these people said 'But we wanted a Patrice Rushen record,'" she recalled in *Keyboard.* "I'm like, 'Well, what are you talking about? What do you want me to do to change it? What can I do to make my record more me?' All they can do is give me the blank look because Patrice Rushen, to them, is just a buzzword. And I'm like, 'Great! I must have a hit on my hands, because the last time somebody at a label said, 'We don't like it,' they were talking about 'Forget-Me-Nots,' the biggest record of my career." Ultimately, Rushen hooked up with the jazz and fusion label Sin-Drome, which released it in 1994. *Cash Box* called it "shameful that this woman has not had a solo contract for so many years."

The musician-composer's recording savvy derives in part from a great deal of experimentation in her home studio. She described her "two setups" in *Home & Studio Recording*: "One is totally acoustic, not a microphone or anything electronic in sight; it's my living room, with a hardwood floor and a grand piano, period. Then there is the MIDI studio, which is like a lab for me. I own Otari 8-track [recording] equipment, but I'm wired for 24 tracks, and now and then we bring in gear to do a real project right there." Because of the options offered by technology, producers--especially in R&B--have taken advantage of their ability to piece together entire recordings by themselves, from rhythm programming to synthesized horns and strings. While Rushen, too, has shown a fondness for such machinery, she admitted that "as a studio musician, I miss the camaraderie of musicians playing together, and the things that come out of that--things that the arranger can't predetermine."

Rushen continued working on a number of fronts, performing sporadically with some of the biggest names in jazz, recording a new album with the Meeting and performing with another group, One + 1, and contributing keyboard work to the soundtrack album for the hit film *Waiting to Exhale.* She also derived satisfaction that a wide range of artists, including Mary J. Blige, R. Kelly, and Shabba Ranks, had begun to sample her records. "It's flattering, because they know what's good," she insisted in *Black Radio Exclusive,* "even if some label executives don't."

> "At some point you hope that a track record like I have, which means at the very least that I know how to make records, would count for something."

Despite her many commitments as producer and music director, Rushen noted in the *Los Angeles Times,* "I love to play, I have to play. So even if I'm playing less in the clubs, I get together with musicians and play. I make time because it's fun and I want to stay sharp so that if someone calls, I'm ready." And despite the ups and downs of the music business, she has maintained her focus. As she told *Mix,* "the biggest thrill for me is the process. So as long as I'm able to be viable and active and doing what I love, which is the process of making music and the playing, then I'll feel okay."

Selected discography

Preclusion, Prestige, 1973.
Before the Dawn, Prestige, 1974.
Shout It Out, Prestige, 1975.
Let There Be Funk, Prestige, 1976.
Patrice (includes "When I Found You"), Elektra, 1978.

Pizzazz (includes "Haven't You Heard"), Elektra, 1979.
Posh (includes "Never Gonna Give You Up"), Elektra, 1980.
Straight from the Heart (includes "Number One" and "Forget- Me-Nots"), Elektra, 1982.
Now, Elektra, 1984.
Watch Out!, Arista, 1986.
Anything But Ordinary, Sin-Drome, 1994.

with the Meeting

The Meeting, 1991.
Update, Hip Bop, 1995.

Also appeared on albums by other artists, including Prince, the Temptations, Sonny Rollins, Wayne Shorter, Carlos Santana, and Sheena Easton.

Sources

Black Radio Exclusive, July 15, 1994; October 21, 1994.
Calgary Sun, May 6, 1994, p. S5.
Cash Box, November 19, 1994.
Entertainment Weekly, December 1, 1995, p.73.
Home & Studio Recording, January 1994, pp. 25-29.
Keyboard, February 1994.
Los Angeles Times (Calendar), January 28, 1994, p. 11.
Mix, June 1994.
Pulse!, October 1995.

Additional information was provided by Sin-Drome publicity materials and the Internet All-Music Guide.

—Simon Glickman

Synthia Saint James

1949—

Author, book illustrator, entrepreneur

The work of self-taught artist Synthia Saint James can not be mistaken for anyone else's. Every painting she creates carries her unmistakeable trademark of brilliant color and lithe body language, and each one spotlights a happy moment captured for her viewers to enjoy. Because she follows her own technical rules she feels free to set her own worthy goal: Synthia Saint James likes to make her viewers feel good.

Saint James chooses to celebrate life--a personal philosophy that could make her art seem superficial if we viewed it on only one level. But gives us many levels to enjoy. Some are the cultural gift of her rich African-American-Cherokee-Haitian heritage. Others come from the different corners of the world to which Saint James has traveled. Yet even this is not all she has to say. She also wants to gather all of us together into one big bouquet of humanity, which she ties together with a vital message: our ancestry may differ but we are all equally valuable.

Despite her intense focus on art there is nothing of the disorderly, otherworldly painter about Synthia Saint James. An eminently practical woman, she is wise enough to protect her own financial security. While learning her craft, she supported herself with all kinds of work, and while she was at it, took care to learn something from everything she undertook. These days, though, no such distractions are necessary, thanks to commissions from such clients as the House of Seagram, Maybelline-Kayser, and *Essence* magazine. Add the beautiful children's books she has written and illustrated, the cards she has created for UNICEF, and the selection of prints that are both sold by her own company and licensed for reproduction on items of clothing, gift bags and decorative items, and it's obvious that she has a comfortable income. Saint James's assorted ventures have made her an international celebrity with little spare time, but thanks to experience in both the legal and the tax fields, she finds time to write all her own contracts. In her own way, she's a living example—the epitome of the American dream.

Quick on the Draw

Synthia Saint James grew up in a blended family of 11 children, four of whom looked upon drawing and paint-

At a Glance...

Born February 11, 1949, in Los Angeles, CA; *Education:* Attended Los Angeles Valley College; Dutchess Community College, Poughkeepsie, New York; Inner City Cultural Center, Los Angeles, CA; and H & R Block, Los Angeles, CA, (certified tax practitioner).

First commissioned paintings, 1969, New York; first one-woman show, 1977, Inner City Cultural Center, New York; Group Exhibition, Paris, France, Musee des Duncans, 1980; House of Seagram commission for Black History Month, 1989; designed cover art for Terry McMillan's *Waiting to Exhale,* international edition, 1992.

Awards: Prix de Paris, 1980; Gentlemen Concerned (An AIDS Foundation) Service Award, 1995; UNICEF Greeting Card Artist Award, 1995.

Addresses: Atelier Saint James, P.O. Box 27683, Los Angeles, CA 90027.

ing as a way of life. All this talent came from her father, William, who had harbored dreams of becoming a professional artist before the responsibilities of marriage and fatherhood led him to steadier ways of earning a living. But he never stopped painting, turning out series after series of pictures in his favorite 4-inch-by 5-inch size.

While a career in art might seem a natural choice for someone from a family like Synthia's, it did not immediately present itself to her as a logical choice. Mother Hattie had taught her the vital importance of financial independence, and Synthia saw no indication that painting could provide it. So instead, she chose to follow this sensible advice and keep her art as a hobby while working at a more lucrative occupation.

Saint James stuck resolutely to this decision after she left Los Angeles at age 18 and went to live in New York City. A succession of jobs helped her to pay her bills and allowed her the after-hours freedom to plunge into art. She experimented with great enthusiasm, creating abstracts and geometrical figures of different types, and applying her colors with sponges of several sizes as well as with brushes. She soon had enough paintings to decorate her apartment, which was much admired by

her coworkers. Before one year was up she had even managed to sell a piece of her work. This modest success proved a turning point. Now she knew that art would be the center of her world forever.

Saint James was 23 when she went back to Los Angeles. There she met a self-taught artist called Richard Jennings, who was happy to pass on some of his vast experience to anyone as meticulous and eager to learn as this young woman was. For her part, she marvelled at his artistic genius. "When he paints a navel," she told *American Visions* magazine in 1992, "you can stick your finger in it!"

Jennings taught her to focus her attention on her art, whether or not she was supporting herself by doing other jobs. By turns she became a biographer, a law firm accountant, and even an actress, but her focus on art did not waver. In time she was able to strengthen her technique and lay the foundation of her creative philosophy. No longer content to stick to the purely abstract, she began to blend elements of both realism and impressionism in a style that seemed ideally suited for animal subjects. Koala bears, lions, and monkeys began to spring to life under her skilful brush.

Success Began in the 1970s

It was not too long before all Saint James's hard work began to pay off. In 1977, she had her first one-woman show. This was an exciting measure of success, but not nearly as thrilling as the joyous experience of winning the prestigious Prix de Paris in 1980. Then, as if even this accolade was not enough, she was invited to exhibit her animal paintings in a prominent Parisian gallery coowned by a niece of dancer Isadora Duncan.

Saint James was now an internationally recognized painter, but she was not content simply to keep to the style that had made her art so highly prized. In the early 1980s, she began to create works in the trademark style that now make her paintings instantly identifiable. She used clear reds, glowing greens, bright blues, and deep yellows—colors that still make her feel good. She used groups of geometric figures that often seemed on the verge of dancing, talking, or swaying towards each other. And, in contrast to the detailed and rather fierce eyes of her painted animals, she used no facial features. "I thought it would be interesting to illustrate character and emotion without eyes and faces, by simply using color blocks and body angles," Saint James explained, in a 1996 interview with *Upscale* magazine.

A Rising Star

Saint James's developing originality was developed further by a 1984 trip to the island of Martinique. By no means her first vacation abroad, she had been to Guyana in the days before it gained its unfortunate association with the 1979 Jim Jones tragedy; and she had also traveled to Barbados. But somehow in the Martinique markets and streets, Saint James found a new magic. And as always, she wanted her viewers to enjoy the vivid colors, the unfamiliar language, and the exotic clothes that had so enchanted her there.

Saint James's fascination with body language as an expression of cultural individuality found another living example some time afterwards, when she visited colorful Tortola in the British Virgin Islands. "People of different cultures walk differently from each other," she observed, after standing in the street one Sunday and watching people streaming out of church. "Someone from Tibet, wearing all those clothes, does not walk like someone from, say, Thailand, whose clothes and culture are dissimilar."

While travel made an intense impression on Synthia Saint James, she derived just as much stimulation from literature and from poetry. In 1989, she read Alice Walker's *The Temple of My Familiar,* which she admired so much that she felt inspired to paint her, dreadlocks and all, in a setting typical of the Ndebele women of South Africa. It was an unusual work representing Saint James's intense interest in all peoples of African descent, and its featured backdrop was singularly appropriate for the prominently feminist Walker, since the artistic Ndebele women have been highly respected feminists for generations.

Walker was enchanted with the photograph. "She had her assistant find me, and she asked whether the picture could be used for a special trilogy edition of her novels, to be published in 1990, by the Book of the Month Club" Saint James noted later. This book cover proved to be the first of a list that, in time, would reach 40 and still be soaring upward.

Saint James's second such venture started with "Ensemble," a 1988 painting of four black women that promptly became one of her best-known works. In one of those serendipitous events that later prove to be pivotal to success, a copy of the print was snapped up in an art gallery by novelist Terry McMillan, who thought it so appropriate as a cover of her novel *Waiting to Exhale* that she contacted Saint James and introduced her to her own publisher's art director. Still one of Saint James's best-beloved works, "Ensemble" has also made an appearance in several other places, including television shows hosted by Arsenio Hall and Oprah Winfrey.

Fresh Fields to Conquer

If ever Saint James could claim 12 months as The Year of the Children's Book, 1994 was it. The idea of illustrating children's books came to her from one of the art directors involved with *Waiting to Exhale,* and, never one to resist a challenge, Saint James lost no time in picking up on it. By the end of the year she had three picture books to her credit. The first, *Tukama Tootles the Flute,* was a folktale from the Antilles retold by Phillis Gershator. It tells the story of Tukama, a "very wild" boy who ducks out on his chores to play his flute on the seashore, despite his grandmother's dire warnings of a two-headed cannibalistic giant on the lookout for small, succulent small boys. The book deals with a universally familiar theme, and Saint James's innovative illustrations cleverly offset her usual featureless faces against a sea painted in such detail that it seems to be heaving under the sun.

However, though it has always been popular for reading aloud, *Tukama* was received with guarded enthusiasm at best. Possibly the unique style of the pictures was too unusual for the young children who were its targeted audience. Perhaps it was the subject-matter, two-headed giants being deemed too scary for young readers. But almost certainly, in these times of drive-by shootings and senseless kidnappings, *Tukama* failed because it twangs too loudly at every parent's nightmare about the child who runs away from adult supervision and gets himself into a desperately dangerous situation.

Saint James's second book of 1994 was *Snow on Snow on Snow.* Kids stuffed into bright winter clothing are painted with irresistible warmth, and Clancy the dog is the comical good-sport pet every child dreams about. *Snow on Snow on Snow* is so appealing that it has since been translated into Spanish. It was also selected for use as an interactive video for first and second grade reading, and Saint James herself was asked to do its introduction.

The third book to appear in 1994 was a most beautiful picturebook called *The Gifts of Kwanzaa,* both illustrated and written by Synthia Saint James herself. While it contains no suggestion of textbook style, it is basically an educational book designed to explain the harvest-based holiday first celebrated in the United States in 1966. *The Gifts of Kwanzaa* tells the story of the festival's seven principles and where they originated. Saint James's illustrations make it clear that all children of African origin should share a bond of tradition and acceptance. It is no surprise that *Kwanzaa* sold 9,000 of its first printing of 10,000, and went into a second printing within three months. Before too long it had become a bookstore staple in every major city in the country.

> "Success only makes me work harder and harder."

While Synthia Saint James's special-occasion cards, illustrations, and prints are becoming well-recognized everywhere, her paintings are especially prized. Important clients now include comedian Richard Pryor and attorney Johnnie Cochran, who owns three of Saint James's works, the first bought at a gallery exhibition held to celebrate Saint James's 40th birthday.

Smile Your Special Smile

Saint James's work is also treasured by *Essence* magazine, which chose to mark its 25th anniversary by commissioning one of her paintings, and by corporate giant Maybelline-Kayser/Roth, whose joint theme "The Shades of You" celebrated African American women during the 1995 Black History Month. The House of Seagram, another satisfied client, featured "Visions" and "The Professor," two of her most arresting artworks in their 1996 calendar.

Though any successful artist might be forgiven for a little secret pride in her own achievements, Saint James is scrupulously careful never to lose sight of reality. "Some people who are successful get a big head. Not me," she told the *Press Telegram,* in 1995; "I'm just a regular person. Success only makes me work harder and harder." To prove it, she takes pride in her own self-reliance, and uses her eight years of experience as a freelance tax consultant to write her own contracts as she has always done.

In the mid-1990s Saint James's art is blossoming in ever-expanding new directions. A children's book called *Sunday,* scheduled for September of 1996 is an exercise in the value of the family and the importance of family time together. *Can I Touch You:Love Poems with Paintings*—a collection of the poetry she has been

writing for the past 20 years--was also due out that year.

The world is more than ready for Synthia Saint James's ideas and enthusiasm, judging by the continual blizzard of requests for licenses to reproduce her works on clocks and watches, clothing, a gift bag, and coffee mugs. On a bleak winter morning, when the call to "wake up and smell the coffee" is a duty rather than a joy, how bracing it is to drink it from a mug painted with the bright colors of "Ensemble." Then, as Saint James herself says, it's easy to "smile your special smile as things begin to come your way."

Selected works

Children's Books Illustrations

Tukama Tootles the Flute, with Phillis Gershator, Orchard Books, 1994.
Snow on Snow on Snow, with Cheryl Chapman, Dial, 1994.
How Mr. Monkey Saw the Whole World, with Walter Myers, Doubleday.
Neeny Coming, Neeny Going, with Karen English, Bridgewater, 1996.

Children's Books Written and Illustrated by Synthia Saint James

Sunday, Albert Whitman, 1996.
The Gifts of Kwanzaa, Albert Whitman, 1994.

Book Covers

Boyd, Julia, *Girlfriend to Girlfriend,* Dutton, Penguin.
Hurston, Zora Neale, *Their Eyes were Watching God,* Scott Foresman.
Johnson, Angela, *Toning the Sweep,* Orchard Books.
McMillan, Terry, *Waiting to Exhale,* Viking, Penguin, 1986.
McMillan, Terry, *Waiting to Exhale,* Pocket Books.
McMillan, Terry, *Disappearing Acts,* Pocket Books.
McMillan, Terry, *Mama,* Pocket Books.
Walker, Alice, *Paperback Trilogy,* Book-of-the-Month Club.

Sources

Periodicals

American Visions, October/November 1992, p. 35.
Carib News, Week Ending March 7, 1995, p.23.
Desert News, February 12, 1995.
Essence, January 1995, p. 97.

L.A. Watts Times, July 20, 1995.

Press-Telegram, July 22, 1995, p. C1.

Publishers Weekly, January 10, 1994; September 19, 1994, p. 27.

School Library Journal, April 1994, 118; September, 1994, p. 182;

October 1994, p. 43.

Sister, Sister, May 1995, p. 59.

Sunday Oaklahoman, March 3, 1996, p. 6.

U.S. Art Magazine, January/February 1993.

Upscale, April 1996, p. 74.

Additional information for this profile was provided by Black Art Gear, Inc; Cornerstone Creative Apparel, Ethnic Reams, Rolls & Bags, July, 1992.

—Gillian Wolf

Augusta C. Savage

1892(?)–1962

Sculptor

The statue called "The Pugilist" says it all. Designed with the head tilted upward, it faces the world calmly with folded arms prepared for whatever challenge the world may present. A late work by an artist renowned for her portrayal of personality and character, "The Pugilist" expresses most clearly the way Augusta Savage's life shaped her personality.

Intent upon showing physical suppleness and humor she often produced works that over-portentous critics labeled "trivial." Concentrating on the aspects of culture shared by black and white Americans alike, she was often castigated by black intellectuals for not drawing inspiration from purely African sources. Shackled by never-ending family responsibilities, plagued by poverty, she also suffered the suspicion and hostility that many black trailblazers of the 1930s experienced, when trying to challenge the established order. In the end her struggles on behalf of others exhausted her, and she simply waited, like "The Pugilist," to deal with life's next challenge.

Augusta Savage was the seventh of fourteen children born to Edward and Cornelia Fells. Sources seem

undecided about whether she was born in 1892 or 1900, but know definitely that five of her siblings did not live to maturity. Savage herself identified her birthplace as Green Cove, Florida, a town whose clay soil made it a thriving brick-making area. Augusta loved the clay from her earliest years, often choosing to slip off to the clay pits to model ducks and birds instead of going to school. This habit infuriated her father, a fundamentalist preacher with a profound belief that frequent whipping would prevent her from "fashioning graven images."

Edward Fells was wrong. Whipping did nothing to stop his daughter from modeling her clay birds. She produced dozens of them during her childhood years, continuing even through her 1907 marriage to John Moore, and the birth of her only child, Irene, the following year. The marriage was a short-lived one—Moore died a couple of years later, so the teenage mother took her child and her clay birds and went back to her parents.

In 1915 Augusta's father was appointed minister of a West Palm Beach Church. The move was good for her.

At a Glance...

Born February 29, 1892, though some dates give 1900, Green Cove Springs, Florida; parents, Edward and Cornelia (Murphy) Fells; thirteen siblings, of whom nine survived to maturity; married John T. Moore, 1907; daughter Irene born 1908; widowed; married James Savage, divorced; married Robert L. Poston 1923, widowed 1924; died: March 26, 1962. *Education:* Florida State Normal School, Tallahassie; Cooper Union, New York City, 1921-1924; Paris, studied with sculptor Hermon MacNeil; Paris, 1929

Career: assistant supervisor of the Federal Arts Project for New York City; Director, Harlem Community Art Center, 1937; taught concurrently president, holding corporation of Salon of Contemporary Negro Art, 1939;

Memberships: National Association of Women Painters and Sculptors.

Awards: Julius Rosenwald Scholarship, 1929; Julius Rosenwald Scholarship, 1930; citation, Salon d' Automne; citation, Salon Printemps at theGrande Palais, Paris; medallion, French Govt. Colonial Exposition.

A mature student who wrote sensitive poetry, she was welcomed by the teachers, and no longer felt the need to play truant. Her modeling, however, did not receive the same encouragement. Withering in the face of her father's disapproval and the scarcity of clay in the area, it came to a stop, until she chanced upon the Chase Potteries on the outskirts of town. Augusta begged a pailful of clay from the owner and modeled a little statue of the Virgin Mary for her over-strict father. This not only impressed him into into allowing her to continue her art undisturbed, but also persuaded the school board to appoint her to teach modeling during her senior year, at a "salary" of one dollar per day.

A Passport to Tomorrow

By now she had begun to broaden her repertoire to include all sorts of farm animals. Sure that some of them would appeal to the town's large number of tourists she showed them to a man named George Graham Currie,

who had recently been appointed the superintendent of an upcoming county fair. Like her school principal, Currie found Augusta's talent exciting. In the face of disapproval from authorities reluctant to encourage a "colored girl," Currie gave her a booth at the fair, where her animals became so popular that she won a $25 prize. She also earned $175—her first real sum of money.

When the fair ended Currie did not abandon Augusta. Believing deeply in her talent, he took the time to write a letter of introduction to Solon Borglum, a New York-based teacher of sculpture whose son Gutzon would one day be famous for his Mount Rushmore carvings of presidents Washington, Jefferson, Lincoln, and Roosevelt. Unfortunately Solon Borglum would not consider accepting Augusta as a non-paying student, but had no objection to writing a recommendation on her behalf to the registrar of Cooper Union, a public institution offering free tuition. This small effort on Borglum's part opened the gateway to her artistic future. His recommendation, as well as the bust of a Harlem minister that she modeled overnight, sent her to the top of a 142-strong waiting list for Cooper Union, then won her immediate entry for a four-year course of study.

Despite Augusta's burning determination to become an artist within six months, she was not able to give her full attention to her studies. The $175 had melted to just $4.60 by the time she arrived in New York, so she was forced to find work immediately in order to support herself. A job as an apartment caretaker tided her over at first but proved as short-lived as her second marriage to carpenter James Savage, who left nothing permanent in her life other than the name she adopted. Still, she was not completely alone with her problems. Noting that this talented, hardworking young woman had completed her first two years of schooling within her first six weeks, the Cooper Union school board voted to supply her with a scholarship to cover her living expenses for the rest of her stay.

Success Tantalizingly Close

Sooner or later life presents every human being with an event that determines their destiny. Augusta Savage's testing time came in 1923, when a committee of distinguished American artists and architects publicised an upcoming summer sculpting school to be held at Fontainbleau, outside Paris, France. Conditions for application were clearly demarcated: Only 100 female students would be considered; tuition was to be provided free of charge; living expenses of $500 would be the responsibility of each candidate, who would also need to furnish two references plus a $35 application fee.

Savage sent the application fee immediately. Shortly thereafter she was in the process of sending the names of her references when she received her application fee back with a note explaining that she had been rejected. At first the committee claimed that the problem lay in her lack of references. However, the true reason soon revealed itself. Apparently two Alabama winners of the scholarship had refused to travel or room with a "colored" girl.

If the committee imagined that this rejection would cause Savage simply to fade away they were very much mistaken. With years of practice born of whippings and poverty she fought grimly for her rights. "How am I to compete with other American artists if I am not given the same opportunity?" she demanded, in a May 20, 1923 letter to *New York World*. But she did not leave matters there. Determined to open every door that was available to her she appealed to the Ethical Culture Society, which in turn wrote to every member of the American committee choosing the applicants. The effects of all this were soon apparent. "Negress Denied Entry to French Art School," shrilled the *New York Times* of April 24, 1923. "Negroes to Ask Harding's Aid in Case of Augusta Savage," ran the newspaper's May 16 headline.

At best, the result was only a partial victory. The ban was upheld, but at least one of the committee members regretted the joint decision. Sculptor Herman MacNeil, then president of the National Sculpture Society, invited Augusta Savage to study privately with him that summer, at his studio on Long Island.

The Tragic Decade

This incident marked the start of a tragic decade for Savage. In October of 1923 she married Robert Poston, an official of black nationalist Marcus Garvey's Universal Negro Improvement Association. The only one of her three marriages that brought her any happiness, it was doomed to an abrupt and far-too-early end. Just five months after the wedding Poston died a mysterious death aboard a steamship returning from Liberia.

In 1925 there was another major setback. Through the efforts of the distinguished W.E.B. Du Bois and the Countess Irene Di Robilant, the manager of the Italian-American Association in New York, Savage received a working scholarship to the Royal Academy of Fine Arts in Rome, Italy. Thrilled, she took a job in a Manhattan steam laundry in order to save the money for the fare, but was forced instead to spend it on bringing her aged parents to New York, so she could care for her paralyzed father.

While these repeated blows would have been enough to discourage anyone, Savage still entertained a small spark of hope that she might, somehow, afford to get to Rome to study. Fanning the ember of hope by keeping her priorities intact, in 1926 she showed 22 works at the Baltimore Federation of Parent Teacher Clubs, in company with paintings by Henry O. Tanner and sculpture by her colleague Meta Warrick Fuller. She also studied incessantly in the public library, her determination to succeed inspiring the Friends of the New York Public Library to commission her for a bust of W.E.B. Du Bois. Savage worked carefully on this piece, intent upon showing the refinement and intelligence that marked the living model. The work of art that resulted drew such admiration that several other orders came her way. Among them was a commission for a bust of Marcus Garvey, who sat for her in his own apartment, on Sunday mornings.

But neither hard work nor determination could break the catalog of calamities that stalked her. In 1928 her brother Fred died while rescuing Florida flood victims. This brought her entire family to New York to live with her. Then, the following year her father died, leaving the responsibility of his funeral expenses for her to shoulder.

Finally defeated, she turned her back on her dreams of Rome to take care of her family. Yet, just when things seemed darkest the tide at last began to turn, courtesy of two unlikely angels in disguise. They were John Nail, a Harlem realtor, and Eugene Kinckle Jones, president of the National Urban League, who brought her work to the attention of a charitable foundation.

The Julius Rosenwald Fund

The Julius Rosenwald Fund dated back to 1917, when the chairman of Sears, Roebuck, had started it specifically for the education of black students. In order to qualify, Savage was asked to assemble a display of her existing work for the review committee. Feverishly she put together a selection of her best works, using a small, jaunty statue of her nephew, Ellis Ford, as the centerpiece. "Gamin" dazzled the scholarship committee into raising their original offer of $1,500 to $1,800, and unlocked the door to her future.

Augusta Savage was now quite well-known among black Americans. Appreciated for the proud black-is-beautiful quality of every character-filled statue she created, she also merited loyalty as the centerpiece of the 1923 racism that had arisen over the summer at Fontainbleau. For both these reasons parties to raise money for her clothes, her fares and her living expenses were held all over Harlem as soon as news of the scholarship became public.

Study in Europe

All the adulation added to the responsibility of trying not to disappoint anyone. But within a short time in Rome, she had proved herself admirably. The Rosenwald Fund was happy enough with her work by 1931 to award her a second scholarship, and the masters at the Academie de la Grande Chaumiere, her chosen place of study. They were so impressed with her eagerness to learn and her outstanding work that they showed her sculptures at both their Autumn and the Spring Salons. In addition she had the satisfaction of having one of her African figures chosen for reproduction on a medallion at the French Colonial Exposition. Then, to crown it all, she received a grant from the Carnegie Foundation, which allowed her to travel through France, Germany, and Belgium to study the classical forms of sculpture revered by her eminent teacher, Charles Despiau.

But if these magic years were sweet they were also short. By 1932 the Rosenwald grant had run out, and the Great Depression left little hope of another scholarship. Savage came back to New York and turned to portrait sculpture in order to make a steady living. Her bust of surgeon Dr. Walter Gray Crump dates from this time, as does her sculpture of statesman and author James Weldon Johnson, a longtime friend and fellow Floridian.

Home to Harlem

But sculpture was a precarious source of income during this time of economic downturn. So Savage turned to teaching, using a basement apartment to house the Savage Studio of Arts and Crafts that was supported by a $1,500 Carnegie Foundation grant. She brought her usual passion and enthusiasm to this task, guiding several young black artists to eventual prominence. Among them were William Artis, Ernest Critchlow, and Norman Lewis, a museum-quality modern painter who was honored at the 1955 Carnegie Exhibition in Pittsburgh.

By all accounts Savage was a spectacular leader—vivid, innovative, and magnetic. She knew well how to apply the power of the press to her cause, and how to raise support from others. During the dark Depression year of 1933 she used these skills to organize the Vanguard Club, an intellectual group that met weekly in order to discuss the social and economic issues of importance to the progress of black artists. Unfortunately this group was not destined to survive. Within a couple of years it became a favorite gathering ground for Harlem-area communists, and Savage immediately withdrew.

Other efforts centered around the Works Projects Administration, a program established by President Franklin Roosevelt to provide work for black artists blocked from the ever-dwindling available work supply. Initially the all-white WPA staff was ignorant of the number and excellence of non-white artists in America, but the socially-concious Savage was happy to bring the total of almost 200 of them to their attention. Tirelessly she led delegations, pressured politicians, and raised all the support she could to ensure that black painters were engaged to paint murals in schools, hospitals, and post offices. In an effort to make it possible for them to supervise their white counterparts on such projects, she also helped to organize the Harlem Artists' Guild.

In 1937 her administrative ability and energy brought her a new kind of challenge. She was appointed the director of the Harlem Community Center, one of the WPA's biggest art programs, which catered to both recreational and serious art students. Characteristically she threw herself into its organization, despite the warnings of well-meaning friends that she was being distracted from her life's work of sculpture. "I have created nothing really beautiful, really lasting," she said, in her usual forthright fashion. "But if I can inspire one of these youngsters to develop the talent I know they possess, then my monument will be in their work. No one could ask more than that." The friends remained unconvinced, but Savage would not be dissuaded.

The New York World's Fair

Soon after assuming this directorship Savage was commissioned to produce a sculpture for the 1939 New York World's Fair. The only black woman invited to participate, she was paid $1,200 by the Design Committee and took a leave of absence from the center to complete what was to be her last major work. The Fair's theme read: "To contribute a Happier Way of American Living by demonstrating how it can be achieved through the growing interdependence of men of every class and function and by showing the things, ideas and forces at work in the world which are the tools of today and with which the better world of tomorrow is to be built."

To link the important idea of a better world being

achieved through the interdependence of humanity's different groups Savage chose to base her sculpture on the lyric "Lift every voice and sing/Till earth and heaven ring …" which had been written in 1900 by her old friend James Weldon Johnson and set to music by his composer brother Rosamond. It was a large piece, consisting of a foundation modeled on a curved human arm whose hand was gently cupped round the top of a soaring, sixteen-foot harp. Jubilantly crowning each harp-string was the head of a singing boy or girl, while the front of the work boasted a kneeling youth whose outstretched hands offered music to all mankind. "The Harp" was a work that seemed the very essence of music, a work that symbolized a universal tenderness found only in artists who have been strengthened by lifelong burdens, as Augusta Savage had been.

> "How am I to compete with other American artists if I am not give the same opportunity?"

The statue was cast in plaster, then painted to resemble basalt, so that it could be shown in the courtyard of the Contemporary Arts Building before being cast for permanence in bronze. But, unfortunately there was no money for such luxuries as bronze castings. Though "The Harp" was seen by countless visitors, and was reproduced as a small souvenir, it was destined to leave only a photographic memory behind. When the Fair was over the bulldozers moved in and reduced it to a heap of rubble.

Stoically Savage returned to familiar Harlem, where her surroundings had always been comfortingly familiar. But she found that her position at the Art Center had been filled by someone else, and that federal funding for the program itself would shortly be diverted to the needs of World War II. These blows finally defeated Augusta Savage, and she retreated to a small town named Saugerties, in the Catskill Mountains of New York. Here she finally found a measure of serenity, though her days as an artist were behind her. With the advent of the 1960s she contracted cancer, so she moved back to New York to live out her final months with her daughter. The end came on March 26, 1962, when she died in Abraham Jacobi Hospital. She is buried in Ferncliff Cemetery in Hartsdale, New York.

Selected works

"Gamin," 1930
"Laughing Boy," 1932
"Reclining Nude," 1932
"Dr. Walter Gray Crump," 1932
"Portrait of Gwendolyn Knight," 1934
"James Weldon Johnson," 1939
"Lift Every Voice and Sing," 1939
"The Pugilist," 1942

Sources

Books

Augusta Savage and the Art Schools of Harlem, Schomburg Center for Black Culture, Exhibition catalog, 1988.

Bearden, Romare and Harry Henderson, *A History of African-American Artists: from 1792 to the Present,* Pantheon Books, 1993.

Bearden, Romare and Harry Henderson, *Six Black Masters of American Art,* Zenith Books, 1972.

Bergman, Peter M, *The Chronological History of the Negro in America,* Harper & Row, 1969.

Ferguson, Blanche E, *Countee Cullen and the Negro Renaissance,* Dodd, Mead & Company, 1966.

Hughes, Langston et al, *A Pictorial History of African Americans,* 6th edition, Crown Publishers, 1995.

Igoe, Lynn Moody, *250 Years of Afro-American Art: An Annotated Bibliography,* R.R. Bowker, 1981.

Lewis, Samella, *Art: African American,* Harcourt, Brace Jovanovich, 1978.

Logan, Rayford and Michael R. Winston, *Dictionary of American Negro Biography,* Norton & Company, 1982.

Sicherman, Barbara, ed., *Notable American Women: The Modern Period,* Belknap Press, 1980.

Smith, Jessie Carney, *Notable Black American Women,* Gale Research, 1992.

Periodicals

Crisis, August 1929, p. 269; June, 1930, p. 209.
New York Times, May 11, 1923; September 9, 1928; December 24, 1933; December 19, 1937.

—Gillian Wolf

Leopold Sedar Senghor

1906—

Political leader, poet, essayist

Achieving major success as a poet, politician, and intellectual, Léopold Senghor has had a truly unique identity among African leaders. His development from tribal member in Senegal, to scholar in France, to head of the government back in Senegal made him a symbol of Africa's shift from colonial domination to self-determination.

Senghor was one of the architects of the philosophy of *négritude,* a movement established in France to raise black consciousness. He was the first black African to receive the equivalent of the American Ph.D. degree in France, as well as the first black African to be elected to the French Academy. As a poet, he generated a body of work that led to his nomination for the Nobel Prize for Literature in 1962. Senghor's poetry often reflected his problems of dual consciousness resulting from his upbringing in Senegal and education in France. In his review of Senghor's *The Collected Poetry* in the *Washington Post,* K. Anthony Appiah wrote, "By themselves these poems would justify giving Senghor a place in the history of our times."

Along with maintaining dual identities as an African and Frenchman, Senghor has remained active as both a poet and a politician during his long career. Janet G. Vaillant summed up Senghor's life in *Black, French, and African: A Life of Léopold Sédar Senghor:* "Just as he [Senghor] refused to choose between his talents as poet and politician, sensing that each added depth to the other, so, too, he refused to choose between his two homelands, France and Africa. He knew their strengths and weaknesses, their darkness and their light, and he loved them both."

Born into Minority Group

Senghor was one of the youngest of some two dozen children of Basile Digoye Senghor, a well-to-do peanut merchant and exporter in Senegal. Senegal at the time was a French colony and part of French West Africa. Senghor's membership in the Christian Serer ethnic group made him a minority in his mostly Muslim country. His minority status made it all the more impressive that he later became head of the country. As Ellen Conroy Kennedy noted in the *Washington Post,* "That Senghor, a Catholic in a country 85 percent Muslim, and from its smallest tribal group, succeeded in governing through

At a Glance...

Born October 9, 1906, in Joal, Senegal; son of Basile Digoye (peanut merchant and exporter) and Nyilane (Bakhoume) Senghor; marriages: Ginette Eboue (divorced); Colette Hubert; children: Francis, Guy (with Eboue); Philippe (with Hubert). *Education:* University of Paris (France), *Diplome d'Etudes Supérieures, agrége.*

Sent to a French missionary school in, 1913; entered a Catholic boarding school, 1914; won many academic prizes; entered a Roman Catholic seminary, 1923; was only African in the graduating class of the French lycée, Dakar, Senegal, 1928 enrolled in Lycée Luis-le-Grand, Paris, France, 1928; entered the Sorbonne campus of the University of Paris, 1931; began espousing theory of négritude; helped launch *L'Edudiant noir* (The Black Student), 1934; began writing poetry, mid-1930s; held series of teaching posts near Paris; drafted into the French army; spent two years as a Nazi prisoner-of-war; published first collection of poetry, *Chants d'ombre* (Shadow Songs), 1945; helped introduce *Présence Africaine* (African Presence), late 1940s; became part of the French Constituent Assemblies, 1945; elected to French National Assembly and General Council of Senegal, 1946; formed Bloc Democratique Sénégalais in Senegal, 1948; helped draft a formal request to officially recognize the Mali Federation, 1959; became first president of independent Senegal, 1961; published *Nocturnes,* 1961; nominated for the Nobel Prize for Literature, 1962; sponsored Third World Festival of Negro Arts in Dakar, 1966; stepped down from presidency of Senegal, 1981; became a member of the Academie Francaise's Dictionary Committee, 1986.

Addresses: *Home*—1 square de Tocqueville, 75017, Paris, France.

the first 20 difficult years of independence was in itself a triumph." Part of Senghor's success story was a talent for compromise that was prevalent in his Serer tribal culture. "To survive in Senegal, Senghor had to go beyond his intellectual achievements in France and call on all the shrewdness of his Serer ancestors," wrote G.

Wesley Johnson in the *American Historical Review.*

Much of Senghor's youth was spent roaming the countryside with local shepherds who taught him about Serer customs. His father did not care for this behavior, and expressed his disapproval by sending his son to a school run by French missionaries in 1913. This proved a pivotal development in Senghor's life, as he proved himself to have superior academic skills. Also playing an important role in Senghor's life as a child was his sister-in-law, Helene. She and Senghor had similar affections for French books and culture, as well as had similar religious views, and she helped promote his scholarly ambition.

While in the missionary school, Senghor was indoctrinated with the French colonial policy of "assimilation." According to this policy, the smartest Senegalese were taught the French language and culture and were urged to support French political interests. Senghor won many academic prizes as a student. He decided to study for the priesthood and enrolled in the Roman Catholic seminary in Dakar. Senghor was then considered unfit for the priesthood after he verbally attacked the director for calling Africans "savages."

Was Outstanding Student

After leaving the seminary, Senghor achieved academic distinction in the French lycée in Dakar by becoming the only African in its graduating class in 1928. This accomplishment made him famous in West Africa. His reputation was further enhanced when he won the book prize in every subject, in addition to receiving the outstanding student award. Senghor's success earned him a scholarship to study in France, and in 1928 he enrolled in Lycée Luis-le-Grand in Paris. While at the Lycée he made key contacts with the Martinican poet Aimé Césaire, the French Guyanan poet Léon Damas, and George Pompidou, who became the president of France in 1969. These friends helped introduce Senghor to theater music, museums, and other aspects of French culture.

Senghor entered the Sorbonne campus of the University of Paris after graduating from the Lycée in 1931. Around this time he began seriously evaluating his self-image and future in the world. He also became more sensitized to what he considered French "cultural arrogance." It was a difficult time for Senghor, and he suffered bouts of depression and anxiety over his financial situation and identity. He began writing poetry as a means of grappling with his emotional distress during this troubled period.

After earning a Diplome d'Etudes Supérieures degree, Senghor began working toward his graduate degree at the University of Paris. Around this time, Senghor, Césaire and other blacks began espousing their theory of négritude, which at the time was interpreted to mean that blacks had intuition superior to that of whites, while whites were better at rational thought. In 1934 Senghor was among those who launched *L'Edudiant noir* (The Black Student), which communicated his ideas and those of his circle. He also helped form the Association of West African Students, whose aim was to promote African culture and embrace French culture without being absorbed into it.

Began Writing Poetry

As he began writing poetry in the mid 1930s, Senghor held a series of teaching posts at Lycées near Paris. After being drafted into the French army during World War II, he was captured by the Nazis and spent two years as a prisoner-of-war. While incarcerated he studied German and organized underground resistance movements in a number of prison camps. He was released in 1942 due to illness, then went back to teaching and continued his resistance activities.

Senghor's poetry was first published in a collection called *Chants d'ombre* (Shadow Songs), which came out in 1945. French critics praised the collection. Containing poems about being torn between France and Africa, as well as ones that supported négritude, the collection made Senghor into somewhat of spokesman for people with mixed consciousness like him. His 1948 publication called *Hosties noires* (*Black Sacrifices*) contained poems that had been written by Senghor in a German prison camp and had been sneaked out of the camp to George Pompidou by a sympathetic guard. These poems dealt with public themes and historical issues, according to Vaillant. "This collection strikes a militant note," she wrote. "The very title *Hosties noires* was carefully chosen for its double meaning. It can be translated into English in two ways, either as 'black victims' or as 'black hosts'—host in the sense of the sacrificial host of Catholic Communion. The title suggests therefore that black people have been both victims and sacrifices for European causes." Also in the late 1940s, Senghor helped introduce *Présence Africaine* (*African Presence*), a journal that became an important voice of literary and sociopolitical thought for black intellectuals.

Formation of Senghor's literary self coincided with development of his political side. In 1945 he became part of the French Constituent Assemblies, as a deputy of Senegal. The following year he was elected to the French National Assembly and General Council of Senegal. His language expertise earned him an invitation to review the accuracy and style of the French constitution drafted in 1946. A dozen years later, he was asked to help write a new French constitution.

Formed Political Party

Staking a political claim in his own country, Senghor formed the Bloc Democratique Sénégalais in Senegal in 1948. His formation of the party resulted partly from a protest against what he considered France's lack of consideration for the interests of Africa. "Senghor now realized that his vision of a free and self-directing African culture could not be realized without attention to political issues," wrote Vaillant. Senghor's friends in Senegal helped gather support for the new party, and Senghor himself spent much time traveling across the country to campaign for the party after its formation. Meanwhile, he continued to retreat regularly to write poetry. In 1949 he published a small compilation of lyric love poems, *Chants pour naett* (Songs for Naett), and another in 1956 called *Ethiopiques,* which dealt with his bonds to his native Senegal.

During the 1950s Senghor made numerous speeches demanding improvements in the life of the Senegalese, while at the same time demonstrating his loyalty to France. As his frustration with France's lack of concern for their African territories grew, he worked to establish a federation of the country's African colonies that would provide the territories more voice for positive change. Vaillant noted, "Without federation, he [Senghor] felt sure, the tiny states of West Africa would be doomed to poverty and perpetual dependence on others, probably France."

As problems with France's African colonies escalated with the revolt in Algeria in 1955, it was clearly that France needed a new relationship with its colonies there. Senghor was appointed by the French government to investigate the problems of overseas territories. He had talks with leaders in Tunisia and Morocco that helped settle unrest there. He also urged France to allow African states to form in loose confederations. By 1956 he was stumping Senegal and calling for autonomy, stopping just short of demanding independence. "I urge you to consider yourselves henceforth as in a state of legal resistance," an increasingly militant Senghor told a meeting of members of a political party he helped to create in Senegal, the Union Progressiste Sénégalaise, according to Vaillant

Became President of Senegal

Senegal was thwarted in his hopes when the new French constitution in 1958 gave only limited autonomy to the territories. Although he agreed to support the document, it added to his dissatisfaction with France as overseer of his homeland and fueled his efforts to create a federation. In 1959 he helped formulate a formal request to officially recognize the Mali Federation, a union of Senegal with the Sudanese Republic (now Mali). Although permission to form the union was granted, disagreements led to Senegal's withdrawal the next year. Senegal then drafted its own constitution, and Senghor was elected its first president in 1961.

> "I urge you to consider yourselves henceforth as in a state of legal resistance."

As president, Senghor made economic development his top priority. However, problems arose due to disagreements between him and his prime minister, Mamadou Dia, a close friend. Senghor supported a tight relationship with France, while Dia wanted to sever these ties. Escalation of the two men's differences led Dia to attempt a coup d'etat in 1962, which was crushed by Senghor. Dia was then convicted to a life sentence in prison. Senghor used this opportunity to make the prime minister part of his own position, and through his presidency continued fostering his relationship with France. He also strove to build cultural exchanges between African nations.

Despite his early promotion of democracy, Senghor became more authoritarian as head of the Senegalese government through the 1960s. In the middle of the decade he declared all parties other than his own illegal. He also helped sidestep potential criticisms by hiring his critics for prestigious government posts. This system of patronage proliferated the bureaucracy and led to a great waste of government funds in a country that could ill afford it.

Political office did not deter Senghor from his poetry writing, and in 1961 he published an acclaimed collection called *Nocturnes*. The following year he was nominated for the Nobel Prize for Literature in honor of his esteemed body of work. Senghor tried to stir up support for his policies by promoting his philosophy of négritude through his writings and by sponsoring events such as the Third World Festival of Negro Arts in Dakar in 1966, but his attempts largely did not succeed. His focus on cultural matters also had an adverse effect on the economy, and by 1970 economic growth was slowing. During his term the country became too dependent on the export of peanuts, and a major drought that hurt the harvest became an economic nightmare for the country. "Convinced as he was that Senegal's economic problems would yield to technology and modern planning, Senghor was slow to see poor performance as a reason to rethink his entire strategy," wrote Vaillant.

Numerous coups were attempted and thwarted during Senghor's term in power. As his support was eroded due to widespread hardship, Senghor responded by shifting away from his authoritarian stance. He re-established the position of prime minister, allowed the existence of competing political parties again, and voiced his support for freedom of the press. Senghor also released Dia and other political prisoners.

Resigned as Head of Government

In 1981 Senghor became the first African chief of government to peaceably step down from power and pass the torch to someone else. He felt at the time that he would not live to see the country he had dreamed of in Senegal. "In the morning when I awake," he wrote, according to Vaillant, "I feel all the world that weighs on me . . . [but] when I open the window and see the sun rising over Gorée, over the island of slavery, I say to myself, all the same, since the end of the slave trade, we have made progress."

In 1986 Senghor became a member of the Academie Francaise's Dictionary Committee to make sure that new words and expressions from Francophone territories would be incorporated into the academy's dictionary. After moving to France following his retirement from political office, Senghor focused more on writing, traveled widely, and became president of an international authors' rights organization. Leaders throughout the world have often turned to him for advice due to his achievement in helping Senegal gain its independence.

Selected writings

Songs for Naeett, 1949.
Ethiopiques, 1956.
Nocturnes, 1961.
The Collected Poetry, 1992.

Sources

Books

Baudet, Henri, *Paradise on Earth: Some Thoughts on*

European Images of Non-European Man, Yale University Press, 1965.

Buell, Raymond Leslie, *The Native Problem in Africa,* Macmillan, 1928.

Hymans, Jacque Louis, *Léopold Sédar Senghor: An Intellectual Biography,* Edinburgh University Press, 1971.

Johnson, G. Wesley, *The Emergence of Black Politics in Senegal,* Stanford University Press, 1971.

Mortimer, Edward, *France and the Africans, 1944–1960,* Faver, 1969.

Vaillant, Janet G., *Black, French, and African: A Life of Léopold Sédar Senghor,* Harvard University Press, 1990.

Periodicals

Chicago Tribune, September 19, 1990, pp. C3, C5.

Macleans, May 29, 1989, p. 17.

New York Review of Books, December 20, 1990, pp. 11–21.

New York Times Book Review, October 21, 1990, p. 7.

Researches in African Literature, Fall 1990, pp. 51–57.

Washington Post Book World, November 11, 1990, pp. 1, 14; July 5, 1992, p. 1.

—Ed Decker

Audrey Smaltz

1937(?)—

Fashion show coordinator

The women's wear trade usually accounts for an annual bottom line of nearly $35 billion in the United States. This huge amount of seasonally generated money covers profits drawn from sales to both the thriftiest clothes shoppers at one end of the spectrum and the wealthiest trendsetters at its opposite edge. Regardless of the market a clothing designer is targeting, he or she runs a fierce race for customer dollars. The life of a designer would be easier if one knew positively whether women would like shorter or longer skirts next winter; whether buyers for department stores would like to offer their customers classic elegance or novel chic for spring, or whether summer's merchandise should feature cool pastels or vivid brights. But predicting trends is a precarious business.

All designers use potent weapons to meet these formidable challenges of bulls-eye forecasting and relentless competition. Heavy advertising is one method. Another is the fashion show, which can be cleverly accessorised with music or strobe lights, or whatever else will suggest the link between the clothes on display and a targeted customer group's innermost longings about their image.

Fashion shows are expensive undertakings guaranteed to bring a designer plenty of praise or ridicule in the all-important trade magazines. So behind every successful show a wise and experienced organizer with a streak of self-confidence wide enough to weather any last-minute crisis, a cutting-edge fashion flair, and a healthy respect for the power of the spotlight must exist. Enter Audrey Smaltz.

Smaltz's first brush with celebrity came in 1951, when *Life* magazine photographed her as a "Say Hey" kid cheerleader for baseball great Willie Mays. But though the memory lingered, her own space in the spotlight waited until 1959, when she started working as a saleswoman at exclusive Bloomingdale's in New York City. Soon thereafter, her six-foot one-inch height and her willowy body earned her the additional assignment of modeling Christmas robes. The two roles blended together well for her—so well that she entered the store's executive training program early the following year.

By 1965, Smaltz was ready for a new challenge. She found one in the Tall Girl division of Lane Bryant, a store that specializes in clothes for women requiring special

At a Glance...

Born c. 1937, in Harlem, New York.

Bloomingdales, saleswoman and model, 1959-65; Lane Bryant's Tall Girl Division, model and buyer, 1965-69; Ebony Fashion Fair, coordinator, 1970-77; The Ground Crew, founder, 1977--.

Selected awards: Best Dressed List, three times.

sizes. She enjoyed her work there, but was surprised to learn that her job description included the unusual request that she give up her wardrobe of designer clothes in order to wear only Lane Bryant merchandise. "But what did I care," she later told *Newsday* magazine, ``I was making $140 a week and getting my wardrobe absolutely free." Smaltz stayed with Lane Bryant until 1969, when she left to marry a Chicago physician. The marriage was shortlived, and she was soon back looking for work on the fashion scene.

The Ebony Fashion Fair

The right job came along in record time. In 1970, Smaltz went to work with Eunice Johnson, wife of the Chicago-based *Ebony* magazine publisher. Already highly experienced in the fashion world, Smaltz was asked to put her expertise to work coordinating the Ebony Fashion Fair, a review that traveled from coast to coast featuring shows for charities, the garment industry, and conventions.

For anyone who enjoyed being on the road, this was an ideal job. The Fair required constant trips to Europe to visit the top couture houses, plus many other jaunts to exotic places, where novel accessories, textiles, and designs could be found. And when Smaltz brought all her treasures back to the United States, she was needed on the tours themselves.

Smaltz found all this highly enjoyable. She also took great pleasure in the commentaries she did for the Fashion Fair performances, though she found that providing a constant interpretation of outfit after outfit could become terminally boring for her. So she took infinite care to find something unusual and interesting to tell each audience. "I'd tell them what they didn't know," she told *Savvy Woman* in 1990, "like what the inside of the Christian Dior boutique in Paris looks like."

40 years old in 1977, Smaltz felt it was high time she stopped working for others. So as a first step she moved back to New York City and used some of her $60,000 savings to buy a 900-square-foot condominium on West 55th Street. Then, using the apartment as both business headquarters and residence, she started planning her business around the fashion shows she understood so well. Smaltz began by comparing the two completely different halves that any show encompasses.

Part one, which the audience sees, is the idyllic runway, down which graceful models parade, dance, or twirl, seemingly without a care in the world. Part two takes place behind the scenes. Inevitably the show consists of a whirlwind rush to get each model out on time with zipper forced into obedience, makeup smudges erased, and matching shoes placed on the right feet. As Smaltz knew from her own experience, the hundreds of details that go into this effort are often complicated by backstage disorganization culminating in frantic hunts for missing earrings, calls for assistants who can sew well enough to sew on a runaway button, or demands for an iron to get rid of an obstinate wrinkle.

Knowing that life behind the fashion show scenes could be made far less stressful for everyone concerned, she decided to change the situation by offering organizers teams of dressers who would work under her personal supervision. She hoped to provide an assistant for each model. That way, the dresser could keep track of the outfits, zip and unzip the model, and make sure that none of the costume jewelry, scarves, or belts matching the clothes were missing when showtime arrived.

The Ground Crew

Smaltz called her new venture "The Ground Crew," after a comment once made by Dr. Martin Luther King. "He was talking about the marvel of the jumbo jets and their pilots and engineers," she recalled, in a November of 1987 interview with *The Wall Street Journal*. "To get that plane off! To fuel it! To keep it clean!" King had said, `You need the ground crew!' Applying this remark to her own business-in-the-making, Smaltz used her own considerable experience in the fashion industry to come up with her own adage: "To get that model out! To dress her! To make sure she has everything the outfit calls for! You need my Ground Crew!"

Smaltz planned her operation so carefully that the rules she formulated in 1977 are still the rules by which she operates in the mid-1990s. She still provides two extra dressers for emergencies, but adds no charge for them.

Each dresser studies photographs of each outfit to be worn by the model who is being helped, so that she knows exactly which earrings, shoes, or lingerie go with each outfit. Smaltz has had to add one further rule: today's dresser understands that she will have to pay for anything that disappears while under her care, and that she will be fired for losing it.

In addition to the dressers, Smaltz provides other assistants to ensure that behind-the-scenes operations at fashion shows happen with the smooth precision which is the audience's view of things. She offers "fashion calculators"—people who track missing accessories; "fashion sleepers" who will spend the night in the room with valuable clothing to be shown the next day, and even "fashion couriers," who lug the huge dress boxes and racks from one venue to the next.

Smaltz herself is always available to burnish a show to perfection from its planning stage to the day of its presentation. And once the great day arrives, she is always the eye in the center of the boiling backstage storm, giving instructions, cobbling sagging hemlines, or producing the capacious bagful of extension cords, staplers, aspirins and whatever else it takes to stave off a possible disaster.

Finding Crew members has never been a problem—Smaltz often finds would-be employees clamoring to work for her. Dressing fashion models is a popular, part-time money spinner for many people with regular jobs in other fields, and she is often contacted by would-be Ground Crew members who may also hold jobs as aerobics instructors, students, and secretaries; on occasion she has even employed public relations executives and writers wanting to experience the business of fashion from this invaluable inside track.

In the mid-1990s, Smaltz's Ground Crew is familiar to most fashion designers in the United States, but business was slow at first. Organizers were accustomed to using secretaries, students, or friends as assistants—in fact anyone interested enough to help for minimal reward. The thought of using trained dressers had simply never occurred to any of them. As *Savvy Woman* dryly noted, "designers such as Arnold Scaasi and Carolyne Roehm weren't exactly wringing their hands without her." Still, Smaltz persevered, adding to her income by writing a regular column for *Vogue,* sending out business cards, and making sure that everyone who tried her service once would find her teams efficient, her own presence reassuring, and her company essential in the future.

In 1966, a civic-minded woman named Lois Alexander founded the Harlem Fashion Institute (HIF), a small private school training milliners, pattern cutters, tailors, and other indispensable members of the fashion industry. Alexander added a museum in 1979, in order to document the contribution that African Americans had made to American fashion from the Colonial times to the present. Prominently noted was the creative genius of Elizabeth Keckley, a former slave who designed and sewed much of Mary Lincoln's official wardrobe; a matter of equal pride was that Jacqueline Kennedy's elegant wedding gown as well as the bridal wear worn by her entire retinue had been sewn by African American seamstress Ann Lowe.

An unofficial but respected hall of fashion fame, the Black Fashion Museum was supported by such prominent members of the African American community as jazz musician Lionel Hampton and Audrey Smaltz, who was employing larger and larger numbers of African American dressers. By 1982, her contribution to New York's black community was acknowledged by the Black Fashion Museum's invitation to join their first Board of Directors—an honor commemorated by a photograph showing her, tall and svelte in shining boots and tailored pantsuit, being sworn in by then-New York City mayor David Dinkins at the Institute's Easter Gala.

The Best Dressed List

This was not the only accolade to come Smaltz's way during the mid-1980s. By 1984, her name had appeared three times on the Best-Dressed List, a fashion phenomenon originally invented to promote fashion in a post-World War II world. According to *Town & Country,* a magazine that chronicles the activities of the wealthy, the Best Dressed List characterizes the world's best-dressed women as "those with slender waists, but never slender means," an observation borne out by such regular listees as Jacqueline Onassis, whose husband's bank account ranked in the world's top three. For this reason alone, Smaltz's name on the Best Dressed List was testimony to her financial success. A second advantage gained by this honor was the chance to improve her business networking by her association with the world's most fashion-conscious women and their designers, many of whom frequently organized fashion shows themselves.

By 1987, Smaltz's Ground Crew members in their trademark black tee shirts were a familiar sight at fashion shows featuring the clothes of fashion legends Calvin Klein and Donna Karan. So the team was a natural choice to smooth the path for the revered French designer Christian Lacroix, who made his American debut in October of that year. This was deemed such an important occasion by fashion cognoscenti that carefully crafted articles about Lacroix appeared in the press as early as February of 1987. Items about his split from the establishment of the immortal Jean Patou became familiar to fashion-lovers nationwide; details of his basic fashion philosophy were widely interpreted in newspaper articles, and speculations about his forthcoming collection increased to a garment-industry crescendo as the time for the debut approached.

> "To get that model out! To dress her! To make sure she has everything the outfit calls for! You need my Ground Crew!"

When the appointed night arrived, New York City rolled out both the red carpet and the Ground Crew for Lacroix at a benefit sponsored by Bergdorf Goodman for the Memorial Sloan-Kettering Cancer Center. It was a spectacular occasion marked by sumptuous food, glittering decor, and even fireworks, but the 600 guests, who included opera diva Beverley Sills, dancer Mikhail Baryshnikov, and actress Faye Dunaway as well as fellow-designers Diane Von Furstenburg and Calvin Klein, intimidated Lacroix to such an extent that he later confessed to greater terror than he had ever before experienced, even at his very first show in Paris.

The authoritative Standard & Poor's Industry Surveys suggested that by 1994, the number of employees in the apparel manufacturing industry had dwindled to 969,000 from a healthy 1,438 million recorded 21 years earlier. Automation and a lurching economy each bore part of the responsibility for this phenomenon, which soon showed up to such an extent in shoppers' close attention to discounts rather than exclusive designs that stores had to start keeping themselves afloat with constant sales and promotions. No doubt lingers that this new taste for austerity also tarnished the glamour and extravagance that characterized the mid-1980s fashion shows.

Comments in *The Wall Street Journal* reported that even the avant-garde Isaac Mizrahi, once a devout show enthusiast, decided to scale back his fall of 1995 show, opting for a simply- organized 25-outfit presentation in his showrooms, with comments about prices, fabrics and availability provided by himself instead of a hired commentator. Despite this change of heart wealthy shoppers always exist who want to see the collections modeled before they choose their own new clothes. For that reason, Audrey Smaltz will be ever in need to keep things humming smoothly.

Smaltz has received hundreds of post-show notes from hundreds of satisfied clients. Among them are the following three: a fervent post-show "thank you" dated October of 1994 from Vera Wang, designer of exclusive wedding dresses; a 1996 note from top designer Carolina Herrerra, and a third from fashion legend Oscar de la Renta. And probably many more are to come.

Sources

Books

Alexander, Lois, *Blacks in the History of Fashion*, Harlem Institute of Fashion, 1982.

Periodicals

Newsday, April 6, 1968, Part II, p. 7.
Essence, March 1984, p. 103.
Wall Street Journal, November 4, 1987, p. 34; May 25, 1995, Section B, p. 1.
New York Times, October 30, 1987.
Savvy Woman, April 1990, p. 48.
Town & Country, January 1994, p. 68.

—Gillian Wolf

Roger Guenveur Smith

1960—

Actor, writer, director

Roger Guenveur Smith is not a famous actor, nor would his face be readily recognized on the street. He is, however, an extremely well-respected actor who makes a point of accepting provocative roles in theater, television, and film. More importantly, when those roles are not immediately forthcoming, Smith creates his own. Without fail, the work he does aims at bringing the black experience into mainstream American entertainment. As a writer, director, and actor, he is making an admirable place for himself in the theatrical world.

Born in Berkeley, CA, but raised in Los Angeles, Smith did not have the acting bug at first; his interests were varied and ever changing. Smith was the first of his family to be born outside of the South. His mother, from South Carolina, and his father, from Virginia, moved to California in order to find opportunities denied to them as blacks in the segregated south. Not coincidentally, the vast majority of Smith's work as an adult addresses the African American's position in society.

As Smith sought his own place, he was drawn to acting, but was afraid he might not be able to make a living at it. He attended Occidental College, a small private college in Los Angeles, from which he received a Bachelors degree in American Studies. Now beginning to toy seriously with the idea of acting as a career, Smith applied for and won a fellowship to do theater abroad for a year. The Thomas J. Watson fellowship allowed him to apprentice at the Keskidee Arts Centre, a small

theater in London that was an African-Caribbean theater center. On returning home Smith went to Yale University, initially into their African American studies program. Acting finally got the best of him, however, and he transferred into and graduated from Yale's prestigious School of Drama.

Gave in to the Acting Bug

Law school had tempted Smith, as had the idea of teaching history at the college level. His strong desire to instruct led to a year spent teaching English at Hollywood High in Los Angeles following graduate school. Although he eventually gave it up to enter the performing sphere full-time, Smith still teaches performance workshops from time to time, including stints at the University of California at Berkeley. As he told Marianne Ruuth in *Players,* "I've had the opportunity to be influential within Academia and yet maintain my independence as an artist. That's a good combination."

Smith began his professional acting career in the mid 1980s. He developed his craft on the stage of the Guthrie Theater in Minneapolis and at the New York Shakespeare festival playing Pinter, Ionesco, Shakespeare, and Dickens. Smith went on to play seasons at the Mark Taper Forum, Mabou Mines, and the Actors' Theatre of Louisville. As Don Snowden wrote in the *New York Times Syndicate,* Smith "also honed his skills in

At a Glance...

Born 1960, in Berkeley, CA; son of Sherman (a judge) and Helen (a dentist) Smith. Wife: Carolina; children: Luna Rae. *Education:* Bachelor's degree in American studies from Occidental College, Los Angeles, CA, c. 1982; Master's degree from Yale School of Drama; apprenticed at the Keskidee Arts Centre, London, England, on a Thomas J. Watson Fellowship.

Actor, writer, and director. Acted in films including *School Daze,* 1988, *Do the Right Thing,* 1989, *King of New York,* 1990, *Deep Cover,* 1992, *Malcolm X,* 1992, *Poetic Justice,* 1993, *Tales from the Hood,* 1995, *Panther,* and *The Bus,* 1996; wrote and starred in stage performances including *Frederick Douglass Now,* 1990, *Inside the Creole Mafia,* 1991, *Christopher Columbus 1992,* 1992, *A Huey P. Newton Story,* 1995; appeared on the stage in *The Birthday Party, Agamemnon, The Task, Suenos, It's a Man's World, That Serious He-Man Bull,* and *Coriolanus*; appeared on television in *A Different World, Cosmic Slop, Murphy Brown,* and *Fallen Angels.*

Awards: The *LA Weekly's* award for Best Two Person Show for *Inside the Creole Mafia;* two NAACP awards for Best Playwright and Best Actor for *A Huey P. Newton Story,* 1995; and the *LA Weekly's* award for Best Solo Performance for *A Huey P. Newton Story,* 1996.

Addresses: *Management*—Kaplan-Adams Entertainment, 8205 Santa Monica Blvd., #1-177, Los Angeles, CA, 90046.

the minimal, make-do-with-what's-at-hand tradition that Smith only half-jokingly refers to as 'the theater of nothing and everything.'"

Began Work in Films

During the late 1980s Smith began to work in films. In 1989 he appeared in Spike Lee's *Do the Right Thing* Although Smith's role as Smiley in this extremely controversial film about racial tension was a small one, it was memorable. Smith was allowed to create the role

himself. What he developed was the stuttering neighborhood idiot who wandered the streets hawking photos of Martin Luther King and Malcolm X shaking hands. Most every review of the film made mention of Smith's part. *Elle* went so far as to note that "Smith pulled off the role of the stuttering militant ... with such chilling finesse that it has obscured the fact that he's passionately articulate."

Smith went on to appear in small roles in many films, especially those directed by a group of rising young African American filmmakers whose films bring realistic and powerful images of black life to the screen. A favorite of Spike Lee, Smith appeared in his *School Daze, Malcolm X,* and worked with him on *Jungle Fever,* although his scenes for that film were cut in the final version. In 1996 Smith played one of the leads in Lee's *The Bus.* Smith has also been in *King of New York, Deep Cover, Poetic Justice, Tales from the Hood,* and *Panther,* a film about the 60s militant group the Black Panthers.

Smith has also tried his hand at television. Many would remember him in the acclaimed Bill Cosby spinoff, *A Different World,* in which Smith had a recurring role as history Professor Randolph. He appeared in Showtime's cable TV adaption of black detective writer Walter Mosley's *Fearless* as well as in Showtime's series *Fallen Angels.* Smith has been seen in highly-rated series as the Hudlin Brother's *Cosmic Slop* on HBO and network television's long-running *Murphy Brown.*

Theater Remained First Love

Roger Smith's first love, however, remains the theater. As he told Snowden, "Theater is my foundation and it's something to which I continually return. It's a source of creativity that's really unparalleled because it's live and direct." Smith is not one to sit around waiting for his agent's call; he creates his own work. Since 1990 Smith has been developing and performing critically acclaimed solo theater pieces around African American historical figures and/or themes.

His first piece, *Frederick Douglass Now,* premiered at the La Mama Theater in New York City in 1990. In it Smith tells the story of this self-educated ex-slave who became an abolitionist leader. In an hour-long performance, Smith combined Douglass's texts with rap, jazz, and reggae, and as *Elle* described "all the historical immediacy that dictaphones, video cameras, and cordless telephones can muster." The reviewer went on to say, "Inscribing the recent racial strife in Bensonhurst and the rape of the Central Park jogger in his piece,

Smith makes Douglass's critique of American life seem tragically relevant. The show is both pedagogical and inspirational in its call to resistance." When *Elle* asked him if he feared this stirring of controversy would hurt his chances in an already intolerant industry, Smith replied, "I'm already under siege in South Africa, in Central America, and in Bensonhurst. *Frederick Douglass Now* is my remedy." *Players* Magazine called the piece "eloquent, passionate."

Smith then created his *Christopher Columbus 1992.* When Ruuth wondered "why Columbus?" in *Players,* Smith replied amused, "It was the 500th anniversary of his alleged discovery of America and I had a statement to make—I didn't make him into a hero but into a kind of lounge entertainer who runs a travel agency on the side…a guy still among us, he's been on the charts for 500 years and has some political aspirations!" In *Venice Magazine* Victoria L. Tilney remarked that Smith had "dazzled audiences" with both *Frederick Douglass* and *Christopher Columbus.*

Smith first performed his next piece, *Inside the Creole Mafia,* in late 1991, and like his other works, often revives it, performing it again and again across the nation. Together with Mark Broyard, a vocalist, composer, choir director, and assemblage artist—with whom Smith has been friends since childhood—Smith created *Inside the Creole Mafia.* He described it as a "not too dark" comedy. It is an assortment of New Orleans memories, skits, performance art, a capella singing, and creole language instruction, and audience spoofing.

Most of the humor in *Mafia* has to do with the color of Creole skin. "As they explain," according to *LA Magazine,* "the plight of Creole actors is that they're not dark enough for black roles but too dark for white roles." *LA Magazine* gave it an "A," calling Smith a "gifted actor," the show "engaging" and remarked that "Two better, more talented representatives would be hard to imagine.…Their show is more fun than Mardi Gras." In the *Los Angeles Times* Jan Breslauer wrote that *Mafia* "isn't just a cut above most performance works about racial identity. It's a cut above most performance works, period." Breslauer called them "consummately skilled performers," and "witty and versatile" writers, calling the whole thing an "exceptional work."

Recreated Huey Newton

In 1994 Smith began preparation on a piece that would be a landmark in his career, *A Huey P. Newton Story.* Huey Newton was one of the founders of the Black Panthers. As an in touch urban African American youth,

Smith could not help having heard of Newton, but he became more and more aware of the man as Smith grew older. He remembered Newton's release from prison in 1970 and, in particular, a 1972 incident involving the black leather jackets that, because of the Panthers influence, had become de rigueur among black youth in LA. A friend of a friend of Smith's had his jacket ripped off of him by gang members in Hollywood. When Smith's friend came to his assistance, he was stomped to death by the gang. Callous adults made remarks like "that'll teach you to wear a black leather jacket." The incident had a profound effect on Smith.

He did not, however, necessarily feel allied to the Panthers—telling *Players* that his "allegiances as an adolescent switched rapidly from year to year, from season to season." But as Smith became more and more drawn to exploring the lives of influential African Americans, he became intrigued by Newton. He wanted to present the Huey Newton that most people knew nothing about. After a year of trust-building with Newton's family, they allowed Smith an unprecedented look at his papers and records. Smith began to understand what it must have felt like to be in Newton's family, to sit in his place. Newton's relatives were at times actually made uncomfortable by Smith's resemblance to Newton.

> "Theater is my foundation and it's something to which I continually return. It's a source of creativity that's really unparalleled because it's live and direct."

The piece developed—and continues to develop—in an improvisational manner. Smith told Snowden, "I had been absorbing all this material for the past year—listening to tapes of Huey, watching video tapes of Huey—and I came to the point when I put all the paperwork to the side and just started doing Huey." The piece eventually involved Smith simply sitting in front of a mike, chain smoking, and speaking words taken directly from Newton's writings. The *San Francisco Focus* called the *Newton Story* an "impressionistic yet razor-sharp portrait of a complex figure." Smith wanted to delve into that complexity, to show more than just what people saw on the famous posters of Newton.

It wasn't easy melding Newton's words into a performance piece. Frederick Douglass had been a great orator, but Newton was not considered a dynamic speaker, a fact that disappointed many of his followers after they'd built a certain image of him. The *Los Angeles Times* wrote, "Smith's meticulously researched solo performance illuminates these diverse facets with laser-like precision, the only common thread being Newton's defiance of the expectations fostered by his own myth." Marianne Ruuth asked Smith if he set out to be controversial. Smith laughed, "Of course not. If I set out to be controversial, I'd just take this bottle and throw it through the window. There are simpler ways of being controversial than going through the agony of putting on a play."

It *is* difficult mounting the sorts of productions that Smith takes on. Although his vehicles for alternative theater strategies fit comfortably in the college circuit or store front gallery spaces, Smith also presents his work at African American Institutions like the Lorraine Hanbury Theater in Oakland, CA, as well as mainstream theaters like the Mark Taper Forum in Los Angeles and New York's Public Theater. It's hard work, but work for which Smith receives the kudos he is due. What he does makes more than just a theatrical statement, he makes important social commentary. Smith admitted to Snowden, "Certainly, I'd like my work to be seen by the widest audience possible. The audience base for so-called legitimate theater in this country is dying. The legitimate theater has not found a way to create a new audience so that the same people packing the Apollo to see [rapper] Ice Cube will come to see *Frederick Douglass Now* or *Inside the Creole Mafia.*"

To spread a message, Roger Smith has to have listeners. In order to develop new audiences, he makes a point of connecting with the people who do come to see him. That's why you'll see Smith standing in front of the theater after every show, sincerely thanking people for coming, encouraging them to come back to the theater—for any show—again and again.

Sources

Booklist, January 1, 1996.
Elle, February 1990.
Essence, June 1991.
Los Angeles Magazine, December 1993.
Los Angeles Times, December 7, 1991; October 2, 1993; January 19, 1995; January 27, 1995.
Nation, July 17, 1989.
New Yorker, June 8, 1987; July 24, 1989.
New York Times, February 19, 1990.
New York Times Syndicate, July 4, 1995.
People Weekly, July 3, 1989.
Players, August 1995.
San Francisco Focus, November 1995.
Variety, November 6, 1995.
Venice (CA), January 1995.

Additional information for this profile was obtained from press materials for *Poetic Justice,* 1993; *Tales From the Hood,* 1995; and from Kaplan-Adams Entertainment, 1995 and 1996.

—Joanna Rubiner

Paul Wilbur Stewart

1925—

Museum curator

Paul Stewart, founder and director of the Black American West Museum and Heritage Center, has dedicated his life to documenting the role that blacks played in settling and shaping the American West. Paul Stewart's own collection forms the nucleus of the museum's holdings, which now total 35,000 items. Based in Denver, Colorado, the museum is considered to be the most comprehensive source of historical material on African Americans in the West.

Paul Wilbur Stewart was born on December 18, 1925, in Clinton, Iowa, the son of Martha and Eugene Stewart. Eugene Stewart was in the trucking business and owned a trucking company during the Depression. The Stewarts were one of the few black families in the predominantly white area.

As a child growing up in the 1930s, Stewart enjoyed playing cowboys and Indians. However, he always had to be one of the Indians, because his white playmates insisted that there was no such thing as a black cowboy. It was not until the early 1960s that Stewart would learn differently. In fact, according to one estimate, nearly one-third of cowboys were black.

Stewart joined the Navy after high school, attaining the rank of seaman first class. When he returned from service, he moved to Evanston, Illinois, along with his brother Eugene. There, Stewart worked as a mail sorter in the post office and took evening classes at Roosevelt University in Chicago. Later, he dropped out of school in order to help his brother with his college expenses. Stewart then trained to be a barber, earning a certificate from Moler Barber College in 1947. For more than a decade, Stewart earned his living as a barber in various places in Illinois, Wisconsin, and New York.

Saw First Black Cowboy

In the early 1960s, Stewart travelled to Denver to visit a relative—a visit that would decide the rest of his career. One day while they were sight-seeing, Stewart noticed a black man dressed as a cowboy. "He was wearing full cowboy regalia—boots, chaps, gun belt, spurs, cowboy hat—I mean everything," Stewart told

At a Glance...

Born Paul Wilbur Stewart, December 18, 1925, Clinton, Iowa; son of Eugene Joseph Stewart and Martha L. Moor Stewart; married Johnnie Mae Davis, 1986; children: Mark, Tracy, Linda, Earl. *Education:* Hampton Institute, Roosevelt College; certificate, Moler Barber College, 1947.

Licensed barber: Illinois, Wisconsin, New York, and Colorado; Curator, Black American West Foundation; Director, Black American West Museum.

Addresses: *Home*—Denver, Colorado. *Office*—Black American West Museum, 3091 California, Denver, CO 80205.

The Smithsonian. ``I said to my cousin, 'Look at that drugstore cowboy. Who's he trying to fool? Everybody knows there are no black cowboys.''

Stewart's cousin explained that the man was a well-known local rancher—and in fact, black cowboys were no rarity in Colorado. Stewart suddenly realized that black people had been left out of the history books about the West, and he set out to correct the omission. Stewart decided that he would dedicate himself to finding out everything he could about black cowboys, so that other children would not be taught the incomplete history that he had learned. "It became a sort of mission," he told *The Smithsonian.*

Stewart moved to Denver and opened a barbershop, which would be the scene of his initial research on African Americans in the West. As he cut black men's hair, Stewart would ask them if they knew or had heard about any black pioneers. A surprising number of them did. Sometimes, Stewart secretly taped these informal interviews. Later, he sought interviews outside the barber shop, convinced that he had found his life's work--collecting oral history about blacks in the days of the frontier. Soon, Stewart was travelling all over the western United States, collecting artifacts and interviews.

As the news spread that he was interested in black Western history, people began to drop by the barbershop, bringing artifacts that had been passed down to them—cowboy boots, miner's helmets, photographs, etc. Stewart initially displayed these items in his shop, until it became so crowded that he decided to look for a

permanent exhibition space.

Founded Black American West Museum

In 1971, Stewart established the collection in an old Denver saloon; but downtown urban renewal soon forced him to look for another location. Denver's Clayton College offered to house the "Paul Stewart collection" in a room on its campus, where it remained for almost ten years. By then, the collection had become a real museum, incorporated and with a board of directors. Stewart was no longer called the curator of the Black American West Foundation, but rather the director of the Black American West Museum. What the museum lacked, however, was a prominent location; visitors often wandered the campus unable to find the collection.

> "I said to my cousin, 'Look at that drugstore cowboy. Who's he trying to fool? Everybody knows there are no black cowboys,'"

In the mid-1980s, the museum was moved to a larger, more accessible site in Denver's Five Points, a largely black neighborhood near the city's downtown area, and the hub of Denver's black community in the 1940s and 1950s. In the early 1990s, the collection was moved to another location in Five Points—the home of the first African American female physician in Colorado.

The 35,000 items in the museum's collection include personal artifacts, clothing, photographs, paintings, letters, newspapers, legal documents, and oral histories. One exhibit—objects used by Colorado homesteader Charlie Rothwell—includes rope and saddles, scales for weighing hay, rifle and pistol holders, a small anvil for making horseshoes, a two-man saw, a Navajo blanket, a hat, and a coffee pot with a two-foot handle, for use over a campfire. An unusual aspect of the museum is that artifacts are not hidden behind glass, but out in the open so that visitors can touch them.

The museum documents the lives of the Younger brothers, outlaws who travelled with Jesse James; cowboy Bill Pickett, who was honored with a US postage stamp; and Mary Fields, the second female ever to drive a US mail coach. It also tells the stories of nameless black American men and women who came to the West in covered wagons, and established themselves in black towns such as Dearfield, Colorado, working as farmers, teachers, barbers, and doctors. There is material on black homesteaders, miners, and enlisted men, or "Buffalo soldiers." "The Indians called them Buffalo soldiers," Stewart explained in *The Smithsonian,* "because they were tough and their hair reminded the Indians of buffalo fur—and the name stuck. The buffalo was sacred to the Indians, so some historians believe the name was also a term of respect."

Open only for limited hours for many years, the museum is now open seven days a week. More than 5,000 visitors from the United States and abroad visit every year. The museum offers education activities and programs, including tours, films, special events, and travelling exhibits. The calendar of events for 1996 includes a celebration of the signing of the Emancipation Proclamation, a youth writing contest, a Western Dance Jamboree, and a 1960s scavenger hunt.

Delivers Lectures on Black History

Stewart often gives lectures about black western history at schools, libraries, churches, or other organizations. At one church event, where Stewart was delivering a lecture on black women pioneers, he met his future wife, gospel singer Johnnie Mae Davis. The couple married in 1986, and have four children--Mark, Tracy, Linda, and Earl.

In addition to his work in establishing and running the Black American West Museum, Stewart is a member of the Historical Records Advisory Board for Colorado and has taught at Metropolitan State College in Denver. In 1972, he coproduced the documentary "Blacks Here and Now," which was shown on Denver's public television channel. He has received several awards for his work, including the Black Educators United Award in 1977.

Now, like the rancher that he saw more than thirty years ago, Stewart often dresses like a cowboy—not to handle cattle, but to educate. "Paul always liked to wear Western-style clothing—he just needed a wife to show him how to put it all together," Johnnie Mae Davis told *The Smithsonian.* "There aren't too many men who can walk around dressed like a cowboy and carry it off. But Western culture is really in Paul's blood—he's presenting an image of something that means a lot to him."

Sources

Books

Who's Who Among African Americans, 1996-97, Gale Research, 1996.

Periodicals

Oakland Post, May 31, 1995, p. 4.
Smithsonian, August 1989, p. 58.

Other

Black American West Museum Web page (http://www.coax.net/people/lwf/bawmus.htm)

—Carrie Golus

Sheryl Swoopes

1971—

Professional basketball player

Her name rhymes with "hoops." Her talent has drawn comparisons with Michael Jordan. More importantly, she has earned that ultimate endorsement contract most athletes only dream about—a line of footwear named in her honor. Sheryl Swoopes is helping to re-define the limits of women's professional basketball in the United States. A prominent member of the U.S. women's national basketball team, Swoopes is the only player—male or female—ever to score 47 points in a collegiate national championship game. She is widely considered one of the finest women's basketball players ever to grace a court. Former basketball phenomenon Nancy Lieberman-Cline told the *Washington Post* of Swoopes: "We're breaking new ground with Sheryl. Women's sports hasn't had a team sport athlete with the star-appeal that Sheryl has. She's young and pretty and articulate…. She's the female Jordan."

Being a "female Jordan" is nice, but the title does not bring with it the kind of salary and opportunities Michael Jordan enjoys. Indeed, Swoopes has been described as a "Legend without a League," since women's professional basketball has never been able to gain a foot-hold

in the American market. In 1993 the engaging Swoopes completely dominated the National Collegiate Athletic Association (NCAA) championships. Had she been a man, she would have cruised into the National Basketball Association draft and landed on a team with a million-dollar salary. Instead she had to embark for Italy, where she faced homesickness, language barriers, and a meager salary by sports standards, just to be able to keep playing. Recent years have been kinder to the emerging star, however. She is an anchor of the women's national team and the first sportswoman ever to get her own signature line of athletic footwear: the Nike "Air Swoopes" basketball shoes. She may make a pittance compared to Jordan, but she is still a wealthy woman with a bright future.

Homesickness Influenced Her Career

Swoopes was born in 1971 in Brownfield, Texas, a small city in the western region of the state. Her parents were divorced, and she grew up with her mother, Louise, and three brothers. Swoopes credits her siblings with helping to hone her game. "At first, they didn't like playing with

At a Glance...

Born Sheryl Denise Swoopes, March 25, 1971, in Brownfield, TX; daughter of Louise Swoopes; married, husband's name Eric Jackson. *Education:* Attended South Plains Junior College, 1989-91; Texas Tech University, B.A., 1994.

Basketball player. Led the Texas Tech Lady Red Raiders to the National Collegiate Athletic Association Final Four, 1993; scored 47 points in the NCAA championship final as Texas Tech defeated Ohio State 84-82. Played professional basketball in Italy, 1993 and 1994. Joined U.S. Women's basketball team, 1994; played in Goodwill Games and 1996 Summer Olympics.

Selected awards: Named collegiate player of the year, 1993; Naismith and Sullivan Awards for amateur athletics, 1993; named Sportswoman of the Year by Women's Sports Foundation, 1993.

Addresses: c/o Nike, Inc., One Bowerman Dr., Beaverton, OR 97005.

me," she admitted in the *Los Angeles Times.* "Then when they did, they wouldn't play hard. But eventually one brother, James, played ball at Murray State. He's 6-4. He wouldn't play hard until he saw how good I was getting, when I beat him a couple of times." With the help of her two older brothers, Swoopes developed into an All-State and All-American high school player—one who was eager to test her skills against any opponent. "It helps to play with the guys," she explained in the *Washington Post.* "They're so much more physical than girls are. Once you go out and you play with guys, and you get in a situation with girls, you think, 'Well, if I scored on that guy, I know I can score on her.'"

The six-foot Swoopes was widely recruited by colleges, including the high-profile University of Texas at Austin. "Texas was the only school I really considered out of high school," Swoopes told the *Los Angeles Times.* "It was a big national basketball power, and I thought they could take my game to another level. But once I got there ... well, I just didn't realize how far it was from home." Austin is 400 miles from Brownfield, and the moment Swoopes arrived on her new campus she began to feel the distance acutely. After four days she relinquished her full scholarship and returned to her mother. Ignoring the

suggestions that she had ruined her career, she enrolled in South Plains Junior College in Levelland, a school within easy driving distance of Brownfield. That institution was glad to have her, especially when she was named National Junior College Player of the Year after her second season.

Making a Mark in the NCAA

In 1991 Swoopes enrolled at Texas Tech University in Lubbock. Still close to home, she nevertheless found a coach and a program that could put her amazing skills to use. With Swoopes's help, the Lady Raiders finally moved out of the shadow of the University of Texas Lady Longhorns, winning back-to-back Southwest Conference titles. Swoopes's coach at Texas Tech, Marsha Sharp, told *Sports Illustrated:* "I can't tell you what Sheryl has meant to this program. She'll be a legend in women's basketball, but not just because of her play. She has a charisma that the crowd loves. You never doubt that she is a team player."

> "I never in my wildest dreams thought I would have as many opportunities as I do to go out and do someg with my life and actually make money so I can help the peple who helped me."

Swoopes's teammates and coach might have considered her a "team player," but their opponents usually came off the court viewing the Brownfield native as a one-woman wrecking crew. Fourteen times over two seasons at Texas Tech she scored 30 or more points in a game. In her senior season she averaged 27.4 points and 9.3 rebounds per game as the Lady Raiders compiled a 31-3 record, including a national championship. Facing the University of Texas at Austin in the Southwest Conference final, she put a phenomenal 53 points on the board. As Swoopes herself observed to the *Washington Post* during those days, "At times, I get it in my mind that there is no way I can miss."

That feeling of invincibility followed Swoopes to the NCAA tournament in 1993. There, in the semifinal match between Texas Tech and Vanderbilt University, she earned 31 points, 11 rebounds, and three steals as the Lady Raiders cruised to a 60-46 victory. Swarmed by reporters after the game, Swoopes predicted that she would play even better in the final, when Texas Tech would meet Ohio State University.

Her predictions proved true in dramatic fashion. As a nation watched, Swoopes and the Lady Raiders beat favored Ohio State in a close game, 84-82, before a sellout crowd at Atlanta's Omni Arena. People had little to say about the final score, however. All anyone talked about was Swoopes's personal performance—47 points, including 16 of 24 field goals, four three-point shots, and a perfect 11-for-11 from the free throw line. "I thought I should personally take control of the game," she explained in the *Washington Post.* "I felt like I needed to score whenever I got [the ball]."

What Swoopes did in her evening at the Omni was break the old record for most points scored in an NCAA final game. The former record of 44 points had belonged for 20 years to Bill Walton, who had gone on from college to become a top-ranked NBA player. "I've been watching a lot of basketball over a lot of years, men and women, professional and amateur," wrote *Atlanta Journal and Constitution* columnist Furman Bisher. "... I've never seen a player take over a game and keep it won for her team like Sheryl Swoopes took over for Texas Tech." Coach Sharp was even more glowing in her appraisal of her star's performance. "There are no words to explain what a great player Sheryl Swoopes is," Sharp exclaimed in the *Washington Post.* "We are just pleased that she got to show the whole nation."

Even the Ohio State coach graciously conceded that Swoopes could not be beaten. "You don't really appreciate Sheryl Swoopes until you try and stop her," Nancy Darsch commented in the *Washington Post.* "She's an absolutely tremendous player. She showed why she's national player of the year."

Tough Times for a Female Pro

In the wake of the NCAA championship, Swoopes was endowed with almost every prestigious collegiate and amateur honor imaginable. She won both the Naismith and the Sullivan Awards, and she was named Sportswoman of the Year by the Women's Sports Foundation. Sports apparel companies—most especially Nike—called about endorsement contracts. What Swoopes wanted to do most was play more basketball. She faced the grim reality that all American women basketball players must face: she would have to go abroad in order to turn pro. Her salary would probably be about a tenth of what her rookie male counterparts could draw from the NBA—and she would have to acclimate to a new

culture, a new language, and a new home in another part of the world.

"People say, if you were a male, you would have gone in the [NBA draft] lottery," Swoopes said in the *Washington Post.* "It's really frustrating to think about it, to think that men have so many more opportunities than women. Going overseas and staying in the United States, those are just two totally different things. The NBA, you watch it on television all the time, but you don't hear anything about women playing overseas, unless you know their college coaches and ask them how so and so is doing. It's sad and frustrating."

Nevertheless, Swoopes signed a contract to play basketball with Bari of the women's Italian professional league. She appeared in only ten games before returning home to America, citing contract disputes, the language barrier, and culture shock as reasons for her quick exit. She had indeed faced the frustrations first-hand. "There I was, right after the championship game, still wanting to play," she recalled in the *Atlanta Journal and Constitution.* "I wanted to play the next day.... On a scale of one to 10, I was at a 10. Then I went overseas, and I was at a one all of a sudden. It was a big drop." She returned to Texas Tech, finished her degree requirements, played in pickup games, and did some volunteer coaching.

A Place on the National Team

Aware that her skills were eroding, Swoopes was relieved when she was invited to try out for the U.S. women's national basketball team. Membership on the team—consisting of a core of America's best female players—offered Swoopes the opportunity to play highly competitive basketball and to stay in the U.S. Her goal, of course, was to represent the U.S. at the 1996 Summer Games in Atlanta. "I almost go crazy thinking about going back to Atlanta for the Olympics," she said in the *Atlanta Journal and Constitution.* "I can't wait."

Joining seasoned professionals such as Teresa Edwards and Lisa Leslie, Swoopes embarked on a busy schedule of exhibition games and appearances at such tournaments as the world championships and the Goodwill Games. Her salary as a Team U.S.A. member—estimated at $50,000—was regally supplemented by the introduction of a Nike "Air Swoopes" basketball shoe for women. Swoopes promoted the shoe—the first ever named for a woman athlete—in a high-profile commercial directed by Spike Lee, as well as by personal appearances across the country. Swoopes saw the publicity as a perfect vehicle to broaden the fan base for women's basketball in America. "Our opportunity to change things for women's basketball is now," she claimed in the *New York Times.*

Swoopes might have been right on target, as usual. The NBA has endorsed the formation of an American women's professional league, and she is assured a starring position on one of the teams. Fan support for a women's league may hinge on the Olympic performance of the women's national team, as well as upon the popularity of products the women basketball players have endorsed. As the new millennium approaches, Swoopes's radiant personality and basketball talent could bring her the level of fame that attends some of the NBA's male players—if not necessarily the extravagant salary. She has also expressed interest in coaching, and this too could provide her with a comfortable future. Rutgers University coach C. Vivian Stringer recently signed a contract that could pay as much as $300,000 per year—incentive enough for any former NCAA star.

All of the acclaim she has received has been a sweet surprise for Swoopes, the small-town Texas girl who grew up shooting hoops with her brothers. "I never in my wildest dreams thought I would have as many opportunities as I do to go out and do something with my life and actually make money so I can help the people who

helped me," she concluded in the *Washington Post.* "Coming from a town of 10,000, it's really unbelievable. It's like I'm in a big old dream."

Sources

Books

Johnson, Anne Janette, *Great Women in Sports,* Visible Ink, 1996, pp. 458-461.

Periodicals

Atlanta Journal and Constitution, April 2, 1993, p. E1; April 5, 1993, pp. D1, D5; April 12, 1993, p. C2; March 27, 1994, p. E9.
Emerge, December/January 1996, p. 12.
Los Angeles Times, April 2, 1993, p. C1.
New York Times, March 30, 1995, p. D9; October 26, 1995, p. B16.
Sports Illustrated, April 12, 1993, p. 42.
Washington Post, April 5, 1993, p. C1; June 15, 1993, p. E1.

—Anne Janette Johnson

Frank Thomas

1968—

Professional baseball player

Frank Thomas is quite possibly the most exciting major league baseball player to emerge in the 1990s. The six-foot-five-inch, 257-pound Thomas carries the nickname "The Big Hurt," which aptly describes his devastating talents as a power hitter for the Chicago White Sox. Thomas is the only player in recent history to have won back-to-back American League Most Valuable Player citations—in 1993 and 1994—after he put together outstanding seasons as a leader in a number of offensive and defensive categories. *Chicago Tribune* reporter Skip Myslenski described Thomas as "a major star, a supernova in his game's constellation of stars." For his part, the hard-working Thomas has only this to say: "I want to make a dent in the game."

Thomas's performance has brought comparison to some of baseball's biggest names. He is one of only five players to bat over .300 with 20 or more home runs, 100 runs batted in, 100 runs, and 100 walks in three consecutive seasons—and the other four players are in the Baseball Hall of Fame. Small wonder that Thomas earned his first Most Valuable Player award by unanimous vote from the always-cantankerous Baseball Writ-

ers' Association of America. As Jerome Holtzman noted in the *Chicago Tribune,* Thomas is "among the very best hitters in baseball history, probably the best of his generation, which is flooded with strong-arm sluggers hitting for both distance and average."

For Thomas, baseball is a serious business. If he performs at the highest levels, he also sets impossible standards for himself and works toward them. "I'm a competitive person," he explained in the *Chicago Tribune.* "I've been involved in athletics all my life, and I don't handle failure well. That's why I try to outwork everyone else." In another *Chicago Tribune* profile, he concluded: "I've learned this much. A player can't take anything for granted. I have a gift. But that means I have to work extra hard to get better."

"Big Baby"

The fifth of six children born to Frank and Charlie Mae Thomas, Frank Edward Thomas Jr. was admittedly spoiled by his doting parents and older siblings. Growing up in Columbus, Georgia, he was called "Big Baby" and

At a Glance...

Full name Frank Edward Thomas Jr.; born May 27, 1968, in Columbus, GA; son of Frank (a bail bondsman) and Charlie Mae (a textile worker) Thomas; married Elise Silver, February 8, 1992; children: Sterling (son), Sloan (daughter). *Education:* Attended Auburn University, 1986-89.

Baseball player with Chicago White Sox organization, 1989—. Signed with White Sox in first round of 1989 college draft (seventh pick overall); member of Class A Sarasota White Sox, 1989; member of Birmingham Barons, 1990; made debut with Chicago White Sox, August 2, 1990, became full-time first baseman for White Sox, 1991.

Selected awards: Southeastern Conference Most Valuable Player and All-SEC Tournament selection (baseball), 1989; named American League Most Valuable Player, 1993 and 1994. Member of American League All-Star Team, 1994 and 1995.

Addresses: *Home*—Burr Ridge, IL. *Office*—Chicago White Sox, 333 W. 35th St., Chicago, IL 60616.

was encouraged to develop his gift for athletics. His parents never pushed him into sports, but they knew that if he was not at home he was playing ball somewhere nearby. As he grew he made little secret of his ambitions to play professional ball—even though his working-class family could hardly imagine such a life. "When I was a kid, probably around 12, I already knew I wanted to be a player," Thomas told the *Chicago Tribune.* "So I was just telling [my parents] what I wanted, and I followed my dream, and I worked hard enough to get it. A lot of people nowadays won't dedicate themselves like that....I was a little different."

Thomas was just nine years old when he convinced his father and the local coaches that he could play football in the Pop Warner league, which catered to 12-year-olds. Sure enough, he easily made one of the teams and won the job of starting tight end. He was equally successful in Little League baseball, where he began seeing the frequent intentional walks that put him on base to this day. His success in sports was put into perspective by a family tragedy. In 1977 his two-year-old sister Pamela died of leukemia. Recalling those days many years later, Thomas told the *Chicago Tribune:* "It

was sad. It affected me. But it's something you don't look back on. The way I've dealt with it is to totally forget about it. As the years went by, it got easier and easier." Thomas has not really forgotten his baby sister, however. For years he has worked closely with The Leukemia Foundation, helping to raise money for research into a cure for the disease.

Thomas's skills won him a scholarship to The Brookstone School, a private college preparatory institution in his home town. He stayed only three years, opting to return to the local public school and its more competitive sports teams. There he lost little time in making his mark. As a Columbus High School sophomore he hit cleanup for a baseball team that won a state championship. As a senior he hit .440 for the baseball team, was named an All-State tight end with the football team, and played forward with the basketball team. He wanted desperately to win a contract to play professional baseball, but he was completely overlooked in the 1986 amateur draft. Baseball teams signed some 891 players on that occasion, and Thomas was not among them.

"I was shocked and sad," Thomas recalled in the *Chicago Tribune.* "I saw a lot of guys I played against get drafted, and I knew they couldn't do what I could do. But I've had people all my life saying you can't do this, you can't do that. It scars you. No matter how well I've done. People have misunderstood me for some reason. I was always one of the most competitive kids around."

A Second Chance in Baseball

In the autumn of 1986, Thomas accepted a scholarship to play football at Auburn University. Even so, his love of baseball drew him to the Auburn baseball team, where the coach immediately recognized his potential. "We loved him," Auburn baseball coach Hal Baird told *Sports Illustrated.* "He was fun to be around—always smiling, always bright-eyed." He was also a deadly hitter, posting a .359 batting average and leading the Tigers in runs batted in as a freshman. During the summer of 1987 he played for the U.S. Pan American Team, earning a spot on the final roster that would compete in the Pan American Games. The Games coincided with the beginning of football practice back at Auburn, so he left the Pan Am team and returned to college—only to be injured twice in early season football games.

Thomas might have lost his scholarship that year because he could no longer play football. Instead the school continued his funding, and baseball became his sole sport. He was good enough as a sophomore to win consideration for the U.S. National Team—preparing for the 1988 Summer Olympics—but he was cut from the final squad. Stung and misunderstood again, he fought back. By the end of his junior baseball season he had hit 19 home runs, 19 doubles, and had batted .403 with a slugging percentage of .801. With another amateur draft looming, the scouts began to comprehend that the big Georgia native could indeed play baseball.

The Chicago White Sox picked Thomas seventh in the first round of the June 1989 draft—after his home state team the Atlanta Braves had chosen someone else. While he would have liked to have played in Georgia, Thomas was thrilled to be with Chicago. He made his minor league debut with the Sarasota, Florida Class-A White Sox. The following year, 1990, he was named Minor League Player of the Year by *Baseball America* magazine after hitting .323 with 18 home runs, 71 runs batted in, and a league-best 112 walks as a member of the Class-AA Birmingham Barons.

Finally prepared to admit that they might have a future star on their hands, the White Sox organization called Thomas to the major leagues on August 2, 1990. Thomas jumped into a tight pennant race and batted .330 with seven home runs and 31 runs batted in over the following two months. He never saw another inning of minor league baseball after that. By the spring of 1991 he had won a position as regular first baseman for Chicago.

The Big Hurt

In his first full season with the White Sox, Thomas batted .318 with 32 home runs and 109 runs batted in. He led the majors in walks, with 138, and on-base percentage (.453). At a stage when most young players are struggling to establish themselves, he finished third in the American League Most Valuable Player voting, behind veterans Cal Ripken Jr. and Cecil Fielder. Chicago fans quickly dubbed Thomas "The Big Hurt," based on his size and his ability to punish opposing pitchers.

Prior to the 1992 season, the *New York Times* released an article about the relative worth of active major league players. Using a formula based on several statistics, the *Times* declared that Thomas was "the biggest bargain in the majors," based on his 1991 salary of $120,000. The White Sox lost little time in placating their emerging star, issuing Thomas a new three-year contract with a base salary more than $1 million, not including performance bonuses. Thomas responded in 1992 by leading the American League in extra-base hits, on-base percentage, walks (a tie at 122), and doubles. Thomas

promised that he could do even better if he could avoid the distractions of superstardom. "Concentration is the key," he explained in the *Chicago Tribune*. "I try not to be distracted. Lately, I've been blowing a lot of people off because they've been getting in the way. I don't like to do that. But to be successful, I've got to have time for myself."

Both Thomas and the White Sox turned in stellar years in 1993. For Thomas it was the unanimous Most Valuable Player award. For the White Sox it was a division title in the competitive American League West. Although the White Sox were beaten in the American League playoffs by the Toronto Blue Jays, Thomas emerged as his team's focal point. He was rewarded accordingly with a four-year contract estimated to be worth $42 million, as well as lucrative product endorsement deals with Reebok, Pepsi-Cola, DonRuss, and Bausch & Lomb. The financial security Thomas achieved with the deal did little to dim his competitive spirit. "I can't afford...not showing up at the ball park mentally," he told the *New York Times*. "I have to be on every night to be a force in the lineup. I'm a humble guy; I've always been humble. But I realize my place."

Back-to-Back MVP

White Sox fans might always moan for what might have been. Frank Thomas was on his way into the history books—and the 1994 baseball season was ended prematurely by a players' strike. No one felt the sting of the strike more than Thomas, who stood poised to achieve one of baseball's most prestigious honors: the Triple Crown. Not since 1967 had any player finished the regular season first in average, home runs, and runs batted in. Thomas was contending for the honor when the strike occurred, and his numbers were good enough to earn him a second American League Most Valuable Player award. Pressed by the media to comment on his accomplishments—and his future—Thomas told the *Atlanta Journal and Constitution:* "I'm not into being known as the best by fans or the media. I care how I'm perceived by my peers. I can settle for the label `one of the best' because that means you're considered an elite player."

This "elite player" has let it be known that baseball comes first and off-the-field activities rank a distant second. For years Thomas has tried to avoid the kind of fish bowl existence that plagues fellow Windy City superstar Michael Jordan. This dedication to his game as a serious business has led to some misunderstandings in Chicago for Thomas, but as the White Sox continue to fare well, he has earned respect for his workmanlike attitude. Thomas is such a lethal hitter that he draws walks—intentional and otherwise—with stunning regularity. Some observers have even speculated that he will some day be walked with the bases loaded, so tremendous is his home run potential. "We're very mindful of his presence," Seattle Mariners manager Lou Piniella told the *Chicago Tribune*. "If we have our druthers, we'll let somebody else beat us."

> "I'm not into being known as the best by fans or the media, I care how I'm perceived by my peers. I can settle for the label 'one of the best' because that means you're considered an elite player."

Thomas has expressed no interest in leaving Chicago, at least in the near future. "I see myself with the Sox my whole career," the slugger told *Sports Illustrated* in 1993. Stability has been part of Thomas's life off the field as well. His 1992 marriage to Elise Silver, the daughter of a minor league baseball team owner, has produced two children, a son and a daughter. Thomas plays an active, if quiet, role in many charities, donating money from autograph signings to a variety of local and national sources. And although he has achieved more in a short major league career than many players do in a lifetime, he still has big ambitions. "I relish the opportunity to rise to the top," he told the *Chicago Tribune*. "When you see the Jordans and guys like that who love that type moment, it takes a special guy to want that. I want to be the guy there with two out and the bases loaded trying to get a hit. I love that situation."

Asked what final mark he would like to leave on the game, Thomas paused and concluded: "I want to be able to…when I leave here, I want people to say, 'Hey, I don't know if some of the things he did can ever be done again.'"

Sources

Atlanta Journal and Constitution, July 30, 1994, p. D7.

Chicago Tribune, March 25, 1992, p. 1 (Sports); November 11, 1993, p. 6 (Sports); March 23, 1994, p. 1 (Sports); August 7, 1994, p. 1 (Sports); September 17, 1995, p. 3 (Sports).

New York Times, March 12, 1992; October 5, 1993, p. B13; October 28, 1993, p. B15; November 11, 1993.

Sports Illustrated, September 16, 1991, p. 30-34; September 13, 1993, pp. 40-44.

—Mark Kram

C. Delores Tucker

1927—

Association executive, activist

C. DeLores Tucker has never shied away from sensitive political issues. A longtime civil rights activist who marched with Dr. Martin Luther King Jr. and raised funds for the National Association for the Advancement of Colored People (NAACP), Tucker has taken her deep convictions and organizing skills into a new arena. Today she is on a crusade to alter the violent, anti-female message in gangsta rap, a message she sees as undermining and even contributing to the early deaths of American youth—especially black youth. Since 1994 Tucker has used her considerable skills as a political figure and public speaker to denounce gangsta rap and to persuade the major entertainment conglomerates not to sell it. "It's an abomination to all of us, after we were taught to sing the songs of faith and hope and freedom in the days of slavery, to let this go on," she told the *Chicago Tribune.* "I'd die before I'd let that music continue to be."

Tucker's crusade has led her into some unlikely alliances. Being a liberal Democrat who has worked diligently for her party, she has joined forces with Bill Bennett, a conservative Republican and former member of the Reagan and Bush administrations who has also in-

veighed against offensive rock and rap lyrics. In 1995 Bennett and Tucker mounted an effective dual campaign aimed primarily at Time Warner, Inc., in order to persuade the media giant to sever its ties to record distributors who sold gangsta rap. Tucker explained in the *Los Angeles Times* that, while she disagreed with Bennett's political views, she was completely in accord with him on the issue of promoting better values among youth. "This [issue] transcends politics," she concluded. "This deals with the most sacred gift God has given the world, and that's the child. We have a responsibility to preserve, protect, and make sure that the child is nurtured with the most positive of virtues and values. Let's make virtues and values something that is a proud badge for everyone to wear."

A Minister's Daughter

Cynthia DeLores Nottage was born in Philadelphia, Pennsylvania in 1927 and was the tenth of 11 children in her family. Her Bahamian-born father and her hard-working mother approached life from a Christian per-

At a Glance...

Born Cynthia DeLores Nottage, October 4, 1927, in Philadelphia, PA; daughter of Whitfield (a minister) and Captilda (Gardiner) Nottage; married William Tucker (a businessman), July, 1951. *Education:* Attended Temple University, Pennsylvania State University, the University of Pennsylvania, and North Philadelphia School of Realty.

Civil rights activist and fundraiser for the National Association for the Advancement of Colored People, ca. 1955—; first female member of the Philadelphia Zoning Board; Secretary of the Commonwealth of Pennsylvania, 1971-77; president, Federation of Democratic Women, 1977; chairman, Democratic National Committee Black Caucus, 1984; founder and vice-chairman, National Political Congress of Black Women, 1984—. Founder, Bethune-DuBois Fund, a scholarship and opportunity program for minority youngsters.

Member: NAACP (board of trustees), Rainbow Coalition, National Organization of Women, Democratic National Committee.

Selected awards: Honorary doctorate degrees from Villa Maria College (Erie, PA), and Morris College (Sumter, SC); NAACP Freedom Fund award, 1961; named one of the 100 most influential black Americans by *Ebony* magazine, 1972-77; Thurgood Marshall Award, 1982.

Addresses: *Office*—National Political Congress of Black Women, 600 New Hampshire Ave. N.W., Washington, DC 20037.

illness that kept her out of college for a year, she changed her course. In 1951 she married William Tucker, a construction company owner who soon built a fortune in Philadelphia real estate. Although the couple never had children of their own, they helped to raise nieces and nephews, and they built a mutually respectful relationship that endures to this day. In the *Washington Post,* William Tucker called his wife "one of the most fearless individuals I have ever known," adding: "She will take on anyone, anything, if that is what she thinks is right.... She is not one who will readily entertain the idea of compromise about anything."

As the civil rights movement gained momentum in the late 1950s and early 1960s, Tucker found the perfect channel for her activism. She joined the NAACP and helped to raise funds for the organization, a task that she still conducts as a member of its board of trustees. She also participated in marches and demonstrations all around the country, joining the Reverend and Mrs. Martin Luther King Jr. in their call for freedom and equality. Tucker recalled those days in the *Washington Post:* "I realized we always started at the church and marched to the political kingdom, whether local or state or national. And I realized that's where we needed to go to make a difference. That's where the decisions were being made that affected our lives, but we weren't in those seats."

As the 1960s progressed, Tucker campaigned for black candidates and served on the Pennsylvania Democratic Committee. She also became the first-ever black member of the Philadelphia Zoning Board. Her ties to the Democratic Party in Pennsylvania served her well when, in January of 1971, she was named Secretary of the Commonwealth by then-governor Milton Shapp. The appointment made Tucker the highest-ranking black woman in state government, an honor not lost in *Ebony* magazine, which listed her as among the "100 most influential" African Americans every year during her tenure. She lost the position in 1977, "after charges that she used state workers and resources to produce speeches for which she received $65,000 in 28 months," as stated in a *Washington Post* report.

Defending the Interests of Democrats, Women

After leaving state government, Tucker turned to national politics. She served as chairman of the Black Caucus of the Democratic National Committee for 11 years and spoke at the Democratic National Convention five times. She also entered the 1992 Congressional race in her Philadelphia district, but she lost in the

spective and encouraged their children to do so as well. Sundays found the close-knit family together in church, where young DeLores directed the choir and played the saxophone. "My mother and father gave us wonderful values," Tucker claimed in *Good Housekeeping.* "They taught us to be good and loving, and to use our lives to help others."

The notion that she was a "child of the king" helped Tucker to deal with racial slights when she was young. She originally intended to become a doctor, but after an primary election. Her private business dealings included real estate ventures and a position with the *Philadelphia Tribune.*

In 1984 Tucker began a new organization that has since grown in power and influence. The National Political Congress of Black Women was formed to advance the interests of the black community, especially its women. The group has devised a 10-point covenant plan to reclaim and improve the African American community--focusing on voter registration, education quality and equity, welfare reform that will not victimize poor people, and fair and adequate legal services for everyone. The NPCBW has involved itself with broad national issues as well as small local ones--throwing its clout behind beleaguered Georgia Congresswoman Cynthia J. McKinney and other black congresswomen, as well as honoring civil rights pioneers such as Myrlie Evers-Williams, Dr. Betty Shabazz, and Coretta Scott King.

Under Tucker's direction the NPCBW has also included the reform of the music industry in the group's agenda. Tucker herself became enraged by gangsta rap after she saw the effect it had on some of her young nieces and nephews. In *Good Housekeeping,* Tucker described the plight on one niece who had parroted the bad language she heard in the songs to the point that she had become "at eighteen... a social leper." When she turned her attention to the lyrics of rap songs--especially those of Snoop Doggy Dogg and Tupac Shakur—Tucker was infuriated. Beginning in 1993 with local demonstrations in front of record shops, she began to fight back.

Crusader Against the Gangstas

With her sharp command of rhetoric and her elegant, turban-clad appearance, Tucker quickly became recognized for her campaign against gangsta rap. Calling the music "sleazy, pornographic smut," she waged war by passing out leaflets containing the lyrics from some gangsta albums and exhorting people to read them out loud. One person who took the challenge was political leader Julian Bond, who, in a column for the *Columbus Times,* expressed agreement with Tucker's stance. "C. DeLores Tucker is convinced that this music and the talent that creates it can be a force for good, and that positive images can be sold to young Americans just as easily as the stereotypical visions of sex-crazed young black women and thuggish young black men some of this music promotes," Bond wrote. "If you agree, maybe you'll pay a little more attention to what goes into your youngster's head.... Maybe you might start by letting him know that if he can't recite it at the breakfast table, he can't import it into his mind or your house any other way."

Just as she had in the civil rights days, Tucker decided to take her fight right into the corporate boardrooms of businesses profiting from gangsta rap. The first and most visible target she chose was Time Warner, Inc., a massive entertainment conglomerate that owns records, magazines, movies, television stations, and other forms of entertainment. In 1995 Tucker bought stock in Time Warner, enabling her to gain entrance to the company's annual shareholders' meeting. There she took the microphone and challenged the executives to read aloud the lyrics from albums sold by Interscope Records, a distributor owned in part by Time Warner.

By that time, Tucker had been joined by Bill Bennett, a conservative author best known for serving as Ronald Reagan's "drug czar." When Bennett and Tucker took their crusade to television in a commercial condemning Time Warner and other purveyors of gangsta rap, the company executives arranged for a series of private meetings. The media reports that these meetings grew heated when the executives defended the sale of gangsta rap because suppressing it would be censorship and a violation of the artists' rights under the First Amendment. In return, Tucker blistered them for "putting profit before principle." She added in *People,* "You can't listen to all that language and filth without it affecting you."

In a bizarre twist, Tucker was sued by Interscope Records and by Death Row Records in the autumn of 1995. The suit contends that Tucker tried to coerce rap recorder Marion Suge Knight, head of Death Row Records, to pull out of his contract with Interscope and distribute his records through a new company that Tucker herself would control. The lawsuit also charges Tucker with conspiracy, threats, extortion, and bribery. Tucker has insisted that the suit is nothing more than an effort to squelch her effective campaign against gangsta rap and its musicians. "I welcome my day in court," she told the *Washington Post.* "My record speaks for itself. Their record and records speak for them."

The Controversy Continues

Tucker has found widespread support for her crusade among African Americans, including such notable entertainers as Dionne Warwick, Melba Moore, and activist Dick Gregory. Her support is far from unanimous, however. Supporters of gangsta rap as art have accused her of being narrow-minded and of seeing the music as the root of the problem, not as a symptom of widespread anger brought on by deplorable social conditions. As

Kevin Alexander Gray noted in *Emerge,* "When Tucker attacks rappers for racial and sexual violence and the denigration of women, she misses the point and the opportunity to do something about that violence. But rather than listen to the conditions described in gangsta rap and work to change them, Tucker is attacking the expression of those feelings." An alternative view was offered by Bakari Kitwana in *The Source:* "Although Tucker often goes overboard with at times blanket and inaccurate ranting and raving, the essence of her beef is reflective of a growing segment in the Black community who are against Black people participating in advancing stereotypical and demeaning portrayals of ourselves....If the hip-hop culture is to develop beyond its 'mainstream age,' the hip-hop community cannot be afraid of such criticism."

> "She will take on anyone, anything, if that is what she thinks is right.... She is not one who will readily entertain the idea of compromise about anything.
> —William Tucker

Tucker too wants to see progress in hip-hop music. She wants the artists to convey positive images, and hope, to listeners. She sees violent and misogynistic rap lyrics as a significant contribution to black-on-black violence and single-parent families, the first step, she claims, toward racial genocide. "If corporate responsibility dictates that we protect the whales, protect the rivers and protect the environment, then the most important of all Earth's resources should be protected," she asserted in the *Los Angeles Times.* At a time when most women have retired to a leisurely life, Tucker is still hard at work at a task she sees as God-given. "We have to try to save these children," she concluded in *People.* "They don't have daddies in the home, they don't have jobs, they don't have a support system. They only have us."

Sources

Books

Notable Black American Women, Gale, 1994, pp. 1155-1157.

Periodicals

Chicago Tribune, September 15, 1995, p. 8.
Columbus Times, September 19, 1995, p. A5.
Ebony, July 1972, pp. 60-62; September 1995, pp. 25-28.
Emerge, November 1995, pp. 64-67.
Good Housekeeping, October 1995, p. 30.
Hyde Park Citizen, July 20, 1995, p. 3.
Los Angeles Times, July 5, 1995, p. A1.
People, June 26, 1995, pp. 105-106.
Richmond Afro-American, July 12, 1995, p. A10.
The Source, November 1995, p. 22.
Washington Afro-American, August 26, 1995, p. A3.
Washington Post, November 29, 1995, p. C1.

—Anne Janette Johnson

Patrice Clarke Washington

1961—

Airline captain

When you live in the Bahamas it's practically a given that you'll do your shopping in Florida. "I remember many, many summers growing up when, as soon as we were done with school, we were on a plane headed for Miami," the now 35-year-old Chicagoan told *CBB* in a telephone interview. Virtually every summer, Christmas, and Easter school breaks, Washington, her mother, and two sisters would board a plane for the short hop across the water to visit with family members in the States to stock up on essentials. Accordingly, airline travel became second nature to this young Bahamian girl. And, somewhere up there in the clouds, above the shimmery blue of the Carribean, the bug bit--Washington decided she was going to fly planes for a living.

More than anything, she was determined to see the world beyond her lush, tropical island. And remarkably, nobody stopped her, nobody discouraged her, nobody said: You're female, you're black, you can't do these things. So Washington pressed on, despite the cultural and economic odds. And she succeeded far beyond anyone's expectations, including her own. In 1994, while working as first officer on DC-8 for United Parcel Service, she was promoted to captain—the nation's, and possibly the world's, first black commercial airline captain.

Washington's "first" was especially significant considering that there are fewer than a dozen black female pilots on major airlines, according to the Organization of Black Airline Pilots. Of UPS's own 1,650 pilots, only 59 percent are black and only 86 are women. Washington is the only one who is both black and female.

Of course, women had been flying planes for six decades, inspired by role models like Amelia Earhart in the 1930s and by the Women's Air Service Pilots of World War II. African Americans, however, had to fight their way in. After WWII ended in 1945, none of the 992 Tuskegee Airmen were able to get a job in commercial aviation. Throughout the 1960s and 1970s, it took a succession of lawsuits by black pilots against airlines—and eventually one brought by the Justice Department against United Airlines—to weed out the entrenched discrimination.

These facts were unknown to the Bahamian teen-ager with her head in the clouds. "Growing up in the Bahamas I didn't have that consciousness about race," Washington said. All around her were black professionals and blacks in government leadership posts. "So when someone said 'no,' as far as I was concerned it was no because 'this is the way it had to be.' I didn't relate to people and life in terms of black, white, male, or female. It was, 'I can do the job or I can't.'" As for the fact that she was a woman entering a man's world, perhaps the chief influence there was the fact that she grew up in an environment where male and female roles were blissfully combined.

At a Glance...

Born Patrice Francise Clarke on September 11, 1961. In Nassau, Bahamas; son of Nathaniel and Peggy Ann (now Lundy) Clarke. Married Ray Washington, February, 1994. *Education:* Attended Embry-Riddle Aeronautical University in Daytona Beach, Fla. Graduated in April 1982 with a commercial pilot's certificate and B.S. in aeronautical science.

Worked as a pilot for a charter company, Trans Island Airways, in the Bahamas, 1982-84. Flew as a first officer with Bahamasair 1984-88. Hired as a flight engineer for United Parcel Service May 1988; promoted to first officer, January 1990; upgraded to captain November, 1994. Believed to be first African American female pilot with a commercial airline.

Awards: Honoree for female trailblazer award, National Coalition of Federal Aviation Employees, 1995; honoree, Organization of Black Airline Pilots, 1995.

Addresses: *Office*—c/o United Parcel Service, 911 Grade Lane, Building 2, Louisville, KY 40213.

A World of Women

Born in Nassau, Bahamas on September 11, 1961, Patrice Clarke was only five-years-old when her parents, Peggy Ann and Nathaniel Clarke, divorced. Her father then faded almost completely from her life. As for her mother, Peggy Ann Lundy would later become involved in a long-term romantic relationship and eventually marry Leo John Lundy when Patrice was almost an adult. But, primarily, hers was a childhood without men. "I think maybe the lack of male role models [in my life] had a little to do with the decision [to become a pilot] because my head was never filled with the boy thing/girl thing," Washington said. "I wasn't told that 'the boys take out the garbage and the girls do the dishes.'" Because there were no boys in our house, we did it all."

Washington's family included her mother and two younger sisters: Natasha, two years her junior, and Lynette (who was adopted), 13 years her junior. There was a big extended family that cared for the girls while Peggy Ann Lundy was away working, first as a nurse's aide and later as the manager of a bar/restaurant. "There were tough

times," Washington remembered. "She seemed to make things work ... She worked her butt off for us. She was always gone. We had one day with her—Sundays." But Nassau "was safe, and being a relatively small island, family were real close ... within two to three miles of our house. The family network is what made the difference."

Washington decided to apply to Embry-Riddle Aeronautical University in Daytona Beach, Florida, her mother, she recalls, was "awestruck." Perhaps it was her career choice, perhaps it was the stratospheric cost flying school combined with a four-year college degree entails. Still, Peggy Ann Lundy never voiced a single objection, Washington remembers; she just worked all the harder to put her daughter through college.

At Embry-Riddle, young Patrice studied aerodynamics, meteorology, and physics along with the usual subjects; besides these subjects, the biggest distinction her campus had was the 210 hours she put in learning to fly. A Bahamian citizen (the Bahamas had already become independent of Great Britain), Washington went through other changes: She felt pulled to her adopted country, the United States and sought and won official residency here shortly after college graduation. Though she ultimately decided not to follow the usual career path pilots do--through the military. To be understood by her American peers, she realized she had to drop some of the British words she used, along with the lilting, broken English of her Bahamian upbringing.

She graduated in April of 1982 with a B.S. in aeronautical science. It was a recession year and a terrible time to be job-hunting. Finally giving up on a United States-based pilot's job, she returned, dejected, to Nassau that summer. But luck was on her side after all; she was hired by Trans Island Airways that September. At Trans Island she found immense satisfaction, flying charters around the Bahamas, South Florida, Haiti, and Grand Cayman. Finally, she was being allowed to fly over open water. And, seated at the helm of tiny six-and-ten-seater Aztecs and Islanders, she couldn't have been happier. The scenery, the new people she was meeting, and even the occasional gut-wrenching thunderstorms—it was the world she wanted.

But eventually Washington realized she wanted a bigger world and the chance to fly to its furthest reaches. So, in October of 1984, she accepted a job with Bahamasair, a much larger airline, where she could fly Boeing 737s to points as far away as Atlanta and New York. She had taken a giant step up to her eventual goal. Yet three-and-a-half years later, she was job-hunting again. "The point in time came when I got tired doing the same thing, which was flying the Bahamas and South Florida. After you've done that so many times, it gets old." So Washington began interviewing at major U.S. airlines, and eventually she landed--at UPS.

The Tough Ascent to the Top

Initially, Washington worked as a flight engineer on three-crew member flights, from UPS's home flight base in Louisville, Kentucky, to places like Anchorage, Alaska; Sydney, Australia, and Cologne, Germany. As a flight engineer, it was her job to check fuel levels and systems operation. But she yearned to get her hands on the controls of the huge cargo DC-8s she was helping to operate.

> "The point in time came when I got tired of doing the same thing, which was flying the Bahamas and South Florida. After you've done that so many times, it gets old."

Still, she was realizing her dream of getting around the globe. Flying to Alaska, for instance, she saw her first glacier, something she had only read about in school in the tropics. "When I saw the glaciers for the first time my mind went back to geography class, my eyes watered, and I was filled with emotion," Washington has written in a short autobiographical article.

In her personal life there was another emotional high. In February of 1994 she married Ray Washington, a pilot for American Airlines whom she met at an Organization of Black Airline Pilots convention. A little over a year later, she was pregnant with their first child.

But her professional career was moving slowly, and the young Bahamian who had rarely thought of race or gender as controlling factors was starting to think about them now. She yearned to be promoted to first officer so she could fly UPS's planes directly. "The hard times," she says, "were when I started to realize I was being treated differently either because of my sex and or because of my race." During an upgrade test flight at UPS, for instance, when she was being considered for a first officer upgrade, she was paired with a trainer who decided she was not capable of the upgrade. She wondered why.

But she still was not making the connection, she remembers. Then she was paired with a second trainer who also refused to pass her. During one flight, she says he told her, "'I understand you only have about 1,000 hours [flight time]. And when he said that, I understood exactly what time it was. I looked at him and said, ``No, sir, I have about 1000 hours flying a Boeing 737.'' In other words, what he was saying to me was ``You're a low-time pilot, you don't deserve this job.' And, `basically we're not going to pass you, so you can go sit as an engineer for a few more years and try it later.'" The male pilot training alongside her passed the course.

Despite the hitches, however, Washington was finally promoted to first officer, in January 1990. Then, in November of 1994 she was promoted again—this time to captain. It was a hard-won first for African Americans. As Washington told *Time* magazine, "Airlines only hired us because they were sued."

According to *Time*, Korean War pilot Marlon Green sued Continental Airlines, winning a favorable ruling from the U.S. Supreme Court in 1962 that opened the door for black pilots to work for commercial airlines. But the fight was not yet won. In 1973 the U.S. Justice Department won its own landmark case against United Airlines when a federal court found entrenched discrimination and ordered United to hire blacks at twice the percentage of black applicants. American Airlines also was affected; it subsequently dropped its 5-foot, 6-inch height requirement which had nothing to do with flying airplanes, but did leave many women in the wings of the profession. And, USAir agreed to drop its nepotism requirements that also left many women out—because they weren't members of the boys club that was the traditional pilots community.

Despite these rulings, enforcement lagged. In 1988 the Equal Employment Opportunities Commission went back to court against United on behalf of hundreds of rejected African Americans and women. United responded, recruiting minority pilots and paying for their training to boost their numbers from 2.6 percent to 8.1 percent of the total. In the female-pilot category, United increased its numbers from 1.5 percent to 5.5 percent. The result? "Things have changed significantly in the airline industry," Washington said. "I'm just going to be 35 [years-old], and I'm a captain—that was basically unheard of [in the recent past]. Particularly for me to be flying with people who are older than me and subordinate to me. So things have changed."

She wants to continue that trend. To young people interested in flying, she advises taking a serious look at the military as the route in; flight training is normally too expensive for most young people, especially those from low-income backgrounds. She also points to some limited scholarship aid from groups like the Organization of Black Airline Pilots.

Most importantly, she advises youths to disregard the lack of black and female role models—particularly in the still largely white male military. She suggests youths hold fast to their dreams, the way she did. "My point of view has always been that if there's something you want to do, go ahead and do it," Washington said. "I've always been pretty well focused and once I decided on something, I did it."

Sources

Periodicals

"The Still Unfriendly Skies," *Time,* August 28, 1995.
"Pilot flies where no other Black woman has flown before," *Emerge,* May 1995, p. 11.
"Pilot inspires others to follow her lead," *Atlanta Constitution,* January 25, 1995, p. D-3.

Other

Personal Interview with Patricia Clarke Washington, April 6, 1995.

—Joan Oleck

Val Washington

1903–1995

Political organizer, entrepreneur

Inside national political circles, Val J. Washington was an influential Republican in an era prior to civil rights victories and affirmative action opportunities. As director of minorities for the Republican National Committee and advisor to President Dwight D. Eisenhower, Washington was responsible for the appointments of several African Americans to government posts during the 1950s. He also helped win electoral victories for Republican candidates in several states. Intensely committed to the political party that had been founded to oppose slavery, Washington resigned when the Democratic administration of John F. Kennedy took office in 1961--ironically, the start of an era that would see passage of significant civil rights legislation.

Gained Political Expertise in Chicago

Washington was born on September 18, 1903, in Columbus, Indiana, son of James and Ella Washington. He graduated from Indiana University in 1924 with two degrees, and soon after became editor and publisher of the Gary (Indiana) *Sun*. He remained in the post two years before leaving to become a freelance political writer. In 1934 Washington returned to the newspaper business when he took a job with Chicago's African American newspaper, the *Chicago Defender*. From 1934 to 1941 he served as the paper's business, advertising, and general manager. During this era he also became active in the Chicago political machine,

working for local elected officials and helping them secure the votes and ongoing support of their constituencies.

Washington's work earned him an appointment to the Illinois Commerce Commission in 1941, where he served for seven years. Within a few years he had become more integrally involved with the Republican National Committee, and in 1946 served as an assistant campaign manager to Herbert Brownell. That same year, Washington was appointed assistant to the chairman of the Republican National Committee, and also became the director of minorities for the GOP. In this capacity, he was responsible for planning and executing strategies to bring African American voters to the Republican side.

Emphasized Commitment to Civil Rights

The Republican ideal and its relation to African American history was of especial import to Washington, and he often spoke eloquently of it. "Historically, 3,000,000 Negro slaves found emancipation through the Republican party eighty-nine years ago," Washington wrote in *The Crisis*. "In 1952, this same party offers the surest and best chance, the most practical, realistic and honest program through which this minority, now multiplied and transformed into 15,000,000 Americans, can achieve their present political potential ambition of full citizenship." It was Republican administrations, Washington liked to assert, that gained passage of the 13th,

At a Glance...

Full name, Valores James Washington; born September 18, 1903, in Columbus, IN; died of a heart attack, 1995, in Washington, DC; son of James Harry and Ella (Patton) Washington; married Sarah Tyler. *Education:* Indiana University, A.B., B.S., 1924. *Politics:* Republican.

Career: Editor and publisher, Gary (Indiana) *Sun,* Gary, IN, 1924-26; freelance writer of political and special articles, 1926-34; business, advertising, and general manager, *Chicago Defender,* Chicago, IL, 1934-41; Illinois Commerce Commission, member, 1941-48; Republican National Committee, assistant to chair, 1946-48, assistant campaign manager to Herbert Brownell, 1948, director of minorities, c. 1946-61; founded Washington, DC-based import/export firm, 1961.

Member: Republican Party.

14th, and 15th amendments that abolished slavery, gave citizenship to African Americans, and also gave them the right to vote. "Despite repeated attempts by Democrats to nullify, to get around, to kill the potency of these amendments, they have remained the hub upon which organizations like the National Association for the Advancement of Colored People have been able to advance the civil rights of Negroes," Washington wrote.

At the time, the Democratic Party was beginning to espouse civil rights issues, though the name had not been traditionally associated with liberal policies in the past century. The Democrats had been a stronghold in white Southern political circles since Reconstruction, when their return to power in the region marked the start of a new and vicious period of segregation and discrimination. As Washington wrote in *The Crisis* as the 1952 election neared: "While the Democratic candidate chose safe New York, and Lincoln's Illinois, to make his pronouncements on civil rights, Ike on his first tour of the South carried the Republican platform to Dixie," the GOP strategist wrote of General Dwight D. Eisenhower's bid for the presidency. "At Tampa, FL, and again at Little Rock, AR, Eisenhower risked the votes he may lose in that section by reminding Dixie that the Declaration of Independence declares that 'all men are created equal.' And again by reminding Dixie that

the 'Founding Fathers had no thought of the color of skin.'" Washington's work helped Eisenhower win 20 percent of the African American vote in the 1952 election.

Served as Counsel to President

During the Eisenhower administration Washington became a prominent figure in Republican politics. He was an advisor to the president and also served as an administrative liaison to Congress in minority affairs, posts that combined to make him a presence in upper-echelon political circles that had until then been exclusively white. In his work for the GOP, he encouraged Republican officials at all levels--federal, state, and local--to appoint African Americans to their staffs. Patronage, or the rewarding of government jobs to political supporters, was one facet of politics in which Washington had certain expertise; this experience came from his tenure in Chicago's ward politics, where the practice had reached a high degree of refinement.

> "Historically, 3,000,000 negro slaves found emancipation through the Republican party eighty-nine years ago."

In one of the more significant achievements of his career, Washington campaigned for several notable appointments of African Americans in the Eisenhower administration, and helped break down the color barriers in the nation's corridors of power. With his help, E. Fred Morrow was named White House administrative officer for special projects; his brother John was named ambassador to Guinea; Carmel Carrington Marr was appointed a United Nations advisor with Washington's help; and J. Ernest Wilkins became assistant secretary of labor. Washington was also responsible for a more integrated guest list at official White House functions during this era. "If an unattached man in the legal field is invited to a state dinner, Mr. Washington is called upon to recommend a woman of equal status," noted *Ebony* in 1955. It was considered quite forward at the time to pair white and black guests at the same dinner table, but it was even more radical in the era of Jim Crow laws for an African American to be seated next to a Southerner, as once happened to Washington. "I've often wondered if she knew I was a Negro," Washington joked with *Ebony.*

Exited From Politics

In 1961, Washington left the Republican National Committee after the party lost the election to Democratic candidate John F. Kennedy. A writer for *Jet* noted at the time insiders hinted that Washington had expressed dissatisfaction at not be relied upon during the 1960 election to bring in the African American vote--and the GOP candidate Richard Nixon lost out by one of the narrowest popular-vote margins in history. After resigning from the Republican National Committee, Washington co-founded an import/export firm. Two decades later, with the election of Republican candidate Ronald Reagan to the Oval Office in 1980, Washington spoke to *Ebony*'s Simeon Booker about the future of African Americans in the nation's capital, and predicted that Reagan would prove to be a significant catalyst in opening those doors further. "He is determined to select a new brand of quality black officials and change the course of politics. President Reagan can prove that minority rhetoric cannot match majority voting power...." Washington died of a heart attack in the spring of 1995 in Washington, DC, and "left a legacy in American politics few in the Republican Party could match," noted his obituary in *Jet*.

Sources

The Crisis, October, 1952, p. 487.
Ebony, June 1955, p. 18; July 1981, p. 24.
Jet, January 12, 1961, p. 3; May 15, 1995, p. 18.
Our World, April 1955, pp. 48-55.

—Carol Brennan

Perry Watkins

1948–1996

Military figure, entertainer

In *My Country, My Right To Serve,* Perry Watkins--an openly homosexual U.S. Army sergeant first class--said, "People have asked me, 'How have you managed to tolerate all that discrimination you had to deal with in the military?' My immediate answer to them was, 'Hell, I grew up black. Give me a break. I mean, to be discriminated against because I was gay was a joke.' I mean, 'Oh, you don't like me because I'm gay? Excuse me, I'm sorry, but *you've* got a problem.'"

Far from being touted by the gay rights movement, U.S. Army sergeant first class Perry Watkins was essentially ignored by groups that championed the cause of gays in the military during the late 1980s and early 1990s. (Watkins himself thought it had to do with how flamboyant he could be at times.) Nonetheless, his battle "still is the only case of an openly gay GI who had gone all the way through the court system and emerged victorious," according to Doug Honig, public education director of the American Civil Liberties Union (ACLU) Washington state chapter, in the *News Tribune* (Tacoma). "The case was not legally groundbreaking. It didn't overturn the military policy. But Perry was a role model, standing up against what he thought was an unfair policy. Perry was a real pioneer."

Watkins grew up hearing how much alike he and his mother, Ola Watkins, were. They not only looked alike but they had similar personalities. According to author Randy Shilts in *Conduct Unbecoming,* "Perry idolized his mother, and she respected his individuality." And Watkins was very much an individual from a very young age. He played with dolls, dressing them up and styling their hair. He played jump rope with his friends, who consisted of the neighborhood girls. "I used to give those girls hell in my neighborhood," he said in *My Country, My Right To Serve.* "I was great. They'd hate to see me coming with the jump rope...."

Watkins was born and raised in Joplin, Missouri, a small city in the southwest corner of the state. After his parents divorced, the three year old's family consisted of his mother, sister, grandmother, and two aunts. He said that he never had the "pressure of a male role model of having to do the male-type things like football, basketball, and all that." Watkin's just seemed to know that he preferred to play with girls and did not care what other kids thought.

When Watkins was in junior high school his mother remarried. Watkin's stepfather was a career military man stationed near Joplin; when he was transferred to Tacoma, Washington, shortly after the marriage, Ola and her children went with him. In Tacoma, Watkins began exploring his sexuality. Following his mother's teachings about not telling lies, he told the truth when someone in his class asked him if he were "queer." Later he claimed to have never been ridiculed or harassed for being gay.

At a Glance...

Born Perry James Henry Watkins on August 20, 1948, in Joplin, Missouri; died March 13, 1996, in Tacoma, Washington; son of Ola Watkins (a nurse). *Education:* B.A. in Business and Theater.

U.S. Army, soldier stationed in Korea, Virginia, Washington, New Jersey, Germany, 1968-84; honorable discharge as Sergeant First Class, 1984. Social Security Administration, employee, 1984-94. Public speaker and lecturer, 1984-95. Subject of the documentary *Sis: The Perry Watkins Story,* 1994. Co-author, with Gary McGill, *Sovereign Immunity* (screenplay).

By the time he had graduated from Tacoma Lincoln High School, Watkins had taken several years of dance classes, including studying with the Tacoma City Ballet Company. He won several awards in speech tournaments and had been a finalist for the school cheerleading squad--as good as he could do because at that time, blacks were not accepted on the Tacoma cheerleading squad. Shortly after graduating, Watkin's stepfather was transferred again, this time to Germany. Watkins hoped the country would be the perfect place to study ballet. The Vietnam War changed his plans, however.

In the Army

In 1967, Watkins was called to the draft board in Frankfort, Germany, for his induction physical. Describing the experience in *My Country, My Right To Serve,* he explained, "I received my little draft notice, went down to the induction center, and checked the 'yes' box for 'homosexual tendencies.' One of the arguments the army made in court was that I didn't [verbally] *say* I was homosexual." Watkins figured that once military personnel saw that he had checked the box, he would be sent home because the military did not accept gays.

Instead, Watkins was sent to a psychiatrist. That doctor referred Watkins to a lieutenant colonel psychiatrist who grilled Watkins about his sexual practices. He also asked Watkins about whether he had a problem serving his country or going to fight in Vietnam, and Watkins explained that he had no problems in regard to serving his country anywhere. According to *Conduct Unbecoming* the colonel then wrote on the back of Watkin's induction form: "This 19-year-old inductee has had

homosexual tendencies in the past.... Patient can go into military service—qualified for induction." Thus, Watkins began his military service as an openly gay man in May of 1968.

Watkins finished basic training, then participated in advanced training at Fort Dix, New Jersey. There he met a white, gay draftee, who was being kicked out of the military because he had told someone he was gay. Watkins demanded he too be dismissed from the army. His commanding officer denied the request. Then, while stationed at Fort Hamilton, New York, Watkins attempted to be dismissed because he was denied a job when a commander saw his military record stated he was gay. Again, he was denied. The army claimed they could not prove he was gay. Even after the U.S. Army Criminal Investigation Division (CID) investigated some of Watkins's sexual partners, the result was the same. At another time Watkins requested CID investigate the fact he had been attacked by a soldier that wanted to rape him. They instead investigated Watkins for his sexual activities. Finding no proof of sexual activities, Watkin's was reassigned to clerk training in Fort Belvoir, Virginia.

The only reason Perry Watkins could surmise for not being discharged was that he was black as other discharges were given to gay men who were white. Shilts later wrote in *Conduct Unbecoming* that "the doctor probably figured Watkins would be drafted, go to Vietnam, get killed, and nobody would ever hear about it again. At least that was how Watkins sized up the situation years later with a wry chuckle." Watkins's two-year stint in the army ended in 1970.

After trying to re-adjust to civilian life, Watkins discovered he would need more education for the type of job he wanted. He knew he could get that education in the army. So Watkins went down to the recruiting station in Tacoma and signed up again. Again, he admitted to being gay, and, once more, he was accepted for duty in Germany. During his second enlistment Watkins acted no differently than in his first time in the army.

"Simone"

One day Watkins was approached by a commanding officer who was planning entertainment for a big celebration on the military base. Watkins volunteered that he had sometimes been a female impersonator in civilian life. The coordinator of the show signed him up. Playing the costumed role of a woman named 'Simone,' Watkins entertained the troops and families of the army. Watkins act was so well received that he had to get an agent to handle the many requests for his performances.

He played at army clubs all over Germany and other bases in Europe.

At the same time Watkins had received a security clearance from the U.S. Army. After initially being turned down because of potential blackmail because he was gay, Watkins received his clearance when he explained that no one could blackmail him since everyone already knew he was gay. He also survived another CID investigation after someone reported him as being gay. Again the army suggested that Watkin's sexuality could not be proven.

Suddenly, after years of immunity, Watkin's commanding officer began discharge proceedings against him. The hearing took place in October of 1975. The commanding officer was quoted as saying in the *News Tribune* (Tacoma), "In my opinion, Specialist Watkins is the best clerk I have known." Still, the officer pressed the case because military rules required him to do so. Others testified that while they knew Watkin's was gay, no trouble had ever arisen out of that fact and nobody anticipated having problems continuing to work with him. On the basis of such testimony, the discharge board voted to retain Watkins in the U.S. Army. According to Shilts in *Conduct Unbecoming,* the board report stated that "there is no evidence suggesting that his [Watkins's] behavior has had either a degrading effect upon unit performance, morale, or discipline, or upon his own job performance."

During his 15 years of service in the military, Watkins received several commendations from his superiors, both for his regular work and the work he did entertaining as 'Simone.' He also served two tours of duty in Korea--once stationed at the demilitarized zone, where shooting occurred frequently. Despite all of his military work and honors, when Watkins's security clearance was up for renewal in 1979, it was denied because of his gay status. In 1981, after two years of trying to get it back, Watkins sued the U.S. Army. That step led to his being brought before the discharge board though he had served nearly 16 years without hiding his sexuality and had been allowed to re-enlist three times. Times had changed, and the military had become increasingly less tolerant of gays and lesbians.

Double Jeopardy

Watkins was finally discharged because of his homosexuality. Citing the unconstitutionality of double jeopardy, a court later overturned the ruling and ordered that he be re-admitted to the military. In other words, the discharge board had tried Watkins twice on the same charge, first finding him innocent, then ruling him guilty. Once found innocent of a charge, no one may be charged a second time with the same offense, known as double jeopardy. When Watkins tried to re-enlist in the army in 1982, he was denied because of his stated homosexuality. Suing again, the army and was ordered to re-enlist him, but the army fought back, and the court battles went on for some time. In 1984, Watkins was formally discharged.

> "I grew up black. I mean, to be discriminated against because I was gay was a joke. I mean 'Oh you don't like me because I'm gay I'm sorry, but you've got a problem.'"

Watkins spent a great deal of time looking for work as a civilian. He had managed to finish college while in the military, and had bachelor's degrees in business administration and theater. Watkins was able to find work at the Tacoma office of the Social Security Administration, meanwhile finding support through the ACLU. Eventually the 9th Circuit Court of Appeals ruled that the army had treated Watkins unfairly in discharging him when they had "plainly acted affirmatively in admitting, re-enlisting, retaining, and promoting," Perry throughout his career.

The U.S. Justice Department appealed the decision, but, in 1990, the U.S. Supreme Court refused to hear the army's appeal of this decision, and Perry was ordered reinstated. "Rather than re-enlist however," the *News Tribune* (Tacoma) reported, "Watkins settled the case ... receiving retroactive pay, full retirement benefits, an honorable discharge and a retroactive promotion from staff sergeant to sergeant first class."

After the settlement, Watkins settled into a fairly quiet life until his death in 1996. He remains the only person ordered by courts to be reinstated to active military duty after being dismissed for homosexuality. In his last years, he lectured and spoke to various groups around the country on topics relating to being gay in the military. Having tested positive for the virus that causes AIDS, he also worked with terminally ill people. In 1994, a documentary entitled *Sis: The Perry Watkins Story,* chronicled his drag queen performing days. Watkins died in Tacoma on March 17, 1996, from complications brought on by AIDS.

Upon his death, Watkin's attorney and friend, Jim Lobsenz, described Watkins as "a very honest guy, a very stubborn guy, and a brave guy," in the *New York Times.* Similarly, Gary McGill, a childhood friend of Watkin's told *The Washington Blade,* "[Watkins] was just a huge character, very intelligent, with an incredibly wry sense of humor." *Sovereign Immunity,* a screenplay based on Watkins's life, coauthored Watkins and McGill, was optioned by a Los Angeles-based film production company in 1996.

Source

Books

Shilts, Randy, *Conduct Unbecoming,* St. Martin's Press, 1993.
Humphrey, Mary Ann, *My Country, My Right to Serve,* HarperPerennial, 1990.

Periodicals

News Tribune (Tacoma), March 21, 1996, p. A1.
New York Times, March 21, 1996, p. B8.
The Washington Blade, March 22, 1996, pp. 1, 32.

—Stephen Stratton

Dorothy West

1907—

Author

Dorothy West's career has been as anomalous as her life. Born to a freed slave, she lived in one of the very few well-to-do black families in Boston, almost a contradiction in terms. As a teenager she won short story prizes and was widely published; her first novel won critical appraise and put her on the literary map. Then she went into an almost 50-year retirement before she published her second novel, which became an overnight success. At 88 years old, she enjoyed a surge in her career that many would speculate should have come 50 years before.

West's father was a slave who had ambition and energy. She told the *New York Times Book Review,* "My father was born a slave. He was freed when he was seven and began saving his money in a cigar box. When he was ten he started a business, and by the time I was born he was in Dun & Bradstreet." He worked hard in the Boston produce distribution business and was soon financially successful. The West family was one of the richest black families in Boston.

As a child, West enjoyed the privilege of being schooled by a private tutor. She recalled in an essay in *The*

Richer, the Poorer: Stories, Sketches and Reminiscences about her precociousness: "When I was a child of four or five, listening to the conversation of my mother and her sisters, I would sometimes intrude on their territory with a solemnly stated opinion that would jerk their heads in my direction, then send them into roars of uncontrollable laughter. I do not now remember anything I said. But the first adult who caught her breath would speak for them all and say, 'That's no child. That's a little sawed-off woman.'" At the age of ten, she was sent off the exclusive Girls' Latin School.

Writing became a hobby of West's and she showed the same precocity there that she did with her comments to her aunts. The *Boston Post* had weekly fiction contests, and her story "Promise and Fulfillment" won when she was only 14. After that, she became a regular competitor and often won. When she was 17, she tied for second prize with Zora Neale Hurston in a contest in *Opportunity* magazine. Her story, "The Typewriter," won her a trip to New York City. Once she had her taste of the big city, she decided to stay, taking up at the YWCA until she received a fellowship.

At a Glance...

Born June 2, 1907, in Boston, MA; daughter of Isaac Christopher (a produce distributor) and Rachel West. Education: Studied journalism and philosophy at Columbia University; attended Boston University.

Career: Novelist, editor, short story writer. Worked for the Martha's Vineyard Gazette, in various roles from billing clerk to contributor. Founded Challenge magazine, 1934, and New Challenge, 1937. Worked as relief investigator in Harlem during 1930s; worked on Federal Writers Project until mid-1940s.

Awards: Regularly won short story contests in the Boston Post, c. 1925-30; tied for second place with Zora Neale Hurston in a short story contest in Opportunity magazine.

Addresses: Home—Martha's Vineyard, MA. Publisher—Doubleday, 1540 Broadway, New York, NY 10036.

West Encountered Langston Hughes

In New York, she met some of the brightest black artists and writers in the country. She also developed a friendship with H. L. Mencken. For a short time, she took up acting, and she ended up touring with a production of *Porgy and Bess*. But always, she returned to writing. While she formed friendships with black poets, Langston Hughes and Countee Cullen, unknowingly her group of friends was growing into the Harlem Renaissance. In 1932, West, Langston Hughes, and 20 other African Americans went to Russia to film a story of American racism to be called *Black and White*. The project was dropped following accusations of association with Communism.

"We were young, naive, and poor. Today's writers live in a different world."

West found herself enchanted with Russia and decided to stay on even though the movie had failed. Hughes remained as her companion. It was never proven if the two were romantically involved, but West did ask Hughes to marry her in a 1933 letter. After a year in Russia, West learned of her father's death, and quickly exited the country for the United States.

Back in the United States, West was convinced that she needed to return to writing. In New York City, West took her savings of $40, and started *Challenge* magazine, a journal of writings by African American authors. This journal became the quintessential one for black writers of the day, publishing such notables as Langston Hughes, Arna Bontemps, Zora Neale Hurston, Claude McKay, and Helene Johnson. Although she received many submissions from young black writers, West did not publish them, believing that they weren't up to the quality of the others. She was accused of creating too tame a voice for the black writer, of not taking a chance on the new and innovative literature that was being created in the African American community. Disappointed with the work she was getting from the younger writers, she closed the journal down in 1937. West commented to *Publisher's Weekly* about the writers of that era: "There can never again be a period like ours. Now people are more sophisticated. We were young, naive, and poor. Today's writers live in a different world."

That same year, West and Richard Wright teamed up to revamp the lapsed periodical and created *New Challenge*. It was plagued with financial problems, and made West uneasy because of its left-leaning politics. The journal didn't last very long. West decided to take a job as a welfare investigator, an unusual choice that had interesting outcomes. She was appalled by the conditions she found in the black homes she investigated. She managed to write a story that was inspired by her work, "Mammy," which was published in *Opportunity*.

Published her First Novel

West joined the Federal Writers' Project, working there until it was disbanded in the 1940s. She completed many short stories, some of which have never been published. It was also during the 1940s that West had a great change in her living environment. Accustomed to traveling to the family's modest summer home on Martha's Vineyard, one summer she went there and never returned home. She began writing her first novel while there. *The Living is Easy* was published in 1948.

The central character, Cleo Judson, is an insecure but beautiful woman who marries an older, financially stable man. Judson invites her extended family of three sisters and their husbands to live with them. The closeness does not make their relationships any easier; in fact, all the marriages soon explode. Some critics have speculated that the novel was autobiographical, drawing from the fact that many of West's mother's 21 siblings spent time at their home.

When the book was issued, Seymour Krim remarked in the *New York Times,* "The important thing about the book is its abundant and special woman's energy and beat." *Commonweal's* Florence Codman praised West's Cleo Judson as "the predatory female on the loose, a wholly plausible, tantalizing creature." Reviewing the reissued 1987 novel in *Ms.,* Susan McHenry compared West's social commentary to that of Theodore Dreiser and Sinclair Lewis and called the author "a brisk storyteller with an eye for ironic detail." In a 1987 review of the book in the *Times Literary Supplement,* Holly Eley commented, "West's sensitive investigation of issues such as miscegenation, racial heritage and colour consciousness … is extremely relevant today."

There was controversy surrounding the release of her novel. Although generally well-received by critics, the *Ladies' Home Journal* scrapped plans to serialize the book. "I was going to get what at that time was a lot of money," West told *Publishers Weekly.* "But weeks went by before my agent called again. The Journal had decided to drop the book because a survey indicated that they would lose many subscribers in the South." West knew that her book was different from much of the protest literature being written at that time. The book "came out at the wrong time," West related to Alexis De Veaux in *Ms.* "Nobody understood it."

The rejection from the magazine took a toll on West. She began another story, but quickly decided she didn't like it. She planned to write a story like *The Wedding,* about generations of a black family where race and class were major themes. She was afraid, however, that what had happened to her with the Journal would happen again. In need of work, she took a position with the *Martha's Vineyard Gazette,* rising from billing clerk to one of the star contributors.

Although she kept up her writing by contributing to the Gazette, she stashed away her hopes of a next novel. She was also uncomfortable with the political climate in the country. West remarked to *Publishers Weekly* that she was particularly upset with the Black Panthers. "I hated them! They scorned the upper middle class. I wanted to write about people like my father, who were ambitious. But people like him were anathema to the Black Panthers, who said that all black people are victims. Every time I turned on the TV there was a black person making a fool of himself. It was a discouraging time."

In fact, West felt out of step with what was going on in the country. She was afraid that a major work by her would be misinterpreted, or ignored. "I had a suspicion that the reviewers, who were white, would not know how

to judge my work in that prevailing climate," she related to *Publishers Weekly.* "In fact, if I had brought the book out then, white people would not have accepted it."

Supported by Jacqueline Onassis

West's novel might have lied stagnant in her head if it had not been for a coincidental turn of events. Jacqueline Onassis also had a summer home on the island, and became familiar with West's work while reading her contributions to the Gazette. A friend of West's told Onassis of the brewing novel. The two women were introduced, and Onassis told West that she would very much like to have her publisher, Doubleday, publish the book. It was this incentive that started her working seriously on the novel again.

Jacqueline Onassis died before *The Wedding* was released, but without her help it might never have seen publication. The book became popular right away, giving West another wave of the popularity she had enjoyed as a younger writer. The novel deals with Shelby Coles, the beautiful, light-skinned daughter of a successful black doctor. Dr. Coles is upset because his first daughter married a successful man with dark skin, and his youngest daughter is marrying an unsuccessful musician who is white. Neither marriage is acceptable in the father's eyes.

The action takes place in 1953, in an exclusive black community on Martha's Vineyard named the Oval. In the book, there this commentary explain's the father's feelings: "Between the dark man Liz had married and the music maker Shelby was marrying, there was a whole area of eligible men of the right colors and the right professions. For Liz and Shelby to marry so contrary to expectations affronted all the subtle tenets of their training." The occasion of the wedding allows for a look back at generations of Coleses, from the rosy-colored, white grandmother who is glad Shelby is marrying a white man, to a whole slew of relatives ranging in color from ebony to butternut.

Critics Loved *The Wedding*

After the publication of *The Wedding,* critical praise was forthcoming. Susan Kenney wrote in the *New York Times Book Review* that "difficult as it may seem at first to separate Dorothy West the survivor and the legend from the author who has finally delivered a long-awaited book, you have only to read the first page to know that you are in the hands of a writer, pure and simple. At the end, it's as though we've been invited not so much to a wedding as to a full-scale opera, only to find the one great artist is belting out all the parts. She brings down the house." A *Publishers Weekly* review claims that "West's first novel in 45 years is a triumph." Margo Jefferson, writing in the *New York Times*, finds exception to the novel, asserting that West "lacks is the true novelist's gift for intricate plots that feel inevitable and intricate talk that feels spontaneous....`The Wedding' falters as a novel; it takes its stand and holds its own as social history."

"We were young, naive, and poor. Today's writers live in a different world."

In 1995 West also came out with a collection of her works titled *The Richer, the Poorer: Stories, Sketches, and Reminiscences*. The book contains 30 pieces, some of which had never been published before. Gwendolyn M. Parker wrote in the *New York Times Book Review* that West "writes unevenly but with verve of petty crooks, old ladies who turn out to be counterfeiters, vacationing executives, clerks, waiters, housekeepers, artists, precocious young girls, quarrelsome children." Her essays look at people she knows and life on Martha's Vineyard, reminiscences from her Boston childhood, and a tribute to her mother. Parker concludes that the book "is best seen as an artifact, one that allows the reader to discount Dorothy West's weakness for melodrama in the plotting of some of the stories and concentrate pleasurably on the themes and insights of a unique American writer."

Asked about her literary silence for so many years, West commented in *Ms.* that "I never gave up writing. Now I know I was right." Her many years of writing stories for newspapers has paid off. "I'm always surprised when someone tells me they've read one of my stories somewhere," West told *Ms.* "I didn't know that if you wrote a story, it could last forever."

Selected writings

The Living is Easy (novel), Houghton Mifflin, 1948, reprinted in paperback, Feminist Press, 1987.

(Contributor of short stories) "The Best Short Stories by Negro Writers: An Anthology from 1899 to the Present," edited by Langston Hughes, Little, Brown, 1967.

(Contributor) "Harlem: Voices from the South of Black America," New American Library, 1970.

The Wedding (novel), Doubleday, 1995.

The Richer, the Poorer: Stories, Sketches and Reminiscences, Doubleday, 1995.

Contributor to *Saturday Evening Quill, Opportunity, Messenger, New York Daily News,* and *Black World.*

Sources

Books

Black Writers, Gale, 1994, pp. 658-659.

Contemporary Authors, Volume 143, Gale, 1994, pp. 487-489.

Dictionary of Literary Biography, Volume 76: Afro-American Writers, 1940-1955, Gale, 1988, pp. 187-195.

West, Dorothy, *The Richer, the Poorer: Stories, Sketches and Reminiscences,* Doubleday, 1995.

West, Dorothy, *The Wedding,* Doubleday, 1995.

Periodicals

Commonweal, June 25, 1948.

Essence, August 1995, p. 46.

Ms., March, 1982, pp. 37-38; May/June, 1995, p. 73.

New York Times, May 16, 1948, p. 5; February 1, 1995, p. C14.

New York Times Book Review, February 12, 1995, pp. 11-12; August 6, 1995, p. 12.

People, March 6, 1995.

Publishers Weekly, September 21, 1994, p. 68; July 3, 1995, pp. 34-35.

Time, July 24, 1995, p. 67.

Times Literary Supplement, April 17, 1987, p. 410.

—Nancy Rampson

Conrad Worrill

1941—

Author, educator, activist

Dr. Conrad Worrill has established himself as a preeminent figure in Black activism through his work as an educator, newspaper columnist, community organizer, and radio talk show host. From his beginnings in the Civil Rights movement of the 1960s through his mobilizing role in the Million Man March, he has consistently probed issues of power in African American life and emphasized the need for greater independence. "The pressure is on for black people in this country to do more for themselves," he told the *Hyde Park Citizen,* and his leadership in organizations like the National Black United Front, the Task Force for Black Empowerment, and the National Board of Education for People of African Ancestry has provided a powerful example. Though Worrill's militancy has provoked the ire of conservatives, he has been a tireless critic of racism and exponent of economic and political enfranchisement for Black people.

He was born in Pasadena, California. His father was active in both the National Association for the Advancement of Colored People (NAACP) and the Young Men's Christian Association (YMCA), and provided an early example for Conrad to follow. "He was one of the leaders of the NAACP in Pasadena that desegregated Brookside Park, which was next to the Rose Bowl [stadium]," he told *CBB.* "They wouldn't let black people swim, except when they drained the water. So my father led a movement for the desegregation of Brookside Park and was also a leader in getting the first blacks hired in the postal service and the police department in Pasadena." Worrill recalled the "organizing meetings, which were held in our home," and noted that his father's influence on his own lifetime activism didn't become clear until many years later "but it was there all the time." Conrad recollected that YMCA events also played a large part in his growing up. His heroes were black sports trailblazers like Jackie Robinson--the first African American to play major league baseball--and boxer Joe Louis. Robinson's older brother, in fact, was a friend of the Worrill family.

Military Experience and College

The elder Worrill's next post for the YMCA led him to move the family to Chicago when Conrad was nine years old. YMCA events framed his adolescence, and in high

At a Glance...

Born August 15, 1941, Pasadena, CA. Son of Walter Worrill, activist and YMCA leader. Married Cynthia Armster (divorced); married Talibah (a clothing designer) c. 1993. Children: Michelle, Femi, Sobenna. *Education:* Attended Pasadena City College, George Williams College (BS, 1968), University of Chicago (MA, 1971), and University of Wisconsin (Ph.D., 1973). Military service: Specialist 4th Class, U.S. Army, 1962-64.

Educator, activist, and writer, c. 1970s-. Instructor at George Williams College, 1973-75; Northeastern University Center for Inner City Studies, 1975- ; author of "Worrill's World" column for *Chicago Defender* newspaper (later syndicated), 1983-; chairman of National Black United Front (NBUF), Chicago chapter, 1985; host of "On Target" call-in program for radio station WVON, Chicago, 1988- ; chairman of the board of African Educators, National Board of Education for People of African Ancestry; co-founder of Task Force for Black Political Empowerment and many other organizations; Special Consultant of Field Operations for Million Man March/Day of Absence march and rally, Washington, DC, 1995.

Addresses: *Home*—Chicago, IL. Center for Inner City Studies—700 East George H. Clements Blvd., Chicago, IL 60653.

school he enthusiastically pursued football, basketball, and track. In 1962 he was drafted into the U.S. military and stationed on the Japanese island of Okinawa; there he witnessed a large-scale buildup of personnel that he subsequently recognized as preparation for the impending war in Vietnam. "I was wondering why so many black people were showing up on the island," he told *CBB*. "I began to run into young men from Chicago that I had known back home." After leaving the military, he noted, "I became active in a lot of movements," some of which organized to end America's involvement in the Vietnam conflict. Among these was the Student Nonviolent Coordinating Committee (SNCC), the pioneering civil rights group, which was one of the first African American organizations against the war. Civil Rights leader Dr. Martin Luther King Jr., among others, opposed the war and other U.S. military adventures.

Though he eventually earned a doctorate, Worrill's first forays into higher education were less than enthralling. "I wasn't a very successful college student," he admitted. "In fact, it was predicted that I'd be one of those kids who zipped through school and came out and got a job and became a professional, following in my father's footsteps. Well, it didn't quite pan out like that." He first entered Pasadena City College, as his father had, but he was expelled due to his poor attendance record. His brief experiences with junior colleges in the Chicago area were interrupted—perhaps mercifully—by his tenure in the military. "After I came out I went to Central YMCA College for a brief time, got my grades up, and transferred to George Williams College" in Chicago, which was named after the YMCA's founder. He majored there in Applied Behavioral Sciences, then received a master's degree at the University of Chicago.

"Institutions and Power"

For his Ph.D., he entered the University of Wisconsin at Madison, focusing on "Curriculum and Instruction in Secondary Social Studies," writing his dissertation on teaching this subject to black teens and simultaneously teaching at a Madison school. His goal was to help students understand the relationship between institutions and power. When he started, they had "no recollection of these concepts and how they related to their daily lives." A combination of academic work and trips to such local institutions as the university, state capital, and city hall ensured that by the end of the class "it was obvious that they had learned tremendously about these particular concepts and how they had affected their lives." After receiving his degree from Madison, Worrill taught for two years at George Williams College; in 1975 he was hired by Northeastern Illinois University. He became a central figure at the Center for Inner City Studies, a department of the College of Education. "We seek to examine the political, economic, social, and cultural forces that impact on people who live inner cities--not only Chicago, but throughout the world," he explained to *CBB*.

Worrill was also involved in the National Black United Front (NBUF), an organization that came together in 1980 after some years of organizational meetings, debates, and other preparatory work. "The leadership of the organization were all children of the 1960s," he noted. "During the 1970s, much of our movement had been disrupted" by assassination and the Federal Bureau of Investigation (FBI)'s counterintelligence work, among other forces, "so many of us began to analyze what we could do to rebuild the movement." The NBUF was started "as a grass-roots organization to address many of the political, economic, social, and cultural forces that impact on people of African ancestry in this country. It grew, and we developed a chapter in Chicago and about 22 other cities across the country." While the leadership was diverse, he added, "most of the people came out of what we would call the Pan-Africanist, Nationalist, and progressive streams, with some progressive religious leadership involved."

He explained to Billy Montgomery of *Chicago Weekend* that the group works "on a wide range of issues. Whether it's police brutality, electoral politics, or fighting against injustices against Black people, we address solutions to our problems." The organization has been especially active in pushing for a school curriculum that emphasizes the role of Africans and African Americans. Worrill's political militancy, both in affiliation with NBUF and elsewhere, has drawn considerable criticism. He has drawn fire particularly for his work with Minister Louis Farrakhan, leader of the Nation of Islam organization and highly visible figure in black politics. African American activists have often been urged to dissociate themselves from Farrakhan due to the minister's negative remarks about Jews and frequent characterization of whites as malevolent. "We are not in the business of denouncing our leaders," Worrill declared categorically to Montgomery. "We stand strong with Minister Louis Farrakhan and we will continue to urge national leaders that the most important thing that we can do is not respond to other people's demands. We must come together and determine for ourselves how we respond collectively."

Columnist "By Accident"

Worrill ventured into journalism--"by accident," he insisted to *CBB*--in 1983. The United States had just invaded the tiny Caribbean republic of Grenada, and coverage of the event in the mainstream media tended to be scant and government-approved. "I was picking up information about the story," Worrill recalled. "People were calling me because [the NBUF] had done work in Grenada and had a relationship with the government of [leader] Maurice Bishop. So I appealed to the *Chicago Defender* newspaper to chronicle it from an African American perspective, since Grenada was 98.9% black island of 100,000 people. And they indicated that they didn't have anyone equipped to write about the region, and that if I wanted to get something in the paper I'd have to write it myself." The challenge posed by the *Defender*'s editor moved Worrill to write not just a single editorial but a series of three installments about "the implications of the U.S. invasion. And I've been

writing a weekly column ever since." Far from restricting himself merely to foreign policy issues, Worrill has held forth in print on Chicago politics, African American heroes, and the subject closest to his heart, education. The column is syndicated by the National Newspaper Publishers Association, which represents over 200 black periodicals around the country.

> "I was one of the main national organizers of the march, worked very closely with the Nation of Islam and National Million Man March organizing committee and helped field operations mobilizing the march across the country."

Talk radio allowed Worrill another platform, and he began hosting a call-in program, "On Target," for the black-owned Chicago station WVON. He described his show to *CBB* as "a classroom on the air, because in many ways it's a tool to teach and learn and engage people in discourse and debate." He added that the program had "really been a tremendous outlet for us to have discussions about issues the mainstream media doesn't discuss. The most memorable shows are when were able to ignite audience participation at the highest level, and the phones were so jammed that nobody could get in." Though the debate at times could become rancorous, he noted, "you manage and learn how to facilitate debate without people taking advantage of the airwaves in a negative manner. And it took some time to learn that skill." Often bringing in scholars and other specialists to enlighten his listeners about specific issues, Worrill has escaped the trap of sensationalism that has ensnared many talk-radio hosts.

Wide-Ranging Activism

Worrill's activities have scarcely been restricted to writing and speaking. In addition to his energetic activism in local politics—particularly surrounding the mayoral aspirations of Harold Washington and those who sought to succeed him--he has ventured into difficult areas of Chicago life. In 1985, the deaths of several young black men at the hands of Arab American shopkeepers moved him to call for a "summit conference," as the *Chicago Tribune* reported, between the aggrieved parties "to let

Arab businessmen know they cannot declare open season on young black males." Columnist Clarence Page expressed approval of Worrill's understanding of economic reality. "It is refreshing to hear a self-professed black nationalist like Worrill put aside hostilities intellectuals often have toward the business community," he wrote.

The 1990s have seen Worrill organizing on a number of fronts. The NBUF's annual convention has been a constant in his work, and among its many goals has been the attempt to fill what the *Hyde Park Citizen* called black America's "leadership gap." Prior to the 16th annual gathering in 1995, Worrill remarked to the publication that the event "will inspire people to evaluate our situation, prepare to organize and mobilize against the forces of oppression not only here in Chicago but throughout the country, and I think this convention will give our communities that kind of inspiration." The NBUF has also helped raise funds and collect donated materials to help victims of the mass slaughter in the African nation of Rwanda. Meanwhile, as chairman of the board of African Educators and member of the National Board of Education for People of African Ancestry, Worrill has been a tireless advocate for curriculum reform. The truth about the contributions of black people to world civilization, he told the *Philadelphia Tribune,* "have challenged the education establishment as African Americans are organizing throughout America to change the racist and white-supremacist-based curriculum within the public schools."

Million Man March Organizer

Perhaps Worrill's highest-profile endeavor has been his participation in the Million Man March/Day of Absence event organized at Farrakhan's behest. As Special Coordinator of Field Operations for the Washington, DC event, he noted to *CBB,* "I was one of the main national organizers of the march, worked very closely with the Nation of Islam and National Million Man March organizing committee and on the executive committee, and helped field operations mobilizing the march across the country." As might be imagined, this was a daunting set of tasks. "To call it complex logistically is an understatement," he reflected, but added that the event "affirmed that if black people decide to do something and work together cooperatively and put our money where our mouth is, that there's a lot we can do to solve a lot of the problems we face as a people." Next to the fact that the march was achieved, commented Worrill, the next most memorable part of the experience was the sight of the crowd on his way to give his speech. "Just to see the sea of black male humanity was awesome."

Worrill told *CBB* that he was collecting and expanding upon his newspaper columns for a book he hoped to publish in 1997. The working title, *African-Centered Essays: Critiques and Commentary,* suggests the breadth of his concerns. Apart from his family, which includes his second wife, four daughters and two grandsons, Worrill noted that he had little time for hobbies. Indeed, he listed his recreational activities as "reading, research, and study," suggesting that the line between his professional and private lives is thin indeed.

Sources

Afrique, April 1996, pp. 4-6.
Chicago Tribune, July 22, 1985; December 18, 1994.
Chicago Weekend, February 6, 1994, p. 2.
Hyde Park Citizen, July 9, 1995, p. 4.
New Pittsburgh Courier, August 27, 1994, p. A-6.
Philadelphia Tribune, October 25, 1994, p. 1-A.

Additional information was provided by Conrad Worrill's press biography and by an interview with Dr. Worrill, May 6, 1996.

—Simon Glickman

Cumulative Indexes

Cumulative Nationality Index

Volume numbers appear in **bold.**

American
Aaron, Hank **5**
Abdul-Jabbar, Kareem **8**
Abernathy, Ralph David **1**
Adams, Floyd, Jr. **12**
Agyeman, Jaramogi Abebe **10**
Ailey, Alvin **8**
Al-Amin, Jamil Abdullah **6**
Ali, Muhammad **2**
Allen, Byron **3**
Amos, John **8**
Amos, Wally **9**
Anderson, Marian **2**
Andrews, Raymond **4**
Angelou, Maya **1**
Archer, Dennis **7**
Armstrong, Louis **2**
Asante, Molefi Kete **3**
Ashe, Arthur **1**
Bailey, Xenobia **11**
Baker, Dusty **8**
Baker, Ella **5**
Baker, Gwendolyn Calvert **9**
Baker, Houston A., Jr. **6**
Baker, Josephine **3**
Baldwin, James **1**
Bambara, Toni Cade **10**
Banks, Tyra **11**
Banks, William **11**
Baraka, Amiri **1**
Barboza, Anthony **10**
Barden, Don H. **9**
Barkley, Charles **5**
Barrett, Andrew C. **12**
Barry, Marion S. **7**
Basquiat, Jean-Michel **5**
Bassett, Angela **6**
Baylor, Don **6**
Beals, Jennifer **12**
Bearden, Romare **2**
Beckford, Tyson **11**
Belafonte, Harry **4**
Bell, Derrick **6**
Bellamy, Bill **12**
Belle, Albert **10**
Belle, Regina **1**
Ben-Israel, Ben Ami **11**
Bennett, Lerone, Jr. **5**
Berry, Bertice **8**
Berry, Halle **4**
Berry, Mary Frances **7**

Bethune, Mary McLeod **4**
Bing, Dave **3**
Bluford, Guy **2**
Bolden, Charles F., Jr. **7**
Bond, Julian **2**
Bonds, Barry **6**
Bontemps, Arna **8**
Borders, James **9**
Bosley, Freeman, Jr. **7**
Bowe, Riddick **6**
Boyd, T. B. III **6**
Bradley, Ed **2**
Bradley, Thomas **2**
Brandon, Barbara **3**
Braun, Carol Moseley **4**
Brimmer, Andrew F. **2**
Bristow, Lonnie **12**
Brooke, Edward **8**
Brooks, Avery **9**
Brooks, Gwendolyn **1**
Brown, Elaine **8**
Brown, Jesse **6**
Brown, Jim **11**
Brown, Lee P. **1**
Brown, Les **5**
Brown, Marie Dutton **12**
Brown, Ron **5**
Brown, Sterling **10**
Brown, Tony **3**
Brown, Willie L., Jr. **7**
Brown, Zora Kramer **12**
Brunson, Dorothy **1**
Bryant, Wayne R. **6**
Bullard, Eugene **12**
Bumbry, Grace **5**
Bunche, Ralph J. **5**
Burroughs, Margaret Taylor **9**
Burton, LeVar **8**
Busby, Jheryl **3**
Butler, Octavia **8**
Butts, Calvin O., III **9**
Byrd, Donald **10**
Byrd, Robert **11**
Callender, Clive O. **3**
Campbell, Bebe Moore **6**
Campbell, Bill **9**
Campbell, Tisha **8**
Cannon, Katie **10**
Carroll, Diahann **9**
Carson, Benjamin **1**
Carter, Mandy **11**

Carter, Stephen L. **4**
Carver, George Washington **4**
Cary, Lorene **3**
CasSelle, Malcolm **11**
Catlett, Elizabeth **2**
Chambers, Julius **3**
Chavis, Benjamin **6**
Chenault, Kenneth I. **4**
Chisholm, Shirley **2**
Chuck D **9**
Clark, Joe **1**
Clark, Kenneth B. **5**
Clark, Septima **7**
Clay, William Lacy **8**
Clayton, Constance **1**
Clayton, Xernona **3**
Cleaver, Eldridge **5**
Cleaver, Emanuel **4**
Clements, George **2**
Clinton, George **9**
Cobbs, Price M. **9**
Cochran, Johnnie L., Jr. **11**
Cole, Johnnetta B. **5**
Coleman, Bessie **9**
Coleman, Leonard S., Jr. **12**
Colemon, Johnnie **11**
Collins, Albert **12**
Collins, Barbara-Rose **7**
Collins, Cardiss **10**
Collins, Marva **3**
Comer, James P. **6**
Cone, James H. **3**
Conyers, John, Jr. **4**
Cooper, Edward S. **6**
Cooper, J. California **12**
Cornelius, Don **4**
Cosby, Bill **7**
Cose, Ellis **5**
Cottrell, Comer **11**
Crockett, Jr., George **10**
Crouch, Stanley **11**
Cullen, Countee **8**
Dandridge, Dorothy **3**
Dash, Julie **4**
Davidson, Jaye **5**
Davis, Allison **12**
Davis, Angela **5**
Davis, Anthony **11**
Davis, Benjamin O., Jr. **2**
Davis, Benjamin O., Sr. **4**
Davis, Miles **4**

Davis, Ossie **5**
Dawes, Dominique **11**
Days, Drew S., III **10**
Dee, Ruby **8**
Delany, Bessie **12**
Delany, Sadie **12**
Delany, Samuel R., Jr. **9**
Dellums, Ronald **2**
Devers, Gail **7**
Dickerson, Ernest **6**
Dinkins, David **4**
Divine, Father **7**
Dixon, Sharon Pratt **1**
Dixon, Willie **4**
Dodson, Howard, Jr. **7**
Douglas, Aaron **7**
Dove, Rita **6**
Dove, Ulysses **5**
Dr. Dre **10**
Drew, Charles Richard **7**
Drexler, Clyde **4**
Driskell, David C. **7**
Driver, David E. **11**
Du Bois, W. E. B. **3**
Ducksworth, Marilyn **12**
Duke, Bill **3**
Dunbar, Paul Laurence **8**
Dunham, Katherine **4**
Dutton, Charles S. **4**
Dyson, Michael Eric **11**
Edelman, Marian Wright **5**
Edley, Christopher **2**
Edmonds, Kenneth "Babyface"
  10
Edwards, Harry **2**
Elder, Lee **6**
Elders, Joycelyn **6**
Ellington, Duke **5**
Ellington, E. David **11**
Ellison, Ralph **7**
Esposito, Giancarlo **9**
Espy, Mike **6**
Europe, James Reese **10**
Evers, Medgar **3**
Evers, Myrlie **8**
Farmer, Forest J. **1**
Farmer, James **2**
Farrakhan, Louis **2**
Fattah, Chaka **11**
Fauntroy, Walter E. **11**
Fauset, Jessie **7**
Feelings, Tom **11**
Fielder, Cecil **2**
Fishburne, Larry **4**
Fitzgerald, Ella **8**
Flipper, Henry O. **3**
Flood, Curt **10**
Foreman, George **1**
Forman, James **7**
Fortune, T. Thomas **6**
Foxx, Redd **2**
Franklin, Aretha **11**
Franklin, Carl **11**
Franklin, Hardy R. **9**
Franklin, John Hope **5**
Franks, Gary **2**
Frazier, E. Franklin **10**
Freeman, Al, Jr. **11**

Freeman, Morgan **2**
Fudge, Ann **11**
Fulani, Lenora **11**
Fuller, Charles **8**
Gaines, Ernest J. **7**
Gantt, Harvey **1**
Garrison, Zina **2**
Gary, Willie E. **12**
Gaston, Arthur G. **4**
Gates, Henry Louis, Jr. **3**
Gaye, Marvin **2**
Gayle, Helene D. **3**
George, Nelson **12**
Gibson, Althea **8**
Gibson, Kenneth Allen **6**
Gibson, William F. **6**
Giddings, Paula **11**
Gillespie, Dizzy **1**
Giovanni, Nikki **9**
Gist, Carole **1**
Givens, Robin **4**
Glover, Danny **1**
Glover, Nathaniel, Jr. **12**
Goldberg, Whoopi **4**
Golden, Thelma **10**
Gomez-Preston, Cheryl **9**
Goode, W. Wilson **4**
Gordon, Ed **10**
Gordy, Berry, Jr. **1**
Gossett, Louis, Jr. **7**
Gourdine, Simon **11**
Graham, Lawrence Otis **12**
Gravely, Samuel L., Jr. **5**
Graves, Earl G. **1**
Gray, William H. III **3**
Green, Dennis **5**
Greene, Joe **10**
Greenfield, Eloise **9**
Gregory, Dick **1**
Gregory, Frederick D. **8**
Grier, Pam **9**
Griffey, Ken, Jr. **12**
Griffin, Anthony P. **12**
Griffith, Mark Winston **8**
Grimké, Archibald H. **9**
Guillaume, Robert **3**
Guinier, Lani **7**
Gumbel, Greg **8**
Gunn, Moses **10**
Guy, Jasmine **2**
Guy, Rosa **5**
Guyton, Tyree **9**
Hale, Lorraine **8**
Haley, Alex **4**
Hall, Lloyd A. **8**
Hamblin, Ken **10**
Hamer, Fannie Lou **6**
Hamilton, Virginia **10**
Hampton, Henry **6**
Handy, W. C. **8**
Hannah, Marc **10**
Hansberry, Lorraine **6**
Hansberry, William Leo **11**
Hardison, Bethann **12**
Harper, Frances Ellen Watkins **11**
Harrell, Andre **9**
Harrington, Oliver W. **9**
Harris, Alice **7**

Harris, Barbara **12**
Harris, E. Lynn **12**
Harris, Leslie **6**
Harris, Patricia Roberts **2**
Harris, Robin **7**
Harvard, Beverly **11**
Hastie, William H. **8**
Hawkins, Coleman **9**
Hayden, Robert **12**
Hayes, James C. **10**
Hayes, Roland **4**
Haynes, George Edmund **8**
Height, Dorothy I. **2**
Hemphill, Essex **10**
Henderson, Gordon **5**
Hendricks, Barbara **3**
Hendrix, Jimi **10**
Henson, Matthew **2**
Hickman, Fred **11**
Hill, Anita **5**
Hilliard, David **7**
Himes, Chester **8**
Hinderas, Natalie **5**
Hines, Gregory **1**
Hinton, William Augustus **8**
Holder, Eric H., Jr. **9**
Holiday, Billie **1**
Holland, Endesha Ida Mae **3**
Holland, Robert, Jr. **11**
Holyfield, Evander **6**
hooks, bell **5**
Hooks, Benjamin L. **2**
Hope, John **8**
Horne, Lena **5**
House, Son **8**
Houston, Charles Hamilton **4**
Houston, Whitney **7**
Howlin' Wolf **9**
Hudlin, Reginald **9**
Hudlin, Warrington **9**
Hughes, Albert **7**
Hughes, Allen **7**
Hughes, Langston **4**
Hunt, Richard **6**
Hunter-Gault, Charlayne **6**
Hurston, Zora Neale **3**
Ice Cube **8**
Ice-T **6**
Iceberg Slim **11**
Ingram, Rex **5**
Innis, Roy **5**
Irving, Larry, Jr. **12**
Jackson, Isaiah **3**
Jackson, Janet **6**
Jackson, Jesse **1**
Jackson, Mahalia **5**
Jackson, Maynard **2**
Jackson, Samuel L. **8**
Jackson, Shirley Ann **12**
Jacob, John E. **2**
Jamison, Judith **7**
Jeffries, Leonard **8**
Jemison, Mae C. **1**
Jenifer, Franklyn G. **2**
Johnson, Beverly **2**
Johnson, Charles **1**
Johnson, Charles S. **12**
Johnson, Earvin "Magic" **3**

Johnson, Eddie Bernice **8**
Johnson, Jack **8**
Johnson, James Weldon **5**
Johnson, John H. **3**
Johnson, Robert **2**
Johnson, Robert L. **3**
Johnson, Virginia **9**
Johnson, William Henry **3**
Jones, Bill T. **1**
Jones, Carl **7**
Jones, Elaine R. **7**
Jones, James Earl **3**
Jones, Quincy **8**
Jones, Star **10**
Joplin, Scott **6**
Jordan, Barbara **4**
Jordan, June **7**
Jordan, Michael **6**
Jordan, Vernon E. **3**
Josey, E. J. **10**
Joyner-Kersee, Jackie **5**
Julian, Percy Lavon **6**
Just, Ernest Everett **3**
Kani, Karl **10**
Karenga, Maulana **10**
Kearse, Amalya Lyle **12**
Kelly, Patrick **3**
Kennedy, Adrienne **11**
Kennedy, Florynce **12**
Keyes, Alan L. **11**
Khan, Chaka **12**
Khanga, Yelena **6**
Kimbro, Dennis **10**
Kincaid, Jamaica **4**
King, B. B. **7**
King, Bernice **4**
King, Coretta Scott **3**
King, Dexter **10**
King, Martin Luther, Jr. **1**
King, Yolanda **6**
Kirk, Ron **11**
Knight, Suge **11**
Komunyakaa, Yusef **9**
Kotto, Yaphet **7**
Kountz, Samuel L. **10**
Kravitz, Lenny **10**
Kunjufu, Jawanza **3**
La Salle, Eriq **12**
Lafontant, Jewel Stradford **3**
Lane, Charles **3**
Lane, Vincent **5**
Larsen, Nella **10**
Latimer, Lewis H. **4**
Lawless, Theodore K. **8**
Lawrence, Jacob **4**
Lawrence, Martin **6**
Lawrence-Lightfoot, Sara **10**
Lawson, Jennifer **1**
Leary, Kathryn D. **10**
Lee, Canada **8**
Lee, Joie **1**
Lee, Spike **5**
Lee-Smith, Hughie **5**
Leffall, LaSalle, Jr. **3**
Leland, Mickey **2**
Leon, Kenny **10**
Lester, Julius **9**
Lewis, Carl **4**

Lewis, David Levering **9**
Lewis, Delano **7**
Lewis, Edmonia **10**
Lewis, John **2**
Lewis, Reginald F. **6**
Lincoln, Abbey **3**
Little, Robert L. **2**
Locke, Alain **10**
Lofton, Kenny **12**
Lorde, Audre **6**
Lott, Ronnie **9**
Louis, Errol T. **8**
Louis, Joe **5**
Love, Nat **9**
Lover, Ed **10**
Lowery, Joseph **2**
Lucas, John **7**
Lyons, Henry **12**
Madhubuti, Haki R. **7**
Major, Clarence **9**
Marable, Manning **10**
Marshall, Paule **7**
Marshall, Thurgood **1**
Massey, Walter E. **5**
Mayfield, Curtis **2**
Maynard, Robert C. **7**
Mays, Benjamin E. **7**
Mays, Willie **3**
McCabe, Jewell Jackson **10**
McCall, Nathan **8**
McCoy, Elijah **8**
McDaniel, Hattie **5**
McDonald, Erroll **1**
McDougall, Gay J. **11**
McEwen, Mark **5**
McGee, Charles **10**
McKay, Claude **6**
McKinney, Cynthia Ann **11**
McKinnon, Isaiah **9**
McKissick, Floyd B. **3**
McMillan, Terry **4**
McNair, Ronald **3**
McNeil, Lori **1**
McPhail, Sharon **2**
McQueen, Butterfly **6**
Mckee, Lonette **12**
Meek, Carrie **6**
Meredith, James H. **11**
Mfume, Kweisi **6**
Micheaux, Oscar **7**
Miller, Bebe **3**
Miller, Cheryl **10**
Mitchell, Arthur **2**
Mitchell, Corinne **8**
Monk, Thelonious **1**
Moon, Warren **8**
Morgan, Garrett **1**
Morgan, Joe Leonard **9**
Morgan, Rose **11**
Morrison, Toni **2**
Moses, Edwin **8**
Moses, Gilbert **12**
Moses, Robert Parris **11**
Mosley, Walter **5**
Motley, Constance Baker **10**
Moutoussamy-Ashe, Jeanne **7**
Mowry, Jess **7**
Muhammad, Elijah **4**

Muhammad, Khallid Abdul **10**
Murphy, Eddie **4**
Murray, Cecil **12**
Murray, Eddie **12**
Murray, Lenda **10**
Myers, Walter Dean **8**
Naylor, Gloria **10**
Nelson, Jill **6**
Newton, Huey **2**
Nichols, Nichelle **11**
Norman, Jessye **5**
Norman, Pat **10**
Norton, Eleanor Holmes **7**
O'Leary, Hazel **6**
O'Neal, Shaquille **8**
Oglesby, Zena **12**
Ogletree, Jr., Charles **12**
Owens, Jesse **2**
Owens, Major **6**
Page, Alan **7**
Page, Clarence **4**
Paige, Satchel **7**
Parks, Gordon **1**
Parks, Rosa **1**
Parsons, Richard Dean **11**
Patrick, Deval **12**
Patterson, Frederick Douglass **12**
Payne, Donald M. **2**
Payton, Walter **11**
Peete, Calvin **11**
Perez, Anna **1**
Perkins, Edward **5**
Person, Waverly **9**
Pickett, Bill **1**
Pinchback, P. B. S. **9**
Pinkett, Jada **10**
Pippin, Horace **9**
Pleasant, Mary Ellen **9**
Poitier, Sidney **11**
Porter, James A. **11**
Poussaint, Alvin F. **5**
Powell, Adam Clayton, Jr. **3**
Powell, Colin **1**
Powell, Maxine **8**
Powell, Mike **7**
Price, Hugh B. **9**
Price, Leontyne **1**
Primus, Pearl **6**
Prothrow-Stith, Deborah **10**
Pryor, Richard **3**
Puckett, Kirby **4**
Quarterman, Lloyd Albert **4**
Queen Latifah **1**
Rand, A. Barry **6**
Randall, Dudley **8**
Randolph, A. Philip **3**
Rangel, Charles **3**
Raspberry, William **2**
Reagon, Bernice Johnson **7**
Reed, Ishmael **8**
Reese, Della **6**
Rhone, Sylvia **2**
Ribbs, Willy T. **2**
Rice, Condoleezza **3**
Rice, Jerry **5**
Rice, Linda Johnson **9**
Rice, Norm **8**
Richardson, Nolan **9**

Riggs, Marlon **5**
Ringgold, Faith **4**
Robeson, Paul **2**
Robinson **11**
Robinson, Eddie G. **10**
Robinson, Frank **9**
Robinson, Jackie **6**
Robinson, Max **3**
Robinson, Randall **7**
Robinson, Smokey **3**
Rock, Chris **3**
Rodgers, Johnathan **6**
Rodman, Dennis **12**
Rogers, John W., Jr. **5**
Roker, Al **12**
Ross, Diana **8**
Rowan, Carl T. **1**
Rudolph, Wilma **4**
Rushen, Patrice **12**
Russell, Bill **8**
Rustin, Bayard **4**
Saint James, Synthia **12**
Sanders, Joseph R., Jr. **11**
Savage, Augusta **12**
Sister Souljah **11**
Smaltz, Audrey **12**
Smith, Barbara **11**
Smith, Roger Guenveur **12**
St. Jacques, Raymond **8**
Sampson, Edith S. **4**
Sanders, Barry **1**
Sanders, Deion **4**
Sanders, Dori **8**
Satcher, David **7**
Sayles Belton, Sharon **9**
Schmoke, Kurt **1**
Schultz, Michael A. **6**
Seale, Bobby **3**
Sears-Collins, Leah J. **5**
Serrano, Andres **3**
Shabazz, Attallah **6**
Shabazz, Betty **7**
Shakur, Assata **6**
Shange, Ntozake **8**
Shaw, Bernard **2**
Shell, Art **1**
Sifford, Charlie **4**
Simmons, Russell **1**
Simpson, Carole **6**
Simpson, Lorna **4**
Sinbad **1**
Singletary, Mike **4**
Singleton, John **2**
Sleet, Moneta, Jr. **5**
Smith, Anna Deavere **6**
Smith, Bessie **3**
Smith, Emmitt **7**
Smith, Joshua **10**
Smith, Will **8**
Smith, Willi **8**
Snipes, Wesley **3**
Sowell, Thomas **2**
Spaulding, Charles Clinton **9**
Stallings, George A., Jr. **6**
Staples, Brent **8**
Staupers, Mabel K. **7**
Stewart, Paul Wilbur **12**
Stokes, Carl B. **10**

Stokes, Louis **3**
Stone, Chuck **9**
Sudarkasa, Niara **4**
Sullivan, Leon H. **3**
Sullivan, Louis **8**
Swoopes, Sheryl **12**
Tanner, Henry Ossawa **1**
Taylor, Kristin Clark **8**
Taylor, Meshach **4**
Taylor, Regina **9**
Taylor, Susan L. **10**
Terrell, Mary Church **9**
Thomas, Clarence **2**
Thomas, Frank **12**
Thomas, Franklin A. **5**
Thomas, Isiah **7**
Thomas, Vivien **9**
Thurman, Howard **3**
Till, Emmett **7**
Tolliver, William **9**
Toomer, Jean **6**
Townsend, Robert **4**
Tribble, Israel, Jr. **8**
Trotter, Monroe **9**
Tubman, Harriet **9**
Tucker, C. DeLores **12**
Turner, Henry McNeal **5**
Turner, Tina **6**
Tyson, Cicely **7**
Underwood, Blair **7**
VanDerZee, James **6**
Van Peebles, Mario **2**
Van Peebles, Melvin **7**
Vereen, Ben **4**
Vincent, Marjorie Judith **2**
Von Lipsey, Roderick K. **11**
Waddles, Charleszetta (Mother)
   10
Walker, Albertina **10**
Walker, Alice **1**
Walker, Herschel **1**
Walker, Madame C. J. **7**
Walker, T. J. **7**
Wallace, Phyllis A. **9**
Wallace, Sippie **1**
Warfield, Marsha **2**
Washington, Booker T. **4**
Washington, Denzel **1**
Washington, Fredi **10**
Washington, Harold **6**
Washington, MaliVai **8**
Washington, Patrice Clarke **12**
Washington, Val **12**
Waters, Ethel **7**
Waters, Maxine **3**
Watkins, Levi, Jr. **9**
Watkins, Perry **12**
Wattleton, Faye **9**
Watts, Rolonda **9**
Wayans, Damon **8**
Weathers, Carl **10**
Weaver, Robert C. **8**
Webb, Veronica **10**
Webb, Wellington **3**
Wells, James Lesesne **10**
Wells-Barnett, Ida B. **8**
Welsing, Frances Cress **5**
West, Cornel **5**

West, Dorothy **12**
Wharton, Clifton R., Jr. **7**
Whitaker, Forest **2**
Whitaker, Pernell **10**
White, Bill **1**
White, Michael R. **5**
White, Reggie **6**
White, Walter F. **4**
Wideman, John Edgar **5**
Wilder, L. Douglas **3**
Wiley, Ralph **8**
Wilkens, Lenny **11**
Wilkins, Roger **2**
Wilkins, Roy **4**
Williams, Billy Dee **8**
Williams, Daniel Hale **2**
Williams, Evelyn **10**
Williams, Gregory **11**
Williams, Joe **5**
Williams, Maggie **7**
Williams, Montel **4**
Williams, Patricia J. **11**
Williams, Paul R. **9**
Williams, Robert F. **11**
Williams, Vanessa **4**
Williams, Walter E. **4**
Williams, William T. **11**
Williams, Willie L. **4**
Wilson, August **7**
Wilson, Nancy **10**
Wilson, Phill **9**
Wilson, Sunnie **7**
Winfield, Dave **5**
Winfield, Paul **2**
Winfrey, Oprah **2**
Wolfe, George C. **6**
Wonder, Stevie **11**
Woodard, Alfre **9**
Woodruff, Hale **9**
Woods, Granville T. **5**
Woodson, Carter G. **2**
Woodson, Robert L. **10**
Worrill, Conrad **12**
Wright, Bruce McMarion **3**
Wright, Louis Tompkins **4**
Wright, Richard **5**
X, Malcolm **1**
Yoba, Malik **11**
Young, Andrew **3**
Young, Coleman **1**
Young, Whitney M., Jr. **4**
Youngblood, Johnny Ray **8**

Angolan
Savimbi, Jonas **2**

Batswana
Masire, Quett **5**

Beninois
   Kerekou, Ahmed (Mathieu) **1**

Brazilian
   da Silva, Benedita **5**
   Nascimento, Milton **2**
   Pelé **7**

British
Abbott, Diane **9**
Campbell, Naomi **1**
Christie, Linford **8**
Davidson, Jaye **5**
Henry, Lenny **9**
Julien, Isaac **3**
Pitt, David Thomas **10**

Burkinabé
Somé, Malidoma Patrice **10**

Burundian
Ndadaye, Melchior **7**
Ntaryamira, Cyprien **8**

Cameroonian
Kotto, Yaphet **7**
Milla, Roger **2**

Canadian
Bell, Ralph S. **5**
Fuhr, Grant **1**
Johnson, Ben **1**
McKegney, Tony **3**
O'Ree, Willie **5**
Richards, Lloyd **2**

Cape Verdean
Evora, Cesaria **12**

Chadian
Habré, Hissène **6**

Costa Rican
McDonald, Erroll **1**

Dominican
Charles, Mary Eugenia **10**

Dutch
Liberia-Peters, Maria Philomena **12**

Ethiopian
Haile Selassie **7**
Meles Zenawi **3**

French
Baker, Josephine **3**
Baldwin, James **1**
Bonaly, Surya **7**
Noah, Yannick **4**
Tanner, Henry Ossawa **1**

Gabonese
Bongo, Omar **1**

Ghanaian
Jawara, Sir Dawda Kairaba **11**
Nkrumah, Kwame **3**
Rawlings, Jerry **9**

Guinean
Conté, Lansana **7**
Touré, Sekou **6**

Haitian
Aristide, Jean-Bertrand **6**
Charlemagne, Manno **11**
Christophe, Henri **9**
Pascal-Trouillot, Ertha **3**

Italian
Esposito, Giancarlo **9**

Ivorian
Houphouët-Boigny, Félix **4**

Jamaican
Belafonte, Harry **4**
Garvey, Marcus **1**
Johnson, Ben **1**
Marley, Bob **5**
McKay, Claude **6**
Patterson, Orlando **4**
Patterson, P. J. **6**
Tosh, Peter **9**

Kenyan
Kenyatta, Jomo **5**
Mazrui, Ali A. **12**
Moi, Daniel **1**

Liberian
Sawyer, Amos **2**

Malawian
Banda, Hastings Kamuzu **6**

Mozambican
Chissano, Joaquim **7**
Machel, Samora Moises **8**
Mutola, Maria **12**

Namibian
Mbuende, Kaire **12**
Nujoma, Samuel **10**

Nigerian
Abacha, Sani **11**
Achebe, Chinua **6**
Babangida, Ibrahim **4**
Fela **1**
Obasanjo, Olusegun **5**
Olajuwon, Hakeem **2**
Rotimi, Ola **1**
Soyinka, Wole **4**

Puerto Rican
Schomburg, Arthur Alfonso **9**

Russian
Khanga, Yelena **6**

Rwandan
Habyarimana, Juvenal **8**

Senegalese
Diop, Cheikh Anta **4**
Diouf, Abdou **3**
Mboup, Souleymane **10**
N'Dour, Youssou **1**
Senghor, Léopold Sédar **12**

Somali
Ali Mahdi Mohamed **5**
Iman **4**

South African
Biko, Steven **4**
Buthelezi, Mangosuthu Gatsha **9**
Hani, Chris **6**
Makeba, Miriam **2**
Mandela, Nelson **1**
Mandela, Winnie **2**
Masekela, Hugh **1**
Mathabane, Mark **5**
Ramaphosa, Cyril **3**
Tutu, Desmond **6**

Sudanese
Bol, Manute **1**

Tanzanian
Mongella, Gertrude **11**
Mwinyi, Ali Hassan **1**
Nyerere, Julius **5**

Togolese
Eyadéma, Gnassingbé **7**

Trinidadian
Carmichael, Stokely **5**
Guy, Rosa **5**
Primus, Pearl **6**

Ugandan
Museveni, Yoweri **4**

West Indian
Innis, Roy **5**
Kincaid, Jamaica **4**
Staupers, Mabel K. **7**
Pitt, David Thomas **10**
Taylor, Susan L. **10**
Walcott, Derek **5**

Zairean
Mobutu Sese Seko **1**
Mutombo, Dikembe **7**
Ongala, Remmy **9**

Zambian
Kaunda, Kenneth **2**

Zimbabwean
Mugabe, Robert Gabriel **10**
Nkomo, Joshua **4**

Cumulative Occupation Index

Volume numbers appear in **bold.**

Art and design
Bailey, Xenobia **11**
Barboza, Anthony **10**
Basquiat, Jean-Michel **5**
Bearden, Romare **2**
Brandon, Barbara **3**
Burroughs, Margaret Taylor **9**
Catlett, Elizabeth **2**
Douglas, Aaron **7**
Driskell, David C. **7**
Feelings, Tom **11**
Gantt, Harvey **1**
Golden, Thelma **10**
Guyton, Tyree **9**
Harrington, Oliver W. **9**
Hope, John **8**
Hunt, Richard **6**
Johnson, William Henry **3**
Lawrence, Jacob **4**
Lee-Smith, Hughie **5**
Lewis, Edmonia **10**
McGee, Charles **10**
Mitchell, Corinne **8**
Moutoussamy-Ashe, Jeanne **7**
Pippin, Horace **9**
Porter, James A. **11**
Ringgold, Faith **4**
Saint James, Synthia **12**
Sanders, Joseph R., Jr. **11**
Savage, Augusta **12**
Serrano, Andres **3**
Shabazz, Attallah **6**
Simpson, Lorna **4**
Sleet, Moneta, Jr. **5**
Tanner, Henry Ossawa **1**
Tolliver, William **9**
VanDerZee, James **6**
Wells, James Lesesne **10**
Williams, Billy Dee **8**
Williams, Paul R. **9**
Williams, William T. **11**
Woodruff, Hale **9**

Business
Abdul-Jabbar, Kareem **8**
Ailey, Alvin **8**
Al-Amin, Jamil Abdullah **6**
Amos, Wally **9**
Baker, Dusty **8**
Baker, Ella **5**
Baker, Gwendolyn Calvert **9**

Banks, William **11**
Barden, Don H. **9**
Barrett, Andrew C. **12**
Bennett, Lerone, Jr. **5**
Bing, Dave **3**
Borders, James **9**
Boyd, T. B. III **6**
Brimmer, Andrew F. **2**
Brown, Les **5**
Brown, Marie Dutton **12**
Brunson, Dorothy **1**
Burroughs, Margaret Taylor **9**
Busby, Jheryl **3**
CasSelle, Malcolm **11**
Chenault, Kenneth I. **4**
Clay, William Lacy **8**
Clayton, Xernona **3**
Cobbs, Price M. **9**
Cornelius, Don **4**
Cosby, Bill **7**
Cottrell, Comer **11**
Delany, Bessie **12**
Delany, Sadie **12**
Divine, Father **7**
Driver, David E. **11**
Ducksworth, Marilyn **12**
Elder, Lee **6**
Ellington, E. David **11**
Evers, Myrlie **8**
Farmer, Forest J. **1**
Fauntroy, Walter E. **11**
Franklin, Hardy R. **9**
Fudge, Ann **11**
Gaston, Arthur G. **4**
Gibson, Kenneth Allen **6**
Gordy, Berry, Jr. **1**
Graves, Earl G. **1**
Griffith, Mark Winston **8**
Hale, Lorraine **8**
Hamer, Fannie Lou **6**
Handy, W. C. **8**
Hannah, Marc **10**
Hardison, Bethann **12**
Harrell, Andre **9**
Harris, Alice **7**
Harris, E. Lynn **12**
Henderson, Gordon **5**
Henry, Lenny **9**
Holland, Robert, Jr. **11**
Houston, Whitney **7**
Hudlin, Reginald **9**

Hudlin, Warrington **9**
Ice Cube **8**
Johnson, Eddie Bernice **8**
Johnson, John H. **3**
Johnson, Robert L. **3**
Jones, Carl **7**
Jones, Quincy **8**
Jordan, Michael **6**
Julian, Percy Lavon **6**
Kelly, Patrick **3**
Kimbro, Dennis **10**
King, Dexter **10**
Knight, Suge **11**
Lane, Vincent **5**
Lawless, Theodore K. **8**
Lawson, Jennifer **1**
Leary, Kathryn D. **10**
Lewis, Delano **7**
Lewis, Reginald F. **6**
Lott, Ronnie **9**
Louis, Errol T. **8**
Lucas, John **7**
Madhubuti, Haki R. **7**
Maynard, Robert C. **7**
McCabe, Jewell Jackson **10**
McCoy, Elijah **8**
McDonald, Erroll **1**
Micheaux, Oscar **7**
Morgan, Garrett **1**
Morgan, Joe Leonard **9**
Morgan, Rose **11**
Nichols, Nichelle **11**
Parks, Gordon **1**
Parsons, Richard Dean **11**
Payton, Walter **11**
Perez, Anna **1**
Pleasant, Mary Ellen **9**
Powell, Maxine **8**
Price, Hugh B. **9**
Rand, A. Barry **6**
Rhone, Sylvia **2**
Rice, Linda Johnson **9**
Rice, Norm **8**
Robinson, Jackie **6**
Robinson, Randall **7**
Rodgers, Johnathan **6**
Rogers, John W., Jr. **5**
Ross, Diana **8**
Russell, Bill **8**
Saint James, Synthia **12**
Sanders, Dori **8**

Simmons, Russell **1**
Smith, Barbara **11**
Smith, Joshua **10**
Smith, Willi **8**
Spaulding, Charles Clinton **9**
Stewart, Paul Wilbur **12**
Sullivan, Leon H. **3**
Taylor, Kristin Clark **8**
Taylor, Susan L. **10**
Thomas, Franklin A. **5**
Thomas, Isiah **7**
Tribble, Israel, Jr. **8**
Trotter, Monroe **9**
Van Peebles, Melvin **7**
VanDerZee, James **6**
Walker, Madame C. J. **7**
Walker, T. J. **7**
Washington, Val **12**
Wattleton, Faye **9**
Wells-Barnett, Ida B. **8**
Wharton, Clifton R., Jr. **7**
White, Walter F. **4**
Wiley, Ralph **8**
Williams, Paul R. **9**
Williams, Walter E. **4**
Wilson, Phill **9**
Wilson, Sunnie **7**
Winfrey, Oprah **2**
Woodson, Robert L. **10**
Yoba, Malik **11**

Dance
Ailey, Alvin **8**
Baker, Josephine **3**
Beals, Jennifer **12**
Byrd, Donald **10**
Dove, Ulysses **5**
Dunham, Katherine **4**
Guy, Jasmine **2**
Hines, Gregory **1**
Horne, Lena **5**
Jamison, Judith **7**
Johnson, Virginia **9**
Jones, Bill T. **1**
McQueen, Butterfly **6**
Miller, Bebe **3**
Mitchell, Arthur **2**
Nichols, Nichelle **11**
Powell, Maxine **8**
Primus, Pearl **6**
Robinson **11**
Vereen, Ben **4**
Washington, Fredi **10**

Education
Achebe, Chinua **6**
Archer, Dennis **7**
Aristide, Jean-Bertrand **6**
Asante, Molefi Kete **3**
Baker, Gwendolyn Calvert **9**
Baker, Houston A., Jr. **6**
Bambara, Toni Cade **10**
Baraka, Amiri **1**
Barboza, Anthony **10**
Bell, Derrick **6**
Berry, Bertice **8**
Berry, Mary Frances **7**
Bethune, Mary McLeod **4**

Bosley, Freeman, Jr. **7**
Boyd, T. B. III **6**
Brooks, Avery **9**
Brown, Sterling **10**
Burroughs, Margaret Taylor **9**
Burton, LeVar **8**
Callender, Clive O. **3**
Campbell, Bebe Moore **6**
Cannon, Katie **10**
Carver, George Washington **4**
Cary, Lorene **3**
Catlett, Elizabeth **2**
Clark, Joe **1**
Clark, Kenneth B. **5**
Clark, Septima **7**
Clayton, Constance **1**
Clements, George **2**
Cobbs, Price M. **9**
Cole, Johnnetta B. **5**
Collins, Marva **3**
Comer, James P. **6**
Cone, James H. **3**
Cooper, Edward S. **6**
Cosby, Bill **7**
Cottrell, Comer **11**
Crouch, Stanley **11**
Cullen, Countee **8**
Davis, Allison **12**
Davis, Angela **5**
Days, Drew S., III **10**
Delany, Sadie **12**
Delany, Samuel R., Jr. **9**
Diop, Cheikh Anta **4**
Dodson, Howard, Jr. **7**
Douglas, Aaron **7**
Dove, Rita **6**
Dove, Ulysses **5**
Driskell, David C. **7**
Dyson, Michael Eric **11**
Edelman, Marian Wright **5**
Edley, Christopher **2**
Edwards, Harry **2**
Elders, Joycelyn **6**
Ellison, Ralph **7**
Fauset, Jessie **7**
Franklin, John Hope **5**
Frazier, E. Franklin **10**
Freeman, Al, Jr. **11**
Gaines, Ernest J. **7**
Gates, Henry Louis, Jr. **3**
Giddings, Paula **11**
Giovanni, Nikki **9**
Greenfield, Eloise **9**
Guinier, Lani **7**
Hale, Lorraine **8**
Handy, W. C. **8**
Hansberry, William Leo **11**
Harris, Alice **7**
Harris, Patricia Roberts **2**
Hayden, Robert **12**
Haynes, George Edmund **8**
Hill, Anita **5**
Hinton, William Augustus **8**
Holland, Endesha Ida Mae **3**
hooks, bell **5**
Hope, John **8**
Houston, Charles Hamilton **4**
Hunt, Richard **6**

Jeffries, Leonard **8**
Jenifer, Franklyn G. **2**
Johnson, James Weldon **5**
Joplin, Scott **6**
Jordan, Barbara **4**
Jordan, June **7**
Josey, E. J. **10**
Just, Ernest Everett **3**
Karenga, Maulana **10**
Kennedy, Florynce **12**
Kimbro, Dennis **10**
Komunyakaa, Yusef **9**
Kunjufu, Jawanza **3**
Lawrence, Jacob **4**
Leffall, LaSalle, Jr. **3**
Lawrence-Lightfoot, Sara **10**
Lester, Julius **9**
Lewis, David Levering **9**
Liberia-Peters, Maria Philomena **12**
Locke, Alain **10**
Lorde, Audre **6**
Madhubuti, Haki R. **7**
Major, Clarence **9**
Marable, Manning **10**
Marshall, Paule **7**
Massey, Walter E. **5**
Maynard, Robert C. **7**
Mays, Benjamin E. **7**
Meek, Carrie **6**
Meredith, James H. **11**
Mitchell, Corinne **8**
Mongella, Gertrude **11**
Moses, Robert Parris **11**
Norton, Eleanor Holmes **7**
Ogletree, Jr., Charles **12**
Owens, Major **6**
Page, Alan **7**
Patterson, Frederick Douglass **12**
Patterson, Orlando **4**
Porter, James A. **11**
Poussaint, Alvin F. **5**
Primus, Pearl **6**
Reagon, Bernice Johnson **7**
Ringgold, Faith **4**
Satcher, David **7**
Schomburg, Arthur Alfonso **9**
Shabazz, Betty **7**
Shange, Ntozake **8**
Smith, Anna Deavere **6**
Soyinka, Wole **4**
Stone, Chuck **9**
Sudarkasa, Niara **4**
Sullivan, Louis **8**
Terrell, Mary Church **9**
Thurman, Howard **3**
Tribble, Israel, Jr. **8**
Tutu, Desmond **6**
Walcott, Derek **5**
Wallace, Phyllis A. **9**
Washington, Booker T. **4**
Wattleton, Faye **9**
Wells, James Lesesne **10**
Wells-Barnett, Ida B. **8**
Welsing, Frances Cress **5**
West, Cornel **5**
Wharton, Clifton R., Jr. **7**
Wilkins, Roger **2**

Williams, Gregory **11**
Williams, Patricia J. **11**
Williams, Walter E. **4**
Woodruff, Hale **9**
Woodson, Carter G. **2**
Worrill, Conrad **12**

Fashion
Banks, Tyra **11**
Beals, Jennifer **12**
Beckford, Tyson **11**
Berry, Halle **4**
Bailey, Xenobia **11**
Barboza, Anthony **10**
Campbell, Naomi **1**
Davidson, Jaye **5**
Henderson, Gordon **5**
Iman **4**
Johnson, Beverly **2**
Jones, Carl **7**
Kani, Karl **10**
Kelly, Patrick **3**
Powell, Maxine **8**
Smaltz, Audrey **12**
Smith, Barbara **11**
Smith, Willi **8**
Walker, T. J. **7**
Webb, Veronica **10**

Film
Amos, John **8**
Baker, Josephine **3**
Banks, Tyra **11**
Bassett, Angela **6**
Beals, Jennifer **12**
Belafonte, Harry **4**
Bellamy, Bill **12**
Berry, Halle **4**
Brown, Jim **11**
Brown, Tony **3**
Byrd, Robert **11**
Campbell, Naomi **1**
Campbell, Tisha **8**
Carroll, Diahann **9**
Cosby, Bill **7**
Dandridge, Dorothy **3**
Dash, Julie **4**
Davidson, Jaye **5**
Davis, Ossie **5**
Dee, Ruby **8**
Dickerson, Ernest **6**
Dr. Dre **10**
Driskell, David C. **7**
Duke, Bill **3**
Dunham, Katherine **4**
Dutton, Charles S. **4**
Esposito, Giancarlo **9**
Fishburne, Larry **4**
Foxx, Redd **2**
Franklin, Carl **11**
Freeman, Al, Jr. **11**
Freeman, Morgan **2**
Fuller, Charles **8**
George, Nelson **12**
Givens, Robin **4**
Goldberg, Whoopi **4**
Gordy, Berry, Jr. **1**

Gossett, Louis, Jr. **7**
Grier, Pam **9**
Guillaume, Robert **3**
Gunn, Moses **10**
Guy, Jasmine **2**
Hampton, Henry **6**
Harris, Leslie **6**
Harris, Robin **7**
Henry, Lenny **9**
Hines, Gregory **1**
Horne, Lena **5**
Houston, Whitney **7**
Hudlin, Reginald **9**
Hudlin, Warrington **9**
Hughes, Albert **7**
Hughes, Allen **7**
Ice Cube **8**
Iman **4**
Ingram, Rex **5**
Jackson, Janet **6**
Jackson, Samuel L. **8**
Johnson, Beverly **2**
Jones, James Earl **3**
Jones, Quincy **8**
Julien, Isaac **3**
Kotto, Yaphet **7**
Kunjufu, Jawanza **3**
La Salle, Eriq **12**
Lane, Charles **3**
Lawrence, Martin **6**
Lee, Joie **1**
Lee, Spike **5**
Lincoln, Abbey **3**
Lover, Ed **10**
McDaniel, Hattie **5**
McQueen, Butterfly **6**
Mckee, Lonette **12**
Micheaux, Oscar **7**
Moses, Gilbert **12**
Murphy, Eddie **4**
Nichols, Nichelle **11**
Parks, Gordon **1**
Pinkett, Jada **10**
Poitier, Sidney **11**
Pryor, Richard **3**
Reese, Della **6**
Riggs, Marlon **5**
Rock, Chris **3**
Ross, Diana **8**
Smith, Roger Guenveur **12**
St. Jacques, Raymond **8**
Schultz, Michael A. **6**
Singleton, John **2**
Smith, Anna Deavere **6**
Smith, Will **8**
Snipes, Wesley **3**
Taylor, Meshach **4**
Taylor, Regina **9**
Townsend, Robert **4**
Turner, Tina **6**
Tyson, Cicely **7**
Underwood, Blair **7**
Van Peebles, Mario **2**
Van Peebles, Melvin **7**
Vereen, Ben **4**
Warfield, Marsha **2**
Washington, Denzel **1**
Washington, Fredi **10**

Waters, Ethel **7**
Wayans, Damon **8**
Weathers, Carl **10**
Webb, Veronica **10**
Whitaker, Forest **2**
Williams, Billy Dee **8**
Williams, Vanessa **4**
Winfield, Paul **2**
Winfrey, Oprah **2**
Woodard, Alfre **9**
Yoba, Malik **11**

Government and politics--
international
Abacha, Sani **11**
Abbott, Diane **9**
Achebe, Chinua **6**
Ali Mahdi Mohamed **5**
Aristide, Jean-Bertrand **6**
Babangida, Ibrahim **4**
Baker, Gwendolyn Calvert **9**
Banda, Hastings Kamuzu **6**
Berry, Mary Frances **7**
Biko, Steven **4**
Bongo, Omar **1**
Bunche, Ralph J. **5**
Buthelezi, Mangosuthu Gatsha **9**
Charlemagne, Manno **11**
Charles, Mary Eugenia **10**
Chissano, Joaquim **7**
Christophe, Henri **9**
Conté, Lansana **7**
da Silva, Benedita **5**
Diop, Cheikh Anta **4**
Diouf, Abdou **3**
Eyadéma, Gnassingbé **7**
Fela **1**
Habré, Hissène **6**
Habyarimana, Juvenal **8**
Haile Selassie **7**
Hani, Chris **6**
Houphouët-Boigny, Félix **4**
Jawara, Sir Dawda Kairaba **11**
Kabunda, Kenneth **2**
Kenyatta, Jomo **5**
Kerekou, Ahmed (Mathieu) **1**
Liberia-Peters, Maria Philomena **12**
Machel, Samora Moises **8**
Mandela, Nelson **1**
Mandela, Winnie **2**
Masire, Quett **5**
Mbuende, Kaire **12**
Meles Zenawi **3**
Mobutu Sese Seko **1**
Moi, Daniel **1**
Mongella, Gertrude **11**
Mugabe, Robert Gabriel **10**
Museveni, Yoweri **4**
Mwinyi, Ali Hassan **1**
Ndadaye, Melchior **7**
Nkomo, Joshua **4**
Nkrumah, Kwame **3**
Ntaryamira, Cyprien **8**
Nujoma, Samuel **10**
Nyerere, Julius **5**
Obasanjo, Olusegun **5**
Pascal-Trouillot, Ertha **3**

Patterson, P. J. **6**
Perkins, Edward **5**
Pitt, David Thomas **10**
Ramaphosa, Cyril **3**
Rawlings, Jerry **9**
Rice, Condoleezza **3**
Robinson, Randall **7**
Sampson, Edith S. **4**
Savimbi, Jonas **2**
Sawyer, Amos **2**
Senghor, Léopold Sédar **12**
Soyinka, Wole **4**
Touré, Sekou **6**
Tutu, Desmond **6**
Wharton, Clifton R., Jr. **7**

Government and politics--U.S.
Adams, Floyd, Jr. **12**
Ali, Muhammad **2**
Archer, Dennis **7**
Barden, Don H. **9**
Barrett, Andrew C. **12**
Barry, Marion S. **7**
Berry, Mary Frances **7**
Bethune, Mary McLeod **4**
Bond, Julian **2**
Bosley, Freeman, Jr. **7**
Bradley, Thomas **2**
Braun, Carol Moseley **4**
Brimmer, Andrew F. **2**
Brooke, Edward **8**
Brown, Elaine **8**
Brown, Jesse **6**
Brown, Les **5**
Brown, Ron **5**
Brown, Willie L., Jr. **7**
Bryant, Wayne R. **6**
Bunche, Ralph J. **5**
Campbell, Bill **9**
Chavis, Benjamin **6**
Chisholm, Shirley **2**
Clay, William Lacy **8**
Cleaver, Eldridge **5**
Cleaver, Emanuel **4**
Collins, Barbara-Rose **7**
Collins, Cardiss **10**
Conyers, John, Jr. **4**
Cose, Ellis **5**
Crockett, George, Jr. **10**
Davis, Angela **5**
Davis, Benjamin O., Jr. **2**
Davis, Benjamin O., Sr. **4**
Days, Drew S., III **10**
Dellums, Ronald **2**
Dinkins, David **4**
Dixon, Sharon Pratt **1**
Du Bois, W. E. B. **3**
Elders, Joycelyn **6**
Espy, Mike **6**
Farmer, James **2**
Farrakhan, Louis **2**
Fattah, Chaka **11**
Fauntroy, Walter E. **11**
Flipper, Henry O. **3**
Fortune, T. Thomas **6**
Franks, Gary **2**
Fulani, Lenora **11**
Gantt, Harvey **1**

Garvey, Marcus **1**
Gibson, Kenneth Allen **6**
Gibson, William F. **6**
Goode, W. Wilson **4**
Gravely, Samuel L., Jr. **5**
Gray, William H. III **3**
Grimké, Archibald H. **9**
Guinier, Lani **7**
Hamer, Fannie Lou **6**
Harris, Alice **7**
Harris, Patricia Roberts **2**
Harvard, Beverly **11**
Hastie, William H. **8**
Hayes, James C. **10**
Holder, Eric H., Jr. **9**
Irving, Larry, Jr. **12**
Jackson, Jesse **1**
Jackson, Maynard **2**
Jackson, Shirley Ann **12**
Jacob, John E. **2**
Johnson, Eddie Bernice **8**
Johnson, James Weldon **5**
Jones, Elaine R. **7**
Jordan, Barbara **4**
Keyes, Alan L. **11**
Kirk, Ron **11**
Lafontant, Jewel Stradford **3**
Leland, Mickey **2**
Lewis, Delano **7**
Lewis, John **2**
Marshall, Thurgood **1**
McKinney, Cynthia Ann **11**
McKissick, Floyd B. **3**
Meek, Carrie **6**
Meredith, James H. **11**
Mfume, Kweisi **6**
Moses, Robert Parris **11**
Norton, Eleanor Holmes **7**
O'Leary, Hazel **6**
Owens, Major **6**
Page, Alan **7**
Patrick, Deval **12**
Payne, Donald M. **2**
Perez, Anna **1**
Perkins, Edward **5**
Pinchback, P. B. S. **9**
Powell, Adam Clayton, Jr. **3**
Powell, Colin **1**
Randolph, A. Philip **3**
Rangel, Charles **3**
Rice, Condoleezza **3**
Rice, Norm **8**
Robinson, Randall **7**
Rustin, Bayard **4**
Sampson, Edith S. **4**
Satcher, David **7**
Sayles Belton, Sharon **9**
Schmoke, Kurt **1**
Sears-Collins, Leah J. **5**
Shakur, Assata **6**
Simpson, Carole **6**
Staupers, Mabel K. **7**
Stokes, Carl B. **10**
Stokes, Louis **3**
Stone, Chuck **9**
Sullivan, Louis **8**
Thomas, Clarence **2**
Tribble, Israel, Jr. **8**

Tucker, C. DeLores **12**
Turner, Henry McNeal **5**
Von Lipsey, Roderick K. **11**
Wallace, Phyllis A. **9**
Washington, Harold **6**
Washington, Val **12**
Waters, Maxine **3**
Weaver, Robert C. **8**
Webb, Wellington **3**
Wharton, Clifton R., Jr. **7**
White, Michael R. **5**
Wilder, L. Douglas **3**
Wilkins, Roger **2**
Williams, Maggie **7**
Wilson, Sunnie **7**
Young, Andrew **3**
Young, Coleman **1**

Law
Archer, Dennis **7**
Banks, William **11**
Barrett, Andrew C. **12**
Bell, Derrick **6**
Berry, Mary Frances **7**
Bosley, Freeman, Jr. **7**
Bradley, Thomas **2**
Braun, Carol Moseley **4**
Brooke, Edward **8**
Brown, Lee P. **1**
Brown, Ron **5**
Brown, Willie L., Jr. **7**
Bryant, Wayne R. **6**
Campbell, Bill **9**
Carter, Stephen L. **4**
Chambers, Julius **3**
Cochran, Johnnie L., Jr. **11**
Conyers, John, Jr. **4**
Crockett, George, Jr. **10**
Days, Drew S., III **10**
Dinkins, David **4**
Dixon, Sharon Pratt **1**
Edelman, Marian Wright **5**
Edley, Christopher **2**
Ellington, E. David **11**
Espy, Mike **6**
Gary, Willie E. **12**
Glover, Nathaniel, Jr. **12**
Gomez-Preston, Cheryl **9**
Graham, Lawrence Otis **12**
Griffin, Anthony P. **12**
Grimké, Archibald H. **9**
Guinier, Lani **7**
Harris, Patricia Roberts **2**
Harvard, Beverly **11**
Hastie, William H. **8**
Hill, Anita **5**
Holder, Eric H., Jr. **9**
Hooks, Benjamin L. **2**
Houston, Charles Hamilton **4**
Jackson, Maynard **2**
Johnson, James Weldon **5**
Jones, Elaine R. **7**
Jones, Star **10**
Jordan, Vernon E. **3**
Kearse, Amalya Lyle **12**
Kennedy, Florynce **12**
King, Bernice **4**
Kirk, Ron **11**

Lafontant, Jewel Stradford **3**
Lewis, Delano **7**
Lewis, Reginald F. **6**
Mandela, Nelson **1**
Marshall, Thurgood **1**
McDougall, Gay J. **11**
McKinnon, Isaiah **9**
McKissick, Floyd B. **3**
McPhail, Sharon **2**
Motley, Constance Baker **10**
Norton, Eleanor Holmes **7**
O'Leary, Hazel **6**
Ogletree, Jr., Charles **12**
Page, Alan **7**
Parsons, Richard Dean **11**
Pascal-Trouillot, Ertha **3**
Patrick, Deval **12**
Robinson, Randall **7**
Sampson, Edith S. **4**
Schmoke, Kurt **1**
Sears-Collins, Leah J. **5**
Stokes, Carl B. **10**
Stokes, Louis **3**
Thomas, Clarence **2**
Thomas, Franklin A. **5**
Washington, Harold **6**
Wilder, L. Douglas **3**
Wilkins, Roger **2**
Williams, Evelyn **10**
Williams, Gregory **11**
Williams, Patricia J. **11**
Williams, Willie L. **4**
Wright, Bruce McMarion **3**

Military
Babangida, Ibrahim **4**
Abacha, Sani **11**
Bolden, Charles F., Jr. **7**
Brown, Jesse **6**
Bullard, Eugene **12**
Chissano, Joaquim **7**
Christophe, Henri **9**
Conté, Lansana **7**
Davis, Benjamin O., Jr. **2**
Davis, Benjamin O., Sr. **4**
Europe, James Reese **10**
Eyadéma, Gnassingbé **7**
Flipper, Henry O. **3**
Gravely, Samuel L., Jr. **5**
Gregory, Frederick D. **8**
Habré, Hissène **6**
Habyarimana, Juvenal **8**
Kerekou, Ahmed (Mathieu) **1**
Obasanjo, Olusegun **5**
Powell, Colin **1**
Rawlings, Jerry **9**
Staupers, Mabel K. **7**
Stokes, Louis **3**
Von Lipsey, Roderick K. **11**
Watkins, Perry **12**

Music
Anderson, Marian **2**
Armstrong, Louis **2**
Baker, Josephine **3**
Belafonte, Harry **4**
Belle, Regina **1**
Brooks, Avery **9**

Bumbry, Grace **5**
Busby, Jheryl **3**
Campbell, Tisha **8**
Carroll, Diahann **9**
Charlemagne, Manno **11**
Chuck D **9**
Clinton, George **9**
Collins, Albert **12**
Crouch, Stanley **11**
Davis, Anthony **11**
Davis, Miles **4**
Dixon, Willie **4**
Dr. Dre **10**
Edmonds, Kenneth "Babyface" **10**
Ellington, Duke **5**
Europe, James Reese **10**
Evora, Cesaria **12**
Fela **1**
Fitzgerald, Ella **8**
Franklin, Aretha **11**
Gaye, Marvin **2**
Gibson, Althea **8**
Gillespie, Dizzy **1**
Gordy, Berry, Jr. **1**
Handy, W. C. **8**
Harrell, Andre **9**
Hawkins, Coleman **9**
Hayes, Roland **4**
Hendricks, Barbara **3**
Hendrix, Jimi **10**
Hinderas, Natalie **5**
Holiday, Billie **1**
Horne, Lena **5**
House, Son **8**
Houston, Whitney **7**
Howlin' Wolf **9**
Ice Cube **8**
Ice-T **6**
Jackson, Isaiah **3**
Jackson, Janet **6**
Jackson, Mahalia **5**
Johnson, Beverly **2**
Johnson, James Weldon **5**
Johnson, Robert **2**
Jones, Quincy **8**
Joplin, Scott **6**
Khan, Chaka **12**
King, B. B. **7**
King, Coretta Scott **3**
Knight, Suge **11**
Kravitz, Lenny **10**
Lester, Julius **9**
Lincoln, Abbey **3**
Lover, Ed **10**
Madhubuti, Haki R. **7**
Makeba, Miriam **2**
Marley, Bob **5**
Masekela, Hugh **1**
Mayfield, Curtis **2**
McDaniel, Hattie **5**
Mckee, Lonette **12**
Monk, Thelonious **1**
Moses, Gilbert **12**
Murphy, Eddie **4**
Nascimento, Milton **2**
N'Dour, Youssou **1**
Norman, Jessye **5**

O'Neal, Shaquille **8**
Ongala, Remmy **9**
Parks, Gordon **1**
Powell, Maxine **8**
Price, Leontyne **1**
Queen Latifah **1**
Reagon, Bernice Johnson **7**
Reese, Della **6**
Rhone, Sylvia **2**
Robeson, Paul **2**
Robinson, Smokey **3**
Ross, Diana **8**
Rushen, Patrice **12**
Simmons, Russell **1**
Sister Souljah **11**
Smith, Bessie **3**
Smith, Will **8**
Tosh, Peter **9**
Turner, Tina **6**
Vereen, Ben **4**
Walker, Albertina **10**
Wallace, Sippie **1**
Waters, Ethel **7**
Williams, Joe **5**
Williams, Vanessa **4**
Wilson, Nancy **10**
Wilson, Sunnie **7**
Wonder, Stevie **11**
Yoba, Malik **11**

Religion
Abernathy, Ralph David **1**
Agyeman, Jaramogi Abebe **10**
Al-Amin, Jamil Abdullah **6**
Aristide, Jean-Bertrand **6**
Banks, William **11**
Bell, Ralph S. **5**
Ben-Israel, Ben Ami **11**
Boyd, T. B. III **6**
Butts, Calvin O., III **9**
Cannon, Katie **10**
Chavis, Benjamin **6**
Cleaver, Emanuel **4**
Clements, George **2**
Colemon, Johnnie **11**
Cone, James H. **3**
Divine, Father **7**
Dyson, Michael Eric **11**
Farrakhan, Louis **2**
Fauntroy, Walter E. **11**
Gray, William H. III **3**
Haile Selassie **7**
Harris, Barbara **12**
Hayes, James C. **10**
Hooks, Benjamin L. **2**
Jackson, Jesse **1**
King, Bernice **4**
King, Martin Luther, Jr. **1**
Lester, Julius **9**
Lowery, Joseph **2**
Lyons, Henry **12**
Mays, Benjamin E. **7**
Muhammad, Elijah **4**
Muhammad, Khallid Abdul **10**
Murray, Cecil **12**
Powell, Adam Clayton, Jr. **3**
Reese, Della **6**
Shabazz, Betty **7**

Somé, Malidoma Patrice **10**
Stallings, George A., Jr. **6**
Sullivan, Leon H. **2**
Thurman, Howard **3**
Turner, Henry McNeal **5**
Tutu, Desmond **6**
Waddles, Charleszetta (Mother) **10**
Waters, Ethel **7**
West, Cornel **5**
White, Reggie **6**
X, Malcolm **1**
Youngblood, Johnny Ray **8**

Science and technology
Banda, Hastings Kamuzu **6**
Bluford, Guy **2**
Bolden, Charles F., Jr. **7**
Bristow, Lonnie **12**
Bullard, Eugene **12**
Callender, Clive O. **3**
Carson, Benjamin **1**
Carver, George Washington **4**
CasSelle, Malcolm **11**
Cobbs, Price M. **9**
Coleman, Bessie **9**
Comer, James P. **6**
Cooper, Edward S. **6**
Davis, Allison **12**
Delany, Bessie **12**
Diop, Cheikh Anta **4**
Drew, Charles Richard **7**
Dunham, Katherine **4**
Elders, Joycelyn **6**
Ellington, E. David **11**
Flipper, Henry O. **3**
Fulani, Lenora **11**
Gayle, Helene D. **3**
Gibson, Kenneth Allen **6**
Gibson, William F. **6**
Gregory, Frederick D. **8**
Hall, Lloyd A. **8**
Hannah, Marc **10**
Henson, Matthew **2**
Hinton, William Augustus **8**
Irving, Larry, Jr. **12**
Jackson, Shirley Ann **12**
Jawara, Sir Dawda Kairaba **11**
Jemison, Mae C. **1**
Jenifer, Franklyn G. **2**
Johnson, Eddie Bernice **8**
Julian, Percy Lavon **6**
Just, Ernest Everett **3**
Kountz, Samuel L. **10**
Latimer, Lewis H. **4**
Lawless, Theodore K. **8**
Leffall, LaSalle, Jr. **3**
Lewis, Delano **7**
Massey, Walter E. **5**
Mboup, Souleymane **10**
McCoy, Elijah **8**
McNair, Ronald **3**
Morgan, Garrett **1**
O'Leary, Hazel **6**
Person, Waverly **9**
Pitt, David Thomas **10**
Poussaint, Alvin F. **5**
Prothrow-Stith, Deborah **10**

Quarterman, Lloyd Albert **4**
Roker, Al **12**
Satcher, David **7**
Shabazz, Betty **7**
Staples, Brent **8**
Staupers, Mabel K. **7**
Sullivan, Louis **8**
Thomas, Vivien **9**
Washington, Patrice Clarke **12**
Watkins, Levi, Jr. **9**
Welsing, Frances Cress **5**
Williams, Daniel Hale **2**
Woods, Granville T. **5**
Wright, Louis Tompkins **4**

Social issues
Aaron, Hank **5**
Abbott, Diane **9**
Abdul-Jabbar, Kareem **8**
Abernathy, Ralph David **1**
Achebe, Chinua **6**
Agyeman, Jaramogi Abebe **10**
Al-Amin, Jamil Abdullah **6**
Angelou, Maya **1**
Archer, Dennis **7**
Aristide, Jean-Bertrand **6**
Asante, Molefi Kete **3**
Ashe, Arthur **1**
Baker, Ella **5**
Baker, Gwendolyn Calvert **9**
Baker, Houston A., Jr. **6**
Baker, Josephine **3**
Baldwin, James **1**
Baraka, Amiri **1**
Belafonte, Harry **4**
Bell, Derrick **6**
Bell, Ralph S. **5**
Bennett, Lerone, Jr. **5**
Berry, Bertice **8**
Berry, Mary Frances **7**
Bethune, Mary McLeod **4**
Biko, Steven **4**
Bond, Julian **2**
Bosley, Freeman, Jr. **7**
Boyd, T. B. III **6**
Braun, Carol Moseley **4**
Brooke, Edward **8**
Brown, Elaine **8**
Brown, Jesse **6**
Brown, Jim **11**
Brown, Lee P. **1**
Brown, Les **5**
Brown, Tony **3**
Brown, Zora Kramer **12**
Bryant, Wayne R. **6**
Bunche, Ralph J. **5**
Burroughs, Margaret Taylor **9**
Butts, Calvin O., III **9**
Campbell, Bebe Moore **6**
Carmichael, Stokely **5**
Carter, Mandy **11**
Carter, Stephen L. **4**
Cary, Lorene **3**
Chavis, Benjamin **6**
Chissano, Joaquim **7**
Christophe, Henri **9**
Chuck D **9**
Clark, Joe **1**

Clark, Kenneth B. **5**
Clark, Septima **7**
Clay, William Lacy **8**
Cleaver, Eldridge **5**
Clements, George **2**
Cobbs, Price M. **9**
Cole, Johnnetta B. **5**
Collins, Barbara-Rose **7**
Comer, James P. **6**
Cone, James H. **3**
Conté, Lansana **7**
Conyers, John, Jr. **4**
Cooper, Edward S. **6**
Cosby, Bill **7**
Cose, Ellis **5**
Crockett, George, Jr. **10**
Crouch, Stanley **11**
Dash, Julie **4**
da Silva, Benedita **5**
Davis, Angela **5**
Davis, Ossie **5**
Dee, Ruby **8**
Dellums, Ronald **2**
Dickerson, Ernest **6**
Diop, Cheikh Anta **4**
Divine, Father **7**
Dodson, Howard, Jr. **7**
Dove, Rita **6**
Drew, Charles Richard **7**
Du Bois, W. E. B. **3**
Dunham, Katherine **4**
Edelman, Marian Wright **5**
Edley, Christopher **2**
Edwards, Harry **2**
Elder, Lee **6**
Elders, Joycelyn **6**
Ellison, Ralph **7**
Esposito, Giancarlo **9**
Espy, Mike **6**
Europe, James Reese **10**
Evers, Medgar **3**
Evers, Myrlie **8**
Farmer, James **2**
Fauntroy, Walter E. **11**
Fauset, Jessie **7**
Fela **1**
Forman, James **7**
Fortune, T. Thomas **6**
Franklin, Hardy R. **9**
Franklin, John Hope **5**
Frazier, E. Franklin **10**
Fulani, Lenora **11**
Fuller, Charles **8**
Gaines, Ernest J. **7**
Garvey, Marcus **1**
Gates, Henry Louis, Jr. **3**
Gayle, Helene D. **3**
Gibson, Kenneth Allen **6**
Gibson, William F. **6**
Gist, Carole **1**
Goldberg, Whoopi **4**
Gomez-Preston, Cheryl **9**
Gossett, Louis, Jr. **7**
Graham, Lawrence Otis **12**
Gregory, Dick **1**
Griffith, Mark Winston **8**
Grimké, Archibald H. **9**
Guinier, Lani **7**

Guy, Rosa **5**
Hale, Lorraine **8**
Haley, Alex **4**
Hamblin, Ken **10**
Hamer, Fannie Lou **6**
Hampton, Henry **6**
Hani, Chris **6**
Hansberry, Lorraine **6**
Hansberry, William Leo **11**
Harper, Frances Ellen Watkins **11**
Harrington, Oliver W. **9**
Harris, Alice **7**
Harris, Leslie **6**
Harris, Patricia Roberts **2**
Haynes, George Edmund **8**
Height, Dorothy I. **2**
Henry, Lenny **9**
Hill, Anita **5**
Hilliard, David **7**
Holland, Endesha Ida Mae **3**
hooks, bell **5**
Hooks, Benjamin L. **2**
Horne, Lena **5**
Houston, Charles Hamilton **4**
Hughes, Albert **7**
Hughes, Allen **7**
Hughes, Langston **4**
Hunter-Gault, Charlayne **6**
Ice-T **6**
Iceberg Slim **11**
Iman **4**
Ingram, Rex **5**
Innis, Roy **5**
Jackson, Janet **6**
Jackson, Jesse **1**
Jackson, Mahalia **5**
Jacob, John E. **2**
Jeffries, Leonard **8**
Johnson, Charles S. **12**
Johnson, Earvin "Magic" **3**
Johnson, James Weldon **5**
Jones, Elaine R. **7**
Jordan, Barbara **4**
Jordan, June **7**
Jordan, Vernon E. **3**
Josey, E. J. **10**
Julian, Percy Lavon **6**
Kaunda, Kenneth **2**
Kennedy, Florynce **12**
Khanga, Yelena **6**
King, B. B. **7**
King, Bernice **4**
King, Coretta Scott **3**
King, Dexter **10**
King, Martin Luther, Jr. **1**
King, Yolanda **6**
Lane, Charles **3**
Lane, Vincent **5**
Lee, Canada **8**
Lee, Spike **5**
Leland, Mickey **2**
Lester, Julius **9**
Lewis, Delano **7**
Lewis, John **2**
Little, Robert L. **2**
Lorde, Audre **6**
Louis, Errol T. **8**
Lowery, Joseph **2**

Lucas, John **7**
Madhubuti, Haki R. **7**
Makeba, Miriam **2**
Mandela, Nelson **1**
Mandela, Winnie **2**
Marable, Manning **10**
Marley, Bob **5**
Marshall, Paule **7**
Marshall, Thurgood **1**
Masekela, Hugh **1**
Mathabane, Mark **5**
Maynard, Robert C. **7**
Mays, Benjamin E. **7**
McCabe, Jewell Jackson **10**
McDaniel, Hattie **5**
McDougall, Gay J. **11**
McKay, Claude **6**
McKissick, Floyd B. **3**
McQueen, Butterfly **6**
Meek, Carrie **6**
Meredith, James H. **11**
Mfume, Kweisi **6**
Micheaux, Oscar **7**
Mongella, Gertrude **11**
Morrison, Toni **2**
Moses, Robert Parris **11**
Mosley, Walter **5**
Motley, Constance Baker **10**
Moutoussamy-Ashe, Jeanne **7**
Mowry, Jess **7**
Muhammad, Elijah **4**
Muhammad, Khallid Abdul **10**
Ndadaye, Melchior **7**
Nelson, Jill **6**
Newton, Huey **2**
Nkrumah, Kwame **3**
Norman, Pat **10**
Norton, Eleanor Holmes **7**
Obasanjo, Olusegun **5**
O'Leary, Hazel **6**
Oglesby, Zena **12**
Owens, Major **6**
Page, Alan **7**
Page, Clarence **4**
Paige, Satchel **7**
Parks, Rosa **1**
Patterson, Frederick Douglass **12**
Patterson, Orlando **4**
Patterson, P. J. **6**
Perkins, Edward **5**
Pitt, David Thomas **10**
Pleasant, Mary Ellen **9**
Poussaint, Alvin F. **5**
Powell, Adam Clayton, Jr. **3**
Price, Hugh B. **9**
Primus, Pearl **6**
Prothrow-Stith, Deborah **10**
Ramaphosa, Cyril **3**
Rand, A. Barry **6**
Randolph, A. Philip **3**
Rangel, Charles **3**
Reagon, Bernice Johnson **7**
Reed, Ishmael **8**
Rice, Norm **8**
Riggs, Marlon **5**
Ringgold, Faith **4**
Robeson, Paul **2**
Robinson, Jackie **6**

Robinson, Randall **7**
Rowan, Carl T. **1**
Rustin, Bayard **4**
Sampson, Edith S. **4**
Satcher, David **7**
Savimbi, Jonas **2**
Sawyer, Amos **2**
Sayles Belton, Sharon **9**
Schomburg, Arthur Alfonso **9**
Seale, Bobby **3**
Senghor, Léopold Sédar **12**
Shabazz, Attallah **6**
Shabazz, Betty **7**
Shakur, Assata **6**
Sifford, Charlie **4**
Simpson, Carole **6**
Sister Souljah **11**
Sleet, Moneta, Jr. **5**
Smith, Anna Deavere **6**
Soyinka, Wole **4**
Stallings, George A., Jr. **6**
Staupers, Mabel K. **7**
Stone, Chuck **9**
Sullivan, Leon H. **3**
Taylor, Susan L. **10**
Terrell, Mary Church **9**
Thomas, Franklin A. **5**
Thomas, Isiah **7**
Thurman, Howard **3**
Till, Emmett **7**
Toomer, Jean **6**
Tosh, Peter **9**
Tribble, Israel, Jr. **8**
Trotter, Monroe **9**
Tubman, Harriet **9**
Tucker, C. DeLores **12**
Tutu, Desmond **6**
Underwood, Blair **7**
Van Peebles, Melvin **7**
Vincent, Marjorie Judith **2**
Waddles, Charleszetta (Mother) **10**
Walcott, Derek **5**
Walker, Alice **1**
Walker, Madame C. J. **7**
Wallace, Phyllis A. **9**
Washington, Booker T. **4**
Washington, Fredi **10**
Washington, Harold **6**
Waters, Maxine **3**
Wattleton, Faye **9**
Wells, James Lesesne **10**
Wells-Barnett, Ida B. **8**
Welsing, Frances Cress **5**
West, Cornel **5**
White, Michael R. **5**
White, Reggie **6**
White, Walter F. **4**
Wideman, John Edgar **5**
Wilkins, Roger **2**
Wilkins, Roy **4**
Williams, Evelyn **10**
Williams, Maggie **7**
Williams, Montel **4**
Williams, Patricia J. **11**
Williams, Robert F. **11**
Williams, Walter E. **4**
Williams, Willie L. **4**

Wilson, August **7**
Wilson, Phill **9**
Wilson, Sunnie **7**
Winfield, Paul **2**
Winfrey, Oprah **2**
Wolfe, George C. **6**
Woodson, Robert L. **10**
Worrill, Conrad **12**
Wright, Louis Tompkins **4**
Wright, Richard **5**
X, Malcolm **1**
Yoba, Malik **11**
Young, Andrew **3**
Young, Whitney M., Jr. **4**
Youngblood, Johnny Ray **8**

Sports
Aaron, Hank **5**
Abdul-Jabbar, Kareem **8**
Ali, Muhammad **2**
Amos, John **8**
Ashe, Arthur **1**
Baker, Dusty **8**
Barkley, Charles **5**
Baylor, Don **6**
Belle, Albert **10**
Bing, Dave **3**
Bol, Manute **1**
Bonaly, Surya **7**
Bonds, Barry **6**
Bowe, Riddick **6**
Brown, Jim **11**
Christie, Linford **8**
Coleman , Leonard S., Jr. **12**
Cottrell, Comer **11**
Dawes, Dominique **11**
Devers, Gail **7**
Drew, Charles Richard **7**
Drexler, Clyde **4**
Edwards, Harry **2**
Elder, Lee **6**
Fielder, Cecil **2**
Flood, Curt **10**
Foreman, George **1**
Fuhr, Grant **1**
Garrison, Zina **2**
Gibson, Althea **8**
Gourdine, Simon **11**
Green, Dennis **5**
Griffey, Ken, Jr. **12**
Gumbel, Greg **8**
Greene, Joe **10**
Hickman, Fred **11**
Holyfield, Evander **6**
Johnson, Ben **1**
Johnson, Earvin "Magic" **3**
Johnson, Jack **8**
Jordan, Michael **6**
Joyner-Kersee, Jackie **5**
Lee, Canada **8**
Lewis, Carl **4**
Lofton, Kenny **12**
Lott, Ronnie **9**
Louis, Joe **5**
Love, Nat **9**
Lucas, John **7**
Mays, Willie **3**
McKegney, Tony **3**

McNeil, Lori **1**
Milla, Roger **2**
Miller, Cheryl **10**
Moon, Warren **8**
Morgan, Joe Leonard **9**
Moses, Edwin **8**
Murray, Eddie **12**
Murray, Lenda **10**
Mutola, Maria **12**
Mutombo, Dikembe **7**
Noah, Yannick **4**
Olajuwon, Hakeem **2**
O'Neal, Shaquille **8**
O'Ree, Willie **5**
Owens, Jesse **2**
Page, Alan **7**
Paige, Satchel **7**
Payton, Walter **11**
Peete, Calvin **11**
Pelé **7**
Pickett, Bill **11**
Powell, Mike **7**
Puckett, Kirby **4**
Ribbs, Willy T. **2**
Rice, Jerry **5**
Richardson, Nolan **9**
Robinson, Eddie G. **10**
Robinson, Frank **9**
Robinson, Jackie **6**
Rodman, Dennis **12**
Rudolph, Wilma **4**
Russell, Bill **8**
Sanders, Barry **1**
Sanders, Deion **4**
Shell, Art **1**
Sifford, Charlie **4**
Singletary, Mike **4**
Smith, Emmitt **7**
Swoopes, Sheryl **12**
Thomas, Frank **12**
Thomas, Isiah **7**
Walker, Herschel **1**
Washington, MaliVai **8**
Weathers, Carl **10**
Whitaker, Pernell **10**
White, Bill **1**
White, Reggie **6**
Wilkens, Lenny **11**
Wilson, Sunnie **7**
Winfield, Dave **5**

Television
La Salle, Eriq **12**
Allen, Byron **3**
Amos, John **8**
Banks, William **11**
Barden, Don H. **9**
Bassett, Angela **6**
Belafonte, Harry **4**
Bellamy, Bill **12**
Berry, Bertice **8**
Berry, Halle **4**
Bradley, Ed **2**
Brooks, Avery **9**
Brown, Les **8**
Brown, Tony **3**
Burton, LeVar **8**
Byrd, Robert **11**

Campbell, Tisha **8**
Carroll, Diahann **9**
Clayton, Xernona **3**
Cornelius, Don **4**
Cosby, Bill **7**
Davis, Ossie **5**
Dee, Ruby **8**
Dickerson, Ernest **6**
Dr. Dre **10**
Duke, Bill **3**
Dutton, Charles S. **4**
Esposito, Giancarlo **9**
Fishburne, Larry **4**
Foxx, Redd **2**
Freeman, Al, Jr. **11**
Freeman, Morgan **2**
Gaines, Ernest J. **7**
Givens, Robin **4**
Goldberg, Whoopi **4**
Gordon, Ed **10**
Gossett, Louis, Jr. **7**
Grier, Pam **9**
Guillaume, Robert **3**
Gumbel, Greg **8**
Gunn, Moses **10**
Guy, Jasmine **2**
Haley, Alex **4**
Hampton, Henry **6**
Harrell, Andre **9**
Harris, Robin **7**
Henry, Lenny **9**
Hickman, Fred **11**
Hinderas, Natalie **5**
Horne, Lena **5**
Hunter-Gault, Charlayne **6**
Iman **4**
Ingram, Rex **5**
Jackson, Janet **6**
Jackson, Jesse **1**
Johnson, Beverly **2**
Johnson, Robert L. **3**
Jones, James Earl **3**
Jones, Quincy **8**
Jones, Star **10**
Kotto, Yaphet **7**
Lawrence, Martin **6**
Lawson, Jennifer **1**
Lover, Ed **10**
McDaniel, Hattie **5**
McEwen, Mark **5**
McQueen, Butterfly **6**
Mckee, Lonette **12**
Miller, Cheryl **10**
Morgan, Joe Leonard **9**
Moses, Gilbert **12**
Murphy, Eddie **4**
Nichols, Nichelle **11**
Pinkett, Jada **10**
Price, Hugh B. **9**
Reese, Della **6**
Robinson, Max **3**
Rock, Chris **3**
Rodgers, Johnathan **6**
Roker, Al **12**
Ross, Diana **8**
Rowan, Carl T. **1**
Russell, Bill **8**
Smith, Barbara **11**

Smith, Roger Guenveur **12**
St. Jacques, Raymond **8**
Schultz, Michael A. **6**
Shaw, Bernard **2**
Simpson, Carole **6**
Smith, Will **8**
Stokes, Carl B. **10**
Stone, Chuck **9**
Taylor, Meshach **4**
Taylor, Regina **9**
Tyson, Cicely **7**
Underwood, Blair **7**
Van Peebles, Mario **2**
Van Peebles, Melvin **7**
Vereen, Ben **4**
Warfield, Marsha **2**
Washington, Denzel **1**
Wattleton, Faye **9**
Watts, Rolonda **9**
Wayans, Damon **8**
Weathers, Carl **10**
Wilkins, Roger **2**
Williams, Billy Dee **8**
Williams, Montel **4**
Williams, Vanessa **4**
Winfield, Paul **2**
Winfrey, Oprah **2**
Yoba, Malik **11**

Theater
La Salle, Eriq **12**
Amos, John **8**
Angelou, Maya **1**
Ailey, Alvin **8**
Baraka, Amiri **1**
Bassett, Angela **6**
Belafonte, Harry **4**
Borders, James **9**
Brooks, Avery **9**
Campbell, Naomi **1**
Campbell, Tisha **8**
Carroll, Diahann **9**
Davis, Ossie **5**
Dee, Ruby **8**
Duke, Bill **3**
Dunham, Katherine **4**
Dutton, Charles S. **4**
Esposito, Giancarlo **9**
Europe, James Reese **10**
Fishburne, Larry **4**
Freeman, Al, Jr. **11**
Freeman, Morgan **2**
Fuller, Charles **8**
Glover, Danny **1**
Goldberg, Whoopi **4**
Gossett, Louis, Jr. **7**
Grier, Pam **9**
Guillaume, Robert **3**
Gunn, Moses **10**
Guy, Jasmine **2**
Hansberry, Lorraine **6**
Harris, Robin **7**
Holland, Endesha Ida Mae **3**
Horne, Lena **5**
Ingram, Rex **5**
Jackson, Samuel L. **8**
Jamison, Judith **7**
Jones, James Earl **3**

King, Yolanda **6**
Kotto, Yaphet **7**
Lee, Canada **8**
Leon, Kenny **10**
Lincoln, Abbey **3**
McDaniel, Hattie **5**
McQueen, Butterfly **6**
Mckee, Lonette **12**
Moses, Gilbert **12**
Powell, Maxine **8**
Primus, Pearl **6**
Reese, Della **6**
Richards, Lloyd **2**
Robeson, Paul **2**
Rotimi, Ola **1**
Smith, Roger Guenveur **12**
St. Jacques, Raymond **8**
Schultz, Michael A. **6**
Shabazz, Attallah **6**
Shange, Ntozake **8**
Smith, Anna Deavere **6**
Snipes, Wesley **3**
Soyinka, Wole **4**
Taylor, Meshach **4**
Taylor, Regina **9**
Townsend, Robert **4**
Tyson, Cicely **7**
Underwood, Blair **7**
Van Peebles, Melvin **7**
Vereen, Ben **4**
Walcott, Derek **5**
Washington, Denzel **1**
Washington, Fredi **10**
Waters, Ethel **7**
Whitaker, Forest **2**
Williams, Billy Dee **8**
Wilson, August **7**
Winfield, Paul **2**
Wolfe, George C. **6**
Woodard, Alfre **9**

Writing
Achebe, Chinua **6**
Al-Amin, Jamil Abdullah **6**
Andrews, Raymond **4**
Angelou, Maya **1**
Aristide, Jean-Bertrand **6**
Asante, Molefi Kete **3**
Ashe, Arthur **1**
Baker, Houston A., Jr. **6**
Baldwin, James **1**
Bambara, Toni Cade **10**
Baraka, Amiri **1**
Bell, Derrick **6**
Bennett, Lerone, Jr. **5**
Berry, Mary Frances **7**
Bontemps, Arna **8**
Borders, James **9**
Bradley, Ed **2**
Brimmer, Andrew F. **2**
Brooks, Gwendolyn **1**
Brown, Elaine **8**
Brown, Les **5**
Brown, Marie Dutton **12**
Brown, Sterling **10**
Brown, Tony **3**
Bunche, Ralph J. **5**
Burroughs, Margaret Taylor **9**

Butler, Octavia **8**
Campbell, Bebe Moore **6**
Carmichael, Stokely **5**
Carter, Stephen L. **4**
Cary, Lorene **3**
Clark, Kenneth B. **5**
Clark, Septima **7**
Cleaver, Eldridge **5**
Cobbs, Price M. **9**
Cole, Johnnetta B. **5**
Comer, James P. **6**
Cone, James H. **3**
Cooper, J. California **12**
Cosby, Bill **7**
Cose, Ellis **5**
Crouch, Stanley **11**
Cullen, Countee **8**
Davis, Allison **12**
Davis, Angela **5**
Davis, Miles **4**
Davis, Ossie **5**
Delany, Samuel R., Jr. **9**
Diop, Cheikh Anta **4**
Dodson, Howard, Jr. **7**
Dove, Rita **6**
Driskell, David C. **7**
Driver, David E. **11**
Du Bois, W. E. B. **3**
Dunbar, Paul Laurence **8**
Dunham, Katherine **4**
Dyson, Michael Eric **11**
Ellison, Ralph **7**
Fauset, Jessie **7**
Feelings, Tom **11**
Forman, James **7**
Fortune, T. Thomas **6**
Franklin, John Hope **5**
Frazier, E. Franklin **10**
Fuller, Charles **8**
Gaines, Ernest J. **7**
Gates, Henry Louis, Jr. **3**
George, Nelson **12**
Gibson, Althea **8**
Giddings, Paula **11**
Giovanni, Nikki **9**
Graham, Lawrence Otis **12**
Greenfield, Eloise **9**
Griffith, Mark Winston **8**
Grimké, Archibald H. **9**
Guinier, Lani **7**
Guy, Rosa **5**
Haley, Alex **4**
Hamblin, Ken **10**
Hamilton, Virginia **10**
Hansberry, Lorraine **6**
Harper, Frances Ellen Watkins **11**
Harrington, Oliver W. **9**
Harris, Leslie **6**
Hayden, Robert **12**
Hemphill, Essex **10**
Henry, Lenny **9**
Henson, Matthew **2**
Hilliard, David **7**
Holland, Endesha Ida Mae **3**
hooks, bell **5**
Hughes, Langston **4**
Hunter-Gault, Charlayne **6**
Hurston, Zora Neale **3**

Iceberg Slim **11**
Johnson, Charles **1**
Johnson, Charles S. **12**
Johnson, James Weldon **5**
Johnson, John H. **3**
Jordan, June **7**
Josey, E. J. **10**
Just, Ernest Everett **3**
Karenga, Maulana **10**
Kennedy, Adrienne **11**
Kennedy, Florynce **12**
Khanga, Yelena **6**
Kimbro, Dennis **10**
Kincaid, Jamaica **4**
King, Coretta Scott **3**
King, Yolanda **6**
Komunyakaa, Yusef **9**
Kotto, Yaphet **7**
Kunjufu, Jawanza **3**
Larsen, Nella **10**
Lawrence, Martin **6**
Lawrence-Lightfoot, Sara **10**
Lester, Julius **9**
Lewis, David Levering **9**
Locke, Alain **10**
Lorde, Audre **6**
Louis, Errol T. **8**
Madhubuti, Haki R. **7**
Major, Clarence **9**
Makeba, Miriam **2**
Marshall, Paule **7**
Mathabane, Mark **5**
Maynard, Robert C. **7**
Mays, Benjamin E. **7**
McCall, Nathan **8**
McKay, Claude **6**
McMillan, Terry **4**
Meredith, James H. **11**
Micheaux, Oscar **7**
Morrison, Toni **2**

Mosley, Walter **5**
Moutoussamy-Ashe, Jeanne **7**
Mowry, Jess **7**
Myers, Walter Dean **8**
Naylor, Gloria **10**
Nelson, Jill **6**
Newton, Huey **2**
Nkrumah, Kwame **3**
Owens, Major **6**
Page, Clarence **4**
Patterson, Orlando **4**
Poussaint, Alvin F. **5**
Powell, Adam Clayton, Jr. **3**
Pryor, Richard **3**
Randall, Dudley **8**
Raspberry, William **2**
Reagon, Bernice Johnson **7**
Reed, Ishmael **8**
Riggs, Marlon **5**
Ringgold, Faith **4**
Rodman, Dennis **12**
Rotimi, Ola **1**
Rowan, Carl T. **1**
Saint James, Synthia **12**
Sanders, Dori **8**
Schomburg, Arthur Alfonso **9**
Seale, Bobby **3**
Senghor, Léopold Sédar **12**
Shabazz, Attallah **6**
Shakur, Assata **6**
Shange, Ntozake **8**
Shaw, Bernard **2**
Simpson, Carole **6**
Singleton, John **2**
Sister Souljah **11**
Smith, Anna Deavere **6**
Smith, Barbara **11**
Somé, Malidoma Patrice **10**
Sowell, Thomas **2**
Soyinka, Wole **4**

Staples, Brent **8**
Stone, Chuck **9**
Taylor, Kristin Clark **8**
Taylor, Susan L. **10**
Thurman, Howard **3**
Toomer, Jean **6**
Townsend, Robert **4**
Trotter, Monroe **9**
Turner, Henry McNeal **5**
Turner, Tina **6**
Tutu, Desmond **6**
Van Peebles, Melvin **7**
Walcott, Derek **5**
Walker, Alice **1**
Wallace, Phyllis A. **9**
Washington, Booker T. **4**
Waters, Ethel **7**
Wattleton, Faye **9**
Wayans, Damon **8**
Webb, Veronica **10**
Wells-Barnett, Ida B. **8**
West, Cornel **5**
West, Dorothy **12**
Wharton, Clifton R., Jr. **7**
White, Walter F. **4**
Wideman, John Edgar **5**
Wiley, Ralph **8**
Wilkins, Roger **2**
Wilkins, Roy **4**
Williams, Patricia J. **11**
Williams, Robert F. **11**
Wilson, August **7**
Wolfe, George C. **6**
Woodson, Carter G. **2**
Worrill, Conrad **12**
Wright, Bruce McMarion **3**
Wright, Richard **5**
Young, Whitney M., Jr. **4**

Cumulative Subject Index

Volume numbers appear in **bold**.

AA
See Alcoholics Anonymous

AAAS
See American Association for the
Advancement of Science

ABC
See American Broadcasting
Company

Academy awards
Freeman, Morgan **2**
Goldberg, Whoopi **4**
Gossett, Louis, Jr. **7**
McDaniel, Hattie **5**
Poitier, Sidney **11**
Washington, Denzel **1**
Wonder, Stevie **11**

A cappella
Reagon, Bernice Johnson **7**

ACDL
See Association for Constitutional
Democracy in Liberia

ACLU
See American Civil Liberties
Union

**Acquired Immune Deficiency
Syndrome (AIDS)**
Ashe, Arthur **1**
Gayle, Helene D. **3**
Hale, Lorraine **8**
Johnson, Earvin "Magic" **3**
Mboup, Souleymane **10**
Moutoussamy-Ashe, Jeanne **7**
Norman, Pat **10**
Riggs, Marlon **5**
Satcher, David **7**
Wilson, Phill **9**

Acting
Ailey, Alvin **8**
Amos, John **8**
Angelou, Maya **1**
Baker, Josephine **3**
Banks, Tyra **11**

Bassett, Angela **6**
Beals, Jennifer **12**
Berry, Halle **4**
Borders, James **9**
Brooks, Avery **9**
Brown, Jim **11**
Campbell, Naomi **1**
Campbell, Tisha **8**
Carroll, Diahann **9**
Cosby, Bill **7**
Dandridge, Dorothy **3**
Davidson, Jaye **5**
Davis, Ossie **5**
Dee, Ruby **8**
Duke, Bill **3**
Dutton, Charles S. **4**
Esposito, Giancarlo **9**
Fishburne, Larry **4**
Foxx, Redd **2**
Freeman, Al, Jr. **11**
Freeman, Morgan **2**
Givens, Robin **4**
Glover, Danny **1**
Goldberg, Whoopi **4**
Gossett, Louis, Jr. **7**
Grier, Pam **9**
Guillaume, Robert **3**
Gunn, Moses **10**
Guy, Jasmine **2**
Harris, Robin **7**
Henry, Lenny **9**
Hines, Gregory **1**
Horne, Lena **5**
Houston, Whitney **7**
Ice Cube **8**
Iman **4**
Ingram, Rex **5**
Jackson, Janet **6**
Jackson, Samuel L. **8**
Jones, James Earl **3**
Kotto, Yaphet **7**
La Salle, Eriq **12**
Lane, Charles **3**
Lawrence, Martin **6**
Lee, Canada **8**
Lee, Joie **1**
Lee, Spike **5**
Lincoln, Abbey **3**
McDaniel, Hattie **5**
McQueen, Butterfly **6**

Mckee, Lonette **12**
Murphy, Eddie **4**
Nichols, Nichelle **11**
Pinkett, Jada **10**
Poitier, Sidney **11**
Pryor, Richard **3**
Reese, Della **6**
Richards, Lloyd **2**
Robeson, Paul **2**
Rock, Chris **3**
Ross, Diana **8**
Smith, Barbara **11**
Smith, Roger Guenveur **12**
St. Jacques, Raymond **8**
Sinbad **1**
Smith, Anna Deavere **6**
Smith, Will **8**
Snipes, Wesley **3**
Taylor, Meshach **4**
Taylor, Regina **9**
Townsend, Robert **4**
Turner, Tina **6**
Tyson, Cicely **7**
Underwood, Blair **7**
Van Peebles, Mario **2**
Van Peebles, Melvin **7**
Vereen, Ben **4**
Warfield, Marsha **2**
Washington, Denzel **1**
Washington, Fredi **10**
Waters, Ethel **7**
Wayans, Damon **8**
Weathers, Carl **10**
Webb, Veronica **10**
Whitaker, Forest **2**
Williams, Billy Dee **8**
Williams, Vanessa **4**
Winfield, Paul **2**
Winfrey, Oprah **2**
Woodard, Alfre **9**
Yoba, Malik **11**

**Active Ministers Engaged in
Nurturance (AMEN)**
King, Bernice **4**

ACT UP
See AIDS Coalition to Unleash
Power

Acustar, Inc.
Farmer, Forest **1**

ADC
See Agricultural Development
Council

Adoption and foster care
Oglesby, Zena **12**

Adoption
Baker, Josephine **3**
Clements, George **2**
Gossett, Louis, Jr. **7**
Hale, Lorraine **8**

Adventures in Movement (AIM)
Morgan, Joe Leonard **9**

Advertising
Barboza, Anthony **10**
Johnson, Beverly **2**

Advocates Scene
Seale, Bobby **3**

AFCEA
See Armed Forces Communica
tions and Electronics
Associations

Affirmative action
Berry, Mary Frances **7**
Carter, Stephen L. **4**
Maynard, Robert C. **7**
Norton, Eleanor Holmes **7**
Rand, A. Barry **6**
Waters, Maxine **3**

AFL-CIO
See American Federation of
Labor and Congress of
Industrial Organizations

African American culture
George, Nelson **12**
Johnson, Charles S. **12**

**African/African-American
Summit**
Sullivan, Leon H. **3**

**African American Catholic
Congregation**
Stallings, George A., Jr. **6**

African American folklore
Bailey, Xenobia **11**
Brown, Sterling **10**
Driskell, David C. **7**
Ellison, Ralph **7**
Gaines, Ernest J. **7**
Hamilton, Virginia **10**
Hughes, Langston **4**
Hurston, Zora Neale **3**
Lester, Julius **9**
Morrison, Toni **2**
Primus, Pearl **6**

African American folk music
Handy, W. C. **8**
House, Son **8**
Johnson, James Weldon **5**
Lester, Julius **9**

African American history
Angelou, Maya **1**
Ashe, Arthur **1**
Bennett, Lerone, Jr. **5**
Berry, Mary Frances **7**
Burroughs, Margaret Taylor **9**
Dodson, Howard, Jr. **7**
Douglas, Aaron **7**
Du Bois, W. E. B. **3**
Dyson, Michael Eric **11**
Feelings, Tom **11**
Franklin, John Hope **5**
Gaines, Ernest J. **7**
Gates, Henry Louis, Jr. **3**
Haley, Alex **4**
Hughes, Langston **4**
Johnson, James Weldon **5**
Lewis, David Levering **9**
Madhubuti, Haki R. **7**
Marable, Manning **10**
Morrison, Toni **2**
Reagon, Bernice Johnson **7**
Ringgold, Faith **4**
Schomburg, Arthur Alfonso **9**
Wilson, August **7**
Woodson, Carter G. **2**

African American Images
Kunjufu, Jawanza **3**

African American literature
Andrews, Raymond **4**
Angelou, Maya **1**
Baker, Houston A., Jr. **6**
Baldwin, James **1**
Bambara, Toni Cade **1**
Baraka, Amiri **1**
Bontemps, Arna **8**
Brooks, Gwendolyn **1**
Burroughs, Margaret Taylor **9**
Campbell, Bebe Moore **6**
Cary, Lorene **3**
Cullen, Countee **8**
Dove, Rita **6**
Du Bois, W. E. B. **3**
Dunbar, Paul Laurence **8**
Ellison, Ralph **7**
Fauset, Jessie **7**
Feelings, Tom **11**
Fuller, Charles **8**
Gaines, Ernest J. **7**
Gates, Henry Louis, Jr. **3**
Giddings, Paula **11**
Giovanni, Nikki **9**
Guy, Rosa **5**
Haley, Alex **4**
Hansberry, Lorraine **6**
Harper, Frances Ellen Watkins **11**
Himes, Chester **8**
Holland, Endesha Ida Mae **3**
Hughes, Langston **4**
Hurston, Zora Neale **3**

Iceberg Slim **11**
Johnson, Charles **1**
Johnson, James Weldon **5**
Jordan, June **7**
Larsen, Nella **10**
Lester, Julius **9**
Lorde, Audre **6**
Madhubuti, Haki R. **7**
Major, Clarence **9**
Marshall, Paule **7**
McKay, Claude **6**
McMillan, Terry **4**
Morrison, Toni **2**
Mowry, Jess **7**
Naylor, Gloria **10**
Randall, Dudley **8**
Reed, Ishmael **8**
Ringgold, Faith **4**
Schomburg, Arthur Alfonso **9**
Shange, Ntozake **8**
Toomer, Jean **6**
Van Peebles, Melvin **7**
Walker, Alice **1**
Wideman, John Edgar **5**
Wilson, August **7**
Wolfe, George C. **6**
Wright, Richard **5**

African dance
Ailey, Alvin **8**
Primus, Pearl **6**

African folk music
Makeba, Miriam **2**
Nascimento, Milton **2**

African history
Diop, Cheikh Anta **4**
Dodson, Howard, Jr. **7**
Hansberry, William Leo **11**
Jawara, Sir Dawda Kairaba **11**
Madhubuti, Haki R. **7**
Marshall, Paule **7**

**African Methodist Episcopal
Church (AME)**
Murray, Cecil **12**
Turner, Henry McNeal **5**
Youngblood, Johnny Ray **8**

**African National Congress
(ANC)**
Baker, Ella **5**
Hani, Chris **6**
Kaunda, Kenneth **2**
Mandela, Nelson **1**
Mandela, Winnie **2**
Nkomo, Joshua **4**
Ramaphosa, Cyril **3**
Tutu, Desmond **6**

**African Women on Tour
conference**
Taylor, Susan L. **10**

Afro-American League
Fortune, T. Thomas **6**

Afrocentricity
Asante, Molefi Kete **3**
Diop, Cheikh Anta **4**
Hansberry, Lorraine **6**
Hansberry, William Leo **11**
Turner, Henry McNeal **5**

Agency for International Development (AID)
Gayle, Helene D. **3**
Perkins, Edward **5**
Wilkins, Roger **2**

A. G. Gaston Boys and Girls Club
Gaston, Arthur G. **4**

A. G. Gaston Motel
Gaston, Arthur G. **4**

Agricultural Development Council (ADC)
Wharton, Clifton R., Jr. **7**

Agriculture
Carver, George Washington **4**
Espy, Mike **6**
Hall, Lloyd A. **8**
Masire, Quett **5**
Obasanjo, Olusegun **5**
Sanders, Dori **8**

AHA
See American Heart Association

AID
See Agency for International Development

AIDS
See Acquired Immune Deficiency Syndrome

AIDS Coalition to Unleash Power (ACT UP)
Norman, Pat **10**

AIDS Health Care Foundation
Wilson, Phill **9**

AIDS Prevention Team
Wilson, Phill **9**

AIDS research
Mboup, Souleymane **10**

AIM
See Adventures in Movement

ALA
See American Library Association

Alcoholics Anonymous (AA)
Hilliard, David **7**
Lucas, John **7**

All Afrikan People's Revolutionary Party
Carmichael, Stokely **5**
Moses, Robert Parris **11**

Alliance Theatre
Leon, Kenny **10**

Alpha & Omega Ministry
White, Reggie **6**

Alvin Ailey American Dance Theater
Ailey, Alvin **8**
Dove, Ulysses **5**
Jamison, Judith **7**
Primus, Pearl **6**

Alvin Ailey Repertory Ensemble
Ailey, Alvin **8**
Miller, Bebe **3**

AME
See African Methodist Episcopal Church

AMEN
See Active Ministers Engaged in Nurturance

American Association for the Advancement of Science (AAAS)
Massey, Walter E. **5**

American Ballet Theatre
Dove, Ulysses **5**

American Book Award
Baraka, Amiri **1**
Clark, Septima **7**
Gates, Henry Louis, Jr. **3**
Lorde, Audre **6**
Marshall, Paule **7**
Walker, Alice **1**

American Broadcasting Company (ABC)
Robinson, Max **3**
Simpson, Carole **6**
Winfrey, Oprah **2**

American Cancer Society
Leffall, LaSalle, Jr. **3**

American Civil Liberties Union (ACLU)
Norton, Eleanor Holmes **7**
Griffin, Anthony P. **12**

American Community Housing Associates, Inc.
Lane, Vincent **5**

American Enterprise Institute
Woodson, Robert L. **10**

American Express Company
Chenault, Kenneth I. **4**

American Express Consumer Card Group, USA
Chenault, Kenneth I. **4**

American Federation of Labor and Congress of Industrial Organizations (AFL-CIO)
Randolph, A. Philip **3**

American Heart Association (AHA)
Cooper, Edward S. **6**

American Library Association (ALA)
Franklin, Hardy R. **9**
Josey, E. J. **10**

American Medical Association (AMA)
Bristow, Lonnie **12**

American Negro Academy
Grimké, Archibald H. **9**
Schomburg, Arthur Alfonso **9**

American Nurses' Association (ANA)
Staupers, Mabel K. **7**

American Red Cross blood banks
Drew, Charles Richard **7**

ANA
Kennedy, Adrienne **11**
See American Nurses' Association

ANC
See African National Congress

Anglican church hierarchy
Tutu, Desmond **6**

Anthropology
Asante, Molefi Kete **3**
Bunche, Ralph J. **5**
Cole, Johnnetta B. **5**
Davis, Allison **12**
Diop, Cheikh Anta **4**
Dunham, Katherine **4**
Hansberry, William Leo **11**
Morrison, Toni **2**
Primus, Pearl **6**

Antoinette Perry awards
See Tony awards

Apartheid
Berry, Mary Frances **7**
Biko, Steven **4**
Makeba, Miriam **2**
Mandela, Nelson **1**
Mandela, Winnie **2**

Masekela, Hugh **1**
Mathabane, Mark **5**
Mbuende, Kaire **12**
McDougall, Gay J. **11**
Ramaphosa, Cyril **3**
Robinson, Randall **7**
Tutu, Desmond **6**

Arab-Israeli conflict
Bunche, Ralph J. **5**

ARCH
See Argonne National
Laboratory-Univ.of Chicago
Devt. Corporation

Architecture
Gantt, Harvey **1**
Williams, Paul R. **9**

Argonne National Laboratory
Massey, Walter E. **5**
Quarterman, Lloyd Albert **4**

**Argonne National Laboratory-
University of Chicago
Development Corporation
(ARCH)**
Massey, Walter E. **5**

Ariel Capital Management
Rogers, John W., Jr. **5**

**Arkansas Department of
Health**
Elders, Joycelyn **6**

**Armed Forces Commun-
ications and Electronics
Associations (AFCEA)**
Gravely, Samuel L., Jr. **5**

Arthritis treatment
Julian, Percy Lavon **6**

Artists for a Free South Africa
Woodard, Alfre **9**

ASALH
See Association for the Study of
Afro-American Life and History

ASH
See Association for the Sexually
Harassed

**Association for Constitutional
Democracy in Liberia
(ACDL)**
Sawyer, Amos **2**

**Association for the Sexually
Harassed (ASH)**
Gomez-Preston, Cheryl **9**

**Association for the Study of
Afro-American Life and
History (ASALH)**
Dodson, Howard, Jr. **7**
Woodson, Carter G. **2**

Astronauts
Bluford, Guy **2**
Bolden, Charles F., Jr. **7**
Gregory, Frederick D. **8**
Jemison, Mae C. **1**
McNair, Ronald **3**

Atco-EastWest
Rhone, Sylvia **2**

Atlanta Baptist College
See Morehouse College

Atlanta Board of Education
Mays, Benjamin E. **7**

Atlanta Braves baseball team
Aaron, Hank **5**
Baker, Dusty **8**
Sanders, Deion **4**

Atlanta City Council
Campbell, Bill **9**

Atlanta city government
Campbell, Bill **9**
Jackson, Maynard **2**
Young, Andrew **3**

Atlanta Falcons football team
Sanders, Deion **4**

Atlanta Hawks basketball team
Wilkens, Lenny **11**

Atlantic Records
Franklin, Aretha **11**
Harvard, Beverly **11**
Rhone, Sylvia **2**

Aviation
Bullard, Eugene **12**
Coleman, Bessie **9**

"Back to Africa" movement
Turner, Henry McNeal **5**

Ballet
Ailey, Alvin **8**
Dove, Ulysses **5**
Johnson, Virginia **9**
Mitchell, Arthur **2**
Nichols, Nichelle **11**
Parks, Gordon **1**

Baltimore city government
Schmoke, Kurt **1**

**Baltimore Orioles baseball
team**
Baylor, Don **6**
Robinson, Frank **9**

Banking
Boyd, T. B., III **6**
Brimmer, Andrew F. **2**
Griffith, Mark Winston **8**
Lawless, Theodore K. **8**
Louis, Errol T. **8**
Morgan, Rose **11**
Parsons, Richard Dean **11**

**Baptist World Alliance
Assembly**
Mays, Benjamin E. **7**

Baseball
Aaron, Hank **5**
Baker, Dusty **8**
Baylor, Don **6**
Belle, Albert **10**
Bonds, Barry **6**
Coleman , Leonard S., Jr. **12**
Cottrell, Comer **11**
Edwards, Harry **2**
Fielder, Cecil **2**
Flood, Curt **10**
Griffey, Ken, Jr. **12**
Lofton, Kenny **12**
Mays, Willie **3**
Morgan, Joe Leonard **9**
Murray, Eddie **12**
Paige, Satchel **7**
Puckett, Kirby **4**
Robinson, Frank **9**
Robinson, Jackie **6**
Sanders, Deion **4**
Thomas, Frank **12**
White, Bill **1**
Winfield, Dave **5**

Basketball
Abdul-Jabbar, Kareem **8**
Barkley, Charles **5**
Bing, Dave **3**
Bol, Manute **1**
Drexler, Clyde **4**
Edwards, Harry **2**
Gossett, Louis, Jr. **7**
Johnson, Earvin "Magic" **3**
Jordan, Michael **6**
Lofton, Kenny **12**
Lucas, John **7**
Miller, Cheryl **10**
Mutombo, Dikembe **7**
Olajuwon, Hakeem **2**
O'Neal, Shaquille **8**
Richardson, Nolan **9**
Russell, Bill **8**
Swoopes, Sheryl **12**
Thomas, Isiah **7**
Wilkens, Lenny **11**

BCALA
See Black Caucus of the
American Library Association

BDP
See Botswana Democratic Party

Beatrice International
See TLC Beatrice International Holdings, Inc.

Bebop
Davis, Miles **4**
Fitzgerald, Ella **8**
Gillespie, Dizzy **1**

Bechuanaland Protectorate Legislative Council
Masire, Quett **5**

Bedford-Stuyvesant Restoraion Corporation
Thomas, Franklin A. **5**

Ben & Jerry's Homemade Ice Cream, Inc.
Holland, Robert, Jr. **11**

BET
See Black Entertainment Television

Bethann Management, Inc.
Hardison, Bethann **12**

Bethune-Cookman College
Bethune, Mary McLeod **4**

BFF
See Black Filmmaker Foundation

BGLLF
See Black Gay and Lesbian Leadership Forum

Billy Graham Evangelistic Association
Bell, Ralph S. **5**
Waters, Ethel **7**

Bing Steel, Inc.
Bing, Dave **3**

Biology
Just, Ernest Everett **3**

Birth control
Elders, Joycelyn **6**
Williams, Maggie **7**

BLA
Cottrell, Comer **11**
See Black Liberation Army

Black Aesthetic
Baker, Houston A., Jr. **6**

Black American West Museum
Stewart, Paul Wilbur **12**

Black and White Minstrel Show
Henry, Lenny **9**

Black Arts movement
Giovanni, Nikki **9**

Black Cabinet
Hastie, William H. **8**

Black Caucus of the American Library Association (BCALA)
Josey, E. J. **10**

Black Christian Nationalist movement
Agyeman, Jaramogi Abebe **10**

Black Consciousness movement
Biko, Steven **4**
Muhammad, Elijah **4**
Ramaphosa, Cyril **3**
Tutu, Desmond **6**

Black culturalism
Karenga, Maulana **10**

Black Enterprise
Brimmer, Andrew F. **2**
Brown, Jim **11**
Graves, Earl G. **1**
Wallace, Phyllis A. **9**

Black Entertainment Television (BET)
Gordon, Ed **10**
Johnson, Robert L. **3**

Black Filmmaker Foundation (BFF)
Hudlin, Reginald **9**
Hudlin, Warrington **9**

Black Gay and Lesbian Leadership Forum (BGLLF)
Wilson, Phill **9**

Black History Month
Woodson, Carter G. **2**

Black Horizons on the Hill
Wilson, August **7**

Black Liberation Army (BLA)
Shakur, Assata **6**
Williams, Evelyn **10**

Black literary theory
Gates, Henry Louis, Jr. **3**

Black Manifesto
Forman, James **7**

Black Muslims
Ali, Muhammad **2**
Farrakhan, Louis **2**
Muhammad, Elijah **4**
X, Malcolm **1**

Black nationalism
Baker, Houston A., Jr. **6**
Baraka, Amiri **1**
Carmichael, Stokely **5**
Farrakhan, Louis **2**
Forman, James **7**
Garvey, Marcus **1**
Innis, Roy **5**
Muhammad, Elijah **4**
Turner, Henry McNeal **5**
X, Malcolm **1**

Black Panther Party (BPP)
Al-Amin, Jamil Abdullah **6**
Brown, Elaine **8**
Carmichael, Stokely **5**
Cleaver, Eldridge **5**
Davis, Angela **5**
Forman, James **7**
Hilliard, David **7**
Newton, Huey **2**
Seale, Bobby **3**
Shakur, Assata **6**

Black Power movement
Al-Amin, Jamil Abdullah **6**
Baker, Houston A., Jr. **6**
Brown, Elaine **8**
Carmichael, Stokely **5**
Dodson, Howard, Jr. **7**
Giovanni, Nikki **9**
McKissick, Floyd B. **3**
Stone, Chuck **9**

Blackside, Inc.
Hampton, Henry **6**

Black theology
Cone, James H. **3**

"Blood for Britain"
Drew, Charles Richard **7**

Blood plasma research/preservation
Drew, Charles Richard **7**

Blues
Collins, Albert **12**
Dixon, Willie **4**
Evora, Cesaria **12**
Handy, W. C. **8**
Holiday, Billie **1**
House, Son **8**
Howlin' Wolf **9**
King, B. B. **7**
Reese, Della **6**
Smith, Bessie **3**
Wallace, Sippie **1**
Waters, Ethel **7**
Williams, Joe **5**
Wilson, August **7**

Blues Heaven Foundation
Dixon, Willie **4**

Blues vernacular
Baker, Houston A., Jr. **6**

Bobsledding
Moses, Edwin **8**

Bodybuilding
Murray, Lenda **10**

Booker T. Washington Business College
Gaston, Arthur G. **4**

Booker T. Washington Insurance Company
Gaston, Arthur G. **4**

Boston Bruins hockey team
O'Ree, Willie **5**

Boston Celtics basketball team
Russell, Bill **8**

Boston Red Sox baseball team
Baylor, Don **6**

Botany
Carver, George Washington **4**

Botswana Democratic Party (BDP)
Masire, Quett **5**

Boxing
Ali, Muhammad **2**
Bowe, Riddick **6**
Foreman, George **1**
Holyfield, Evander **6**
Johnson, Jack **8**
Lee, Canada **8**
Louis, Joe **5**
Whitaker, Pernell **10**

BPP
See Black Panther Party

Brazilian Congress
da Silva, Benedita **5**

Breast Cancer Resource Committee
Brown, Zora Kramer **12**

British House of Commons
Abbott, Diane **9**
Pitt, David Thomas **10**

British House of Lords
Pitt, David Thomas **10**

British Parliament
See British House of Commons

Broadcasting
Allen, Byron **3**
Banks, William **11**
Barden, Don H. **9**
Bradley, Ed **2**
Brown, Les **5**
Brown, Tony **3**
Brunson, Dorothy **1**

Clayton, Xernona **3**
Cornelius, Don **4**
Davis, Ossie **5**
Gumbel, Greg **8**
Hamblin, Ken **10**
Hickman, Fred **11**
Hunter-Gault, Charlayne **6**
Johnson, Robert L. **3**
Jones, Star **10**
Lawson, Jennifer **1**
Lewis, Delano **7**
McEwen, Mark **5**
Miller, Cheryl **10**
Morgan, Joe Leonard **9**
Robinson, Max **3**
Rodgers, Johnathan **6**
Russell, Bill **8**
Shaw, Bernard **2**
Simpson, Carole **6**
Stokes, Carl B. **10**
Watts, Rolonda **9**
White, Bill **1**
Williams, Montel **4**
Winfrey, Oprah **2**

Broadside Press
Randall, Dudley **8**

Brooklyn Academy of Music
Miller, Bebe **3**

Brooklyn Dodgers baseball team
Robinson, Jackie **6**

Brotherhood of Sleeping Car Porters
Randolph, A. Philip **3**

Brown v. Board of Education of Topeka
Bell, Derrick **6**
Clark, Kenneth B. **5**
Franklin, John Hope **5**
Houston, Charles Hamilton **4**
Marshall, Thurgood **1**
Motley, Constance Baker **10**

Busing (anti-busing legislation)
Bosley, Freeman, Jr. **7**

Cabinet
See U.S. Cabinet

Cable News Network (CNN)
Shaw, Bernard **2**
Hickman, Fred **11**

California Angels baseball team
Baylor, Don **6**
Robinson, Frank **9**
Winfield, Dave **5**

California State Assembly
Brown, Willie L., Jr. **7**
Waters, Maxine **3**

Calypso
Belafonte, Harry **4**

Canadian Football League (CFL)
Moon, Warren **8**
Weathers, Carl **10**

Cancer research
Leffall, LaSalle, Jr. **3**

Cardiac research
Watkins, Levi, Jr. **9**

CARE
Gossett, Louis, Jr. **7**
Stone, Chuck **9**

Caribbean dance
Ailey, Alvin **8**
Dunham, Katherine **4**
Nichols, Nichelle **11**
Primus, Pearl **6**

Cartoonists
Brandon, Barbara **3**
Harrington, Oliver W. **9**

Catholicism
See Roman Catholic Church

CBEA
See Council for a Black Economic Agenda

CBC
See Congressional Black Caucus

CBS
See Columbia Broadcasting System

CBS Television Stations Division
Rodgers, Johnathan **6**

CDC
See Centers for Disease Control and Prevention

CDF
See Children's Defense Fund

CEDBA
See Council for the Economic Development of Black Americans

Celebrities for a Drug-Free America
Vereen, Ben **4**

Censorship
Butts, Calvin O., III **9**
Ice-T **6**

Centers for Disease Control and Prevention (CDC)
Gayle, Helene D. **3**
Satcher, David **7**

CFL
See Canadian Football League

CHA
See Chicago Housing Authority

Challenger
McNair, Ronald **3**

Chama cha Mapinduzi (Tanzania; Rev. Party)
Nyerere, Julius **5**
Mongella, Gertrude **11**

Chamber of Deputies (Brazil)
da Silva, Benedita **5**

Chanteuses
Baker, Josephine **3**
Dandridge, Dorothy **3**
Horne, Lena **5**
Reese, Della **6**

Che-Lumumba Club
Davis, Angela **5**

Chemistry
Hall, Lloyd A. **8**
Julian, Percy Lavon **6**

Chemurgy
Carver, George Washington **4**

Chesapeake and Potomac Telephone Company
Lewis, Delano **7**

Chicago Bears football team
Page, Alan **7**
Payton, Walter **11**
Singletary, Mike **4**

Chicago Bulls basketball team
Jordan, Michael **6**
Rodman, Dennis **12**

Chicago city government
Washington, Harold **6**

Chicago Eight
Seale, Bobby **3**

Chicago Housing Authority (CHA)
Lane, Vincent **5**

Chicago Tribune
Page, Clarence **4**

Chicago White Sox baseball team
Thomas, Frank **12**

Child abuse prevention
Waters, Maxine **3**

Child psychiatry
Comer, James P. **6**

Child psychology
Hale, Lorraine **8**

Children's Defense Fund (CDF)
Edelman, Marian Wright **5**
Williams, Maggie **7**

Child Welfare Administration
Little, Robert L. **2**

Choreography
Ailey, Alvin **8**
Brooks, Avery **9**
Byrd, Donald **10**
Dove, Ulysses **5**
Dunham, Katherine **4**
Jamison, Judith **7**
Johnson, Virginia **9**
Jones, Bill T. **1**
Miller, Bebe **3**
Mitchell, Arthur **2**
Primus, Pearl **6**

Christian Science Monitor
Khanga, Yelena **6**

Chrysler Corporation
Farmer, Forest **1**

Church for the Fellowship of All Peoples
Thurman, Howard **3**

Church of God in Christ
Hayes, James C. **10**

Cincinnati Reds baseball team
Morgan, Joe Leonard **9**
Robinson, Frank **9**

Cinematography
Dickerson, Ernest **6**

Citadel Press
Achebe, Chinua **6**

Citizens Federal Savings and Loan Association
Gaston, Arthur G. **4**

City government--U.S.
Archer, Dennis **7**
Barden, Don H. **9**
Barry, Marion S. **7**
Bosley, Freeman, Jr. **7**
Bradley, Thomas **2**
Brown, Lee P. **1**
Campbell, Bill **9**
Clayton, Constance **1**
Cleaver, Emanuel **4**
Dinkins, David **4**

Dixon, Sharon Pratt **1**
Evers, Myrlie **8**
Fauntroy, Walter E. **11**
Gibson, Kenneth Allen **6**
Goode, W. Wilson **4**
Hayes, James C. **10**
Jackson, Maynard **2**
Johnson, Eddie Bernice **8**
Kirk, Ron **11**
McPhail, Sharon **2**
Powell, Adam Clayton, Jr. **3**
Rice, Norm **8**
Sayles Belton, Sharon **9**
Schmoke, Kurt **1**
Stokes, Carl B. **10**
Washington, Harold **6**
Webb, Wellington **3**
White, Michael R. **5**
Young, Andrew **3**
Young, Coleman **1**

CityKids Foundation
Yoba, Malik **11**

Civil rights
Abernathy, Ralph **1**
Abbott, Diane **9**
Agyeman, Jaramogi Abebe **10**
Al-Amin, Jamil Abdullah **6**
Ali, Muhammad **2**
Angelou, Maya **1**
Aristide, Jean-Bertrand **6**
Baker, Ella **5**
Baker, Houston A., Jr. **6**
Baker, Josephine **3**
Belafonte, Harry **4**
Bell, Derrick **6**
Bennett, Lerone, Jr. **5**
Berry, Mary Frances **7**
Biko, Steven **4**
Bond, Julian **2**
Brown, Elaine **8**
Brown, Tony **3**
Campbell, Bebe Moore **6**
Carmichael, Stokely **5**
Carter, Mandy **11**
Carter, Stephen L. **4**
Chambers, Julius **3**
Chavis, Benjamin **6**
Clark, Septima **7**
Clay, William Lacy **8**
Cleaver, Eldridge **5**
Cobbs, Price M. **9**
Cosby, Bill **7**
Crockett, George, Jr. **10**
Davis, Angela **5**
Days, Drew S., III **10**
Dee, Ruby **8**
Divine, Father **7**
Dodson, Howard, Jr. **7**
Du Bois, W. E. B. **3**
Edelman, Marian Wright **5**
Ellison, Ralph **7**
Evers, Medgar **3**
Evers, Myrlie **8**
Farmer, James **2**
Fauntroy, Walter E. **11**
Forman, James **7**

Fortune, T. Thomas **6**
Franklin, John Hope **5**
Gaines, Ernest J. **7**
Gibson, William F. **6**
Gregory, Dick **1**
Griffin, Anthony P. **12**
Grimké, Archibald H. **9**
Guinier, Lani **7**
Haley, Alex **4**
Hamer, Fannie Lou **6**
Hampton, Henry **6**
Hansberry, Lorraine **6**
Harper, Frances Ellen Watkins **11**
Harris, Patricia Roberts **2**
Hastie, William H. **8**
Height, Dorothy I. **2**
Hilliard, David **7**
Holland, Endesha Ida Mae **3**
hooks, bell **5**
Hooks, Benjamin L. **2**
Horne, Lena **5**
Houston, Charles Hamilton **4**
Hughes, Langston **4**
Innis, Roy **5**
Jackson, Jesse **1**
Johnson, Eddie Bernice **8**
Johnson, James Weldon **5**
Jones, Elaine R. **7**
Jordan, Barbara **4**
Jordan, June **7**
Jordan, Vernon E. **3**
Julian, Percy Lavon **6**
Kennedy, Florynce **12**
Kenyatta, Jomo **5**
King, Bernice **4**
King, Coretta Scott **3**
King, Martin Luther, Jr. **1**
King, Yolanda **6**
Lee, Spike **5**
Lester, Julius **9**
Lewis, John **2**
Lorde, Audre **6**
Lowery, Joseph **2**
Makeba, Miriam **2**
Mandela, Nelson **1**
Mandela, Winnie **2**
Mays, Benjamin E. **7**
McDougall, Gay J. **11**
McKissick, Floyd B. **3**
Meek, Carrie **6**
Meredith, James H. **11**
Morrison, Toni **2**
Moses, Robert Parris **11**
Motley, Constance Baker **10**
Mowry, Jess **7**
Ndadaye, Melchior **7**
Nelson, Jill **6**
Newton, Huey **2**
Nkomo, Joshua **4**
Norman, Pat **10**
Norton, Eleanor Holmes **7**
Parks, Rosa **1**
Patrick, Deval **12**
Patterson, Orlando **4**
Perkins, Edward **5**
Pinchback, P. B. S. **9**
Pleasant, Mary Ellen **9**
Poitier, Sidney **11**

Powell, Adam Clayton, Jr. **3**
Price, Hugh B. **9**
Ramaphosa, Cyril **3**
Randolph, A. Philip **3**
Reagon, Bernice Johnson **7**
Riggs, Marlon **5**
Robeson, Paul **2**
Robinson, Jackie **6**
Robinson, Randall **7**
Rowan, Carl T. **1**
Rustin, Bayard **4**
Seale, Bobby **3**
Shabazz, Attallah **6**
Shabazz, Betty **7**
Shakur, Assata **6**
Sleet, Moneta, Jr. **5**
Staupers, Mabel K. **7**
Sullivan, Leon H. **3**
Thurman, Howard **3**
Till, Emmett **7**
Trotter, Monroe **9**
Turner, Henry McNeal **5**
Tutu, Desmond **6**
Underwood, Blair **7**
Washington, Booker T. **4**
Washington, Fredi **10**
Weaver, Robert C. **8**
Wells, James Lesesne **10**
Wells-Barnett, Ida B. **8**
West, Cornel **5**
White, Walter F. **4**
Wideman, John Edgar **5**
Wilkins, Roy **4**
Williams, Evelyn **10**
Williams, Robert F. **11**
Williams, Walter E. **4**
Wilson, August **7**
Wilson, Sunnie **7**
Woodson, Robert L. **10**
X, Malcolm **1**
Yoba, Malik **11**
Young, Andrew **3**
Young, Whitney M., Jr. **4**

Classical singers
Anderson, Marian **2**
Bumbry, Grace **5**
Hayes, Roland **4**
Hendricks, Barbara **3**
Norman, Jessye **5**
Price, Leontyne **1**

**Cleveland Browns football
team**
Brown, Jim **11**

**Cleveland Cavaliers basketball
team**
Wilkens, Lenny **11**

Cleveland city government
Stokes, Carl B. **10**
White, Michael R. **5**

**Cleveland Indians baseball
team**
Lofton, Kenny **12**
Murray, Eddie **12**

Paige, Satchel **7**
Belle, Albert **10**
Robinson, Frank **9**

Clothing design
Henderson, Gordon **5**
Bailey, Xenobia **11**
Jones, Carl **7**
Kani, Karl **10**
Kelly, Patrick **3**
Smith, Willi **8**
Walker, T. J. **7**

CNN
See Cable News Network

Coaching
Baylor, Don **6**
Gibson, Althea **8**
Green, Dennis **5**
Greene, Joe **10**
Miller, Cheryl **10**
Richardson, Nolan **9**
Robinson, Eddie G. **10**
Russell, Bill **8**
Shell, Art **1**

COHAR
See Committee on Appeal for
Human Rights

Collage
Bearden, Romare **2**
Driskell, David C. **7**

**Colorado Rockies baseball
team**
Baylor, Don **6**

**Columbia Broadcasting System
(CBS)**
Bradley, Ed **2**
McEwen, Mark **5**
Rodgers, Johnathan **6**
Taylor, Meshach **4**

Comedy
Allen, Byron **3**
Amos, John **8**
Bellamy, Bill **12**
Berry, Bertice **8**
Campbell, Tisha **8**
Cosby, Bill **7**
Foxx, Redd **2**
Goldberg, Whoopi **4**
Gregory, Dick **1**
Harris, Robin **7**
Henry, Lenny **9**
Lawrence, Martin **6**
McEwen, Mark **5**
Murphy, Eddie **4**
Pryor, Richard **3**
Reese, Della **6**
Rock, Chris **3**
Schultz, Michael A. **6**
Sinbad **1**
Smith, Will **8**
Taylor, Meshach **4**

Townsend, Robert **4**
Warfield, Marsha **2**
Wayans, Damon **8**

Comer Method
Comer, James P. **6**

Comic Relief
Goldberg, Whoopi **4**

Commission for Racial Justice
Chavis, Benjamin **6**

**Committee on Appeal for
Human Rights (COHAR)**
Bond, Julian **2**

Communist party
Davis, Angela **5**
Du Bois, W. E. B. **3**
Wright, Richard **5**

Computer graphics
Hannah, Marc **10**

Computer science
Hannah, Marc **10**

Conceptual art
Bailey, Xenobia **11**
Simpson, Lorna **4**

Concerned Black Men
Holder, Eric H., Jr. **9**

Conductors
Jackson, Isaiah **3**

**Congressional Black Caucus
(CBC)**
Clay, William Lacy **8**
Collins, Cardiss **10**
Conyers, John, Jr. **4**
Dellums, Ronald **2**
Fauntroy, Walter E. **11**
Gray, William H. III **3**
Johnson, Eddie Bernice **8**
Mfume, Kweisi **6**
Owens, Major **6**
Rangel, Charles **3**
Stokes, Louis **3**

**Congressional Black Caucus
Higher Education Braintrust**
Owens, Major **6**

**Congress of Racial Equality
(CORE)**
Dee, Ruby **8**
Farmer, James **2**
Innis, Roy **5**
Jackson, Jesse **1**
McKissick, Floyd B. **3**
Rustin, Bayard **4**

Conservatism
Keyes, Alan L. **11**

**Convention People's Party
(Ghana; CPP)**
Nkrumah, Kwame **3**

Cook County Circuit Court
Sampson, Edith S. **4**

CORE
See Congress of Racial Equality

**Corporation for Public Broad
casting (CPB)**
Brown, Tony **3**

Cosmetology
Cottrell, Comer **11**
Morgan, Rose **11**
Powell, Maxine **8**

**Council for a Black Economic
Agenda (CBEA)**
Woodson, Robert L. **10**

**Council for Social Action of
the Congregational
Christian Churches**
Julian, Percy Lavon **6**

**Council for the Economic
Development of Black
Americans (CEDBA)**
Brown, Tony **3**

Count Basie Orchestra
Williams, Joe **5**

Cow hand
Love, Nat **9**
Pickett, Bill **11**

CPB
See Corporation for Public
Broadcasting

CPP
See Convention People's Party

**Cress Theory of Color-
Confrontation and Racism**
Welsing, Frances Cress **5**

Crisis
Du Bois, W. E. B. **3**
Fauset, Jessie **7**
Wilkins, Roy **4**

Cross Colours
Jones, Carl **7**
Kani, Karl **10**
Walker, T. J. **7**

Crucial Films
Henry, Lenny **9**

CTRN
See Transitional Committee for
National Recovery (Guinea)
Williams, Robert F. **11**

Cubism
Bearden, Romare **2**

Cultural Criticism
Crouch, Stanley **11**

Cultural pluralism
Locke, Alain **10**

Cumulative voting
Guinier, Lani **7**

Curator/exhibition designer
Golden, Thelma **10**
Sanders, Joseph R., Jr. **11**

Curator\exhibition designer
Stewart, Paul Wilbur **12**

Cytogenetics
Satcher, David **7**

Dallas city government
Johnson, Eddie Bernice **8**
Kirk, Ron **11**

Dallas Cowboys football team
Smith, Emmitt **7**

Dance Theatre of Harlem
Johnson, Virginia **9**
Mitchell, Arthur **2**
Tyson, Cicely **7**

DAV
See Disabled American Veterans

David M. Winfield Foundation
Winfield, Dave **5**

Daytona Institute
See Bethune-Cookman College

**Dayton Philharmonic
Orchestra**
Jackson, Isaiah **3**

D.C. Black Repertory Theater
Reagon, Bernice Johnson **7**

Death Row Records
Knight, Suge **11**

De Beers Botswana
Knight, Suge **11**
See Debswana

Debswana
Masire, Quett **5**

**Defense Communications
Agency**
Gravely, Samuel L., Jr. **5**

Def Jam Records
Simmons, Russell **1**

Democratic National Committee (DNC)
Brown, Ron **5**
Brown, Willie L., Jr. **7**
Dixon, Sharon Pratt **1**
Fattah, Chaka **11**
Hamer, Fannie Lou **6**
Jordan, Barbara **4**
Waters, Maxine **3**
Williams, Maggie **7**

Democratic National Convention
Brown, Ron **5**
Brown, Willie L., Jr. **7**
Dixon, Sharon Pratt **1**
Hamer, Fannie Lou **6**
Jordan, Barbara **4**
Waters, Maxine **3**
Williams, Maggie **7**

Democratic Socialists of America (DSA)
West, Cornel **5**
Marable, Manning **10**

Dentistry
Delany, Bessie **12**

Denver city government
Webb, Wellington **3**

Denver Nuggets basketball team
Mutombo, Dikembe **7**

Depression/The Great Depression
Hampton, Henry **6**

Desert Shield
See Operation Desert Shield

Desert Storm
See Operation Desert Storm

Detective fiction
Himes, Chester **8**
Mosley, Walter **5**

Detroit City Council
Collins, Barbara-Rose **7**

Detroit city government
Archer, Dennis **7**
Crockett, George, Jr. **10**
Young, Coleman **1**

Detroit entertainment
Wilson, Sunnie **7**

Detroit Golden Gloves
Wilson, Sunnie **7**

Detroit Lions football team
Sanders, Barry **1**

Detroit Pistons basketball team
Bing, Dave **3**
Thomas, Isiah **7**

Detroit Police Department
Gomez-Preston, Cheryl **9**
McKinnon, Isaiah **9**

Detroit Tigers baseball team
Fielder, Cecil **2**

Diamond mining
Masire, Quett **5**

Diplomatic Corp
Parsons, Richard Dean **11**
See U.S. Diplomatic Corp

Disabled American Veterans (DAV)
Brown, Jesse **6**

DNC
See Democratic National Committee

Documentary film
Byrd, Robert **11**
Dash, Julie **4**
Davis, Ossie **5**
Hampton, Henry **6**
Henry, Lenny **9**
Hudlin, Reginald **9**
Hudlin, Warrington **9**
Julien, Isaac **3**
Riggs, Marlon **5**

Donald Byrd/The Group
Byrd, Donald **10**

Drug abuse prevention
Brown, Les **5**
Clements, George **2**
Hale, Lorraine **8**
Harris, Alice **7**
Lucas, John **7**
Rangel, Charles **3**

Drug synthesis
Julian, Percy Lavon **6**

DSA
See Democratic Socialists of America

Dunham Dance Company
Dunham, Katherine **4**

DuSable Museum of African American History
Burroughs, Margaret Taylor **9**

Earthquake Early Alerting Service
Person, Waverly **9**

Ebenezer Baptist Church
King, Bernice **4**

Ebony
Bennett, Lerone, Jr. **5**
Johnson, John H. **3**
Rice, Linda Johnson **9**
Sleet, Moneta, Jr. **5**

Ebony Museum of African American History
See DuSable Museum of African American History

Economic Community of West African States (ECOWAS)
Sawyer, Amos **2**

Economic Regulatory Administration
O'Leary, Hazel **6**

Economics
Boyd, T. B. III **6**
Brimmer, Andrew F. **2**
Brown, Tony **3**
Divine, Father **7**
Dodson, Howard, Jr. **7**
Gibson, William F. **6**
Hamer, Fannie Lou **6**
Hampton, Henry **6**
Masire, Quett **5**
Robinson, Randall **7**
Sowell, Thomas **2**
Sullivan, Leon H. **3**
Van Peebles, Melvin **7**
Wallace, Phyllis A. **9**
Wharton, Clifton R., Jr. **7**
White, Michael R. **5**
Williams, Walter E. **4**

ECOWAS
See Economic Community of West African States

Edelman Public Relations
Barrett, Andrew C. **12**

Edmonton Oilers hockey team
Fuhr, Grant **1**

Educational Testing Service
Stone, Chuck **9**

EEC
See European Economic Community

EEOC
See Equal Employment Opportunity Commission

Egyptology
Diop, Cheikh Anta **4**

Elder Foundation
Elder, Lee **6**

Emmy awards
La Salle, Eriq **12**
Amos, John **8**
Ashe, Arthur **1**
Belafonte, Harry **4**
Bradley, Ed **2**
Brown, Les **5**
Clayton, Xernona **3**
Cosby, Bill **7**
Dee, Ruby **8**
Foxx, Redd **2**
Freeman, Al, Jr. **11**
Goldberg, Whoopi **4**
Gossett, Louis, Jr. **7**
Guillaume, Robert **3**
Gumbel, Greg **8**
Hunter-Gault, Charlayne **6**
Jones, James Earl **3**
McQueen, Butterfly **6**
Parks, Gordon **1**
Robinson, Max **3**
Stokes, Carl B. **10**
Tyson, Cicely **7**
Wayans, Damon **8**
Williams, Montel **4**
Woodard, Alfre **9**

Endocrinology
Elders, Joycelyn **6**

Energy studies
Cose, Ellis **5**
O'Leary, Hazel **6**

Engineering
Gibson, Kenneth Allen **6**
Hannah, Marc **10**
McCoy, Elijah **8**

Environmental issues
Chavis, Benjamin **6**

Epidemiology
Gayle, Helene D. **3**

Episcopal Diocese of Massachusetts
Harris, Barbara **12**

EPRDF
See Ethiopian People's Revolutionary Democratic Front

Equal Employment Opportunity Commission (EEOC)
Hill, Anita **5**
Lewis, Delano **7**
Norton, Eleanor Holmes **7**
Thomas, Clarence **2**
Wallace, Phyllis A. **9**

Essence
Parks, Gordon **1**
Taylor, Susan L. **10**

Essence Communications
Taylor, Susan L. **10**

Essence, the Television Program
Taylor, Susan L. **10**

Ethiopian People's Revolutionary Democratic Front (EPRDF)
Meles Zenawi **3**

Eugene O'Neill Theater
Richards, Lloyd **2**

European Economic Community (EEC)
Diouf, Abdou **3**

Exiled heads of state
Aristide, Jean-Bertrand **6**

Exploration
Henson, Matthew **2**

Eyes on the Prize series
Hampton, Henry **6**

Fairbanks city government
Hayes, James C. **10**

FAIRR
See Foundation for the Advancement of Inmate Rehabilitation and Recreation

Fair Share Agreements
Gibson, William F. **6**

Famine relief
See World hunger

Famous Amos Cookie Corporation
Amos, Wally **9**

FAN
See Forces Armées du Nord (Chad)

Fashion
Smaltz, Audrey **12**

FCC
See Federal Communications Commission

Federal Bureau of Investigation (FBI)
Harvard, Beverly **11**

Federal Communications Commission (FCC)
Barrett, Andrew C. **12**
Hooks, Benjamin L. **2**

Federal Energy Administration
O'Leary, Hazel **6**

Federal Reserve Bank
Brimmer, Andrew F. **2**

Fellowship of Reconciliation (FOR)
Farmer, James **2**
Rustin, Bayard **4**

Feminism
Cannon, Katie **10**

Fiction
Cooper, J. California **12**

Figure skating
Bonaly, Surya **7**

Film direction
Byrd, Robert **11**
Dash, Julie **4**
Davis, Ossie **5**
Dickerson, Ernest **6**
Duke, Bill **3**
Franklin, Carl **11**
Freeman, Al, Jr. **11**
Harris, Leslie **6**
Hudlin, Reginald **9**
Hudlin, Warrington **9**
Hughes, Albert **7**
Hughes, Allen **7**
Julien, Isaac **3**
Lane, Charles **3**
Lee, Spike **5**
Micheaux, Oscar **7**
Moses, Gilbert **12**
Poitier, Sidney **11**
Riggs, Marlon **5**
Smith, Roger Guenveur **12**
St. Jacques, Raymond **8**
Schultz, Michael A. **6**
Singleton, John **2**
Townsend, Robert **4**
Underwood, Blair **7**
Van Peebles, Mario **2**
Van Peebles, Melvin **7**
Wayans, Damon **8**

Film scores
Jones, Quincy **8**

Finance
Griffith, Mark Winston **8**
Lawless, Theodore K. **8**
Louis, Errol T. **8**
Rogers, John W., Jr. **5**

Fisk University
Johnson, Charles S. **12**

Florida state government
Meek, Carrie **6**
Tribble, Isreal, Jr. **8**

Flouride chemistry
Quarterman, Lloyd Albert **4**

Folk music
Charlemagne, Manno **11**

Football
Amos, John **8**

Brown, Jim **11**
Edwards, Harry **2**
Green, Dennis **5**
Greene, Joe **10**
Lott, Ronnie **9**
Moon, Warren **8**
Page, Alan **7**
Payton, Walter **11**
Rice, Jerry **5**
Robinson, Eddie G. **10**
Sanders, Barry **1**
Sanders, Deion **4**
Shell, Art **1**
Singletary, Mike **4**
Smith, Emmitt **7**
Walker, Herschel **1**
Weathers, Carl **10**
White, Reggie **6**

FOR
See Fellowship of Reconciliation

Forces Armées du Nord (Chad; FAN)
Habré, Hissène **6**

Ford Foundation
Thomas, Franklin A. **5**

Foreign policy
Bunche, Ralph J. **5**
Rice, Condoleezza **3**
Robinson, Randall **7**

Forest Club
Wilson, Sunnie **7**

40 Acres and a Mule Filmworks
Lee, Spike **5**

Foster care
Hale, Lorraine **8**

Foundation for the Advancement of Inmate Rehabilitation and Recreation
King, B. B. **7**

Freedom Farm Cooperative
Hamer, Fannie Lou **6**

Free Southern Theater (FST)
Borders, James **9**

FRELIMO
See Front for the Liberation of Mozambique

French West Africa
Diouf, Abdou **3**

FRODEBU
See Front for Democracy in Burundi

FROLINAT
See Front de la Libération

Nationale du Tchad (Chad)

FRONASA
See Front for National Salvation (Uganda)

Front de la Libération Nationale du Tchad (Chad; FROLINAT)
Habré, Hissène **6**

Front for Democracy in Burundi (FRODEBU)
Ndadaye, Melchior **7**
Ntaryamira, Cyprien **8**

Front for National Salvation (Uganda; FRONASA)
Museveni, Yoweri **4**

Front for the Liberation of Mozambique (FRELIMO)
Chissano, Joaquim **7**
Machel, Samora Moises **8**

FST
See Free Southern Theater

Funk music
Clinton, George **9**

Fusion
Davis, Miles **4**
Jones, Quincy **8**

Gary, Williams, Parenti, Finney, Lewis & McManus
Gary, Willie E. **12**

Gary Enterprises
Gary, Willie E. **12**

Gay Men of Color Consortium
Wilson, Phill **9**

Genealogy
Dash, Julie **4**
Haley, Alex **4**

Geometric symbolism
Douglas, Aaron **7**

Geophysics
Person, Waverly **9**

George Foster Peabody Broadcasting Award
Bradley, Ed **2**
Hunter-Gault, Charlayne **6**
Shaw, Bernard **2**

Georgia state government
Bond, Julian **2**

Georgia State Supreme Court
Sears-Collins, Leah J. **5**

Glaucoma treatment
Julian, Percy Lavon **6**

Glidden Company
Julian, Percy Lavon **6**

Golden Globe awards
Carroll, Diahann **9**
Taylor, Regina **9**

Golden State Warriors basketball team
Edwards, Harry **2**
Lucas, John **7**

Golf
Elder, Lee **6**
Gibson, Althea **8**
Peete, Calvin **11**
Sifford, Charlie **4**

Goodwill Games
Swoopes, Sheryl **12**

Gospel music
Franklin, Aretha **11**
Jackson, Mahalia **5**
Mayfield, Curtis **2**
Reagon, Bernice Johnson **7**
Reese, Della **6**
Walker, Albertina **10**

Grammy awards
Belafonte, Harry **4**
Cosby, Bill **7**
Davis, Miles **4**
Edmonds, Kenneth "Babyface" **10**
Ellington, Duke **5**
Fitzgerald, Ella **8**
Franklin, Aretha **11**
Gaye, Marvin **2**
Goldberg, Whoopi **4**
Houston, Whitney **7**
Jones, Quincy **8**
Makeba, Miriam **2**
Murphy, Eddie **4**
Norman, Jessye **5**
Price, Leontyne **1**
Reagon, Bernice Johnson **7**
Robinson, Smokey **3**
Smith, Will **8**
Turner, Tina **6**
Wilson, Nancy **10**
Wonder, Stevie **11**

Green Bay Packers football team
White, Reggie **6**

Groupe de Recherche Choréographique de l'Opéra de Paris
Dove, Ulysses **5**

Guardian
Trotter, Monroe **9**

Guitar
Hendrix, Jimi **10**
House, Son **8**
Howlin' Wolf **9**
Johnson, Robert **2**
King, B. B. **7**
Kravitz, Lenny **10**
Marley, Bob **5**
Mayfield, Curtis **2**
Ongala, Remmy **9**

Gulf War
Powell, Colin **1**
Shaw, Bernard **2**
Von Lipsey, Roderick K. **11**

Gurdjieff Institute
Toomer, Jean **6**

Gymnastics
Dominique Dawes **11**

Hair care
Cottrell, Comer **11**
Walker, Madame C. J. **7**

Haitian refugees
Dunham, Katherine **4**
Robinson, Randall **7**

Hale House
Hale, Lorraine **8**

Harlem Renaissance
Cullen, Countee **8**
Ellington, Duke **5**
Fauset, Jessie **7**
Frazier, E. Franklin **10**
Hughes, Langston **4**
Hurston, Zora Neale **3**
Johnson, James Weldon **5**
Johnson, William Henry **3**
Larsen, Nella **10**
Locke, Alain **10**
McKay, Claude **6**
Toomer, Jean **6**
VanDerZee, James **6**

Harlem Writers Guild
Guy, Rosa **5**

Harlem Youth Opportunities Unlimited (HARYOU)
Clark, Kenneth B. **5**

Harmonica
Howlin' Wolf **9**

Harriet Tubman Home for Aged and Indignet Colored People
Tubman, Harriet **9**

Harvard Law School
Bell, Derrick **6**
Ogletree, Jr., Charles **12**

HARYOU
See Harlem Youth Opportunities Unlimited

Head Start
Edelman, Marian Wright **5**

Health care reform
Brown, Jesse **6**
Cooper, Edward S. **6**
Davis, Angela **5**
Gibson, Kenneth A. **6**
Norman, Pat **10**
Satcher, David **7**
Williams, Daniel Hale **2**

Heart disease
Cooper, Edward S. **6**

Heidelberg Project
Guyton, Tyree **9**

HEW
See U.S. Department of Health, Education, and Welfare

HHS
See U.S. Department of Health and Human Services

Historians
Berry, Mary Frances **7**
Diop, Cheikh Anta **4**
Dodson, Howard, Jr. **7**
Du Bois, W. E. B. **3**
Franklin, John Hope **5**
Gates, Henry Louis, Jr. **3**
Giddings, Paula **11**
Hansberry, William Leo **11**
Marable, Manning **10**
Patterson, Orlando **4**
Reagon, Bernice Johnson **7**
Schomburg, Arthur Alfonso **9**
Woodson, Carter G. **2**

Hockey
Fuhr, Grant **1**
McKegney, Tony **3**
O'Ree, Willie **5**

Homosexuality
Carter, Mandy **11**
Delany, Samuel R., Jr. **9**
Hemphill, Essex **10**
Julien, Isaac **3**
Lorde, Audre **6**
Norman, Pat **10**
Riggs, Marlon **5**
Wilson, Phill **9**

House of Representatives
See U.S. House of Representatives

Houston Astros baseball team
Morgan, Joe Leonard **9**

Houston Oilers football team
Moon, Warren **8**

Houston Rockets basketball team
Lucas, John **7**
Olajuwon, Hakeem **2**

Howard University
Jenifer, Franklyn G. **2**
Locke, Alain **10**
Mays, Benjamin E. **7**
Porter, James A. **11**
Wells, James Lesesne **10**

HRCF
See Human Rights Campaign Fund

HUD
See U.S. Department of Housing and Urban Development

Hugo awards
Butler, Octavia **8**
Delany, Samuel R., Jr. **9**

Hull-Ottawa Canadiens hockey team
O'Ree, Willie **5**

Human Rights Campaign Fund (HRCF)
Carter, Mandy **11**

Hurdles
Devers, Gail **7**

IBF
See International Boxing Federation

Ice skating
See Figure skating

Igbo people/traditions
Achebe, Chinua **6**

IHRLG
See International Human Rights Law Group

Illinois state government
Braun, Carol Moseley **4**
Washington, Harold **6**

Illustrations
Saint James, Synthia **12**

Imani Temple
Stallings, George A., Jr. **6**

IMF
See International Monetary Fund

Indianapolis 500
Ribbs, Willy T. **2**

Information technology
Smith, Joshua **10**

In Friendship
Baker, Ella **5**

Inkatha
Buthelezi, Mangosuthu Gatsha **9**

Institute for Black Parenting
Oglesby, Zena **12**

Institute for Journalism Education
Maynard, Robert C. **7**

Institute for Research in African American Studies
Marable, Manning **10**

Institute of Positive Education
Madhubuti, Haki R. **7**

Institute of Social and Religious Research
Mays, Benjamin E. **7**

Institute of the Black World
Dodson, Howard, Jr. **7**

Insurance
Spaulding, Charles Clinton **9**

International Boxing Federation (IBF)
Whitaker, Pernell **10**

International Free and Accepted Masons and Eastern Star

International Human Rights Law Group (IHRLG)
Banks, William **11**
McDougall, Gay J. **11**

International Monetary Fund (IMF)
Babangida, Ibrahim **4**
Chissano, Joaquim **7**
Conté, Lansana **7**
Diouf, Abdou **3**
Patterson, P. J. **6**

Inventions
Julian, Percy Lavon **6**
Latimer, Lewis H. **4**
McCoy, Elijah **8**
Morgan, Garrett **1**
Woods, Granville T. **5**

Investment management
Rogers, John W., Jr. **5**

Jamison Project
Jamison, Judith **7**

Jazz
Armstrong, Louis **2**
Belle, Regina **1**
Brooks, Avery **9**
Crouch, Stanley **11**
Davis, Anthony **11**
Davis, Miles **4**
Ellington, Duke **5**
Ellison, Ralph **7**
Fitzgerald, Ella **8**
Gillespie, Dizzy **1**
Hawkins, Coleman **9**
Holiday, Billie **1**
Jones, Quincy **8**
Lincoln, Abbey **3**
Madhubuti, Haki R. **7**
Monk, Thelonious **1**
Nascimento, Milton **2**
Reese, Della **6**
Ross, Diana **8**
Smith, Bessie **3**
Williams, Joe **5**
Wilson, Nancy **10**

Jet
Bennett, Lerone, Jr. **5**
Johnson, John H. **3**
Sleet, Moneta, Jr. **5**

John Lucas Enterprises
Lucas, John **7**

Johnson Publishing Company, Inc.
Bennett, Lerone, Jr. **5**
Johnson, John H. **3**
Rice, Linda Johnson **9**
Sleet, Moneta, Jr. **5**

Joint Chiefs of Staff
See U.S. Joint Chiefs of Staff

Journalism
Bennett, Lerone, Jr. **5**
Barden, Don H. **9**
Borders, James **9**
Bradley, Ed **2**
Brown, Tony **3**
Campbell, Bebe Moore **6**
Cose, Ellis **5**
Crouch, Stanley **11**
Cullen, Countee **8**
Dunbar, Paul Laurence **8**
Forman, James **7**
Fortune, T. Thomas **6**
Giddings, Paula **11**
Gordon, Ed **10**
Grimké, Archibald H. **9**
Gumbel, Greg **8**
Hansberry, Lorraine **6**
Harrington, Oliver W. **9**
Hickman, Fred **11**
Hunter-Gault, Charlayne **6**
Johnson, James Weldon **5**
Khanga, Yelena **6**
Maynard, Robert C. **7**
McCall, Nathan **8**
McKay, Claude **6**

Nelson, Jill **6**
Page, Clarence **4**
Parks, Gordon **1**
Perez, Anna **1**
Price, Hugh B. **9**
Raspberry, William **2**
Reed, Ishmael **8**
Robinson, Max **3**
Rodgers, Johnathan **6**
Rowan, Carl T. **1**
Shaw, Bernard **2**
Simpson, Carole **6**
Sowell, Thomas **2**
Staples, Brent **8**
Stokes, Carl B. **10**
Stone, Chuck **9**
Taylor, Kristin Clark **8**
Trotter, Monroe **9**
Watts, Rolonda **9**
Webb, Veronica **10**
Wells-Barnett, Ida B. **8**
Wiley, Ralph **8**
Wilkins, Roger **2**
Williams, Patricia J. **11**

Journal of Negro History
Woodson, Carter G. **2**

Kansas City Athletics baseball team
Paige, Satchel **7**

Kansas City government
Cleaver, Emanuel **4**

KANU
See Kenya African National Union

Karl Kani Infinity
Kani, Karl **10**

KAU
See Kenya African Union

KCA
See Kikuyu Central Association

Kenya African National Union (KANU)
Kenyatta, Jomo **5**

Kenya African Union (KAU)
Kenyatta, Jomo **5**

Kikuyu Central Association (KCA)
Kenyatta, Jomo **5**

King Center
See Martin Luther King Jr. Center for Nonviolent Social Change

Kraft General Foods
Fudge, Ann **11**

Ku Klux Klan
Griffin, Anthony P. **12**

Kwanzaa
Karenga, Maulana **10**

Kwazulu Territorial Authority
Buthelezi, Mangosuthu Gatsha **9**

**Ladies Professional Golfers'
Association (LPGA)**
Gibson, Althea **8**

LAPD
See Los Angeles Police Depart
ment

Latin American folk music
Nascimento, Milton **2**

Law enforcement
Bradley, Thomas **2**
Brown, Lee P. **1**
Glover, Nathaniel, Jr. **12**
Gomez-Preston, Cheryl **9**
Harvard, Beverly **11**
McKinnon, Isaiah **9**
Schmoke, Kurt **1**
Thomas, Franklin A. **5**
Williams, Willie L. **4**

LDF
McDougall, Gay J. **11**
See NAACP Legal Defense Fund

League of Nations
Haile Selassie **7**

Leary Group Inc.
Leary, Kathryn D. **10**

"Leave No Child Behind"
Edelman, Marian Wright **5**

Lee Elder Scholarship Fund
Elder, Lee **6**

Legal Defense Fund
See NAACP Legal Defense Fund

Les Brown Unlimited, Inc.
Brown, Les **5**

Lexicography
Major, Clarence **9**

Liberation theology
West, Cornel **5**

Library science
Bontemps, Arna **8**
Franklin, Hardy R. **9**
Josey, E. J. **10**
Larsen, Nella **10**
Owens, Major **6**
Schomburg, Arthur Alfonso **9**

Lincoln University
Randall, Dudley **8**
Sudarkasa, Niara **4**

LISC
See Local Initiative Support
Corporation

Literacy Volunteers of America
Amos, Wally **9**

Literary criticism
Baker, Houston A., Jr. **6**
Brown, Sterling **10**
Reed, Ishmael **8**
West, Cornel **5**

Lobbying
Brooke, Edward **8**
Brown, Elaine **8**
Brown, Jesse **6**
Brown, Ron **5**
Edelman, Marian Wright **5**
Lee, Canada **8**
Robinson, Randall **7**

**Local Initiative Support
Corporation (LISC)**
Thomas, Franklin A. **5**

Long jump
Lewis, Carl **4**
Powell, Mike **7**

Los Angeles city government
Bradley, Thomas **2**
Evers, Myrlie **8**

**Los Angeles Dodgers baseball
team**
Baker, Dusty **8**
Robinson, Frank **9**

**Los Angeles Lakers basketball
team**
Abdul-Jabbar, Kareem **8**
Johnson, Earvin "Magic" **3**

**Los Angeles Police
Department (LAPD)**
Williams, Willie L. **4**

**Los Angeles Raiders football
team**
Lott, Ronnie **9**
Shell, Art **1**

Lost-Found Nation of Islam
Farrakhan, Louis **2**
Muhammad, Elijah **4**
Muhammad, Khallid Abdul **10**
X, Malcolm **1**

Louisiana state government
Pinchback, P. B. S. **9**

Louisiana State Senate
Pinchback, P. B. S. **9**

LPGA
See Ladies Professional Golfers'
Association

**Lynching (anti-lynching
legislation)**
Johnson, James Weldon **5**
Till, Emmett **7**

Lyricist
Dunbar, Paul Laurence **8**
Fitzgerald, Ella **8**
Johnson, James Weldon **5**

MacNeil/Lehrer NewsHour
Hunter-Gault, Charlayne **6**

**Madame C. J. Walker
Manufacturing Company**
Walker, Madame C. J. **7**

Malawi Congress Party (MCP)
Banda, Hastings Kamuzu **6**

Manhattan Project
Quarterman, Lloyd Albert **4**

MARC Corp.
See Metropolitan Applied
Research Center

**March on Washington/
Freedom March**
Baker, Josephine **3**
Belafonte, Harry **4**
Bunche, Ralph J. **5**
Davis, Ossie **5**
Fauntroy, Walter E. **11**
Forman, James **7**
Franklin, John Hope **5**
Horne, Lena **5**
Jackson, Mahalia **5**
King, Coretta Scott **3**
King, Martin Luther, Jr. **1**
Lewis, John **2**
Meredith, James H. **11**
Randolph, A. Philip **3**
Rustin, Bayard **4**
Sleet, Moneta, Jr. **5**
Wilkins, Roy **4**
Young, Whitney M., Jr. **4**

Marie Brown Associates
Brown, Marie Dutton **12**

**Martin Luther King Jr. Center
for Nonviolent Social
Change**
Dodson, Howard, Jr. **7**
King, Bernice **4**
King, Coretta Scott **3**
King, Dexter **10**
King, Martin Luther, Jr. **1**
King, Yolanda **6**

Marxism
Baraka, Amiri **1**

Machel, Samora Moises **8**
Nkrumah, Kwame **3**

Massachusetts state government
Brooke, Edward **8**

Masters Tournament
Elder, Lee **6**

MAXIMA Corporation
Smith, Joshua **10**

Maxwell House Coffee Company
Fudge, Ann **11**

McCall Pattern Company
Lewis, Reginald F. **6**

MCP
See Malawi Congress Party

Medicine
Banda, Hastings Kamuzu **6**
Bristow, Lonnie **12**
Callender, Clive O. **3**
Carson, Benjamin **1**
Comer, James P. **6**
Cooper, Edward S. **6**
Drew, Charles Richard **7**
Elders, Joycelyn **6**
Gayle, Helene D. **3**
Gibson, William F. **6**
Hinton, William Augustus **8**
Jemison, Mae C. **1**
Kountz, Samuel L. **10**
Lawless, Theodore K. **8**
Leffall, LaSalle, Jr. **3**
Pitt, David Thomas **10**
Poussaint, Alvin F. **5**
Satcher, David **7**
Sullivan, Louis **8**
Thomas, Vivien **9**
Watkins, Levi, Jr. **9**
Welsing, Frances Cress **5**
Williams, Daniel Hale **2**
Wright, Louis Tompkins **4**

Melanin theory of racism
See also Cress Theory of Color Confrontation and Racism
Jeffries, Leonard **8**

Men's movement
Somé, Malidoma Patrice **10**

Merce Cunningham Dance Company
Dove, Ulysses **5**

MESBICs
See Minority Enterprise Small Business Investment Corporations

Metropolitan Applied Research Center (MARC Corp.)
Clark, Kenneth B. **5**

MFDP
See Mississippi Freedom Democratic Party

Miami Dolphins football team
Greene, Joe **10**

Michael Jordan Foundation
Jordan, Michael **6**

Michigan House of Representatives
Collins, Barbara-Rose **7**

Michigan State Supreme Court
Archer, Dennis **7**

Michigan State University
Wharton, Clifton R., Jr. **7**

Millinery
Bailey, Xenobia **11**

Million Man March
Worrill, Conrad **12**

Milwaukee Braves baseball team
Aaron, Hank **5**

Milwaukee Brewers baseball team
Aaron, Hank **5**
Baylor, Don **6**

Milwaukee Bucks basketball team
Abdul-Jabbar, Kareem **8**
Lucas, John **7**

Minneapolis City Council
Sayles Belton, Sharon **9**

Minneapolis city government
Sayles Belton, Sharon **9**

Minnesota State Supreme Court
Page, Alan **7**

Minnesota Twins baseball team
Baylor, Don **6**
Puckett, Kirby **4**
Winfield, Dave **5**

Minnesota Vikings football team
Green, Dennis **5**
Moon, Warren **8**
Page, Alan **7**
Walker, Herschel **1**

Minority Enterprise Small Business Investment Corporations (MESBICs)
Lewis, Reginald F. **6**

Minstrel shows
McDaniel, Hattie **5**

Miss America
Vincent, Marjorie Judith **2**
Williams, Vanessa **4**

Mississippi Freedom Democratic Party (MFDP)
Baker, Ella **5**
Hamer, Fannie Lou **6**
Norton, Eleanor Holmes **7**

Mississippi state government
Hamer, Fannie Lou **6**

Miss USA
Gist, Carole **1**

MLA
See Modern Language Association of America

Model Inner City Community Organization (MICCO)
Fauntroy, Walter E. **11**

Modeling
Beckford, Tyson **11**
Berry, Halle **4**
Banks, Tyra **11**
Campbell, Naomi **1**
Hardison, Bethann **12**
Houston, Whitney **7**
Iman **4**
Johnson, Beverly **2**
Powell, Maxine **8**
Smith, Barbara **11**
Tyson, Cicely **7**
Webb, Veronica **10**

Modern dance
Ailey, Alvin **8**
Byrd, Donald **10**
Dove, Ulysses **5**
Jamison, Judith **7**
Miller, Bebe **3**
Primus, Pearl **6**
Vereen, Ben **4**

Modern Language Association of America (MLA)
Baker, Houston A., Jr. **6**

Montgomery bus boycott
Abernathy, Ralph David **1**
Baker, Ella **5**
Jackson, Mahalia **5**
King, Martin Luther, Jr. **1**
Parks, Rosa **1**
Rustin, Bayard **4**

Morehouse College
Hope, John **8**
Mays, Benjamin E. **7**

Morna
Evora, Cesaria **12**

Moscow World News
Khanga, Yelena **6**
Sullivan, Louis **8**

Mother Waddles Perpetual Mission, Inc.
Waddles, Charleszetta (Mother) **10**

Motivational speaking
Brown, Les **5**
Kimbro, Dennis **10**

Motown Records
Busby, Jheryl **3**
Gaye, Marvin **2**
Gordy, Berry, Jr. **1**
Powell, Maxine **8**
Robinson, Smokey **3**
Ross, Diana **8**
Wonder, Stevie **11**

Mouvement Revolutionnaire National pour la Developpement (Rwanda; MRND)
Habyarimana, Juvenal **8**

MOVE
Goode, W. Wilson **4**
Wideman, John Edgar **5**

MRND
See Mouvement Revolutionnaire National pour la Developpement

"MTV Jams"
Bellamy, Bill **12**

Multimedia art
Bailey, Xenobia **11**
Simpson, Lorna **4**

Murals
Douglas, Aaron **7**
Lee-Smith, Hughie **5**

Musical composition
Charlemagne, Manno **11**
Davis, Anthony **11**
Davis, Miles **4**
Ellington, Duke **5**
Europe, James Reese **10**
George, Nelson **12**
Gillespie, Dizzy **1**
Gordy, Berry, Jr. **1**
Handy, W. C. **8**
Jones, Quincy **8**
Joplin, Scott **6**
King, B. B. **7**
Lincoln, Abbey **3**

Reagon, Bernice Johnson **7**
Rushen, Patrice **12**
Van Peebles, Melvin **7**

Music publishing
Gordy, Berry, Jr. **1**
Handy, W. C. **8**
Ice Cube **8**
Knight, Suge **11**
Mayfield, Curtis **2**
Ross, Diana **8**

Muslim Mosque, Inc.
X, Malcolm **1**

Mysteries
Himes, Chester **8**
Mosley, Walter **5**

NAACP
See National Association for the Advancement of Colored People

NAACP Legal Defense Fund (LDF)
Bell, Derrick **6**
Chambers, Julius **3**
Edelman, Marian Wright **5**
Guinier, Lani **7**
Jones, Elaine R. **7**
Julian, Percy Lavon **6**
Marshall, Thurgood **1**
Motley, Constance Baker **10**

NABJ
See National Association of Black Journalists

NAC
See Nyasaland African Congress

NACGN
See National Association of Colored Graduate Nurses

NACW
See National Association of Colored Women

NAG
See Nonviolent Action Group

NASA
See National Aeronautics and Space Administration

Nation
Wilkins, Roger **2**

National Aeronautics and Space Administration (NASA)
Bluford, Guy **2**
Bolden, Charles F., Jr. **7**
Gregory, Frederick D. **8**
Jemison, Mae C. **1**
McNair, Ronald **3**

Nichols, Nichelle **11**

National Afro-American Council
Fortune, T. Thomas **6**

National Alliance Party (NAP)
Fulani, Lenora **11**

National Association for the Advancement of Colored People (NAACP)
Baker, Ella **5**
Bell, Derrick **6**
Bond, Julian **2**
Bontemps, Arna **8**
Brooks, Gwendolyn **1**
Bunche, Ralph J. **5**
Chambers, Julius **3**
Chavis, Benjamin **6**
Clark, Kenneth B. **5**
Clark, Septima **7**
Days, Drew S., III **10**
Dee, Ruby **8**
Du Bois, W. E. B. **3**
Edelman, Marian Wright **5**
Evers, Medgar **3**
Evers, Myrlie **8**
Farmer, James **2**
Gibson, William F. **6**
Grimké, Archibald H. **9**
Harrington, Oliver W. **9**
Hooks, Benjamin L. **2**
Horne, Lena **5**
Houston, Charles Hamilton **4**
Johnson, James Weldon **5**
Jordan, Vernon E. **3**
Marshall, Thurgood **1**
McKissick, Floyd B. **3**
McPhail, Sharon **2**
Meredith, James H. **11**
Moses, Robert Parris **11**
Motley, Constance Baker **10**
Owens, Major **6**
Rustin, Bayard **4**
Terrell, Mary Church **9**
Tucker, C. Delores **12**
White, Walter F. **4**
Wilkins, Roger **2**
Wilkins, Roy **4**
Williams, Robert F. **11**
Wright, Louis Tompkins **4**

National Association of Black Journalists (NABJ)
Stone, Chuck **9**

National Association of Colored Graduate Nurses (NACGN)
Staupers, Mabel K. **7**

National Association of Colored Women (NACW)
Bethune, Mary McLeod **4**
Harper, Frances Ellen Watkins **11**
Terrell, Mary Church **9**

National Baptist Convention USA
Lyons, Henry **12**

National Baptist Publishing Board
Boyd, T. B., III **6**

National Baptist Sunday Church School and Baptist Training Union Congress
Boyd, T. B., III **6**

National Bar Association
Archer, Dennis **7**
McPhail, Sharon **2**

National Basketball Associaion (NBA)
Abdul-Jabbar, Kareem **8**
Barkley, Charles **5**
Bing, Dave **3**
Bol, Manute **1**
Drexler, Clyde **4**
Gourdine, Simon **11**
Johnson, Earvin "Magic" **3**
Jordan, Michael **6**
Lucas, John **7**
Mutombo, Dikembe **7**
Olajuwon, Hakeem **2**
O'Neal, Shaquille **8**
Rodman, Dennis **12**
Russell, Bill **8**
Thomas, Isiah **7**
Wilkens, Lenny **11**

National Basketball Players Association
Gourdine, Simon **11**

National Black Arts Festival (NBAF)
Borders, James **9**
Brooks, Avery **9**

National Black Gay and Lesbian Conference
Wilson, Phill **9**

National Black Gay and Lesbian Leadership Forum (NBGLLF)
Carter, Mandy **11**

National Book Award
Ellison, Ralph **7**
Haley, Alex **4**
Johnson, Charles **1**
Patterson, Orlando **4**

National Broadcasting Company (NBC)
Allen, Byron **3**
Cosby, Bill **7**
Hinderas, Natalie **5**
Jones, Star **10**
Simpson, Carole **6**
Stokes, Carl B. **10**

Williams, Montel **4**

National Center for Neighborhood Enterprise
Woodson, Robert L. **10**

National Coalition of 100 Black Women
McCabe, Jewell Jackson **10**

National Commission for Democracy (Ghana; NCD)
Rawlings, Jerry **9**

National Council of Negro Women (NCNW)
Bethune, Mary McLeod **4**
Cole, Johnnetta B. **5**
Hamer, Fannie Lou **6**
Height, Dorothy I. **2**
Horne, Lena **5**
McDougall, Gay J. **11**
Sampson, Edith S. **4**
Staupers, Mabel K. **7**

National Defence Council (Ghana; NDC)
Rawlings, Jerry **9**

National Democratic Party (Rhodesia)
Mugabe, Robert Gabriel **10**

National Earthquake Information Center (NEIC)
Person, Waverly **9**

National Endowment for the Arts (NEA)
Hemphill, Essex **10**
Serrano, Andres **3**
Williams, William T. **11**

National Equal Rights League (NERL)
Trotter, Monroe **9**

National Football League (NFL)
Green, Dennis **5**
Greene, Joe **10**
Lott, Ronnie **9**
Moon, Warren **8**
Page, Alan **7**
Rice, Jerry **5**
Sanders, Barry **1**
Sanders, Deion **4**
Shell, Art **1**
Singletary, Mike **4**
Smith, Emmitt **7**
Walker, Herschel **1**
White, Reggie **6**

National Football League (NFL)
Brown, Jim **11**
Payton, Walter **11**

National Hockey League (NHL)
Fuhr, Grant **1**

McKegney, Tony **3**
O'Ree, Willie **5**

National Information Infrastructure (NII)
Lewis, Delano **7**

National Institute of Education
Baker, Gwendolyn Calvert **9**

National League
Coleman , Leonard S., Jr. **12**

National Minority Business Council
Leary, Kathryn D. **10**

National Museum of American History
Reagon, Bernice Johnson **7**

National Negro Congress
Bunche, Ralph J. **5**

National Negro Suffrage League
Trotter, Monroe **9**

National Organization for Women
Kennedy, Florynce **12**

National Political Congress of Black Women
Chisholm, Shirley **2**
Tucker, C. DeLores **12**
Waters, Maxine **3**

National Public Radio (NPR)
Lewis, Delano **7**

National Resistance Army (Uganda; NRA)
Museveni, Yoweri **4**

National Resistance Movement
Museveni, Yoweri **4**

National Revolutionary Movement for Development
See Mouvement Revolutionnaire National pour la Developpment

National Science Foundation (NSF)
Massey, Walter E. **5**
Williams, Robert F. **11**

National Security Council
Powell, Colin **1**
Rice, Condoleezza **3**

National Union for the Total Independence of Angola (UNITA)
Savimbi, Jonas **2**

National Union of Mineworkers (South Africa; NUM)
Ramaphosa, Cyril **3**

National Urban League
Brown, Ron **5**
Haynes, George Edmund **8**
Jacob, John E. **2**
Jordan, Vernon E. **3**
Price, Hugh B. **9**
Young, Whitney M., Jr. **4**

National Women's Political Caucus
Hamer, Fannie Lou **6**

National Youth Administration (NYA)
Bethune, Mary McLeod **4**
Primus, Pearl **6**

Nation of Islam
See Lost-Found Nation of Islam

Nature Boys Enterprises
Yoba, Malik **11**

NBA
See National Basketball Association

NBAF
See National Black Arts Festival

NBC
See National Broadcasting Company

NBGLLF
See National Black Gay and Lesbian Leadership Forum

NCD
See National Commission for Democracy

NCNE
See National Center for Neighborhood Enterprise

NCNW
See National Council of Negro Women

NDC
See National Defence Council

NEA
See National Endowment for the Arts

Nebula awards
Butler, Octavia **8**
Delany, Jr., Samuel R. **9**

Negro American Labor Council
Randolph, A. Philip **3**

Negro American Political League
Trotter, Monroe **9**

Negro Digest
Johnson, John H. **3**

Negro Ensemble Company
Schultz, Michael A. **6**
Taylor, Susan L. **10**

Negro History Bulletin
Woodson, Carter G. **2**

Negro Leagues
Paige, Satchel **7**

Negro World
Fortune, T. Thomas **6**

NEIC
See National Earthquake Information Center

Neo-hoodoo
Reed, Ishmael **8**

Nequai Cosmetics
Taylor, Susan L. **10**

NERL
See National Equal Rights League

Netherlands Antilles
Liberia-Peters, Maria Philomena **12**

NetNoir Inc.
CasSelle, Malcolm **11**
Ellington, E. David **11**

Neurosurgery
Carson, Benjamin **1**

Newark city government
Gibson, Kenneth Allen **6**

Newark Housing Authority
Gibson, Kenneth Allen **6**

New Concept Development Center
Madhubuti, Haki R. **7**

New Dance Group
Primus, Pearl **6**

New Jersey Family Development Act
Bryant, Wayne R. **6**

New Jersey General Assembly
Bryant, Wayne R. **6**

New Negro movement
See Harlem Renaissance

New York Age
Fortune, T. Thomas **6**

New York City government
Dinkins, David **4**

New York Daily News
Cose, Ellis **5**

New York Drama Critics Circle Award
Hansberry, Lorraine **6**

New York Freeman
Fortune, T. Thomas **6**

New York Giants baseball team
Mays, Willie **3**

New York Globe
Fortune, T. Thomas **6**

New York Institute for Social Therapy and Research
Fulani, Lenora **11**

New York Jets football team
Lott, Ronnie **9**

New York Public Library
Dodson, Howard, Jr. **7**
Schomburg, Arthur Alfonso **9**

New York Shakespeare Festival
Gunn, Moses **10**
Wolfe, George C. **6**

New York State Senate
Motley, Constance Baker **10**
Owens, Major **6**

New York State Supreme Court
Wright, Bruce McMarion **3**

New York Sun
Fortune, T. Thomas **6**

New York Times
Hunter-Gault, Charlayne **6**
Price, Hugh B. **9**
Wilkins, Roger **2**

New York Yankees baseball team
Baylor, Don **6**
Winfield, Dave **5**

NFL
See National Football League

Nguzo Saba
Karenga, Maulana **10**

NHL
See National Hockey League

Niagra movement
Du Bois, W. E. B. **3**
Hope, John **8**
Trotter, Monroe **9**

Nigerian Armed Forces
Abacha, Sani **11**
Babangida, Ibrahim **4**
Obasanjo, Olusegun **5**

Nigerian literature
Achebe, Chinua **6**
Rotimi, Ola **1**
Soyinka, Wole **4**

NII
See National Information
Infrastructure

1960 Masks
Soyinka, Wole **4**

Nobel Peace Prize
Bunche, Ralph J. **5**
King, Martin Luther, Jr. **1**
Tutu, Desmond **6**

Nobel Prize for literature
Soyinka, Wole **4**
Walcott, Derek **5**

**Nonviolent Action Group
(NAG)**
Al-Amin, Jamil Abdullah **6**

**North Carolina Mutual Life
Insurance**
Spaulding, Charles Clinton **9**

North Pole
Henson, Matthew **2**

NPR
See National Public Radio

NRA
See National Resistance Army
(Uganda)

NRA
See National Rifle Association

NSF
See National Science Foundation

Nuclear energy
O'Leary, Hazel **6**
Quarterman, Lloyd Albert **4**

**Nuclear Regulatory
Commission**
Jackson, Shirley Ann **12**

Nucleus
King, Yolanda **6**

Shabazz, Attallah **6**

NUM
See National Union of
Mineworkers (South Africa)

Nursing
Johnson, Eddie Bernice **8**
Larsen, Nella **10**
Shabazz, Betty **7**
Staupers, Mabel K. **7**

Nutrition
Gregory, Dick **1**

NYA
See National Youth
Administration

**Nyasaland African Congress
(NAC)**
Banda, Hastings Kamuzu **6**

**Oakland Athletics baseball
team**
Baker, Dusty **8**
Baylor, Don **6**
Morgan, Joe Leonard **9**

Oakland Tribune
Maynard, Robert C. **7**

OAU
See Organization of African Unity

OECS
See Organization of Eastern
Caribbean States

Office of Civil Rights
See U.S. Department of
Education

Ohio House of Representatives
Stokes, Carl B. **10**

Ohio state government
Brown, Les **5**
Stokes, Carl B. **10**

Ohio State Senate
White, Michael R. **5**

OIC
See Opportunities
Industrialization Ctrs. of America

Olympics
Ali, Muhammad **2**
Bonaly, Surya **7**
Bowe, Riddick **6**
Christie, Linford **8**
Dawes, Dominique **11**
Devers, Gail **7**
Edwards, Harry **2**
Garrison, Zina **2**
Holyfield, Evander **6**
Johnson, Ben **1**

Joyner-Kersee, Jackie **5**
Lewis, Carl **4**
Miller, Cheryl **10**
Moses, Edwin **8**
Mutola, Maria **12**
Owens, Jesse **2**
Powell, Mike **7**
Rudolph, Wilma **4**
Russell, Bill **8**
Swoopes, Sheryl **12**
Whitaker, Pernell **10**
Wilkens, Lenny **11**

Oncology
Leffall, LaSalle, Jr. **3**

One Church, One Child
Clements, George **2**

OPC
See Ovambo People's Congress

Opera
Anderson, Marian **2**
Brooks, Avery **9**
Bumbry, Grace **5**
Davis, Anthony **11**
Hendricks, Barbara **3**
Joplin, Scott **6**
Norman, Jessye **5**
Price, Leontyne **1**

Operation Desert Shield
Powell, Colin **1**

Operation Desert Storm
Powell, Colin **1**

OPO
See Ovamboland People's
Organization

**Opportunities Industrialization
Centers of America, Inc.
(OIC)**
Sullivan, Leon H. **3**

Organization of African States
Museveni, Yoweri **4**

**Organization of African Unity
(OAU)**
Diouf, Abdou **3**
Haile Selassie **7**
Kaunda, Kenneth **2**
Kenyatta, Jomo **5**
Nkrumah, Kwame **3**
Nujoma, Samuel **10**
Nyerere, Julius **5**
Touré, Sekou **6**

**Organization of Afro-American
Unity**
X, Malcolm **1**

**Organization of Eastern
Caribbean States (OECS)**
Charles, Mary Eugenia **10**

Orisun Repertory
Soyinka, Wole **4**

Orlando Magic basketball team
O'Neal, Shaquille **8**

**Ovambo People's Congress
(South Africa; OPC)**
Nujoma, Samuel **10**

**Ovamboland People's Org.
(South Africa; OPO)**
Nujoma, Samuel **10**

Page Education Foundation
Page, Alan **7**

PAIGC
See Partido Africano da
Independencia da Guine e
Cabo Verde

Painting
Basquiat, Jean-Michel **5**
Bearden, Romare **2**
Douglas, Aaron **7**
Driskell, David C. **7**
Flood, Curt **10**
Guyton, Tyree **9**
Johnson, William Henry **3**
Lawrence, Jacob **4**
Lee-Smith, Hughie **5**
Major, Clarence **9**
McGee, Charles **10**
Mitchell, Corinne **8**
Pippin, Horace **9**
Porter, James A. **11**
Ringgold, Faith **4**
Tanner, Henry Ossawa **1**
Tolliver, William **9**
Wells, James Lesesne **10**
Williams, Billy Dee **8**
Williams, William T. **11**
Woodruff, Hale **9**

Pan-Africanism
Carmichael, Stokely **5**
Du Bois, W. E. B. **3**
Garvey, Marcus **1**
Haile Selassie **7**
Kenyatta, Jomo **5**
Madhubuti, Haki R. **7**
Marshall, Paule **7**
Nkrumah, Kwame **3**
Nyerere, Julius **5**
Touré, Sekou **6**
Turner, Henry McNeal **5**

**Pan African Orthodox Chris
tian Church**
Agyeman, Jaramogi Abebe **10**

Parents of Watts (POW)
Harris, Alice **7**

**Parti Démocratique de Guinée
(Guinea Democratic Party;
PDG)**
Touré, Sekou **6**

**Parti Démocratique de la Côte
d'Ivoire (Democratic Party
of the Ivory Coast; PDCI)**
Houphouët-Boigny, Félix **4**

**Partido Africano da
Independencia da Guine e
Cabo Verde (PAIGC)**

**Party for Unity and Progress
(Guinea; PUP)**
Conté, Lansana **7**

PATC
See Performing Arts Training
Center

Patriot Party
Fulani, Lenora **11**

PBS
See Public Broadcasting Service

PDCI
See Parti Démocratique de la
Côte d'Ivoire (Democratic Party
of the Ivory Coast)

PDG
See Parti Démocratique de
Guinée (Guinea Democratic
Party)

Peace and Freedom Party
Cleaver, Eldridge **5**

Peace Corps
See U.S. Peace Corps

Peace Mission
Divine, Father **7**

Pediatrics
Carson, Benjamin **1**
Elders, Joycelyn **6**

**People Organized and
Working for Economic
Rebirth (POWER)**
Farrakhan, Louis **2**

**People's Association Human
Rights**
Williams, Robert F. **11**

**People's Liberation Army of
Namibia (PLAN)**
Nujoma, Samuel **10**

**People's National Party
(Jamaica; PNP)**
Patterson, P. J. **6**

**People's Progressive Party
(Gambia; PPP)**
Jawara, Sir Dawda Kairaba **11**

**People United to Serve
Humanity (PUSH)**
Jackson, Jesse **1**

**Performing Arts Training
Center (PATC)**
Dunham, Katherine **4**

PGA
See Professional Golfers'
Association

Phelps Stokes Fund
Patterson, Frederick Douglass **12**

Philadelphia city government
Goode, W. Wilson **4**

**Philadelphia Eagles football
team**
White, Reggie **6**

**Philadelphia Phillies baseball
team**
Morgan, Joe Leonard **9**

Philadelphia public schools
Clayton, Constance **1**

**Philadelphia 76ers basketball
team**
Barkley, Charles **5**
Bol, Manute **1**
Lucas, John **7**

Philanthropy
Cosby, Bill **7**
Pleasant, Mary Ellen **9**
Thomas, Franklin A. **5**
Waddles, Charleszetta (Mother)
10
Walker, Madame C. J. **7**
White, Reggie **6**
Wonder, Stevie **11**

Philosophy
Baker, Houston A., Jr. **6**
Davis, Angela **5**
Toomer, Jean **6**
West, Cornel **5**

Phoenix Suns basketball team
Barkley, Charles **5**

Photography
Barboza, Anthony **10**
Lester, Julius **9**
Moutoussamy-Ashe, Jeanne **7**
Parks, Gordon **1**
Serrano, Andres **3**
Simpson, Lorna **4**
Sleet, Moneta, Jr. **5**
Tanner, Henry Ossawa **1**
VanDerZee, James **6**

Photojournalism
Moutoussamy-Ashe, Jeanne **7**
Parks, Gordon **1**
Sleet, Moneta, Jr. **5**

Physical therapy
Elders, Joycelyn **6**

Physics
Jackson, Shirley Ann **12**
Massey, Walter E. **5**

Piano
Ellington, Duke **5**
Hinderas, Natalie **5**
Joplin, Scott **6**
Monk, Thelonious **1**

Pittsburgh Pirates baseball team
Bonds, Barry **6**

Pittsburgh Steelers football team
Greene, Joe **10**

PLAN
See People's Liberation Army of Namibia

Planned Parenthood Federation of America Inc.
Wattleton, Faye **9**

Playwright
Kennedy, Adrienne **11**

PNP
See People's National Party (Jamaica)

Poet laureate (U.S.)
Dove, Rita **6**

Poetry
Dove, Rita **6**
Harper, Frances Ellen Watkins **11**
Hayden, Robert **12**
Lorde, Audre **6**
Randall, Dudley **8**
Senghor, Léopold Sédar **12**

Politics
Adams, Floyd, Jr. **12**
Charlemagne, Manno **11**
Kearse, Amalya Lyle **12**
Liberia-Peters, Maria Philomena **12**
Mazrui, Ali A. **12**
McKinney, Cynthia Ann **11**

Pop music
Edmonds, Kenneth "Babyface" **10**
Franklin, Aretha **11**
Houston, Whitney **7**
Jackson, Janet **6**
Jones, Quincy **8**

Khan, Chaka **12**
Robinson, Smokey **3**
Senghor, Léopold Sédar **12**
Turner, Tina **6**
Washington, Val **12**
Williams, Vanessa **4**
Wilson, Nancy **10**
Wonder, Stevie **11**

Portland Trail Blazers basketball team
Drexler, Clyde **4**
Wilkens, Lenny **11**

POW
See Parents of Watts

POWER
See People Organized and Working for Economic Rebirth

PPP
See People's Progressive Party (Gambia)

Presbyterianism
Cannon, Katie **10**

Pride Economic Enterprises
Barry, Marion S. **7**

Printmaking
Wells, James Lesesne **10**

Prison ministry
Bell, Ralph S. **5**

Pro-Line Corp.
Cottrell, Comer **11**

Professional Golfers' Association (PGA)
Elder, Lee **6**
Sifford, Charlie **4**

Psychiatry
Cobbs, Price M. **9**
Comer, James P. **6**
Poussaint, Alvin F. **5**
Welsing, Frances Cress **5**

Psychology
Fulani, Lenora **11**
Staples, Brent **8**

Public Broadcasting Service (PBS)
Brown, Les **5**
Davis, Ossie **5**
Duke, Bill **3**
Hampton, Henry **6**
Hunter-Gault, Charlayne **6**
Lawson, Jennifer **1**
Riggs, Marlon **5**
Wilkins, Roger **2**

Public housing
Hamer, Fannie Lou **6**

Lane, Vincent **5**

Public relations
Barden, Don H. **9**
McCabe, Jewell Jackson **10**
Perez, Anna **1**
Rowan, Carl T. **1**
Taylor, Kristin Clark **8**
Williams, Maggie **7**

Public television
Brown, Tony **3**

Publishing
Achebe, Chinua **6**
Barden, Don H. **9**
Boyd, T. B. III **6**
Brown, Marie Dutton **12**
Driver, David E. **11**
Ducksworth, Marilyn **12**
Giddings, Paula **11**
Graves, Earl G. **1**
Johnson, John H. **3**
Jones, Quincy **8**
Kunjufu, Jawanza **3**
Lawson, Jennifer **1**
Lorde, Audre **6**
Madhubuti, Haki R. **7**
Maynard, Robert C. **7**
McDonald, Erroll **1**
Morgan, Garrett **1**
Myers, Walter Dean **8**
Parks, Gordon **1**
Perez, Anna **1**
Randall, Dudley **8**
Walker, Alice **1**
Wells-Barnett, Ida B. **8**
Williams, Patricia J. **11**

Pulitzer prize
Brooks, Gwendolyn **1**
Dove, Rita **6**
Fuller, Charles **8**
Haley, Alex **4**
Komunyakaa, Yusef **9**
Lewis, David Levering **9**
Morrison, Toni **2**
Page, Clarence **4**
Sleet, Moneta, Jr. **5**
Walker, Alice **1**
Wilkins, Roger **2**
Wilson, August **7**

PUP
See Party for Unity and Progress (Guinea)

PUSH
See People United to Serve Humanity

Quiltmaking
Ringgold, Faith **4**

Race car driving
Ribbs, Willy T. **2**

Race relations
Abbott, Diane **9**
Achebe, Chinua **6**
Asante, Molefi Kete **3**
Baker, Ella **5**
Baker, Houston A., Jr. **6**
Baldwin, James **1**
Bell, Derrick **6**
Bennett, Lerone, Jr. **5**
Bethune, Mary McLeod **4**
Bosley, Freeman, Jr. **7**
Boyd, T. B. III **6**
Brown, Elaine **8**
Bunche, Ralph J. **5**
Butts, Calvin O., III **9**
Carter, Stephen L. **4**
Cary, Lorene **3**
Chavis, Benjamin **6**
Clark, Kenneth B. **5**
Clark, Septima **7**
Cobbs, Price M. **9**
Cochran, Johnnie L., Jr. **11**
Cole, Johnnetta B. **5**
Comer, James P. **6**
Cone, James H. **3**
Conyers, John, Jr. **4**
Cosby, Bill **7**
Davis, Angela **5**
Davis, Benjamin O., Jr. **2**
Davis, Benjamin O., Sr. **4**
Dee, Ruby **8**
Dellums, Ronald **2**
Divine, Father **7**
Dunbar, Paul Laurence **8**
Dyson, Michael Eric **11**
Edelman, Marian Wright **5**
Elder, Lee **6**
Ellison, Ralph **7**
Esposito, Giancarlo **9**
Farmer, James **2**
Farrakhan, Louis **2**
Fauset, Jessie **7**
Franklin, John Hope **5**
Fuller, Charles **8**
Gaines, Ernest J. **7**
Gibson, William F. **6**
Goode, W. Wilson **4**
Graham, Lawrence Otis **12**
Gregory, Dick **1**
Grimké, Archibald H. **9**
Guinier, Lani **7**
Guy, Rosa **5**
Haley, Alex **4**
Hampton, Henry **6**
Hansberry, Lorraine **6**
Harris, Alice **7**
Hastie, William H. **8**
Haynes, George Edmund **8**
Henry, Lenny **9**
hooks, bell **5**
Hooks, Benjamin L. **2**
Hope, John **8**
Ingram, Rex **5**
Innis, Roy **5**
Jeffries, Leonard **8**
Johnson, James Weldon **5**
Jones, Elaine R. **7**
Jordan, Vernon E. **3**

Khanga, Yelena **6**
King, Bernice **4**
King, Coretta Scott **3**
King, Martin Luther, Jr. **1**
King, Yolanda **6**
Lane, Charles **3**
Lee, Spike **5**
Lee-Smith, Hughie **5**
Lorde, Audre **6**
Mathabane, Mark **5**
Maynard, Robert C. **7**
Mays, Benjamin E. **7**
McDougall, Gay J. **11**
McKay, Claude **6**
Meredith, James H. **11**
Micheaux, Oscar **7**
Mosley, Walter **5**
Muhammad, Khallid Abdul **10**
Norton, Eleanor Holmes **7**
Page, Clarence **4**
Perkins, Edward **5**
Pitt, David Thomas **10**
Poussaint, Alvin F. **5**
Price, Hugh B. **9**
Robeson, Paul **2**
Sampson, Edith S. **4**
Shabazz, Attallah **6**
Sifford, Charlie **4**
Simpson, Carole **6**
Sister Souljah **11**
Smith, Anna Deavere **6**
Sowell, Thomas **2**
Spaulding, Charles Clinton **9**
Staples, Brent **8**
Till, Emmett **7**
Tutu, Desmond **6**
Walcott, Derek **5**
Washington, Booker T. **4**
Washington, Harold **6**
Wells-Barnett, Ida B. **8**
Welsing, Frances Cress **5**
West, Cornel **5**
Wideman, John Edgar **5**
Wiley, Ralph **8**
Wilkins, Roger **2**
Wilkins, Roy **4**
Williams, Gregory **11**
Williams, Patricia J. **11**
Williams, Walter E. **4**
Wilson, Sunnie **7**
Wright, Richard **5**
Young, Whitney M., Jr. **4**

Radio
Banks, William **11**
Dee, Ruby **8**
Dr. Dre **10**
Fuller, Charles **8**
Gumbel, Greg **8**
Hamblin, Ken **10**
Keyes, Alan L. **11**
Lewis, Delano **7**
Lover, Ed **10**

Ragtime
Europe, James Reese **10**
Joplin, Scott **6**

Rainbow Coalition
Jackson, Jesse **1**

Rap music
Baker, Houston A., Jr. **6**
Butts, Calvin O., III **9**
Chuck D. **9**
Dr. Dre **10**
Dyson, Michael Eric **11**
Harrell, Andre **9**
Ice Cube **8**
Ice-T **6**
Jones, Quincy **8**
Knight, Suge **11**
Lover, Ed **10**
O'Neal, Shaquille **8**
Queen Latifa **1**
Simmons, Russell **1**
Sister Souljah **11**
Smith, Will **8**
Tucker, C. DeLores **12**

**Rassemblement Démocratique
   Africain (African
   Democratic Rally; RDA)**
Houphouët-Boigny, Félix **4**
Touré, Sekou **6**

Rastafarianism
Haile Selassie **7**
Marley, Bob **5**
Tosh, Peter **9**

RDA
See Rassemblement
   Démocratique Africain (African
   Democratic Rally)

Real estate development
Barden, Don H. **9**
Brooke, Edward **8**
Lane, Vincent **5**

Recording executives
Busby, Jheryl **3**
Gordy, Berry, Jr. **1**
Harrell, Andre **9**
Jones, Quincy **8**
Knight, Suge **11**
Mayfield, Curtis **2**
Rhone, Sylvia **2**
Robinson, Smokey **3**
Simmons, Russell **1**

Record producer
Edmonds, Kenneth "Babyface"
   10
Ice Cube **8**
Jones, Quincy **8**

Reggae
Marley, Bob **5**
Tosh, Peter **9**

**Revolutionary Party of
   Tanzania**
See Chama cha Mapinduzi
Smith, Barbara **11**

Rhythm and blues/soul music
Belle, Regina **1**
Busby, Jheryl **3**
Campbell, Tisha **8**
Clinton, George **9**
Edmonds, Kenneth "Babyface" **10**
Franklin, Aretha **11**
Gaye, Marvin **2**
Houston, Whitney **7**
Jackson, Janet **6**
Johnson, Robert **2**
Jones, Quincy **8**
Mayfield, Curtis **2**
Robinson, Smokey **3**
Ross, Diana **8**
Turner, Tina **6**
Williams, Vanessa **4**
Wilson, Nancy **10**
Wonder, Stevie **11**

RNA
Republic of New Africa (RNA)

Rock and Roll Hall of Fame
Franklin, Aretha **11**

Rockefeller Foundation
Price, Hugh B. **9**
Wonder, Stevie **11**

Rock music
Clinton, George **9**
Hendrix, Jimi **10**
Ice-T **6**
Kravitz, Lenny **10**
Turner, Tina **6**

Rodeo
Pickett, Bill **11**

Roman Catholic Church
Aristide, Jean-Bertrand **6**
Clements, George **2**
Guy, Rosa **5**
Stallings, George A., Jr. **6**

Royal Ballet
Jackson, Isaiah **3**

Royalty
Christophe, Henri **9**

RPT
See Togolese People's Rally

Rush Artists Management Co.
Simmons, Russell **1**

SAA
See Syndicat Agricole Africain

SACC
See South African Council of
Churches

**Sacramento Kings basketball
team**
Russell, Bill **8**

SADCC
See Southern African
Devt Coordination Conference

Seattle Mariners baseball team
Griffey, Ken, Jr. **12**

Senate Confirmation Hearings
Ogletree, Jr., Charles **12**

Silicon Graphics Incorporated
Hannah, Marc **10**

Social disorganization theory
Frazier, E. Franklin **10**

**Southern African Development
Community (SADC)**
Mbuende, Kaire **12**

**Southern Christian Leadership
Conference (SCLC)**
Moses, Robert Parris **11**

**St. Louis Browns baseball
team**
Paige, Satchel **7**

**St. Louis Cardinals baseball
team**
Baylor, Don **6**
Flood, Curt **10**

St. Louis city government
Bosley, Freeman, Jr. **7**

**St. Louis Hawks basketball
team**
See Atlanta Hawks basketball
team

**San Antonio Spurs basketball
team**
Lucas, John **7**

San Diego Gulls hockey team
O'Ree, Willie **5**

San Diego Hawks hockey team
O'Ree, Willie **5**

**San Diego Padres baseball
team**
Winfield, Dave **5**

**San Francisco 49ers football
team**
Edwards, Harry **2**
Green, Dennis **5**
Lott, Ronnie **9**
Rice, Jerry **5**

**San Francisco Giants baseball
team**
Baker, Dusty **8**
Bonds, Barry **6**
Mays, Willie **3**
Morgan, Joe Leonard **9**
Robinson, Frank **9**

Sankofa Film and Video
Julien, Isaac **3**

Saturday Night Live
Murphy, Eddie **4**
Rock, Chris **3**

Saxophone
Hawkins, Coleman **9**

**Schomburg Center for
Research in Black Culture**
Dodson, Howard, Jr. **7**
Schomburg, Arthur Alfonso **9**

School desegregation
Fortune, T. Thomas **6**
Hamer, Fannie Lou **6**

Science fiction
Bell, Derrick **6**
Butler, Octavia **8**
Delany, Samuel R., Jr. **9**

SCLC
See Southern Christian
Leadership Conference

Sculpture
Catlett, Elizabeth **2**
Guyton, Tyree **9**
Hunt, Richard **6**
Lewis, Edmonia **10**
McGee, Charles **10**
Ringgold, Faith **4**
Savage, Augusta **12**
Shabazz, Attallah **6**

Seattle city government
Rice, Norm **8**

**Seattle Supersonics basketball
team**
Lucas, John **7**
Russell, Bill **8**
Wilkens, Lenny **11**

Second Republic (Nigeria)
Obasanjo, Olusegun **5**

Seismology
Person, Waverly **9**

Sexual harassment
Gomez-Preston, Cheryl **9**
Hill, Anita **5**
Thomas, Clarence **2**

Shrine of the Black Madonna
Agyeman, Jaramogi Abebe **10**

Sickle cell anemia
Satcher, David **7**

Slavery
Asante, Molefi Kete **3**
Bennett, Lerone, Jr. **5**
Douglas, Aaron **7**
Du Bois, W. E. B. **3**
Dunbar, Paul Laurence **8**
Gaines, Ernest J. **7**
Haley, Alex **4**
Harper, Frances Ellen Watkins **11**
Johnson, Charles **1**
Morrison, Toni **2**
Muhammad, Elijah **4**
Patterson, Orlando **4**
Pleasant, Mary Ellen **9**
Tubman, Harriet **9**
X, Malcolm **1**

SNCC
See Student Nonviolent
Coordinating Committee

Soccer
Milla, Roger **2**
Pelé **7**

Socialist Party of Senegal
Diouf, Abdou **3**

Social science
Berry, Mary Frances **7**
Bunche, Ralph J. **5**
Clark, Kenneth B. **5**
Cobbs, Price M. **9**
Frazier, E. Franklin **10**
Haynes, George Edmund **8**
Lawrence-Lightfoot, Sara **10**
Marable, Manning **10**
Woodson, Robert L. **10**

Social work
Berry, Bertice **8**
Dunham, Katherine **4**
Hale, Lorraine **8**
Harris, Alice **7**
Haynes, George Edmund **8**
Little, Robert L. **2**
Waddles, Charleszetta (Mother) **10**
Young, Whitney M., Jr. **4**

Soul City, NC
McKissick, Floyd B. **3**

Soul Train
Cornelius, Don **4**

South African Communist Party
Hani, Chris **6**

South African Council of Churches (SACC)
Tutu, Desmond **6**

South African Defence Force (SADF)
Nujoma, Samuel **10**

South African literature
Mathabane, Mark **5**

South African Students' Organization
Biko, Steven **4**

Southern African Development Coordination Conference (SADCC)
Masire, Quett **5**
Numjoma, Samuel **10**

Southern African Project
McDougall, Gay J. **11**

Southern Christian Leadership Conference (SCLC)
Abernathy, Ralph **1**
Angelou, Maya **1**
Baker, Ella **5**
Chavis, Benjamin **6**
Dee, Ruby **8**
Fauntroy, Walter E. **11**
Hooks, Benjamin L. **2**
Jackson, Jesse **1**
King, Martin Luther, Jr. **1**
Lowery, Joseph **2**
Rustin, Bayard **4**
Young, Andrew **3**

South West African People's Organization (SWAPO)
Nujoma, Samuel **10**

Space Shuttle
Bluford, Guy **2**
Bolden, Charles F., Jr. **7**
Gregory, Frederick D. **8**
Jemison, Mae C. **1**
McNair, Ronald **3**

Spectroscopy
Quarterman, Lloyd Albert **4**

Spelman College
Cole, Johnnetta B. **5**

Spingarn medal
Aaron, Hank **5**
Ailey, Alvin **8**
Anderson, Marian **2**
Bethune, Mary McLeod **4**
Bradley, Thomas **2**
Brooke, Edward **8**
Bunche, Ralph J. **5**
Carver, George Washington **4**
Clark, Kenneth B. **5**
Cosby, Bill **7**
Drew, Charles Richard **7**
Du Bois, W. E. B. **3**
Ellington, Duke **5**
Evers, Medgar **3**
Grimké, Archibald H. **9**

Haley, Alex **4**
Hastie, William H. **8**
Hayes, Roland **4**
Hinton, William Augustus **8**
Hooks, Benjamin L. **2**
Horne, Lena **5**
Houston, Charles Hamilton **4**
Hughes, Langston **4**
Jackson, Jesse **1**
Johnson, James Weldon **5**
Johnson, John H. **3**
Jordan, Barbara **4**
Julian, Percy Lavon **6**
Just, Ernest Everett **3**
King, Martin Luther, Jr. **1**
Lawless, Theodore K. **8**
Lawrence, Jacob **4**
Marshall, Thurgood **1**
Mays, Benjamin E. **7**
Parks, Gordon **1**
Parks, Rosa **1**
Powell, Colin **1**
Price, Leontyne **1**
Randolph, A. Philip **3**
Robeson, Paul **2**
Robinson, Jackie **6**
Staupers, Mabel K. **7**
Sullivan, Leon H. **3**
Weaver, Robert C. **8**
White, Walter F. **4**
Wilder, L. Douglas **3**
Wilkins, Roy **4**
Williams, Paul R. **9**
Woodson, Carter **2**
Wright, Louis Tompkins **4**
Wright, Richard **5**
Young, Andrew **3**
Young, Coleman **1**

Spirituals
Anderson, Marian **2**
Hayes, Roland **4**
Jackson, Mahalia **5**
Norman, Jessye **5**
Reese, Della **6**
Robeson, Paul **2**

Sports psychology
Edwards, Harry **2**

State University of New York System
Wharton, Clifton R., Jr. **7**

Stonewall 25
Norman, Pat **10**

Structural Readjustment Program
Babangida, Ibrahim **4**

Student Nonviolent Coordinating Committee
Al-Amin, Jamil Abdullah **6**
Baker, Ella **5**
Barry, Marion S. **7**
Bond, Julian **2**
Carmichael, Stokely **5**

Clark, Septima **7**
Crouch, Stanley **11**
Davis, Angela **5**
Forman, James **7**
Hamer, Fannie Lou **6**
Holland, Endesha Ida Mae **3**
Lester, Julius **9**
Lewis, John **2**
Moses, Robert Parris **11**
Norton, Eleanor Holmes **7**
Poussaint, Alvin F. **5**
Reagon, Bernice Johnson **7**

Sundance Film Festival
Harris, Leslie **6**

Supreme Court
See U.S. Supreme Court

Supreme Court of Haiti
Pascal-Trouillot, Ertha **3**

Surrealism
Ellison, Ralph **7**
Lee-Smith, Hughie **5**

SWAPO
See South West African People's
Organization

Sweet Honey in the Rock
Reagon, Bernice Johnson **7**

Syndicat Agricole Africain
Houphouët-Boigny, Félix **4**

Synthetic chemistry
Julian, Percy Lavon **6**

**Tanga Consultative Congress
(Tanzania)**
Nujoma, Samuel **10**

**Tanganyikan African National
Union (TANU)**
Nyerere, Julius **5**

TANU
See Tanganyikan African
National Union

**Tanzanian African National
Union**
See Tanganyikan African
National Union

Tap dancing
Hines, Gregory **1**

TBS
See Turner Broadcasting System

**Teachers Insurance and
Annuity Association and the
College Retirement Equities
Fund (TIAA-CREF)**
Wharton, Clifton R., Jr. **7**

Teaching
Delany, Sadie **12**

TEF
See Theological Education Fund

Television
Banks, William **11**

Television scores
Jones, Quincy **8**

Tennis
Ashe, Arthur **1**
Garrison, Zina **2**
Gibson, Althea **8**
Lucas, John **7**
McNeil, Lori **1**
Noah, Yannick **4**
Washington, MaliVai **8**

**Texas House of
Representatives**
Johnson, Eddie Bernice **8**

Texas Rangers baseball team
Cottrell, Comer **11**

Texas State Senate
Johnson, Eddie Bernice **8**
Jordan, Barbara **4**

**Theological Education Fund
(TEF)**
Tutu, Desmond **6**

Third World Press
Madhubuti, Haki R. **7**

Threads 4 Life
Jones, Carl **7**
Kani, Karl **10**
Walker, T. J. **7**

TIAA-CREF
See Teachers Insurance and
Annuity Association and the
College Retirement Equities
Fund

Time-Warner Inc.
Parsons, Richard Dean **11**

**TLC Beatrice International
Holdings, Inc.**
Lewis, Reginald F. **6**

TLC Group L.P.
Lewis, Reginald F. **6**

Togolese Army
Eyadéma, Gnassingbé **7**

Togolese People's Rally (RPT)
Eyadéma, Gnassingbé **7**

Tony awards
Belafonte, Harry **4**

Carroll, Diahann **9**
Fishburne, Larry **4**
Horne, Lena **5**
Jones, James Earl **3**
Richards, Lloyd **2**
Vereen, Ben **4**
Wilson, August **7**
Wolfe, George C. **6**

**Toronto Blue Jays baseball
team**
Winfield, Dave **5**

**Toronto Raptors basketball
team**
Thomas, Isiah **7**

Track and field
Christie, Linford **8**
Devers, Gail **7**
Joyner-Kersee, Jackie **5**
Lewis, Carl **4**
Moses, Edwin **8**
Mutola, Maria **12**
Owens, Jesse **2**
Powell, Mike **7**
Rudolph, Wilma **4**

TransAfrica, Inc.
Robinson, Randall **7**

Transition
Soyinka, Wole **4**

**Transitional Committee for
National Recovery (Guinea;
CTRN)**
Conté, Lansana **7**

Transplant surgery
Callender, Clive O. **3**
Kountz, Samuel L. **10**

Trinidad Theatre Workshop
Walcott, Derek **5**

Trumpet
Armstrong, Louis **2**
Davis, Miles **4**
Ellison, Ralph **7**
Gillespie, Dizzy **1**

**Turner Broadcasting System
(TBS)**
Clayton, Xernona **3**

Tuskegee Airmen
Patterson, Frederick Douglass **12**

Tuskegee Experiment Station
Carver, George Washington **4**

U. S. Postal Service
Davis, Allison **12**

U.S. Court of Appeals
Kearse, Amalya Lyle **12**

UCC
See United Church of Christ

UFBL
See Universal Foundation for Better Living

UGA
See United Golf Association

Umkhonto we Sizwe
Hani, Chris **6**
Mandela, Nelson **1**

UN
See United Nations

UNCF
See United Negro College Fund

Uncle Nonamé Cookie Company
Amos, Wally **9**

Unemployment and Poverty Action Committee
Forman, James **7**

UNESCO
See United Nations Educational, Scientific, and Cultural Organization

UNIA
See United Negro Improvement Association

UNICEF
See United Nations Children's Fund

Unions
Clay, William Lacy **8**
Crockett, George, Jr. **10**
Europe, James Reese **10**
Farmer, James **2**
Hilliard, David **7**
Ramaphosa, Cyril **3**
Randolph, A. Philip **3**
Touré, Sekou **6**

UNIP
See United National Independence Party

UNITA
See National Union for the Total Independence of Angola

United Church of Christ (UCC)
Chavis, Benjamin **6**

United Golf Association (UGA)
Elder, Lee **6**
Sifford, Charlie **4**

United National Independence Party (UNIP)
Kaunda, Kenneth **2**

United Nations (UN)
Bunche, Ralph J. **5**
Diouf, Abdou **3**
Lafontant, Jewel Stradford **3**
Mongella, Gertrude **11**
Perkins, Edward **5**
Sampson, Edith S. **4**
Young, Andrew **3**

United Nations Children's Fund (UNICEF)
Baker, Gwendolyn Calvert **9**
Belafonte, Harry **4**

United Nations Educational, Scientific, and Cultural Organization (UNESCO)
Diop, Cheikh Anta **4**
Frazier, E. Franklin **10**

United Negro College Fund (UNCF)
Boyd, T. B. III **6**
Edley, Christopher **2**
Gray, William H. III **3**
Jordan, Vernon E. **3**
Mays, Benjamin E. **7**
Patterson, Frederick Douglass **12**

United Negro Improvement Association (UNIA)
Garvey, Marcus **1**

United Parcel Service
Washington, Patrice Clarke **12**

United Somali Congress (USC)
Ali Mahdi Mohamed **5**

United States Football League (USFL)
White, Reggie **6**

United Workers Union of South Africa (UWUSA)
Buthelezi, Mangosuthu Gatsha **9**

Universal Foundation for Better Living (UFBL)
Colemon, Johnnie **11**
Reese, Della **6**

University of California administration
Massey, Walter E. **5**

University of Colorado administration
Berry, Mary Frances **7**

Urban League (regional)
Clayton, Xernona **3**
Jacob, John E. **2**
Mays, Benjamin E. **7**

Young, Whitney M., Jr. **4**

Urban renewal
Archer, Dennis **7**
Barry, Marion S. **7**
Bosley, Freeman, Jr. **7**
Collins, Barbara-Rose **7**
Harris, Alice **7**
Lane, Vincent **5**
Waters, Maxine **3**

US
Karenga, Maulana **10**

U.S. Air Force
Davis, Benjamin O., Jr. **2**
Gregory, Frederick D. **8**

U.S. Armed Forces Nurse Corps
Staupers, Mabel K. **7**

U.S. Army
Davis, Benjamin O., Sr. **4**
Flipper, Henry O. **3**
Powell, Colin **1**
Watkins, Perry **12**

U.S. Attorney's Office
Lafontant, Jewel Stradford **3**

U.S. Basketball League (USBL)
Lucas, John 7

USBL
See U.S. Basketball League

USC
See United Somali Congress

U.S. Cabinet
Brown, Ron **5**
Elders, Joycelyn **6**
Espy, Mike **6**
Harris, Patricia Roberts **2**
O'Leary, Hazel **6**
Sullivan, Louis **8**
Weaver, Robert C. **8**

U.S. Circuit Court of Appeals
Hastie, William H. **8**

U.S. Commission on Civil Rights
Berry, Mary Frances **7**

USDA
See U.S. Department of Agriculture

U.S. Department of Agriculture (USDA)
Espy, Mike **6**

U.S. Department of Commerce
Brown, Ron **5**
Irving, Larry, Jr. **12**
Person, Waverly **9**

Wilkins, Roger **2**

U.S. Department of Defense
Tribble, Israel, Jr. **8**

U.S. Department of Education
Hill, Anita **5**
Thomas, Clarence **2**
Tribble, Israel, Jr. **8**

U.S. Department of Energy
O'Leary, Hazel **6**

U.S. Department of Health and Human Services (HHS)
See also U.S. Department of Health, Education, and Welfare
Sullivan, Louis **8**

U.S. Department of Health, Education, and Welfare (HEW)
Bell, Derrick **6**
Berry, Mary Frances **7**
Harris, Patricia Roberts **2**
Johnson, Eddie Bernice **8**

U.S. Department of Housing and Urban Development (HUD)
Harris, Patricia Roberts **2**
Weaver, Robert C. **8**

U.S. Department of Justice
Bell, Derrick **6**
Campbell, Bill **9**
Days, Drew S., III **10**
Guinier, Lani **7**
Holder, Eric H., Jr. **9**
Lafontant, Jewel Stradford **3**
Lewis, Delano **7**
Patrick, Deval **12**
Wilkins, Roger **2**

U.S. Department of Labor
Crockett, George, Jr. **10**

U.S. Department of Social Services
Little, Robert L. **2**

U.S. Department of State
Bethune, Mary McLeod **4**
Bunche, Ralph J. **5**
Keyes, Alan L. **11**
Lafontant, Jewel Stradford **3**
Perkins, Edward **5**
Rice, Condoleezza **3**
Wharton, Clifton R., Jr. **7**

U.S. Department of the Interior
Person, Waverly **9**

U.S. Department of Veterans Affairs
Brown, Jesse **6**

U.S. Diplomatic Corp
Grimké, Archibald H. **9**
Harris, Patricia Roberts **2**
Stokes, Carl B. **10**

USFL
See United States Football League

U.S. Geological Survey
Person, Waverly **9**

U.S. House of Representatives
Chisholm, Shirley **2**
Clay, William Lacy **8**
Collins, Barbara-Rose **7**
Collins, Cardiss **10**
Conyers, John, Jr. **4**
Crockett, George, Jr. **10**
Dellums, Ronald **2**
Espy, Mike **6**
Fauntroy, Walter E. **11**
Franks, Gary **2**
Gray, William H. III **3**
Jordan, Barbara **4**
Leland, Mickey **2**
Lewis, John **2**
Meek, Carrie **6**
Mfume, Kweisi **6**
Norton, Eleanor Holmes **7**
Owens, Major **6**
Payne, Donald M. **2**
Pinchback, P. B. S. **9**
Powell, Adam Clayton, Jr. **3**
Rangel, Charles **3**
Stokes, Louis **3**
Washington, Harold **6**
Waters, Maxine **3**
Young, Andrew **3**

U.S. Joint Chiefs of Staff
Powell, Colin **1**

U.S. Marines
Bolden, Charles F., Jr. **7**
Brown, Jesse **6**
Von Lipsey, Roderick K. **11**

U.S. Navy
Gravely, Samuel L., Jr. **5**

U.S. Peace Corps
Days, Drew S., III **10**
Lewis, Delano **7**

U.S. Senate
Braun, Carol Moseley **4**
Brooke, Edward **8**
Dodson, Howard, Jr. **7**
Johnson, Eddie Bernice **8**
Pinchback, P. B. S. **9**

U.S. Supreme Court
Marshall, Thurgood **1**
Thomas, Clarence **2**

U.S. Surgeon General
Elders, Joycelyn **6**

U.S. Virgin Islands government
Hastie, William H. **8**

UWUSA
See United Workers Union of South Africa

Vaudeville
Johnson, Jack **8**
McDaniel, Hattie **5**
Robinson, Bill "Bojangles" **11**
Waters, Ethel **7**

Veterinary science
Jawara, Sir Dawda Kairaba **11**
Patterson, Frederick Douglass **12**
Thomas, Vivien **9**

Vibe
Jones, Quincy **8**

Village Voice
Crouch, Stanley **11**

Virginia state government
Wilder, L. Douglas **3**

Voodoo
Dunham, Katherine **4**
Guy, Rosa **5**
Hurston, Zora Neale **3**

Voting rights
Clark, Septima **7**
Forman, James **7**
Guinier, Lani **7**
Hamer, Fannie Lou **6**
Harper, Frances Ellen Watkins **11**
Johnson, Eddie Bernice **8**
Moses, Robert Parris **11**
Terrell, Mary Church **9**
Trotter, Monroe **9**
Tubman, Harriet **9**
Wells-Barnett, Ida B. **8**
Woodard, Alfre **9**

Vulcan Realty and Investment Company
Gaston, Arthur G. **4**

War Resister's League (WRL)
Carter, Mandy **11**

Washington Bullets basketball team
Lucas, John **7**

Washington, DC City Council
Fauntroy, Walter E. **11**

Washington, DC city government
Barry, Marion S. **7**
Dixon, Sharon Pratt **1**
Fauntroy, Walter E. **11**
Norton, Eleanor Holmes **7**

Washington Post
Maynard, Robert C. **7**
McCall, Nathan **8**
Nelson, Jill **6**
Raspberry, William **2**
Wilkins, Roger **2**

WBA
See World Boxing Association

WBC
See World Boxing Council

WBF
See World Boxing Federation

WCC
See World Council of Churches

Weather
McEwen, Mark **5**

Welfare reform
Bryant, Wayne R. **6**
Williams, Walter E. **4**

West Indian folklore
Walcott, Derek **5**

West Indian folk songs
Belafonte, Harry **4**

West Indian literature
Guy, Rosa **5**
Kincaid, Jamaica **4**
Marshall, Paule **7**
McKay, Claude **6**
Walcott, Derek **5**

West Point
Davis, Benjamin O., Jr. **2**
Flipper, Henry O. **3**

West Side Preparatory School
Collins, Marva **3**

White House Conference on Civil Rights
Randolph, A. Philip **3**

Whitney Museum of American Art
Golden, Thelma **10**

WHO
See Women Helping Offenders

William Morris Talent Agency
Amos, Wally **9**
Yoba, Malik **11**

WillieWear Ltd.
Smith, Willi **8**

Wilmington 10
Chavis, Benjamin **6**

WOMAD
See World of Music, Arts, and Dance

Women Helping Offenders (WHO)
Holland, Endesha Ida Mae **3**

Women's issues
Angelou, Maya **1**
Baker, Ella **5**
Berry, Mary Frances **7**
Brown, Elaine **8**
Campbell, Bebe Moore **6**
Charles, Mary Eugenia **10**
Clark, Septima **7**
Cole, Johnnetta B. **5**
Dash, Julie **4**
Davis, Angela **5**
Edelman, Marian Wright **5**
Elders, Joycelyn **6**
Fauset, Jessie **7**
Giddings, Paula **11**
Goldberg, Whoopi **4**
Grimké, Archibald H. **9**
Hale, Lorraine **8**
Hamer, Fannie Lou **6**
Harper, Frances Ellen Watkins **11**
Harris, Alice **7**
Harris, Leslie **6**
Harris, Patricia Roberts **2**
Height, Dorothy I. **2**
Hill, Anita **5**
Holland, Endesha Ida Mae **3**
hooks, bell **5**
Jordan, Barbara **4**
Jordan, June **7**
Larsen, Nella **10**
Lorde, Audre **6**
Marshall, Paule **7**
McCabe, Jewell Jackson **10**
McMillan, Terry **4**
Meek, Carrie **6**
Mongella, Gertrude **11**
Morrison, Toni **2**
Naylor, Gloria **10**
Nelson, Jill **6**
Nichols, Nichelle **11**
Norman, Pat **10**
Norton, Eleanor Holmes **7**
Ringgold, Faith **4**
Shange, Ntozake **8**
Simpson, Carole **6**
Terrell, Mary Church **9**
Tubman, Harriet **9**
Walker, Alice **1**
Waters, Maxine **3**
Wattleton, Faye **9**
Winfrey, Oprah **2**

Women's Strike for Peace
King, Coretta Scott **3**

Worker's Party (Brazil)
da Silva, Benedita **5**

Workplace equity
Hill, Anita **5**

Clark, Septima **7**
Nelson, Jill **6**
Simpson, Carole **6**

Works Progress Administration (WPA)
Baker, Ella **5**
Douglas, Aaron **7**
Dunham, Katherine **4**
Lawrence, Jacob **4**
Lee-Smith, Hughie **5**
Wright, Richard **5**

World African Hebrew Israelite Community
Ben-Israel, Ben Ami **11**

World beat
Belafonte, Harry **4**
Fela **1**
N'Dour, Youssou **1**
Ongala, Remmy **9**

World Boxing Association (WBA)
Whitaker, Pernell **10**

World Boxing Council (WBF)
Whitaker, Pernell **10**

World Council of Churches (WCC)
Mays, Benjamin E. **7**
Tutu, Desmond **6**

World Cup
Milla, Roger **2**
Pelé **7**

World hunger
Belafonte, Harry **4**
Iman **4**
Jones, Quincy **8**
Leland, Mickey **2**
Masire, Quett **5**
Obasanjo, Olusegun **5**

World of Music, Arts, and Dance (WOMAD)
Ongala, Remmy **9**

World peace
Bunche, Ralph J. **5**

World War I
Bullard, Eugene **12**

World War II
Bullard, Eugene **12**

WPA
See Works Progress Administration

WRL
See War Resister's League

Xerox Corp.
Rand, A. Barry **6**

Yale Child Study Center
Comer, James P. **6**

Yale Repertory Theater
Dutton, Charles S. **4**
Richards, Lloyd **2**
Wilson, August **7**

Yale School of Drama
Dutton, Charles S. **4**
Richards, Lloyd **2**

YMCA
See Young Men's Christian
Associations

Yoruban folklore
Soyinka, Wole **4**

**Young Men's Christian
Association (YMCA)**
Butts, Calvin O., III **9**

Hope, John **8**
Mays, Benjamin E. **7**

**Young Negroes' Cooperative
League**
Baker, Ella **5**

**Young Women's Christian
Association (YWCA)**
Baker, Ella **5**
Baker, Gwendolyn Calvert **9**
Clark, Septima **7**
Height, Dorothy I. **2**
Sampson, Edith S. **4**

Youth Pride Inc.
Barry, Marion S. **7**

Youth Services Administration
Little, Robert L. **2**

YWCA
See Young Women's Christian
Association

ZANLA
See Zimbabwe African National
Liberation Army

ZAPU
See Zimbabwe African People's
Union

**Zimbabwe African National
Liberation Army (ZANLA)**
Mugabe, Robert Gabriel **10**

**Zimbabwe African People's
Union (ZAPU)**
Mugabe, Robert Gabriel **10**
Nkomo, Joshua **4**

ZTA
See Zululand Territorial Authority

**Zululand Territorial Authority
(ZTA)**
Buthelezi, Mangosuthu Gatsha **9**

Cumulative Name Index

Volume numbers appear in **bold.**

Aaron, Hank 1934-- **5**
Aaron, Henry Louis
  See Aaron, Hank
Abacha, Sani 1943-- **11**
Abbott, Diane (Julie) 1953-- **9**
Abdul-Jabbar, Kareem 1947-- **8**
Abdulmajid, Iman Mohamed
  See Iman
Abernathy, Ralph David 1926-
  1990 **1**
Achebe, (Albert) Chinua(lumogu)
  1930-- **6**
Adams, Floyd, Jr. 1945-- **12**
Agyeman, Jaramogi Abebe 1911-
  - **10**
Ailey, Alvin 1931-1989 **8**
Al-Amin, Jamil Abdullah 1943-- **6**
Alcindor, Ferdinand Lewis
  See Abdul-Jabbar, Kareem
Ali Mahdi Mohamed 1940-- **5**
Ali, Muhammad 1942-- **2**
Allen, Byron 1961-- **3**
Amos, John 1941-- **8**
Amos, Wally 1937-- **9**
Anderson, Marian 1902-- **2**
Andrews, Raymond 1934-1991 **4**
Angelou, Maya 1928-- **1**
Anna Marie
  See Lincoln, Abbey
Archer, Dennis (Wayne) 1942-- **7**
Aristide, Jean-Bertrand 1953-- **6**
Armstrong, (Daniel) Louis 1900-
  1971 **2**
Asante, Molefi Kete 1942-- **3**
Ashe, Arthur 1943-- **1**
Atkins, David
  See Sinbad
Babangida, Ibrahim (Badamasi)
  1941-- **4**
Babyface
  See Edmonds, Kenneth
  "Babyface"
Bailey, Xenobia 1955(?)-- **11**
Baker, Constance
  See Motley, Constance Baker
Baker, Dusty 1949-- **8**
Baker, Ella 1903-1986 **5**
Baker, George
  See Divine, Father
Baker, Gwendolyn Calvert 1931--
  9

Baker, Houston A(lfred), Jr. 1943-
  - **6**
Baker, Johnnie B., Jr.
  See Baker, Dusty
Baker, Josephine 1906-1975 **3**
Baldwin, James 1924-1987 **1**
Bambara, Toni Cade 1939-- **10**
Banda, (Ngwazi) Hastings Kamuzu
  1898(?)-- **6**
Banks, Tyra 1973-- **11**
Banks, William (Venoid) 1903-
  1985 **11**
Baraka, Amiri 1934-- **1**
Barboza, Anthony 1944-- **10**
Barden, Don H. 1943-- **9**
Barkley, Charles (Wade) 1963-- **5**
Barrett, Andrew C. 1942(?)-- **12**
Barrow, Joseph Louis
  See Louis, Joe
Barry, Marion S(hepilov, Jr.)
  1936-- **7**
Basquiat, Jean-Michel 1960-1988
  5
Bassett, Angela 1959(?)-- **6**
Baylor, Don(ald Edward) 1949-- **6**
Beals, Jennifer 1963-- **12**
Bearden, Romare (Howard) 1912-
  1988 **2**
Beasley, Myrlie
  See Evers, Myrlie
Beck, Robert
  See Iceberg Slim
Beckford, Tyson 1970-- **11**
Belafonte, Harold George, Jr.
  See Belafonte, Harry
Belafonte, Harry 1927-- **4**
Bell, Derrick (Albert, Jr.) 1930-- **6**
Bell, Ralph S. 1934-- **5**
Bellamy, Bill 1967-- **12**
Belle, Albert (Jojuan) 1966-- **10**
Belle, Regina 1963-- **1**
Ben-Israel, Ben Ami 1940(?)-- **11**
Bennett, Lerone, Jr. 1928-- **5**
Berry, Bertice 1960-- **8**
Berry, Halle 1967(?)-- **4**
Berry, Mary Frances 1938-- **7**
Bethune, Mary (Jane) McLeod
  1875-1955 **4**
Biko, Stephen
  See Biko, Steven (Bantu)
Biko, Steven (Bantu) 1946-1977

4
Bing, Dave 1943-- **3**
Blair, Maxine
  See Powell, Maxine
Bluford, Guion Stewart, Jr.
  See Bluford, Guy
Bluford, Guy 1942-- **2**
Bol, Manute 1963-- **1**
Bolden, Charles F(rank), Jr. 1946-
  - **7**
Bonaly, Surya 1973-- **7**
Bond, (Horace) Julian 1940-- **2**
Bonds, Barry (Lamar) 1964-- **6**
Bongo, Albert-Bernard
  See Bongo, (El Hadj) Omar
Bongo, (El Hadj) Omar 1935-- **1**
Bontemps, Arna(ud Wendell)
  1902-1973 **8**
Borders, James (Buchanan, IV)
  1949-- **9**
Bosley, Freeman (Robertson), Jr.
  1954-- **7**
Bowe, Riddick (Lamont) 1967-- **6**
Boyd, T(heophilus) B(artholomew)
  III 1947-- **6**
Bradley, Ed(ward R.) 1941-- **2**
Bradley, Thomas 1917-- **2**
Brandon, Barbara 1960(?)-- **3**
Braun, Carol (Elizabeth) Moseley
  1947-- **4**
Breedlove, Sarah
  See Walker, Madame C. J.
Brimmer, Andrew F(elton) 1926--
  2
Bristow, Lonnie 1930-- **12**
Brooke, Edward (William, III)
  1919-- **8**
Brooks, Avery 1949-- **9**
Brooks, Gwendolyn 1917-- **1**
Brown, Andre
  See Dr. Dre
Brown, Elaine 1943-- **8**
Brown, H. Rap
  See Al-Amin, Jamil Abdullah
Brown, Hubert Gerold
  See Al-Amin, Jamil Abdullah
Brown, James Nathaniel
  See Brown, Jim
Brown, James Willie, Jr.
  See Komunyakaa, Yusef
Brown, Jesse 1944-- **6**

Brown, Jim 1936-- **11**
Brown, Lee P(atrick) 1937-- **1**
Brown, Les(lie Calvin) 1945-- **5**
Brown, Marie Dutton 1940-- **12**
Brown, Ron(ald Harmon) 1941-- **5**
Brown, Sterling (Allen) 1901-- **10**
Brown, Tony 1933-- **3**
Brown, William Anthony
   See Brown, Tony
Brown, Willie L., Jr. 1934-- **7**
Brown, Zora Kramer 1949-- **12**
Brown Bomber, The
   See Louis, Joe
Brunson, Dorothy 1938-- **1**
Bryant, Wayne R(ichard) 1947-- **6**
Bullard, Eugene Jacques 1894-
   1961 **12**
Bullock, Anna Mae
   See Turner, Tina
Bumbry, Grace (Ann) 1937-- **5**
Bunche, Ralph J(ohnson) 1904-
   1971 **5**
Burnett, Chester Arthur
   See Howlin' Wolf
Burroughs, Margaret Taylor 1917-
   - **9**
Burton, LeVar(dis Robert Martyn)
   1957-- **8**
Busby, Jheryl 1949(?)-- **3**
Buthelezi, Mangosuthu Gatsha
   1928-- **9**
Butler, Octavia (Estellle) 1947-- **8**
Butts, Calvin O(tis), III 1950-- **9**
Byrd, Donald 1949-- **10**
Byrd, Robert (Oliver Daniel, III)
   1952-- **11**
Byron, JoAnne Deborah
   See Shakur, Assata
Cade, Toni
   See Bambara, Toni Cade
Callender, Clive O(rville) 1936-- **3**
Campbell, Bebe Moore 1950-- **6**
Campbell, Bill 1954-- **9**
Campbell, Charleszetta Lena
   See Waddles, Charleszetta
   (Mother)
Campbell, Naomi 1970-- **1**
Campbell, Tisha 1969-- **8**
Canegata, Leonard Lionel
   Cornelius
   See Lee, Canada
Cannon, Katie 1950-- **10**
Carmichael, Stokely 1941-- **5**
Carroll, Diahann 1935-- **9**
Carson, Benjamin 1951-- **1**
Carson, Josephine
   See Baker, Josephine
Carter, Ben
   See Ben-Israel, Ben Ami
Carter, Mandy 1946-- **11**
Carter, Stephen L(isle) 1954-- **4**
Carver, George Washington
   1861(?)-1943 **4**
Cary, Lorene 1956-- **3**
CasSelle, Malcolm 1970-- **11**
Catlett, Elizabeth 1919-- **2**
Chambers, Julius (LeVonne)
   1936-- **3**

Charlemagne, Emmanuel
   See Charlemagne, Manno
Charlemagne, Manno 1948-- **11**
Charles, Mary Eugenia 1919-- **10**
Chavis, Benjamin (Franklin, Jr.)
   1948-- **6**
Chenault, Kenneth I. 1952-- **4**
Chesimard, JoAnne (Deborah)
   See Shakur, Assata
Chisholm, Shirley (Anita St. Hill)
   1924-- **2**
Chissano, Joaquim (Alberto)
   1939-- **7**
Christie, Linford 1960-- **8**
Christophe, Henri 1767-1820 **9**
Chuck D 1960-- **9**
Clark, Joe 1939-- **1**
Clark, Kenneth B(ancroft) 1914--
   5
Clark, Kristin
   See Taylor, Kristin Clark
Clark, Septima (Poinsette) 1898-
   1987 **7**
Clarke, Patrice Francise
   See Washington, Patrice Clarke
Clay, Cassius Marcellus, Jr.
   See Ali, Muhammad
Clay, William Lacy 1931-- **8**
Clayton, Constance 1937-- **1**
Clayton, Xernona 1930-- **3**
Cleage, Albert Buford
   See Agyeman, Jaramogi Abebe
Cleaver, (Leroy) Eldridge 1935--
   5
Cleaver, Emanuel (II) 1944-- **4**
Clements, George (Harold) 1932--
   2
Clinton, George (Edward) 1941--
   9
Cobbs, Price M(ashaw) 1928-- **9**
Cochran, Johnnie L., Jr. 1937--
   11
Cole, Johnnetta B(etsch) 1936-- **5**
Coleman, Bessie 1892-1926 **9**
Coleman , Leonard S., Jr. 1949--
   12
Colemon, Johnnie 1921(?)-- **11**
Collins, Albert 1932-1993 **12**
Collins, Barbara-Rose 1939-- **7**
Collins, Cardiss 1931-- **10**
Collins, Marva 1936-- **3**
Comer, James P(ierpont) 1934-- **6**
Cone, James H. 1938-- **3**
Conté, Lansana 1944(?)-- **7**
Conyers, John, Jr. 1929-- **4**
Cooper, Edward S(awyer) 1926--
   6
Cooper, J. California 19(?)(?)-- **12**
Cornelius, Don 1936-- **4**
Cosby, Bill 1937-- **7**
Cosby, William Henry, Jr.
   See Cosby, Bill
Cose, Ellis 1951-- **5**
Cottrell, Comer 1931-- **11**
Crockett, George (William), Jr.
   1909-- **10**
Crouch, Stanley 1945-- **11**
Cullen, Countee 1903-1946 **8**

Dandridge, Dorothy 1922-1965 **3**
Dash, Julie 1952-- **4**
da Silva, Benedita 1942-- **5**
Davenport, Arthur
   See Fattah, Chaka
Davidson, Jaye 1967(?)-- **5**
Davis, Allison 1902-1983 **12**
Davis, Angela (Yvonne) 1944-- **5**
Davis, Anthony 1951-- **11**
Davis, Benjamin O(liver), Jr.
   1912-- **2**
Davis, Benjamin O(liver), Sr.
   1877-1970 **4**
Davis, Miles (Dewey III) 1926-
   1991 **4**
Davis, Ossie 1917-- **5**
"Deadwood Dick"
   See Love, Nat
Dawes   , Dominique Margaux
   1976-- **11**
Days, Drew S(aunders, III) 1941--
   10
Dee, Ruby 1924-- **8**
Delany, Annie Elizabeth 1891-
   1995 **12**
Delany, Samuel R(ay), Jr. 1942--
   9
Delany, Sarah (Sadie) 1889-- **12**
Dellums, Ronald (Vernie) 1935-- **2**
Devers, (Yolanda) Gail 1966-- **7**
Devine, Major J.
   See Divine, Father
Dickerson, Ernest 1952(?)-- **6**
Dinkins, David (Norman) 1927-- **4**
Diop, Cheikh Anta 1923-1986 **4**
Diouf, Abdou 1935-- **3**
Divine, Father 1877(?)-1965 **7**
Dixon, Sharon Pratt 1944-- **1**
Dixon, Willie (James) 1915-1992
   4
Dodson, Howard, Jr. 1939-- **7**
Domini, Rey
   See Lorde, Audre (Geraldine)
do Nascimento, Edson Arantes
   See Pelé
Douglas, Aaron 1899-1979 **7**
Dove, Rita (Frances) 1952-- **6**
Dove, Ulysses 1947-- **5**
Dr. Dre **10**
Drew, Charles Richard 1904-
   1950 **7**
Drexler, Clyde 1962-- **4**
Driskell, David C(lyde) 1931-- **7**
Driver, David E. 1955-- **11**
Du Bois, W(illiam) E(dward)
   B(urghardt) 1868-1963 **3**
Ducksworth, Marilyn 1957-- **12**
Duke, Bill 1943-- **3**
Dunbar, Paul Laurence 1872-
   1906 **8**
Dunham, Katherine (Mary)
   1910(?)-- **4**
Dutton, Charles S. 1951-- **4**
Dyson, Michael Eric 1958-- **11**
Early, Deloreese Patricia
   See Reese, Della
Edelman, Marian Wright 1939-- **5**
Edley, Christopher (Fairfield, Sr.)

1928-- **2**
Edmonds, Kenneth "Babyface"
1958(?)-- **10**
Edwards, Eli
See McKay, Claude
Edwards, Harry 1942-- **2**
Elder, (Robert) Lee 1934-- **6**
Elders, Joycelyn (Minnie) 1933-- **6**
El-Hajj Malik El-Shabazz
See X, Malcolm
Ellington, Duke 1899-1974 **5**
Ellington, E. David 1960-- **11**
Ellington, Edward Kennedy
See Ellington, Duke
Ellison, Ralph (Waldo) 1914-1994
7
El-Shabazz, El-Hajj Malik
See X, Malcolm
Espy, Alphonso Michael
See Espy, Mike
Esposito, Giancarlo (Giusseppi
Alessandro) 1958-- **9**
Espy, Mike 1953-- **6**
Europe, (William) James Reese
1880-1919 **10**
Everett, Ronald McKinley
See Karenga, Maulana
Evers, Medgar (Riley) 1925-1963
3
Evers, Myrlie 1933-- **8**
Evora, Cesaria 1941-- **12**
Eyadéma, (Étienne) Gnassingbé
1937-- **7**
Farmer, Forest J(ackson) 1941-- **1**
Farmer, James 1920-- **2**
Farrakhan, Louis 1933-- **2**
Fattah, Chaka 1956-- **11**
Fauntroy, Walter E(dward) 1933--
11
Fauset, Jessie (Redmon) 1882-
1961 **7**
Feelings, Thomas 1933-- **11**
Fela 1938-- **1**
Fielder, Cecil (Grant) 1963-- **2**
Fishburne, Larry 1962-- **4**
Fishburne, Laurence III
See Fishburne, Larry
Fitzgerald, Ella 1918-- **8**
Flipper, Henry O(ssian) 1856-
1940 **3**
Flood, Curt(is) 1963-- **10**
Folks, Byron
See Allen, Byron
Foreman, George 1949-- **1**
Forman, James 1928-- **7**
Fortune, T(imothy) Thomas 1856-
1928 **6**
Foxx, Redd 1922-1991 **2**
Franklin, Aretha 1942-- **11**
Franklin, Carl 1949-- **11**
Franklin, Hardy R. 1929-- **9**
Franklin, John Hope 1915-- **5**
Franks, Gary 1954(?)-- **2**
Frazier, Edward Franklin 1894-
1962 **7**
Freeman, Al(bert Cornelius), Jr.
1934-- **11**
Freeman, Morgan 1937-- **2**

Fresh Prince, The
See Smith, Will
Fudge   , Ann (Marie)
1951(?)-- **11**
Fuhr, Grant 1962-- **1**
Fulani, Lenora (Branch) 1950--
11
Fuller, Charles (Henry) 1939-- **8**
Gaines, Ernest J(ames) 1933-- **7**
Gantt, Harvey (Bernard) 1943-- **1**
Garrison, Zina 1963-- **2**
Garvey, Marcus 1887-1940 **1**
Gary, Willie Edward 1947-- **12**
Gaston, Arthur G(eorge) 1892-- **4**
Gates, Henry Louis, Jr. 1950-- **3**
Gay, Marvin Pentz, Jr.
See Gaye, Marvin
Gaye, Marvin 1939-1984 **2**
Gayle, Helene D(oris) 1955-- **3**
George, Nelson 1957-- **12**
Gibson, Althea 1927-- **8**
Gibson, Kenneth Allen 1932-- **6**
Gibson, William F(rank) 1933-- **6**
Giddings, Paula (Jane) 1947-- **11**
Gillespie, Dizzy 1917-1993 **1**
Gillespie, John Birks
See Gillespie, Dizzy
Gist, Carole 1970(?)-- **1**
Giovanni, Nikki 1943-- **9**
Giovanni, Yolande Cornelia, Jr.
See Giovanni, Nikki
Givens, Robin 1965-- **4**
Glover, Danny 1948-- **1**
Glover, Nathaniel, Jr. 1943---- **12**
Goldberg, Whoopi 1955-- **4**
Golden, Thelma 1965-- **10**
Gomez-Preston, Cheryl 1954-- **9**
Goode, W(oodrow) Wilson 1938--
4
Gordon, Ed(ward Lansing, III)
1960-- **10**
Gordy, Berry, Jr. 1929-- **1**
Goreed, Joseph
See Williams, Joe
Gossett, Louis, Jr. 1936-- **7**
Gourdine, Simon (Peter) 1940--
11
Graham, Lawrence Otis 1962--
12
Gravely, Samuel L(ee), Jr. 1922--
5
Graves, Earl G(ilbert) 1935-- **1**
Gray, Frizzell
See Mfume, Kweisi
Gray, William H. III 1941-- **3**
Green, Dennis 1949-- **5**
Greene, Joe 1946-- **10**
Greenfield, Eloise 1929-- **9**
Gregory, Dick 1932-- **1**
Gregory, Frederick D(rew) 1941--
8
Grier, Pam(ala Suzette) 1949-- **9**
Griffey, George Kenneth, Jr.
1969-- **12**
Griffin, Anthony P. 1954-- **12**
Griffith, Mark Winston 1963-- **8**
Grimké, Archibald H(enry) 1849-
1930 **9**

Guarionex
See Schomburg, Arthur Alfonso
Guillaume, Robert 1927-- **3**
Guinier, (Carol) Lani 1950-- **7**
Gumbel, Greg 1946-- **8**
Gunn, Moses 1929-1993 **10**
Guy, Jasmine 1964(?)-- **2**
Guy, Rosa 1925(?)-- **5**
Guyton, Tyree 1955-- **9**
Habré, Hissène 1942-- **6**
Habyarimana, Juvenal 1937-
1994 **8**
Haile Selassie 1892-1975 **7**
Hale, Lorraine 1926(?)-- **8**
Haley, Alex (Palmer) 1921-1992
4
Hall, Lloyd A(ugustus) 1894-1971
8
Hamblin, Ken 1940-- **10**
Hamer, Fannie Lou (Townsend)
1917-1977 **6**
Hamilton, Virginia 1936-- **10**
Hampton, Henry (Eugene, Jr.)
1940-- **6**
Handy, W(illiam) C(hristopher)
1873-1937 **8**
Hani, Chris 1942-1993 **6**
Hani, Martin Thembisile
See Hani, Chris
Hannah, Marc (Regis) 1956-- **10**
Hansberry, Lorraine (Vivian)
1930-1965 **6**
Hansberry, William Leo 1894-
1965 **11**
Hardison, Bethann 19(?)(?)-- **12**
Harper, Frances Ellen Watkins
1825-1911 **11**
Harrell, Andre (O'Neal) 1962(?)--
9
Harrington, Oliver W(endell)
1912-- **9**
Harris, Alice 1934-- **7**
Harris, Barbara 1930-- **12**
Harris, E. Lynn 1957-- **12**
Harris, Leslie 1961-- **6**
Harris, Patricia Roberts 1924-
1985 **2**
Harris, Robin 1953-1990 **7**
Harris, "Sweet" Alice
See Harris, Alice
Harvard, Beverly (Joyce Bailey)
1950-- **11**
Hastie, William H(enry) 1904-
1976 **8**
Hawkins, Adrienne Lita
See Kennedy, Adrienne
Hawkins, Coleman 1904-1969 **9**
Hayden, Robert Earl 1913-1980
12
Hayes, James C. 1946-- **10**
Hayes, Roland 1887-1977 **4**
Haynes, George Edmund 1880-
1960 **8**
Height, Dorothy I(rene) 1912-- **2**
Hemphill, Essex 1957-- **10**
Henderson, Gordon 1957-- **5**
Henderson, Natalie Leota
See Hinderas, Natalie

Hendricks, Barbara 1948-- **3**
Hendrix, James Marshall
　See Hendrix, Jimi
Hendrix, Jimi 1942-1970 **10**
Hendrix, Johnny Allen
　See Hendrix, Jimi
Henry, Lenny 1958-- **9**
Henson, Matthew (Alexander)
　1866-1955 **2**
Hickman, Fred(erick Douglass)
　1951-- **11**
Hill, Anita (Faye) 1956-- **5**
Hilliard, David 1942-- **7**
Himes, Chester 1909-1984 **8**
Hinderas, Natalie 1927-1987 **5**
Hines, Gregory (Oliver) 1946-- **1**
Hinton, William Augustus 1883-
　1959 **8**
Holder, Eric H., Jr. 1951(?)-- **9**
Holiday, Billie 1915-1959 **1**
Holland, Bob 1940-- **11**
Holland, Endesha Ida Mae 1944--
　3
Holyfield, Evander 1962-- **6**
hooks, bell 1952-- **5**
Hooks, Benjamin L(awson) 1925--
　2
Hope, John 1868-1936 **8**
Horne, Lena (Mary Calhoun)
　1917-- **5**
Houphouët, Dia
　See Houphouët-Boigny, Félix
Houphouët-Boigny, Félix 1905-- **4**
House, Eddie James, Jr.
　See House, Son
House, Eugene
　See House, Son
House, Son 1902-1988 **8**
Houston, Charles Hamilton 1895-
　1950 **4**
Houston, Whitney 1963-- **7**
Howard, Corinne
　See Mitchell, Corinne
Howlin' Wolf 1910-1976 **9**
Hudlin, Reginald 1962(?)-- **9**
Hudlin, Warrington, Jr. 1953(?)--
　9
Hughes, Albert 1972-- **7**
Hughes, Allen 1972-- **7**
Hughes, (James Mercer) Langston
　1902-1967 **4**
Hunt, Richard (Howard) 1935-- **6**
Hunter, Charlayne
　See Hunter-Gault, Charlayne
Hunter-Gault, Charlayne 1942-- **6**
Hurston, Zora Neale 1891-1960
　3
Ice Cube 1969(?)-- **8**
Ice-T 1958(?)-- **6**
Iceberg Slim 1918 -1992 **11**
Iman 1955-- **4**
Ingram, Rex 1895-1969 **5**
Innis, Roy (Emile Alfredo) 1934-- **5**
Irving, Clarence (Larry) 1955-- **12**
Jackson, Isaiah (Allen) 1945-- **3**
Jackson, Janet 1966-- **6**
Jackson, Jesse 1941-- **1**
Jackson, Mahalia 1911-1972 **5**

Jackson, Maynard (Holbrook, Jr.)
　1938-- **2**
Jackson, O'Shea
　See Ice Cube
Jackson, Samuel L. 1949(?)-- **8**
Jackson, Shirley Ann 1946-- **12**
Jacob, John E(dward) 1934-- **2**
Jamison, Judith 1943-- **7**
Jawara, David Kairaba 1924-- **11**
Jeffries, Leonard 1937-- **8**
Jemison, Mae C. 1957-- **1**
Jenifer, Franklyn G(reen) 1939-- **2**
Johnson, Ben 1961-- **1**
Johnson, Beverly 1952-- **2**
Johnson, Carol Diann
　See Carroll, Diahann
Johnson, Caryn E.
　See Goldberg, Whoopi
Johnson, Charles 1948-- **1**
Johnson, Charles Arthur
　See St. Jacques, Raymond
Johnson, Charles Spurgeon 1893-
　1956 **12**
Johnson, Earvin "Magic" 1959-- **3**
Johnson, Eddie Bernice 1935-- **8**
Johnson, Jack 1878-1946 **8**
Johnson, James Weldon 1871-
　1938 **5**
Johnson, James William
　See Johnson, James Weldon
Johnson, John Arthur
　See Johnson, Jack
Johnson, John H(arold) 1918-- **3**
Johnson, Virginia (Alma Fairfax)
　1950-- **9**
Johnson, "Magic"
　See Johnson, Earvin "Magic"
Johnson, Marguerite
　See Angelou, Maya
Johnson, Robert 1911-1938 **2**
Johnson, Robert L. 1946(?)-- **3**
Johnson, William Henry 1901-
　1970 **3**
Jones, Bill T. 1952-- **1**
Jones, Carl 1955(?)-- **7**
Jones, Elaine R. 1944-- **7**
Jones, James Earl 1931-- **3**
Jones, Le Roi
　See Baraka, Amiri
Joplin, Scott 1868-1917 **6**
Jones, Quincy (Delight) 1933-- **8**
Jones, Star(let Marie) 1962(?)-- **10**
Jordan, Barbara (Charline) 1936--
　4
Jordan, June 1936-- **7**
Jordan, Michael (Jeffrey) 1963-- **6**
Jordan, Vernon E(ulion, Jr.) 1935-
　- **3**
Josey, E. J. 1924-- **10**
Joyner, Jacqueline
　See Joyner-Kersee, Jackie
Joyner-Kersee, Jackie 1962-- **5**
Julian, Percy Lavon 1899-1975 **6**
Julien, Isaac 1960-- **3**
Just, Ernest Everett 1883-1941 **3**
Kamau, Johnstone
　See Kenyatta, Jomo
Kani, Karl 1968(?)-- **10**

Karenga, Maulana 1941-- **10**
Kaunda, Kenneth (David) 1924--
　2
Kearse, Amalya Lyle 1937-- **12**
Kelly, Patrick 1954(?)-1990 **3**
Kelly, Sharon Pratt
　See Dixon, Sharon Pratt
Kennedy, Adrienne 1931-- **11**
Kennedy, Florynce Rae 1916-- **12**
Kenyatta, Jomo 1891(?)-1978 **5**
Kerekou, Ahmed (Mathieu) 1933-
　- **1**
Keyes, Alan L(ee) 1950-- **11**
Khan, Chaka 1953-- **12**
Khanga, Yelena 1962-- **6**
Kimbro, Dennis (Paul) 1950-- **10**
Kincaid, Jamaica 1949-- **4**
King, B. B. 1925-- **7**
King, Bernice (Albertine) 1963-- **4**
King, Coretta Scott 1929-- **3**
King, Dexter (Scott) 1961-- **10**
King, Martin Luther, Jr. 1929-
　1968 **1**
King, Riley B.
　See King, B. B.
King, Yolanda (Denise) 1955-- **6**
Kirk, Ron 1954-- **11**
Knight, Marion, Jr.
　See Knight, Suge
Knight, Suge 1966-- **11**
Komunyakaa, Yusef 1941-- **9**
Kotto, Yaphet (Fredrick) 1944-- **7**
Kountz, Samuel L(ee) 1930-1981
　10
Kravitz, Lenny 1964-- **10**
Kravitz, Leonard
　See Kravitz, Lenny
Kunjufu, Jawanza 1953-- **3**
Kuti, Fela Anikulapo
　See Fela
La Salle, Eriq 1962-- **12**
Lafontant, Jewel Stradford 1922--
　3
Lane, Charles 1953-- **3**
Lane, Vincent 1942-- **5**
Larsen, Nella 1891-1964 **10**
Latimer, Lewis H(oward) 1848-
　1928 **4**
Lawless, Theodore K(enneth)
　1892-1971 **8**
Lawrence, Jacob (Armstead)
　1917-- **4**
Lawrence, Martin 1965-- **6**
Lawrence-Lightfoot, Sara 1944--
　10
Lawson, Jennifer (Karen) 1946--
　1
Leary, Kathryn D. 1952-- **10**
Lee, Canada 1907-1952 **8**
Lee, Don L(uther)
　See Madhubuti, Haki R.
Lee, Gabby
　See Lincoln, Abbey
Lee, Joie 1962(?)-- **1**
Lee, Shelton Jackson
　See Lee, Spike
Lee, Spike 1957-- **5**
Lee-Smith, Hughie 1915-- **5**

Leffall, LaSalle (Doheny), Jr. 1930-- **3**
Leland, George Thomas
  See Leland, Mickey
Leland, Mickey 1944-1989 **2**
Leon, Kenny 1957(?)-- **10**
Lester, Julius 1939-- **9**
Lewis, (Frederick) Carl(ton) 1961--**4**
Lewis, (Mary) Edmonia 1845(?)-1911(?) **10**
Lewis, David Levering 1936-- **9**
Lewis, Delano (Eugene) 1938-- **7**
Lewis, John (Robert) 1940-- **2**
Lewis, Reginald F. 1942-1993 **6**
Lincoln, Abbey 1930-- **3**
Little, Malcolm
  See X, Malcolm
Little, Robert L(angdon) 1938-- **2**
Locke, Alain (LeRoy) 1886-1954 **10**
Lofton, Kenneth 1967-- **12**
Lord Pitt of Hampstead
  See Pitt, David Thomas
Lorde, Audre (Geraldine) 1934-1992 **6**
Lott, Ronnie 1959-- **9**
Louis, Errol T. 1962-- **8**
Louis, Joe 1914-1981 **5**
Love, Nat 1854-1921 **9**
Lover, Ed **10**
Lowery, Joseph E. 1924-- **2**
Lucas, John 1953-- **7**
Lyons, Henry 1942(?)-- **12**
Machel, Samora Moises 1933-1986 **8**
Madhubuti, Haki R. 1942-- **7**
Madikizela, Nkosikazi Nobandle Nomzamo Winifred
  See Mandela, Winnie
Major, Clarence 1936-- **9**
Makeba, (Zensi) Miriam 1932-- **2**
Malcolm X
  See X, Malcolm
Mandela, Nelson 1918-- **1**
Mandela, Winnie 1934-- **2**
Marable, Manning 1950-- **10**
Marley, Bob 1945-1981 **5**
Marley, Robert Nesta
  See Marley, Bob
Marrow, Tracey
  See Ice-T
Marshall, Gloria
  See Sudarkasa, Niara
Marshall, Paule 1929-- **7**
Marshall, Thurgood 1908-- **1**
Marshall, Valenza Pauline Burke
  See Marshall, Paule
Masekela, Hugh (Ramopolo) 1939-- **1**
Masire, Quett (Ketumile Joni) 1925-- **5**
Massey, Walter E(ugene) 1938-- **5**
Mathabane, Johannes
  See Mathabane, Mark
Mathabane, Mark 1960-- **5**
Mayfield, Curtis (Lee) 1942-- **2**
Maynard, Robert C(lyve) 1937-1993 **7**

Mays, Benjamin E(lijah) 1894-1984 **7**
Mays, William Howard, Jr.
  See Mays, Willie
Mays, Willie 1931-- **3**
Mazrui, Ali Al'Amin 1933-- **12**
Mboup, Souleymane 1951-- **10**
Mbuende, Kaire Munionganda 1953-- **12**
McCabe, Jewell Jackson 1945-- **10**
McCall, Nathan 1955-- **8**
McCoy, Elijah 1844-1929 **8**
McDaniel, Hattie 1895-1952 **5**
McDonald, Erroll 1954(?)-- **1**
McDougall, Gay J. 1947-- **11**
McEwen, Mark 1954-- **5**
McGee, Charles 1924-- **10**
McIntosh, Winston Hubert
  See Tosh, Peter
McKay, Claude 1889-1948 **6**
McKay, Festus Claudius
  See McKay, Claude
McKegney, Tony 1958-- **3**
McKinney, Cynthia Ann 1955-- **11**
McKinnon, Ike
  See McKinnon, Isaiah
McKinnon, Isaiah 1943-- **9**
McKissick, Floyd B(ixler) 1922-1981 **3**
McMillan, Terry 1951-- **4**
McNair, Ronald (Ervin) 1950-1986 **3**
McNeil, Lori 1964(?)-- **1**
McPhail, Sharon 1948-- **2**
McQueen, Butterfly 1911-- **6**
McQueen, Thelma
  See McQueen, Butterfly
Mckee, Lonette 1952-- **12**
Meek, Carrie (Pittman) 1926-- **6**
Meles Zenawi 1955(?)-- **3**
Meredith   , James H(oward) 1933-- **11**
Messenger, The
  See Divine, Father
Meyer, June
  See Jordan, June
Mfume, Kweisi 1948-- **6**
Micheaux, Oscar (Devereaux) 1884-1951 **7**
Milla, Roger 1952-- **2**
Miller, Bebe 1950-- **3**
Miller, Cheryl 1964-- **10**
Mitchell, Arthur 1934-- **2**
Mitchell, Corinne 1914-1993 **8**
Mobutu, Joseph-Desire
  See Mobutu Sese Seko (Nkuku wa za Banga)
Mobutu Sese Seko (Nkuku wa za Banga) 1930-- **1**
Mohamed, Ali Mahdi
  See Ali Mahdi Mohamed
Moi, Daniel (Arap) 1924-- **1**
Mongella, Gertrude 1945-- **11**
Monk, Thelonious (Sphere, Jr.) 1917-1982 **1**

Moon, (Harold) Warren 1956-- **8**
Morgan, Garrett (Augustus) 1877-1963 **1**
Morgan, Joe Leonard 1943-- **9**
Morgan, Rose (Meta) 1912(?)-- **11**
Morris, Stevland Judkins
  See Wonder, Stevie
Morrison, Toni 1931-- **2**
Moseka, Aminata
  See Lincoln, Abbey
Moseley-Braun, Carol
  See Braun, Carol (Elizabeth) Moseley
Moses, Edwin 1955-- **8**
Moses, Gilbert III 1942-1995 **12**
Moses, Robert Parris 1935-- **11**
Mosley, Walter 1952-- **5**
Motley, Constance Baker 1921-- **10**
Moutoussamy-Ashe, Jeanne 1951--**7**
Mowry, Jess 1960-- **7**
Mugabe, Robert Gabriel 1928-- **10**
Muhammad, Elijah 1897-1975 **4**
Muhammad, Khallid Abdul 1951(?)-- **10**
Murphy, Eddie 1961-- **4**
Murphy, Edward Regan
  See Murphy, Eddie
Murray, Cecil (Chip) 1929-- **12**
Murray, Eddie 1956-- **12**
Murray, Lenda 1962-- **10**
Museveni, Yoweri (Kaguta) 1944(?)-- **4**
Mutola, Maria de Lurdes 1972-- **12**
Mutombo, Dikembe 1966-- **7**
Mwinyi, Ali Hassan 1925-- **1**
Myers, Walter Dean 1937-- **8**
Myers, Walter Milton
  See Myers, Walter Dean
Nascimento, Milton 1942-- **2**
Naylor, Gloria 1950-- **10**
Ndadaye, Melchior 1953-1993 **7**
N'Dour, Youssou 1959-- **1**
Nelson, Jill 1952-- **6**
Nettles, Marva Deloise
  See Collins, Marva
Newton, Huey (Percy) 1942-1989 **2**
Ngengi, Kamau wa
  See Kenyatta, Jomo
Nichols, Grace
  See Nichols, Nichelle
Nichols, Nichelle 1933(?)-- **11**
Nkomo, Joshua (Mqabuko Nyongolo) 1917-- **4**
Nkrumah, Kwame 1909-1972 **3**
Noah, Yannick (Simon Camille) 1960-- **4**
Norman, Jessye 1945-- **5**
Norman, Pat 1939-- **10**
Norton, Eleanor Holmes 1937-- **7**
Nottage, Cynthia DeLores
  See Tucker, C. DeLores
Ntaryamira, Cyprien 1955-1994 **8**

Nujoma, Samuel 1929-- **10**
Nyerere, Julius (Kambarage)
    1922-- **5**
O'Neal, Shaquille (Rashaun) 1972-
    - **8**
Obasanjo, Olusegun 1937-- **5**
Oglesby, Zena 1947-- **12**
Ogletree, Jr., Charles 1933-- **12**
Olajuwon, Akeem
    See Olajuwon, Hakeem (Abdul
    Ajibola)
Olajuwon, Hakeem (Abdul Ajibola)
    1963-- **2**
O'Leary, Hazel (Rollins) 1937-- **6**
O'Ree, William Eldon
    See O'Ree, Willie
O'Ree, Willie 1935-- **5**
Ongala, Ramadhani Mtoro
    See Ongala, Remmy
Ongala, Remmy 1947-- **9**
Owens, Dana
    See Queen Latifah
Owens, James Cleveland
    See Owens, Jesse
Owens, J. C.
    See Owens, Jesse
Owens, Jesse 1913-1980 **2**
Owens, Major (Robert) 1936-- **6**
Page, Alan (Cedric) 1945-- **7**
Page, Clarence 1947-- **4**
Paige, Leroy Robert
    See Paige, Satchel
Paige, Satchel 1906-1982 **7**
Parks, Gordon (Roger Alexander
    Buchanan) 1912-- **1**
Parks, Rosa 1913-- **1**
Parsons, Richard Dean 1948-- **11**
Pascal-Trouillot, Ertha 1943-- **3**
Patrick, Deval Laurdine 1956--
    12
Patterson, Frederick Douglass
    1901-1988 **12**
Patterson, Orlando 1940-- **4**
Patterson, P(ercival) J(ames)
    1936(?)-- **6**
Payne, Donald M(ilford) 1934-- **2**
Payton, Walter (Jerry) 1954-- **11**
Peete, Calvin 1943-- **11**
Pelé 1940-- **7**
Perez, Anna 1951-- **1**
Perkins, Edward (Joseph) 1928--
    5
Person, Waverly (J.) 1927--- **9**
Peters, Maria Philomena 1941--
    12
Pickett, Bill 1870-1932 **11**
Pinchback, P(inckney) B(enton)
    S(tewart) 1837-1921 **9**
Pinkett, Jada 1971-- **10**
Pippin, Horace 1888-1946 **9**
Pitt, David Thomas 1913-1994
    10
Pleasant, Mary Ellen 1814-1904
    9
Poitier, Sidney 1927-- **11**
Poole, Elijah
    See Muhammad, Elijah
Porter, Countee Leroy

See, Cullin, Countee
Porter, James A(mos) 1905-1970
    11
Poussaint, Alvin F(rancis) 1934-- **5**
Powell, Adam Clayton, Jr. 1908-
    1972 **3**
Powell, Colin (Luther) 1937-- **1**
Powell, Maxine 1924-- **8**
Powell, Michael Anthony
    See Powell, Mike
Powell, Mike 1963-- **7**
Pratt Dixon, Sharon
    See Dixon, Sharon Pratt
Price, Leontyne 1927-- **1**
Price, Hugh B. 1941-- **9**
Primus, Pearl 1919-- **6**
Prothrow, Deborah Boutin
    See Prothrow-Stith, Deborah
Prothrow-Stith, Deborah 1954--
    10
Pryor, Richard (Franklin Lennox
    Thomas) 1940-- **3**
Puckett, Kirby 1961-- **4**
Quarterman, Lloyd Albert 1918-
    1982 **4**
Queen Latifah 1970(?)-- **1**
Ramaphosa, (Matamela) Cyril
    1952-- **3**
Rand, A(ddison) Barry 1944-- **6**
Randall, Dudley (Felker) 1914-- **8**
Randolph, A(sa) Philip 1889-
    1979 **3**
Rangel, Charles (Bernard) 1930--
    3
Raspberry, William 1935-- **2**
Ras Tafari
    See Haile Selassie
Rawlings, Jerry (John) 1947-- **9**
Reagon, Bernice Johnson 1942--
    7
Reed, Ishmael 1938-- **8**
Reese, Della 1931-- **6**
Rhone, Sylvia 1952-- **2**
Ribbs, William Theodore, Jr.
    See Ribbs, Willy T.
Ribbs, Willy T. 1956-- **2**
Rice, Condoleezza 1954-- **3**
Rice, Jerry 1962-- **5**
Rice, Linda Johnson 1958-- **9**
Rice, Norm(an Blann) 1943-- **8**
Richards, Lloyd 1923(?)-- **2**
Richardson, Elaine Potter
    See Kincaid, Jamaica
Richardson, Nolan 1941-- **9**
Richardson, Pat
    See Norman, Pat
Ridenhour, Carlton
    See , Chuck D.
Riggs, Marlon 1957-- **5**
Ringgold, Faith 1930-- **4**
Roberts, James
    See Lover, Ed
Robeson, Paul (Leroy Bustill)
    1898-1976 **2**
Robinson, Luther
    See Robinson
Robinson 1878-1949 **11**
Robinson, Eddie G. 1919-- **10**

Robinson, Frank 1935-- **9**
Robinson, Jackie 1919-1972 **6**
Robinson, Jack Roosevelt
    See Robinson, Jackie
Robinson, Max 1939-1988 **3**
Robinson, Randall 1942(?)-- **7**
Robinson, Smokey 1940-- **3**
Robinson, William, Jr.
    See Robinson, Smokey
Rock, Chris 1967(?)-- **3**
Rodgers, Johnathan (Arlin) 1946--
    6
Rodman, Dennis Keith 1961-- **12**
Rogers, John W., Jr. 1958-- **5**
Roker, Albert Lincoln, Jr. 1954(?)-
    - **12**
Ross, Araminta
    See Tubman, Harriet
Ross, Diana 1944-- **8**
Rotimi, (Emmanuel Gladstone)
    Ola(wale) 1938-- **1**
Rowan, Carl T(homas) 1925-- **1**
Rudolph, Wilma (Glodean) 1940--
    4
Rushen, Patrice 1954-- **12**
Russell, Bill 1934-- **8**
Russell, William Felton
    See Russell, Bill
Rustin, Bayard 1910-1987 **4**
Saint James, Synthia 1949-- **12**
Sanders, Joseph R(ichard), Jr.
    1954-- **11**
Savage, Augusta Christine
    1892(?)-1962 **12**
Senghor, Léopold Sédar 1906--
    12
Sheffey, Asa Bundy
    See Hayden, Robert Earl
Sister Souljah 1964-- **11**
Smaltz, Audrey 1937(?)-- **12**
Smith, Barbara 1949(?)-- **11**
Smith, Roger Guenveur 1960-- **12**
St. Jacques, Raymond 1930-1990
    8
SAMO
    See Basquiat, Jean-Michel
Sampson, Edith S(purlock) 1901-
    1979 **4**
Sanders, Barry 1968-- **1**
Sanders, Deion (Luwynn) 1967--
    4
Sanders, Dori(nda) 1935-- **8**
Sanford, John Elroy
    See Foxx, Redd
Satcher, David 1941-- **7**
Satchmo
    See Armstrong, (Daniel) Louis
Savimbi, Jonas (Malheiro) 1934--
    2
Sawyer, Amos 1945-- **2**
Sayles Belton, Sharon 1952(?)-- **9**
Schmoke, Kurt (Lidell) 1949-- **1**
Schomburg, Arthur Alfonso 1874-
    1938 **9**
Schomburg, Arturo Alfonso
    See Schomburg, Arthur Alfonso
Schultz, Michael A. 1938-- **6**
Scott, Coretta

See King, Coretta Scott
Seale, Bobby 1936-- **3**
Seale, Robert George
  See Seale, Bobby
Sears-Collins, Leah J(eanette)
  1955-- **5**
Selassie, Haile
  See Haile Selassie
Serrano, Andres 1951(?)-- **3**
Shabazz, Attallah 1958-- **6**
Shabazz, Betty 1936-- **7**
Shakur, Assata 1947-- **6**
Shange, Ntozake 1948-- **8**
Shaw, Bernard 1940-- **2**
Shell, Art(hur, Jr.) 1946-- **1**
Sifford, Charlie (Luther) 1922-- **4**
Simmons, Russell 1957(?)-- **1**
Simpson, Carole 1940-- **6**
Simpson, Lorna 1960-- **4**
Sinbad 1957(?)-- **1**
Singletary, Michael
  See Singletary, Mike
Singletary, Mike 1958-- **4**
Singleton, John 1968-- **2**
Sleet, Moneta (J.), Jr. 1926-- **5**
Smith, Anna Deavere 1950-- **6**
Smith, Arthur Lee, Jr.
  See Asante, Molefi Kete
Smith, Bessie 1894-1937 **3**
Smith, Emmitt (III) 1969-- **7**
Smith, Joshua (Isaac) 1941-- **10**
Smith, Will 1968-- **8**
Smith, Willi (Donnell) 1948-1987
  8
Snipes, Wesley 1962-- **3**
Somé, Malidoma Patrice 1956--
  10
Sowell, Thomas 1930-- **2**
Soyinka, (Akinwande Olu)Wole
  1934-- **4**
Spaulding, Charles Clinton 1874-
  1952 **9**
Stallings, George A(ugustus), Jr.
  1948-- **6**
Staples, Brent 1951-- **8**
Staupers, Mabel K(eaton) 1890-
  1989 **7**
Stevens, Yvette
  See Khan, Chaka
Stewart, Paul Wilbur 1925-- **12**
Stokes, Carl B(urton) 1927-- **10**
Stokes, Louis 1925-- **3**
Stone, Charles Sumner, Jr.
  See Stone, Chuck
Stone, Chuck 1924-- **9**
Sudarkasa, Niara 1938-- **4**
Sullivan, Leon H(oward) 1922-- **3**
Sullivan, Louis (Wade) 1933-- **8**
Swoopes, Sheryl Denise 1971--
  12
Tafari Makonnen
  See Haile Selassie
Tanner, Henry Ossawa 1859-
  1937 **1**
Taylor, Kristin Clark 1959-- **8**
Taylor, Meshach 1947(?)-- **4**
Taylor, Regina 1959-- **9**
Taylor, Susan L. 1946---- **10**

Terrrell, Mary (Elizabeth) Church
  1863-1954 **9**
Thomas, Clarence 1948-- **2**
Thomas, Frank Edward, Jr. 1968-
  - **12**
Thomas, Franklin A(ugustine)
  1934-- **5**
Thomas, Isiah (Lord III) 1961-- **7**
Thomas, Vivien (T.) 1910-1985 **9**
Thurman, Howard 1900-1981 **3**
Till, Emmett (Louis) 1941-1955 **7**
Tolliver, William (Mack) 1951-- **9**
Toomer, Jean 1894-1967 **6**
Toomer, Nathan Pinchback
  See Toomer, Jean
Tosh, Peter 1944-1987 **9**
Touré, Sekou 1922-1984 **6**
Townsend, Robert 1957-- **4**
Tribble, Isreal, Jr. 1940-- **8**
Trotter, (William) Monroe 1872-
  1934 **9**
Trouillot, Ertha Pascal
  See Pascal-Trouillot, Ertha
Tubman, Harriet 1820(?)-1913 **9**
Tucker, C. DeLores 1927-- **12**
Ture, Kwame
  See Carmichael, Stokely
Turner, Henry McNeal 1834-
  1915 **5**
Turner, Tina 1939-- **6**
Tutu, Desmond (Mpilo) 1931-- **6**
Tyson, Cicely 1933-- **7**
Underwood, Blair 1964-- **7**
VanDerZee, James (Augustus
  Joseph) 1886-1983 **6**
Vann, Harold Moore
  See Muhammad, Khallid Abdul
Van Peebles, Mario (Cain)
  1957(?)-- **2**
Van Peebles, Melvin 1932-- **7**
Vereen, Ben(jamin Augustus)
  1946-- **4**
Vincent, Marjorie Judith 1965(?)--
  2
Von Lipsey, Roderick 1959-- **11**
Waddles, Charleszetta (Mother)
  1912-- **10**
Waddles, Mother
  See Waddles, Charleszetta
  (Mother)
Walcott, Derek (Alton) 1930-- **5**
Walcott, Louis Eugene
  See Farrakhan, Louis
Walker, Albertina 1929-- **10**
Walker, Alice (Malsenior) 1944-- **1**
Walker, Herschel (Junior) 1962--
  1
Walker, Madame C. J. 1867-
  1919 **7**
Walker, Nellie Marian
  See Larsen, Nella
Walker, Thomas "T. J."
  See Walker, T. J.
Walker, T. J. 1961(?)-- **7**
Wallace, Phyllis A(nn) 1920(?)-
  1993 **9**
Wallace, Ruby Ann
  See Dee, Ruby

Wallace, Sippie 1898-1986 **1**
Wamutombo, Dikembe Mutombo
  mpolondo Mukamba Jean
  Jacque
  See Mutombo, Dikembe
wa Ngengi, Kamau
  See Kenyatta, Jomo
Warfield, Marsha 1955-- **2**
Washington, Booker T(aliaferro)
  1856-1915 **4**
Washington, Denzel 1954-- **1**
Washington, Fred(er)i(cka Carolyn)
  1903-1994 **10**
Washington, Harold 1922-1987 **6**
Washington, MaliVai 1969-- **8**
Washington, Patrice Clarke 1961-
  - **12**
Washington, Valores James 1903-
  1995 **12**
Waters, Ethel 1895-1977 **7**
Waters, Maxine 1938-- **3**
Watkins, Frances Ellen
  See Harper, Frances Ellen
  Watkins
Watkins, Gloria Jean
  See hooks, bell
Watkins, Levi, Jr. 1945-- **9**
Watkins, Perry James Henry
  1948-1996 **12**
Wattleton, (Alyce) Faye 1943-- **9**
Watts, Rolonda 1959-- **9**
Wayans, Damon 1961-- **8**
Weathers, Carl 1948-- **10**
Weaver, Robert C(lifton) 1907-- **8**
Webb, Veronica 1965-- **10**
Webb, Wellington, Jr. 1941-- **3**
Wells, James Lesesne 1902-1993
  10
Wells-Barnett, Ida B(ell) 1862-
  1931 **8**
Welsing, Frances (Luella) Cress
  1935-- **5**
West, Cornel (Ronald) 1953-- **5**
West, Dorothy 1907-- **12**
Wharton, Clifton R(eginald), Jr.
  1926-- **7**
Whitaker, "Sweet Pea"
  See Whitaker, Pernell
Whitaker, Forest 1961-- **2**
Whitaker, Pernell 1964-- **10**
White, Bill 1933(?)-- **1**
White, Michael R(eed) 1951-- **5**
White, Reggie 1961-- **6**
White, Reginald Howard
  See White, Reggie
White, Walter F(rancis) 1893-
  1955 **4**
White, William DeKova
  See White, Bill
Wideman, John Edgar 1941-- **5**
Wilder, L(awrence) Douglas 1931-
  - **3**
Wiley, Ralph 1952-- **8**
Wilkens, Lenny 1937-- **11**
Wilkens, Leonard Randolph
  See Wilkens, Lenny
Wilkins, Roger (Wood) 1932-- **2**
Wilkins, Roy 1901-1981 **4**

Williams, Billy Dee 1937-- **8**
Williams, Carl
  See Kani, Karl
Williams, Daniel Hale (III) 1856-
  1931 **2**
Williams, Evelyn 1922(?)-- **10**
Williams, Gregory (Howard) 1943-
  -**11**
Williams, Joe 1918-- **5**
Williams, Maggie 1954-- **7**
Williams, Margaret Ann
  See Williams, Maggie
Williams, Montel (B.) 1956(?)-- **4**
Williams, Patricia J. 1951-- **11**
Williams, Paul R(evere) 1894-
  1980 **9**
Williams, Paulette Linda
  See Shange, Ntozake
Williams, Robert F(ranklin) 1925--
  11
Williams, Robert Peter
  See Guillaume, Robert
Williams, Vanessa 1963-- **4**

Williams, Walter E(dward) 1936--
  4
Williams, William December
  Williams, Billy Dee
Williams, William T(homas) 1942--
  11
Williams, Willie L(awrence) 1943--
  4
Williamson, Lisa
  See Sister Souljah
Wilson, August 1945-- **7**
Wilson, Nancy 1937-- **10**
Wilson, Phill 1956-- **9**
Wilson, Sunnie 1908-- **7**
Wilson, William Nathaniel
  See Wilson, Sunnie
Winfield, Dave 1951-- **5**
Winfield, David Mark
  See Winfield, Dave
Winfield, Paul (Edward) 1941-- **2**
Winfrey, Oprah (Gail) 1954-- **2**
Wofford, Chloe Anthony
  See Morrison, Toni

Wolfe, George C. 1954-- **6**
Wonder, Stevie 1950-- **11**
Woodard, Alfre 1953-- **9**
Woodruff, Hale (Aspacio) 1900-
  1980 **9**
Woods, Granville T. 1856-1910 **5**
Woodson, Carter G(odwin) 1875-
  1950 **2**
Woodson, Robert L. 1937---- **10**
Wooldridge, Anna Marie
  See Lincoln, Abbey
Worrill, Conrad 1941-- **12**
Wright, Bruce McMarion 1918-- **3**
Wright, Louis Tompkins 1891-
  1952 **4**
Wright, Richard 1908-1960 **5**
X, Malcolm 1925-1965 **1**
Yoba, (Abdul-)Malik (Kashie)
  1967-- **11**
Young, Andrew (Jackson, Jr.)
  1932-- **3**
Young, Coleman 1918-- **1**
Young, Whitney M(oore), Jr.
  1921-1971 **4**